MW00487544

When the newly consecrated monk-Archbishop of Milan visited his seminary in 1929 he was invited to explain Benedictine spirituality. "There is no such thing," he replied. "It is nothing other than the spirituality of the Church: the praying of the Sacred Liturgy." For Blessed Ildefonso Schuster—monk, abbot, cardinal and archbishop—that reality was a constant. The Sacred Liturgy was the source and summit of his entire Christian life and work, as these volumes testify.

Scholarship has progressed in the century since higher duties called Schuster from the classroom, certainly. Yet in these pages his thirst for learning is as palpable as is the true liturgical spirit—indeed sanctity—that animates his exposition of the nature of the liturgy and his meditations on the seasons and feasts of the liturgical year. From these we can learn a great deal, not only in respect of our approach to liturgical study and celebration, but also regarding the fundamental nature of Christian life and spirituality. That these volumes are once again in print is a singular grace.

—DOM ALCUIN REID, Prior, Monastère Saint-Benoît, Fréjus-Toulon, France, Author, *The Organic Development of the Liturgy*

In addition to having been a worthy son of Saint Benedict and, later, successor of Saint Ambrose, Blessed Ildefonso Schuster (1880–1954) was a notable figure of the early Liturgical Movement, one whose scholarship deserves to be better known in the anglophone world. Arouca Press has done a great service toward that end by republishing the English translation of his long out-of-print seminal work. Although scholarship has progressed in some areas in the last century, it remains a valuable commentary on the living tradition that is the older Roman Rite, on a par with Dom Guéranger's magnum opus, *The Liturgical Year*.

—FR. THOMAS KOCIK, KHS, Author, *Singing His Song: A Short Introduction to the Liturgical Movement*

The achievement of Blessed Ildefonso's Schuster *Liber sacramentorum* was to build a bridge between liturgical scholarship and spiritual commentary on the Mass. The reprint of this great contribution to liturgical renewal in the twentieth century is most welcome at a time when the older form of the Roman Rite is rediscovered by new generations of Catholics. Anyone diving into this monumental work of erudition and piety will find it an inspiring guide to the riches of the liturgical year.

—FR UWE MICHAEL LANG, Cong.Orat., Mater Ecclesiae College, St Mary's University, Twickenham, London

Ildefonse Schuster was among the towering figures of the Liturgical Movement in its healthy phase, where the overriding concern was to study the family history in the spirit of descendents keen to know their glorious heritage, so that they might carry on long-standing customs with grateful understanding, and rediscover lost, forgotten, or neglected treasures. In his own life, he combined a scholar's diligent attention to primary sources with a pastor's warm-hearted embrace of all the gifts the Holy Spirit has bestowed on the Church over the ages. This carefully limned commentary, spacious and leisurely, plunges us into the pure font of tradition and intensifies our participation in the life-giving mysteries of Christ.

—DR. PETER KWASNIEWSKI, author of *Noble Beauty, Transcendent Holiness: Why the Modern Age Needs the Mass of Ages*

THE SACRAMENTARY

The Sacramentary

(LIBER SACRAMENTORUM)

Historical & Liturgical Notes on the Roman Missal

BY ILDEFONSO SCHUSTER

Abbot of the Monastery of St Paul's Without the Walls. Translated from the Italian by ARTHUR LEVELIS-MARKE, M.A.

VOLUME I

(Parts 1 and 2)

AROUCA PRESS

Volume 1 originally translated from the Italian
by Arthur Levelis-Marke
© Burns Oates & Washbourne Ltd.
1924

Reprinted by Arouca Press 2020
Foreword © Gregory DiPippo

ISBN: 978-1-989905-03-6 (pbk)
ISBN: 978-1-989905-04-3 (hardcover)

Arouca Press
PO Box 55003
Bridgeport PO
Waterloo, ON N2J3G0
Canada
www.aroucapress.com

Send inquiries to info@aroucapress.com

NIHIL OBSTAT:

    Fʀ. INNOCENTIUS APAP, S.Th.M., O.P.
                    Censor Deputatus.

IMPRIMATUR:

    EDM. CAN. SURMONT,
                    Vicarius Generalis.

WESTMONASTERII,
    die 20ᵃ Octobris, 1924.

FOREWORD

by Gregory DiPippo

DESPITE his last name, which he received from his Bavarian father, and the ancestry of his mother, who was from the German-speaking Sudtirol region (then part of the Austrian Empire, but now in Italy), the early life of the Blessed Ildephonse Schuster was entirely Roman. His father had worked as a tailor for a military corps of the Papal State, and remained in Rome even after it had fallen to the Kingdom of Italy in 1870; the son was born there in 1880, on January 18th, a date which was then "the feast of St Peter's Chair in Rome." In youth, he entered the community of the Roman basilica and Benedictine abbey of St Paul Outside-the-Walls, and after completing his studies, was ordained a priest on the feast of St Joseph in 1904, in the cathedral of Rome. Before he had reached the age of 40, he had served his religious family as procurator general, prior, and then abbot of St Paul, and had taught at two Pontifical schools in Rome, the Higher School for Sacred Music and the Oriental Institute; he was appointed rector of the latter in 1919, a position in which he served for three years.

It was in this first part of his life that Schuster compiled the lecture notes on the Roman liturgy that would later become the fives volumes of *Liber Sacramentorum*, known to us in English as *The Sacramentary*, and here presented for the first time in a modern reprint. In his original preface, Schuster himself described his goal in transforming his notes into a book as "that of sharing with devout and studious souls, especially among my brother priests, whatever sentiments of faith and reverence Our Lord may have deigned to grant me, his unworthy servant, in the course of my daily meditation on the Roman Missal." The work is neither "exclusively for the learned," nor "a mere manual of piety"; the author approaches his subject as a scholar and a teacher, but also "with the fearful reverence of the believer."

The first volume begins with a long series of topical essays, on matters such as "Christian Initiation," "The Papal Mass at the Roman Stations," "Holy Orders," and so forth. This is followed by a systematic exposition of the various features of the liturgical year, from Advent to the end of the season after Epiphany. The second volume covers the period from Septuagesima to Pentecost, the third finishes the liturgical year, and begins with the feasts of Saints, from St Andrew at the beginning of Advent

ix

to the end of February, while the fourth and fifth volumes are occupied with the rest of the calendar of Saints. Each volume also includes a number of other topical excursuses, and appendices with examples of liturgical texts.

Schuster was not the first modern author to write a commentary on the whole of the liturgical year, and his work inevitably invites comparison with that of his fellow Benedictine and predecessor in the field of liturgical study, Dom Prosper Guéranger. In 1841, the latter published the first part of his great project *The Liturgical Year*, a fifteen-volume series which he did not live to complete. While it is not a *mere* manual of piety, it is a manual of piety nonetheless; alongside many other prayers, each volume contains the full Order of Mass, Vespers for Sundays and major feasts, and Compline, such that one can actually assist at these liturgies with his book in hand. He often includes liturgical texts from other rites and uses, hoping to inspire in his readers love for the full richness of the Christian liturgy, and thus also of the Faith which it proclaims. The *Catholic Encyclopedia* calls it "a mystical work," one aimed at "arous(ing) the faithful from their spiritual torpor," and it is on account of this work that he is rightly regarded as the father of the Liturgical Movement.

Given its genesis as a series of lecture notes, it is no surprise that Schuster's work is more academic, and, we might well say, more scientific. It is a book to be kept handy in the library for frequent consultation, but not really a book that one brings to church for a liturgical celebration. It is also very much focused on the Mass, as indicated by the title *Liber Sacramentorum*, the ancient name for a Roman liturgical book containing only the priest's parts of the Mass. Each entry offers explanation and commentary not just on the liturgical day, but also on the individual texts of the Mass, with many useful and interesting insights into the development and past history of the Roman Rite. In keeping with its purpose, it says very little about the Divine Office, or about other Eastern and Western rites and their texts, except where they may occasionally be brought in to illustrate a point about the Roman Rite. It is not, however, only a reference work. Schuster himself, as we have seen, described his work as the fruit of daily meditation, and it is certainly also a work one can read daily, to foster one's own further meditation on the texts of the liturgy. The balance between scholarship and prayer which he achieves gives us a work from which the learned man can take his spiritual readings, and the man at prayer can immerse himself in the history of his Church's tradition of liturgical prayer.

At the same time, however much we may and should revere this author and respect his work, we should not expect that everything he writes will prove to be true, or equally valuable, after a further hundred years of study. The scholarly study of the liturgy was still in its youth in Schuster's time, and the reader of *The Sacramentary* should therefore be aware that many of his assumptions about the past history of liturgy can no longer be accepted in the light of more recent study. It is also unfortunately true that in his time, it was not uncommon for authors to state as *facts* about the liturgy things which were really just *speculations*. This overconfidence was perhaps inevitable, given the eagerness of scholars of his era to "return to the sources" of early Christianity, together with the scarcity and incomplete state of early sources for the liturgy. Schuster also falls into this trap, although rather less often than many of his contemporaries.

One therefore often finds that his "reverential fear" for his subject does not prevent him from looking at it with a critical, and indeed skeptical eye (more so, sometimes, than is merited). This has both advantages and disadvantages. For example, he does not shy away from saying that a particular Mass (that of the Seven Sorrows in Passiontide), "though very devout, does not show much liturgical talent in the composer"—something Guéranger does not say and would never have said. At the same time, he avoids Guéranger's Romantic and often rather fanciful presentations, especially when speaking of the more devout ages of the past, and his classically Romantic "purple" prose.

It remains to say something of the rest of Schuster's career, the most prominent part of it, which involved a permanent departure from his Roman origins in more than one sense. In the original preface cited above, he says that he had intended to expand *The Sacramentary* into "a full exposition and commentary," but was called "away...from books and libraries" to the office of abbot. In addition to his teaching responsibilities and position as rector of the Oriental Institute, he served the Holy See from 1924–28 as apostolic visitor to the seminaries of Lombardy, Campagna, and Calabria. In the light of his success in this mission, in 1929 he was appointed archbishop of Milan by Pius XI, who had held that See briefly before his election to the Papacy. The appointment was made on June 26th, the feast of two of the most prominent ancient Roman martyrs, Ss John and Paul.

Within the month, he was elevated to the cardinalate, and consecrated bishop by the Pope personally in the Sistine Chapel; on September 7th, he formally took possession of the See in which he would serve the Church for the rest of his life. In accepting the pastoral governance of one of the largest cities in Italy (and this, in the days of Italian Fascism, followed by the disasters of the Second World War), he was required to leave behind not only his native city, and the quiet, studious life of a monastic, but also the Roman Rite to which he had dedicated so much of his energy as a priest and scholar.

Alone in western Christendom, the See of Milan has never adopted the Roman Rite, but rather, kept its ancient liturgical tradition, known from one of its greatest bishops as the Ambrosian Rite. Schuster embraced this rite as wholeheartedly as if it had always been his own. During his tenure as archbishop, he enacted many measures to preserve and promote its authentic traditions, commissioning new editions of the chant books, and leading by example through his assiduous celebration of and attendance at the major services in the cathedral. He also wrote an Ambrosian version of *The Sacramentary*, entitled *Il libro della preghiera antica* ("the book of ancient prayer"), and many articles about the rite in the diocesan review *Ambrosius*. In his time, the church of Milan saw in many ways the realization of the goals of the Liturgical Movement, a true flourishing of liturgical piety among both the clergy and the laity.

In August of 1954, worn out by his constant labors, Schuster finally granted himself a period of rest at the advice of his doctors, and repaired to the diocesan seminary of Milan in the town of Venegono. Fr Giovanni Colombo, then professor of Italian literature at the seminary (later Schuster's successor but one as archbishop), left a moving account of these days, which would prove to be Schuster's last. He writes that on arriving, "exhausted, wan, in pain, walking towards the elevator with difficulty, the archbishop said, 'I would like to read some of the recent publications on archeology, liturgy, church history, while I am here'"—a scholar to the very end. Early in the morning of August 30th, he took a sudden turn for the worse, and having receiving the Last Rites, died after three hours of agony.

The cause for his canonization was begun on the third anniversary of his death; he was beatified by Pope St John Paul II in 1996.

PREFACE

THESE hasty notes were originally intended by me for the limited circle of my own pupils, whether at the Pontifical Higher School of Sacred Music, or later at the Pontifical Oriental Institute in Rome. In thus yielding to the persuasion of influential persons desirous of a wider field for my efforts, I have, in giving them to the Press, no other end in view save that of sharing with devout and studious souls, especially among my brother-priests, whatever sentiments of faith and reverence our Lord may have deigned to grant me, his unworthy servant, in the course of my daily meditation on the Roman Missal.

It has not been my wish either to write a book exclusively for the learned, or to compose a mere manual of piety. The whole of theology will be found contained in the revered and time-honoured Roman formulas of the holy Sacrifice; and faith, moreover, reminds me that our divine Saviour has constituted the Church to be the depositary of the mystical science of prayer, and has given her, through the unspeakable groanings of the Spirit, the key to the very heart of God himself. *Omnipotentia supplex!* I have, therefore, guarded against analyzing the eucharistic formularies with that critical indifference which would fail to estimate at its true value the venerable antiquity of the documents under consideration. Rather have I approached their study with the fearful reverence of the believer, who feels, in those sublime pages, the heart-beat of a thousand generations of martyrs, doctors, and saints, who have not alone conceived nor merely recited the words they contain, but have actually experienced them in their own lives.

It is a fact without doubt that the Roman Missal represents in its entirety the loftiest and most important work in ecclesiastical literature, being that which shows forth with the greatest fidelity the life-history of the Church, that sacred poem in the making of which *ha posto mano e cielo e terra.*[1]

To bring out clearly the subject-matter in its historical and archæological aspect, by rapid but accurate touches, to illustrate it by expressive comparisons, to point out the theological authority for its most important statements, whilst

---

[1] Dante, *Paradiso,* xxv, 1-2.—Tr.

at the same time drawing attention to the artistic beauty of its mystical aspect—such has been the aim that I have ever kept in view. Some would, perhaps, have wished me to be less concise, preferring a full exposition and commentary to a work of private study and spiritual preparation for the intelligent recitation of the prayers in the Missal—*Psallam spiritu, psallam et mente,* as says St Paul. This was likewise my own original idea, but I had to condense my scheme when, with barely a third of the work completed, our Lord thought fit to call me away from books and libraries to take up the pastoral rule of this ancient and world-renowned church, which, in place of the pen, now claims the whole of my strength. The notes which follow represent, consequently, but the scanty fruit of those rare moments of leisure that a shepherd of souls may find at his disposal. Yet the wishes expressed by friend and disciple alike will, I trust, in some measure be satisfied by the publication of this *Liber Sacramentorum,* and in dedicating it to them in particular I will make my own the prayer of that great Apostle near whose sacred tomb its teachings were first uttered : *Et nunc commendo vos Deo et verbo gratiae ipsius, qui potens est aedificare et dare hereditatem in sanctificatis omnibus* (Acts xx, 32).

† ILDEFONSO,
Abbot and Ordinary.

PATRIARCHAL BASILICA OF ST PAUL, ROME,
   In Natali Apostolorum, 1919.

CONTENTS

PAGE

FOREWORD BY GREGORY DiPippo ix

PREFACE xiii

PART I

SONGS OF ZION BESIDE THE WATERS OF REDEMPTION

(GENERAL CONCEPTIONS OF SACRED LITURGY)

CHAPTER

    I. THE SACRED LITURGY : ITS DIVISIONS AND SOURCES   ·   3

    II. CHRISTIAN INITIATION · · · · · · 12

    III. ECCLESIASTICAL PRAYER IN THE EARLY CHURCH · · 26

    IV. THE HISTORICAL SETTING OF ST GREGORY'S REFORM OF THE
         ROMAN LITURGY · · · · · · 39

    V. " FRACTIO PANIS " · · · · · · 53

    VI. THE PAPAL MASS AT THE ROMAN STATIONS · · · 66

    VII. POETRY AND MUSIC IN THE EUCHARISTIC SYNAXIS · · 72

  VIII. THE PART OF THE LATERAN MUSICAL " SCHOLA " IN THE
         DEVELOPMENT OF THE ROMAN LITURGY · · · 78

    IX. SINNERS AND PENITENTS UNDER ANCIENT ECCLESIASTICAL
         DISCIPLINE · · · · · · 116

    X. HOLY ORDERS · · · · · · · 126

    XI. THE CONSECRATION OF BASILICAS IN EARLY CHRISTIAN TIMES 136

    XII. SACRED ART IN THE HOUSE OF GOD · · · 161

  XIII. RELIGIOUS CONSECRATION · · · · · 173

  XIV. THE CHURCH'S CONSECRATION OF STATES AND RULERS · 180

    XV. THE NUPTIAL BLESSING · · · · · 190

  XVI. THE LITURGY ON THE THRESHOLD OF ETERNITY · 198

PART II
THE INAUGURATION OF THE KINGDOM OF THE MESSIAH

INTRODUCTION

PAGE

CHAPTER I. HIERARCHY AND WORSHIP IN ROME IN THE EARLY CENTURIES OF CHRISTIANITY - - - 211

,, II. THE ROMAN CALENDAR - - - - - 230

,, III. THE ORIGIN AND EVOLUTION OF THE "ORDINARIUM MISSAE" - - - - - - 262

THE SACRED LITURGY FROM ADVENT TO SEPTUAGESIMA

FIRST SUNDAY OF ADVENT: STATION AT ST MARY MAJOR - - 319

SECOND SUNDAY OF ADVENT: STATION AT HOLY CROSS IN JERUSALEM - - - - - - - - 323

THIRD SUNDAY OF ADVENT: STATION AT ST PETER'S - - 325

WEDNESDAY IN EMBER WEEK: COLLECTA AT THE TITLE OF EUDOXIA. STATION AT ST MARY MAJOR - - - - 329

FRIDAY IN EMBER WEEK: COLLECTA AT ST MARK'S. STATION AT THE TWELVE HOLY APOSTLES - - -, - 333

SATURDAY IN EMBER WEEK: STATION AT ST PETER'S - - 337

FOURTH SUNDAY OF ADVENT: STATION AT THE TWELVE HOLY APOSTLES - - - - - - - 352

CHRISTMAS EVE: STATION AT ST MARY MAJOR - - - 356

CHRISTMAS DAY:

THE FIRST MASS—AT MIDNIGHT. STATION AT ST MARY AD PRAESEPE - - - - - - 361

THE SECOND MASS—AT DAWN. STATION AT ST ANASTASIA 368

THE THIRD MASS—IN DAYLIGHT. STATION AT ST MARY MAJOR (AT ST PETER'S) - - - - 373

ST STEPHEN THE PROTOMARTYR: STATION AT ST STEPHEN'S ON THE CŒLIAN HILL - - - - - - 378

ST JOHN, APOSTLE AND EVANGELIST: STATION AT ST MARY MAJOR 381

THE HOLY INNOCENTS: STATION AT ST PAUL'S - - 385

PAGE

SUNDAY WITHIN THE OCTAVE OF THE NATIVITY · · · 388

DECEMBER 29. ST THOMAS OF CANTERBURY, BISHOP AND MARTYR · 391

DECEMBER 31. ST SYLVESTER, POPE AND CONFESSOR: STATION AT
THE CEMETERY OF PRISCILLA · · · · · · 393

JANUARY 1. OCTAVE OF OUR LORD: STATION AT ST MARY IN
TRASTEVERE · · · · · · · · · 395

JANUARY 2. OCTAVE OF ST STEPHEN · · · · · 398

JANUARY 3. OCTAVE OF ST JOHN · · · · · 398

JANUARY 4. OCTAVE OF THE HOLY INNOCENTS · · · 398

JANUARY 5. VIGIL OF THE EPIPHANY: STATION AT ST PETER'S · 399

JANUARY 6. THE EPIPHANY OF OUR LORD: STATION AT ST PETER'S 400

SUNDAY WITHIN THE OCTAVE OF THE EPIPHANY: STATION AT THE
TITLE OF PAMMACHIUS · · · · · · · 405

OCTAVE OF THE EPIPHANY · · · · · · 408

SECOND SUNDAY AFTER THE EPIPHANY: STATION AT ST EUSEBIUS · 409

THIRD SUNDAY AFTER THE EPIPHANY · · · · 412

FOURTH SUNDAY AFTER THE EPIPHANY · · · · 414

FIFTH SUNDAY AFTER THE EPIPHANY · · · · 415

SIXTH SUNDAY AFTER THE EPIPHANY · · · · 416

PART I

SONGS OF ZION BESIDE THE WATERS OF REDEMPTION

(GENERAL CONCEPTIONS OF SACRED LITURGY)

CHAPTER I

THE SACRED LITURGY : ITS DIVISIONS AND SOURCES

THE sacred Liturgy, in its widest sense, has for its objective the religious and supernatural polity of Christianity in its various expressions, whether sacramental, euchological, ritual, literary or artistic. It embraces, therefore, as in a vast combination, the highest efforts of the human mind to grasp and express that which is indescribable and divine.

Nor is this all. As children of the Catholic Church, and heirs of the truths revealed to the former patriarchs and prophets of Israel, our religious polity not only dates in its fundamental principles from before the coming of the Son of God, but is many centuries older than the oldest civilizations recorded in history, and by this fact alone commands the respect and veneration of the learned. Indeed, it is impossible to speak of its origin as merely natural and human, both because the dogmatic element in Christianity emanates from a direct and positive divine revelation, and because the life and action of the Church are derived from the Spirit of Christ, which dwells and works within her.

The Church's Liturgy may, therefore, be considered as a sacred poem, in the framing of which both heaven and earth have taken part, and by which our humanity, redeemed in the blood of the Lamb without spot, rises on the wings of the Spirit even unto the throne of God himself. This is more than a mere aspiration, for the sacred Liturgy not only shows forth and expresses the ineffable and the divine, but also, by means of the sacraments and of its forms of prayer, develops and fulfils the supernatural in the souls of the faithful, to whom it communicates the grace of redemption. It may even be said that the very source of the holiness of the Church is fully contained in her Liturgy; for, without the holy sacraments, the Passion of our Lord, in the existing dispensation instituted by almighty God, would have no efficacy in us, since there would be no channels capable of conveying its treasures to our souls.

The domain of liturgy is unsurpassed in range by any other science, embracing as it does the origin of man, his essential relations with his Creator, the Redemption, the sacraments, divine grace, Christian eschatology; in fact, whatever is most sublime and beautiful, most necessary and important in

3

the whole world. For the sake of order, however, this vast field may be divided into various sections, each of which concerns one special aspect of Catholic worship.

The division may be made thus :

Sacred Liturgy

(a) Sacramental Liturgy { Essential Rites / Ceremonial Rites

(b) Psalmody (Divine Office) { Heortology / Hymnody / Sacred Music { Antiphonal Psalmody / Responsorial Psalmody / Direct Psalmody

(c) Extraordinary or Occasional Liturgy { Dedication of Churches { Altars / Cemeteries { Architecture / Painting / Sacred Arts

Consecration or Blessing of { Virgins / Abbots / Sovereigns

(d) Liturgy of the Dead.

As a science, sacred Liturgy has its canons, its laws, its subdivisions, in the same manner as the other sciences, especially that of dogmatic theology, to which it is closely related both in its method and in its object. It aims, in fact, at a systematic study of Christian worship, distinguishing and classifying the various liturgical forms according to the type which marks each family, arranging them in accordance with the date of their institution, examining and comparing the various types, in order to trace them back to a common origin. Thus only does it become possible to follow out the development from a single stock of liturgies apparently so unconnected as, for instance, the Roman, the Gallican, and the Mozarabic. Yet, unless this were done, we should fail to understand how it was that the unity of the faith did not have as its immediate consequence a like unity in its primitive liturgical expression; whereas recent careful study and patient research have discovered in all liturgies, even in those which differ most from one another, a common foundation. Occasionally the same idea is expressed by wholly different forms and wording; but there is no longer room for doubt that the Eastern and Western liturgies all spring from one and the same root of great antiquity, which forms, as it were, the foundation and support of Catholic unity in religious worship.

The sources from which we gain information about the sacred Liturgy are both direct and indirect.

To the first category belong the ancient and modern publications of Eastern Anaphoras and of the various Latin Sacramentaries. Prince Maximilian of Saxony has recently undertaken the publication in successive parts of the different texts of the Oriental liturgies, including the Syro-Maronite, Chaldaic, Greek, Armenian, and Syro-Antiochene; but there is no lack of good illustrative examples and annotations on almost all the Oriental liturgical books edited up to the present time.[1] Among the Western sources, the Leonine, Gelasian and Gregorian Sacramentaries call for special notice, as well as the *Ordines Romani,* the *Missale Gothicum,* the ancient Gallican Missal and the Mozarabic liturgical books.

The various liturgies, taking into account their chronological development and their ethnographical relationship, may be roughly grouped as shown on p. 6.

This table indicates merely the main outlines of classification of the various liturgical families; and, in some cases, the relationships suggested have a purely approximate value, as, for instance, in deriving from the Roman all the other Latin liturgies.

Particular mention should be made of the ancient Roman Sacramentaries, although they are far from giving us the actual state of the Liturgy in Rome in its primitive period, as they have all, more or less, been affected by Gallican influences in adapting them to local usage.

The Gregorian Sacramentary.—This is the title given by Pope Adrian I (784-791) to a collection of Masses said at the " Stations," some of which are undoubtedly anterior to the pontificate of Gregory the Great. The collection, however, contains many elements of a decidedly later date. The compiler has evidently based his work on a Sacramentary attributed to St Gregory, but as we do not know to what extent he modified the original, we should, perhaps, be more accurate in calling it after Pope Adrian I. This Sacramentary contains only the stational Masses at which the Pope usually assisted, omitting all other feasts and solemnities to which no station was attached.[2]

The Gelasian Sacramentary.—This name was formerly given in France to a Roman liturgical collection, which found its way into Gaul between the years 628 and 731, long after the time of Gregory the Great, but considerably before that of Adrian I. The original Roman work, however, suffered many alterations in France, on account of which it needs to be examined with much discrimination before it can be cited as a witness to the liturgical customs of Rome before the time of Charlemagne. The introduction of the Gregorian

[1] The most important work on this subject is still that of F. E. Brightman, *Liturgies Eastern and Western,* vol. i, Oxford 1896.

[2] *Cf.* Duchesne, *Christian Worship: its Origin and Evolution,* 5th ed., London 1919, pp. 120 *sq.*

Sub-Apostolic Sources—
{
(a) Διδαχή
(b) *Epistola I. Clementis*
(c) *Epistola S Ignatii*
}

Second Century. { Western Liturgies. St Justin. Fragmentary Latin Palimpsest of Verona. Tertullian

Third Century.   *Canones Hippolyti*

Fourth Century. Liturgies

Eastern Antiochene

Syriac
- Catecheses of St Cyril
- Apostolic Constitutions[1]
- Liturgy of St James (Greek)
- Liturgy of St James (Syriac)
- Liturgy of St Basil
- Liturgy of St John Chrysostom } Greek { Armenian

Nestorian of Persia and Mesopotamia
- Anaphora of Bickel (Sixth Century)
- Liturgy of SS Addai and Mari
- Anaphora of Theodore of Mopsuestia, of Nestorius, etc.

Alexandrine
- Euchology of Serapion { Greek Liturgy of St Mark
- Coptic Liturgies
  - St Cyril of Alexandria { Abyssinian Liturgy of the Twelve Apostles
  - St Gregory Nazianzen
  - St Basil

Latin { Roman
- Milanese { Aquileia / Ravenna
- Gallican
- Mozarabic
- Celtic

Sacramentary into France threatened for a time to overshadow the Gelasian collection, but the former, having been found wholly inadequate to the Church's daily requirements, was amplified and enriched from that attributed to Pope

[1] *Cf.* Funk, *Didascalia et Constitutiones Apostolorum*, Paderborn 1905.

Gelasius, which, as a result of this fusion, has left many marks of its influence even in the Romano-French Liturgy of the present day.[1]

Missale Francorum.—This is represented by a single fragmentary uncial codex of the seventh century, originally preserved in the Abbey of St Denis, and now in the Vatican Library. The eleven Masses which it contains are all Roman in form, but the collection is not free from Gallican interpolations, especially in the rubrics.[2]

The Leonine Sacramentary.—This is the fullest and most ancient of the Sacramentaries; but, unfortunately, the very nature of the matter brought together by the compiler and the unusual disorder in its arrangement show that it could never have borne an official character. It contains, for instance, vigorous denunciations of false zealots, who *sub specie gratiae* deceive the simple, and insists upon the necessity of guarding against their craftiness. Some of the Masses would appear to have been inspired by the misery and anguish of the Romans whilst their city was being besieged by the Ostrogoths (537-539), and one of the collects for the dead has reference to the burial of Pope Simplicius (died 483). In any case, the collection is prior to the time of St Gregory, and seems to be the only Roman source untainted by extraneous additions. Perhaps the fortunate preservation of this text is due to the strictly private nature of the collection, which was therefore kept wholly within the confines of the basilica or titular church for which it was destined. The material collected by the compiler has every mark of authenticity, but the hypothesis is not to be dismissed that the collection, as a whole, never had an official character nor any practical aim, for the very reason that it was never actually brought into use. According to some authorities, the compiler had in view merely the literary interest of the contents.[3]

The Ravenna Roll.—The document bearing this name is an opistographical scroll in large uncial characters which belonged, in all probability, to the metropolitan archives of Ravenna. It contains in all forty prayers of the Roman type in preparation for Christmas, but it is extremely difficult to

---

[1] *Cf.* Duchesne, *Christian Worship*, 5th ed., pp. 125 *sq.*

[2] *op. cit.*, pp. 134 *sq.*

[3] This Sacramentary was first published by Bianchini from an uncial codex of the seventh century, preserved in the Chapter Library of Verona (*Liber Pontifical.*, vol. iv). Muratori re-edited it in *Liturgia Romana vetus* I; but the brothers Ballerini brought out later a more correct edition, which is reproduced in Migne, *P.L.*, vol. lv. An excellent edition is that recently published by Feltoe, *Sacramentarium Leonianum*, Cambridge Univ. Press 1896. *Cf.* Duchesne, *op. cit.*, pp. 135 *sq.*

determine their date, which might be as early as the time of St Peter Chrysologus.[1]

Ordines Romani.—These form a very important collection of ceremonials of various periods, enabling us to follow, step by step, the development of the papal liturgy in Rome from the eighth to the fifteenth century. The first of these Ordines, which is the most ancient, appears to date from the eighth century, but not all the matter which it contains is of the same period, nor has it the same right to be considered exclusively Roman. As in the case of the Sacramentaries, so here, when introduced into other episcopal sees, these forms become modified and are adapted to local usage, without maintaining any further connection with that development which the Liturgy was continuing to show even in Rome itself. Thus we read of the curious case of Amalarius,[2] who, after having recognized the authority of the *Ordo Romanus* as unquestioned, found, to his great amazement, on the occasion of his journey to Rome in 832, that the clergy there were completely ignorant of the very existence of the said *Ordo*.[3]

The most important documents of the Gallican Liturgy are the *Missale Gothicum* of the Church of Autun, dating from the end of the seventh century;[4] the *Missale Gallicanum vetus* of the same period;[5] the eleven Masses discovered by Mone in a palimpsest of 760-781, formerly belonging to John II, Bishop of Constance;[6] the Lectionary of Luxeuil (seventh century); the Homilies of St Germanus of Paris; and the Missal of Bobbio (seventh century).

The Spanish or Mozarabic Liturgy has left us a greater number of documents, but these have not yet all been published. Dom Morin brought out in 1893 the *Liber Comicus* or *Comes*, containing the lessons of the Mass with very important rubrics. Dom Férotin has published the *Liber Ordinum*, a kind of prayer-book or ritual; but a careful study of the Sacramentary and Antiphonary is still required, for the Mozarabic rite, as revived in the fifteenth century by Cardinal Ximenes for use in a chapel of the Cathedral of Toledo, contains many additions borrowed from the Roman Liturgy; consequently the Mozarabic Missal and

---

[1] It was first edited by Ceriani: *Il rotolo opistografo del principe Antonio Pio di Savoia*, Milan 1883. Later this article was republished in *Archiv. Stor. Lombardo*, 1884, vol. i *sq.*

[2] Amalarius Fortunatus, Bp. of Treves, *ob.* 846.—Tr.

[3] Duchesne, *op. cit.*, 146 *sq.*

[4] *Cf.* Delisle in *Mémoires de l'Académie des Inscriptions*, Part I, vol. xxxii, in which the author has collected and catalogued all the Latin Sacramentaries known to him.

[5] *Cf.* Duchesne, *op. cit.*, pp. 152 *sq.*

[6] Mone, *Lateinische und griechische Messen aus dem zweiten bis sechsten Jahrhundert*, Frankfurt 1850; *P.L.*, vol. cxxxviii, 863.

Breviary reproduced by Migne in his *Latin Patrology* (vol. lxxxv) are of no real scientific use.

The Liturgy of Milan, too, has its own documentary sources, among which the most important are the tenth-century Sacramentary of Biasca and that of Bergamo of the eleventh. The monks of Solesmes have brought out an Ambrosian Antiphonary accompanied by a minute and exhaustive treatise by Cagin. Magistretti also has published the *Beroldus* of the twelfth century, showing the great historical and liturgical importance of these collections of ceremonial usages, recalling as they do the *Ordines Romani*. Lastly, Ceriani edited the ancient text of the Ambrosian Missal, and since his death, Magistretti and Ratti,[1] continuing the work of the great master, have completed the materials for a critical study of that most precious heirloom of the Church of Milan.

Regarding the word " Missal," it should be noted that this name, as well as the liturgical work thus designated, dates only from the Middle Ages, towards the Carlovingian period. The faithful of earlier times were acquainted with the Sacramentaries, but these correspond as to their contents in part only to the *Missale plenarium*.

In order to understand the question more clearly, it is necessary to bear in mind the special character of religious worship in the primitive Church. Unlike modern Christians, who are content in church to unite their intention with that of the priest, without understanding the words of the prayer, the ancient Christians were desirous that the *actio* should be truly shared by all, and be eminently dramatic, so that not only the bishop, but the priests, deacons, and other clergy, the singers and the people should have their own distinct parts to perform. From this arose the necessity of having separate texts for these various parts. Thus, while the bishop or the priest had for his use the *Liber Sacramentorum*, the soloist would have the Responsorial, the pupils of the *schola* their Antiphonary, the sub-deacon his *Epistolarium*, and so on.

The Sacramentary, or *Liber Sacramentorum*, therefore, contained all the prayers to be recited by the bishop or by the priest, not only in the Mass, but in the administration of all the other sacraments, which were, in fact, intimately connected with the eucharistic *actio*. Thus the forms for the administration of Baptism and of Confirmation were part of the liturgy of Easter Eve; those of Absolution were contained in the rites for reconciling penitents on Maundy Thursday. The prayers in that of Extreme Unction followed the Absolution of the Sick *ad succurrendum* before the Mass and the

---

[1] Now Pope Pius XI.

Viaticum; the rites of Ordination were contained in the ceremonies of the nocturnal Station at St Peter's on Ember Saturday, while the nuptial benediction was to be found in a sort of appendix containing the Masses for special occasions —*e.g.*, marriages, funerals, the dedication of churches, the anniversaries of the consecration of bishops and priests, etc. The whole is so intimately linked together and disposed in such order as to show, even in its bibliographical arrangement, that the holy Eucharist is the true centre of Christian worship, whereby all the other sacraments are co-ordinated with it, either by preparing the soul to receive it worthily, or by preserving the grace conferred by it. Consequently all those parts of the service intended for the minor orders of ministers, such as introits, lessons, antiphons, and graduals, were excluded from the Sacramentary, which comprised, on the other hand, all those which are used by the priest in the administration of the sacraments, and are now scattered through the Missal, the Pontifical, and the Roman Ritual. In such manner did the Sacramentary completely justify its ancient title of *Liber Sacramentorum.*

This system, however, though possible in Rome and in other metropolitan churches, where a special place was set apart in the sanctuary for the liturgical codices, in order to have them close at hand, presented grave difficulties in country parishes and in churches where, for want of clergy and of funds, the Roman stational liturgy had been reduced to its most simple expression.

We can well imagine the case of a poor country priest, somewhat advanced in years, assisted only by three or four fidgety boys acting as *lectores*. He would require an entire library for the celebration of Mass—to wit, the Sacramentary, the book of the Gospels, that of the Epistles, the Antiphonary, the Responsorial; and would, moreover, have the trouble of searching through the collection in order to find the collects, the scriptural readings, the proper chants; in a word, the various parts required in the service. The simplest solution of his difficulties would have been to combine all these compilations into one, by copying out for each day at full length the entire Mass belonging to the different feasts of the year. This is the origin of the *Missale plenarium* of the Carlovingian epoch. It was entitled *plenarium* because, unlike the early Sacramentaries, it contained the whole of the eucharistic liturgy, without the need of employing any other book.

When we compare the Missal in use in our churches since the Tridentine reform with the medieval Missal and with the Gregorian Sacramentary, the difference is by no means fundamental. Ours is richer and more varied in the proper of the

Saints, but the stational Masses of the Sunday, of Advent, of Lent, and of the saints' days comprised in the Sacramentary of St Gregory are, with few exceptions, almost identical. We can, therefore, say that our eucharistic codex, taking into account the natural development continued through several centuries of existence, is the same in substance as that used by the great doctors of the Church in the Middle Ages, under the name of Gregory the Great.

We have said that it is in substance the same, but by this we do not mean that there is an absolute identity. Alterations and additions have been made, the greater number of them before the time of the Council of Trent; but, happily, the severe standard of liturgical reform which inspired the Popes of the latter half of the sixteenth century purified the Roman Missal of many additions, tropes, sequences, collects and Masses of the later Middle Ages, which detracted from the harmony of the marvellous liturgical structure erected by the Popes who ruled from the fourth to the eighth century. The Masses of the *auxiliatorum* were suppressed, together with those for the judgements of God, as also the custom of celebrating on Sundays the Mass *de Trinitate* in place of the proper of the Sunday. There were further abolished the festivals of fools, of asses, etc., and other grotesque abuses which had crept into the sanctuary. Some valuable material, however, which might perhaps have been reintroduced was omitted, owing, no doubt, to the want of documents at the disposal of the liturgists of the sixteenth century. Thus among the gaps in the Missal of to-day we deplore the suppression of the various prefaces in which both the Leonine and Gregorian Sacramentaries were so rich; so much so that each feast in the year, and each Sunday of special importance, had its own proper preface. The Middle Ages, in order to economize time and paper, had too readily cast away all this Roman accumulation, barely retaining some ten or twelve special prefaces for Lent, Easter, Pentecost, etc., while the *praefatio communis* still in daily use sufficed for all other occasions.

May we be permitted to hope that in some future revision of the Missal the supreme authority will restore to its former place of honour this venerable and beautiful portion of the liturgical treasure bequeathed to us by SS Leo, Gelasius, and Gregory the Great? It is true that primitive Roman tradition showed itself somewhat adverse from admitting into the actual *Canon Missae* all those changing and variable portions which found so much favour with the Gallican mind; but it is certain that the tradition of the prefaces proper to the feast dates back in Rome at least as far as the time of Leo I.

CHAPTER II

CHRISTIAN INITIATION

BAPTISM is not merely a form by which one is admitted to the fellowship of the faithful, but is the sacrament which contains and confers on the soul supernatural life itself. Wherefore, whatever may be the degree of holiness to which that soul is eventually raised by God, whatever spiritual gifts may afterwards adorn it, these graces will only develop and confirm in it the pristine sanctity infused by the sacrament of Baptism. As the tree is virtually contained in the seed, so Baptism is the very life of the Christian soul. It is the chaste and fruitful womb of holy Mother Church, in which she conceives and brings forth for Christ all the peoples of the earth. A clear understanding of this is necessary in order to raise our minds to the sublime ideal which inspired the rites that we are about to describe. By grasping their spiritual sense we shall be better able to comprehend the mind of those men of true genius, those builders of an earlier age, who raised the grand baptisteries of the Lateran, of Ravenna, Pisa, Florence, Siena and many other cities of Italy.

From the very earliest dawn of Christianity initiation into the Faith has comprised two distinct rites—Baptism and the infusion of the Holy Spirit through the laying on of hands. The administration of the latter sacrament was ordinarily reserved to the Apostles and to the heads of the Christian communities, whereas Baptism could be conferred by a deacon or even by one of the laity.

Our earliest sources of information do not describe, it is true, the discipline of the catechumens as we find it fully practised in the third century, but the very nature of things leads us to suppose that, even from the beginning, there must have been a special rule for those who, whilst preparing for Christian Baptism, could not yet be partakers of the holy sacraments. A period of instruction must certainly have preceded such a final conversion as the ancients justly defined Baptism to be; and, as the Διδαχή attests, fasting and confession of sins accompanied the catechetical instruction from the very first.

St Justin is our most authoritative witness to the baptismal rites as they were performed about the year 150, when he wrote his first *Apologia*. There we find the profession of

faith : μετὰ τὸ οὕτως, λοῦσαι τὸν πεπεισμένον καὶ συγκατατεθειμέ-
νον;[1] the special prayers recited publicly by the whole
assembly, and the fasting and confession which preceded the
sacramental immersion. (Εὔχεσθαι τε καὶ αἰτεῖν νηστεύοντες
παρά τοῦ θεοῦ προημαρτημένων ἄφεσιν διδάσκονται, ἡμῶν συνευχο-
μένων καὶ συννηστευόντων αὐτοῖς.)[2] As we find no trace of any
other public and solemn fast except that which took place
before Easter, we may be almost certain that from then
onwards the solemn administration of Baptism was reserved
for the Paschal season.   This rule was not, however, strictly
adhered to, as among the works of Hippolytus there is a
sermon attributed to him and addressed to those about to be
baptized "εἰς τα ἄγια θεοφάνεια," whence it would appear that,
in those very early days, even in Rome, according to Eastern
custom, solemn Baptism could be administered also at the
feast of the Epiphany.[3]   The form of prayer referred to by
St Justin has not been preserved, but, on the other hand, we
have many versions of the baptismal creed which catechumens had to recite publicly before going down into the
font.

Some writers have wished to see in the words with which
St Paul compares the Holy Spirit to an unction diffused in the
soul an allusion to the *Chrismatio* of Baptism, for which we
have no certain testimony earlier than the third century; but
more modern exegetes reject this materialistic interpretation
of the Pauline text, as also a similar gloss on a passage from
Theophilus of Antioch (*circa* A.D. 180)—*Tu vero non vis ungi
oleo Dei? nos enim ideo Christiani vocamur, quod Dei oleo
ungamur.*[4]

By far the greater part of the information we possess
concerning the baptismal rites in Rome and in Carthage
at the time of Septimius Severus is undoubtedly derived
from Tertullian.   In a special treatise of his on Baptism he
describes in glowing colours, in his rude but vigorous African
style, the ceremonies of the Christian initiation, the minister,
the prayers, and the fasts preceding it; the solemn renunciation of Satan, the sacramental immersion, the anointing
with chrism, the imposition of the Bishop's hands, together
with the invocation of the Holy Ghost; the participation in
the eucharistic banquet, and the redemption of the cup of milk
and honey which brought the ceremony to a close.   In his
treatise *de Resurrectione* this prolific writer thus sums up the
baptismal ceremony : *Caro abluitur ut anima emaculetur;
caro ungitur ut anima consecretur; caro signatur ut et anima*

---

[1] *Apolog. I*, c. lxiii ; *P.G.* VI, col. 428.
[2] c. lxi, *P.G.* VI, col. 420.
[3] Ed. Achelis, pp. 257-58 (Leipzig 1897).
[4] *Lit. I, ad Autolycum* 12; *P.G.* IV, col. 1042.

*muniatur, caro manus impositione adumbratur, ut et anima
Spiritu illuminetur; caro Corpore et Sanguine Christi vescitur
ut et anima Deo saginetur.*[1]

The Canons of Hippolytus, whether they represent an
ancient disciplinary document of Rome, or whether, as seems
more probable, they belong to Alexandria and are of the
time of Bishop Dionysius, contain the most complete liturgical description of the rites of Baptism at the close of the
third century. The catechumen was to be presented to the
Bishop by persons who would vouch for the genuineness of
his intention, after which he was admitted to Confession;
then, having listened to the reading of a passage from the
Gospels suitable to the occasion, he made a public profession
of his desire for *Conversion.*[2] On Thursday in the great
Paschal week[3] the catechumens were allowed to bathe and
to take a meal, but during the two following days they had
to observe a strict fast, which lasted until after they had
received Baptism. An ecclesiastic—at Rome and in Africa
it was the exorcist—was specially entrusted with their
instruction.

The Paschal night having come, the Bishop laid his hands
on them, whilst reciting the last exorcisms, so that, Satan
being now driven out, their soul should henceforth acknowledge the supreme dominion of Christ. Kneeling at the feet
of the Bishop, the aspirants turned towards the East, the
region of light and the symbol of divine indwelling, and
promised always to obey the holy law of God. He then
breathed upon their faces and signed them with the sign of
the cross on the forehead, the lips, the ears, and the breast.
Next followed the solemn Paschal vigils, during which a
certain number of scriptural passages were read, with explanations, probably, by the Bishop or by the priests, and a
like number of collects recited. At length, when day was
about to break, the catechumens, laying aside their garments,
turned to the West to mark their renunciation of Satan.
Then, having been anointed with holy oil, as though the
supreme moment of their fight with the Evil One had come,
they descended full of faith into the holy font, showing thus
in symbol their death and burial with Christ himself, as
St Paul has so well explained to us. The Bishop then
questioned them in this manner : " Dost thou believe in God
the Father almighty?" " I do believe." " Dost thou believe

---

[1] c. viii, *P.L.* II, col. 806.

[2] Early monachism used this word in its pristine Christian signification, applying it to the religious state and the profession of a monk, in
so far as it implies the renewal of the promises made when a catechumen, and a return to the innocence of Baptism.

[3] Our Holy Week.

in Jesus, the Son of God?" "I do believe." "Dost thou believe in the Holy Ghost?" "I do believe." Then, after this threefold profession of faith, the sacred minister baptized them in the name of the blessed Trinity. On coming out of the water their bodies were again anointed by a priest with oil mixed with balm—*Chrismatio*. Then the Bishop laid his hands upon their heads, invoking the Holy Ghost, and making the sign of the cross on their foreheads—*Consignatio*. The holy sacrifice was then offered up, at which the neophytes were admitted for the first time to share in the sacred mysteries. *Corpus Christi*, proclaimed the Bishop as he gave into their hands the particle of consecrated bread, and then, testifying their faith anew in the sacramental presence of our Lord in the Eucharist, answered solemnly : *Amen. Sanguis Christi*, repeated the deacon as he brought to their lips the sacred chalice, and the neophytes again replied : *Amen*. After the Communion they were given a cup of milk and honey, to signify that henceforth they were citizens of the heavenly kingdom, that true Land of Promise flowing with milk and honey, of which prophetic mention is made in Holy Writ.

The baptismal rites of Jerusalem are known to us through the *Peregrinatio* of Egeria,[1] and the explanations of the mysteries attributed to St Cyril. At the beginning of Lent the candidates gave in their names to the Bishop, and if the inquiries made as to their manner of living proved satisfactory they were admitted to the instructions given every morning by the Bishop or by his delegate.

During Lent other clergy of lesser rank recited the exorcisms, and breathed upon the faces of the candidates; and three weeks before Easter they were taught the Creed—*Traditio symboli*—in order that they might be able to repeat it to the Bishop at the commencement of Holy Week.

The days commemorating the Passion of our Lord at Jerusalem were too much taken up with the contemplation of his sufferings to allow of the clergy devoting themselves in any special way to the catechumens. Therefore these were collected together in the porch of the baptistery only on the night preceding Easter Sunday, when the very suggestive rite of the renouncing of Satan, common to all liturgies, was to take place. Pointing with his forefinger towards the West, the region of darkness, the candidate said : "I renounce thee, O Satan, thee and thy worship." Then, pointing to the East, he recited the sacred symbol of the Faith. After laying aside his garments, the new Christian athlete was anointed all over with holy oil previously exor-

---

[1] Etheria.—Tr.

cized. He then went down into the font, where he received Baptism by a threefold immersion, followed at once by the anointing with chrism as in the Canons of Hippolytus.[1] The ceremony ended with the celebration of the eucharistic Sacrifice on Golgotha in the Basilica of the *Martyrium,* when the neophytes were admitted for the first time to the holy table.[2]

The baptismal rite in use in the Western Churches of Rome and Milan, of Gaul, and of Spain, agrees in its main features with that of the Eastern Churches. The initiation of the catechumen comprised three distinct ceremonies—the exorcism, the breathing on the face and the anointing. In Spain the anointing of the body followed immediately upon the first exorcism, whilst at Milan and in Rome it was deferred until the actual moment of Baptism. This diversity of custom perturbed the Bishops of Gaul for a time, so they consulted the Holy See on this question towards the year 400. Rome replied that it was immaterial on which day the anointing was administered as long as it took place after the third scrutiny.

We know too little about the order and number of these scrutinies or examinations, the prayers preparatory to which are recorded in the Gallican Missal. On the other hand, we possess a good deal of information concerning the ceremony of the *traditio symboli* on the Sunday before Easter, when it was the custom in France to bless the holy oils—*dies unctionis.* On Maundy Thursday the catechumens recited the Creed in the presence of the Bishop, but they did not then make their renunciation of Satan, as was done in the Roman rite. This was put off until the vigil of Easter.

Notwithstanding these slight differences, the baptismal rite of the Gallican Church is identical in all its essential features with that of Rome. After the exorcism of the water, without further anointing, except at Milan, the candidates proceeded to their threefold immersion in the font. On emerging from the water, they were led before the Bishop, who anointed them on the head with chrism, clothed them in a white tunic, and, at Milan and in Gaul, also washed their feet. This last rite, inspired no doubt by that passage in the Gospel where our Lord washes the feet of Peter, saying, *He that is washed needeth not but to wash his feet, for he is clean wholly,* was customary also in Spain until it was abolished by the forty-eighth canon of the Council of Elvira.

The baptismal ceremonies in Rome were not less grand in any way than those of the other liturgies. The supreme Power of the Keys, the memory of the Baptism of those early

---

[1] Cf. *Canones Hippolyti* in Duchesne, *Christian Worship,* p. 533.
[2] Duchesne, *op. cit.,* p. 512.

Roman Christians conferred by the Apostles Peter and Paul, the historical traditions attached to the ancient catacombs of the Via Nomentana, where was preserved the memory of the chair and font used by St Peter; all these things contributed to give a peculiar solemnity to the rite of Baptism when administered in that privileged spot, which still retains a special atmosphere of devotion unlike any other.

When the custom of baptizing at the Epiphany fell into disuse, Easter and Pentecost were the only days on which Baptism was solemnly administered at Rome. It took place at Easter because the font, according to St Paul, symbolizes the tomb into which the soul descends with the crucified Christ, in order to rise again therefrom to a new life of grace; and at Pentecost because the coming down of the Holy Ghost upon the Apostles represents our *consignatio* and the infusion of the Holy Spirit into the Christian soul. The anointing with chrism was, in fact, a sacramental rite intimately connected with that of Baptism, of which it was considered to be the natural complement—*confirmatio sacramenti.* When, later on, under Eastern influence, the Churches of Spain and Sicily attempted to revive the usage of administering Baptism at the Epiphany, the Popes did not fail to condemn this practice as constituting in their eyes a dangerous innovation in the Roman Patriarchate.

As in the East, so also in the Eternal City, those catechumens who were desirous of completing their initiation presented themselves at the beginning of Lent to the Pope, in order to be inscribed in the list of the *electi* or *competentes,* and undertook from that moment to follow earnestly the course of instruction prepared for them. There were, however, many in those days, especially among the nobility, who preferred to postpone the receiving of Baptism until that moment when the near approach of death should render its obligations less onerous and its privileges more certain. The rite of initiation to the order of catechumens—*ordo ad christianum faciendum*—was very simple in Rome, consisting as it did of the breathing on the face of the candidate by the priest, of an exorcism, of the signing of the cross on the forehead, and of the placing of a grain of salt on the lips. Then followed during Lent the long catechetical preparation of the *electi,* with at least three scrutinies, and a very complicated but imposing order of rites and instructions.

According to the *Ordines Romani* of the seventh century, there were seven scrutinies, none of which took place on Sundays; but from the Gelasian Sacramentary, from a record of the Chapter at Naples[1] and from a question put by

---

[1] *Anecd. Mareds.*, pp. 427, 428.

Senarius, *vir illustris,* to the Roman deacon John,[1] we gather
that in the fourth century there were only three scrutinies,
and that these were, as a matter of fact, held on the Sunday
itself.

Duchesne observes that in the seventh century these
scrutinies must have lost the greater part of their early
significance, since Baptism was then administered only to
infants. He is, therefore, at a loss to understand how it was
that the rite, instead of becoming shortened, continued to
develop in such an elaborate manner that the number of the
scrutinies was doubled, thus making the ceremony still more
complicated. This constitutes a problem which that learned
liturgist prefers to leave unsolved.[2] To us, however, this
development of the baptismal liturgy in the seventh century
seems quite natural. The Baptism of adults had become by
that time a mere memory, and survived in the Liturgy only
as a ceremony. Having passed out of the region of actuality
into that of symbolism, the rite developed therein exceedingly. This development may be compared to that which
we notice in the Lenten liturgy of the seventh and eighth
centuries, when Gregory I and Gregory II introduced the
three Sundays in preparation for Lent, the four Stations in
Quinquagesima week, those of the Thursdays in Lent, and
of the Sundays following the great vigils of the Saturdays
in Ember week, celebrated at St Peter's (*dominica vacat*).

Of the seven great scrutinies of the *Ordo Romanus VII,*
four are, in fact, only a repetition of the first *ante auris
aperitionem,* showing that this one, too, as the others, had
been introduced at a later date for a symbolical purpose,
merely in order to bring the number of the scrutinies up to
that of the seven gifts of the Holy Ghost.[3] The first
examination began on the Wednesday of the third week in
Lent, when, about the hour of Terce, an acolyte, after calling
over the names of the catechumens, arranged the youths on
the right hand and the maidens on the left. A priest then
passed along the ranks and signed them with the sign of the
cross on their foreheads, laid his hands upon them, and
placed salt, which had been previously blessed, on their lips,
in order to symbolize the doctrine of the new knowledge
which was to give, as it were, a supernatural savour to their
future lives. At the beginning of the Mass the catechumens
withdrew; but after the first collect the deacon called them
once more before the Bishop, who said to them: *Orate,
electi, flectite genua.* They then knelt in prayer, and after
a short pause the prelate continued: *Levate, complete orna-*

---

[1] *Joannis Diaconi Epist. ad Senarium, P.L.* LIX, p. 401.
[2] *op. cit.,* p. 305.
[3] *Ord. Rom. VII; P.L.* LXXXVII, col. 998.

tionem vestram, et dicite: Amen. The godfathers and god-
mothers now signed their future godchildren once more on
the forehead with the sign of the cross; next came three
other acolytes for the recitation of the exorcisms, which
were accompanied by the imposition of hands; and lastly a
priest repeated the same rite and recited a final prayer. The
first Christian initiation was now accomplished. After a
reading from Ezechiel—*Haec dicit Dominus: effundam super
vos aquam*—the candidates were formally dismissed; but at
the Offertory the godparents made the oblations on their
behalf, causing their names to be inscribed on the diptychs
of those who gave offerings.

The same rites were repeated on the following Saturday,
but the third scrutiny in the following week—*in aperitione
aurium*—had special importance, for then the disciplinary
veil guarding the mysteries was carefully removed, so that
the catechumens might be initiated into the secrets of the
sons of God, and might come to the full knowledge of the
holy Gospel, of the Creed, and of the Lord's Prayer. Up to
that time they had learnt only the outlines of the Gospel
teaching; but now Christ, by means of his Church, presents
to them the tables of the new law of love: *Dominus legem
dat.* These words are inscribed in the open book held by the
figure of the Saviour seated in majesty on his throne in the
apse of many an ancient Roman basilica; and it is more than
probable that this solemn and triumphal representation of the
divine Lawgiver is intended to commemorate the touching
ceremony of the Christian initiation *in aperitione auris.*

After the singing of the Gradual, four deacons appeared
carrying the books of the Gospels, which they placed on the
four corners of the altar. A few verses were read from each
and a brief explanation given by the Bishop; then the
catechumens were taught the Creed and the Lord's Prayer.
Qua lingua confitentur Dominum nostrum Jesum Christum?
asked the Bishop; and two acolytes, each carrying in his
arms a little child, the one Byzantine and the other Roman,
recited in both languages the symbol of faith. The *Credo*
and *Pater* having been explained, the catechumens retired,
and the Mass continued as in the first scrutiny. The fourth,
fifth, and sixth examinations had no special importance, but
the seventh was held in the Lateran about the hour of Terce
on the morning of Holy Saturday. After the usual exorcisms
the priest touched with saliva the principal organs of the
senses of the catechumen, thus recalling the *Ephpheta* of the
Gospel narrative. The supreme conflict with the Evil One is
now about to begin. After the manner of athletes descending
into the arena, the candidates for Baptism lay aside their
garments and are anointed on the breast and on the

shoulders with blessed oil—*oleum eatechumenorum.* At Rome in the fourth century the renouncing of Satan and the profession of faith were repeated by the aspirants themselves as they stood on the ambo; in later times it was sufficient for a priest to recite the *Credo* in the name of all present. This profession of faith being completed, the candidates were dismissed until sunset, when the great Paschal vigil began.

The holy oils used in Baptism had been consecrated by the Pope on the preceding Thursday. On that day, before the Chrismal Mass—distinct in Rome both from that of the reconciliation of penitents and from the third *in Coena Domini*—the subdeacons had prepared in the sacristy two vases, the one of pure oil, the other of oil with an admixture of balm poured into it by the Pope himself. The rite of the blessing of the holy oils proceeded thus: Towards the end of the Canon of the Mass the faithful presented to the Pope their own little glass phials filled with oil for the anointing of the sick—*oleum infirmorum.* Of these he blessed a few, which were brought to the altar by the deacons; the others, placed by the people on the *podium* enclosing the sanctuary, were blessed at the same time by the Bishops and priests who celebrated with him on that day, and who recited together with him the prayers prescribed for the blessing of the holy oils. This first blessing being finished, the Mass was continued at the words of the canon *per quem haec omnia.* After the Communion of the Pope, and before the clergy received the holy Eucharist from his hands, the ministers brought to the papal throne the large vessels containing the chrism and the oil of the catechumens. The Pope breathed three times on the first, made the sign of the cross over it and recited a lengthy eucharistic prayer, *praefatio,* in which all the scriptural allusions to the *Chrismatio* were recorded, from the anointing of Aaron, of the kings of Juda, and of the prophets, down to that of the martyrs of the new dispensation who were anointed with the inward grace of the Paraclete. The blessing of the oil of catechumens was much less impressive, but it comprised the breathing, the signing of the cross, and the eucharistic prayer with the Preface.

Now that all was made ready for the Baptism, at the first dawning of the joyful day of the resurrection of the Lord, the catechumens prepared themselves to rise again with him, after having first descended into the symbolical tomb of the baptismal font. That night had been passed in reading the most striking passages from the Scriptures having reference to Baptism, each lesson being followed by a prayer; and, to break the monotony of the reading, the choir, from time to time, had sung some of the most beautiful from among their

many canticles.[1]   After the twelfth reading, the Pope and
the candidates, to the singing of the psalm *Sicut cervus,*
moved in procession to the baptistery, while the *Schola*
within the Basilica of the Lateran sang the Litany alternately
with the people, reciting first seven petitions, then five, and
lastly three, until such time as the Pope returned.

The ancient Lateran Baptistery still exists, though bare of
all that once adorned it.   We know, however, that a golden
lamp, in which burned a mixture of asbestos and balm, once
stood on a column of porphyry in the centre of the font.   On
one side was a silver group representing our Lord and
St John the Baptist with a lamb, from the feet of which
gushed forth a fountain of water, while seven other fountains
flowed from as many stags' heads arranged around the
interior of the piscina.

The Lateran Baptistery, however, is not the only one in
Rome, nor is it even the most ancient.   Besides that one *ad
nymphas beati Petri* which remained in use at least until the
fifth century, there was another very celebrated baptistery
erected by Pope Damasus near the Basilica of St Peter;
while a third one, probably for the use of the rural population,
was situated in the cemetery of Pontian in the Via Portuense.
Moreover, there was a baptistery at San Lorenzo in Damaso;
one also known under the title of Anastasia, another under
that of Marcellus; in fact, most of the urban parishes possessed their own baptistery.

The blessing of the water of Baptism, like the consecration
of the holy oils, inspired in Rome one of the most sublime
eucharistic prayers to be found in the whole Sacramentary.
The Pope first breathed on the water, as in the beginning the
Spirit of God hovered over chaos to infuse life into its depths;
then, in accordance with the *Ordines Romani* of the eighth
century, he repeatedly traced the sign of the cross over the
font and in the water, in which, after the ninth century, it
became the custom to dip the Paschal candle.   The blessing
being ended, a phial of perfumed chrism was poured into the
font.

When all was in readiness for the baptism, the archdeacon
presented to the Pope the candidates who, after the threefold
profession of faith, were immersed in the holy font while the
Pope pronounced the sacramental forms.   In order to
shorten the ceremony when the catechumens were numerous,
priests, deacons and acolytes all took off their shoes and went
down into the water to assist in the baptizing.   The Pope
after a while left the baptistery, and, entering the *consignatorium,* awaited the neophytes, to whom he administered the

---

[1] They were usually taken from the traditional collection of " odes,"
or scriptural canticles, reserved exclusively for the Office of Matins.

Consignatio, the first *Chrismatio,* on the head, being given immediately after Baptism by one of the priests. In consequence of the concession permitting priests to perform the baptismal anointing, this solemn *consignatio* by the Pope— in addition to the invocation of the Holy Ghost upon the neophytes—involved a second unction with chrism on the forehead, accompanied by the words: *In nomine Patris et Filii et Spiritus Sancti.* With this the *sacramentum regenerationis christianiae* was complete, and the Church had now only to associate the spiritual resurrection of her children with the bodily resurrection of the Lord by celebrating the universal feast, the *Pascha nostrum,* in the joy of the Holy Ghost. When, therefore, the newly baptized Christians, clothed in white garments, returned in procession to the Lateran Basilica, the solemn Paschal sacrifice at once commenced, at which the neophytes communicated for the first time. It was customary, moreover, up to the seventh century, to bless a draught of milk and honey for their consumption.

During all the seven days of Easter week the grand conception of the resurrection of the human race by means of holy Baptism dominated the whole liturgy. Each morning Mass was said expressly for the neophytes. In the evening, after Vespers in the Lateran, the procession returned *ad fontes*—that is, to the baptistery and to the *consignatorium,* to venerate those holy places which, next to the altar of their first Communion, would henceforth remain in the eyes of all the faithful of Rome as the sanctuaries of their redemption.

Out of consideration for the Byzantine colony, which at that time was very numerous, Greek canticles alternated with the Latin ones, and the whole Church seemed as if she wished, like a loving mother, to rock these newborn children of hers, Heaven's latest recruits, to the strains of her sweetest *melos,* as they visited during those first Easter days the great Roman sanctuaries of St Peter, St Paul and St Laurence. Thus they went ever surrounded by that same atmosphere of mystic enthusiasm which had inspired the Popes of old to enrich the Paschal liturgy with such profound and suggestive symbolic rites.

If the minds of those early generations—raised by the sacred rites to the full comprehension of those sublime words of St Peter, who called the neophytes *gens sancta, genus electum, regale sacerdotium,* clothed as it were in the white garment of the sanctity and merits of Christ the Redeemer— were penetrated by the theological teaching which pervades the ancient baptismal liturgy, we too should be inspired thereby to a high ideal of the dignity of our vocation, who, as Christians, have participated in the same baptism. *Una fides, unus Christus, unum baptisma,* whose waters are indeed poured forth upon the earth, but which spring *de praecordiis divinitatis,* from the very heart of God himself.

Some examples of ancient inscriptions taken from the Roman baptisteries will help us to realize more fully the supreme importance given in early Christian doctrine to the holy sacrament of Baptism, and to the symbolism connected therewith.

1. Inscription by Sixtus III on the architrave of the Lateran Baptistery (432-440):

> Gens sacranda polis hic semine nascitur almo,
>   quam foecundatis Spiritus edit aquis.
> Virgineo foetu genitrix Ecclesia natos
>   quos, spirante Deo, concipit, amne parit.
> Coelorum regnum sperate, hoc fonte renati
>   non recipit felix vita semel genitos.
> Fons hic est vitae, qui totum diluit orbem,
>   sumens de Christi vulnere principium.
> Mergere, peccator, sacro purgande fluento;
>   quem veterem accipiet proferet unda novum.
> Insons esse volens, isto mundare lavacro,
>   seu patrio premeris crimine, seu proprio.
> Nulla renascentum est distantia, quos facit unum
>   unus fons, unus Spiritus, una fides.
> Nec numerus quemquam scelerum, nec forma suorum
>   terreat, hoc natus flumine sanctus erit.

This may be translated as follows :

In this spot a holy race destined to Heaven is born begotten by the Spirit who gives life to these waters. Here Mother Church brings forth her pure offspring, conceived by the virtue of the Holy Ghost.

O ye who have been born again in this fount, aspire to the heavenly kingdom ! For its bliss is not for those who live for the world alone. This is the living spring which refreshes all the earth, whose source is in the Wounds of Christ. Come, O sinner, desirous of washing away the stains of sin, bathe thyself in this sacred stream ! The water that receives thee grown old will restore the innocence of thy former youth. O thou who longest for purity, whether weighed down by original sin or thine own wrongdoing, bathe in this font and be made clean !

All who receive life here are made equal by one Baptism, one Spirit, one Faith. Let neither the guilt nor the number of thy sins appal thee—he who is born again in these waters shall surely be holy.

2. Inscription placed in the Baptistery of the Apostles, probably in the Vatican :

> Sumite perpetuam sancto de gurgite vitam;
>   Cursus hic fidei, mors ubi sola perit.
> Roborat hic animos divino fonte lavacrum,
>   et dum membra madent, mens solidatur aquis.
> Auxit apostolicae geminatum sedis honorem
>   Christus, et ad coelos hanc dedit esse viam;
> Nam cui siderei commisit limina regni,
>   Hic habet in templis altera claustra poli.

Draw from this holy fount life eternal. Here faith comes forth and death alone is vanquished. The stream which flows from Heaven strengthens the heart, and whilst it bathes the limbs, confirms the mind. Christ gave a double glory to the Apostolic See, permitting that this should be the way to eternal bliss, so that he to whom were entrusted the keys of the heavenly kingdom should in this sanctuary also be guardian of a second Gate of Life.[1]

3. Inscription placed in the *Consignatorium,* probably in the Vatican Baptistery, where stood the chair of wood said to be that of St Peter :

> Istic insontes coelesti flumine lotas,
> pastoris summi dextera signat oves.
> Huc undis generate veni, quo Sanctus ad unum
> Spiritus ut capias te sua dona vocat.
> Tu, cruce suscepta, mundi vitare procellas
> disce, magis monitus hac ratione loci.

Here the innocent lambs, washed clean in the heavenly fount, are signed by the right hand of the Chief Shepherd. Hasten hither, O newly born in the waters of Life! The Holy Spirit calls thee to become one of a blessed family and to rejoice in his gifts. Having received on thy forehead the sign of the cross, do thou learn to flee the dangers of the world, keeping thyself in special control by the memories of this place.[2]

4. In the Baptistery of the Basilica of San Lorenzo in Damaso :

> Iste salutaris fons continet inclitus undas
> et solet humanum purificare luem.
> Munia sacrati quae sint vis scire liquoris :
> dant regeneratricem flumina sancta fidem.
> Ablue fonte sacro veteris contagia vitae,
> o nimium felix, vive renatus aqua.
> Hunc fontem quicumque petit, terrena relinquit,
> subicit et pedibus coeca ministeria.

---

[1] The meaning of this inscription is not altogether clear. The two-fold honour conferred on the Apostolic See is evidently the evangelizing, with the martyrdom and burial places, of the two Princes of the Apostles. The additional privilege, therefore, granted to the Roman Church would be the circumstance that the holder of the keys of heaven guards a second door of paradise in his own baptistery. In order, however, that this latter privilege may constitute a special glory for the Apostolic See, it is not sufficient that baptism should open to everyone the gate of heaven—all other churches had their baptistery too—but it is further necessary that this baptism should have special historical connection with the Apostle Peter. Either he himself in-augurated the baptistery, if the inscription refers to the cemetery *ad nymphas beati Petri ubi baptizabat,* or he consecrated it by his martyrdom ; or again because his successors, the Popes, make use of it in his name, all which circumstances are true of the baptistery of St Damasus in the Vatican.

[2] To what circumstances does this refer? The same problem arises with regard to this as in the case of the former inscription, of which this one is, as it were, the continuation. *Monitus hac ratione loci—* that is, by the very spot on which St Peter was crucified.

From this noble source a health-giving river flows, cleansing every human stain. Wouldst thou know the virtue of these holy waters? Behold, through faith art thou born again. Wash away the sins of thy past life at this holy spring. O happy one, born to a new life through these waters, live in gladness! Who seeks this fount abandons earthly thoughts and tramples underfoot the servitude of darkness.

5. In the Roman Baptistery of the *Titulus Anastasiae*:

> Qui peccatorum sordes abolere priorum,
>   Terrenisque optas maculis absolvere vitam,
> Huc ades ad Christi fontem sacrumque liquorem,
>   Corpus ubi ac mentes pariter sensusque lavantur,
> Aeternumque datur casto baptismate munus.
>   Hanc autem fidei sedem construxit ab imis
> Militiae clarus titulis aulaeque fidelis
>   Romanaeque urbis praefectus Longinianus.[1]

Thou who seekest to wash away the pollution of thy sins, and to cleanse thy life from every earthly stain, draw near to the fount of Christ, to this sacred stream in which the soul with all its powers is bathed together with the body, and a pure baptism is rewarded by eternal gain.

Longinianus, prefect of the Eternal City, high in military rank, and faithful adherent of the Imperial House, raised from its foundation this holy shrine.

---

[1] Flavius Macrobius Longinianus was prefect of Rome in 403.

CHAPTER III

ECCLESIASTICAL PRAYER IN THE EARLY CHURCH

THE custom of the synagogue, confirmed by the example of the prophets and Apostles,[1] led the first Christians to pray at dawn, at noon, and at sunset, and occasionally also at night,[2] whether in order to honour the blessed Trinity by a daily threefold praise, or perhaps to consecrate the entire day to God by dedicating to him the three chief periods into which it is commonly divided. In later days theology wished to give, in addition to these ascetic reasons, a more dogmatic meaning to this pious custom by pointing out that, as the constant presence of the Blessed Sacrament preserved always upon the altar adds to the unbloody sacrifice of the Mass a sense of continuity, so the *laus perennis* unites the Church closely to the divine Victim who is in heaven *semper vivens ad interpellandum pro nobis*.[3]

The eucharistic Agape, celebrated at sunset on Saturday and carried on well into the night,[4] was the starting-point of the primitive Christian liturgy. From this soon followed the substitution of Sunday for Saturday as the weekly holy day, and the institution of that most ancient of all liturgical rites, the Vigil of the Sunday Feast. With the exception of these sacramental rites, the Church in Jerusalem remained attached, for some time longer, to the ceremonies and prayers of the synagogue,[5] until after the destruction of the Temple, when the faithful of Ælia Capitolina, on their return from Pella, felt themselves to be wholly freed from the yoke of the Israelitish Law, and in exactly the same position as the faithful of Antioch and other churches founded by St Paul.

In spreading the Gospel among the Gentiles, the Apostles had reduced to a minimum the obligations of the new religion. The Council of Jerusalem and the Epistles of St Paul enlighten us sufficiently[6] as regards the general principles of Christian conduct and their application to the innumerable exceptional cases to which contact with idolaters gave rise, whilst the Διδαχή furnishes even to-day the most abundant source from which we derive our knowledge of the ceremonies of those very early times.

---

[1] Dan. vi, 10; Acts ii, 15; x, 9; xvi, 25.
[2] Psalm cxviii. [3] Heb. vii, 25. [4] Acts xx, 7 *sq.*
[5] Acts ii, 42; v, 42. [6] Acts xv, i *sq.*; Gal. ii *sq.*

In this we find that two days of fasting in the week are counselled—the Wednesday and the Friday.[1] The Lord's Prayer and the Doxology are to be recited three times a day.[2] Sunday is especially set aside for the eucharistic synaxis, but the faithful are exhorted to meet together and to keep vigil even more frequently.[3] The whole work, in fact, evidences the widest divergence from the spirit of the synagogue as dominated by the Pharisees.

Besides the Διδαχή and its obscure indications of a form of prayer distinct from the Mass which the faithful were wont to recite at certain fixed hours, St Clement,[4] St Ignatius[5] and Pliny in his letter to Trajan, all speak of public prayers apart from the eucharistic sacrifice as ordained by the Apostles. There is, further, an allusion to the above-mentioned prayer in the first Epistle of St Paul to Timothy,[6] where the terminology used by the Apostle is that which the Hebrews adopted to distinguish the different parts of their daily prayer.

On certain days two kinds of meetings were held, the one at night devoted to prayer, the other at close of day for the celebration of the Agape. The ignorant pagan commonly accused the Christians of eating human flesh, but the apostates who gave information to the Governor of Bithynia were honest enough to bear willing testimony to the perfect morality of that feast, so that the *cibum promiscuum tamen et innoxium* of Pliny[7] not only contains no allusion to the eucharistic bread, but proves, on the contrary, that the Agape, in those places where its use continued, was already completely separate from the sacrificial rite of the Mass.

We have already noted Justin's detailed description of this nocturnal meeting in his first *Apologia.* On Sunday at dawn the faithful of the countryside and the various parts of the town all came together in an appointed place, where the reading of the Scriptures, the chanting of prayers, and the ardent words of the Bishop prepared their souls for a worthy reception of the holy Sacrament, whilst the deacons carried forth the Bread of Life to those few who were prevented from being present. Here the *Vigilia dominicalis,* as in the time of St Paul, consists in the celebration of Mass only,[8] whereas with Hermas the history of the Liturgy advances another step. Besides the Sunday observance, other days

---

[1] Διδαχή c. viii.   [2] *op. cit.,* c. xiv.
[3] *op. cit.,* c. xvi.   [4] Clem., *Ep. ad Cor.,* xl, xlii.
[5] Ignat., *Ep. ad Ephes,* xiii.   [6] c. ii, 1-2.
[7] Plinii *Epist. ad Traianum* X, xcvii. The text according to some critics is not altogether trustworthy, but the arguments which they produce do not appear to establish the apocryphal character of the letter.
[8] *Apolog.* I, lxvii ; *P.G.* VI, p. 427.

were set apart for prayer and fasting (*statio*).[1] Although from the text of the *Pastor* the *statio* would appear to be a matter of private devotion only; still, by comparing the words of Hermas with the testimony of Tertullian and of St Cyprian, we come to the conclusion that, although it was not obligatory, it was of a public character, beginning like the vigil before the Sunday at dawn,[2] and lasting until None, when the fast ended. During those early days of Christianity the Paschal *Vigilia* alone had the privilege of being obligatory upon all the faithful, and of taking up the whole of the night, whereas the other vigils were usually left to the piety of the people and began only towards dawn.

Gradually, as the Church extended her conquests, and as the light of theology revealed more and more to her children that *sublimitas et profundum* which the Apostle contemplated in our Lord, it naturally followed that this clearer knowledge or *gnosis* was reflected in the Liturgy. In the second century other feasts besides that of Easter began to be kept in honour of the mysteries of our Redemption, Good Friday, Pentecost and the Ascension.[3] The birthdays of the martyrs[4] were celebrated; nocturnal vigils were multiplied, and private prayer three times a day was no longer enough to satisfy the devotion of the faithful. Terce and None were, therefore, kept distinct from morning and evening prayer; in Christian households psalms were sung in common, and the ancient chant, being considered too simple, was already adorned with the harmonies of the responsorial Alleluia.

Clement of Alexandria often speaks of prayer at fixed hours; he also draws attention to the nocturnal vigil; but from the context it would appear that he considered these as purely private acts of piety, only practised by the more devout.[5]

Tertullian is the most prolific and talented author of his day. In his various works, apologetic, ascetical, and polemic, besides giving evidence of vast learning—unlike Justin or Clement—he shows himself familiar with the ecclesiastical traditions, not only of Carthage, but of Rome and the other churches of Italy, Africa and Greece. After his separation from the Catholics, with whom he disagreed on matters almost entirely of discipline, he often found himself,

---

[1] *Similit.* V.: τί ὀρθρινὸς ὧδε ἐλήλυθας; ὅτι φημί, κύριε, στατίωνα ἔκω. Edit. A. Hilgenfeld, Leipzig 1866, p. 84.

[2] Hermas, *id.*, ὀρθρινός.

[3] Pentecost is mentioned by St Paul (1 Cor. xvi, 8). *Cf.* Acts xiii, 2. Tertullian affirms that in his time Baptism was administered on that day (*De Baptismo*, c. xix; *P.L.* I, 1331). *Cf.* P. de Meester, *L'Ascensione del Signore*, in *Rassegna Gregoriana*, May 1902, pp. 76-77.

[4] *Cf.* S. Baümer, *Hist. du Bréviaire*, Paris 1905, pp. 77 *sq.*

[5] *op. cit.*, pp. 62-64.

by the position he had adopted, forced into opposition to their
rites and usages. Hence it is that his writings contain so
much information concerning ecclesiastical discipline in the
third century.

Besides the Easter παννυχίς,[1] *the nocturnae convocationes*[2]
often brought the faithful together to watch and pray,
especially during the night preceding the Sundays and the
festivals of the martyrs, as well as in times of persecution,[3]
when it was not possible for them to assemble in the daytime.
There existed as yet no law which should compel Christians
to pray at fixed hours,[4] therefore assisting at the *stationes,*
where[5] the offering of the divine Sacrifice at the commencement of the hour of None put an end to *the semi-jejunium,*[6]
was regarded as a pious custom, of counsel only. Later,
when Tertullian had joined the Montanists, these devout
practices, which were in no sense obligatory, became the
subject of bitter contention on the part of that learned but
scathing teacher, who wished to see them universally en-
forced, and considered it extremely lax not to prolong the
fast beyond the hour of None.[7] Even then there were some
Christians who, according to ancient custom, kept the
stations privately, and did not assist at the Mass. Others
considered the Kiss of Peace unsuitable on such days; while
some, in order to lengthen the period of fasting, even
abstained from receiving Holy Communion until quite late in
the day.

The stational prayers alone were recited kneeling,[8] this
symbol of penitence being especially forbidden during the
Paschal season and on Sundays, although Tertullian con-
cedes that everyone might kneel at morning prayers if he
wished to do so; from which we infer that these, at least,
were said privately in the home.

Morning and evening prayers, he says, are so generally
in use as to be almost obligatory (*legitimatae orationes*);[9]
but, besides these, the habit of sanctifying the hours of
Terce, Sext and None by the singing of psalms is right and
proper, as these hours call to mind the blessed Trinity, and
also mark the divisions of the secular day.[10]

Tertullian remarks also on the various liturgical abuses
which he considers he ought to combat sharply. There were
some persons who were causing scandal in church because
they did not kneel on Saturdays;[11] others went to the *statio*

[1] *Ad uxorem* II, c. iv; *P.L.* I, 1407. [2] *l.c.*
[3] *De fuga,* xiv; *P.L.* II, 141.
[4] *De oratione,* xxiii; *P.L.* I, 1299.
[5] *op. cit.,* c. xix, p. 1287.
[6] *De jejun.,* x; *P.L.* II, 1017. [7] *op. cit.,* x, pp. 1017 *sq.*
[8] *De oratione,* xxiii, 1298-99. [9] *De oratione,* xxviii, 1304.
[10] *op. cit.,* xxviii, 300. [11] *op. cit.,* xxiii, 1298.

in their oldest clothes.[1] Some threw off their cloaks during prayer, after the manner of the pagans, whilst others sat down as soon as the prayer was over,[2] as though the act of praying for some time with arms raised and extended in the form of a cross had utterly exhausted them. Although Tertullian writes so fully on the liturgical usages of his time, yet he never mentions that the prayers used at various hours of the day were said publicly in church. Indeed, the persecution of the year 202 had already begun; the hierarchy was dispersed, and the faithful were obliged to bribe the agents of the police to ignore the rare occasions when it was possible for them to meet for worship under cover of darkness. On such occasions as these the Mass regained its original place—viz., at the conclusion of the night vigil.

Unlike Justin, who describes the ceremonies of the eucharistic sacrifice, Tertullian dilates on the simplicity of the Christian " love-feasts."[3] These charitable repasts, preceded and followed by prayer, were extremely frugal in character, and were especially prepared for the poor; for in Rome, at Carthage and Alexandria, wherever, in fact, there were to be found several thousands of Christians, one common table could not suffice for all the faithful. The religious spirit of the Christians made these intimate and cordial meetings an opportunity for exercising their musical and poetic talents by reciting poems and singing psalms composed for the occasion (*in medio canere . . . de proprio ingenio*). This, however, is not the only reference to music contained in the works of Tertullian. He also tells us that the more zealous were accustomed even then to insert the Alleluia in their private prayers,[4] and that, when they assembled together, they preferred the responsorial psalms to those *in directum*.

Clement of Alexandria had already laid down rules on the matter in his *Stromata*, allowing, indeed, such chants with responsorial hemistichs (ἀκροστίχια ὑποψάλλειν), but pointing out at the same time that the chant should merely embellish the psalmody, and avoid for that reason the chromatic tones, τὰς χρωματικάς ἁρμονιάς.[5]

Whilst in his *De anima* Tertullian speaks of the psalmody which followed the scriptural lesson[6] at Mass, in his *Apologeticus*—with reference rather to the Agape—he says, speak-

---

[1] *op. cit.*, xviii, 1280-1.   [2] *op. cit.*, xvi, 1375.

[3] *Apol.*, xxxix; *P.L.* I, 538 *sq.*

[4] *De oratione*, xxviii, 1302.

[5] *Stromata* I, i; *P.G.* VIII, 708; *Paedag.* II, c. iv; *P.G.* XIII, 445. *Cf.* also de Nourry's notes in *P.G.* IX, 469, n. 84.

[6] *De anima*, c. ix; *P.L.* II, 701. The text is important, especially for its mention of the litany which always followed the homily in the Mass. *Scripturae leguntur*, aut *psalmi canuntur*, aut *adlocutiones proferuntur* aut *petitiones delegantur*.

ing generally : *Fidem sanctis vocibus pascimus*.[1] We know, however, from Justin that the consecratory anaphora also was modulated upon definite inflexions of the voice, intended to express the emotion of the priest while performing that holy rite.[2]

Origen, ever unyielding, seems, with his spirit of pure devotion, to attach very slight importance to the traditional prayers of Terce, Sext and None. It is true that he speaks of prayers (τὰς προσταχθεῖσας τε εὐχάς)[3] as appointed for these hours of the day, but the ideal which he desires for his gnostic (ascete) is that of prayer far more exalted and continuous than that established by tradition. There is a close resemblance to Tertullian in the discipline embodied in the *Canones Hippolyti*, that document of doubtful origin and much controverted authorship.[4] Here we find the night vigils to be neither daily nor obligatory; the liturgical hours of Terce, Sext and None are celebrated in church on days when the Station is held, whilst on other days the faithful are counselled at least to consecrate them in their homes by private prayer; the same being done in the case of night devotions. The evening or Vesper prayer bears the same private character, except, perhaps, on the evening of Saturday, when it was joined to the Agape and to the prayer of the *Lucerna*[5] which ushered in the vigil of the Sunday. The possible absence of the bishop or the priest from the Agape is foreseen and provided for; it would in such a case be the deacon's duty to distribute the portions and to pronounce the various formulas of the blessing.

St Cyprian, alluding to the original hours set aside for prayer according to Hebrew tradition, observes that *orandi nunc et spatia et sacramenta creverunt* . . . and speaks of morning and evening prayers in honour of Christ risen from the dead and become the Light of the World.[6] He repeatedly insists on the night prayer,[7] and his very insistence would induce us to believe that, especially during the period of persecution mentioned above, there was no strict ecclesiastical law on the subject. During the night preceding St Cyprian's martyrdom the faithful of Carthage watched before the procurator's house where he was kept under arrest, and the deacon Pontius, in narrating the circumstance, points out very touchingly that the people wished by this vigil to pay him in advance, as it were, the honour due to a martyr on his natal day.

---

[1] *Apolog.*, xxxix, p. 532.   [2] *Apolog. I*, lxvii ; *P.G.* VI, 427-29.
[3] *Contr. Celsum* VI, xli ; *P.G.* XI, 1359-60.
[4] *Cf.* Baümer, *op. cit.*, 69 *sq.*
[5] *Canon.*, 26, 27, 25. Baümer, *op. cit.*, 72.
[6] Cypr., *De Domin. Orat.*; *P.L.* IV, 542.
[7] *op. cit.*, xxix ; *P.L.* IV, 538 ; xxxvi, p. 543.

It is strange that the Council of Elvira, which laid down so many canons concerning the Liturgy and ecclesiastical discipline in Spain, is entirely silent on the subject of the divine Office; while Eusebius of Caesarea, in his *Commentary on the Psalms* (327-340) repeatedly speaks of psalm-singing as occurring both at morning and evening and during the night, as if it were a public and universal custom throughout the Church.[1] We must remember, however, that Eastern ecclesiastical traditions would take a long time to reach the far-off Iberian Peninsula, and that the silence of the Council of Elvira with regard to the divine Office can easily be explained if we admit the hypothesis that, owing to its recent introduction into Spain, abuses would hardly have had time to arise, and it was upon such that the Fathers of the Council were called together to give their judgement.

The *Canon Psalmorum,* attributed to Eusebius, but perhaps the work of some contemporary writer, is still more explicit. At Vespers, as in the Vigils, twelve psalms are to be sung, three at dawn and three others in the evening.[2] From this last document it would appear that the first period of arranging and fixing the form of liturgical prayer is now to close with the era of the persecutions. By this time the discipline of the Church has tended to become uniform, and there is need only of some great event or some powerful institution to seal the sacred rite with the lasting impress of worldwide stability. For the Latin peoples this was essentially the task of the Church of Rome alone.

* * * * *

The evidence we have just considered, though it bears witness to the custom of public prayer as distinct from the Eucharistic sacrifice, tells us very little indeed about the rites and elements of which such prayer was composed.

At the close of the Apostolic Age, when, during the pontificate of Clement, the *Pastor* of Hermas described his first visions, there were, besides the Sunday feast, days consecrated to fasting and prayer, the latter beginning very early in the morning and ending at the hour of None, after the offering of the holy sacrifice. Very probably this rite (borrowed from the synagogue, where the Pharisee of the Gospel fasted *bis in sabbato* each Monday and Thursday) was carried out on Wednesdays and Fridays, since the most ancient Roman lectionaries still show traces of the scriptural lessons assigned throughout the year to these stational Masses during the week. There was not, however, any

[1] *Comment. in psalm.* xci, *P.G.* XXIII, 1772; Ps. cxlii, *P.G.* XXIV, 9; Ps. lxiv, *P.G.* XXIII, p. 649.
[2] *P.G.* XXIII, 1395.

ecclesiastical law obliging the faithful to assist at them; on the contrary, when the Montanists were desirous of making the practice obligatory, the Church insistently defended its true characteristic of voluntary worship.

Let us now turn our attention to the liturgical heritage of Rome in the Middle Ages—at a period, that is, when the divine Office in the Eternal City had embodied such features as originated in Palestine and Egypt, where the monks had established a weekly *cursus* of psalmody, by day and by night. Here we find our attention arrested by another form of night prayer, still surviving in the Roman Missal, which on certain more solemn feasts regularly precedes the Mass of the Vigil celebrated at dawn. Since then we know that the most ancient form of the divine Office, its very nucleus, as it were, is certainly to be found in the παννυχίς of the Sunday or of the nights preceding the natal day of the more famous martyrs, and also that this *vigilia,* according to the testimony just cited from Pliny, Justin and Tertullian, terminated with holy Mass, we may well believe that in the *vigilia* of the Gelasian and Gregorian Sacramentaries the most ancient type of the Roman *vigilia* lies hidden.

Besides the *oratio lucernaris,* preserved only in the Easter Vigil, we find this rite ordinarily made up of scriptural lessons—twelve in the Gelasian Sacramentary and six in the Gregorian—interspersed with prophetic odes (*cantica*) and with the collects recited by the presiding ecclesiastic. Formerly these collects were preceded by the private prayers of the people, and these with their relative forms of appeal and various insertions were bound considerably to lengthen the service, which then concluded with the Litany, the purpose of which was to serve as an introduction to the solemn celebration of the Eucharist.

It is noteworthy that the psalmody of this παννυχίς is not taken from the psalms, but from the prophetic books, thus corresponding to those chants or morning odes so general throughout the East. A passage of the *Liber Pontificalis* referring to Pope Symmachus, who is believed to have inserted in the Sunday Mass the Great Doxology, placed elsewhere at the end of Matins, would cause us to see in this liturgical displacement a disordering of the ancient rite of the vigil; and this is all the more likely when we reflect that the Church of Rome would hardly have modelled her *cursus* on the Eastern type, had she still preserved her own in the fourth or fifth century.

In the life of St Melania the Younger there are to be found some valuable indications concerning the Roman Liturgy. Among other things, mention is made of the παννυχίς preceding the Feast of St Lawrence held in his basilica by the Tiber.

Here, too, we find the custom of daily Communion carried back to the time of SS Peter and Paul, together with the rite of giving Communion for the last time to those lying at the point of death. The passages describing the round of duties instituted by St Melania among her nuns at Jerusalem are much more doubtful. Some writers are desirous of seeing here a source of derivation of the Roman *cursus,* but it is much safer to presume that in an environment where, according to Cassian, almost every monastery boasted its own *cursus,* Melania, too, would have availed herself of that liberty of liturgical eclecticism which obtained in Palestine, in order to draw up a *canon* on her own account. This does not mean that the Roman tradition may not henceforth have had its own canon—we know, as a matter of fact, that in the Convent of Hippo Melania used to recite her own special canon at night, after the *cursus* of the nuns was finished— but simply that we must plead ignorance of any connection that there may be between Melania's liturgy and the Roman *cursus,* supposing such a *cursus* to have been in existence at that time.

The solemn rites of Easter; the Sunday; the Stations on Wednesday and Friday, and, in very early days, on Saturday also; the three weeks' fast preceding Easter; possibly the three Ember seasons, with Pentecost, Ascensiontide and Christmas (243-336); and after the second century some feasts of martyrs also; in these we have the original elements from which the ancient Roman Liturgy developed.

Although in the fourth century the people flocked in great numbers to the occasional night assemblies, we gather from a letter of Pelagius to Demetrias the Virgin, who was living in retirement in Rome, that towards the year 414 there existed as yet no fixed and ancient tradition, even among ecclesiastics, regarding the daily *cursus* (*Debet aliquis esse determinatus et constitutus horarum numerus. . . . Optimum est ergo huic operi matutinum deputari tempus . . . usque ad horam tertiam . . . in secretiori domus parte*);[1] so much so that Pelagius himself had to instruct Demetrias concerning it. From the way, too, in which St Jerome speaks in his letter to Læta, it may be concluded that the *cursus* was a matter left still to the private devotion of the faithful.

The early responsorial psalmody remained for a long time the only choral form used in Rome. Even after the antiphony of Syria had spread by way of Antioch, Constantinople, Neocæsarea, Milan, Carthage and Hippo throughout the entire Western world, the capital of Christendom re-

[1] *P.L.* XXXIII, 1115.

mained among the last to accept it. Thus the antiphonal melodies of the Gregorian Antiphonary indubitably betray a late origin as regards the Gradual, Tract, and Alleluiatic *jubilus*. If Augustine, moreover, in order to justify the introduction of antiphony in the Offertory and during the Holy Communion at Hippo, was obliged to appeal to the custom of Carthage, it is probable that the Roman practice was not on his side, since otherwise he would scarcely have failed to cite it. Indeed, even to-day the Mass for the Easter Vigil is wholly without antiphonal psalmody.

The deacons, therefore, for a long period acted as soloists in the Roman basilicas, several of them attaining to great skill in their art, and even finding opportunity therein to gratify the natural vanity of musicians. Pope Damasus sometimes praises their *placidum modulamen,* but the austere Jerome disapproves of their operatic trills, as also of their aromatic applications to the throat, in order to render the sound of the voice more affected.

To Pope Damasus, familiar from childhood with the archives of the Roman Church, poet of the catacombs and the martyrs, and patron of Jerome's biblical studies, ancient tradition points as the true founder of the daily *cursus* in Rome. It is true that his correspondence with St Jerome regarding the introduction of the *Graecorum psallentiam* into the Holy City is apocryphal—the παννυχίs of the Sunday had by this time fallen into disuse, *nec psallentium mos tenetur, nec hymni decus in ore nostro cognoscitur*[1]—but it was at any rate earlier than the sixth century, when these letters found their way (about 530) into the *Liber Pontificalis,* their witness being further confirmed by other important documents.

It was certainly Damasus who commissioned Jerome to correct the Psalter by the *Itala* text, and as the new version soon penetrated into the responsorial books of Rome, such a change as this could hardly take place without an entire revision of the whole heritage, liturgical and musical, of the Pontifical Church. Furthermore, according to the evidence of St Gregory I, it was Damasus, too, who first introduced into Rome the custom of singing the Alleluia in the Sunday Mass, as was done at Jerusalem : *Ut alleluia hic diceretur, de Jerosolymorum Ecclesia, e beati Hieronymi traditione, tempore beatae memoriae Damasi papae traditur tractum.*[2] Amid so many liturgical changes taking place in Rome, Damasus is not likely to have been reluctant to introduce there the ecclesiastical *cursus* also, at a time when, through the

[1] Cf. *Liber Pontif.*, ed. Duchesne, i, 215.
[2] *Ep. Greg. I*, ix, n. xii; *P.L.* LXXVII. col. 956.

initiative of St Ambrose at Milan, it was being adopted everywhere in Italy.

The *Graecorum psallentiam* of the apocryphal text of Damasus is, then, in agreement with the *canendi mos orientalium partium*[1] of St Augustine, when indicating the first beginnings of the Milanese Office; and Paulinus the priest, the biographer of Ambrose, in describing the very same rite, explains even more clearly the significance of the *Graecorum psallentiam* when he says that the saintly bishop instituted *hoc in tempore primum antiphonae, hymni ac vigiliae in Ecclesia.*[2] St Augustine, Paulinus, and the letters attributed to Damasus all agree, therefore, in describing the rapid spread of these rites of psalmody in the West. Although no single passage explicitly affirms it, yet a concurrence of reasons leads us to the conclusion that the introduction of the divine Office into Rome dates back, in all probability, to the end of the fourth century—that is, to the time of Pope Damasus and of St Jerome.

We may call to mind once more the tragic circumstances which caused Ambrose to introduce the *canendi mos orientalium partium* into Milan, so that he might resist the tyranny of the Arians who wanted to seize his basilica. The intrepid prelate shut himself up therein with his people and sustained a siege of several days, until his firmness obliged the Court party to abandon their hateful designs. Moreover, so that the people should not be overborne by such great distress, and that their courage might be proof against the wiles of the Arians, Ambrose introduced into the Milanese Liturgy, together with the *cursus,* that special collection of psalmody in the form of acrostics, refrains and doxologies, together with processions at night, preceded by crosses illuminated with candles, which in Antioch and Constantinople had already commonly acquired the name of *antiphonia.* We shall doubtless not be diverging from the truth if, while bearing in mind the origin of the Roman Antiphon from Milan and Antioch, we reconstruct the history of the Gregorian " Cento " after this fashion.

A certain passage in the *Liber Pontificalis,* which attributes the custom of reciting the Psalter before the Mass to Pope Celestine I (422-432), is capable of several different explanations. While the compiler of the second edition of this Pope's *Life* (written some time before the latter half of the sixth century) maintains such psalmody to have been antiphonal, Duchesne and others have seen in it the beginning of the Roman *cursus.* Amid such diversities of opinion it is not easy to see one's way clearly, for the *Liber Pontificalis*

[1] *Confess.* I, ix, c. vii; *P.L.*, XXXII, 770.
[2] *P.L.* XIV, 31.

seems to speak of the entire recital of the Psalter before the Mass; while in the Milanese rite and in that of the other churches of Lombardy we have precisely this same recital of the Psalter, after the first portion of the solemn vigils. This coincidence is too significant for us to reject absolutely the theory which sees in Celestine's *Life* a further confirmation of the dependence of the Roman Antiphonal Liturgy on that of the metropolis of Lombardy.

The fact that Hormisdas, according to his biographer,[1] *composuit clerum et psalmis erudivit,* does not greatly elucidate the history of the Roman *cursus.* Yet since the Roman *schola cantorum* is certainly prior to the pontificate of Gregory I, we might possibly see in this passage evidence for the origin, or at least the survival, of that pontifical school of music; unless, indeed, the document simply alludes to the distribution and ordering of the clergy for the different urban titles where the *cursus* was to be followed, in obedience to Justinian's new law of the year 528.

It is well known that the Apostolic See prescribed the observance of the *cursus* in all the dioceses immediately dependent on the metropolis, so that the bishops, in the actual course of their consecration in Rome, had to promise in writing to carry out its observance in accordance with the formula laid down in the *Liber Diurnus.*[2] Now it happened that a certain Eleutherius, on returning to his own church after his episcopal ordination, met with strong opposition on the part of his clergy to the introduction of daily vigils; so he appealed to the Pope, who strongly supported him in his task of bringing his rebellious clergy into submission. The passage gives the name of the Pope sometimes as Gelasius and sometimes as Pelagius, but the critics are agreed in recognizing the document as contemporary with Justinian, or at most only a little later in date.

We may turn also to the famous decree *De libris recipiendis et non recipiendis,* which, as regards its primitive elements, may well go back to the time of Damasus (366-384), and which treats of the readings from Holy Writ then customary during the night vigils. It mentions that in Rome, *ob singularem cautelam,* the Acts of the Martyrs were not read, and that it was deemed advisable to substitute for them the *opuscula atque tractatus orthodoxorum patrum.*

This liturgical movement was by no means confined to the Italian Peninsula, but spread throughout Gaul and Africa, where, in 393, the bishops assembled at Council of Hippo forbade that, without the approval of the local ordinary,

---

[1] *Lib. Pontif.* I, p. 269.
[2] Batiffol, *History of the Roman Breviary* (London 1912), p. 38.

*quicumque sibi preces aliunde describit . . . ex regionibus
vel ecclesiis transmarinis.*[1]

Freedom in liturgical matters and individual initiative in
Christian worship, dating from primitive times, were already
threatening to become excessive; hence, to prevent disorders,
it was now time that the Roman Church, while duly respect-
ing the almost paternal rights of Milan, should legislate for
all the faithful, and herself become the vindicator of the *lex
supplicandi.* She fulfilled this mission mainly through the
work of St Gregory the Great.

[1] *Op. S. Leonis, P.L.* III, c. 426.

CHAPTER IV

THE HISTORICAL SETTING OF ST GREGORY'S REFORM OF THE ROMAN LITURGY

THE spell of the *sacra Urbs* which, in the Leonine Sacramentary, still continued to link the world's destinies with its own, was definitely broken by the Lombard invasion. The ancient dread of the *parousia* and of the end of the world weighed more fearfully upon the minds of those who, even more than the Romans of old, could now repeat with their distant ancestors :

Fuimus Troes, fuit Ilium et ingens gloria Teucrum.

Rome herself had been so inured to the occupations and the plunderings which she had suffered under Alaric and Genseric that now, in the sixth century, she could consider her own downfall at the hands of the *nefandissima gens Langobardorum,* as the official documents call them, as inevitable.

Such was the gloomy disposition of the public mind about the year 546, when, with Totila already threatening the capital, Sabinus, the blind Bishop of Canosa, caused himself to be conveyed to the summit of Monte Cassino, in order that he might both comfort his soul, distracted by earthly woes, with the contemplation of a better and heavenly kingdom, and renew the bond of an old friendship with St Benedict. One day, as the prelate was dining in the refectory of the monastery, and the great Patriarch with his disciples was cheering him with gentle and affectionate attentions, the talk fell upon Rome. Equally with St Benedict, Sabinus had been the recipient of many marks of esteem and respect from Totila, but nevertheless he did not conceal his fear lest the barbarian's cruelty should utterly crush the ancient queen of the world.

Benedict, who in that very spot had seen the King of the Goths prostrate at his feet, and had foretold to him that his occupation of Rome would be the beginning of his own overthrow, smiled at such fears. Gazing with prophetic vision into the dim future, he assured the good Sabinus that it would not be Totila who would lay waste the Holy City, but that Rome would destroy herself, and fall a victim to her own decrepitude, under an onrush of disasters, earthquake, pestilence and famine.

At that prophecy, the fame of which reached generations as yet unborn, Sabinus and the monks may well have shuddered. Five centuries after the death of St Benedict, Monte Cassino still reminded her guests, upon their entering her refectory, that—

> *in refectorio qui est*
> *justa ipsum dormitorium, profeta*
> *vid de roma.*

Totila did, indeed, occupy the Eternal City; but deeply impressed by the prediction of St Benedict, he gave to her inhabitants such signal proofs of pity and justice that the *Liber Pontificalis* was able to record of him that he bore himself towards them as a father among his own children.

At a time nearly contemporary with these events, whilst already the Patriarch of Monte Cassino was causing to be prepared that tomb which was to receive his worn-out body, there was born in Rome, in the ancestral palace on the Cœlian Hill beside the Clivus Scaurus, a child, chosen in accordance with the far-seeing designs of Providence to be at once the authoritative interpreter of the teaching of St Benedict, the chronicler of his life, the depositary of his world mission, and the resplendent glory of his spiritual posterity. This was Gregory the Great, from whose writings we have taken the particulars set down above.

If it be true that the Middle Ages begin with St Gregory, then the old scholastic axiom that death is the source of life has never met with more fatal verification; for the end of the world, so much dreaded in the Byzantine period, and so often menacingly foretold by the holy Pontiff in his homilies to the people, was truly an awful and living reality, a spectacle witnessed by the world at large.

For, indeed, the Lombard invasion, and, outside of the Roman dukedom, the mingling of oppressors with oppressed, caused a profound change in all that unity of institutions, artistic, literary, juridical and religious, which at that time comprised the Christian polity of the *romanum imperium.* Cities and townships, episcopal palaces and monasteries were destroyed by hundreds in the first onrush of blind fury; the aqueducts were broken, the land laid waste, commerce paralyzed, municipal government overturned, civil and ecclesiastical laws set at defiance, while in their stead arose a formless conglomeration of barbarian Germanic edicts, having no clear conception of civil liberty, personal property or hereditary right. Italy was thus more than sunk in barbarism; her very existence was to all appearance annihilated. To such material woes as these, scarcity and want, the horrors of war, floods, famine and disease, and the deceitful desertion of the Byzantines, lent still further bitterness; while the haughty bearing of the *Ecumenical Faster* in his patriarchal see of Constantinople, and the Aquileian schism of the " Three Chapters " seemed as if they wished to take advantage of the universal distress to involve Italy and the Holy See in one common ruin. The subject is so involved that we can scarcely do more than touch upon it here; yet it is necessary to take due note of all these outward circumstances in order the better to understand the spirit of the reform brought about by Gregory the Great.

When the Saint, at first Praetor in Rome, next a monk at the Clivus Scaurus, then delegate at Constantinople, and finally Abbot of Sant' Andrea, was lamenting the cruel fate that flung him constantly hither and thither in the world, when by natural disposition he was given to the tranquil reflections of philosophy, neither he nor any of his contemporaries could have foreseen how by means of that hard training divine Providence was preparing the future Pontiff to be the saviour of the Roman people. Hence it was that on September 3, 590, upon the death of Pelagius II, he did his utmost to evade the yoke of pastoral cares, finally invoking the imperial veto, that last refuge of the desperate; but the united will of the people overcame his humility, and he was obliged to bow his head in resignation under the hands of the bishops assembled for his consecration.

The Lombard incursion into Italy had threatened to shake the very foundations of Catholic social life; hence Gregory needed, before all else, to set himself to their reconsolidation. Truly our divine Redeemer desired to establish among mankind in the supernatural order also that arrangement which he had devised from the beginning in the course of Nature, when he created man a social being, and decreed that only by means of society would he be able to attain to that perfection to which he was called. For this reason, also, the structure of a perfect society has been given by our Lord to the whole body of the redeemed; a society supernatural in origin and aim, but visible by reason of the members that compose it, as also of its actions and the means which it employs. Consequently, since our Saviour has made his Church the one depository of all the treasures of redemption, outside of her there is no salvation.

A society without authority and without directive means of action moves like the blind rush of a crowd; hence our Lord has bestowed upon his Church that form of government most in harmony with human nature. Peter, with the keys of heaven, has the sovereignty of all powers on earth also:

Hic habet in terris altera claustra poli.

Since, however, the exclusive and universal rule of one person alone, though it has its advantages, is in practice unsuitable to the good government of whole nations, the other bishops derive through him their own lofty mission as individual shepherds of particular churches.

This is the reason, in the Church's hierarchical constitution, for the specific separation into dioceses, vital cells in a single organism, characterized by a systematic variety which harmonizes admirably with the unity of the supreme pontificate and carries the spiritual life-stream, at once single and multiform, to every member of the corporate body.

It was this fundamental realization of the nature of the Church which inspired Gregory in his great task of religious reform. The well-being of a whole, he argued, results from the well-being of its parts; and since God has decreed that these parts, too, should each occupy the position of an organic whole, having clearly defined and specific functions with absolutely distinct characteristics, the Pontiff made it his special care to reanimate the Christian consciousness in the life of the diocese.

The Lombards had thrown into confusion the boundaries of the dioceses; Gregory consequently set them again in order. In some cases the few remaining relics from episcopal treasuries had been carried away by stealth across the sea, so he caused inventories of these to be drawn up before persons who would act as sureties, with the intention that when peace was restored they might be given back to the bishop. He also exercised every caution before approving the nomination of prelates to vacant sees; but when once they were enthroned he would not suffer even the smallest arbitrary lessening of their authority, being ever ready to confirm to each diocese its customary rites and privileges. Having been an abbot of monks before he was Pope, Gregory liked to consider the bishops of his metropolitan province somewhat in the light of his own monks, treating them with all that firm yet gentle kindness which had distinguished his abbatial rule.

Thus to one who was ill-provided against the winter's cold he sends a mantle and a horse; another, of a nature lacking somewhat in straightforwardness, he reproves; a third was a little close-fisted and gouty, and is exhorted, therefore, to greater liberality; a fourth, who was weakly, he forbids to fast more than five times a year, while enjoining upon him to come, with the return of warmer weather, to Rome, to the Palace of the Lateran, either that he may be nursed back to health, or otherwise die in the arms of his old master, Pope Gregory himself.

Remorselessly vigilant over the discipline of the monasteries of Italy, Gregory, while very remotely preparing the way for monastic exemption from episcopal authority by direct appeal to the Apostolic See, was careful to guard himself against disturbing in any way the peace of the dioceses, and laid down, with wise judgement, the first rules of what we might almost call the *Jus Regularium*. Nothing escaped his attention, and as he had at heart the maintaining of a good understanding between Abbots and Bishops, he displayed a prudent reserve on occasions of abbatial elections, when the choice fell upon persons who were not altogether praiseworthy. Nor did he disdain to concern himself with the material needs of the young novices, and during a winter of bitter cold and distressing scarcity he caused all the religious under seventeen years of age to be sent from the Tuscan Archipelago to Rome, so that they might suffer less from hunger, and have him at hand to minister to their wants.

Thanks to this prudent watchfulness, which does honour to his name, for *Gregory* signifies "vigilant," a new stream of spiritual vitality now flowed through all the churches of Italy. It was not long before Agilulf and his Lombards conformed to the Catholic polity of the Latin peoples and received the orthodox Roman baptism. Once within the bosom of holy Church, her former persecutors set themselves, with all the fiery energy peculiar to their race, to rebuild the ruined churches and monasteries, and to set up schools, hospitals and clerical communities, to such an extent that every noble Lombard, in the century following St Gregory's death, would have considered himself unworthy of his spiritual lineage if he had not erected on his own domain some church or convent *ob redemptionem animae suae*. In Italy, especially in the rural districts, they are so numerous that the entire countryside is bedecked with them as with jewels.

Gregory, however, began his work of reform with the head before he attempted the revival of the whole body. His starting-point was the *episcopium lateranense*, and since the reform which he contemplated was not to be a mere official act, but was rather to consist in a real deepening of the Christian spirit, he removed from the dwelling-place of Christ's Vicar on earth the whole of the lay element, placing the various offices of his household under the care of ecclesiastics or of monks of exemplary life.

It was a colossal building, or, rather, group of buildings, that Lateran palace, which, in the night of the Middle Ages,

" *a le cose mortali andò di sopra.*"[1]

---

[1] *Cf.* Dante, *Paradiso*, xxxi, 36.—TR.

In the sacred precincts of the Basilica of the Saviour and of the Baptistery of Sylvester, beside the Palace of Pope Vigilius and the Synodal Hall with its eleven apsidal recesses rich in mosaics, there arose the pontifical residence, with its chapels and library, its baths and towers, and whatever else of cultural treasure the Popes of old had been able to collect therein as in a very ark of refuge. Encircled though it was by a girdle of monasteries on its inner side, along the Cœlian and Esquiline Hills, yet the patriarchal see of Rome possessed, too, its own *monasterium lateranense,* founded probably in the lifetime of St Benedict, but in any case before the era of Pelagius II and the destruction of Monte Cassino by the Lombards.

Close to the Baptistery was to be seen the orphanage of the papal choir, just then awaiting its re-establishment at the hands of St Gregory. There the young clerics were taught, not only music, but theology and the sciences, so that not a few of the former pupils of that conservatorium passed from it to be raised later to the papal throne itself.

Every day, but more lavishly at certain fixed seasons, the widows, orphans and poor of Rome received in free gift from Gregory their necessary supplies, clothing, beds and coverings. Daily about 4,000 nuns claimed relief from the papal exchequer, and at the solemn feasts of Easter and of SS Peter and Paul the nobles, together with the monks and the clergy, assembled to receive a token of the unfailing lovingkindness of their supreme Pastor—a kiss from the Pope himself—and also a little gift of precious perfumes as a slight remembrance of the goodwill of St Peter towards them.

A reform carried out on a purely legal basis may be too violent in its mode of action, and therefore may often meet with but indifferent success. It is the intellect which must determine the will; whence it comes that, in order to promote the good, we have to begin by making it loved, and especially by educating the mind to its reception. To allure the heart with mere feeling is not sufficient, for it is a blind force not easily controlled; we must turn, rather, to the mind if we wish to persuade and convince. For some time after the peace of Constantine, the Christians in their private liturgical worship had filled for themselves the void caused by the temporary interruption of that episcopal teaching which, in the beginning, had formed an integral part of the eucharistic synaxis. St Leo I had, indeed, in a period of exceptional disturbance, restored the old custom, but after his day it was abandoned, to be again revived by St Gregory, who had been already accustomed when Abbot to speak daily to his monks, commenting, as in his *Moralia,* upon the Book of Job or some other part of the sacred Scriptures.

The Roman people, gathered together for the stations or

for the feasts of the martyrs, had thus frequent opportunity of beholding with admiration their Pontiff, who, personally when his health allowed him, or otherwise by proxy through his deacon, expounded the Gospel to the faithful, seated on his marble throne in the hemicycle of the apse at the end of the sanctuary. His manner of speech was simple and easy, at once free from the rhetorical subtleties which at times characterized St Augustine, and from the somewhat pompous mannerism displayed by St Leo. He expressed himself in faultless, grammatical Latin, as pure as his own soul, and, like a father teaching his children, was careful for the eternal welfare of each separate individual.

Gregory, through his sermons, has contributed more than any other to the development of the various forms of that popular devotion which was so well marked in the Middle Ages, by dwelling on the devotion to the holy angels, the apparitions of souls detained in Purgatory, the offering of Masses on their behalf, and finally by the little edifying stories of which the Pontiff had always such a plentiful collection.

Now that we have seen the destinies of Italy restored by the infusion of the Lombard stock with noble Latin blood, diocesan life revived in the peninsula, and the Christian consciousness awakened in Rome and throughout all Italy, the moment has at length come to study St Gregory's liturgical reform, of which we have so far traced out merely the foundations.

The Saint's liturgical standards are well known. He writes to Augustine of Canterbury that he is to choose freely from the Frankish churches those ritual customs which he may consider the most suitable for his English neophytes, since *non pro locis res, sed pro rebus loca amanda sunt;* and in another letter, addressed to Bishop John of Syracuse, he declares himself ready to apply this eminently eclectic principle to the Roman Liturgy itself. In this he was faithfully following the tradition of his predecessors, so that the Roman Liturgy did not definitely enter upon its period of *stasis* until after the death of the great teacher. Note his words to the Bishop of Syracuse : *Si quid boni vel ipsa[1] vel altera ecclesia habet, ego et minores meos quod ab illicitis prohibeo, in bono imitari paratus sum. Stultus est enim qui in eo se primum existimat, ut bona quae viderit, discere contemnat.*

Happily the liturgical heritage of the Apostolic See is unrivalled in splendour and suitableness by that of any other church ; hence the holy Pope, as if to reassure us against his own theories, which might prove somewhat disastrous for the history of the ancient Liturgy, affirms that his innova-

---

[1] *i.e.*, of Constantinople.

tions in the Mass were in reality nothing else than a return to the purest Roman tradition. *In nullo aliam ecclesiam secuti sumus*, he asserts, not even when he put the Alleluia back into its place of honour on all Sundays except in Lent, since this was the actual Roman tradition inaugurated by Pope Damasus under the auspices of St Jerome. *Et ideo magis in hac re illam consuetudinem amputavimus, quae hic a Graecis fuerat tradita.*

Nor was it a real innovation when he gave greater importance to that last relic of the primitive Litany (*Kyrie eleison*), which originally followed the Office of the Vigil before the commencement of the eucharistic Anaphora. Moreover, between the time of the earliest watchings in the *cubicula* of the martyrs in the suburban cemeteries and that of Constantine's splendid basilicas, many circumstances had arisen to modify the ancient sacrificial rite. The early παννυχίς with its final litany had almost disappeared, while the solemn entrance of the Pope into the church for the celebration of the divine mysteries had grown vastly more imposing, thanks to the *schola cantorum* and its musical prelude to the whole eucharistic *actio*—a prelude that was called simply *introitus*. It was to this introit that Gregory reattached the Kyrie, thus insuring that the priest's collect should not be said without at any rate some sort of introductory formula.

It was Gregory, likewise, who placed the singing of the *Pater Noster* before the fraction of the consecrated species, in order that it might form, as it were, the conclusion of the eucharistic Canon; since originally, so he argued, the consecratory Anaphora could have been nothing else than a free paraphrase of the prayer which our Lord himself had taught the Apostles.

Gregory had, perhaps, heard vaguely of the tradition laid down in the *Didache*, according to which the threefold daily prayer of the Christians consisted of a triple *Pater Noster*, recited at the morning, noon and evening hour.

In the Apostolic Age, he added, the Lord's Prayer was the starting-point of the whole Liturgy; it was therefore altogether unsuitable that the Canon, composed by *scholasticus quidam*, should wholly supplant the Gospel prayer, which was recited, not indeed at the altar, *in fractione*—that is to say, at the moment of the sacrifice—but only after the fraction of the Host, when, the offering of the Eucharist having ended with the Anaphora, the Pope returned to his throne to prepare for Holy Communion. It was then no mere rubrical nicety, no question of a moment sooner or later, which led Gregory to give the *Pater Noster* a place within the Roman consecratory Anaphora, but rather a profound theological reason, resting upon the primitive liturgical tradition of the Apostolic Age.

Ever since the days of St Paul the unity of the Christian family under the rule of its lawful pastors was symbolized by the unity of the altar—of the eucharistic bread and wine—in which all alike shared. Almost down to the time of Justin Martyr the faithful from every quarter of the city and its suburbs made their way on the Saturday, as it was growing dusk, to the Esquiline, to the *titulus Pastoris,* in order to celebrate, together with the Pope and his clergy, the solemn vigil of the ensuing Sunday. It was only later that, taking example, perhaps, from the great capitals of Antioch and Alexandria, the various urban *tituli* assigned to the different presbyteries became so many reproductions in the *Urbs* of the original sole title of the Shepherd, where the faithful of the district received the holy sacraments at the hands of the clergy of that particular title.

But in order that the sense of unity of the *ecclesia romana* should not be weakened by this system of parochial division, which bore a purely administrative character, not only did there obtain for a long period the use of a single baptistery in which every one was born again into Christian life at the hands of the Holy Father—the *sponsus ecclesiae;* but, more than this, every Sunday the Pontiff used to send to the presbyteries attached to the different titles a consecrated particle from his *eucharistia,* so that, being placed in their chalices as a *sacrum fermentum,* it might typify the identity of the Sacrifice and the Sacrament which united both Shepherd and sheep in the one and only faith. We see the last remaining memento of this rite in the eucharistic particle which is still at this day placed in the chalice after the breaking of the Host.

Thanks to these rites, the parochial Mass of the titular priests did not obscure the memory of the single primitive papal synaxis formerly held in the house of the family of Pudens. The recollection, too, of the earlier stations at the cemeteries always lived on in Rome, even after the pestilence, notwithstanding the danger of venturing beyond the shelter of the city walls on account of the Lombards. Gregory, however, with that wonderful adaptability to circumstances which revealed in him the former Roman praetor under the papal pallium, substituted the titular churches within the walls for the extra-mural basilicas of the martyrs. His idea of having popular processions was a stroke of genius, fostered, doubtless, for many years past, during the processions in which, as monk and abbot, he had taken part within the enclosure of his monastery on the Cœlian. This wish of Gregory's was realized on the morrow of the death of Pope Pelagius, when, while still simply a candidate for the Holy See, he announced his famous *litania septiformis,* in which the faithful from all parts of the city, moving in seven companies and chanting the *Kyrie eleison,* were to go in procession to the Vatican Basilica, to implore from almighty God the cessation of the pestilence by which all Rome was being devastated.

When that scourge had ceased, famine, war and earthquake succeeded each other until finally the Pontiff offered himself to God as a victim in expiation of the sins of the people. In those tragic days, as John the Deacon relates, Gregory was to be seen at the head of his clergy, leading the way from one Roman sanctuary to another, to entreat the martyrs for the safety of his people. Decimated though they were by famine and disease, yet they ever followed him, drawn onwards by the attractive holiness of their *episcopus,* who now, since the shameful flight of the Byzantine governor, had become the Consul of God also—*Dei Consul factus.* In seeing and listening to their Father the Pope, the Roman people even became oblivious of the ring of hostile swords drawn now so close about the city as to hem her in within a wall of steel. Their case appeared wellnigh desperate, since the treacherous malice of the Exarchs, jealous of Gregory's political success with the Lombards, broke truce and armistice, in order to enrage the barbarians and thus deprive Gregory of the honour of being the saviour of Italy. The Pontiff himself, regarding all this with the scrutinizing gaze of a philosopher, realized on the one hand the utter impossibility of any resistance to the invaders on the part of the Italians, and, on the other, already foresaw that *vita nova* which should arise, full of vigour and strength, from the fusion of the two races; and so he insistently defended the cause of peace, though not openly daring as yet to put forward publicly the conditions it might entail. He commended Italy, therefore, to the care of divine Providence, and in the eucharistic prayer, just before the consecration of the holy mysteries, at the place where the Roman Liturgy was wont to make mention of the particular intentions for which the sacrifice was being offered, he inserted those words so expressive of the great yearning of his pastoral heart— *diesque nostros in tua pace disponas*—which the *Canon Missae* has for ever kept as the precious legacy of St Gregory the Great.

Meanwhile the besiegers were pressing ever closer and closer. Gregory just then was commenting to his people upon the Prophet Ezechiel, but there came a day when the lamentations broke down the eloquence of the venerable teacher. "Let no one be angry with me," he said to his assembled hearers, " if henceforth I say no more, since you all see how our tribulation has reached its height. From the Roman eagle, once so proud, they have stripped all the feathers. Where is the Senate now? Where are the legions which carried the terror of our power to the ends of the earth? Instead of these, refugees come fleeing to us daily, some driven from their homes and despoiled of their every possession; others wounded, mutilated and horribly ill-used."

At length there dawned, if not a definite peace, at any rate an honourable settlement with the Lombard host, and the penitential stations were changed into festivals of gratitude and thanksgiving. Gregory again took up his interrupted teaching, and, acting on the suggestion of his friends, arranged in definite shape the collection of his homilies *in Evangelia* which began from this time to be read at the recitation of the divine Office.

These homilies, forty in number, represent in all probability but a very small part of St Gregory's sermons—only those, in fact, which treat of the Gospel; but, besides commenting upon Job and Ezechiel, he must have dealt in like manner with other books of Holy Scripture—the Books of Kings, for instance—and must very frequently have addressed the Roman *presbyterium* gathered together in the *consistorium* of the Lateran.

Gregory's homiletic style is clear and smooth : first of all, he gives a succinct explanation of the literal meaning of the Gospel passage read at Mass, without losing himself, as St Jerome does, amid digressions into textual criticism. Then he proceeds to the moral application of the text, and it is here that the former Abbot of St Andrew makes himself felt as a great master with mature experience of the ways of the spiritual life. Yet even in his highest flights he desires above all things to be approved of the people; so he does not fail to add some edifying anecdote, nearly always drawn from personal experience, calling his hearers themselves to witness.

In the sermons of St Gregory the theological argument appears indubitably less profound than in those of St Leo; but the forty homilies far surpass in moral effect the discourses of Attila's conqueror, who lingers too long amid lofty speculations and dogmatic abstractions for one whose audience is but an ignorant multitude. When Gregory speaks we feel that he is well accustomed to the giving of many ascetic addresses and dissertations, and that he has many things to say to his flock, who are desirous of assuring him of their own anxiety for their common salvation; so much so, indeed, that while he is preaching the stational Mass becomes too long, and the less fervent are found complaining of the untiring eloquence of the one-time Prætor. This sign of discontent displayed on the faces of the more impatient does not escape St Gregory, but because, as a person of much experience, in choosing between the traditional chants of the Mass and the sermon, he gives preference to the latter, he therefore decides to curtail the ancient melodies which now for several centuries past had accompanied the eucharistic synaxis, thus leaving more time for the Word of God. According to John the Deacon, we have here the motive which caused the Saint to rearrange the collection of the chants of the Mass, the *Cantatorium,* which, taken probably from Milan in the time of St Damasus, had been gradually recast, developed and amplified by Roman hands.

We cannot exactly determine the part in this development of the Roman liturgical chant taken respectively by Leo I, Symmachus, John and Boniface, whom an anonymous writer of the eighth century calls the co-authors of the *cantus annualis*. Yet from all sources the conclusion is reached that the exact meaning of the *Antiphonarium Centonem,* as John the Deacon calls the Gregorian version, is explained for us in those lines written in honour of St Gregory, which of old were usually inscribed on the first page of his Antiphonary :

Ipse Patrum monumenta sequens, renovavit et auxit,
Carmina in officiis retinet quae circulus anni.

He did, in fact, revise all that vast collection of music, compressing, correcting, beautifying and reducing to more harmonious proportions the exuberant growth of those religious melodies which, originating in the East and transferred to Milan, retained many elements little suited to the more sober and orderly taste of the Westerns in general, and of the Romans in particular.

Did Gregory accomplish such a task alone? It is necessary for us to bear in mind the great work of abbreviation already going on for more than a century at the hands of the *magistri romanae ecclesiae,* as Amalarius styles them; but the ancients are agreed in attributing to the Pontiff the completed edition of the *Antiphonarium.* We know from another source that, after the Saint had reorganized his two *scholae* of singers at St Peter's and in the Lateran, an authentic copy of St Gregory's musical recension was still preserved in the latter palace, in the time of John the Deacon, together with the rod with which, when confined at times to his bed by gout, he would recall the wandering attention of his too lively pupils.

There are some writers who have wished to see in a canon of the Roman Council of July 5, 595, the *terminus a quo* of the *schola* of the Roman singers, and even the date of foundation of the musical institution. It was an ancient custom in Rome for the deacon to sing the responsorial solo at the Mass from the steps of the ambo—*responsorium graduale*. It resulted from this that in choosing the deacon for this purpose more attention was paid to musical skill than to holiness of life; and the deacons, anxious to sing with taste, neglected the other duties of their ministry. In order, therefore, to do away with this abuse, St Gregory forbade the Roman deacons to exercise any longer the office of solo singers, reserving it henceforth to the subdeacons, or failing them, to clerics of lower degree.

Some authorities have deduced from this rule that in 595 the *schola* of singers did not as yet exist in Rome. This conclusion, however, does not hold. It is not said that the subdeacons are to carry out the entire singing of every kind, antiphonal or responsorial, in Mass and Office; they are merely charged exclusively with the duty of executing the responsorial *solo,* which, by reason of the importance attached to it, was formerly reserved to the deacon, and sometimes even to the bishop. On this account Gregory wished to entrust its execution to an acolyte, in the absence of a subdeacon, rather than give it to the younger lectors, as would have seemed the more likely course to pursue. More-over, the Canon of the Roman Council of 595, far from excluding the existence of the *schola,* presupposes it, since without the *schola* musical skill sufficient for the rendering of solos could hardly have been expected of the subdeacons, much less from the inferior clerics. The Introit, Offertory and Communion Antiphons, too, date back at least to the time of Celestine I, a type of chant which necessarily demands a choir of singers and takes for granted, therefore, the establishment of a *schola.* On this point we have a further piece of evidence which contains a definite solution of the problem, witnessing as it does to the existence of the *schola* at least fifty years before the pontificate of St Gregory. It is the epitaph on the tomb of Pope Deusdedit, who died in 618, fourteen years after St Gregory, in which occur these lines, calling attention to the *cursus honorum* of the deceased :

> *Hic vir ab exortu Petri est nutritus ovili,*
> *Excuvians Christi cantibus hymnisonis.*

If Pope Deusdedit was brought up from early childhood in the musical conservatorium of St Peter's, it follows that this must be very much older than the Roman Council of 595, and probably goes back to the era of Pope Celestine I. The establishment of the two choir schools, the Vatican and the

Lateran, attributed to St Gregory by John the Deacon, does not necessarily imply a foundation *ad imis,* but only a re-establishment and reorganization, seeing that pestilence, famine and siege would have scattered far and wide the orphan children received therein.

With Gregory's work of critically revising the liturgical chants went hand in hand his recension of the Roman Sacramentary, in which, taking into account the hardships which evil times had imposed upon the faithful, the Pope shortened both prayers and ceremonies, arranged in a different manner the course of eucharistic stations, and finally suppressed whatever was superfluous and unsuitable in the old collections. To rescue in proportion as the former Imperium decayed all classes of society; to inoculate the Latin blood with the new and eager zeal of the Catholic Lombards; to make them Italians in their turn; to rebuild on the foundations of the diocesan ecclesiastical life the dislocated hierarchical system, inspiring it anew with spiritual energy; to shed the light of the Church's inner holiness upon the outside world by means of processions, in which priests, monks and virgins poured forth the psalms in exquisite harmony; to make all this vast movement of reform a permanent one by means of books or of lasting institutions; to mould the new polity of the Middle Ages, so essentially Christian, out of the ruins of the ancient world—such was Gregory's great work.

Some may call him the Apostle of England, others may even give to him the glory of having laid the foundation of the temporal power of the Popes; but these are only side issues in that manifold and stupendous achievement of his, so intimately realized by the Roman people on the morrow of his passing from them, that they, after their own special manner, saluted him as the Consul of God.

> *Hisque Dei Consul factus, laetare triumphis,*
> *Nam mercedem operum jam sine fine habes.*

CHAPTER V

"FRACTIO PANIS"

THE coming of our Lord into this world constitutes the fulfilment of the divine promises made to the patriarchs and prophets;[1] hence the New Testament, far from abrogating the Old Law, completes it and gives it its final perfection.[2] It is for this reason that the Catholic Liturgy, inasmuch as it is the expression of the Church's perfect and essential worship of almighty God, neither annulled nor wholly proscribed the former Israelitish ritual with its joyous songs of Sion, but rather, reanimating these with the light of the Gospel, and engrafting thereon her own prayers and intercessions, brought them to the knowledge of redeemed humanity in like manner as the flower which blossomed upon the stem of Jesse.

The worship of the Father in spirit and in truth, which was from the beginning the essential end and aim of the creation of the world, was also that of the incarnation of the Word of God and of the founding of his Church. To adore in spirit means nothing less than to lift up oneself to God with the soaring flight of a pure soul, clear of every stain, and free from every earthly attachment. It is the gift of the Holy Ghost. To adore in truth—what is it save worthily to acknowledge the divine perfections, without needless searchings regarding the object of our worship, in thanksgiving for that Catholic revelation which recognizes Jesus Christ our Lord, the Truth himself, as its source?

The prayer of no mortal creature, indeed, can fully satisfy this twofold condition; it is the privilege of the eternal and divine High Priest alone to adore the Father with a perfect adoration. Yet so that humanity may neither remain deprived of the efficacy of this prayer, nor shut out from participating in the glory of this adoration by which alone it can reach its true goal, our Lord has willed by means of his Church to associate our nature closely with his own life of sanctity and prayer. Hence all the faithful, inasmuch as they are true members of the mystical body of Christ, have a share in his sacerdotal dignity, and the Spirit of the Lord adores and prays in them in a manner so exalted and so worthy of God that St Paul is at a loss to explain this intimate intercourse of the soul with its Creator, save by calling it the " unspeakable groanings " of the Spirit.

[1] Rom. i, 2. [2] Matt. v, 17.

53

Yet the individual life of the mystical members of Christ is to be distinguished from that of the whole Body, his Church. This latter is One, Holy, Catholic, Apostolic, united to the Saviour by an eternal and perfect marriage-bond, whereas the individual faithful only share in this endowment proportionately to the faith and love which joins them to Christ and the Church. For this reason the holiness of Christendom and its social worship are also quite distinct from the holiness and piety of the faithful as individuals; these last being, as it were, a reflection and consequence of the Church's sanctity. The devotion and personal goodness of the members of the Church may vary indefinitely, and may depend upon a number of contingencies, but the devotion and goodness of the mystical body of Christ are inherent and eternal. It follows from this that the piety of the faithful as individuals bears a wholly different stamp from the piety of the Church. This last claims the special name of Liturgy, which defines it as the essential and perfect worship which Christian society, as such, renders to God through Christ. In practice the sanctity of Christendom and its supernatural life consist mainly of this worship offered to the sacred Trinity, just as the life of the soul expresses itself principally in operations of intellect and will.

Of the entire number of the rites and formulas comprised in Christian worship some are of divine institution,[1] as the sacraments; others, such as certain parts of the canonical Office and other extra-sacramental rites, are ordained by the Church, always acting, however, under the guiding and vivifying influence of the Holy Ghost. The history of the ancient Christian Liturgy is exceedingly obscure, owing to the lack of necessary documents; and one might almost think that a kind of mysterious cloud were hiding from the eyes of men the footprints of our Saviour along the pathway of redemption. Though we may feel only too strongly that the most natural attitude for a soul confronted by God's lovingkindness is that of prayer, we have, nevertheless, to lament the almost total loss of primitive Christian euchology, of prayers frequently extemporary and expressive of thanksgiving, often handed down by oral tradition, just as the ἄγραφα,[2] the λογία of Jesus and the axioms of the early elders mentioned by Papias[3] and Irenæus.[4]

The eucharistic sacrifice was instituted by the Saviour at

---

[1] *Cf.* Probst, *Liturgie der drei ersten christlichen Jahrhunderte*, Part I, Tübingen 1870. Fouard, *Vie de J.C.*, 2, appendix.

[2] A. Resch, *Agrapha, Texte und Untersuchungen*, etc., Leipzig 1889, v, 4. *Cf.* I. H. Ropes, *Die spräche Jesu, die in den kanonischen Evangelien nicht überliefert sind*, 1896. (*Ibid.*, xiv, 2.)

[3] Cf. *Fragmenta beati Papiae ep.*, in Routh, *Reliquiae Sacrae*, i, 9-44.

[4] *Seniores apud Irenæum* (*op. cit.*, 47-68).

a meal, purely religious in character, the ceremonial of which it is not difficult to reconstruct. We know also from the New Testament writers that the sacrament of Confirmation was conferred by means of an episcopal invocation, accompanied by the imposition of hands;[1] to Extreme Unction was joined the *oratio fidei* of the presbyters;[2] while Episcopal Ordination demanded a preparatory fast, the Invocation and the imposition of hands by the celebrant.[3] St Paul mentions also a *bonam confessionem coram multis testibus;*[4] but it is doubtful whether this is to be taken as meaning a preparatory profession of faith.

In any case, it is certain that from the earliest times there existed certain well-defined catechetical formulas, known in all the churches. Moreover, the inspired mind of the Apostles must have determined these formulas very early, together with the ceremonies and the whole setting of the sacramental rites which constitute the predominating element in our worship; and this becomes the more certain when we reflect that the extra-sacramental assemblies, being based on the customs of the synagogue, had the model for their ceremonial close at hand. For the celebration of the sacraments, on the other hand, the Apostles had recourse almost solely to the gifts infused into the Church by her heavenly Bridegroom, so that they might translate into tangible forms and noble words the new emotions welling up in every heart.

Those were the true songs *pro torcularibus*, when the strong new wine in the new skins fermented, as it were, under the action of the divine Spirit.[5] The Epistles of St Paul, especially those to the Corinthians,[6] the pastorals addressed to Timothy,[7] the Διδαχὴ,[8] the Song of Solomon,[9] the Canticles in the Apocalypse;[10] these, with some few phrases of Clement I[11] and of Ignatius,[12] furnish us with

---

[1] Acts viii, 15-17.
[2] James v, 14-15.
[3] Acts xiii, 3.
[4] 1 Tim. iv, 14; i, 18.
[5] Matt. ix, 17-18.
[6] 1 Cor. x, 16.
[7] 1 Tim. iii, 16. *Cf.* Th. Innitzer, *Der "hymnus" in Epheserbriefe*, i, 3, 14. (*Zeitschr. f. Kathol. Theolog.*, 1904, iii, 612-21.)
[8] *Cf.* P. Cagin, *L'Euchologie latine étudiée dans la tradition de ses formulaires*, ii; *L'Eucaristia, Canon primitif de la Messe, ou Formulaire essentiel et premier de toutes les liturgies*, Desclée, 1912, viii; "*L'Eucaristia*" *primitive et la* Διδαχὴ, 252-288.
[9] *Cf.* I. Labourt et P. Batiffol, *Les Odes de Salomon. Une œuvre chrétienne des environs de l'an* 101-120. *Traduct. française et introduction historique*, Paris, Lecoffre, 1911.
[10] *Cf.* G. Morin, *Un texte préhieronymien du Cantique de l'Apocalypse; l'hymne* "*Magna et Mirabilia*," in *Rev. Bénédict.*, 1909, pp. 644-9.
[11] S Clement Roman., *Epist. I ad Corinth.*, c. xl *sq.*, Edit. Funk, Tübingen 1887, pp. 110 *sq.*
[12] *Cf.* I. Nirschl, *Die Theologie des hl. Ignatius*, Mainz 1880; E. Car. v. d. Goltz, *Ignatius von Antiochien als Christ und Theologe*, Leipzig 1894 (*Text. und Untersuchungen*, etc., xii, 3).

materials as scanty as they are precious for a slight reconstruction of the original scheme of the Liturgy, although
they scarcely suffice for sketching its bare outline.

Once we allow for the judaizing tendency of the early
Church of Jerusalem[1] when, under the sole episcopal rule of
James, "the Lord's brother," even St Paul had, for an
instant, to adapt himself to the harmless ritual of the
Temple,[2] it is not strange that the ceremonial of the
synagogue should have been willingly adopted in the extra-
sacramental gatherings of the first Christians.　Moreover,
since we know that, prior to the episcopate of James, Peter
and John also used to frequent the Temple services,[3] following therein the example of our Lord himself,[4] it seems
needful to conclude that the grafting of the Hebrew ceremonial upon the Christian rites took place by the authority
of the twelve Apostles, rather than merely through the
individual initiative of the *frater Domini* with his strictly
judaizing surroundings.[5]　Without, however, exaggerating
the value of such euchological borrowings, the obstinate
persistence of certain Aramaic elements in all liturgies[6]—
Amen, Alleluia, Anathema, Maran Atha, etc.[7]—cannot be
explained, especially in the Roman and Greek world in which
St Paul lived, otherwise than by taking into account the
almost hieratic importance attached by Christian tradition
until this time to those formulas which had their origin in
Jerusalem.[8]

We have spoken of the influence of the Jewish capital upon
the Christian Liturgy, but we must reckon also with the
other numerous synagogues scattered throughout East and
West.[9]　These existed under the protection of the law, and
were represented juridically by a community partly religious,
partly national in character, having benefactors, a treasury
and common burial-grounds, and maintaining more or less
cordial relations with the great Sanhedrin at Jerusalem.
St Paul, when on his missionary journeys, always made his
headquarters at the local synagogue,[10] where his role of
stranger and disciple of Gamaliel gave him the privilege of

---

[1] " *Vides, frater, quot millia sunt in Judaeis qui crediderunt et
omnes aemulatores sunt legis.*" Acts xxi, 20.

[2] Acts xxi, 20-27.　　　　　[3] Acts iii, 1.

[4] John vii, 10-11, 37; v, 1.

[5] The feasts mentioned by New Testament writers are those ordained
under the law. *Cf.* Acts xiii, 2 = Feast of Tabernacles (?); Lev. xvi, 29.

[6] 1 Cor. xvi, 22; Rom. viii, 15.　　　[7] *Apoc.* xix, 1-7; Διδαχὴ ix, x.

[8] Cf. *Paléograph, musicale*, v. vi; v. d. Goltz, E., *Neue Fragmente
aus der Ägyptischen Liturgie nach der Veröffentlichung von Dom P. de
Puniet*, Zeitschrift für Kirchengeschichte, 1909, vol. xxx, pp. 352-61.

[9] *Cf.* O. Marucchi, *Manuale d'Archeologia cristiana*, II, c. i, pp.
25 *sq.*

[10] *Acts* xiii, 46.

interpreting the law to the people,[1] and only when his words were not received did he separate his first disciples from the synagogue, to reassemble them in the house of one of the more wealthy among the faithful.[2] Theological and historical reasons would naturally establish a prejudice in favour of Israel, and her rites occupied such a place of honour among the early Christians that even to-day the first part of the eucharistic ceremonial corresponds exactly to that which was observed in the houses of prayer of the Dispersion.[3]

We may fairly affirm that the Jewish euchology penetrated into the Christian Church vested in the fulness of its musical setting, with its traditional alleluiatic melodies,[4] and with its living and popular forms of psalmody, both responsorial and antiphonal, although we are not at present able to determine more accurately the harmonic elements from whence all this was derived.[5]

In order to realize better the historical conditions which influenced the development of the Christian Liturgy, especially in the Latin world, a knowledge of the surroundings in which it grew up is of capital importance.[6]

It is in the town or country homes of the more prosperous Christians among whom the preaching of St Peter, St John[7] and St Paul at Rome bore such marvellous fruit, that we find the first " cenacles " of the Roman Church. We can still recognize the sites of some of these places of resort, *domesticae ecclesiae,* on the Aventine and the Viminal, as well as in the suburban estates of the Acilii Glabriones and the Flavii along the Salarian and Ardeatine Ways.[8] The pastoral administration within the city was early divided into seven districts and placed under the charge of the presbyteral college and of the seven regionary deacons, whose dependence upon the *episcopus* was very much more complete than at Alexandria. The prerogatives of the pontifical primacy,

[1] Acts xvii, 2; *cf.* C. Fouard, *Saint Paul, ses Missions,* Paris, Lecoffre, c. ii, pp. 31 *sq.*

[2] Acts xix, 8, 9.

[3] Mark xii, 38, 39; Luke xx, 46; Acts xiii, 14 *sq.*

[4] P. Wagner, *Origine e sviluppo del canto liturgico,* Versione italiana del Sacerdote M. R., riveduta dall'autore, Siena, Tipografia Pontificia S. Bernardino, 1910, c. i, pp. 34 *sq.*

[5] P. Cagin, *Archaisme et progrès dans la restauration des Mélodies Grégoriennes,* in *Rassegna Gregor.,* iv, 1905, pp. 295 *sq. Cf.* A. Gastoue, *Les Origines du Chant Romain—L'Antiphonaire Grégorien,* Picard et Fils, Paris.

[6] Tertull., *Apolog.* XLII, *P.L.* I, 557-8; *De Fuga* XIV, *P.L.* II, 141-2; O. Marucchi, *op. cit.,* III, c. v, p. 388.

[7] " Ista quam felix ecclesia . . . ubi Petrus passioni dominicae adaequatur, ubi Paulus Joannis exitu coronatur, ubi apostolus Joannes, posteaquam in oleum igneum demersus, nihil passus est, in insulam relegatur." Tertull., *De Praescr., P.L.* II, 59.

[8] O. Marucchi, *op. cit.,* p. 387.

universally acknowledged, even by those heretics who were trying to wrest from it its protection, rendered altogether harmless this early presbyteral oligarchy[1]—scarcely mentioned by Hermas[2]—while it left the Popes full opportunity to extend that efficacious influence over the churches of the whole world to which all ancient writers bear witness.

The tangible symbol of this supreme authority of the Popes was probably, for some time at least, the *ecclesia Pudentiana* in the house of Pudens on the Viminal. The connection of St Peter with this family is indeed shrouded in the obscurity of legend, but recent excavations and researches have given further probability to the hypothesis that the Apostle was in actual relation with the *gens Cornelia* of the Aventine and also with the family of Pudens, all of whose monumental records converge upon the cemetery of Priscilla, where ancient tradition has preserved the remembrance of the baptism administered by St Peter himself.[3]

The history of the *ecclesia Pudentiana* or *Titulus Pastoris* makes mention in its records of that enigmatical Hermas, brother of Pius I,[4] who dedicates the early chapters of his visions to Pope Clement, that he may communicate them to the churches. Near this spot Justin set up his school, and perhaps also Tatian.[5] It would seem, indeed, that the theological tradition lingered long in that locality, since, close by, a *memoria martyris Hippolyti* of the fourth century preserved also the record of the famous antipope, one of the most powerful minds of Christian antiquity.[6] We are still far from arriving at a *didascaleion,* properly speaking, such as flourished at Alexandria, yet the existence of a catechetical school on the Viminal near the *vicus patricius* remains highly probable.

In spite, however, of the great importance of the *titulus pastoris,* the faithful could not all assemble on every occasion in the stately atrium before the *tablinium* where the Pope celebrated Mass; and though Justin, in his first *Apologia,* seems to assert positively that the Christians were wont to gather on the Sunday in one single place of assembly,[7] yet in the interrogatory to which he was afterwards subjected by

---

[1] O. Marucchi, *op. cit.*, pp. 391 *sq.*

[2] An account of the literature relating to this celebrated work is to be found in Bardenhewer, *Patrologia,* Italian trans. by Rev. Prof. A. Mercati, i, 238-9.

[3] De Rossi, *Bullettino d'Archeol. Crist.*, 1867, pp. 49 *sq.*; Marucchi, *op. cit.*, pp. 27-8.

[4] *Cf.* Marani, *Ad opera S. Justini praefatio,* c. iii; *P.G.* VI, p. 122.

[5] Euseb., *Histor.*, v, 13.

[6] *Cf.* de Rossi, *Bullet.*, ser. III, ann. 6º (1818), 5·55; ser. IV, ann. 1º (1882) 9-76; ann. 2º (1883), 60-65.

[7] *Apolog. I,* c. lxvii; *P.L.* VI, 429.

Rusticus, the Roman Prefect, he maintains the exact opposite: *An existimas omnes nos in unum locum convenire? Minime res ita se habet.*   Indeed, some centuries later the Pope on festival days was still accustomed to send to the priests of the titular churches a particle of his own *Eucharistia,*[1] to be placed in the chalice as a *sacrum fermentum,* to signify the union of the Christian flock with their pastor and the identity of the eucharistic sacrifice, which, celebrated in many places, was yet always offered in the name and in the stead of the one *Episcopus* of the capital of the world.[2]

Justin preserves to us the fullest account of a eucharistic assembly in the second century.[3]   In the cemetery of Priscilla the so-called Greek chapel and the adjoining baptistery offer very suggestive points of comparison for the identifying of them with the places described by the celebrated martyr; but the question is foreign to our purpose here, for which it will suffice to reproduce the text of the Martyr-Philosopher.

I.

Κοινὰς εὐχὰς ποιησόμενοι ὑπέρ τε ἑαυτῶν καὶ τοῦ φωτισθέντος, καὶ ἄλλων πανταχοῦ πάντων εὐτόνως ... Ἀλλήλους φιλήματι ἀσπαζόμεθα παυσάμενοι τῶν εὐχῶν. Ἔπειτα προσφέρεται τῷ προεστῶτι τῶν ἀδελφῶν ἄρτος καὶ ποτήριον ὕδατος καὶ κράματος· καὶ οὗτος λαβὼν αἶνον καὶ δόξαν τῷ πατρὶ τῶν ὅλων διὰ τοῦ ὀνόματος τοῦ Υἱοῦ καὶ τοῦ Πνεύματος τοῦ Ἁγίου ἀναπέμπει καὶ εὐχαριστίαν ὑπὲρ τοῦ κατηξιῶσθαι τούτων παρ' αὐτοῦ ἐπὶ πολὺ ποιεῖται· οὗ συντελέσαντος τὰς εὐχὰς καὶ τὴν εὐχαριστίαν, πᾶς ὁ παρὼν λαὸς ἐπευφημεῖ λέγων· Ἀμήν ... Εὐχαριστήσαντος δὲ τοῦ προεστῶτος, καὶ ἐπευφημήσαντος παντὸς τοῦ λαοῦ, οἱ καλούμενοι παρ' ἡμῖν Διάκονοι δι-

A

Post preces modulamine fusas pro nobis, pro eo qui illuminatus est, pro aliis omnibus ubivis degentibus, ab orationibus desis-

B

timus, nosque invicem osculo com-

C

plectimur.   Affertur dein ei qui fratribus praeest panis poculusque aquae et vini; qui (ea) accipiens

D •

laude et gloria Patrem omnium prosequitur per Filii et Spiritus Sancti nomen, et pro iis quibus ab Eo dignamur abunde gratias

E

reddit.   Postquam preces et Gratiarum Actionem compleverit, omnis qui adest populus gratiose

F

dicit.   Amen.

... Cum vero praeses egerit grates et "Eucharistiam," et omnis qui adest populus adclamaverit, qui a nobis diaconi

---

[1] Innocentii I, *Ep. ad Decentium ep. Eugub. P.L.* XXVI, 553-4.
[2] *Cf.* Cagin, *L'Euchologie Latine;* II, *L'Eucharistie,* c. viii, 252 *sq.*
[3] *Cf.* P. de Puniet, *Le nouveau papyrus d'Oxford,* in *Rev. Bénédict.* XXVI, 1909, pp. 34-51.

δβασι ἑκάστῳ τῶν παρόντων μεταλά-
βειν ἀπὸ τοῦ εὐχαριστηθέντος ἄρτου καὶ
οἴνου καὶ ὕδατος, καὶ τοῖς οὐ παροῦσιν
ἀποφέρουσιν . . . Τὴν δι' εὐχῆς λόγου
τοῖ παρ' αὐτοῦ εὐχαρισθεῖσαν τροφήν. . .
'Ἰησοῦ καὶ σάρκα καὶ αἷμα ἐδιδάχθη
μὲν εἶναι. . . Ἐπὶ πᾶσί τε προσφερό-
μεθα εὐλογοῦμεν τὸν ποιητὴν τῶν παν-
τῶν διὰ τοῦ Υἱοῦ αὐτοῦ Ἰησοῦ Χριστοῦ
καὶ διὰ Πνεύματος τοῦ Ἀγίου . . .

G

vocantur dant unicuique praesen-
tium (ut accipiant) de pane
Eucharistiae et de vino aqua
(mixto); (quaeque) vero etiam iis
qui minime adsunt deferunt.
. . . Docemur vero escam
eucharisticam esse corpus et
sanguinem Iesu, propter verba
precis. . . . Postquam omnibus

H

attulerimus, benedicimus omnium
rerum factorem per Filium eius
Iesum Christum et Spiritum
Sanctum.[1]

II.

Τὰ ἀπομνημονεύματα τῶν Ἀποστόλων, ἢ τὰ συγ γράμματα τῶν προ-
φετῶν ἀναγινώσκεται μέχρις ἐγχωρεῖ:
Εἶτα παυσαμένου τοῦ ἀναγινώσκοντος,
ὁ προεστὼς διὰ λόγου τὴν νουθεσίαν
καὶ πρόκλησιν . . . . . ποιεῖται. Ἔπειτα
ἀνιστάμεθα κοινῇ πάντες, καὶ εὐχὰς
πέμπομεν . . . καὶ . . ., παυσαμένων ἡμῶν
τῆς εὐχῆς, . . . ὁ προεστὼς εὐχὰς ὁμοίως
καὶ εὐχαριστίας, ὅση δύναμις αὐτῷ
ἀναπέμπει, καὶ ὁ λαὸς ἐπευφημεῖ λέ-
γων· Ἀμήν.

a

. . . Leguntur Commentaria

β

Apostolorum et aliae Prophetarum
Scripturae, prout vacat; cumque

γ

lector desierit, praeses exhortans
alloquitur. Hinc omnes simul

δ

surgimus et preces fundimus, . . .
a quibus postquam destiterimus,

ε

iterum pro suis viribus praeses
precatur et grates reddit, (cui) et
populus iure adclamat. Amen.[2]

In Justin's account of the Eucharist we have kept the same
order as that followed in his first *Apologia,* where the author
sketches twice over in different circumstances the scheme of
the Mass in his day, describing first the Anaphora properly
so called, and then, some pages further on, the explanatory
or preparatory portion of the Mass, consisting of readings
from the Scriptures and the homily of the bishop. From the
text of the apologist we can clearly establish the following
elements as composing the eucharistic liturgy of the second
century. (The letters employed in this outline refer to the
different portions analyzed in the preceding text.)

[1] Justini, *Apolog. I, P.G.* VI, 427.
[2] *op. cit.,* 429.

I	II
Mass of the Catechumens.	*Mass of the Faithful.*
α Readings from the Gospel (New Testament, including the Pauline Epistles, etc.).	A. δ Litany for the various needs of the Church.
β Readings from the Prophets (Old Testament).	B. Kiss of Peace.
γ Homily of the Bishop.	C. Offertory.
	D. ε Eucharistic Anaphora with Invocation of the Trinity, predominately christological.
Mass of the Faithful.	E. Final doxology.
δ Litany for the various needs of the Church.	F. Popular acclamation.[1]
ε Eucharistic Anaphora recited by the Bishop.	G. Communion.
	H. Thanksgiving.

The author of the *Apologia*, in order to attain his object, had to treat the preparatory portion of the Mass as being of secondary importance, so that he could develop his dogmatic arguments regarding the eucharistic transubstantiation and maintain the position laid down by him in such precise terms against the common calumnies of the pagans.

The sacramental theology of Tertullian calls, on the other hand, for greater reserve, laying, as it does, special stress upon the ethical aspect of Christian worship. Among the rites of the Mass he mentions the *commemoratio litterarum divinarum*,[2] the psalmodic prayer (*fidem sanctis vocibus pascimus*), and the bishop's address (*ibidem etiam exhortationes*); but, passing rapidly over the description of the eucharistic gatherings, the sharp-tongued apologist insists above all upon the ethical end of the Christian Agape,[3] which Justin does not so much as mention. This points to the conclusion that also in the West, in Africa and at Rome, these love-feasts had been already separated from the eucharistic sacrifice, as we find in the Διδαχή and in Pliny's letter to Trajan. It was in the Agape, in all probability, that those New Testament psalms mentioned by St Paul and the early writers had found place, though always excluded from the eucharistic liturgy, properly so called. *Non prius discumbitur quam oratio ad Deum praegustetur; editur . . . ita saturantur, ut qui meminerit etiam per noctem adorandum sibi Deum esse; post aquam manualem et lumina, ut quisque de scripturis sanctis vel de proprio ingenio potest, provocatur in medium Deo canere. Hinc probatur quomodo biberis.*

[1] With reference to this final " Amen " *cf.* Διδαχή c. ix, xxxix; Tertullian, *De Spectaculis, P.L.* I, 733.

[2] *Apolog.*, c. xxxix; *P.L.* I, 531 *sq.*

[3] *Cf.* E. F. v. der Goltz, *Unbekannte Fragmente altchristlicher Gemeindeordnungen. Nach C. Horpers englischer Ausgabe des Æthiopischen Kirchen Rechtsbuchs.* (Sitzungsberichte der K. Preuss. Akad. der Wissenschaften, 1906, pp. 141-57.)

Aeque oratio convivium dirimit. Inde disceditur.[1] St Cyprian adds far more gracefully: *Quidquid, inclinato jam sole in vesperam, diei superest, ducamus hunc diem laeti, nec sit vel hora convivii gratiae coelestis immunis. Sonet psalmos convivium sobre; et, ut tibi tenax memoria est, vox canora, aggredere hoc munus, ex more. . . . Prolectet aures religiosa mulcedo.*[2]

Tertullian points out also some further liturgical features of his time. Thus, during the Litany, after the Bishop's sermon . . . *oramus . . . manibus expansis, quia innocui, capite nudo, quia non erubescimus; denique sine monitore, quia de pectore, oramus pro omnibus imperatoribus; vitam illi prolixam, imperium securum, domum tutam, exercitus fortes, senatum fidelem, populum probum, orbem quietem, et quaecumque hominis et Caesaris sunt.*[3] It is not impossible that the author is here paraphrazing a portion of that same Litany of which traces remain in the one recited on Good Friday after the lessons in the Office of the Presanctified. Other references of Tertullian are no less important for the history of the Latin Liturgy in the second century. *Si colligere interdiu non potes, habes noctem, luce Christi luminosam. Non potes discurrere per singulos; sit et in tribus ecclesia.*[4] *Quale est, ex ore quo Amen in Sanctum protuleris*—the final acclamation of the Anaphora—*gladiatori testimonium reddere;* εἰς αἰῶνας ἀπ' αἰῶνας *alii omnino dicere, nisi Deo Christo?*[5] Describing once more the heretical assemblies, he says, *In primis, quis catechumenus, quis fidelis incertum est: pariter adeunt, pariter audiunt, pariter orant,*[6] making evident allusion to the Litany which regularly followed the reading of the Scriptures, and the homily of the Bishop.[7]

Before proceeding to speak of the liturgies, Eastern and Western, posterior to the peace of Constantine, we must at any rate draw attention to the important studies made by Dom Cagin upon the reconstruction of the Roman Canon of the Mass and the fixing of the text of the eucharistic Anaphora, which from apostolic times has formed the common foundation of all other Christian liturgies. The close reasoning of this learned monk, joined to the vast and minute analysis to which he has subjected the eucharistic text of the Egyptian Apostolic Statutes, renders at least highly probable,

[1] *Apolog.,* xxxix.
[2] Cypriani, *Epist. ad Donatum, P.L.* IV, 227.
[3] *Apolog.,* xxx; *P.L.* I, 504.
[4] *De Fuga, P.L.* II, p. 142.
[5] *De Spectaculis, P.L.* I, 733. Cf. *De Corona, P.L.* II, c. iii, 99.
[6] *De Praescript., P.L.* II, cxli, 68.
[7] Cf. *Monumenta Ecclesiae Liturgica* I, *Reliq. liturgicae vetustissimae.*

if not quite certain, his theory that in the Latin text of the palimpsest of Verona we possess what is actually the most ancient type of the *hymnus eucharisticus* previous to the interpolations of the second century. While referring the reader for explanation to Dom Cagin's own work, we will here transcribe the venerable formulary from the edition issued by Hauler.[1]

Gratias tibi referimus, Deus,
Per dilectum puerum tuum
Jesum Christum,
Quem in ultimis temporibus
Misisti nobis
Salvatorem
Et Redemptorem
Et angelum voluntatis tuae,
Qui est verbum tuum inseparabile,
Per quem omnia fecisti,
Et beneplacitum tibi fuit;
Misisti de coelo in matricem virginis,
Quique in utero habitus, incarnatus est
Et filius tibi ostensus est;
Et Spiritu Sancto
Et virgine natus;
Qui voluntatem tuam complens,
Et populum sanctum tibi adquirens,
Extendit manus cum pateretur,
Ut a passione liberaret
Eos qui in te crediderunt;
Qui, cumque traderetur voluntariae passioni
Ut mortem solvat \
Et vincula diaboli dirumpat,
Et infernum calcet,
Et justos illuminet,
Et terminum figat,
Et resurrectionem manifestet,
Accipiens panem,

Gratias tibi agens,
Dixit : Accipite, manducate;
Hoc est corpus meum
Quod pro vobis confringetur.
Similiter et calicem
Dicens : Hic est sanguis meus
Qui pro vobis effunditur ;
Quando hoc facitis,
Meam commemorationem facitis.
Memores igitur mortis
Et resurrectionis ejus,
Offerimus tibi panem et calicem,
Gratias tibi agentes,
Quia nos dignos habuisti
Adstare coram te
Et tibi ministrare.
Et petimus,
Ut mittas Spiritum tuum Sanctum
In oblationem sanctae Ecclesiae ;
In unum congregans, des omnibus,
Qui percipiunt, sanctis
In repletionem Spiritus Sancti,
Ad confirmationem fidei in veritate,
Ut te laudemus et glorificemus
Per puerum tuum Jesum Christum,
Per quem tibi gloria et honor
Patri et Filio cum Sancto Spiritu,
In sancta Ecclesia tua,
Et nunc et in saecula saeculorum.
Amen.

The latter part of the Epistle of Clement I to the Corinthians offers a very significant instance of an abrupt transition from the epistolary and hortative manner to this lyrical style inspired by our Anaphora, thus demonstrating the extreme antiquity of this literary form, of which there are so many traces in the Roman Pontifical. After exhorting his readers to peace and submission, the Pontiff *ex abrupto* goes on : *Inspector omnium Deus, et Dominus spirituum, et herus universae carnis, qui elegit Dominum Jesum Christum et nos per eum in populum peculiarem, det omni animae quae gloriosum et sanctum nomen ejus invocaverit, fidem, timorem,*

---

[1] Cagin, *op. cit.*, pp. 147 *sq.*

pacem, patientiam, aequanimitatem, continentiam, castitatem et pudicitiam, ut nomini ejus recte placeat per summum sacerdotem et patronum nostrum Jesum Christum, per quem illi gloria, majestas, potestas, honor et nunc et in saecula saeculorum. Amen. The beautiful prayers contained in sections IX and X of the Διδαχὴ, though drawing their inspiration from the dominating idea of the eucharistic mystery, are simply for the Agape and constitute no part of any liturgical Anaphora.

Two famous documents of the fourth century, the one Italian, the other from Palestine, describe at length the ceremonies of the Mass as they were carried out in Italy and at Jerusalem. In the Easter week of the year 348, St Cyril, who was then only a simple priest under Bishop Maximus of Jerusalem, gave a course of explanatory conferences, the very model of their kind, to the neophytes whom he had already initiated into the Christian faith during the preceding Lent. There remained to be explained only that portion of the Catechism which the *disciplina arcani* kept hidden at that time from the uninitiated, and Cyril set to work to lift the veil in five conferences—"πρὸς τοὺς νεοφωτίστους."[1] In the fifth conference, the only one which concerns us, he describes the *missa fidelium,* since the Mass of the Catechumens must have been quite familiar to his hearers, seeing that the abuse of remaining in this class up to the end of one's life in order to be baptized on one's deathbed was only too widespread. Cyril first explains the meaning of the bishop washing his hands before commencing the Anaphora; then, passing over the *cherubicon,* he comes to the dialogue between the celebrant and the people, "Ανω τὰς καρδίας, followed by the splendid eucharistic hymn preceding the Trisagion. The Invocation he regards ideally, in one single view, inclusive of the sacramental formula *Christi verba continens,* as Justin words it. The Litany follows with the Commemoration of the Dead and the final *Amen* of the people. To the priest's invitation, 'Αγιᾶ ἁγίοις, already mentioned in the Διδαχὴ, the choir at the moment of Communion reply that one only is holy, Christ Jesus; then to the singing of the verse of the psalm *Gustate et videte quoniam suavis est Dominus,* as a solo, μετὰ μέλους Θείου, the faithful approach to receive the Holy Eucharist. The consecrated particle is placed in the hand of each; then, drawing near to the sacred chalice, they sign themselves with the sign of the cross on eyes and forehead.

The thanksgiving pronounced by the bishop in the name of

---

[1] Some MSS. attribute the " Mystagogic Catecheses " to Bishop John. This authorship is not unlikely, as, strictly speaking, it would fall to Cyril to give only the instructions preparatory to baptism.

all present sums up that more intimate thanksgiving already made by each one in the secrecy of his own heart, during such time as the sacred ministers were occupied in distributing the holy mysteries to the faithful.[1]

The account of the Eucharist given in the *De Sacramentis* makes only a passing illusion to the rites of the Mass without giving any real description of them. The author, who is evidently accustomed to the Ambrosian rite, is desirous of showing that the transubstantiation of the eucharistic elements of bread and wine into the body and blood of Christ takes place through the all-powerful efficacy of our Lord's own words. To this end he says that that which precedes the consecration—viz., *Laus Deo, oratio pro populo, pro regibus, pro caeteris,* is offered up in the name of the priest and of the assembly, adding : *at ubi venitur ut conficiatur . . . sacramentum, jam non suis sermonibus sacerdos, sed utitur sermonibus Christi,* and ends by calling to mind the formula used by the priest in giving the Holy Communion : *Dicit tibi sacerdos: Corpus Christi. Et tu dicis: Amen.*[2]

[1] S. Cyrilli Hierosol, *Catech. Mystagog.*, v; *P.G.* XXXIII, 1110 *sq.*
[2] L. IV, c. iv; *P.L.* XVI, col. 460.

CHAPTER VI

THE PAPAL MASS AT THE ROMAN STATIONS

FROM the commencement of the eighth century rituals and explanations of the ceremonies of the Mass begin to be less rare, but no document exceeds in importance the collection known as the *Ordines Romani*, by means of which we are able to follow the development of the papal liturgy in Rome all through the Middle Ages. It is not easy, indeed, always to fix the exact date of these ceremonials, which often amount to no more than mere aids to memory compiled at different times from ancient sources. There is nothing more impersonal than the Liturgy, and it is this which makes it difficult to recognize the successive emanations of these documents and correctly to establish their chronology.[1] The *Ordo Romanus I*, to which we now refer, was finally revised in the eighth century, but there are older elements in it, showing clearly the state of the papal Liturgy after the reform of St Gregory. This was the period of the great stational processions, revived by him, after a century of wars, sieges and civil trouble had caused them to be temporarily abandoned.[2]

When the Mass was not preceded by a procession, the Pope went straight to the stational church and vested in the *secretarium*, aided by the chief persons of the Apostolic Palace; while the bishops, clergy and monks took their places within the building. When all was ready, one of the regionary subdeacons approached the sacristy door, calling out, *Schola*, upon which the paraphonist presented himself before the Pope and announced the names of those soloists who were to sing the Epistle and the Gradual. The *Ordo* adds that when this was once done, no change was allowed to be made in the persons of the singers, under penalty of being excluded from holy Communion on that day.

The papal retinue, in their many-coloured mantles, their paenulas, mappulas and white tunics, now arranged themselves in order for their triumphal entry into the basilica, while, at a sign from the Pope, a subdeacon bade the paraphonist intone the antiphon of the Introit.

The latter bowed to the prior of the *schola: domne jubete,*

---

[1] Cf. *P.L.* LXXVIII, 937 *sq.*

[2] *Cf.* H. Grisar, *La più antica descrizione della Messa pontificia solenne,* Civiltà Cattol., 20 magg. 1905, pp. 463 *sq.*

and the choir, placed on either side before the altar, sang the melody from the Gregorian Antiphonary. The seven deacons then went into the *secretarium* to escort the Pope, who made his entrance into the basilica in procession, supported by the chief dignitaries of the Lateran Court. Before proceeding up the sanctuary, however, the cortège paused to allow the Pontiff to adore a particle of the Holy Eucharist reserved for that purpose in a pyx from a previous Mass. This was retained on the altar during the ensuing ceremony, as a symbol of the eternal sacrifice of Calvary, ever perpetuated in the Church until the day of the final παρουσία of the Lord,[1] *donec veniat.*

Traversing the marble enclosure reserved for the singers, the Pope went up to the *tribunal,* where the episcopal throne was set facing the altar. There he at once exchanged the Kiss of Peace with the bishop of the week, the archpriest and the deacons; and while, at a sign from him, the prior of the *schola* was bringing the Introit to an end with the Doxology, he knelt in prayer for a moment at the altar, kissing in conclusion the holy table and the Book of the Gospels. The church was already re-echoing with the plaintive strains of the ever-repeated *Kyrie,* in which the people also might join; and, when all was ready, the Pope intoned the *Gloria,* which was taken up by the bishops and priests, thus becoming from a simple morning hymn, as it was at first, a specially sacerdotal chant.

After the *oratio* and the reading of the first lesson from the Old Testament by the subdeacon, a solo singer went up into the ambo *cum cantatorio* and intoned the Gradual. After the second or New Testament lesson, usually taken from St Paul's Epistles, there followed, according to the season of the year, the Tract or Alleluiatic Verse; lastly, the deacon ascended the ambo with the Book of the Gospels, and read from it a short passage which the Pope, as a rule, commented upon and explained to the people, using very simple thoughts and familiar words.

Formerly the catechumens were dismissed at this point, as also those who for their transgressions had been excluded from communion with the Church. The Eastern and Ambrosian Liturgies still retain the formulas for this dismissal,

---

[1] "*Salutat Sancta.*" The rite is parallel with that described by S Germanus of Paris in his "Expositio Missae," *P.L.* LXXII, 92, 3, and by Gregory of Tours in the "De Gloria Martyrum," c. lxxxv. It was also common to the Greek liturgy; in fact, the obeisance made by the faithful when the priest passed with the "holy Gifts" during the great Introit seems to have arisen from the custom of carrying the Holy Eucharist in procession, as was done by the Latins, whatever explanation may be given to it nowadays by the Easterns. S Germanus, too, mentions this obeisance, "*incurvati adorarent.*"

but the rite itself, together with the Great Litany which then
ushered in the *missa fidelium* properly so called, have long
disappeared from the Roman Liturgy.   In the first half of the
sixth century, in a church in the neighbourhood of Monte
Cassino, the deacon, as St Gregory relates,[1] still used to
pronounce the formula for dismissing those who were excom-
municated, but the later Roman sources are entirely silent on
this point.

Meanwhile the sacred ministers spread the linen cloth on
the altar, and the Pope, accompanied by the deans of the
notaries and by the *defensores,* approached the enclosure
reserved to the great nobles, in order to receive personally
their offerings for the holy sacrifice.   The archdeacon followed
him, ready to pour the *ampullae* of wine one by one as they
were presented to him by the faithful into a large two-handled
chalice held by a subdeacon.   After the men, came the turn
of the women.   The Pope then went to the *matroneum* to
receive the offerings of the ladies, pausing for a while at the
foot of the steps leading to the tribunal to take over also
those of the high officials of the Lateran Court.   The bishops
and priests in the meantime collected the offerings of the
people at the *pergula,* which shut off the space reserved for
the clergy.   Thus the sacrifice about to be offered to almighty
God bore a thoroughly collective and social character, inasmuch as each one took his part in it, bringing his own contribution for supplying the material elements of bread and wine;
as one of the oldest prayers in the Gregorian Sacramentary so
well expresses it : *Ut quod singuli obtulerunt ad honorem
nominis tui, cunctis proficiat ad salutem.*   The Pope himself
was not exempt from taking with his people his share in the
offerings for the sacrifice, and very pathetic for this reason
was the privilege accorded to the orphaned singers of the
Lateran, who, on account of their poverty, used to bring as
their offering only the ampulla containing the water, which
the archdeacon poured into the chalice in the form of a cross.

Here originally followed the reading of the diptychs with
the *oratio super nomina,* preserved in the Gallican Liturgy and
in the *secreta* of the prayer *A cunctis* in the Roman Missal;
but at Rome, in 410, it had already been transposed to just
before the Consecration.   The various chalices of wine, together with the loaves of unleavened bread, were arranged on
the altar for the Communion; and whilst the *schola* repeated
the last neums of the antiphon *ad offertorium,* the Pope went
up to the altar to begin the eucharistic *actio* itself.   Up to
this point there has been nothing that rightly belongs to the
sacrifice as such; the choir therefore remain seated until the

[1] *Dialog.,* lib. II, 23.

priest begins the *praefatio*. The bishops and priests now range themselves in a double line behind the Pope; the sub-deacons take up their position near the gates separating the tribunal of the clergy from the people, and all remain in their places motionless and bowed down until the end of the Canon. Just before the *Pater Noster,* the archdeacon goes up to the Pope, and when the latter elevates the Host in the sight of all and recites the final doxology *per ipsum,* he, too, lifts up on high one of the eucharistic chalices from the altar. This was the solemn showing of the sacred mysteries to the people common to nearly all liturgies, of which our medieval elevation is merely a reflex.

The eucharistic particles which are detached at this point in the *actio* from the Host consecrated by the Pope are given to the acolytes, who bear them to the priests of the titular churches in their several parishes to be placed in the chalice at the conclusion of the canon of their own Mass, thus sym-bolizing the identity of the Sacrifice and Sacrament by which pastor and flock alike are nourished and sanctified.

Before the Pope completes the *fractio* of the sacred mysteries, which symbolizes the violent death of the divine Victim, he gives a last greeting to the people as an augury of peace—*Pax Domini sit semper vobiscum;* and the peace thus invoked by the pastor is at once passed on to the clergy, nobles and people by means of the apostolic embrace, the *osculum sanctum.* The archdeacon receives it from the Pope and exchanges it with the chief among the bishops; the men and the women embrace separately, while the nobles and the great ladies do the same in the *senatorium* and *matroneum.* The *consecratio* and the sacrifice are complete at the end of the canon; here, in the Gallican rite, the bishops used even to bless the people, so as to allow those to depart who did not intend to receive holy Communion. At Rome the Pope used now to leave the altar to return to his throne, whence he gave instructions to the *nomenclator,* to the *sacellarius* and to the notary of the *majordomus* concerning those whom he wished to invite to dinner, either at his own table, or at that prepared in his name in the apartments of the majordomus. To those who were thus invited the Holy Communion was forthwith imparted in the Church; so closely was the memory of the agape still bound up with that of the eucharistic feast.

While this is being done, the bishops, priests and deacons, from around the papal throne, proceed with all solemnity to the *fractio panis*. They break up the eucharistic bread, pre-sented to them by the acolytes in small linen bags, and place the particles on the patens, to the singing of the *schola* who meanwhile intone the *Agnus Dei*—that eloquent chant, in which, from the time of Pope Sergius I (687-701), the people also joined—thus investing with solemn dignity this symbolical *fractio,* which after the Consecration and the Invocation is the most characteristic moment of the eucharistic *actio.*

It appertained to the second of the seven deacons to give the sacred particle for Communion to the Pope, who, upon taking it, first broke off a fragment which the archdeacon replaced in the large two-handled chalice, from which the Pontiff then received the precious Blood.

The chalice having been placed again on the altar, the archdeacon announced to the people the date and place of the next station; and as one chalice alone would not have sufficed for the Communion of so great a number of the faithful as presented themselves it was customary, in order to show also in a tangible form the oneness of the sacrifice in which all participated, to pour some few drops of the eucharistic wine from the Pope's chalice into the large cup (σκύφος) of the people. The bishops and priests received their particle of the consecrated bread from the hands of the Pope; they then drew near to receive Communion from the Pope's chalice, which was presented to them by the archdeacon, while that which still remained over after their Communion was also poured into the σκύφος of the people. To facilitate the reception by the faithful of the Holy Communion under both kinds with greater reverence, and with less difficulty, a regionary subdeacon, so as to avoid any danger of spilling, placed in the chalice a tube of precious metal, such as is still in use at the Papal Mass.

When the Communion of the higher clergy was finished, the Pope, with the bishops and priests, distributed the Blessed Sacrament to the nobles and the people, while the choir chanted the Communion psalm with its antiphon. The deacons, bearing the two-handled chalices, assisted the Pope and the bishops; and of the priests, some distributed the sacred particles, while others carried the σκύφος.

As soon as the nobles and great ladies had received the Communion, and while the holy Sacrament was still being administered to the people, the Pope returned to his throne in order to give Communion to the regionary subdeacons; and on feast days also to twelve children chosen from the *schola* of the singers. Therefore the subdeacons, who had previously received the holy Communion, came to the assistance of the *schola,* so that they sang the Antiphon and Communion psalm in alternate verses until the distribution of the holy mysteries was completed. Then, standing before the altar, alone, but in the name of all, the Pope recited the collect *ad complendum* in thanksgiving for the holy gifts received; a deacon sang the formula of dismissal, *ite, missa est,* to which the people having answered *Deo gratias,* the pontifical procession began to return towards the *secretarium.* Seven acolytes with lighted candles went in front; a subdeacon gently waved the smoking thurible, then came the Pope, followed by the bishops, priests and monks, the *schola,* the standard-bearers, and all the other high officials of the Patriarchate. Everyone bowed down as the Pontiff passed by, saying, *Jube, domne, benedicere,* to which he responded : *Benedicat nos Dominus.*[1]

[1] *Ordo Romanus I; P.L.* LXXVIII, 937 *sq.*

CHAPTER VII
POETRY AND MUSIC IN THE EUCHARISTIC SYNAXIS

HAVING thus far studied the elements of our subject, we are now ready to differentiate and arrange in chronological order the component parts of this splendid assemblage of eucharistic rites. If it is true that in them the bridegroom utters a language of love so ineffable that it can scarcely be translated into human speech, it may equally be said that the bride soars to such sublimity of thought as can only be understood by those chosen souls who, through a spotless life, realize in themselves the ideal of grace and sanctity possessed in all its fulness by the Church. Hence, to be fully understood, the sacred Liturgy must above all be realized in union with the one, holy, Catholic and Apostolic Church.

Litanies, collects, scriptural readings, eucharistic prayers and general acclamations, all these we have found in sufficient number from the second half of the first century onwards in the writings of St Paul and St John, and above all in the Διδαχή. Moreover, which is more remarkable, they maintained the same order in liturgical use as they had formerly occupied in the προσευχή of Palestine and Greece.

Perhaps it will be thought singular that we have at once brought our readers to assist at the holy sacrifice in the Roman catacombs at the time of Justin and Tertullian, and then carried them off to Jerusalem, to Milan, and to the great Constantinian basilicas of the Lateran and of St Peter, without first of all furnishing them with any introductory explanation of the ritual and euchological constituents of the sacred *actio*. Here we must plead guilty to a little artifice on our part, arising from the wish to give an immediate impression of the lyrical sublimity of Christian worship, before proceeding to analyze its separate formulas, since these latter are as little able as the human skeleton to convey to us the full joy and beauty of the actual living body.

Nevertheless it is time to examine more in detail various elements which go to make up our Missal, especially now that we are in a position to appreciate the beauty of them and to realize the place which each has occupied in the arrangement and development of liturgical ceremonial. The eminently dramatic character of the *actio sacra* being granted, we will begin by distinguishing the various musical types to which the psalm-chants in the Mass belong.

The Psalter, the book of ecclesiastical prayer *par excellence,* furnished our Saviour and his Church with the accents of that sublime supplication which, foretold in different forms and at different times in the songs of David, found its true completion in the vesper prayer uttered upon Calvary on the first Good Friday.

We know of four different kinds of psalmody in the early Church :

(*a*) A solo singer chanting in an assembly of persons a psalm which is interrupted after every verse or group of verses by a refrain sung by those present ; this is the *psalmus responsorius.* It has the great advantage of closely uniting the feelings of the cantor with those of the congregation, arousing their mutual attention and ensuring that the two alternate parts shall be closely interwoven and shall complete each other. This intimate bond and inter-connection, as well in the melodies of the psalmody as in the scriptural readings to which the psalmody served as ornament and setting, is one of the most striking features of the ancient liturgy, emphasised by the eminently dramatic forms which unfolded themselves with a regular and natural dignity, just as in a great drama or in the scenic representation of a sacred poem.

For a right understanding of the beauty of the Roman Liturgy, and especially of the Missal, too great an emphasis cannot be laid upon the fact that all these prayers, chants and ceremonies were originally intended and arranged to be carried out in a spacious basilica. Low Masses took their rise much later, and simply constitute an adaptation of the grandeur of the stational Liturgy, which had been purposely so drawn up as to be participated in by a very large number of persons.

The origin of the *responsorius* is bound up with that of the Psalter itself ; indeed, some psalms demand exclusively this form of rendering with refrains, such as Psalm cxxxv, which was sung by the great choir at the dedication of the Temple of Jerusalem, while the people cried out *Quoniam in aeternum misericordia ejus.* Christian antiquity took over this custom from the synagogue, where it still flourishes ; it even found its way beyond the strictly liturgical rite into the private devotion of the faithful, as when Evodius at the deathbed of St Monica chanted Psalm c, to which Augustine and the other members of her family replied with the refrain : *Misericordiam et judicium cantabo tibi, Domine.*[1]

---

[1] August., *Confess.,* lib. IX, c. xii, n. 3. St Jerome in his life of St Paul, the first Hermit, relates how St Anthony buried his friend "hymnos quoque et psalmos de christiana traditione decantans" (c. xiii), and the responsorial psalm sung at Ostia at St Monica's deathbed was probably one of those which belonged to this collection of traditional funeral psalms.

(*b*) Akin to the responsorial psalm is that which is recited without interruptions by a soloist, the persons assembled answering him only by some formula or final doxology, such as *Amen, Benedictus Deus, Alleluia,* or something similar. Psalms xl, lxxi, lxxxviii, and especially Psalm cv—*Benedictus Dominus Deus Israel a saeculo et usque in saeculum. Et dicet omnis populus: Fiat, fiat*—all bear witness to this custom among the Hebrew people. In the time of Cassian the rite of the Gallican monasteries, unlike that of the Eastern monasteries, required that the assembly should sing the *Gloria Patri* immediately upon the termination of the psalm by the soloist; whereas in Egypt and in Palestine this doxology was reserved for the conclusion of the antiphonal psalm only.[1]

(*c*) Antiphonal psalmody differs from responsorial in that the original soloist's part having been done away with, the people were divided into two choirs for the execution of, as it were, a duet, singing alternate verses to different melodies, sometimes even in different languages, and coming into unison again at intervals of an octave.[2] Later on, when the polyphonic element with its consonance in octaves had become of secondary importance, and had been forgotten, it was the double choir and the answering in turn which came to be considered as the characteristic of the antiphonal psalm. The people's refrain[3] was not necessarily chosen from the psalm itself, as was done in the case of the responsorial chant (the Alleluia inserted in the alleluiatic psalms came, however, to be regarded as a true psalmodic element), but might also be taken from other parts of the Scriptures; and in this case it bore some particular application or indicated the special meaning given by the Liturgy to a psalm in certain circumstances. Thus at Pentecost the antiphon of the Introit is taken from the Book of Wisdom (i, 7) *Spiritus Domini replevit orbem terrarum,* and the psalm which follows, Psalm lxvii—*Exsurgat Deus et dissipentur inimici ejus*—alludes directly to the mission of the Holy Ghost—namely, to glorify our Lord and to humble his foes. It very soon became the custom—earlier in the East than in the West—to make the doxology (*Gloria Patri*) the conclusion of the antiphonal psalm, thus giving to this latter a markedly Trinitarian and anti-Arian character.

The origin of the antiphon is generally considered to date back to the years 344-357, when the monks Flavian and Diodorus brought it to Antioch in order to combat the Arian antiphony then dominant in that city. Yet its introduction into the Eastern Liturgy is very much older than the fourth century, since in the time of St Basil the Antistrophe was

---

[1] Cassian, *Institut.* II, c. viii. [2] Wagner, *op. cit.,* 23.
[3] Cassian, *op. cit.,* II, c. xi.

universally known, and even before his day Eusebius Pamphilus discoursed on it at length.[1] We shall return later on to speak of the sources of the antiphony.

(*d*) Related to antiphonal and responsorial psalmody is that which may be called the psalmody of the Litany, consisting of verses repeated alternately by priest and people; traces of which Baümer thinks may be found as far back as the first century. The early Christians in general gave to this type of chant the name of *Litania*. Unlike the preceding kinds of psalmody, the Litany was not derived exclusively from the Psalms, and, even when emanating thence, the paraphrase was so free that it quite lost its literary unity (unalterably preserved on the other hand in antiphonal and responsorial psalmody), and became rather a lively dialogue between the people and the celebrant.[2] In proportion then as the Litany broke away from the text of the Psalter, it gained in freshness of inspiration, spiritual vitality and sense of reality. The last part of our *litania major* or Litany of the Saints, together with the *preces* of the Breviary at Prime and at Compline, are among the best examples of this Litany, which originally marked the transition between the *Vigilia* and the Mass which followed it at daybreak. Very characteristic of the *litania* was the Collect, which united and summed up the common thought of the worshippers. The Gloria, which is now interposed in the Mass between the Litany and the Collect, represents an insertion of much later date.

(*e*) Altogether different from this alternating psalmody was the psalm known as *in directum* or *tractus*, which was entrusted exclusively to the skill of a soloist. Cassian relates how the monks of Egypt used, when keeping their night vigils, to recite twelve psalms *in directum: parili pronunciatione, contiguis versibus*, and St Benedict ordains this psalmody *in directum* for the day hours whenever the small number of monks would make antiphonal chanting too great a burden. The *in directum* is the easiest and most convenient kind of psalmody, and is that which has in the end prevailed over the other kinds in ecclesiastical use. It is remarkable, too, that both Cassian and St Benedict attached peculiar importance to it, observing that it was the only sort of psalmody suitable to a very small community, whose members, moreover, would probably be tired out after a hard day's work.[3]

The *in directum* was called also the *tractus*, unless we are to

---

[1] *Cf.* Wagner, *op. cit.*, 21, 22; *La petite antiphone* in *Dictionnaire d'archéologie chrétienne et de liturgie*, edited by Dom F. Cabrol, I, 2, col. 2473.
[2] F. Cabrol, *Liturgical Prayer*, p. 35.
[3] Cassian, *Institut.* II, 12.

understand by this latter term a special kind of psalmody *in directum,* one enriched with more solemn and more ornate melodies. Some derived the name *tractus* from the slow manner of its execution, while others held that it simply meant the psalmodic continuity proper to this type of psalmody, without the interpolation of any refrain whatsoever.

The fact is, that while the *directaneum* of the soloist was preferred by the monks of ancient Egypt just because it was more rapid and less fatiguing, in the Rule of St Benedict, on the other hand, the *subtrahendo,* attached to the responsorial invitatory of the vigils, has become synonymous with *morose,*[1] and marks an entirely different type of performance.

In more recent times certain liturgists have sought to recognize in the *tractus* the sadness proper to penitential seasons. We would, however, observe that the tract *Laudate Dominum* of the Easter vigil, and the eighth Gregorian tone, to which many tracts belong, are not in the least melancholy or mournful in character, and we shall see later on that the *tractus* was the Sunday and Feast day chant of the Roman Liturgy, previous, that is, to the introduction of the alleluiatic verse for all the Sundays outside of Lent. The characteristics of the *tractus* were the solo singing and the continuity of psalmodic modulation without any interruption or refrain on the part of the congregation. It would seem to be a fact of much less importance, on the other hand, that, in the eucharistic Liturgy, the *tractus* is intimately connected with the Scripture lesson which precedes it. (Compare, for instance, the *Cantemus Domino* of Holy Saturday and the *Benedictiones* of Ember Saturday, coming after the lesson about the three children in the fiery furnace.)

(*f*) The *psalmus gradualis* is not strictly speaking a distinct kind of psalmody; it merely signifies a responsorial chant with solos sung from the steps of the ambo. It is derived by some from a transformation of the *tractus,* after this latter had taken on a much more ornate type of melody of an antiphonal character, becoming thus a true responsorial antiphony; yet we know that the responsorial gradual was already in use long before the time of Leo I, and that it was co-existent with the gradual.

Before concluding this short summary of the different psalmodic forms anciently in use in the early Church, we must point out, however briefly, the æsthetic law which measures and determines all these prolonged melodies and refrains. We allude to parallelism, which is a kind of echo between the

---

[1] *Regula S Benedicti,* c. xliii, " Propter hoc omnino *subtrahendo et morose* volumus dici."

two parts of one and the same psalmodic verse. Biblical parallelism has been defined by Dom Cabrol as the rhythm of thought;[1] it thus preserves for us, as it were, the last trace of the original poetical form of the Psalms and Canticles, composed according to metrical laws which have only been brought to light by recent study.

Parallelistic redundancy resembles a gentle lulling of the mind in devout affections, from which the entranced spirit is for ever drawing forth fresh sweetness; and this is the effect of an intense comprehensiveness of thought seeking repeated individual expression, thus prolonging the spiritual joy of the faithful soul. Antithetic parallelism, on the other hand, unlike redundancy, provides strong contrasts of light and shade, at times carrying the sacred lyric to heights hardly attainable by any kind of profane literature. In both these kinds of parallelism the characteristic element which it concerns us most to notice is the alternating unison and the mutual refrain of the various members of the verse or parts of a psalm, for this constitutes the æsthetic basis of responsorial and strophic psalmody. While Psalm lxx offers us several examples of parallelism in half-verses, Psalm cvi gives us, on the other hand, four little sketches,[2] matchless in their purity of outline, and separated the one from the other by means of one and the same eucharistic verse: *Confiteantur Domino misericordiae ejus et mirabilia ejus filiis hominum,* with which also the psalm is brought to a conclusion as with a kind of doxology.

We have thus traced the sources of our psalmodic forms, beyond the mere custom of the synagogue, back to the fundamental laws of artistic literary perceptions among the Semitic peoples, from whom we ourselves, *aedificati super fundamentum Apostolorum et Prophetarum,* have with full right inherited, together with the sacred legacy of the Scriptures, the artistic setting in which they were contained. The time has now come in which to examine the use which the Church has made of her treasures; for, like the mystical bride presaged in the song of Debbora,[3] she gives out most joyfully to the faithful the rich booty brought to her by her divine bridegroom, returning from battle as victor over death and hell.

---

[1] *op. cit.,* p. 14.
[2] They are those of a man lost in the desert and about to die of hunger, a prisoner, a sick person, and lastly a ship caught in a storm and in danger of foundering.
[3] Judg. v, 30.

CHAPTER VIII

THE PART OF THE LATERAN MUSICAL "SCHOLA" IN THE DEVELOPMENT OF THE ROMAN LITURGY

THE INTROIT.—That which has been remarked concerning the origin of so many other ecclesiastical rites is equally true of the Introit—viz., that having been first introduced into the liturgy of one particular Church, it gradually spread everywhere until at last it became an integral part of Catholic ceremonial.

We have already stated the reasons why there could be neither Introit nor any psalmodic antiphony as such, during the first three centuries, so long as the condition of the Church did not allow of the bishop entering his basilica in state accompanied by a triumphal escort. Yet it seems that there must have been some kind of initial greeting or acclamation uttered by the celebrant to those present before the beginning of the scriptural lessons, since besides a text from the pseudo-Dionysius, which describes how the priest, having censed the altar and choir, returns to the *vima* and ἀπάρχεται τῆς ἱερᾶς ψαλμῶν μελῳδίας,[1] a passage in St Basil mentions a Euchology which preceded the readings from the prophets. Οὐ γάρ δέ τούτοις ἀρχούμεθα ὧν ὁ'Απόστολος, ἤ τὸ Εὐαγγέλιον ἐπεμνήσθη, ἀλλά προλέγομεν, καὶ ἐπιλέγομεν ἕτερα, ὡς μεγάλην ἔχοντα πρὸς τὸ μυστήριον τὴν ἰσχύν.[2]

Whatever may have been the custom in the East, at Rome a silent prayer, *ante altare, super oratorium*,[3] is inserted before the lessons in the Liturgy for Good Friday, which, better than any other, preserves the primitive type of the papal Liturgy; but the Mass for that day has no Introit, a peculiarity common in Rome to all Masses of the vigils, in which, the lessons being ended, the *actio* is begun with the Litany only. It is to be noted that in the Roman rite the Litanies were sung on the night preceding Easter, while the bishop was occupied in the baptistery, so that his solemn entrance with the neophytes into the church should take place during the final Κύριε of the Litany, which on that night, therefore, constituted a real Introit.

The passages from St Ambrose[4] and from St Gregory of

---

[1] *De Eccles. Hier.*, c. iii.
[2] *De Spiritu Sancto ad Amphilochium*, c. xxvii.
[3] Cf. *Ordines Romani, P.L.* LXXVIII, 953.
[4] *Epist.*, i, 20; *P.L.* LXXVIII, 986.

Tours (?) in his *Life* of St Nicetius of Trèves,[1] which are commonly cited to prove the absence of the Introit in the Ambrosian Liturgy (fourth century) and in the Gallican (sixth century), are inconclusive, since they do not profess to describe the ceremonies of the Mass in detail, and, while they record the reading of passages from the Scriptures, make no mention at all of the responsorial psalms which at that time certainly followed such reading.

The authority of the *Liber Pontificalis,* on the other hand, is more explicit, in that it attributes the origin of the anti-phonal psalmody of the Introit to Pope Celestine (died 432),[2] adding that at first there was nothing read but the Gospel and the Epistles of St Paul.

The introduction of the Introit into the Roman Liturgy cannot therefore be prior to the fifth century, though it may possibly have been earlier elsewhere; but there at once arises the scarcely less important question of its primitive form.[3] Dom Morin, who considers the Introit to be far older than the time of Celestine, sees in it a parallel to the Ambrosian *ingressa,* which is without any psalm, even at the present day. Here we have a twofold difficulty—namely, that not only does the chanting of a single verse in no way fulfil the purpose for which the melody of the Introit was intended; that is to say, it would not occupy the whole of the time required for the processional entry of the Pope into the basilica; but also no other corresponding form is to be found in any ancient liturgical chant consisting exclusively of a hymn or of a psalm. Again, as Ceriani justly observes,[4] the Ambrosian *ingressa* is certainly of far later origin than what is called the *missa canonica* in the Milanese rite, and if to-day the *ingressa* has no psalm, this abridgement may well be owing to the fact that, contemporaneously with its introduc-tion into Milan, the Introit was shortened also in Gaul and elsewhere; in fact, in every place where, there being no papal procession to unfold itself through the aisles of the church, the antiphonal psalm became more and more a mere formality (eighth century). This is one of the many instances of atrophy to be met with in the history of the Liturgy. The antiphonal Introit was executed in Rome so that the refrain (*antiphona ad introitum*) alternated with the verses of the psalm in the following manner: *Incipit prior scholae anti-phona ad introitum . . . (pontifex) annuit (priori) ei ut dicat Gloriam, et prior . . . ; et pontifex orat . . . usque ad*

---

[1] *Vita S Nicetii ep., P.L.* LXXI, 1080. *Cf.* Duchesne, *Christian Worship,* c. vii, pp. 189 *sq.*

[2] *Liber Pontif.* (ed. Duchesne), i, 230. *Cf.* Duchesne *Christian Wor-ship,* c. vi, pp. 161 *sq.*

[3] *Veritables origines du chant grégorien.*

[4] *Notitia liturgiae Ambrosianae,* Milan 1895, p. 3.

*repetitionem versus. Nam diaconi surgunt quando dicturi:
Sicut erat . . . Schola vero, finita antiphona, intonet
Kyrie.*[1]

Recent study of the texts of these antiphons *ad introitum*
has established several very important results.[2] It is known
that some ten years or so after the death of St Gregory I a
sort of stagnation was already affecting the musical inspiration of the Roman *schola,* a stagnation or deadness partly
due, doubtless, to the current belief in the miraculous origin
of St Gregory's Antiphonary. This being a work produced
by St Gregory through the inspiration of the Holy Ghost, to
alter it in any way would be equivalent to pronouncing it to
be less than perfect. It was for this reason that the stational
Masses instituted by Pope Gregory II for the Thursdays of
Lent had to take their chants from other feasts found in the
Gregorian Cento.

Since the elaboration of the melody of the Introit did not
affect the length of the ceremony—for the psalm ended at the
moment when the celebrant went up to the altar—this melody
could be freely developed without paying much heed as to
whether the antiphon had any special reference, or not, to the
text of the psalm—as was usual in the case of the psalm *in
directum*—or as to whether, after the manner of the alleluiatic
psalms, it had merely a vague and distant connection with it.
We see this exactly in the case of the historical Introits, where
text and melody so wonderfully harmonize that with a sure
and graceful touch they at once sound the leading note of the
feast and embody its most characteristic features. The *Viri
Galilei*—the Introit for Ascension Day—is a striking example
of this, in which it is easy to see that the psalmodic element
is relegated to a secondary place by the desire of the composer to introduce a sacred prelude which should crystallize
in a single phrase both the triumphs of the Ascension and
those of the Second Coming of our Lord.

The choice of certain Introits drawn from the extra-
canonical books of Scripture is somewhat perplexing at the
first glance. We know that, at least from the time of
Pope Damasus, the Roman Church has cherished a marked
antipathy to the Fourth Book of Esdras, and yet several
antiphons and liturgical texts can be traced to this tainted
fount, amongst them the famous Reproaches of Good
Friday,[3] the Easter Antiphons for Martyrs (*Sancti tui*

---

[1] *P.L.* LXXVIII, 942; *Ordo Romanus I.*

[2] *Origine e sviluppo del canto liturgico sino alla fine del medio evo.*
Italian translation by M. R., revised by the author. Tip. San
Bernardino, Siena 1910, c. iv, pp. 64 *sq.*

[3] " Ego vos per mare transmeavi . . . lucem vobis per columnam ignis
praestiti, et magna mirabilia feci in vobis. . . . Ego dolui gemitus
vestros, et dedi vobis manna in escam." 4 Esd. i, 13, 14-24.

Domine and *Lux Aeterna lucebit sanctis*[1]), and, best known of all, the acclamation in the Office for the Dead (*Requiem aeternam*[2]).

The Responsory of the Night Office *modo coronatur et accipiunt palmam*,[3] the Introit *Exclamaverunt*,[4] with *Accipite jucunditatem gloriae vestrae*[5] and probably also *In excelso throno*,[6] all come from the same source. It is more difficult to establish the origin of the Introit *Ecce advenit*,[7] to the strains of which the Byzantines advanced to meet Pope John I when he made his solemn entry into the capital of the Bosphorus; but this contact of the extra-canonical Roman Introits with the parallel formulas of Byzantium does not seem to have been merely fortuitous, since the extra-canonical Introits would have found favour in Rome simply through the Greek Liturgy.[8] As a matter of fact, the Introit *Exclamaverunt* for the Feast of SS Philip and James distinctly alludes to an episode in Byzantine history—namely, the liberation of Rome by the Greek Narses, when the *Apostoleion* at the foot of the Quirinal was dedicated as a votive church in commemoration of the victory of the Byzantines over the Goths (553?).

The Introits of the Mass, which, though they bear no special character, yet follow one another in a certain fixed order in the Gregorian Antiphonary, help us to realize more clearly the standard of compilation adopted in the Gregorian Cento and to distinguish its successive developments. The Lenten Introits sometimes correspond to the psalms at Prime for the respective ferias,[9] while those of Pentecost fall into two groups. The first group comprises the Sundays from the first to the seventeenth and includes Psalms xii, xvii,

---

[1] " Lux perpetua lucebit vobis per aeternitatem temporis." Ch. ii, v. 35.

[2] " Requiem aeternitatis dabit vobis . . . quia lux perpetua lucebit vobis." ii, v. 34-5.

[3] ii, 45.   [4] ii, 9-28.

[5] " Accipite jucunditatem gloriae vestrae. Commendatum domum accipite et jucundamini gratias agentes ei qui vos ad coelestia regna vocavit." ii, 36-7.

[6] 4 Esd. viii, 21. "Domine . . . cujus thronus inaestimabilis et gloria incomprehensibilis; cui adstat exercitus angelorum."

[7] This is found as a *versus* to the second Responsory of Matins for the Second Sunday of Advent with the following variation : " Ecce Dominus cum virtute veniet; et regnum in manu ejus et potestas et imperium . . ."

[8] This intrusion of the Apocryphal Fourth Book of Esdras at Rome is parallel to the anomaly found in the mosaics of Sta Maria Maggiore, where, contrary to all Roman tradition, the Life of the Virgin is taken to a considerable extent from the *Protevangelium Jacobi*.

[9] Feria VI post Dom. II Quadrag. : *Ego autem* taken from Psalm xvi, assigned to Prime of that day according to the Benedictine *Cursus*; Sabb. post Dom. II Quadrag. : *Lex domini* taken from Psalm xviii, assigned to Prime of that day by the Benedictine *Cursus*.

xxiv, xxvi, xxvii, xlvi, xlvii, liii, liv, lxvii, lxix, lxxiii, lxxxiii, lxxxv, cxviii; the second group extends from the Wednesday of the autumn Ember Days to the twenty-fourth Sunday after Pentecost, and shows a wholly different plan of arrangement, since only once is the Introit taken from the Psalms (Ps. cxxix); in every other case it is chosen from the other canonical books of Scripture.

Still, one cannot as yet speak of an ordered scheme properly so called, since the Introits derived from the Psalms belong as a rule to the same period as those taken from the other books of Scripture, and occasionally to a later date, as is shown by the very ancient feasts of Christmas, Whitsuntide, and Epiphany, also by Easter Week and that of Pentecost, all of which have Introits of an eminently historical character.[1]

It is not without interest in this connection to examine into the reasons that determined the choice of the antiphon *ad introitum* for the stational Masses, which almost always contain hagiographical or historical allusions of great interest. Thus the Introit for the fourth Sunday of Lent, *Laetare Jerusalem,* makes a graceful allusion to the Church of *Jerusalem,* as the Sessorian Basilica was called, in which the Station took place. On the following Wednesday the Introit *Cum sanctificatus* has reference to the great scrutinies for the admission of the catechumens to Baptism, while the Introits of Easter Week and of Pentecost allude nearly all of them to the regeneration of the neophytes in the baptismal font. The Introit of the Dedication of the *Apostoleion* refers to the victory of Narses, the *Laudate pueri* to St Felicitas and her seven martyred sons, the *Confessio et pulchritudo* for St Lawrence to the Basilica *speciosa* erected over the tomb of the martyr by Gelasius I, and finally the *Sapientiam* for the martyrs SS Cosmas and Damian is connected with their profession of doctor, under which title the " two holy moneyless ones " were venerated by the Byzantines.

* * * * *

THE LITANY.—The provision of a concise formula by means of which the whole assembly of the faithful may unite themselves with the prayer of the sacred minister and share in his

---

[1] It is not at all unlikely that the author or compiler of certain of the Gregorian melodies may sometimes have taken into special account the building in which the composition would be performed. Thus in the Midnight Mass of Christmas the Introit *Dominus dixit,* on the second Tone, is very simple, because it was to be sung in the Crypt *ad Praesepe* of Santa Maria Maggiore, where the very limited space would allow of only a small gathering of persons, whilst the Introit *Scio cui credidi,* on the other hand, sung to the first Tone on the feast of the *Translatio* of St Paul, January 25, produced a marvellous effect in the spacious and imposing Ostian Basilica.

holy intentions; such is the benefit we derive from prayer in the form of a litany. *Let us call upon God on behalf of the catechumens, that he who is all goodness and full of love of all men, mercifully hearing our prayers . . . may reveal to them the Gospel of Christ, may enlighten them with divine wisdom, may admonish them in his precepts, may inspire them with pure and salutary fear, and may open the ear of their hearts.* And the people answer : *Kyrie eleison.* This is one of the most ancient forms of litany in existence.[1]

It is not, then, to be wondered at if this euchological formula, so easy in expression and so popular in character, penetrated from the very earliest times into all liturgies. Bäumer thinks that he has found traces of it in the very first century; but even if the arguments which he adduces to this end are not always clear and convincing, we must nevertheless agree with this eminent liturgiologist in recognizing the great antiquity of the Litany, so minutely described for us in the Apostolic Constitutions and in the *Peregrinatio of Etheria,* and so constantly met with in all liturgies whether Eastern or Western.

When the use of Greek as a liturgical language disappeared from Rome about the fourth century, the popular refrain in the Litany, *Kyrie eleison,* still maintained its place, having passed, doubtless through the influence of Rome, into the various Latin liturgies. The Mass of Holy Saturday (the Easter Vigil) still keeps in its old place—at the end of the Vigils and before the eucharistic sacrifice—one of the finest examples of the Litany, which in the fifth century was recited also in other parts of the liturgical Office, regularly preceding the collect of the priest. A canon of the Council of Vaison orders it to be sung at Mass, at Vespers, and at the morning Office (Lauds),[2] while the *Regula Sancta*[3] extends its use also to the end of each canonical hour, and the *Ordo Romanus I* even ordered the use of the Kyrie of the Litany at the beginning of the Easter Vespers.[4]

It would seem, however, that there are two distinct forms of Litany, the one much developed and very stately, represented to some extent by our *Litaniae Sanctorum,* and carefully preserved in the Oriental liturgies, the other so greatly condensed and simplified as to consist merely of the single acclamation *Kyrie eleison,* repeated a definite number of times. The fact of the Council of Vaison introducing the use

---

[1] *Cf.* S. Bäumer, *Histoire du Bréviaire,* vol. ii, 434, Traduction française par Dom R. Biron.

[2] *Cf.* Hefele, *Summ. Concil.,* pp. 740-42; *cf.* Bäumer, *op. cit.,* vol. i, pp. 221-22.

[3] Cf. *Regula S. Benedicti,* c. ix, xii, xiii, xvii.

[4] *Ordo Romanus I; P.L.* LXXVIII, 915. *Cf.* P. Wagner, *Origine e sviluppo del canto liturgico,* p. 69.

of the Litany into Gaul shows that it was already customary in Rome and in other churches, both in the East and in the West. Yet how and when the shorter Litany developed from the longer form cannot be clearly determined. In the sixth century the two forms already appear side by side, the longer one almost constituting a euchology in itself, and sometimes rendered much more solemn by being sung during the processions—*litania septiformis, quina, terna*—whilst the shortened form was recited in the Mass and in the divine Office simply as a preparation for the *collecta* of the priest.

The *Ordo Romanus I* mentions the sevenfold litany, then the fivefold and the threefold sung by the *schola* in the Lateran Basilica, while the Pope was administering Baptism *ad fontes ;*[1] but the Gregorian Regest and John the Deacon reserve the title of sevenfold for the other celebrated litany or penitential procession instituted by St Gregory in 590, when the people of Rome in seven groups repaired in mournful array to the Vatican Basilica.

The *Kyrie eleison* of the *Ordo Romanus I,* if it be not taken from the evening liturgy of the Byzantines, is, perhaps, a last relic of the processional litany[2] chanted by the *schola* while the clergy were going up to the *vima*—a rite identical with the chanting of the antiphons *Lapidem,* etc., when, after the Easter Vespers, the choir went from the Basilica of the Saviour to sing the lesser Vespers also in other adjacent oratories.

The great feature of the shortened Litany, on the other hand, seems to have been that it preceded the priest's *collecta,* thus approximating in some degree to the *oratio dominica* or to the *Pater Noster* which took the place of the collect at the Lateran down to the later Middle Ages. This is still, in a measure, the monastic custom, according to which every liturgical Office concluded normally with the Litany followed by the *Pater Noster* and by the *benedictio* or final *collecta* of the priest.

The place of the *Kyrie* in the eucharistic *actio* was not everywhere the same. The Greeks sang it after the Angelic Hymn, after the Gospel, and after the Communion; the early Milanese rite approached closely to the Eastern use, whilst in the Gallican the Litany followed the *Trisagion.* In all probability the Mozarabic rite also had felt the Eastern influence, in a great measure through the Gallican Liturgy, while Rome, on the other hand, remained more faithful to the earlier custom.

A very difficult question now presents itself—namely, that of the innovations which St Gregory made with regard to the

[1] *Ordo Romanus I; P.L.* LXXVIII, 957.
[2] *Ordo Romanus I; P.L.* LXXVIII, 965.

Litany in the Mass.   The Litany is undoubtedly very much
older than his restorative work : the canon of the Council of
Vaison, among other authorities, witnesses to this, as does
St Gregory himself, who, in a letter relating to such liturgical
innovations, does not, indeed, justify himself for having introduced the *Kyrie* into the Mass, but merely defends the new
way of reciting it, which was somewhat different from that of
the Greeks.   From this letter—the only existing document on
the question—we arrive at three facts : (*a*) Contrary to the
Eastern custom, according to which clergy and people together sing the *Kyrie,* at Rome they chanted it alternately ;
(*b*) unlike the Greeks in this also, the Romans inserted in
the *Kyrie* the invocation *Christe eleison;* (*c*) in the daily
Masses, in order to give full scope to the melody of the
Litany, the other invocations *quae dici solent*[1] had been
suppressed.   Here, then, is the crux of the whole question.
In what way did the solemn Masses, with the prayers *quae
dici solent,* differ from those daily Masses containing only the
shortened litany?

The Gregorian Sacramentary is our best authority upon the
structure of those daily Masses, almost private in character,
in which the Litany took on a more humble guise, in contrast
to the stational Masses, in which the clergy of Rome, together with a numerous following of the people, took part
together with the Pope.   On the occasion of the *missa
publica* some church adjacent to the one appointed for the
Statio was usually chosen as a preliminary place of meeting ;
then, when all were assembled, after the recital of a collect,
the whole body set forth, to the chanting of litanies, in
devout procession towards the stational Basilica, so that the
term *litanias facere* became synonymous with a processional
cortège.

Besides the *litania septiformis* of St Gregory, a decree of
Arcadius to the Prefect Clearchus, in which heretics are forbidden *ad litaniam faciendam . . . profanis coire conventi-
bus,* also bears evidence to the custom of employing the word
litania in this later meaning of procession.[2]

The divergence between the stational and the daily Masses
seems, therefore, to have involved also a twofold manner of
singing the litany, the *litania prolixa* being reserved for the
processional entry, whilst the *litania brevior* gave rise to
Masses of a more private character.   Occupying an intermediate position between these two were the *missae publicae*
of less solemn feasts, when the stational procession was
omitted, and the Introit took the place at Rome of the
preliminary *litania prolixa* at the beginning of the Mass.   On

[1] S. Gregorii I, *Regist.,* Epist. ix, 42 (26).
[2] *P.L.* LXXVIII, 867 *sq.*

such occasions, too, the shortened form of the Litany followed the Introit, as we have already seen; but in any case the innovation introduced by St Gregory had especially in view the daily Mass, from which, if we understand aright the words of the holy Pontiff, he had deleted the Introit, as being superfluous, in order to prolong somewhat the shorter litany in its stead.

Such instances of the lengthening out of the litanies are not, indeed, very unusual in the early Church, since medieval documents occasionally mention a *litania* consisting of the single invocation *Kyrie eleison* repeated a hundred times. *In assumptione S Mariae . . . exeunt cum litania ad S Mariam Maiorem . . . ibique in gradibus . . . omnis chorus virorum ac mulierum . . . una voce per numerum dicunt centies: Kyrie eleison . . . centies: Christe eleison item centies: Kyrie.* So speaks a Roman ritual of the eleventh century, preserved in the archives of Monte Cassino.[1]

It is true that the interpretation here placed upon St Gregory's letter seems at first sight inconsistent with the rubric of the Sacramentary, which prescribes the Introit and the Litany also, *sive diebus festis seu quotidianis;* so much so that the Introit in its shortened form is found unaltered in all the medieval sacramentaries. It is to be noticed, however, that St Gregory's innovation may well have reference to a time later than that at which a Sacramentary would be revised, so that among the things omitted *quae dici solent* the Introit itself may be included. Thus the Introit in Rome, at least from the seventh century, would appear to have been condensed by the supreme authority of the Sovereign Pontiff himself to the antiphonal chanting of a single verse of a psalm, immediately followed by the doxology.

Being a chant for the people, the Litany could not develop any very elaborate forms of melody, and the Ambrosian rite to-day still retains it in its primitive and almost syllabic form. At Rome, nevertheless, after the *schola* had appropriated to itself the execution of all the choral parts of the Mass, the *Kyrie* also came to be enriched by vocalizations, especially upon its final syllable, thus giving rise to the tropes of later centuries.

* * * * *

THE ANGELIC HYMN.—This indeed is the triumphal song of the Church, and one so sublime as perfectly to justify its appellation of *Angelic,* or of the *Great Doxology,* since here the mystical Bride of Christ joins with the angels of heaven in uttering an ineffable canticle of praise.

Much more so than the *Te Deum* is the *Gloria* truly the

[1] *P.L.* LXXVIII, 868.

eucharistic hymn, the great thanksgiving song, and it was as such that the holy Fathers sang it in all the most solemn circumstances of life.

Its origin reaches back to the earliest beginnings of Christian literature,[1] some writers even going so far as to identify it with that primitive *carmen* in honour of our Lord mentioned by Pliny, and with the hymn πολυώνυμος preserved to us by Lucian the Satirist.[2] There is absolutely nothing against such a supposition, since the rhythm to which the hymn is set, its literary form[3] and the theological conceptions underlying it would all equally carry it back to the very earliest sources of ecclesiastical literature. The Angelic Hymn, with its rhythmic harmony and its modulated phrases, that seem to answer one another in a species of rhyme—much more noticeable in the Greek text than in the Latin version—as it is as yet unaware of any Arian controversy, so is it still less concerned with the keen Trinitarian disputes of the time of Hippolytus. The Holy Ghost—whose divinity Origen considered a legitimate subject for controversy among theologians—is not even mentioned, and our Lord himself, just as in the Διδαχή and in the writings of St John, appears in the light of his mission of redemption, rather as High Priest and Lamb of God than as being consubstantial with the Father.

After the third century such language would certainly have seemed most equivocal, and favouring by its very reticence the Arian heresy, while the fact that during the Trinitarian polemics of the third and fourth centuries no heretic ever appealed to the hymn as an authority or tried to distort its meaning to give colour to his own doctrines, is in itself an indirect proof of the remoteness of its origin and of the completeness of its orthodoxy, too well known ever to have been called in question. The text falls naturally into three divisions. The Angelic Doxology forms, as it were, the introduction, after which comes the first part in praise of the Father; then follows that in praise of Jesus Christ, and lastly the mention of the Cherubim in the Greek text comes as a kind of Trisagion, *Sanctus-Dominus-Altissimus*, preparatory to the final doxology, in which, however, there is no mention at all of the Holy Ghost.

The oldest document which gives us the full text of the Angelic Hymn is the Seventh Book of the Apostolic Constitutions (fourth to fifth centuries), but there are allusions to it in the *De virginitate*, attributed—with some hesitation—to St Athanasius, but not later than the fifth to the sixth

[1] *Cf.* Batiffol, *History of the Roman Breviary, ed. cit.*, pp. 6 *sq.*
[2] Dom Cabrol, *Liturgical Prayer*, c. xi.
[3] Cf. *Paléograph. musicale*, 34, 45, p. 17 (1897).

centuries, and also in St John Chrysostom. In the West, besides a very doubtful note contained in the *Liber Pontificalis*, attributing the introduction of the hymn into the Roman Mass to Pope Telesphorus (died 154 ?), we know that Pope Symmachus (died 514) ordered it to be sung on Sundays and all feasts of martyrs; and as in the Alexandrine Codex of the Psalms (fifth century) the hymn is already found written after the Psalms, together with the other scriptural canticles, so also the Celtic Antiphonary of Bangor (end of seventh century), and later still the entire series of medieval psalters always keep a place of honour for the " Great Doxology " at the end of the Davidic Psalter.

THE COLLECT.—The Angelic Hymn forms a parenthesis between the Litany and the Collect on certain rare feast days; ordinarily, however, the prayer of the priest concludes the Litany of the people, which thus constitutes a natural prelude to his intercession. In the Roman Liturgy the Collect, which now precedes the reading of the Scriptures at Mass, dates at least from the time of St Leo; but it is doubtful if this was its original position, since the place of the Litany has also been changed. Indeed, in the ferial Masses for Good Friday and for the vigils of Easter and of Pentecost, in which so many archaic elements are preserved to us, the sacred *actio* begins at once with the lessons, without either Introit or Collect, exactly as is seen in the *Liber Pontificalis* prior to the reform of Celestine I, and this would seem to be the ancient Roman use. The Collect would thus be connected with the introduction of the Litany into the Mass, and would embody a sort of compromise between the suppression of the Παννυχίς and the institution of the Introit. Anciently, as a matter of fact, the Mass followed immediately upon the Office of the Vigil, and as this latter consisted of a series of lessons, the Mass—without other Epistles or Gospels —began at once with the Litany, which immediately preceded the Offertory. When, however, the custom of the vigil gradually died out and gave place to the stational procession, the Litany, on the other hand, was recited in anticipation during the passage from the church chosen as the place of assembly to that of the *statio;* and the three scriptural lessons—the last relics of the rite of the παννυχίς—followed, instead of preceding, the Litany and its normal conclusion, the Collect.

In order, however, to explain the presence of the Collect at this point in the Mass, another circumstance has to be taken into account. The meaning originally attached by the faithful to this prayer of the priest was that of a kind of final benediction or leave-taking; hence they named it indifferently *oratio super populum, benedictio,* or *fit missa catechumenis,* etc. It therefore presupposes a prayer of the people, so that the sacred minister may be said to gather together, as it were (*collecta*), the desires of the whole people and lift them up on the wings of his own prayer to the throne of almighty God. Hence it is not impossible that the original position of the Collect may have been at the very beginning of the Office, at a time when St Gregory had not as yet introduced the Litany as a form of prayer. We have, however, to note another circumstance which, putting on one side the Litany, might have brought the Collect into close connection with the Introit. As is well known, when the stational Mass was celebrated in Rome, the clergy and people first of all assembled in an adjacent church, and from there set out in procession, singing the Litany, for the basilica where the station was to be held. During the time that the people were assembling and the procession was being formed, the *schola* sang a psalm as Introit, which, according to the Sacramentaries and the *Ordines Romani,* was followed by a Collect said by the Pope, who thus concluded this preparatory ceremony, which was itself called *collecta.* We know that when the procession had arrived at its destination neither Introit nor Litany was sung; but as soon as the dust of the road had been removed from his feet (for the Pontiff had been walking barefooted) he at once recited the Collect at the conclusion of the Litany. Here, then, there were not one but two Collects, preceding the lessons in the Roman stational rite. Now, since we know that both daily and festal Masses are an abbreviation of the stational Mass, we can well understand the reason for the Introit and the Collect, even when there was no procession, and consequently no previous gathering or *collecta.* They are simply adjustments and contractions of other rites and ceremonies much more lengthy and solemn.

In analogy with that which we still see in the Masses of the vigils, of Embertide, Good Friday, Holy Saturday and of the Saturday of Pentecost, after the psalmody or responsorial canticle—the prayer of the people—there followed regularly the priest's Collect, which, therefore, always sought its inspiration in the preceding passage of Scripture. Those preserved in the Missal for the Easter Vigil are among the finest examples of this kind. The lesson, the psalmodic chant and the Collect were thus three elements so closely related that the one was not made use of without the others. The Roman Missal, which has now for many centuries lost its original Collects between one lesson and the next, exhibits in this an obvious lacuna, dating, perhaps, from the time of St Gregory himself, seeing that the Leonine Sacramentary for the most part takes note of it.

We must here call to mind that, notwithstanding Tertullian's declaration that the faithful of his day used to pray *sine monitore, quia de corde,* yet, in later times at any rate, the deacon was charged with the duty of recalling the attention of the people and inviting them to pray. *Humiliate capita vestra Deo, Humiliate vos ad benedictionem, Flectamus genua,* were the most usual formulas, and the people prostrated themselves in silent prayer until the sacred minister bade them rise up again—*levate, surge, electe, comple orationem tuam*—to listen to the recitation of the Collect by the priest, who prefaced it by one of the biblical salutations, *Dominus vobiscum,*[1] *Pax vobis, Pax omnibus,* all of which are found in use from the second century onwards.

When the special character of the *oratio* which ended the responsorial melody is realized it is easy to understand why the rhythm exactly followed the rules of the *cursus* and why its style is clear-cut, terse and almost austere. It is precisely for this reason that the ancient Collects of the Roman Missal, for loftiness of conception, force of expression and harmony of rhythm, are placed among the finest compositions of Latin literature, often supplying the Fathers of the Church with the text of their homilies to the people on days of festival.

We will quote some examples :

Dominica XI post Pentecosten.

Omnipotens, sempiterne Deus, qui abundantia pietatis tuae et merita supplicum excedis et vota; effunde super nos misericordiam tuam, ut dimittas quae conscientia metuit et adjicias quod oratio non praesumit. Per Dominum nostrum, etc.

11th Sunday after Pentecost.

Almighty, everlasting God, who, in the abundance of thy lovingkindness, dost exceed both the merits and the desires of thy suppliants, pour down upon us thy mercy, forgiving us the things whereof our conscience is afraid, and granting us those which our prayer presumeth not to ask. Through Jesus Christ, thy Son, our Lord, etc.

This little gem of Roman euchology embodies a whole treatise upon prayer. It begins, first of all, with an invocation and with divine praise (*Omnipotens sempiterne Deus*); then it rises to the contemplation of the inner reason why God listens favourably to the prayer of his creatures (*abundantia pietatis tuae*), excluding, therefore, any direct connection in justice between God's gifts and man's deserving. Moreover, since, according to the Apostle, we ourselves are ignorant of what is for our real good, for it is the Holy Ghost the Paraclete infused into our souls who obtains it for us, so the Collect adds that God's bountiful mercy surpasses our every expectation and all our desires. The object of prayer is here

---

[1] Ruth ii, 4.

placed in its rightful order. If the just gift that God makes to us is that of loving us, so that his love has for its immediate effect the kindling in our souls of the fire of charity, which destroys sin and restores grace, it can well be understood that the primary object of our prayer can be nothing else than the remission of sin through this infusion of grace (*ut dimittas quae conscientia metuit*). But when the fault has been pardoned and its eternal punishment remitted, there still remains the temporal penalty depriving the soul of her share in certain special gifts reserved to the friends of God alone. It would be presumptuous for anyone else to aspire to these, and the faithful soul who is still filled with a deep sense of contrition, while she longs for those further graces which shall raise her to perfect union with God, nevertheless does not dare to beg directly, as does the Spouse in the Canticle, for the kiss of the Bridegroom's lips. Rather does she make her petition indirectly, with tender reverence, having recourse to that ineffable mercy and divine loving-kindness which is, in truth, the very reason why God, the Uncreated Good, gives himself to us, and allows us to share in his blessings. How great a knowledge of God and what profound lessons are contained in one short prayer !

Feria Sexta post Pascha.

Omnipotens, sempiterne Deus, qui Paschale sacramentum in reconciliationis humanae foedere contulisti; da mentibus nostris, ut quod professione celebramus, imitemur effectu. Per Dominum nostrum, etc.

Friday in Easter Week.

Almighty, everlasting God, who hast bestowed the Paschal Mystery as a part of the covenant of man's reconciliation; grant that what we profess in this celebration, our inner life may imitate in action. Through Jesus Christ, thy Son, our Lord, etc.

Here, too, we have the opening invocation and the divine praise; then calling again to mind the ancient pact sealed by Moses in the blood of the covenant, the soul is lifted up to contemplate a far more acceptable and universal Sacrifice—one which confirms the covenant made by God, not merely with a small people of Palestine, but with the whole human race (*in reconciliationis humanae foedere*).

This covenant, or, rather, the blood of this New Testament, is in the eucharistic chalice, which commemorates the sacrifice of Calvary and the glorious resurrection of the divine victim. It constitutes the true pasch of redeemed humanity, a pasch and covenant that can never more be abrogated as were the offerings of the Mosaic Law, since it is sealed by the death of the Lamb of God *slain from the foundation of the world.* This divine and intimate sacrifice, conclusive and complete, dominates all human history; it pervades and sanctifies every other act of worship, whether exterior or interior, and by means of the eucharistic oblation, it is being daily offered upon our altars *donec veniat*, until our Lord shall reappear on the day of the final *Parousia* and of the resurrection of all mankind. Then truly shall the Paschal Sacrifice have its consummation, when the Church, already sharing in her Redeemer's sacrifice, shall be likewise made by him partaker in the glory of the Resurrection. This will be the true *Pascha nostrum* in the fullest sense of the word.

But our *religio*—that is, that which *binds* and unites us to God—is a thing essentially interior and spiritual. The external rite is its outward sign and manifestation, and to be a real and true bond, it must correspond with the inmost feeling of the soul. Nor is this enough : if faith is not to faint and perish from inanition, it must live through good works informed by charity ; therefore it is that we pray that not only may our hearts be attuned to the outward rite (*da mentibus nostris, ut quod professione celebramus imitemur effectu*), but that the feast by means of which we make public profession of our faith may be continued and carried out into the actions of our lives. The prayer concludes by invoking the merits of our High Priest, Christ Jesus, in whose name we present to the heavenly Father our acts of adoration and our petitions.

✳ ✳ ✳ ✳ ✳

THE SCRIPTURAL LESSONS.—This first part of the sacred *actio* bears a pre-eminently catechetical character ; this is the reason why it was afterwards called the *Mass of the Catechumens*. It is arranged on the plan of the liturgical service of the synagogue, in which, on the Sabbath Day, the *Torah* and the Prophets were read, and passages from the Psalms sung, followed by a homily from the president of the gathering. Such was the order of worship from the earliest days in all the various Christian churches, and we know, too, that in the Roman Liturgy, from the very beginning, there were at least three lessons at Mass—one from the Old Testament, one from the Apostolic writings, and a third from the Gospels, commented upon in an easy, simple style by the presiding member of the assembly. The alleluiatic psalmody, which now follows close upon the responsorial Gradual, and which is therefore musically unpleasing, because of the abrupt transition it involves from one kind of melody to another, points to some part of the Liturgy having disappeared at this point in the Mass.

It is the second lesson which has thus been suppressed, probably with the sanction, at least, of St Gregory the Great, who himself, according to John the Deacon, shortened the Mass, *multa subtrahens, pauca convertens, nonnulla vero super adjiciens,*[1] so as to allow the Pontiff more time to expound the Gospel to the people. This suppression was, however, not absolute at first. The great feast days, on which the people were too well accustomed to hear read those fixed portions of Scripture not to have been troubled at their disappearance, were excepted; hence the old indexes of the Roman lessons of the eighth, ninth and tenth centuries always mention the three ancient lessons for the greater festivals.

Although in the early centuries the choice of passages for reading was left to the bishop, ordered arrangements, cycles and series of readings made their appearance, often to be met with in marginal indications in the biblical manuscripts. In the Roman Missal their order is sometimes interrupted, but there, too, especially in the case of the Epistles, a regular and systematic course of readings is disclosed, dating back to remote antiquity. Taking these as the standard when any one lesson breaks into a series, it is easy to identify the exceptional and occasional character of the Mass in which it occurs; as, for instance, on the Thursday of the fourth week of Lent, and that of Passion Week also, in which the reading of St John's Gospel is interrupted; also on the Sunday following the autumn Ember Days, when the Epistle to the Ephesians is left half read and a reversion is made to that of the Corinthians, which had already been read two months earlier. We know, indeed, that all the Masses for the Thursdays of Lent, save that in *Coena Domini,* were introduced by Gregory II; moreover, the *Ordines Romani* witness to the late character of the Sunday Mass which follows the Office of the Vigil on Ember Saturday. At Rome, down to the eighth century, that Sunday was always *vacant—Dominica vacat*—since the Mass celebrated in St Peter's at dawn, which brings to a conclusion the παννυχίs of the Saturday, also took the place of the Sunday Mass.

As is the case with the Introit, so also do the lessons of the Mass sometimes contain important historical allusions. Thus, on the Feast of St Apollinaris, St Peter's Epistle, with its precept addressed to the bishops *non dominantes in cleris,* was intended for the proud Metropolitans of Ravenna, who, puffed up by the favour they enjoyed at the Court of the Exarchs, not only endeavoured to free themselves from the Primacy of St Peter (whence also came the choice of the Gospel reading for the day, with its account of the dispute among the disciples—*Quis eorum videretur esse major?*), but also used to tyrannize over their clergy and their own suffragan bishops. These latter they

---

[1] *Vita S Greg. I,* lib. II, ch. xvii, xxi ; *P.L.* LXXV, col. 94.

had compelled to abandon their dioceses in order to act as weekly chaplains in the Cathedral of Ravenna, just as the suburbicarian bishops were accustomed to do for the Pope in the Lateran Basilica. In the same way, for the natal day of St Cecilia, the lesson from Ecclesiasticus begins *Domine exaltasti super terram habitationem meam*, and the Station was, in fact, celebrated in the basilica of the martyr, which had been erected on the site of her house where she suffered the extreme penalty. Other special allusions will be noted later on.

* * * * *

THE SOLO ON THE STEPS OF THE AMBO AND THE RESPON-SORIAL REFRAIN.—The monotony of the threefold Scriptural reading was broken, as we have said, by the singing of responsorial psalms—a custom borrowed by the Church from the similar traditions of the synagogue. Besides serving a euchological purpose all its own—the other musical portions of the Mass, the Introit, Offertory, and Communion being merely ornamental in character or intended for the filling up of time—the Responsory claims consideration also as being one of the earliest elements of the Christian Liturgy, inasmuch as it forms the original nucleus of the collection of Gregorian chants.

This chanting with refrains bore various names : in Africa it was simply the *psalmus*, from the fact of its being taken regularly from the Psalter of David; in the Mozarabic Liturgy it was styled *psallenda;* at Milan—perhaps when the primitive form of psalmodic chant gave place to the abbreviated method—it was called *psalmellus cum versu;* whilst at Rome it was known as the *psalmus responsorius,* or Responsory Gradual, on account of the special method of chanting it.

The manner of its execution indeed, as the Fathers attest, seems to have been precisely that described above—viz., the alternation of the refrain of the people with the psalmodic modulations of the soloist. Originally, perhaps, the psalm was sung all through; but very soon, as the ceremonial grew more elaborate, and the Introit and Offertory chants were introduced, these developed at the expense of the Responsory, which was left mutilated and reduced to a single hemistich, *Responsorium breve,* inserted in the verse of the psalm. It is, nevertheless, doubtful whether the material integrity of the psalm was so far respected from early times that the mutilation which it suffered dates only from the time of St Leo I, as some writers would maintain.[1]

We must not, however, confine our observations only to the responsorial chants of the Mass; those of the night vigils have also to be considered, and here we find that the

[1] Wagner, *op. cit.,* pp. 80 *sq.*

texts are often connected with the scriptural reading which precedes them. Hence the Responsory of the Vigil at one time appears as a short prophetic ode, and at another as a marvellous interweaving of intercessions, but often, too, as a striking little historical sketch. This is particularly the case from Septuagesima to Easter, and from Pentecost to the first Sunday in August. If we did not know the Responsory to be taken from the synagogue, we would unhesitatingly attribute it to the influence of Greek tragedy, in which it devolved upon the chorus to give expression to the common feeling aroused in the minds of the audience. It is, in fact, the true characteristic of the Responsory to be so closely connected with the scriptural lesson as to give utterance to the devout feelings which this reading has aroused in the heart. This might well, therefore, be compared to that of the resulting action which follows on the working of the intellect in a spiritual meditation.

Thus it is very doubtful if the Responsory always comprised the singing of a whole psalm. The passages adduced by writers to prove that it did so seem at first sight conclusive, but when examined more closely, they evidently point to some very short psalmodic composition. Thus St Augustine, on one occasion when a lector had intoned a very long psalm in mistake for the shorter one which he had been told to sing, apologized for this to the people;[1] an action which would lead us to suppose that ordinarily the responsorial psalmody, though clothed in a sufficiently elaborate form of melody, was nevertheless not at all lengthy.

Cassian, indeed, relates that it was the ancient custom of the monks of Egypt to divide the longer psalms into two or three portions,[2] a custom which penetrated thence into the West, where it was sanctioned and accepted by the *Regula Sancta*.

This connection of the Gregorian Antiphonary, which never has a whole psalm for the Responsory, with Cassian and the Rule of St Benedict is very striking, while the latter leads us to suppose that from the first half of the sixth century the *Responsorium* had already been considerably curtailed. St Benedict, in fact, distinguishes the *Responsorium breve* from the other one (which we shall for this reason call the long Responsory), followed sometimes by the doxology. For the psalms of the night vigils, St Benedict, faithful to the traditions of the Fathers of the East, wished to keep strictly to the number twelve, even at the cost of dividing some of the psalms into several portions. We must conclude from this that from his time the short responsories after the lessons were abbreviated to such a degree that they could not in any

---

[1] *P.L.* XXXVII, col. 1784.   [2] *Institut.* l. II, c. xi.

way be regarded as forming part of the twelve traditional psalms. Moreover, the Benedictine cursus presupposes the existence of a regular *liber antiphonarius* or responsorial, since every time that the Responsories are there mentioned they are always connected with the singing of the lessons : *Lectiones cum responsoriis suis.* Then there are also historical and instructive Responsories, drawn from the Book of Genesis, from the Machabees, etc. ; hence the Responsory did not necessarily involve the singing of a part of a psalm, much less of a psalm in its entirety.

When, therefore, did the responsorial psalmody of the Mass adopt its present form of the short Responsory? With good reason do we exclude the period later than St Gregory the Great, ánd suggest instead some date between 450-550 as that of a possible condensation of the Gradual at the hands of the *schola cantorum,* instituted by Celestine I (died 432).[1] By embellishing the words of the psalm with musical chants, the choir of child singers would in time have usurped also the part allotted to the people, thus taking upon themselves the entire execution of the psalm. This is a perfectly possible hypothesis ; all the more so because from this time forward the faithful would have ceased to *respond* to the solo of the lector, as is proved by the simple fact that the melodies assigned to the responsorial verse in the Antiphonary are too elaborate ever to have been executed by a large number of persons assembled together.

Little by little, however, as musical art displayed the splendour of its chaste beauty in the solos of the Gradual, the actual text of the psalm came almost to occupy a secondary place, so much so that not only was the psalm still further abbreviated, but the wording was sometimes even borrowed from other books of Scripture.[2]

Characteristic of the responsorial Gradual is the absence of the doxology, but the manner of rendering the responsorial Gradual was not always the same. .The *Ordo Romanus I* directs the soloist first to sing the refrain, and then, after the choir has replied, to intone the verse of the psalm, which is followed by a second " response " on the part of the choir. Later on, even in Rome itself, this final repetition came to be reserved exclusively for those days on which there was not sung any Alleluiatic verse or Tract, and

---

[1] *op. cit.,* 81 *sq.*

[2] It is generally held that the verse *Locus iste a Deo* for the Feast of the Dedication of Santa Maria *ad Martyres* is later than the time of St Gregory, but such a supposition presents very great difficulties. It would seem that the musical composition had been originally written for a Christian Basilica, built by Christian hands (*Locus iste a Deo factus est*), and that it was only afterwards adapted to the Dedication of the Basilica of the Martyrs.

for this reason in the later Middle Ages all the cantor had to do was simply to pre-intone the responsorial refrain together with the verse of the psalm which followed it.

The execution of the *psalmus-responsorium,* entrusted from the first to a soloist, came, in time, to devolve upon several singers, especially in places other than Rome. The difficulty of its rendering and the importance attached to the singing of the Gradual tended to confine its performance only to the most skilful singers; at Rome to the senior member of the *schola;* at St Germanus of Paris to the children; elsewhere to the subdeacons and deacons (it had already been forbidden to these last, however, by St Gregory, who, in so doing, reformed a liturgical abuse of long standing). At Milan on Holy Saturday it was sung by the Archbishop himself. We should need to enter deeply into the mind of those ancient days in order to realize the full vigour of the protest made by Pope Zacharias to Pepin, the Mayor of the Palace, regarding certain nuns who had dared to take upon themselves in their convents the rendering of the melodies of the Gradual.

According to the *Regula Sancta,* the Alleluia was inserted in the responsorial Gradual during Eastertide; a custom which was continued even when the Gradual had altogether lost its responsorial form.

*   *   *   *   *

THE ALLELUIATIC SONG.—The story of the Alleluia, as Cardinal Pitra said, is a poem in itself. Inserted by the Hebrews in certain joyful psalms, repeated by our Lord and his Apostles at the last Paschal Supper, sung in heaven by the angels of the Apocalypse, the Alleluia not only found its way into all liturgies from the very first, but even outside of the liturgical rite its sweet strains echoed joyfully in the fourth century over the fields of Bethlehem and along the shores of the Mediterranean, alleviating the toil of the Christian peasant and solacing the cares of the mariner as he steered his way homewards. It appears that in this instance also the East was before the West in introducing the Alleluiatic song into the Mass; and, indeed, according to St Gregory, it was only Pope Damasus who, at the instance of St Jerome, caused it to be introduced at Rome[1] in all the Sundays of the year, except in Lent.

Sozomen[2] relates that at Rome originally the Alleluia was reserved exclusively for Easter Sunday, so that to be able to hear it again and yet again was deemed by the Romans to be a kind of augury of long life. The story related by Victor Vitensis has reference to this Paschal

[1] L. viii, 15.   [2] S Gregorii I, *Reg., Epist.* ix, 42 (26).

custom, when he tells of a lector killed in Africa by an arrow which pierced his throat as he was standing in the ambo on Easter Day, chanting the Alleluia *from the book*.

St Jerome, on the other hand, in his life of Fabiola, describes how the Roman people bore her dead body to the grave amid the festive chanting of psalms and Alleluias, and St Gregory himself witnesses that through the influence of the Greeks the custom was introduced of singing the Alleluia even during Lent and also at funeral services.

The use of the alleluiatic chant gave rise in the seventh century to a strange anomaly, because although generally excluded from the Mass, except on Easter Sunday and perhaps during the fifty days of the Paschal solemnity,[1] yet in the office of the vigil of the Sunday it was regularly sung by the monks of St Benedict throughout the whole year, save in Lent. This rite, indeed, would seem to go back much farther than the sixth century, since Cassian remarks that the anchorites of Egypt, unlike those of Gaul and Italy, were not in the habit of inserting the Alleluia except in those special psalms taken from the Psalter of David, in which the refrain actually recurred. Hence in the West from the fourth century onwards it was customary to sing the Alleluia as part of the weekly office.

Yet already towards the middle of the fourth century there was a tendency in the West to suppress the alleluiatic melodies during Lent, so as to resume them at Easter as something new and special. This was a compromise between the prevalent custom and the primitive rite. What part, then, did Gregory take in the matter?

Without changing anything in the divine Office, he simply sanctioned the ancient Roman custom of excluding the Alleluia in the Lenten season from funeral ceremonies, while extending it to all the other Sundays of the year, not excepting those after Pentecost, so that when, in Sicily, he was blamed for these innovations, as if he had sought to imitate the Greeks in so doing, he could claim, on the contrary, that he had revived once more the genuine Roman traditions of Pope Damasus and of St Jerome, freeing them at the same time from all the later Byzantine accretions.

It is exceedingly difficult to decide with certainty whether or no the alleluiatic melodies were originally followed by a verse from the psalms. The uncertainty of the Gregorian tradition concerning the text of the verses would seem to point to a negative answer. Such a judgement is confirmed also by the Easter custom of chanting the Alleluia simply as the doxology to the Gospels, like the *Te decet* of the monastic vigils; yet the derivation of the Alleluia in the

---

[1] S Augustini, *Epist.* cxix.

Mass from the alleluiatic antiphony of the divine Office, in which the psalm certainly followed, leaves our decision in doubt.

Like the Gradual, the alleluiatic psalmody in the Mass is very distinctly responsorial in character, and this feature of it is maintained almost unaltered down to the Tridentine reform, thus constituting a strong argument in favour of the antiquity of the verse from the psalms.

The singing of the Alleluia in Rome was reserved exclusively to a soloist : *Cantor qui inchoat alleluia, ipse solus cantat versum de alleluia. Ipse iterum alleluia dicit, stans in eodem gradu, id est inferiore.*[1]

After the Gregorian reform, and through the influence of the Greeks, the Lenten season of mourning came to be anticipated in Rome by three weeks, causing it, that is, to begin with Septuagesima Sunday. This consequently involved the suppression of the Alleluia in the Office and in the Mass of these three preparatory weeks of the Lenten fast also, giving rise in France and Germany to special Offices, in which a farewell, as it were, was taken of this melodious alleluiatic canticle.

The position allotted to the alleluia in the eucharistic *actio* was not everywhere the same. In the Roman Liturgy it precedes the Gospel, and it is only after the disappearance of the second lesson that we find the responsorial Gradual brought into such strange connection with the alleluiatic psalm. In the East, on the other hand, in Gaul and in Spain—wherever, in fact, the Oriental Liturgies have left traces of their influence—the Alleluia follows regularly the reading of the Gospel, and has always the character of a festive acclamation, unaccompanied by any verse from the psalms.

*   *   *   *   *

DIRECT PSALMODY, OR " TRACTUS."—The Roman *Tractus* replaces the alleluiatic chant during Lent, and when the idea underlying the solo *in directum* was lost, the medieval liturgists sought countless reasons by which to explain at least its etymology. The question was worth the trouble spent on it, since it concerned one of the oldest forms of psalmody, the *psalmus in directum,* or solo, which originally followed the second scriptural lesson in the Mass. The text of the Tract is taken regularly from the Davidic Psalter (three times only from the Canticles), but its melody is very simple, alternating exclusively between the first and the eighth mode. The Tract, as a psalmodic composition, is reckoned to be one of the longest contained in the Mass.

Wagner traces Greek influence in the Tract, basing his

---

[1] *Ordo Romanus II; P.L.* LXXVII, 971.

opinion upon the fact that in the Easter Vigils some *Tractus* were also sung in Greek;[1] but his argument proves nothing, since we know that, in deference to the high Byzantine nobility, the lessons of the Mass themselves, together with the processional antiphony of Vespers during the Easter Octave and the processional responsory of the Feast of the Hypapante were similarly rendered in Greek. Must we then conclude that the whole of the Latin Liturgy is derived from the East, and that the Latin mind always felt itself unfitted to aspire to worthy converse with its Creator?

*   *   *   *   *

THE GOSPEL LESSON.—The two initial scriptural lessons with the inserted psalm come from the liturgy of the synagogues of the *Diaspora,* but the Gospel lesson, on the other hand, is a purely Christian institution, or, rather, an apostolic one, seeing the universality and antiquity of this rite, which can only have originated before the various Gnostic sects had separated themselves from the " Great Church," as Celsus calls her.

As regards the Roman Liturgy, the earliest witness to the public reading of the holy Gospels in the Mass is St Justin, where he records, as we have already seen, that before the prayer and the Kiss of Peace there were read " τὰ ἀπομνημον-εύματα τῶν Ἀποστόλων ἢ τὰ συγγράμματα τῶν προφητῶν . . . μέκρις ἐγκωρεῖ." These *Memoirs* or *Commentaries* cannot be anything else than the Gospels, the authorship of which is always attributed to the Apostles, so much so that the early Christians considered the writings of St Mark to be a summary of the preaching of St Peter, and those of St Luke to be the Gospel of St Paul.

In Justin's time the portions to be read were not yet fixed; they varied according to the time available for the reading; but the custom and tradition of the different churches quite early elaborated and definitely fixed those lists or *Capitularia Evangeliorum* which are now of such great value for the history of the Church's festivals. The ideas governing these selections are very dissimilar: sometimes the order of the Gospel Codex was followed without any reference to the special feast which was being kept; at other times, on the contrary, the portions for reading were quite appropriate to the different festivals of the year, and were chosen here and there out of all the four Evangelists. From the second century onwards there were in the East various *Concordantiae Evangeliorum,* merging into a single text the different Gospel narratives, and this *mixed Gospel,* as it was called in Syria, met with wide acceptance. A similar system was not unknown in the West, for we find it actually in use at Farfa towards the middle of the eleventh century. In the Roman Missal the Gospel lessons for the Sundays and Ferias of the year are taken freely from any part of the sacred text without any systematic connection or order among them.

It is only in the fourth week of Lent, with the Gospel of St John, that a real scheme of lessons makes its appearance, being regularly followed to the close of Eastertide. Before Easter the teachings of our Lord and his disputations with the Pharisees are read, and the hatred of the Synagogue against the divine Redeemer is seen gradually increasing, until it finally bursts forth in open fury on the day before the Feast of the Azymes. After Easter, both on Sundays and on the feasts of martyrs, the Roman Church reads our Lord's discourse at the Last Supper, dividing it into portions; hence the Masses for Rogationtide, St Mark, the Finding of the Cross, etc., are at once seen not to be of early origin, but to belong to a later date, because in the Gospel lesson they ignore this rule and break the sequence of the readings from St John.

The custom of bringing in lighted candles when the deacon reads the holy Gospel dates from the early centuries of the Church, and was made the subject of a bitter polemic on the part of the heretics. It is a mark of deep reverence for the word of God, and comes from the Roman ceremony of bearing lighted candelabra before the emperor, to mark the *numen* and the *sacra majestas* of the august successor of the Cæsars.

* * * * *

THE " REGULA FIDEI," OR CREED.—Although from the very first a concise formulary was found necessary by which the whole of Catholic theology might be summarized, under authority, for the instruction of the catechumens, on whose account it soon came to form part of the baptismal liturgy, nevertheless, its recitation seemed for a long period unnecessary and altogether inappropriate to the eucharistic rite, which as the Sacrifice of Praise and the Bread of the Strong presupposes the Christian conscience already enlightened by a strong and lively faith. Only later, when the Byzantines, with their love of theological subtleties, had made these professions of faith part of the accepted order in the East, did the *Regula Fidei*, in its intermediate form between the Creed of Nicæa and that of Constantinople (325-381), constitute part of the liturgy of the Mass, spreading from the shores of the Bosphorus into Gaul and Spain, and thence into the more recently founded churches of Germany. Rome was the last to accept such an innovation,

not doing so until its use had already become universal (in
the eleventh century); nor did she even then without a compromise, shown by excluding the Creed from the *Ordinarium
Missae* and giving it rather the character of a festive
catechesis in place of the usual Sunday homily.

On the introduction of the Creed into the Mass, Eastern
influence is further noticeable in the position allotted to it in
the different Latin liturgies. The Churches most affected by
this influence, such as the Gallican, Mozarabic and Ambrosian, placed the symbol in the *Missa Fidelium* itself; in Spain
it was inserted after the Consecration, at Milan after the
Offertory—but in Rome the position chosen shows at once
a finer and more correct liturgical taste, since it is the *Regula
Fidei* which sets the seal upon the *Didascalia* of the catechumens of the Eternal City.

A further peculiarity of the Creed is its bilingual recitation
in Latin and in Greek; a custom derived from the baptismal
rite of Rome during the Byzantine period, and retained in
some places down to the later Middle Ages.

❋   ❋   ❋   ❋   ❋

THE PROTHESIS OF THE MISSA FIDELIUM AND THE PRE-
SENTATION OF THE OFFERINGS.—The catechumens and penitents having been dismissed at the close of the *catechetical*
liturgy, the Church can now express herself freely before her
children; and, when the veil of the scriptures and psalms
of the Old Covenant which hid the Mystery of Christ from
the uninitiated is lifted, she can speak in more lofty language
to the faithful *palam de Patre*.

For this reason not only is all the ancient poetry of
rejected Zion now hushed in silence, but one might even
say that, on the coming of the Word of God into the midst
of the faithful, the priest also shuts himself up in a mysterious
silence, softly uttering a short prayer, so that, without dis-
traction, the soul may the better contemplate the sublimity of
the mystery about to be enacted upon the altar of sacrifice.

It is thus that the *Missa Fidelium*, without readings,
psalms, or homilies, differs so fundamentally from the *Missa
Catechumenorum*—the latter learns; the former contemplates; the *Missa Fidelium* turns in preference to almighty
God, while the Mass of the catechumens, on the contrary,
seems to occupy itself largely with human interests.

Neither the lapse of centuries, nor the deterioration of
liturgical taste in the ecclesiastical world, availed substantially to modify this character of the two *Missae*, and, as the
priest, when once he has gone up finally to the altar to
offer the holy Sacrifice, does not afterwards leave his post
until the sacred *actio* is completed, so also the people,

even when in process of time they began to interrupt the mysterious silence of his contemplation with the *Hosanna* and the *Agnus Dei,* did so almost on their own account without disturbing in any way the priest in the silent prayer of the canon.

The Mass of the faithful has undergone many more serious modifications than the Mass of the catechumens, changes which have often disturbed the order of its parts and disarranged that natural and logical sequence which constituted one of the most striking features of the primitive Anaphora or eucharistic *hymnus.* This, however, we shall see more clearly in the following pages.

*   *   *   *   *

THE OBLATION.—Both the name and character of the Offertory were determined by its liturgical signification. Anciently all the faithful provided the elements for the Sacrifice, which was therefore offered to God in the name of the whole Christian community making the presentation, just as it is offered for those who give a pecuniary " alms " instead of the former oblations of bread and wine. This custom (already mentioned by St Cyprian when he reproves the niggardly, who go empty-handed to church and share in the Communion of the eucharistic Bread provided by the charity of the poor), is of great antiquity, and is borrowed from the apostolic *agapai,* at which the faithful used to contribute to the common feast by bringing their own personal gifts.

The offering of the eucharistic elements upon the altar was regarded by the Christians of old as a first oblation, introductory to that most holy Oblation of the " Mystery of the Death of Christ "; and since both priests and people were fully occupied during this ceremony—the former in presenting and the latter in receiving the sacred gifts—it seemed fitting that the prayer of the orphan singers should fill in this interval of time, or, rather, sanctify it with the melodies of the Offertory.

With the florid character of the Gregorian Offertories is closely bound up the peculiarity of the very frequent repetitions both of music and of words to be met with in the manuscripts. This is an astonishing anomaly, especially when we reflect that the grandeur of Gregorian musical art consists in the intimate union of the melody with the liturgical rite and its text, so that we know not whether to admire more the skill of the artist who, without obscuring or obliterating the theological idea, adorns it with all the charms of melody and tone, or the lofty flight of the musical phrase, which, more than merely translating it, serves to emphasize and bring out more strongly the eloquence of the sacred text. The Offertory, on the other hand, constitutes an exception, as it were, in the series of eucharistic melodies. It is the least ancient of all the chants, and was produced in the *schola* itself, so that it has easily been the means of fostering the artistic pride of the leading singers by providing them with an opportunity to display therein all the skill of their musical art.

The repetitions, so noticeable in the Gregorian Offertories, are really less strange than might at first sight appear. They must be viewed in the light of the responsorial class to which they belong. The only anomaly in regard to them will then be seen to be that, besides the verse or antiphon which is repeated by the *schola* after each half-verse of the psalm in a more florid form of melody, the same antiphonal verse is reflected, so to speak, upon itself, thus prolonging the sweet and pleasing echo of its harmonies.

Much more than the desire of prolonging the musical theme, in one form or another, in order to fill in the time, does the study of these rhythmical Offertory melodies very clearly reveal to us the dramatic aim of their composer. A good example of this is seen in the Lamentations of Job on the twenty-first Sunday after Pentecost, in which the ninefold repetition of the phrase *ut videam bona* so wonderfully expresses the yearning desire of all humanity towards this sovereign and inconceivable good. It was in this sense that the early Church interpreted these repetitions so dear to Alcuin and Amalarius, both of whom declare their enthusiastic admiration for the beauties of this Offertory.

Akin to the Introit in origin, purpose and manner of execution, the Offertory develops somewhat in the same way; the psalm, unlike the Introit which followed its due course, did not maintain a strict order in the verses. At the solemn Masses in Rome, the Pope himself gave the word for the psalmody to end, but elsewhere than in the papal surroundings—in the manuscripts, for instance—no more than four verses are ever indicated. Very early an increasing tendency towards shortening this responsorial psalmody also began to make itself felt. The oldest Ambrosian musical manuscript gives ordinarily one verse only; in other codices sometimes there are more, as at St Gall; sometimes there are fewer, as in the greater part of the antiphonaries later in date than the twelfth century.

What had occurred to cause this abbreviation? The people had gradually ceased to offer the oblations to the priest, and with the lessening of faith and generosity, the Communion of the laity beginning to be somewhat infrequent, the Church had been obliged to resign herself to supplying the priest with the sacramental elements for the Consecration out of her own resources. This custom, of which the first traces appear in the third century, must have become almost universal by the sixth, when Pope John III prescribed that the Lateran Patriarchate should provide *oblationes, amulae et luminaria* for those priests who were charged with offering the holy Sacrifice every Sunday in the suburban cemeteries. Gregory III confirmed his predecessor's statute, and, with a special Bull, fixed the amount of the oblations to be supplied daily by the monks of St Paul's for the celebration of the holy Sacrifice on the various altars of that basilica.

In the East, too, the faith of the people was sensibly diminishing. Thus, in the Edict of the Empress Irene, it was ordered that every day not less than seven oblations were to be made at the altar, an ordinance which clearly assumes that the greater part of the people did not communicate and consequently did not make any offering.

It is hardly necessary to add that the existing prayers which are recited by the priest in a low voice during the offering of the Host and the Chalice, the incensing of the Holy Table and the washing of hands, although derived, at least in part, from the old Sacramentaries, are of medieval origin in regard to the place they now occupy. At first the sacred minister recited them as a matter of private devotion, then, having become customary, they ended by forming part of the canonical rite.

* * * * *

THE COMMENDATIO OBLATIONUM, OR THE PRAYER DEDICATING THE OFFERINGS.—Without attempting to thread the labyrinth of disquisitions concerning the primitive form of the eucharistic Canon, we shall merely remark that, according to the text of Justin previously examined, after the Kiss of Peace and the Litany of the faithful which preceded the presentation of the oblations on the altar, the priest at once resumed the prayer of the Consecration. In the time of St Jerome, on the other hand, we find the custom somewhat widely spread of reading out publicly the names of those who made the offerings, and by comparing the various Western liturgies, we learn that these diptychs were read just before the *praefatio*. This is confirmed by a letter from Innocent I to Decentius[1] in which to the question—*de nominibus . . . recitandis antequan precem sacerdos faciat, atque eorum oblationes quorum nomina recitanda sunt sua prece commendet,* the Pope replies that the custom is unreasonable, and orders that: *Prius ergo oblationes sunt commendandae (Secreta?) ac tunc eorum nomina quorum sunt edicenda, ut*

---

[1] *Epist.* **xxv**; *P.L.* XX, col. 553.

inter sacra mysteria nominentur non inter alia quae ante praemittimus, ut ipsis mysteriis viam futuris precibus aperiamus. It appears from this extract that at Rome the priest first recited one or more prayers commending to God the oblations of his people, and then entered upon the Canon of the *sacra mysteria,* during which the recital of the diptychs took place. This, at least, is the most probable explanation of the rescript of Pope Innocent.

Yet it cannot be denied that the earlier custom was precisely that to which the correspondent of the Pope refers, not only because such was the discipline of the Gallican churches, where the prayer with which, as Innocent says, *oblationes sunt commendandae,* was simply called *oratio post nomina,* but also because the insertion of the diptychs in the Roman Canon was just that which upset and dislocated the primitive order of this venerable eucharistic text.

Moreover, it is not easy to understand the rhythm of a priestly prayer of recommendation of the oblations to God being embedded at that place between the Collect which concludes the litany of the faithful and the *prex canonica* of consecration, when the diptychs ought, without any doubt, to form an integral part of the eucharistic Canon itself. To what purpose, then, was this separation of the *commendatio* from the names of those who made the offerings? We may suppose that originally the *commendatio oblationum* of the priest followed at Rome, as it did at Gubbio, in France and elsewhere, the reading of the diptychs by the deacon; before, that is, the sacred minister began the chanting of the consecratory *prex canonica,* which admitted of no other interruption than the Trisagion.

For some reason which now eludes us—St Jerome had already begun an attack upon the diptychs—Rome at a certain moment either suppressed or brought directly into the canon itself this reading of the names of those who made offerings, the ancient *commendatio inter alia quae ante praemittimus* remaining intact and undisturbed in its original position. Among the churches of Italy, some followed the example of Rome, whilst others continued faithful to the older rite, so that Bishop Decentius of Gubbio, troubled by such a diversity of custom, referred the matter to Pope Innocent I. The Pontiff justified the Roman use, pronouncing the contrary practice to be superfluous, since in the canon, according to the text of the Apostolic See, the priest had of necessity to pray once again for those who made the oblations: *Pro Ecclesia quam adunare, regere, custodire digneris,* etc., as Pope Vigilius (537-555)[1] also

---

[1] *Ep. ad Justinianum, P.L.* LXIX, col. 22.

testifies in his day. Rome had altogether forgotten the changes brought about in her canon during the fourth and fifth centuries.

After the *Oratio post nomina,* or the *Commendatio oblationum,* as Innocent I would say—which comes, however, practically to the same thing—the Anaphora or eucharistic Canon at last begins. Up to this point the principal part has been borne by the lectors, the *schola,* the deacon and the faithful, but now that it comes to reciting the venerable *prex,* which is to renew on the altar with an unbloody rite the sacrifice of Golgotha, every human tongue is silent save that of the sacred minister, who speaks in the name of the eternal High Priest of our confession.

The eucharistic hymn, as it was called, is preceded by a short introduction or *praefatio,* beginning with the greeting to the people, *Dominus vobiscum,* characteristic of the Alexandrine rite, and then the *Sursum corda,* already mentioned by Cyprian, and the *Gratias agamus—*εὐχαριστῶμεν*— Domino Deo nostro.* This is the *Eucharistia,* which gives to the whole of the song that follows its true and primitive significance of a hymn of thanksgiving, paraphrasing the *Tibi gratias agens* of the Gospel. The people give answer by using the classical formula of acclamation and assent : *Dignum et justum est. Vere dignum et justum est,* continues the priest, and calling to mind the blessings of the Creation and of the Redemption, he prays for his faithful flock, who are to be partakers of the divine Victim, that they may receive the gifts of the Paraclete in all their fulness—the Eastern Epiclesis.

The Canon, or eucharistic *actio,* began, according to the ancient idea, with the sacerdotal greeting *Dominus vobiscum,* and ended with the doxology *omnis honor et gloria,* etc., which accompanied the *fractio panis.* Notwithstanding the intermittent and fragmentary condition in which it has come down to us, but one which, nevertheless, can show excellent documentary evidence from the sixth and seventh centuries onwards, the canon was originally of such a pronouncedly continuous character that not only was the *Pater Noster* excluded from it, but the very Trisagion manifestly shows itself to be an interpolation, due possibly to Pope Pius I.

The rhythmic idea underlying the canon is Trinitarian. The *prex* is addressed to God the Father, as in the Great Doxology, and after exalting the divine attributes of holiness, perfection and mercy—just as in the *Great Hallel* of the Paschal Supper—his compassion in the sending forth of the Word as Redeemer becomes the subject of our praise. Now is unfolded the great work of the Saviour, just as in the *Gloria in excelsis.* Jesus Christ is incarnate by the Holy

Ghost in the womb of a virgin, and appears on earth to crush the serpent of old, to enlighten mankind, and to open to us the way of life and resurrection. He who, on the night before his Passion, took bread, blessed it, and broke it, etc., thus there is inserted into the canon with the sacramental words of the eucharistic consecration, the whole of the Gospel narrative.

The *Anamnesis* continues, having as its central point the Saviour's last command : *Do this in remembrance of me. Wherefore now commemorating, O God, his Birth, Death, Resurrection and Ascension into heaven, we pray thee to accept the offering of our priesthood*—it is the whole body of priests who pray, and who in the canon itself, at this same point of the Mass, speak collectively, placing themselves in a category apart, distinct from the faithful : *Nos servi tui, sed et plebs tua sancta*—*and that of thy holy people, as thou didst accept the sacrifices of Abel, Abraham, etc., so that thou mayest send down upon this sacred altar*—here is proclaimed the office of the Holy Ghost—*thy sevenfold Spirit* (epiclesis) *that he may fill with every grace and blessing all those who worthily draw near to partake of the body and blood of thy Son Jesus Christ, in whom and in thy holy Church may there be to thee, O Father almighty, together with the Paraclete, all honour and glory for ever.* To which the people reply : *Amen.*

Such, if not the actual wording, is at least the rhythm and substance of the early eucharistic Canon, a rhythm hardly disturbed even in the existing Roman Anaphora, composed though it be of shreds and ancient fragments.

Although not a few liturgical scholars have made the attempt, we nevertheless consider the task of making a reconstruction to be an exceedingly difficult one. It would be necessary to join the Preface to the canon by means of the Trisagion, and perhaps of some other connecting link, such as the *Vere Sanctus . . . qui pridie quam pateretur*, etc., of the Gallican liturgies, while the diptychs, *Memento . . . qui nos praecesserunt, Nobis quoque*, would have to be removed and placed before the Secreta. After the Trisagion the canon would be continued in this manner :

(a) *Te igitur* (*hanc igitur oblationem* as an alternative text).
(b) *Communicantes.*
(c) *. . . mitte Spiritum Sanctum . . . et fac nobis hanc oblationem adscriptam, ratam, quod figura est Corporis et Sanguinis Jesu Christi, qui pridie.*[1]
(d) *Unde et memores.*
(e) *Supra quae.*

[1] *De Sacramentis* IV, c. v, 21 ; *P.L.* XVI, 462-3.

(f) *Supplices te rogamus . . . gratia repleamur.*

(g) Blessing of the oil for the sick and of the new fruit.

(h) *Per quem haec omnia . . . per ipsum . . . omnis honor et gloria per omnia saecula saeculorum.* R7. *Amen.*

(i) *Pax Domini*, etc.

(l) *Oremus, Praeceptis salutaribus*, etc. *Pater Noster.* Communion.

How and when did the dislocation of the ancient Roman Canon take place? This is another problem for the solution of which we have not sufficient data. At Rome the Liturgy has shared in a measure the outward history of the world's capital; thus it came about that during the first three centuries its language was Greek whilst afterwards it became Latin. In the time of Pope Gelasius the canon included a preconsecratory *epiclesis*, after the manner of the Eastern liturgies and of the Alexandrine Anaphora itself—*nam quomodo ad divini Mysterii consecrationem coelestis Spiritus invocatus adveniet, si sacerdos et qui eum adesse deprecatur, criminosis plenus actionibus reprobetur?*[1]—an *epiclesis* which has disappeared for many centuries from the Roman Missal, having been completely obscured by the prayer : *Quam oblationem . . . ut nobis fiat Corpus et Sanguis Filii tui*, etc. Pope Vigilius wrote in 538 to Bishop Profuturus that in Rome the *prex canonica* never admitted of any variation whatsoever, *sed semper eodem tenore oblata Deo munera consecramus,*[2] and that on feast days a short phrase only was added commemorative of the actual festival. These additions, with the exception of those at Easter, Pentecost, Christmas, Ascension and Epiphany, now no longer exist, nor are they to be found in the Leonine Sacramentary; whilst, on the other hand, it is clear from the letter of Vigilius that all the many *praefationes* were regarded from that time forward as something extraneous to the canon. We have already mentioned the letter of Pope Celestine to Bishop Decentius. From it we gather the following to have been the order of the sacred *actio* at Rome, excluding Offertory prayers of all kinds : (1) *prius ergo oblationes sunt commendandae;* (2) *alia quae ante praemittimus* (Preface), *ut ipsis futuris mysteriis viam, fusis precibus aperiamus;* (3) *nomina . . . sunt edicenda, ut inter sacra mysteria nominentur.*[3]

One of the last of the innovations made in the canon was the anticipation of the *Pater Noster* by St Gregory I, who placed it before the *fractio panis.*[4] The Lord's Prayer was the first Christian prayer which, at the time of the *Didache*, when

---

[1] *Ep. ad Elpidium; cf.* Thiel, *Epist. Rom. Pontif.* i, 486.
[2] *P.L.* LXIX, 18.   [3] *Epist.* xxv; *P.L.* XX, 553.
[4] *Epist.*, l. IX, n. xii; *P.L.* LXXVII, 956-7.

as yet neither the divine Office nor any other prayers were in existence, was prescribed for recital by each of the faithful three times a day—morning, noon and evening. St Gregory himself tells us that the Apostles, when offering the holy Sacrifice, confined themselves to the *Pater Noster,* and made use of no other Anaphora, so that very soon the tradition arose in the Church of reciting this prayer of the Saviour at the close of the consecratory *prex,* immediately after the fraction of the sacramental species, and before the Communion itself. The *Pater Noster* sealed the canon, as it were, and furnished the final and immediate preparation for the Communion; so much so that in the Roman embolism which introduces it, the dignity and specially sacred character of the prayer are strongly emphasized, as if it were the mind of the Church that the *missa catechumenorum* (*praeceptis salutaribus moniti*) and the sacramental Anaphora (*divina institutione formati*) which precede it should prepare the soul for its devout recitation (*audemus dicere*). St Gregory, however, was not satisfied that the *Pater Noster* should remain in this place of honour. According to him, the Apostles *ad ipsam solummodo orationem oblationis hostiam consecrarent;*[1] and as to recite the *Pater Noster* after the *fractio* was equivalent to doing so after the *mysterium* which ended the sacrificial part of the Mass before the Communion (that this was so is seen in the Gallican rite, wherein, the canon being ended, the bishop blessed the people and dismissed those who were not about to communicate; and at Rome, too, not only did the Pope give the order to the deacon, *Si quis non communicat, det locum,*[2] but he himself withdrew from the altar, as if the Sacrifice were completed, and went back to his throne to receive the Communion) the Pontiff therefore enacted that the Lord's Prayer should precede the eucharistic *fractio,* so that it might be said in some sense to form part of the consecratory canon.

This was the last modification made in the Roman Canon, which from that time has been preserved unchanged in the form in which the Gregorian age handed it down to us. Pope Sergius I, indeed, ordained that during the *fractio panis* the people should sing the invocation *Agnus Dei,* but this innovation in no way affected the Anaphora, since it was simply a chant of the people, the counterpart of the Trisagion of which we are now to speak.

* * * * *

THE OLDEST INTERPOLATION IN THE CANON — THE " SANCTUS."—It is necessary for us to distinguish, as do

---

[1] *Epist.,* l. IX, n. xii; *P.L.* LXXVII, 957; *P.L.* LXVI, 178.
[2] S Gregorii I, *Dialog.,* lib. II, c. xxiii.

the Greeks, the *Song of Victory*, ἐπινίκιον, which ends the *praefatio*, from the Trisagion properly so called, which in the East begins the liturgical *actio,* and which among the Latins is confined to the ceremony of the Adoration of the Cross on Good Friday. This last acclamation was inserted in the liturgical formularies of the Mass in Constantinople only in the fourth century, and through the addition of Peter the Fuller, patriarch of Antioch, Ὁ σταυρωθεὶς δι' ὑμᾶς gave rise to serious disputes among the Easterns on account of the interpolated phrase ἁγία Τριάς, ἐλέησον ἡμᾶς. Acacius of Constantinople and Pope Felix III intervened in the controversy, and though they censured both the formula itself and the meaning attached to it by Peter the Fuller, yet they failed to restore to the Trisagion its original Trinitarian signification, so that later on it was even inserted in the Latin Liturgy of Good Friday; but this was done only with a definitely christological aim, and with special reference to the crucified Redeemer. In the East, according to the testimony of Theodore the Lector, the somewhat ambiguous meaning of this reference was made clearer by adding the words : ρίστε βασιλεῦ.

The mention of the Trisagion which recurs in St Cæsarius, brother to St Gregory Nazianzen,[1] "ουδὲ πάλιν ἡμῶν ἐν τρισαγίῳ ἅγιος ὁ Θεός, ἅγιος ἰοχυρός, ἅγιος ἀθάνατος ἐκβοώντων, ἁγιασμόν ἢ ἰσχύν, ἢ ἀθανασίαν ὁ Θειὸν ἀνίεται," establishes for it an origin prior to the earthquake which devastated Byzantium under the Patriarch Proclus, when, according to St John Damascene, a child rapt in ecstasy is said to have received this Canticle from the angels, that he might teach it to his fellow-citizens and so enable them to escape from well-deserved disasters.

The Epinikion, or *Song of Victory,* on the other hand, is of far greater antiquity. The *Liber Pontificalis* gives to Sixtus I (120) the credit of having introduced the singing of it into the Mass, but such a statement would be destitute of any solid foundation, owing to the dubious authority on which it is based, had not Dom Cagin shown that the Sanctus corresponds exactly with the first interpolation in the eucharistic prayer, which had taken place towards the first half of the second century.

As regards its execution, the Preface in itself seems to invite the whole assembly to take part in the singing of this *supplex confessio;* and such a custom is confirmed by the *Liber Pontificalis,* as well as by a canon of the Council of Vaison; by St Gregory of Nyssa,[2] *Me tui pudet, quod cum senueris, adhuc ejiciaris cum catechumenis . . . unire populo mystico et arcanos disce sermones . . . dic nobiscum ea*

---

[1] *Dialog.* I, int. 29.   [2] *Serm. de non differendo Baptismo.*

quae sex alas habentia Seraphim cum Christianis dicunt; and also by St Cyril of Jerusalem : *Sanctus, sanctus,* etc., *propterea enim traditam nobis hanc seraphicam theologiam dicimus, ut cum coelesti militia in hymnodia communicemus.*[1]

Sublime as is this Trisagion, re-echoing through earth and heaven, an acute observer will, nevertheless, at once perceive that it represents an interpolation, on account of which the ancient *illatio*—originally a true *Symbolum Fidei* expressed in the most sublime lyrical form—is now suddenly arrested, strangled, indeed, in order to join on again in an unnatural manner the account of the Last Supper to the text of the *praefatio* by means of the Gallican *Vere Sanctus.* Thus the Trisagion now divides the eucharistic prayer into two parts, without making it in any way clear how the Trisagion, which precedes the Canon, can ever have come to be excluded from the prayer *infra actionem,* whilst on the evidence[2] of the Διδαχή it was the Sanctus which regularly formed its conclusion.

The text of the Trisagion, or ἐπινίκιον—almost the same in all liturgies—suggests that of Isaias, except for the mention of the *heavens,* which does not occur in the text of the prophet. Another invariable and almost universal interpolation is the enumeration—more or less uniform and detailed—of the hierarchy of the celestial spirits, as also the unending nature of their praise. The acclamation *Benedictus* is found universally in every liturgy.

In the time of St Justin the people concluded the *Epinikion* with the acclamation *Amen.* Soon, however, the idea of the angelic choirs singing the Trisagion seemed to invite the whole assembly to join in the song of the celebrant, until, towards the twelfth century, the *schola* again appropriated the part of the clergy who were present.

*　　*　　*　　*　　*

THE SINGING OF THE " AGNUS DEI " DURING THE FRACTION OF THE EUCHARISTIC BREAD.—The *Agnus Dei* is generally considered to be of Eastern origin, and to be derived from the angelic hymn or from the Litany, and introduced into the Roman Liturgy by Pope Sergius I towards the end of the seventh century (687-701). This chant is, in fact, unknown to the Gelasian Sacramentary and to the *Ordo* of the Ambrosian Mass; the earliest sources which make mention of it are two passages of the *Liber Pontificalis* in the Life of Sergius I, and in the *Ordo Romanus I,* where, however, the choral execution of the *Agnus Dei* is entrusted to the *schola.* According to the *Liber Pontificalis,* Sergius I had committed to the clergy and people the singing of the

---

[1] *Catech. Mystag.* v.　　　　　　　　[2] *Apolog.* i, 6.

Agnus Dei, which in the *Ordo* is reserved to the *schola.* The lack of documentary evidence prevents us from duly accounting for the divergence between the two sources, and perhaps we should not be far wrong if, instead of attributing the introduction of the *Agnus Dei* into the Mass to Sergius I, we were to credit him merely with having popularized its use against the opposing tendencies of the Council in Trullo.

The ceremony of the Kiss of Peace which the faithful exchanged with one another at this point suggests a later interpolation with its allusion to peace : *dona nobis pacem.* This phrase came to be universally adopted, save in the Lateran Basilica; yet it affected the liturgical meaning of the *Agnus Dei,* turning it almost into an invocation preparatory to the Kiss of Peace, while previously it had been closely connected with the *Fractio panis,* which took place during the execution of this chant.

*   *   *   *   *

THE " COMMUNIO."—The singing of the verse *Gustate et videte* from Psalm xxxiii during the distribution of the holy Mysteries is common in all Eastern liturgies; but in the West the first indications of any singing during the Communion are to be found in St Augustine, who introduced at Hippo the recently adopted custom of Carthage. This innovation was at first disapproved of, but later on it gained favour, and became at last so universal as to penetrate into the Roman, Ambrosian, Mozarabic and Gallican liturgies, with this difference, that while in these last the *Communio* is derived directly from the Eastern Anaphoras, and invariably consists of verses taken from Psalm xxxiii, at Rome, on the other hand, it preserves better the marks of its characteristically Latin origin, and as in the case of the Introit and of the Offertory, consists of an antiphon and a psalm, both of them varying in accordance with the different feasts of the year.

By careful examination of the texts of the antiphons *ad Communionem* for Lent, Dom Cagin has made out their original progressive order in its entirety up to the time of Gregory I. The sequence of the psalms is broken only by a few antiphons drawn from the Gospels, this very circumstance betraying their somewhat later origin.

Sometimes in the *Sanctorale* there appear extracts from other scriptural books, and instances are not wanting of the *Communio* being taken from non-canonical writings (for the feasts of St Agatha, St Ignatius of Antioch, Holy Cross Day).

The *Communio* having been introduced with the same intention as that which had suggested the *Offertory,* it shares

8

with this latter its antiphonal form and its later history; since with the lessening of popular devotion in regard to the practice of frequent Communion, the psalm was first reduced to a single verse, with a responsorial acrostic inserted in it, and then was shortened to such an extent that it consisted only of an antiphon.

* * * * *

THE EUCHARIST, OR THANKSGIVING.—During the singing of the *Communio* the clergy and the people partook of the Sacred Mysteries. Far into the Middle Ages the people were still admitted to Communion under both kinds; little by little, however, the custom arose of no longer consecrating the chalice destined for the people, but of merely sanctifying the wine by the infusion of a few drops of the eucharistic Blood from the chalice of the priest. This practice, for reasons of convenience, and because it involved less risk of profanation, extended further and further, until its final cessation in the fourteenth century, since which time the Communion of the laity under one sacramental species only has practically become the traditional custom of the Latin Church.

Originally the consecrated particle was placed in the hand of the faithful; the priest said to them *Corpus Christi,* and they replied *Amen.* Women, out of greater reverence, received it on the palm of the hand covered with a veil. In the third century, and even later, the custom of taking home the particle in order to partake of the Communion on a liturgical day was fairly common. The law of the natural fast which must precede Holy Communion was, however, in full force from the time of Tertullian. In the houses of the faithful the Holy Eucharist was preserved devoutly in a little pyx, and was conveyed thither suspended round the neck within a box or casket. It was even placed upon the body of a dead person and buried with him in the grave. At Jerusalem, St Cyril exhorts the neophytes that as soon as they have put their lips to the sacred chalice they should dip therein a finger and with it make the sign of the cross upon their eyes. We know also of certain Councils at which the bishops, when about to sign their names to an anathema against heretics, dipped their pens in the eucharistic chalice; not to mention the frequent gifts of eucharistic Bread exchanged in sign of friendship by the bishops and priests of the fourth and fifth centuries. All these customs fell into disuse or were abolished by the Church as soon as abuses arose, and the ardent and vigorous faith which had initiated them began to grow cold.

As our Lord at the end of the Paschal Supper had sung

with his Apostles the Great Hallel, to which allusion is made by St Mark in his Gospel,[1] so the Communion in every liturgy was always followed by the thanksgiving, *Eucharistia,* which gave its name to the whole of the sacred *actio.*   The *Didache* preserves to us the very ancient prayers with which the Agape was concluded at the end of the first century, and those of the Mass could not have been very different.   At Rome, in the Sacramentaries, besides the Collect *post Communionem,* there was another, *ad compléndum,* now preserved only on the ferias of Lent.   So long as the custom of pronouncing the euchological formula, *Benedicat vos omnipotens,* over the faithful was not yet in force, this prayer *ad complendum* was the last blessing which the priest imparted to the people before dismissing them.   It is known that anciently the imposition of hands, *Oratio super hominem,* and the benediction were synonymous terms.   No one was ever dismissed from church without the blessing, so much so that when the Byzantines, on the feast of St Cecilia, after the Communion, dragged Pope Vigilius from the altar of the Martyrium on the Trastevere, and carried him off to the ship which was in waiting on the river near by in order to convey him to Constantinople, the people, by whom the Pope was much disliked, clamoured for him at least to be granted time to finish the stational Mass and to recite the last prayer *ad complendum,* so as to leave his blessing on the multitude. It was thought wise to yield to the popular demand; Pope Vigilius, standing on the deck of the ship, recited the last Collect, to which the bystanders replied *Amen.*   Only then did the vessel sail away, carrying the Pontiff into exile upon the faithless shores of the Bosphorus.

[1] xiv, 26.

CHAPTER IX

SINNERS AND PENITENTS UNDER ANCIENT ECCLESIASTICAL DISCIPLINE

THE theological schools of Christian antiquity were for some time exercised over the question of penance for sins committed after Baptism.

The faith of itself implied a real change of habits, and the subject of the controversy was not therefore either the existence of the sacrament or the power of the Church to open and shut the gates of heaven, but rather concerned the suitableness of employing this power indiscriminately towards all classes of sinners.

Since, in Tertullian's phrase, *Christiani non nascuntur sed fiunt*—that is to say, one was not born a Christian, but became such by means of a sincere conversion of the heart—Baptism *in remissionem peccatorum* was the first sacrament of penance, and one which, in the mind of holy Church, involved for the convert the obligation to such an eminent sanctity of life that there would ordinarily be no need for any further penitential rite. We must believe, moreover, that this was generally the case, since in some churches the faithful did not even know of any sacrament of penance distinct from Baptism, and in many more whole classes of believers were actually excluded from participation in this benefit, so lofty was the conception which had been formed of what the Christian life should be.

It is no part of our task to write the history of the dogma; thus we shall merely point out the different tendencies regarding penance which manifested themselves during the first three centuries of the Church's life, so as to pass at once to the description of the rites which accompanied the administration of this sacrament.

The distinction between sins *ad mortem* and *non ad mortem* first occurs in St John's Epistles.[1] Upon the first class of sins, the Church ordinarily refrains from passing any public judgement, referring them directly to that of God; whilst as regards the second, she avails herself of the power to forgive sins granted to her by our Lord. The matter is exceedingly obscure, and to the famous passage in the *Pastor* of Hermas, from which it would seem that penance after Baptism was granted only as a great exception and as a kind of jubilee,[2] was given a wholly different meaning by the early Christians,

---

[1] 1 Joan. v, 16.   [2] *Mandat.* iv, 3; *P.G.* II, 919.

so much so that while to us now it seems a prelude to the severities of the heresy of Montanus, the Catholics of the second century appealed to its authority against the Montanists.[1]

Towards the beginning of the third century, when the weakening of fervour among the faithful, together with persecutions and consequent apostasies, caused the need of some sort of unity among the various churches with regard to the discipline of penance to be felt, Rome asserted her authority and intervened in the discussion, and the decision of Callixtus I (217-222), although fiercely opposed by Hippolytus and Tertullian, finally triumphed at Nicæa, and became a general rule for the whole Western Church. It was on this occasion that Tertullian wrote his *De Poenitentia* and a little later his *De Pudicitia*, and that Hippolytus vented his spleen against Pope Callixtus in his famous *Philosophumena*.[2]

The earliest account of the reconciliation of penitents is, in fact, contained in Tertullian's *De Pudicitia*, in which he caricatures the ceremony. The occasion of this libellous attack was afforded by Pope Callixtus, who had promulgated a decree in which, while keeping a just mean between the severity of the ancient canons and the new situation, which called for greater leniency towards sinners, he declared that he would grant absolution even to those guilty of adultery, provided they had first performed the penance imposed upon them : *Exit edictum et quidem peremptorium . . . pontificis maximi, id est episcopi episcoporum: ego et moechiae et fornicationis delicta, poenitentia functis, dimitto.*[3]

Hippolytus, on his part, fearing lest the mild measures of the Pope should open the way for laxity, inveighed against the decree in these terms : " He (the Pope) had from the first the intention to be easy-going with men in regard to sensual transgressions, saying that he would pardon the sins of everyone." Tertullian adds these particulars : *Tu quidem moechum ad exorandam fraternitatem in Ecclesiam inducens, conciliatum et concineratum cum dedecore et horrore compositum, prosternis in medium ante viduas, ante presbyteros, omnium lacinias invadentem, omnium vestigia lambentem, omnium genua detinentem, inque cum hominis exitum quantis potes misericordiae illecebris, bonus pastor et benedictus papa concionaris, et in parabola ovis capras tuas quaeris, tua ovis ne rursus de grege exiliat; quasi non exinde iam liceat quod semel licuit; coeteras etiam metu comples cum maxime indulgeas.*[4]

---

[1] Tert., *De Pudicitia*, c. x; *P.L.* II, 1052.
[2] *Philosophumena* IX, c. xi-xiii.
[3] *De Pudicitia*, c. i; *P.L.* II, 1032-33.
[4] *op. cit.*, c. xiii; *P.L.* II, 1056.

The innovation of Callixtus met with derision from the Montanists and heretics and even from the Catholics, and was also most strongly opposed in Rome itself. In Africa several bishops *in totum poenitentiae locum contra adulteria clauserant*, as Cyprian records;[1] and Origen himself considers as inopportune the toleration which was then proposed to be shown. "Someone has sinned," he says, "and, after incurring the debt of guilt, demands to be admitted to Communion. To concede to the request and grant the pardon would be the occasion of much harm, for once the restriction is removed the way is opened for every crime. If, on the other hand, the judge, on going seriously into the case, so as not to show himself either too lenient or too severe, will be willing to consider the welfare of the community as well as the good of the individual, whenever to pardon the sinner will give occasion for social harm, there is no doubt that, in order to save the many, he will shut out the one from communion with the Church."[2] In the history of this controversy, however, it is all-important to emphasize the fact that all Catholics, as a rule, presuppose and acknowledge the power of the Church to remit sins; hence the whole question had for them an eminently practical and disciplinary character, and mainly concerned itself with the advisability of making use of this power in favour of sinners, or of exercising it against them.

Tertullian at times explicitly owns: *Sed habet, inquis, potestatem Ecclesia delicta donandi " hoc ego magis agnosco et dispono."*[3] It is therefore not surprising that, as time went on, the disciplinary conditions regarding the administration of this sacrament should have changed and become so lenient that Celestine I could write to the Gallican bishops, who were obstinately cleaving to the old rigorous standard, even as regards the dying: *Horremus, fateor, tantae impietatis aliquem reperiri ut de Dei pietate desperet, quasi non possit ad se quovis tempore concurrenti succurrere. . . . Quid hoc, rogo, aliud est, quam morienti mortem addere, ejusque animam, sua crudelitate, ne absoluta esse possit occidere.*[4]

Such was the course of development followed by the sacrament of penance before it arrived at the discipline of to-day, which is substantially the same as that described by Pope Celestine. In order, however, to realize better the reasons and circumstances which led the bishops of the first three centuries to take up such a far more severe stand in

---

[1] *Epist.* x, n. xxi; *P.L.* III, 811.
[2] *Homil. in Jerem.* xii, 5; *P.G.* XIII, 386.
[3] *De Pudicitia*, xxi; *P.L.* II, 1078.
[4] Coelestini I, *Epist.* iv, 3; *P.L.* L, 472.

the matter, we must distinguish between two kinds of sins and two kinds of penance : the public and solemn penance for the grave sins contemplated in the penitential canons, and the private and secret penance for hidden transgressions. These last were confessed privately to the priest, and could always obtain sacramental absolution, while the first kind had to be publicly expiated once for all : (*Deus*) *collocavit in vestibulo poenitentiam secundam quae pulsantibus patefaciat. Sed jam semel, quia jam secundo, sed amplius numquam, quia proxime frustra* (Tertull., *De Poenitentia*). Origen is even more explicit (*Homil.* XV *in Levit.*) : *In gravioribus enim criminibus semel tantum poenitentiae conceditur locus. Ita vero communia quae frequenter incurrimus super poenitentiam recipiunt et sine intermissione redimuntur.* It is to this public penance that certain texts of the early Fathers refer, when, for instance, they state that ecclesiastics cannot undergo it.

Monastic fervour largely contributed to spreading the custom of seeking priestly absolution even for daily and venial faults. Thus the monks of St Columbanus used to go to confession every day; and in the Rule of St Benedict, besides mention being made of the private sacrament of auricular confession[1] as being a daily means of advancing in the spiritual life, one is advised to confess one's sins openly to the abbot or to the *seniores spirituales*.[2] The custom of the Church ordained that Lent should be the season especially set apart for confession ; later on Christmas and the Rogation Days were made of equal importance with Easter, so that in the Middle Ages the faithful approached the sacrament of penance three or four times a year.

The two rites of public and private confession differed entirely from one another. As a rule, public sins involved the guilty person's separation from the body of the Church in such a manner that reconciliation naturally signified the return of the penitent to ecclesiastical unity. Secret faults, on the other hand, even though they might be grave—not being generally contemplated by the penitential canons—did not of necessity exclude the guilty person from communion with the Church. For this reason, when the bishops of Campania, Samnium and Picenum assumed to themselves the right of compelling the faithful to public confession even for secret shortcomings, St Leo the Great forbade the practice, declaring it to be contrary to apostolic tradition.[3]

The elements which go to make up penance as a sacramental rite are twofold—the confession of the sin and the

---

[1] c. xlvi.   [2] c. iv.
[3] *Epist.* clxviii, c. ii ; *P.L.* LIV, 1210.

priestly absolution.   As regards the first of these, the *Ordines Romani* prescribe that, at the beginning of Lent, the penitents should go to the priest in humble guise, barefooted, without staves or arms, and cast themselves at his feet.

The priest usually recited some prayers over the penitent before his confession, then, bidding him sit down, he questioned him on the principal truths of the Faith, after which he heard his confession, assisting him by suitable questions or by means of a written formulary in which, under the guise of a prayer, was embodied a closely detailed list of sins.

Then followed the absolution in deprecatory form, accompanied by the imposition of hands.   This deprecatory form of absolution was usual, even among the Latins, until towards the twelfth century the indicatory form gained ground in the West, showing as it does so much more clearly than the other the judiciary power exercised by the priest in this sacrament.

Among the Greeks the rite is far less simple.   According to the *Euchologion,* the penitent presents himself to the priest, who first intones a Litany imploring the divine mercy to forgive the penitent all his sins, whether committed through frailty or through malice.   A prayer follows in which the power granted to the Church to absolve from sins is called to mind, and supplication is made to him who alone is without sin to free the sinner from his bonds.   The Trisagion having been sung three times with the Psalms *Venite exultemus* and *Miserere,* the penitent, lying prostrate on the ground, says, "I have sinned, O Lord, have mercy on me," and, rising up, he continues, "O God, be merciful to me, a sinner."   The priest then recites over him another prayer, in which mention is made of the penitence of David and Manasses, and the divine mercy implored for the guilty person, who then lifts up his hands to heaven, and says : "Lord, thou knowest all the secrets of my heart."   The priest next questions him upon the different kinds of sins which he may have committed, and then continues : *Fili mi, abjectus sum et humilis peccator; eius propterea qui apud me confitetur, non valeo dimittere peccata; sed Deus est qui illa condonat.   Propter illam autem divinitus prolatam . . . apostolis . . . vocem: Quorum dimiseritis, etc. . . . et nos confisi dicimus: Quaecumque tenuissimae meae humilitati . . . enarrasti . . . condonet tibi Deus in praesenti saeculo et in futuro.*   Two other prayers follow, in which are expressed in deprecatory form both the pardon of sins and the special nature of the priestly office in this sacrament : *per me peccatorem . . . Deus tibi parcat.*

Among the Latins also, in the Middle Ages, a similar rite

was used. Before the confession, the priest said a prayer; then, when the penitent had ended the recital of his sins, the absolution was pronounced—unless it was referred to the bishop or put off until Holy Thursday—accompanied by various penitential psalms with special collects and prayers.

After public penance had fallen into disuse the conciliary and penitential canons came, in the Middle Ages, to be of great importance, even in those private confessions in which, for each different sin committed, the priest imposed the corresponding penance as laid down in the penitentiary table proper to the diocese.

The priest did not always confer absolution himself; this was sometimes reserved to the bishop or the Pope, in which case the guilty person set out for his episcopal city, or for Rome itself, taking with him a letter from his own confessor. To render the sacramental absolution more solemn, it was often repeated for several days, or else several priests and bishops assembled, who, after the confession had been heard, pronounced collectively the words of absolution over the repentant sinner.

The rite of public penance in those countries which came under Celtic influence was, down to the tenth century, very imposing. The guilty persons, clad in sackcloth and sprinkled with ashes, received the imposition of hands and were turned out of the church. With hair shorn, and feet bared, and clad in the mourning garments which they wore throughout the whole period of their penance, they had to abstain from their usual avocations in order to devote themselves to prayer and fasting. Sometimes they were detained in the ecclesiastical prisons, and were forbidden to eat meat or drink wine, or they were sentenced to undertake weary pilgrimages, loaded, in the case of homicides, with heavy chains. Confessors were not lacking who imposed severe beatings and disciplines upon their penitents, and among the early Cistercians it was the custom to prescribe to their novices the observance of the monastic rule as a sacramental penance.

No trace has been left in the Sacramentaries of the dismissal of the penitents in the Latin Liturgy at the beginning of the *missa fidelium*. St Gregory appears to refer to it as an obsolete ceremony; but the view of some liturgists, who maintain that the reason for this change is to be sought in the Roman discipline of the Middle Ages, by which penitents were shut up in monasteries, is a very doubtful one, since the penance in question was but rarely imposed, and chiefly in the case of ecclesiastical dignitaries.

The first ceremony for the readmission of sinners into communion with the Church followed on their petition to be admitted to canonical penance. After the fourth century this petition was usually granted, and the priest laid his hands upon the head of the sinner and delivered to him a garment of sackcloth. At Rome the ceremony assumed very grand proportions, and Sozomen relates that after the Mass the penitents prostrated themselves on the ground before the bishop and the people, bewailing their sins. The scene called for pity, and the Pontiff himself, prostrate on the ground with his people, joined in their lamentations and implored pardon of almighty God. Rising again to his feet, he invited the penitents to do likewise, and after the recitation of a prayer, he sent them away from the church so that each one might perform privately the penance imposed upon him. This varied according to the transgressions committed, and everything points to the conclusion that, from the time of Origen, before the public confessions took place, matters were arranged privately between the penitent and the bishop, or priest penitentiary, upon whose judgement the decision rested, as to whether or not it was fitting that the sinner should display the wounds of his soul before his assembled fellow-Christians.

It must be made clear at this point that, as regards her disciplinary rules, the Church constantly declared herself to be ever less and less in favour of that public confession and open revelation so dear to the faithful of early times, so that very soon it was not only abolished at Constantinople and censured at Rome by Pope Gelasius I, but even in the monastic rules it was expressly limited to open sins and ordinary breaches of discipline. St Benedict explicitly lays it down that hidden sins shall be confessed to the abbot alone, or to those spiritual fathers who know how to heal their own wounds and those of others without in any way disclosing them.[1]

Towards the ninth century public penance had become steadily more rare; hence, in the absence of penitents, the ancient ceremony of imposing ashes *in capite jejunii* came to be performed upon the clergy and upon the faithful indiscriminately, who thus took the place of public sinners. Such a substitution reveals at once a strange state of disciplinary confusion, and as regards the clergy it is absolutely irreconcilable with the earlier Roman mode of thought, and with the ancient law of the sacred canons, according to which the mediator between God and the sinner ought to be endowed with every virtue and with all perfection. Yet the custom became general, especially through the influence of the Gallican liturgies, which eventually prevailed also in Spain and at Rome.

[1] *Regula S Benedicti*, c. xlvi.

The ceremony described in the existing Roman Pontifical for the expulsion of penitents from the church is very dramatic, and is taken from the Gallican customs of the tenth and eleventh centuries, since it is in the Sacramentaries of that time that the first mention of it is to be found. At the beginning of Lent, the bishop blesses the sackcloth and ashes and places them upon the guilty persons; then, having sung the Penitential Psalms and the Litanies with the people, he reminds the penitents of the sin and penance of Adam, drawing an analogy between his expulsion from Eden and their temporary banishment from the church. The penitents, holding a candle in their right hand, took each other by the hand, and the bishop, having in like manner taken the hand of the one who headed the line, led them forth from the church, while the *schola* in the meantime executed a magnificent responsory, describing the sin of our first parents in Paradise and the divine sentence of expulsion pronounced upon them.

In the medieval Liturgy three Masses were formerly offered on Holy Thursday: the first for the reconciliation of penitents, the second for the blessing of the holy oils and the third for the holy Communion.

The penitents took up their positions betimes before the door of the church. The bishop, the archdeacon, a deacon, and four subdeacons then put on the sacred vestments and recited together with the clergy and the people the Penitential Psalms and the Litany of the Saints. When the choir had come to the invocation of the Patriarchs, at a sign from the bishop, two subdeacons, carrying lighted candles, went out to the penitents at the threshold of the church and sang: *Vivo ego, dicit Dominus, nolo mortem peccatoris, sed ut magis convertatur et vivat.* Then, the lights having been put out, the doors were barred and the Litany continued. When the invocation of the holy martyrs was reached, two other subdeacons repeated the same ceremony, singing: *Dicit Dominus, poenitentiam agite; appropinquavit enim regnum coelorum.* At a third pause, one of the older deacons announced to the penitents their approaching pardon, and lighted their candles in readiness for the ending of the Litany. Then the archdeacon spoke, reminding the bishop that the moment of universal salvation was at hand, the day on which the Redeemer vanquished sin upon the cross and regenerated the Church into newness of life. She is now about to extend her conquests by means of the neophytes and penitents; the water of Baptism washing away the sins of the first, while the second are purified by tears. The bishop replied, exhorting the guilty in no way to doubt the mercy of God; then the *schola* gave a threefold invitation to the wretched sinners to draw nigh to the prelate so as to learn from him the ways of the Lord.

When the psalm *Benedicam Dominum* (xxxiii) had been sung, the penitents re-entered the church and threw themselves at the feet of the bishop. The archpriest then pleaded for their reconciliation, making himself responsible for the sincerity of their new resolutions. Finally, yielding to entreaty, the Pontiff gave his assent, and taking the foremost of the penitents by the hand, brought them all into the basilica. At this point, the Pontifical of to-day shows itself to be a compilation made up from various Sacramentaries, since different forms of absolution follow, wholly independent of one another, and even mutually exclusive. The first and finest has a splendid deprecatory formula with a preface, recalling the divine mercies towards Achab, Peter and the Good Thief, and praying our Lord to make the penitents worthy of the eucharistic banquet. It would seem that the rite should end here, as it did originally, but in the existing Pontifical, on the contrary, a sudden reversion takes place, and clergy and people having prostrated themselves, the psalms *Miserere mei, Deus* (l) and *Miserere mei, Deus, miserere mei* (lvi) are sung, with seven prayers for absolution, not at all Roman in form. Some of these prayers now form part of the *Ordo commendationis animae* (*Deus misericors, Deus clemens*, etc.).

Lastly—and here the rite seems still more strange, almost as if the penalty has still to be paid—the Pontiff grants to the penitents a partial remission of their sins, and then, joining people and penitents together in the same pronouncement of plenary absolution, he gives to all those present his pastoral benediction.

The final part of the reconciliation, after it had taken on a somewhat general character, survived for a long time, even when the ancient discipline of public penance had fallen entirely into disuse. At Rome, indeed, on Holy Thursday, the Pope, down to 1870, was accustomed to bless the people from the loggia of the Vatican basilica, granting them a plenary indulgence; this was the last remnant of one of the most ancient and venerable ecclesiastical traditions.

The medieval custom, at first very limited, of granting indulgences, is closely connected with the discipline of public penance. As the canons became still more strict, and prescribed so many years of punishment that a lifetime would not suffice to wipe out the debt, the custom arose of commuting canonical penances for almsgiving, pilgrimages, disciplines and sometimes, in the Crusades, for the taking of the cross against the infidel in the Holy Land. It is known that St Peter Damian expiated in a few months the very long canonical penance imposed on him by reason of his renunciation of the bishopric of Ostia, by singing psalms and scourging himself with osier rods.[1]

It was, then, the very excess of the penitential canons which largely contributed to the cessation of canonical penance in its old form, for which in the later Middle Ages indulgences and jubilees were substituted.

Rome, with her traditional discretion and good sense, had taken no part either in these strange complications of ritual or in these acts of excessive severity. The ancient Roman rite for the reconciliation of penitents shows a mild and prudent spirit, far in advance of the penitential formulas of the Celtic and Gallican Churches.

[1] S Petri Dam., *Opusc.* xx; *Apol. ob dimissum Episcopat.*, c. i; *P.L.* CXLV, col. 444.

CHAPTER X

HOLY ORDERS

ALTHOUGH the holy Council of Trent teaches us that the priesthood was bestowed upon the Apostles at the Last Supper, yet it does not tell us whether the sacramental rite of Holy Orders was instituted at that time or only after the Resurrection. We read that on the evening of Easter Day our Lord confirmed anew to his Apostles the power to forgive sins, breathing on them and endowing them with the gift of the Holy Ghost; but we are nowhere told that they afterwards copied this ceremony in the bestowal of Holy Orders. Hence it is to be concluded that our Lord himself revealed to them at least the dominant idea of the euchological formulas to be observed when the time should come for them in their turn to raise others to the dignity of the priesthood by means of the imposition of hands.

This thesis is theologically sound, and the sacred books of the New Testament themselves furnish us with historical proof of it when they record the prayers and imposition of hands of the Apostles on ordaining the first deacons; when they speak of the prayer, fasting and imposition of hands in the episcopal ordination of Paul and Barnabas, and, finally, when the great Apostle himself reminds Timothy of the grace which had been conferred upon him through the laying-on of hands.

The imposition of hands and the episcopal "epiclesis" thus constitute the essential mark of the sacrament of Holy Orders, which must be retained intact in all rites and in every age. The fast, of apostolic origin, always and everywhere preceded the sacred rite; but the rest—litanies, anointings, bestowal of outward insignia, etc.—were from the first merely ecclesiastical ceremonies varying in origin and arising at different periods, having as their object the embellishment of the outward sign of the sacrament, and, by means of external things, the explanation of its hidden meaning.

As the existing rite of ordination prescribed in the Pontifical is the result of a fusion of Frankish and Roman customs, it will not be irrelevant to speak of the local customs in more detail. In ordination, as in the Mass, the Gallican and Mozarabic Churches had ceremonies altogether different from those of Rome. The *Statuta Ecclesiae antiqua,* the *Missale Francorum* and the Gelasian

Sacramentary all agree with the *De Officiis* of St Isidore and with the Mozarabic *Liber Ordinum*.

As to the Minor Orders in the Gallican Church, the archdeacon first of all instructed those about to be ordained regarding the functions proper to their state; then the bishop consigned to them the insignia of their office, pronouncing a short form of benediction, which was preceded in the Frankish rite, as was customary, by an invitation to prayer addressed to the people. These instructions of the archdeacon, now contained in the Roman Pontifical, are some of the most interesting liturgical compositions that we have. It is difficult to determine their origin, since, though they claim to be very ancient as to style, yet they sometimes show traces of ideas and customs of so late a date that we must place their definite recension somewhere about the sixth or seventh century. The admonition of the door-keeper, for instance, would seem to imply that bells were in general use, which circumstance takes us back as far as the eighth century; while elsewhere mention is made of the people taking their part in the singing of the divine Office, a custom which in Gaul was not older than the seventh century.

The rite of the ordination of readers is still more singular. The bishop addresses the candidate in the words, *eligunt te fratres tui, ut sis lector,* etc., thus implying that a popular election had preceded this ceremony. He then exalts before all the people the newly chosen reader and the office with which he is about to honour him, finally presenting him with the codex of the Holy Scriptures. The manuscripts do not ordinarily contain any formula for these extemporary addresses; only the existing Roman Pontifical has preserved to us one for each order, which has certainly been derived from the Gallican rite. Thus in the address to the reader mention is made of the fact that the sermon always follows the scriptural lesson. The last prayer at the end of the ordination ceremony is so much mutilated in all the manuscripts as to be almost unintelligible: *Ut assiduitate electionum* (= *lectionum*) *distinctus atque ordinatus* (= *ornatus*) *curis modolis spiritali* (*is*) *devotione* (*i*) (*adde gratiae*) *lingua resonet ecclesiae*—unless this may be in connection with the office of *Cantor,* long since merged into that of the *Lector.*

The rite for ordaining exorcists presents no less difficulty. The gift of casting out devils from those possessed had become already rare in the fourth century, and would seem to have been confined to monks of exceptionally holy life or to the bodies of martyrs resting peacefully in their graves. The *energumens* also were no longer so numerous as to call for the institution of a special order with fixed and permanent gifts in order to meet a need so uncertain and irregular. Therefore—in agreement with the documents—it seems to us probable that from the first the office of exorcist was bound up with the discipline of the catechumenate, and that the breathings and adjurations, afterwards reserved to the acolytes in the great scrutinies before baptism, were originally the function of the exorcists. It was natural, when in the sixth century the catechumenate had lost its primitive character, that the order of exorcists should also become bereft of all importance, so that its primary significance underwent, especially in Gaul, a strange displacement which almost amounted to confusing it with the free gift of liberating those possessed (*gratia curationum*) from the power of the evil spirits.

It would seem that in France the order of acolytes did not meet with universal approval, since the Gelasian Sacramentary and the *Missale Francorum,* while preserving to us the text of the opening prayers of the rite, show much hesitation regarding the place in the hierarchy to which the acolytes belonged. The functions also attributed to the acolyte in the *admonitio* of the present Pontifical are by no means those to be found in Rome, since to prepare the wine and water for the Mass belonged in Rome exclusively to the deacon, who was unassisted by any cleric of lower rank.

The ordination of a subdeacon among the Franks was quite simple. The bishop gave him the chalice and paten, then the archdeacon presented the basin and napkin for drying his hands, and the prelate instructed him upon the importance of the office which he was to fill—*Si usque nunc ebriosus,* etc.—whence it is to be inferred that the Gallican clergy were just that which St Gregory of Tours and St Boniface described them to be—a mixture of good and bad qualities, of lofty piety and barbaric ways.

The candidate chosen for the diaconate was presented by the bishop to the assembly of the faithful, who expressed their approval by the acclamation *Dignus est.* A kind of introductory or general prayer followed—*communis oratio*—of which, however, the documents that we possess do not give the text, but which very likely may have been a *praefatio* or a litany. After this, the bishop laid his hand upon the head of the newly ordained deacon, and pronounced the sacramental *benedictio.* Elsewhere, and especially among the Anglo-Saxons, it was customary to anoint the hands of the deacons as well as those of the priests with holy oil, a rite which about the eighth century was introduced also into France, but the very fact that it was the oil of catechumens and not the sacred chrism which was used for this anointing, shows this ceremony to have been of late origin.

The ordination of priests in the Gallican rite did not differ much from that of deacons, except that the body of priests who were present joined with the bishop in laying their hands on the head of the chosen candidate, who was also anointed with chrism.

The consecration of bishops took place, for the most part, in the city over which the elected prelate was chosen to rule. Long negotiations were first of all entered into between the clergy, the metropolitan bishop and the royal court, and when at last all were agreed regarding the person of the candidate, the metropolitan presented him officially to the clergy and people, so that by their acclamations they might confirm the choice which had been made. The assembly at once replied *Dignus est,* and then the bishop in a long preamble invited the people to join their supplications to his consecratory prayer.

Two bishops held open the codex of the holy Gospels over the head of the bishop elect, while the others, together with the metropolitan, laid their hands on him, after which followed the anointing of the hands with sacred chrism, the only anointing used in France in the Merovingian period, as that of the head was unknown till about the ninth century.

Throughout this Gallican Liturgy there is a very curious tendency to confuse the primitive stretching-out of hands—essential to the sacrament of Holy Orders—with other ceremonies, the object of which is to express outwardly the inner and sacramental meaning. Moreover, it is not altogether clear why the Minor Orders assumed, among the Franks, an importance so great that admission to them was hedged about with such an imposing array of formulas, whilst in Rome the rite was extremely simple. Another striking peculiarity is the consecratory prayer at the conferring of Major Orders in the deprecatory form of a simple *oratio;* whereas the same prayer in Rome was of a grand and majestic character.

The Frankish rituals often omit to mention the laying-on of hands, but this was understood in the very title of *oratio super diaconum, presbyterum,* etc., since, as St Augustine says, *quid aliud est manuum impositio, quam oratio super hominem?*

Let us now pass on from the Gallican to the Eastern customs.

By a strange coincidence, the more the rites of the Gallican Mass differ from Roman uses, the more closely do they assimilate to the Byzantine; but the contrary is the case regarding the ceremonies for ordination, in which it is Rome rather than Gaul or Spain which is in full agreement with the East. Nothing is simpler than ordination among the Greeks and Syrians, as it is described, for example, in the

Apostolic Constitutions and the writings of the pseudo-Dionysius. The bishop-elect is presented to the people, who bear witness to the metropolitan of his suitability for the office; then two deacons hold the holy Gospels over his head while the bishops place their hands on him and pronounce the consecratory *epiclesis* in deprecatory form. The new prelate is then enthroned, and after exchanging the Kiss of Peace with his consecrators, he himself celebrates the solemn Mass. The ordination of priests and deacons is not very different; it begins with the presentation to the people, and then the bishop lays his hands on the candidate and recites the consecratory prayer.

While in the East the *ministerium* was becoming disintegrated, giving rise to two other Minor Orders, the lectorate and the subdiaconate—the other religious offices of less importance, doorkeepers, grave-diggers, cantors, etc., not being reckoned in the ecclesiastical hierarchy—in the West, from the period immediately following the Apostolic Age, we find the first traces of five Minor Orders, which, however, did not always and everywhere meet with the same subsequent fortune. The *sacerdotium* included the episcopate and the priesthood; the deacon shared his eucharistic functions with the subdeacon and the acolyte, while the other three Minor Orders were responsible for the preparing of the catechumens for baptism, the reading of the Scriptures from the ambo and the taking charge of the *dominium* or church.

The historical origin of the Minor Orders is still very obscure. It seems that originally the public reading was entrusted indifferently to anyone the bishop might choose, so that not even the holy Gospel was exclusively reserved to the deacon. The doorkeepers are very rarely mentioned, and, indeed, as long as the Christian assemblies in the first century were held in private houses, it is difficult to understand how the duty of guarding the door could have been given to anyone other than the usual slaves of the patrician *domus* which fostered the infant Church. In the correspondence of St Cyprian, in which the other six ecclesiastical Orders are mentioned, that of the doorkeeper never appears.

St Cornelius, in 251, says that there were in Rome forty-six priests, seven deacons, seven subdeacons, forty-two acolytes and fifty-two other lesser clerics; but it is extremely doubtful if these last included the doorkeepers, since on apportioning these figures among the various urban titles and the seven ecclesiastical districts into which Pope Fabian had divided the city, there would result two priests for each title, and at the head of each of the seven ecclesiastical districts—which, moreover, included two civil districts—a deacon, a subdeacon and six acolytes. If now the other fifty-two lesser clerics were divided among exorcists, readers and door-keepers, this would give an average of six exorcists, thirteen readers and thirteen doorkeepers—a somewhat small number when we reflect that, apart from possible cases of illness, etc., the actual care of the church and the singing demanded that there should be more than one cleric to each title capable of filling this office.

If we were to set aside the doorkeepers altogether, we could then double the number of readers for each title. It is true that the *Liber Pontificalis* assigns Romanus the door-keeper as companion in martyrdom to St Laurence, but the text of this narrative is not altogether reliable. Moreover, the Roman documents enumerating the various ecclesiastical grades very rarely include that of the doorkeeper, who, in the fifth century, had already been superseded by the *mansionarius*, a kind of sacristan, who had, however, no place in the ecclesiastical hierarchy.

Ordinarily the initiation into the ecclesiastical state began, in Rome, with the lectorate, to which even children might be admitted. Later on, the readers were gathered together in a kind of seminary, from which afterwards sprang St Gregory's *schola cantorum*. One of the earliest grades in the hierarchy was that of the exorcist, but it declined with the decay of the discipline of the catechumenate, while the order of acolytes went on increasing in importance until it finally absorbed rights and functions hitherto reserved to the deacon. In fact, in Rome it was the acolytes and no longer the deacons who, at any rate from the fourth century onwards, carried the *eucharistia* consecrated by the Pope to the various urban titular churches; moreover, the *Ordines Romani* give them a very important share in the scrutinies of the catechumens and in the administration of baptism.

In contrast to the Gallican Liturgies—regarding which we have lamented that the ceremonies of the sacrament of Holy Orders seriously compromise the precise meaning of the essential rite, leaving it somewhat confused and obscured by all those admonitions, popular acclamations, conveying of the outward symbols of office and anointing of hands and head—the Roman ordinations are fully in keeping with the char-acter of the *Urbs,* the classic seat of the law and the home of a people destined to rule the world. This characteristic quality consists of concise and solemn formulas, free from all those symbolical wrappings which, instead of bringing out the full meaning of the sacrament, only confuse it, and constitutes a sober, yet magnificent, rite of pure classic outline.

The holy rite of ordination from apostolic days was always preceded by fasting; hence, according to the Roman custom, it was at first confined to the night vigil of the December

Embertide; we know not whether on account of some connection with the approaching Christmas festival or for some
other more practical reason. Consequently Gelasius I in a
letter to the Bishops of Lucania and the Abruzzi, modified
this practice and enjoined that the other Saturdays also
should be recognized as suitable times for the carrying out
of this sacred rite, with the result that his successors, down
to the ninth century, very rarely indeed went beyond this
rule. It is known that St Leo II and St Gregory I alone
occasionally held ordinations in the months of May and
September, whilst the other Popes had held them either in
December or on the first or fifth Saturday of Lent, excluding
of course the great Paschal vigil.

We have spoken of Saturday so as to conform to the present
day terminology, although in reality the Pope conferred Holy
Orders almost at the end of the vigil preceding the Sunday
when outside the church dawn was already breaking. The
ordination of a Pope—at least, after the Byzantine period—
alone took place at the altar of the Apostle; the others were
ordained in the adjacent rotunda of St Andrew. When
ordinations are made mention of at Rome, only those of
bishops, priests and deacons are meant, as the lesser ministers
did not undergo any solemn initiation, and their *benedictio,*
which was quite private and without the presence of any of
the faithful, could be conferred by the bishop on any day of
the year, and even outside of the stational Mass. After the
Communion, the future acolyte or subdeacon knelt at the
feet of the Pope, or the officiating bishop, receiving from
the hands of the archdeacon, in the case of the acolyte, a
small linen bag, and in that of the subdeacon, a chalice.
What may have been the ancient formula of their inaugural
benediction is a matter of doubt, but towards the sixth
century the following was in use: *Intercedente beata et
gloriosa semperque virgine Maria et beato Apostolo Petro,
salvet et custodiat et protegat te Dominus.* We know nothing
of the doorkeepers, and as for the other Minor Orders, either
they had no special rite of initiation, or, if there were one,
then it was carried out within the *schola* of the singers.

The great ordinations which were held on the night of
Ember Saturday were announced to the Roman people on
the previous Wednesday during the stational Mass at
St Mary Major. The faithful were invited to say what
they knew regarding those about to be ordained, stating
whether they were guilty of any serious failing; but already,
previous to this appeal to the judgement of the people, a
secret scrutiny had been conducted by the members of the
clerical body on their own account, before whom the candidates had to swear that they had never stained their souls

with any of those transgressions against morality which, according to the law of that time, excluded those guilty of such sins from Holy Orders. From the eighth century onwards, the ordinations of the Saturday night were carried out on the preceding afternoon. After the chanting of the lessons, and before the Gospel was read, the archdeacon presented the candidates to the Pope, who invited the people to prayer and caused the litanies to be sung. When the ceremony was over, the newly ordained received the Kiss of Peace from the Pope and the clergy present, after which they took their places beside the Pontiff.

As a ceremony, the ordination of priests and bishops hardly differed at all from that of deacons, except that the election of bishops was held in their own episcopal city, and that, after the papal confirmation had been received, the consecration could be performed on any Sunday of the year. Unlike the other bishops, who could only bestow episcopal ordination when assisted by at least two other prelates, as if to represent the whole body of the episcopate, at Rome, the Pope, although surrounded by his suburbicarian bishops, yet performed the sacred rite by himself, wishing by so doing to emphasize the universality of his power. So also the holy Gospel, which elsewhere was unfolded over the head of each episcopal candidate, became at Rome a privilege distinctive of papal consecration, the only one performed at the altar of St Peter, purposely to mark the divine mission and the universal authority of the Sovereign Pontiff. On such an occasion as this the Pope put on the sacred vestments—with the exception of the pallium—in the *secretarium;* whence, while the Introit was being sung, he approached the altar and remained prostrate before it during the chanting of the Litany. Then the Bishops of Albano, Porto and Ostia recited over him the usual consecratory prayers, while two deacons supported above his head the codex of the Gospels.

When the consecration was completed, the archdeacon placed the pallium upon his shoulders, and the newly elected Pope celebrated his first pontifical Mass amid the pomp of bishops, of prelates from the pontifical court and of legates from the different dioceses, who stood around him. Then, after the offering of the holy Sacrifice, there followed the solemn procession to the Lateran, which, in the Middle Ages, attained the proportions of a real triumphal progress. The higher clergy wore their most precious vestments, and it was not unusual for kings and emperors to take part in the function. Later on, under the influence of the Gallican Liturgy, this primitive and eminently dogmatic Roman simplicity was complicated by the addition of accessory formulas which detracted from the dignity of the rite. It was the custom in France to present the pastoral staff to the new bishop, and his enthronement was accomplished by the assistant bishops themselves placing him upon a gilded throne. As a sign of the special bond of affection uniting the consecrated prelate and his consecrator, the latter presented him with a large consecrated Host, so that for a whole month he might break off from it every day a particle to place in his own chalice at Mass.

It was the Roman custom that bishops newly consecrated by the Pope should receive a copy of the pontifical decrees concerning the right administration of their diocese, whence in Gaul also it became usual to present the codex of the Gospels together with the *Pastorale* of St Gregory the Great as an ordination offering.

There is a very curious tradition, recorded by St Jerome and other ecclesiastical writers, to the effect that the ordination of the Bishop of Alexandria was originally performed by the priests of that city. Perhaps it came from a story circulated by the Arians against St Athanasius, unless we prefer to think that at first the Alexandrian hierarchy knew no " monarchist " episcopate, and that under St Mark the presbyteries were all endowed with the episcopal character and with the fulness of the priesthood.

We have already said that from remotest antiquity the consecration of the Pope was the prerogative of the Bishop of Ostia, who for this reason enjoyed the privilege of investing him with the sacred pallium. Afterwards, in the Middle Ages, the consecration and coronation of the Pope were accompanied by a magnificent array of ceremonies which illustrated very clearly the spiritual and political status of the Papacy. Instead of vesting in the *secretarium,* the new Pontiff put on the sacred garments in the Chapel of St Gregory, formerly close to the ancient *secretarium,* and when the long function of the consecration and Mass was over, the procession returned in triumph to the Lateran, traversing, in order to reach it, the *Via Papalis* and the Roman Forum. At the narrowest places, a timely shower of largesse opened a passage through the crowd, which was wont to be especially boisterous at Monte Giordano on account of the Jews, since it was there that on such an occasion as this the Chief Rabbi used to present the new Pontiff with the codex of the Law, requesting at the same time respect and protection for his people. The Pope replied that he reverenced the sacred Scriptures, though he rejected the rabbinical interpretation of them, and as for protection, he was giving them an immediate proof of it by a generous distribution of money.

Then followed in the atrium of the Lateran Basilica the rite of the *sedes stercorea,* so called because, as the Pope took his seat in an ancient chair from one of the *thermae,* the choir chanted the verse *Suscitat . . . et de stercore elevat pauperem,* etc. On rising again to his feet, the Pontiff threw money to the people three times, saying, *Argentum et aurum non est mihi,* and having entered the church, he took possession successively of the Papal throne in the apse of the Lateran and of the two other marble chairs in front of the Oratory of St Sylvester, where he received the keys of the Palace from the prior of the Papal Chapel of St Laurence, and then reconsigned them to him. A further bestowal of largesse to clergy and people brought the strictly liturgical portion of the papal coronation to a close and gave the court an opportunity to partake of refreshment. The banquet was spread in the magnificent Triclinium of Leo III, the Pope taking part in it with all the higher clergy, who continued to wear their sacred vestments and even their mitres. The Pope sat at a table somewhat higher than the rest, glistening with costly plate. One of the cardinal bishops poured out the water for the washing of hands, while two deacons presented the towel. When the dinner was over, the members of the Lateran Court accompanied the Pontiff to his apartments and assisted him to lay aside his state apparel.

CHAPTER XI

THE CONSECRATION OF BASILICAS IN EARLY CHRISTIAN TIMES

THE Sacraments and the Liturgy preceded the altar and the Church, and this for many reasons. In the first two centuries of the Church's history, when she was not yet recognized by the State as a legally constituted *corpus* capable of possessing civil rights, and had to accept the hospitality offered her by the more wealthy among her children in their suburban villas or in their patrician houses within the city, there could be no thought as yet of creating any special and exclusive type of building and of liturgical surroundings. It was, therefore, deemed fitting for the Christian Church to adapt herself as best she might to the customary forms of the Greek and Roman society of that time, with which even Jewish monotheism had eventually found a common ground of agreement in matters artistic, literary and religious, even though strange to her. Our liturgical rites were from the first so little different from the ordinary ceremonial customs in use in the synagogues and religious assemblies of Greece and of Asia Minor, that the eucharistic feast itself differed but slightly in outward appearance from the Jewish Paschal Supper, or from the religious repasts taken in common by priestly associations and burial societies. In contrast to the repellent materialism of the pagans the Christians gloried in the greater spirituality of their worship, which did not imprison the Deity within the dusty chamber of a temple or in a rude and impure Asiatic idol of stone; and therefore, saying that they had neither altar nor incense, they proclaimed themselves to be the temple of a divine being, to whom the most acceptable sacrifice was the prayer of an innocent heart lifted up to God under the blue vault of heaven.

THE CHRISTIAN ALTAR.—The accusation made by Celsus against the Christians, that they had neither temples nor altars, is so fully confirmed in the works of Origen, Tertullian and Lactantius that it has given rise to strange misapprehensions on the part of more recent historians. It must be admitted that in the first two centuries of the Church, the Fathers, possessed with a horror of idolatry and concerned above everything with the spiritual aspect of Christian worship, assigned far less importance to its external setting, whether architectural, artistic or æsthetic; hence, unlike the pagans, they could in all sincerity deny the possession of temples, altars and idols in the materialistic sense attached to them by the heathens; for them, prayer and the sacraments were everything. Out of this arose the accusation of atheism brought against the Christians in the second century. Scarcely, however, had that extraordinary period of spiritual gifts, with its exceptional hierarchy of apostles, prophets, evangelists, doctors, etc., ceased, when the steady expansion of the Church demanded a more stable and normal organization. The customs and traditions of early years naturally became legal ceremonies and obligatory rites, emphasizing more and more the outward aspect of the Christian body.

Besides the banqueting hall in the catacombs of the Flavii, where even to-day we can picture vividly to ourselves how, on the morrow of the persecution of Trajan, the *agape,* the feast of brotherly love, must have developed in Rome, a painting in the so-called Greek Chapel in the catacombs of Priscilla preserves for us the oldest representation of the eucharistic feast in existence (first half of the second century). The guests, among whom is a woman, are reclining upon couches arranged in the form of a *sigma,* all along the table, on which is placed a fish. In the post of honour, seated upon a stool, another figure of mature age, towards whom the rest are looking with respect and veneration, is breaking bread upon which is marked the cross; and before him is the cup of wine. The Priscillian picture blends together symbolical and realistic elements, since the eucharistic feast at this time was certainly distinct from the *agape,* and would therefore be celebrated upon an altar and not upon the *stibadium.* Moreover, the person at the head of the table exhibits realistic features of very great importance, for not only does he occupy the place of honour at the banquet, but is actually performing the characteristic ceremony from which the early Christians derived the name *fractio panis,* which they gave to the eucharistic sacrifice. Noteworthy, too, is the table, placed in the form of a *sigma* and covered with a cloth, although this form of festive table has left no trace in the artistic development of the Christian altar.

A painting, perhaps a little later in date, though still of the second century, in the catacombs of St Callixtus, represents a further development of the eucharistic rite. According to the custom which then obtained, the couches with their occupants have disappeared, the *stibadium* has also vanished, and nothing is left of the ancient *triclinium* except a small three-legged table on which is seen a loaf and a fish.

A person vested with the pallium (reserved in catacomb paintings to our Lord or to the Apostles and Prophets) spreads his hands over them in prayer (*epiclesis super oblata*), and in front of him there is the veiled figure of a woman stretching out her arms in the attitude of supplication. It is probable that after the disappearance of all the ancient *triclinium* ritual of the Mass, the form of the tripod table alone remained for a time in favour in the catacombs and in the Roman titular churches of the second century.

It was the offering of the holy Sacrifice *pro dormitione* on the anniversaries of the dead and of the martyrs which approximated the eucharistic table to the actual tomb, with the result that they often ended by being one and the same thing. The *Liber Pontificalis* attributes the custom of celebrating Mass upon the tombs of the martyrs to Felix I (274), but in Asia Minor it would seem to have been very much older, so perhaps the Pope merely restricted such celebration to the tombs of those who had died a violent death for the Faith. Thus the altars in the catacombs, placed on the most venerated among the tombs, tended gradually to become permanent, especially towards the end of the second century, when, even before the persecution of Diocletian, we see arising apsidal oratories and basilicas with triple choirs not only in Asia, Greece and Dalmatia, but also in Rome and along the Appian Way itself, the *Regina Viarum*.

An altar in the wall is still clearly recognizable in the nameless little basilica of the third century near the catacombs of St Callixtus, to which De' Rossi gave the title of Santa Sotere; while the same may be verified in the building discovered not long ago near the Platonia Apostolica on the Appian Way.

That other *cella,* too, with its triple choir above ground at St Callixtus, which we have the strongest reasons for identifying with the oratory *ubi decollatus est Xystus,* so greatly venerated by medieval pilgrims, undoubtedly had—from the third century onwards—its own isolated altar like that one which was erected lower down in the Papal crypt, and like those others noticed by Boldetti and Bosio in the catacombs of St Peter, St Marcellinus and St Priscilla.

From chapels in the catacombs or in private houses to urban basilicas the transition was an easy one. There the fixed altar rather than the bloodstained tomb of the martyr symbolized the peaceful *mensa Domini*, the centre of the Church's liturgical worship and the very reason for the building of a church; so that it is not to be wondered at if already under Constantine we find the Christian altar adorned with wondrous examples of embroidery and goldsmith's work. On a stone from the catacombs now in the

Lateran Museum we can see the *pergula* or railing that separates the *vima* and the altar from the nave of the church. Two columns support the architrave; right and left, between the columns and the wall, on two low latticed screens are placed branched candlesticks; while higher up the *velarium*, intended to hide the altar from the faithful, is half-raised. Two steps at the intersection of the transepts lead up to the *sacrum vima*. A very similar kind of altar was to be seen at Naples in the catacombs of St Januarius, except that there the columns of the *cancellum,* too, were excavated in the rock itself.

The form and substance of the ancient altars varied with differing localities, periods and tastes. The wooden altar preserved in the Lateran Basilica is described as being concave in shape *ad modum arcae,* just like the medieval altar erected over the tomb of St Nicholas of Bari, of a form somewhat analogous to that of the pagan altars, which also were scooped out in the upper part and had both rim and border. Usually the altar was supported by four or five columns, or even by a single central column or pillar only; sometimes the sides were closed in by openwork marble panels as a protection to the inner sarcophagus containing the relics, but in other instances the pillars rested directly upon the flat surface of the tomb underneath, which thus served as a foundation.

When this was the case, in order to satisfy the devotion of the faithful, a little door, *fenestrella confessionis,* was made in the fore part of the altar, by means of which veils (*brandea*) and other devotional objects might be laid on the funeral urn of the martyr; sometimes also censers were inserted, as was customarily done as late as the fourteenth century in the *confessio* of St Paul's.

*　　*　　*　　*　　*

THE CHRISTIAN BASILICA.—More involved than the history of the Christian altar is that of the basilica, which contains features borrowed, on the one hand, from the civil basilicas of Rome, and, on the other, from the patrician *domus.* The form of the civil basilica is known to us accurately. The name and aisles—two or four in number—of which it consists, are divided from one another by colonnades terminating in an apsidal tribunal and enclosed in front by low openwork marble screens. The plan of the Roman house is a little more complex, but with slight modifications it, too, can easily be approximated to that of the basilica. For this purpose it would suffice, for instance, to roof over the *atrium* or *impluvium* at the entrance, turning the rectangular *tablinum* into a semicircular tribunal; thus the portico becomes the narthex, the side spaces are converted into two lesser aisles, the *atrium displuviatum* forms the nave, the *tablinum* the sanctuary, and the two reception rooms on either side would then be the antechamber and the *diaconicon* for the safe keeping of the sacred vestments. Among the Easterns, the round or octagonal basilica found great favour, either with or without a dome, like San Vitale at Ravenna and Santa Sophia at Constantinople; but this style of building did not accord with the Latin taste, whose liturgy demands for its normal development a church in the form of the Roman basilica.

The precarious fate of the earliest places of assembly destined for Christian worship during the first ages of persecution forbade their being definitely consecrated to God by a special rite; the more so as the Christians held in abhorrence the consecration of the tombs by heathen priests, a ceremony required, however, by Roman law, so that the tomb should become not only a " religious " but a " sacred " spot. Satisfied with the security offered them by the religious character belonging of right to all tombs, they did not trouble themselves at all about the *consecratio,* which would bring with it the subsequent intervention of the heathen priests should it be necessary to make any alteration in the tomb. Even after the peace of Constantine, the first consecrations of churches of which we have any record resemble rather the solemn inauguration of a religious building than a true consecration in the sense afterwards given to it in the liturgies of the Frankish people.

At the first glance it appears very strange that the Christians of early times should have attached such slight importance to a rite which seemed to be suggested by the Holy Scriptures themselves, in that part where the dedication of the tabernacle is described. This anomaly, however, corresponds to that other of the absence at first of any distinctive dress or outward sign marking the clergy in the administration of the sacred mysteries; so that even to-day the Roman Pontifical in the rite for the consecration of bishops remarks : *Pontificalem gloriam, non jam nobis honor commendat vestium, sed splendor animarum.*

In order the better to understand what follows, it will be a help if we first carefully realize the point of view of the ancients regarding the relations between the temple and the Deity to whom it was consecrated.

The need of honouring the Deity through symbols and in fixed places arises from the relativity of man's worship of an infinite being, whom he can adore only by means of tangible forms corresponding to the degree of civilization to which he has attained and to the conception, more or less sublime, which he has of the divine being. Thus we find that even in the lowest depths of ignorance among savages, trees, fountains, caves and fetishes are honoured as symbols representative of a natural power, while altars are raised to them and sacrifices offered. The idea of building a temple in order to protect the Deity from the inclemency of the weather sprang from this very same materialization of the religious instinct among the ancient idolatrous peoples; hence the *naos* of the Greeks and the *cella* of the Romans, unlike the Christian basilica and *ecclesia,* essentially represent the inaccessible shrine of a Deity abiding in the midst of his people within his own house, because, like all other mortals, he too has need of a dwelling-place.

The laws regulating sacrifices fixed at a very early date, especially in the East, the character of this worship offered by man to the Deity. Beginning with the libation of oil poured out by Jacob upon the stone of his vision, and going on to the accounts of the religious rites recorded in the acts and inscriptions of the numerous priestly societies in Asia, Greece and Rome, we might draw very interesting comparisons for the history of religions. Through all these varied ceremonies there is seen, however, one grand idea which always stands out pre-eminent, and which indeed contains, as their ultimate *raison d'être,* other acts of worship, whose office, therefore, is simply to proclaim it and to explain it to the multitude. This majestic conception is that of the essential and ethical transcendence of the Deity, by reason of which man does not dare to approach him until, by a preparatory rite, he has purified his garments and his offerings; until it seems clear to him that even his very words are fully pleasing in the sight of God. For this reason it was that the pagan priest at Rome was wont to admonish the people, *Favete linguis,* lest some word of ill omen should chance to escape their lips.

From the Books of Kings we learn of the great festal celebrations of Solomon when the Temple at Jerusalem was consecrated, and from those of the Machabees we gather also the rite of expiation performed after the Temple had been violated under Antiochus; but it is remarkable that in both these cases there is no real consecration, but rather a solemn inauguration of the ordinary sacrificial worship, without any special sanctification of the structure; and since the old altar which had been defiled could no longer be used, Judas caused it to be removed to another place until a prophet should arise who in the name of God should decide upon its fate.

We find, on the other hand, traces of true expiatory lustrations among the heathen, to which the *lapis niger* of the Roman Forum, among others, bears testimony. Under-neath this stone the ancient *stele* with the *lex sacrificiorum,* which had been thrown down and broken, perhaps during the Gallic invasion, was carefully expiated by a grand sacrifice of many tens of bullocks, sheep, goats and wild boars, while hundreds of little funeral urns were thrown into the cleansing fire, together with small figures of bone or clay, dice, coins, glass beads, weights, personal orna-ments in bronze and weapons, all which things have been discovered intermingled in a layer of ashes, charcoal and gravel.

De Rossi has written about the heathen rites for the con-secration of sepulchres, by means of which the tomb from being merely "religious," as it was in the eyes of the law, became a spot looked upon as *sacer,* being placed thence-forth under the protection of the priests. In Rome, with the decline of the Empire, little by little—as the mystic senti-mentality of the Asiatics profited by the general corruption of manners to win over the popular conscience, vaguely feeling the need of a Deity, to the rites initiating them into the mysteries of Mithras and Isis—this idea of the purifica-tion and consecration of buildings intended for public worship spread further and further; so much so that under Julian the Apostate the pagan official priesthood itself adopted an attitude of ultra-puritanism, grotesquely imitat-ing the Christian hierarchy and ceremonies.

If there be anything specially disconcerting to the modern mode of thought when treating of the history of primitive Christianity, it is the charge of atheism brought from the very first against the followers of Christ, an accusation which the Apologists, as we have already seen, did not flatly deny, but were content merely to explain away and interpret in a kindlier sense, confirming, as they did so, the absence of images, churches and altars in Christian worship. "We have no altars," Origen frankly declares, "but the temple of our God is the whole world, and the altar most acceptable to him is a pure and innocent heart." We could multiply testimony to the same effect, but it is sufficient for our purpose to point out how the Fathers, when confronted with heathen idolatry, insisted above everything upon the sublime transcendence of the Christian faith, which instead of materializing the Deity by hiding him in the dark recesses of a temple shrine, adores the Father "not upon Mount Garizim nor upon Mount Moriah," but in spirit and in truth, with all the transport of an undefiled heart.

The dread inspired in the first generations of Christians by the unclean ritual of the heathen priesthood for a long time hindered the introduction into the Church of rites, ceremonies and religious accessories which were afterwards allowed when the disappearance of idolatry rendered them altogether harmless. Thus, in the time of Tertullian, incense, "intended to fumigate the gods," as that bitter controversialist expresses it, was strongly objected to, while the Greek Church to this day retains all her old aversion from statues, admitting no other sacred representations into the Church than such as are painted or slightly engraved on wood.

These reasons—taken together with the fact pointed out above that during the first three centuries of persecution the Church could not have fixed and permanent places exclusively destined to religious worship—explain why the rite of the consecration of churches could not develop until after the "Peace of Constantine." At this point documents abound, and from Eusebius, who describes enthusiastically the consecration of Constantine's basilicas at Tyre and Jerusalem, down to Ambrose and Paulinus, who embellished Milan and Cemitile with new churches, we can easily enumerate the various consecrations performed in the fourth century, noticing as especially remarkable the immense concourse of the faithful and of bishops who usually took part in them. "It was a splendid and consoling spectacle," says Eusebius, "to see the solemn consecrations of Christian churches and oratories which were springing up everywhere as if by magic, a spectacle rendered still more imposing and worthy of respect because honoured by the presence of the bishops of the whole province." Numerous, however, as are the documents which relate to these early consecrations, the rituals which prescribe the rite are altogether vague. The first condition for carrying out the ceremony in a legal manner was, at least for some time in Africa and the East, the imperial consent—a condition, moreover, parallel to the calling together of councils by the civil authorities and of the bestowal of the pallium by the Byzantine Basileus. This consent was more especially necessitated by the public and almost synodal character assumed by the ceremony on account of the provincial bishops taking part therein. It happened one year at Alexandria that the Patriarch Athanasius undertook during Lent the yearly catechetical preparation for baptism, but the people, who found themselves too crowded in the old church of Theona when it came to Easter Day, began to insist that the bishop should carry out the ceremonies in the basilica then newly completed, but which had not as yet been consecrated. Athanasius hesitated, but was obliged to yield to the popular demand; and when, later on, he was accused by the Arians of having inaugurated the new basilica without the imperial consent, he simply excused himself on the plea of the necessity under which the urgency of the people had placed him, without in any way questioning the privilege of the emperor.

It was on the initiative of Constantine that the Fathers of the Council of Tyre repaired to Jerusalem to consecrate there the basilicas of the *Martyrion* and the *Anastasis,* as related by Eusebius and Sozomen. In like manner, Constantius, acting on the suggestion of Eusebius of Nicomedia, on the completion of the basilica at Antioch, summoned thither a numerous concourse of bishops, who duly carried out its consecration.

This imperial privilege in regard to the consecration of new churches, of which there are no other traces except in the East, was for some time exercised in Italy by the Pope. Hence it was that Pelagius I forbade the Bishops of Lucania, the Abruzzi and Sicily to consecrate new churches unless they had previously *ex more* asked for and obtained a faculty for so doing from the Holy See. This papal right and custom was repeatedly confirmed by the Regesta of St Gregory I, from which we gather that, in Italy and within the metropolitan area of Rome, no bishop, without the consent of the Pontiff, could erect any altar, nor consecrate any church or baptistry whatsoever. Outside the boundaries of the papal province, however—which was so extensive as to include even Ravenna, although its bishop was, on his own account, the metropolitan of the surrounding churches— we never find the Popes exercising such a right; thus, St Ambrose at Milan, St Gaudentius of Brescia, St Columbanus and St Gregory of Tours all consecrated their own basilicas of their own free will, without any necessity for special papal permission.

From the first the rite for the consecration of churches, though it left ample scope for the personal initiative of the bishop, was a somewhat simple matter, without the addition of any anointings or aspersions, such as arose at a later date in Gaul, and thence penetrated into the Roman Liturgy. The ceremony being of a solemn and public character was reserved to the bishop of the diocese or to the provincial bishops invited by him; hence the case to which Walafrid Strabo refers in his *Life of St Gall: Beatus autem Columbanus iussit aquam afferri, et benedicens illam adspersit ea templum, et dum circumirent psallentes dedicavit ecclesiam. Deinde, invocato nomine Domini, unxit altare et B. Aureliae reliquias in eo collocavit, vestitoque altari, missas legitime compleverunt*[1] is altogether sporadic, and similar to that other instance of the Irish St Columba, who, though only

---

[1] *Vita sancti Galli,* vi.

a simple priest, performed for the first time among his people the rite of the consecration of a king. It is known, however, that in Ireland in early times priests and abbots possessed very great influence over the people.

Eusebius, in describing the glories of the consecration festival of Constantine's basilicas at Jerusalem, seems to make its chief splendour consist in long discourses, uttered either in honour of the emperor or to enunciate some theological argument, reserving to the least capable ecclesiastics the office of reciting the written formulary of prayers : *At sacerdotes Dei partim precationibus, partim sermonibus festivitatem ornabant. Alii siquidem comitatem religiosi imperatoris erga omnium Servatorem laudibus celebrabant, et martyrii magnificentiam oratione prosequebantur. Alii sacris theologiae dogmatibus ad praesentem celebritatem accommodatis spirituale quoddam epulum audientibus praebebant. Quidam sacrorum voluminum lectiones interpretabantur. . . . Qui vero ad haec aspirare non poterant, incruentis sacrificiis et mysticis immolationibus Deum placabant.*

Besides the discourse of Eusebius on the occasion of the consecration of the basilica of Tyre (314) we possess the celebrated sermons of St Ambrose and St Gaudentius of Brescia when they inaugurated respectively the churches of their episcopal cities. The existing rite for the consecration of churches, given in the Roman Pontifical, did not spring from a single source, but is a skilful combination of the Gallican and Roman rituals dating from the later Middle Ages.

The oldest document dealing with the consecratory rite at Rome is a letter from Pope Vigilius to Bishop Profuturus of Braga, from which it appears that a twofold form of consecration was then in use, according to whether or not there were sacred relics to be placed in the church. If there were no relics, then no holy water was necessary, *quia consecrationem cujuslibet ecclesiae in qua sanctuaria non ponuntur, celebritatem tantum scimus esse missarum; et ideo, si qua sanctorum basilica a fundamentis etiam fuerit innovata sine aliqua dubitatione, cum in ea missarum fuerit celebrata solemnitas, totius sanctificatio consecrationis impletur.*

It appears that St Ambrose at Milan was the first to popularize in Italy the custom of depositing the relics of martyrs in the basilicas on the occasion of their consecration. In a letter to his sister Marcellina, the Saint narrates that upon his people asking him when he would consecrate the " Basilica Romana " as the others, he replied : *Faciam, si martyrum reliquias invenero.* As a matter of fact, we do know of basilicas consecrated without relics, not only at Rome and in Spain, but also in Gaul, where St Gregory of

Tours states that the altar of the *vico priscianicense* in his diocese was sanctified with relics only during his own Pontificate.[1]

In Africa, the fifth Council of Carthage implies that the same system held good, since it orders that such old altars without relics shall be destroyed, a judgement absolutely contrary to the regulations of the Council of Ephesus (Canon 25) in which it is forbidden that relics be placed in country oratories where there are no local clergy to celebrate the divine office daily, by night as well as by day. In the East also the same rule was in force, and we know from Theophanes that under Justinian, when the *Apostoleion* at Constantinople was consecrated, *recondita sunt λείψανα Andreae et Lucae Apostolorum. Et transiit Menas episcopus cum sanctis λειψάνοις sedens in carruca aurea imperatoris, lapidibus insignita, tenens tres thecas sanctorum Apostolorum in genibus suis et ita encaenia celebravit.* At Jerusalem, in the same way, according to St Cyril of Scythopolis, when Bishop Martyrius consecrated the oratory of St Euthymius, he deposited in the altar the relics of the martyrs Taracus, Probus and Andronicus.

With the increase in devotion to the martyrs it came to be looked upon as almost illegal to erect any altar or church elsewhere than over their tombs; and, as these could only be in certain defined places, the devotion of the faithful ingeniously substituted for them other tombs which might almost claim to be legitimate and genuine from the depositing therein of some small portion of their bones, or of a veil or some other object which had been laid upon their funeral urns. The triumphal *depositiones* of these relics increased to a very great extent in the fifth and sixth centuries, and gave rise to the most characteristic features of the existing rite for the consecration of churches. The second portion of the ceremony, wholly distinct from the first, but evincing a far deeper theological meaning, comes from a completely different source, and includes the consecration of the altar and of the sacred edifice itself. We shall examine these two ceremonies in due order, beginning with the *depositio* of relics.

*   *   *   *   *

When the worship in the catacombs of the first three centuries was transferred to the new basilicas, which arose immediately upon the " Peace of Constantine," the custom of more than a hundred years had closely connected the sacred *mensa* with the tomb, so that it was no longer possible to separate the one from the other. The remembrance

---

[1] *De Vitis Patrum* VIII, n. xi; *P.L.* LXXI, c. 1049.

of the martyrs was the supreme thought which filled the Liturgy of that time, and had originated the great ferias and the vigils. The reading of their *passiones,* the urban titular churches, the catacombs, all awakened their memory; so that when the new works of decoration in the ancient catacombs and the splendid churches of the fourth century demanded that certain of their bodies should be transferred from their first tombs to more fitting resting-places, these translations were carried out with a splendid ceremonial and a great concourse of the faithful, as if it were the real *depositio* or triumphal burial of a martyr. Moreover, when, as in the case of country churches, it was not possible to have the whole body of some heroic champion of the Faith, but only some small relic with which to sanctify the new parochial altar, Christian sentiment surrounded the depositing of such a relic with the same ceremonial of solemn psalmody and processions as would have been used with regard to the actual body of the martyr itself.

An African inscription of 359 is one of the first to mention, among the relics placed in an oratory or *memoria, de ligno Crucis, de terra promissionis ubi natus est Christus (pignora), Apostoli Petri et Pauli,* but towards the close of the same century the custom had become so universal that St Ambrose could call it *antiquissima et ubique recepta consuetudo.*

Various accounts have come down to us of these early translations of the bodies of martyrs, among which, in the East, that of St Babylas of Antioch has remained famous. It took place in 362, when, at the instigation of the pagan oracle, Julian sought to purify Daphne from the pollution of the dead bodies. The faithful, so Theodoret relates, having placed the urn of the martyr upon a triumphal car, competed with one another in taking turns to draw it themselves into the city, keeping up their courage by the singing of psalms. The route covered six miles, but the procession was so solemn throughout that, as Chrysostom says, it seemed as if the martyr himself were returning to his own episcopal city, adorned for the second time with a crown of glory. The dancers (*saltantes*) went first with the singers, followed by the whole assembly of the people, who repeated the verse (*responsorius*), *Confundantur omnes qui adorant sculptilia et qui gloriantur in simulacris suis,* directed against Julian, who took his revenge the next day by condemning the more fervent among them to prison and to torture.

The translation of the martyrs Gervase and Protase was carried out at Milan under happier auspices. When asked by his people to consecrate the new " Roman " church, Ambrose declared that he must first await the discovery of some relics of martyrs; and these were eventually found, not far from the altar of SS Nabor and Felix. For two days the people thronged the basilica to venerate the sacred remains; then, towards sunset on the third day, having caused them to be placed in two separate coffers, Ambrose brought them to the basilica of Fausta, accompanied by the singing of joyful psalms, of which ceremony St Augustine has recorded his impressions in his *Confessiones*. The night was spent in keeping solemn vigil, in the course of which many Arians were converted and made their abjuration; on the following morning, when the two bodies were transferred to the Ambrosian basilica, some sick persons were healed on touching the pall which covered the funeral urns; the energumens bore witness by their cries to the power of the saints, and, while the people were pressing eagerly in their devotion to touch the bier with their linen cloths, a blind man miraculously recovered his sight.

When the procession had arrived at the basilica and the caskets were laid beside the altar, the Mass began, during which, after the scriptural lessons, Ambrose addressed the people, and, making reference to the Psalms xviii (*Coeli enarrant*) and cxii (*Laudate pueri*) which had just been sung, explained to them the defensive significance of the translation and of the miracles accompanying it as against the pretensions of the Arians. *Succedant victimae triumphales,* he exclaimed, *in locum ubi Christus ostia est. Sed ille super altare qui pro omnibus passus est; isti sub altare qui illius redempti sunt passione. Hunc ego locum praedestinaveram mihi; dignum est enim ut ibi requiescat sacerdos, ubi offerre consuevit; sed cedo sacris victimis dexteram portionem. Locus iste martyribus debebatur. Condamus ergo reliquias sacrosanctas et dignis sedibus invehamus totumque diem fida devotione celebremus.*

The people, however, were unwilling to lose sight of the holy remains so soon; they therefore begged Ambrose to postpone the *depositio* to the following Sunday. The bishop stood firm, but at last with great difficulty persuaded them to agree to a postponement of the ceremony to the following day at the latest. When night fell, the Milanese again kept watch before the coffers of the martyrs, whilst on the following morning Ambrose reconciled some more penitents, and, having addressed the people anew, placed the two bodies under the right side of the altar,[1] reserving the left side for his own burial.

St Ambrose describes for us the translation of the bodies of SS Vitalis and Agricola, which took place at Bologna about Eastertide in the year 393. The remains of these two

---

[1] *Epist. ad Marcellinam; P.L.* XVI, 1062 *sq.*

martyrs were lying among Jewish tombs in private property, but when Ambrose miraculously discovered the bodies the Jews themselves repeated the words of the canticle: *Flores apparuerunt in terra nostra.* Having carefully collected the nails and the cross of Agricola, together with the blood of the two martyrs and their sacred bones, the faithful bore them in procession to the basilica, to the chanting of Psalm xviii (*Coeli enarrant gloriam Dei*), frequently interrupted by the chorus of the people, applying to the festival the same sacred words: *Flores apparuerunt . . . tempus incisionis adest.* From Bologna Ambrose went on to Florence, in order to consecrate the basilica built by the widow Juliana in that city, and from the discourse on virginity which he delivered on that occasion we gather that he placed under the new altar some fragments of the cross, together with some of the nails and blood of the martyrs which had been found at Bologna.

In the Epistles of St Paulinus the relics of the martyrs often find mention, especially in connection with the consecration of churches or of altars. Thus, in the basilica of Fondi, which formed part of the patrimony of his family, he placed relics of SS Andrew, Luke, Nazarius, Protase and Gervase; and when about the same time Sulpicius Severus asked him for some relic with which to consecrate his own domestic basilica of *Primuliacum*, Paulinus, who had already destined all of these for his own church, apologized for not being able to send him anything except a fragment of the wood of the holy Cross enclosed in a golden box. From a letter of Paulinus to Bishop Delphinus of Bordeaux we learn that, besides the canticles mentioned by Ambrose, the rite for the consecrating of churches included at that time Psalms lxxx (*Exsultate Deo adjutori nostro*), xcv (*Tollite hostias*), cxxxi (*Surge, Domine in requiem*) and cxvii: *Ita exultasse (ad dedicationis diem) spiritum nostrum in Deo salutari nostro, ut tamquam in praesenti dedicantium coetibus interessemus, illa de psalmis . . . caneremus: Exsultate Deo adjutori nostro, sumite psalmum et date tympanum, tollite hostias et introite in atria Domini; adorate Dominum in aula sancta ejus. Vel illud ejusdem prophetae: Surge, Domine, in requiem tuam, tu et arca sanctificationis tuae. Sacerdotes tui induant salutarem et sancti tui exultent. Constituant diem suum.*

The finding of the body of St Stephen in the fifth century, and the distribution of his relics, gave rise to the numerous basilicas erected in his honour in Palestine, Italy and Africa. St Augustine has described the triumphal processions with which the bishops brought these relics to their churches, the great crowds that took part in them, the flowers which were heaped upon the coffer containing the *pignora,* as if to evoke their wonder-working power, and finally the miracles that accompanied the translation.[1] The noble lady Demetrias also received from Augustine some fragments of the relics of the protomartyrs, which, being afterwards conveyed to Rome, constituted the origin of the convent of nuns at Santo Stefano in the Via Latina as well as of the Vatican oratories of Santo Stefano Minore and Maggiore (*Kata Galla Patricia*).

We do not know what ceremonies accompanied the translation from Nomentum to Rome of the martyrs Primus and Felician, under Pope Vitalian, but, on the other hand, we have some details of that of St Petronilla when her body was brought from the Flavian catacomb to the Vatican basilica under Paul I in 757. When, headed by the Pope, the clergy and people had assembled, the marble sarcophagus containing the body of the saint was taken out of the catacomb, and, having been placed upon a new car, as the Philistines did with the Ark of the Israelites, *in ecclesiam beati Petri apostoli in hymnis et canticis spiritualibus ejus beatitudo deportavit; et in mausoleo illo juxta ecclesiam beati Andreae . . . ipsum sanctum collocavit corpus. Ubi et coronamentum tam in auro quam in argento et palleis sufficienter tribuit.*

An ivory from Trèves gives us an exact representation of these triumphal translations of relics. Seated on a decorated *biga*, like those used at the court of Byzantium, are two bishops, probably Menna of Constantinople and Apollinaris of Alexandria, who support the coffer containing the relics. The procession is wending its way towards the new church of St Irene at Galata between two crowded lines of onlookers who swing censers as the patriarchs pass, whilst others, in order to get a better view of the procession, have climbed upon the roofs of the adjacent buildings.[2]

There is a painting in the lower Church of San Clemente which, though much later than this ivory, since it is of the eleventh century, yet preserves with sufficient accuracy the Roman rite of the translation of martyrs. It represents the transferring of the relics of St Clement from the Vatican to the basilica bearing his name at the foot of the Caelian Hill. The two prominent phases of the translation—the one the triumphal procession, the other the solemn Mass of the *depositio*—are here compressed into a single scene. On the right of the bier borne by four deacons reposes the body of the martyr vested with the pallium; his head is surrounded by a nimbus, and a rich coverlet embroidered all over with crosses half covers the sacred body. Two deacons each wave a censer in one hand, and with the other hold the *acerra* of incense, while a third deacon near the Pontiff supports the

---

[1] *De Civit. Dei*, lib. XXII, c. viii.
[2] De Rossi, *Bullet.*, ser. III, ann. v, 105-6.

Papal cross which dominates all those of the various titular churches, and of the workers' guilds, who make a great display with their banners richly embossed in silk. At the side of Nicholas I, clad in a chasuble and the pallium, and wearing the *regnum* on his head, stand the two bishops, Cyril and Methodius, vested in *paenula* and stole, but without the pallium—their pastoral staffs being borne by deacons— while behind follows a great concourse of clergy and people, above whose heads appear the banners of the guilds of arts and crafts embroidered with the cross.

On the left of the picture is represented the second characteristic phase of the translation—the Mass of the *depositio*— in which, through an error in perspective, the *pergula,* from the top of which are suspended five lamps, appears behind the altar and at the back of the figure of Pope Nicholas I, who is seen with two deacons, in the act of pronouncing the words of the ritual : *Pax Domini sit semper.* Underneath the painting is the following inscription : *Huc a Vaticano fertur PP. Nicolao imnis divinis, quod aromatibus sepelivit.*

The *Ordines Romani* give us many further details when describing, with certain interpolations, the rite *ad reliquias levandas sive deducendas seu condendas.* We can distinguish several of these interpolations ; their very titles are significant, as Duchesne justly observes, for they speak only of the translation of the relics and never of the consecration of the church. This is in full agreement with the letter of Pope Vigilius to Bishop Profuturus and shows that no other consecratory rite was in use in Rome. The Gelasian Sacramentary has preserved the text of the *Denunciatio cum reliquiae ponendae sunt martyrum,* which ordinarily preceded the great stational Masses; after a eulogy of the martyrs the deacon continued : *Et ideo commonemus dilectionem vestram quoniam (illa) feria (illo) loco reliquiae sunt sancti (illius) martyris conlocandae. Quaesumus ut vestram praesentiam, nobis admonentibus, non negetis.*

On the appointed day the bishop, clergy and people repaired to the church where the relics had been deposited. An introit was first sung, followed sometimes by the Litany, at other times merely by a Collect ; the Pontiff then took into his hands the little case containing the *pignora,* which was covered with a cloth, and, surrounded by the deacons who supported his arms, set out at the head of the procession. The cantors sang the antiphon *Cum jucunditate exhibitis* preserved in the Pontifical of to-day, and, if the way were long, other psalms and antiphons also, as indicated in the ancient antiphonaries. Next came the clergy and the people in large numbers, with lighted candles and fragrant censers which they waved all along the route. Just before reaching the appointed destination the singing of the litanies began, and was continued outside the church door, while the bishop went in alone and washed the new altar with holy water. Having accomplished this rite, he came forth again and sprinkled the people also with holy water, the Litany being brought to a conclusion by the recitation of a second Collect.

Then the doors of the church open as if by divine power, the cantors intone a magnificent introit, *Sacerdos magne, pontifex summi Dei, ingredere templum Domini, et hostias pacificas pro salute populi offeres Deo tuo. Hic est enim dies dedicationis sanctorum Domini Dei tui,* and the whole assembly, preceded by the sacred relics, pours into the building to the chanting of a third litany. After another collect the veils are drawn aside which hide the view of the sanctuary from the people, the *schola* sing the psalm *Beati immaculati,* with the antiphon *Sub altare Dei,* while the bishop, having laid aside his *paenula,* places the relics in their new tomb, anointing with chrism both the stone which covers it and the four corners of the altar. This first part of the *dedicatio* ends with the blessing of the altar cloths and the sacred ornaments. As the bishop re-enters the sacristy in order to change his vestments and put on others more fitting for the solemn offering of the eucharistic Sacrifice, a *mansionarius* approaches with a lighted candle, saying, *Jube domne benedicere,* to which the prelate replies, *Illuminet Dominus domum suam in sempiternum,* and from this candle are now lighted the other lamps and candlesticks of the church. All being now ready for the Mass, the paraphonist intones the introit, while the procession of sacred ministers comes out of the sacristy and, traversing the nave of the church, goes up to the sanctuary, there to offer with customary rites the divine sacrifice which, according to the ancient Roman point of view, constituted the true and actual consecration of the church.

It is very strange how the whole ceremony just described is in reality a funeral rite. The relics are borne in procession to the chanting of litanies, just as when to-day the dead are brought into the church at Milan; the tomb is washed, the incense supplies the place of the embalming, and only the chrism with which the four corners of the altar are anointed distantly recalls the consecration of the votive stone of Jacob. (We may here remark that the anointing of the breast with holy oil formed part of the funeral liturgy of the Roman monks in the seventh century.) In Italy and at Rome there was no tracing of the alphabet, no sprinkling of the walls (they were sanctified by the eucharistic sacrifice alone); even the holy water, when not all sprinkled over the people, was poured out at the foot of the altar, as if to prevent any superstitious use being made of it. The tomb of the relics was, indeed, washed and then anointed with chrism, but the reason for this was that the deposition of any dead body requires a previous blessing of the tomb.

This perfect simplicity of the ancient Roman rite should cause no surprise when we compare it with the magnificent Gallican *dedicatio,* so rich in symbolism and suggestive ceremonial. The practical Roman mind would fain preserve the ancient tradition unchanged, and to the many minute details of the Gallican ritual prefers vigorous and outstanding features, which, free from excessive symbolical wrappings, shall at once indicate lucidly and accurately the theological idea hidden within.

We have said that the sprinkling of the building itself with holy water in the time of Pope Vigilius formed no part of the Roman rite of consecration; yet the custom was so general outside Rome, as the same Pope attests, that St Gregory caused the pagan temples in England to be consecrated for Christian worship by sprinkling them with exorcised water, called, from this, "Gregorian." The rite of sprinkling private dwellings with holy water was already known in Rome before the fifth century, and nothing could be simpler than to extend this blessing from the private house to the Church—to the common home, as it were, of the *sancta plebs Dei.*

*   *   *   *   *

We have now to examine the rite of consecrating churches in the Gallican Liturgy.

For lack of other documents this rite can only be reconstructed by eliminating from the rituals of the eighth and ninth centuries, in which the Roman and Gallican uses are merged into one, the accretions and all the features peculiar to the papal Liturgy. This is no easy undertaking, but it is facilitated by the sidelights thrown upon the subject by the numerous lives of Frankish saints of the later Middle Ages.

The Commentary on the rite of the *dedicatio,* attributed to Remigius of Auxerre, even if it cannot rightly claim him as its author, shows us, nevertheless, the Gallican use of the ninth century, confirmed by the *Ordo* of Verona, by the Sacramentaries of Angoulême and Gellone, by the Gelasian Sacramentary and the *Missale Francorum,* all of which contain more or less identical prayers, so that with these documentary authorities as its basis, the reconstruction which we shall attempt will be a sufficiently sound one.

Notwithstanding the fact that the idea prevailed at Rome that the sanctity of the Church arose entirely from the divine Sacrifice therein offered, in practice, however, there was felt the need of some accidental and preparatory sanctification, such as the deposition of relics, which should together furnish the motive for the erection of a new altar or tomb.   Once this principle was admitted, the Gallican Liturgy, perhaps under Eastern influence, set about developing it with marvellous rapidity.

The Frankish documents of the *dedicatio* show us two rites of quite distinct origin, amalgamated to form one single ceremony.   The *depositio martyris* of the Roman rite is here preceded by the consecration of the church and altar, which, as the symbol of Christ and his faithful people, are sanctified with the same baptismal rites as those by which the catechumens are initiated into the Christian life.   Hence the preliminary exorcisms pronounced upon the salt, ashes, wine and water, followed by the purifying *aspersio* and the chrismal *confirmatio;* thus only after being consecrated can the altar become the tomb of the martyrs over whose sacred bones Jesus Christ, both Priest and Victim, will unite in one sacrifice their sufferings and his own.   We will examine more in detail the various elements of the Gallican *dedicatio.*

*   *   *   *   *

The *Ordines Romani* nowhere mention the *vigiliae* preceding the *dedicatio,* but the Gallican liturgical documents, in agreement with the Milanese and Eastern uses, always place them before the solemn consecration of a church, ordaining that they shall be held in a church, or under a tent, in the presence of the relics which are to be placed in the new building.   Thus Gregory of Tours, when he consecrated the basilica of St Julian, placed the relics of that saint in St Martin's Church on the previous evening, and spent the night singing the Psalter.   This same Gregory, when he wished to turn into an oratory the hall which St Euphronius had already destined for a store-room, erected there an altar and spent the night preceding the consecration in his own episcopal basilica before the relics of SS Saturninus, Julian and Illydius, causing them to be transported on the following day to the new chapel with candles and crosses and the singing of psalms.

*   *   *   *   *

In the Gallican rite of the *dedicatio* the preparatory prayers and the entrance of the bishop constitute one of the most suggestive features of the ceremony.   The new church is lighted by twelve branched candlesticks placed along its deserted nave and aisles, which, being as yet unexorcised, still lie under the influence of evil spirits hostile to the reign of Christ and the martyrs.   The bishop, escorted by clergy and people, approaches the door, which he finds locked, and knocks: *Attollite portas, principes, vestras et elevamini, portae aeternales, et introibit Rex gloriae.* (The liturgical meaning here attached to this psalm is, perhaps, the same as that given to it in the East, where at the consecration of churches, according to Theophanes, they sang the verse: Ἄρατε πύλας, οἱ ἄρχωντες, ὑμῶν. From within comes the answer: *Quis est iste rex gloriae?* And the bishop continues: *Dominus virtutum, ipse est rex gloriae.* Then the doors open and the *schola*, singing the antiphon *Pax huic domui et omnibus habitantibus in ea; pax ingredientibus et egredientibus, Alleluia,* accompanies the Pontiff to the altar, before which all prostrate themselves and chant the litanies. The bishop then traces out the Greek and Latin alphabets in ashes in the form of a double diagonal right across the floor of the church. Following De' Rossi, most authorities consider this ceremony to signify the formal taking possession of the new building. Just in this same way the Roman surveyors used to fix the dimensions of a property, by means of alphabetical letters.

It is curious, however, this taking possession of the ground when the space has been already covered by the erection of a building; so, putting aside the interesting classical reminiscence of the augur fixing the boundaries of the holy ground by means of a " decussated " X, we should be rather inclined to see in the " 'ecussations " on the pavement in the Christian basilica ine monogram of Christ, which, accompanied at first by the apocalyptic letters A and Ω, was joined to these and was so developed as to call in time for the use of the whole alphabet. The Gallican rite of consecration of churches is indeed strikingly influenced by that of the Christian baptismal initiation, and we know that not only was it usual at Milan up to the eleventh century solemnly to show the catechumens the monogram of Christ between the letters A and Ω, but that the alphabet, with obvious reference to the baptismal rite, was sometimes engraved on the tombs of neophytes and upon the vessels destined for use in this sacred rite.[1] The alphabet traced by the bishop on the *decussis* of the church was in Greek and Latin, and more rarely in Hebrew.[2] The choir sang the antiphon, *Fundamentum aliud nemo potest ponere praeter illud denique quod positum est a Christo Domino,* and the psalm, *Fundamenta ejus,* which explains still better the liturgical meaning of the " decussated " monogram, which was equivalent to the impressing of the name of Christ on the floor of the church, as if to sanctify the foundation-stone of the building. Here,

[1] *Cf.* De Rossi, *Bullet.*, pp. 128 *sq.*, 1881.
[2] *Cf.* Martène, *De antiquis Eccles. Ritibus,* ii, 678-9.

then, there is no question of either Roman soothsayers or surveyors with their " decussated " X, nor of any ceremony of taking possession of the ground, but only the blessing of the church floor, on which, as upon the walls, a great sign of the cross is traced.

When the blessing of the sacred ground for the new church was completed—it sometimes constituted a rite altogether distinct from the consecration, and often took place before the building was erected—then began the actual consecratory ceremony. The bishop, standing before the altar, intones the verse, *Deus in adjutorium,* followed by the doxology as in the divine Offices; then he blesses the water and the salt, with which, when mingled with ashes and wine, the altar is to be sprinkled and the cement moistened for the sealing up of the tomb of the relics. Dipping his finger into this mixture, he first traces a cross on the four corners of the altar; then, while the *schola* sings the *Miserere,* interspersed with the seven times repeated antiphon, *Asperges,* he passes as many times around the *mensa,* sprinkling it with a bundle of hyssop. Then follows a very striking prayer, evoking memories of the altar of Abel, sanctified by his own blood, and of those of Melchisedech, Abraham, Jacob and Moses. After this, while the clergy sprinkle the outer walls of the church, the bishop performs three lustrations of the inner walls and of the floor, on which he finally pours out the exorcised water in the form of a cross. In the meanwhile the *schola* chants the psalm, *Exsurgat Deus,* emphasizing anew the idea of Christ as the foundation-stone of the whole building : *Fundamenta templi hujus sapientiae*[1] *suae fundavit Deus, in quo . . . si ruant venti et pluant flumina, non possunt ea movere umquam, fundata enim erat supra petram. . . .*

The final lustration being completed, the Pontiff, standing in the middle of the church, chants a eucharistic prayer (*praefatio*), with which the baptism, as we may call it, of the new church is concluded, to be followed by the *confirmatio* of the altar with the sacred chrism. The holy table becomes first of all wrapped in a fragrant cloud of incense, and, when the bishop's censing is over, a priest takes his place, and, waving the thurible, goes unceasingly round the altar throughout the remainder of the ceremony. It is indeed a solemn moment. The *schola* with its melodious antiphons recalls the memory of Jacob pouring oil on the stone of his

---

[1] Was not this antiphon originally composed for a basilica called Santa Sophia? And since so many elements of the Gallican consecratory rite are derived from the Byzantine, have we not to do here with Justinian's famous church, of which Gassisi has lately discovered the Greek dedicatory chants?

vision, and of Solomon dedicating the altar of the Temple, and finally, in allusion to the fragrance of the chrism sprinkled by the celebrant on the altar, sings : *Ecce odor filii mei sicut odor agri pleni . . . Crescere te faciat Deus meus,* thus attaining, by this scriptural analogy of the smell of Jacob's garments and of the last blessing of the dying Isaac applied to the Christian altar, such a loftiness of conception as no profane literature can approach. This anointing with chrism was customary also at Rome and in the East. It is mentioned by the pseudo-Dionysius and is described in the Byzantine Rituals, where we find that the walls, too, of the church were anointed after the altar, just as in Gaul, no such use being known at Rome. At Constantinople this second anointing was entrusted to a priest, whereas in the Gallican rite only a bishop could perform it, the *schola* singing in the meanwhile, *O quam metuendus est locus iste!* . . .

A second oblation of incense follows, which, however, is wholly consumed on the altar itself, while the bishop recites a consecratory prayer, preceded by the introductory formula, *Oremus dilectissimi.* The altar cloths, the candlesticks, the chalice and the paten receive each in turn their special benediction, the paten being anointed with chrism, but not the chalice.

* * * * *

The translation of the relics to the new church about to be consecrated resembles the triumphal deposition of the body of a martyr in the new tomb destined to be its resting-place.

The basilica and the altar have now been purified and made worthy of the holy mysteries, and through that close relationship which unites the sacrifice of the Cross with the sufferings of the martyrs, the holy table is at the same time a sepulchre, wherein the bones of the saints rest in peace under the sacred body of the Lamb without spot, who immolates himself for them and deigns to associate them with his sacrifice. Since, therefore, it is fitting that the martyrs should go before their Lord into the new church, the bishop and the people repair in procession to the spot where the sacred relics were placed on the preceding evening, and, to the singing of psalms and antiphons, bear them solemnly to their new sepulchre. These chants betray their early Roman origin, for one of them has inspired the inscription (*graffito*) in the Papal crypt of St Callixtus of a pilgrim who has written, *Jerusalem civitas . . . et ornamentum martyrorum . . . Jerusalem civitas . . . ornamento martyrum decorata;* another was sung by St Augustine and his choir of forty monks at the moment of their first setting foot in England. On this occasion the people also are permitted to cross the sacred threshold and to take part in the procession, but when the bishop has reached the sanctuary the veil of the *pergula* is drawn, so that the clergy alone can witness the actual entombment of the relics.   While the *schola* sings *Sub altare Dei sedes accepistis* and other appropriate antiphons, the deacons within the sanctuary assist the celebrant to cover the sacred tomb with the marble slab of the altar, securing it with the cement, previously blessed.   When the altar has been covered again with its cloths the *dedicatio* proper is over, the candles are lighted, and the clergy, having returned to the sacristy, prepare to celebrate the solemn Mass.

If the Roman and Gallican rites be compared, the latter indubitably excels the former, both in richness and in dramatic and suggestive power.   Rome supplied Gaul with the ideal outline of the ceremony and with some of the more striking prayers, but the Frankish Liturgy so elaborated and enlarged this early papal foundation that the very Mass itself, the first and essential condition at Rome for the consecration of a church, was stifled in France by other far more showy rites and relegated to the last place, ceasing to form any more a part of the *dedicatio* which it presumes to be already completed.   It would be invidious in such a case as this to prefer one rite to another; we will merely remark that the Gallican rite would certainly be more impressive than the Roman if only that persistent idea of the satanic presence in the Church, involving so many episcopal lustrations, did not cause its inferiority to the grandeur of the Roman conception which, without so many exorcisms and expiations, simply " dedicates " the new basilica as the living expression of its religious polity, resting content that in the divine Sacrifice almighty God himself fills the church with the sanctity of his own sacramental presence.   The liturgical terminology also reveals the two different points of view; for while the Gallican rite *consecrates* the new church, the Roman, on the other hand, *dedicates* or *inaugurates* it.

Was, then, the Gallican rite a direct development from the ancient Roman *augurial* form, or were the elements in its development derived from other sources?   It is difficult to decide this question with certainty, since it has been shown that the very same Gallican eucharistic rites, which were supposed to come from the East, belong in reality to the ancient Roman Liturgy, and a like hypothesis might be shown to be true in the case of the *dedicatio*.   Yet the agreement of the *Ordines Romani* with the ancient and only dedicatory form of the fourth century—consisting simply of the deposition of the relics and the Mass following it—and much more the famous passage of Vigilius quoted above, seem to exclude altogether from Roman influence both the rite itself and the idea which inspired the Gallican *dedicatio*.

We would rather be inclined to seek in the East the early origin of the ceremonies used in Gaul.

At the first glance it seems extraordinary that Columbanus, in order to "reconcile" the Church of St Aurelia, *jussit aquam afferri et benedicens illam adspersit ea templum, et dum circumirent psallentes dedicavit ecclesiam. Deinde, invocato nomine Domini, 'unxit altare et beatae Aureliae reliquias in eo collocavit, vestitoque altari, missas legitime compleverunt,* since we know that the liturgy of the Irish was precisely the ancient Roman Liturgy. Yet the monks of Luxeuil, during their sojourn in France, must have made more than one compromise between the Frankish rites and those of their mother country; besides, why should we necessarily see the Gallican *lustratio* in the description of Walafrid Strabo when St Gregory himself caused the pagan temples in England to be "reconciled" by the very same expiation as that of Columbanus, which differs so profoundly in conception from the simple Roman *dedicatio?* In the first case, indeed, it was a question of purifying by exorcisms a place formerly a heathen temple, perhaps actually profaned by the presence of the evil spirit; and the very adaptation of pagan religious buildings to the service of the Christian faith may possibly have caused the Roman ceremony of lustral reconciliation, confined at first exclusively to buildings contaminated by idolatry, to become general outside Italy.

Another strange feature of the Gallican formula of the *dedicatio* is the complete independence of the consecration of the church from the deposition of the relics, which, in Rome, was closely connected with the Mass and the chrismal anointings of the altar. In this case also the Frankish use again shows astonishing analogies with the Byzantine Liturgy, in which the consecration of the altar and the deposition of the relics take place sometimes on different days. The Greek bishop begins by washing the holy table with baptismal water and with wine, then he anoints it with chrism and envelops it in a cloud of incense. After the consecration of the altar he goes round the church, waving the thurible, whilst a priest anoints the walls with chrism.

In the East the deposition of the relics is a very much more solemn function than the simple consecration of the altar; the clergy keep watch before the *pignora*, and when the procession arrives at the church in which they are to be placed, the singers intone the verse, Ἄρατε πύλας, οἱ ἄρχωντες, ὑμῶν, just as is done among the Franks.

Later on the introduction of the Roman Liturgy into Gaul at the hands of Pepin and Charlemagne, and the imperial favour bestowed upon the liturgical studies of the "Schola Palatina," had the effect of impairing its simplicity by interspersing it with Frankish customs, especially where the concise formulas of Rome appeared too rigid or incomplete. Thus the two rites of the *dedicatio* and the *consecratio* ended by being merged into one, giving rise in this way to the existing ceremony as we find it in the Roman Pontifical. According to an ancient Pontifical of Narbonne, the alphabet was traced three times on the outer walls of the new church[1] and the relics carried in procession round the outside of the edifice in the exact manner prescribed in the Pontifical. Formerly, following a rite which was so widespread that it was even adopted at one time at Rome itself, three particles of the holy Eucharist were placed with the relics, also a parchment on which were written the titles and the opening verses of the four Gospels.

The Gallican rite for the blessing of bells is very remarkable. In imitation of the ceremonial of baptism and of the *dedicatio,* the bells are first washed with baptismal water (water, oil and salt), and then anointed with chrism seven times on the outside and four times within, while the *schola* sings seven psalms. When it comes to the censing of the bell, it is suspended over the thurible, so as to be filled with the smoke of the incense. The idea is a beautiful one, especially by reason of its connection with the Gallican rite for conferring the office of doorkeeper who *oportet percutere cymbalum et campanam;* but whereas at Rome not even was the chalice consecrated with chrism, in France, from the eighth century onwards, there begins to be felt that tendency to destroy the original balance of the Latin Liturgy, a tendency which, developing to such a remarkable degree the extra-sacramental rites, ends by giving us in the eighteenth century the capricious and seemingly endless Gallican liturgies.

Medium tutissimum iter. Charlemagne had already foreseen this by ordering, in the eighth capitulary of the year 789, *Ut cloccae non baptizentur.*

---

[1] *Cf.* Martène, *De ant. Eccl. Rit.,* Ed. II, vol. ii, p. 734, Antwerp 1736.

CHAPTER XII

SACRED ART IN THE HOUSE OF GOD

FROM a general survey of sacred buildings, beginning with those of Egypt, Greece, Etruria and Latium, down to Christian basilicas, whether Romanesque, Gothic or of the Renaissance, two common features emerge, evolving a twofold sublime conception which dominates all those architectural and decorative forms, however much they may differ among themselves. These two features are the transcendent majesty of the Deity whose seat is in the sacred edifice, and the comparative nothingness of man, who only dares to approach him after a fitting purification.

Among ancient peoples the temple is usually regarded as the earthly *domus* of the Deity, and religious art has realized from the very beginning that her function is to express this great idea, whether through the design of the architect, the palette of the painter, or the chisel of the sculptor. Hence arises that unity of conception and inspiration which everywhere influences the building of the temples of antiquity, pervading every part of them from the *pronaos* to the decorated *cella* of the unapproachable divinities of Greece or Egypt, to the *Sancta Sanctorum* of the Israelites, and to the *bema* of the Byzantine basilicas.

Almighty God fills the entire sacred building with his majesty, but he does not actually " dwell " therein, save in its more secret and sacred portion, so that the other parts— the transept, nave, aisles, narthex, pronaos, atrium or *paradisus*—each forms, as it were, an annex to the original home of the Deity, an extension and amplification of his glory. It is God who, as by an act of condescension, comes forth from the sacred *limen* of his seat, in order to stretch out his arms across the *naos* towards us poor mortals.

For this reason, while the *bema* is always reserved to the Deity or to the priests who represent him, the other parts of the church are also for men, in so far as these advance in the work of their interior purification and render themselves fitted to approach almighty God. This necessity for cleansing is expressed in all ancient religious art. The expiatory lustration begins outside the temple, where the pagan places his altar of sacrifice, and the Christian his fount of lustral water; but it is continued also within the *naos,* where God himself completes it through the rites and ceremonies of divine worship.

These ideas, common to all ancient religions alike, influenced Christian art as much more forcibly as the Gospel story excelled all mythology. For the Christian, God does not merely dwell in the church by the all-pervading irradiation and omnipotence of his love, but the Word himself, made Man and become Emmanuel—that is, God with us—abides there sacramentally in his humanity, as Priest and Victim of the New Covenant. All Christianity, then, centres round the altar—as has been so clearly expressed by the genius of Raphael—and while the ancient Jewish ritual wearied the souls of men by a series of sacrifices repeated *ad infinitum* before the tent of Jahveh without any substantial result, the New Testament offers only the one sacrifice of the Immaculate Lamb, whose precious blood flows for the effective purification of all the ages.

Moreover, while other religions failed to express and *operare* with fitting rites the worship due to almighty God, Jesus Christ, Priest and Victim, offers to the divine Trinity in our temples an adoration perfect in spirit and in truth, the very adoration, indeed, which God seeks from us.

It follows that as the eucharistic Sacrifice is the centre of the Catholic Liturgy—in such a way that all other rites, singing of psalms, processions, etc., either prepare the soul for the offering of the holy Sacrifice, or make due thanksgiving for participation therein—so the architectural and artistic forms of the Christian temple draw all their inspiration and unity of conception from Jesus Christ, who through these sacred rites achieves the redemption of humanity and applies to the souls of men the merits of his sacrifice. Hence in the Christian basilica the altar of sacrifice is the central and culminating point in the edifice; we might almost say the essential motive and *raison d'être* of the whole building. The early Christians, therefore, had but one altar in the church, which they placed either isolated in the centre of the rotunda, as at Sancta Sophia, or in the middle of the transept, between the mosaics of the apse and those of the central arch leading from the nave to the sanctuary. This latter position was well chosen, because the height of the intersection in regard to the *naos* lent greater prominence to the sacred *mensa,* and caused the resplendent mosaics of the concave apse and those of the arch to encircle it like a golden diadem set with Eastern gems.

There alone was offered the eucharistic sacrifice; there, suspended by precious chains from the vaulting of the *tegurium* or ciborium which covered the altar, hung the dove with wings of gold, typifying the gifts of the Paraclete. Upon that holy table was kept the codex of the Gospels, the letter of the New Law, while above it hovered the lifegiving

Spirit who was to breathe into it the breath of life. That volume, and that eucharistic dove, holding hidden within its breast the consecrated species, signified the whole New Testament whose law is love, for love is the supreme law of the believing soul. The sum of the Christian religion was there upon that altar, the Gospel of the Word and the gifts of the Paraclete. For this reason, in the minds of the early Christians, the altar could never be without the halo of its sacred nature—that is, the ciborium or baldacchino in marble or in silver. The altar in its entirety constituted the true tabernacle of the most High, who assuredly could not dwell *sub divo* without a special roof of his own under the lofty vaulting of the *naos*.

This central and culminating position of the altar dominating the vast edifice of the *domus Dei* was, nevertheless, by no means wanting in that character of mystical secrecy which enveloped the inaccessible seat of the Holy One. As at the moment of the Saviour's death, when the sanctuary of the Temple at Jerusalem was desecrated in sign of reprobation, its rent curtain allowing profane eyes to penetrate within the sanctuary, so in ancient Christian symbolism an altar without the artistic crown of its *tegurium*, and consequently exposed to the unrestricted gaze of the multitude, would have seemed almost a profanation. We can still see at Ravenna in the mosaics of Sant' Apollinare Nuovo and of San Vitale how before the *palatium* of Theodoric, as well as before the *porticum* of Justinian's basilica, *velaria* are hung to protect the sanctity of those buildings, and especially the imperial *sacrum cubiculum*, from the rash approach of the curious. These curtains were even used to protect the *basileus* of Byzantium on those occasions when he did not deign to bless the wretched mortals over whom he ruled with the majesty of his countenance. As at Rome the Lateran Court adopted something of Byzantine ceremonial, so St Gregory the Great, when dictating his mystical elucidations of the Scriptures to Peter the Deacon, was protected by a *velarium* which hid the supernaturally inspired doctor from the view of his Levite secretary. Thus it was impossible that the divine Emmanuel on the altar should not have his own *velarium*, which, while not altogether concealing the artistic outlines of the tabernacle, yet to some extent hindered the full view of it.

The laity, for that matter, and even the inferior clergy, beginning with the exorcists, had no right of access to the *bema*, which was divided from the nave not only by the marble *plutei* of the *schola cantorum*, but also by a balustrade of metal or of marble, which in the East at once became a dividing wall, shutting off the sanctuary, with three doors, each framed with representations of saints—the *ikonostasis*.

The Latins in general have stopped short of this excess of hieratic mysticism, which would reduce the people almost to the condition of pariahs; but the primitive elements whence the Byzantine *ikonostasis* developed are found in the Latin basilicas from the fifth century onwards, at which period it became customary to stretch curtains between the columns of the *podium* in order to hide the sanctuary from the sight of the curious multitude.

Upon the holy table, covered at the time of the sacrifice with a plain white cloth, the oblations alone were laid, as if to place them in the lap of God himself. Hence it was not possible that the *mensa* should serve as a place on which to put crosses, or candlesticks, or indeed anything else. During the sacred *actio* the acolytes deposited the *cereostata* on the steps òf the altar or around the *podium,* while for the lighting of the sanctuary several rows of lamps, fed with fragrant oil mixed with perfumes from the East, were usually suspended either from the vaulting or from the silver architrave of the *pergula.*

The most natural place for the sacred relics was under the *mensa* of the altar. In contrast to the piety of the Greeks, the devout Latin mind for many centuries shrank from opening the tombs of the martyrs in order to divide their remains and place them in caskets for purposes of private devotion. The Roman sense of the *sacrum jus sepulchri* was still far too strong not to deem it the greatest of all disasters to be deprived of a last resting-place in kindly mother earth. To open a tomb would have seemed a desecration; to take out the bones therefrom and disperse them a sacrilege.

   ✳   ✳   ✳   ✳   ✳

The spot destined for pictures and sacred representations was on the wide wall spaces of the *naos,* on the great arch of the *bema* and on the semicircle of the apse. Even before any direct veneration was paid by the faithful to such representations, they were used by the Church for the catechetical instruction of the people, so that the choice of the artist was naturally directed towards the scenes of our Lord's life. It was therefore requisite that there should be perfect agreement between the plan of the architect who traced the outline of the *naos* and the conception of the painter or the mosaicist who adorned it with colour. Many a time has one and the same artist planned, builded and decorated the entire church.

From the ever-flowing fountain of purification in the *atrium,* where the public penitents, like so many Adams driven out of Paradise, awaited redemption and pardon, it was necessary to go right up to the sacred *bema* and to the figure of the *Pantocrator,* represented in all his awful majesty in the centre of the apse, with saints and angels round about him in fear and trembling. The road was long and difficult. The various scenes of the Old Testament were contrasted with those of the Gospel narrative; Cain killing Abel, and Judas betraying Christ; Isaac under his burden of wood for the sacrifice, and Jesus carrying his cross; Moses feeding the people with the celestial manna, and our Lord multiplying the loaves in the desert, etc.; and all this, whether pointing out to the people the value of those ancient prophetic episodes or inculcating the idea that the whole story of man's salvation, its remote preparation under the Old Covenant and its fulfilment in the New, must have its own special realization in the life of each Christian soul.

Before reaching, therefore, the golden vault of the sanctuary where the saints raise glad hosannas to the divine *Pantocrator* and offer him their golden crowns, it is necessary to undergo many spiritual purifications, to renew the faith of the patriarchs and prophets, to be spiritually born again with Jesus Christ, and with him to die unto sin in order to rise again in him to the holiness of the children of the resurrection. Thus only can the soul become worthy to enjoy here below a foretaste of the joys of the divine vision; thus only, in response to the invitation of the priest at Mass, *sancta sanctis*, can the Christian present himself with a clean conscience at the *solea* of the *bema*, there to put his lips to the chalice of salvation and stretch out his hand to receive upon the bare palm the heavenly food. *Corpus Christi*, says the priest to him with all solemnity, and he, glowing with faith, replies like those celestial spirits who enjoy the Beatific Vision, *Amen*. Yes, thou art the Christ, the Son of the living God.

This communion of man with God, which has ever been the eternal desire of believing humanity, is interpreted by the Christian artist in a special cycle of paintings adorning the walls of the sanctuary. These are the ancient *Theophania* of the Blessed Sacrament, the true records of the Eucharist, which, in the guise of rays of purest light, emanate from the nimbus which surrounds the pendent eucharistic dove and illuminate the long periods of eucharistic history.

Here, too, as in the scriptural cycles, the artist draws his inspiration from the prayer in the Liturgy. " Vouchsafe, O Lord, to accept these gifts," exclaims the priest in the Mass, " as thou wert graciously pleased to accept the gifts of thy just servant Abel, the sacrifice of our Patriarch Abraham, and that which thy High Priest Melchisedech offered up to thee," and the sacred artist for his inspiration needs but to recollect himself and to feel the reality of his faith, for him at once to reproduce these eucharistic scenes on the walls of the sanctuary.

In the narrow *cubicula* and on the sepulchral *arcosolia* of the catacombs space was lacking for the Christian painter to represent this heavenly epic in all its inexhaustible richness. He was obliged, for the most part, to rest content with merely indicating his theme by means of symbols—the fish on the trident, the seven baskets with loaves marked with a cross, the anchor, the Lamb with the pastoral *pedum,* and the vessel for holding milk. But after the Peace of Constantine had brought the Church out of the dark recesses of the catacombs into the bright light of the noonday sun, all need for secrecy ceased; was there less reason for the symbolism designed hitherto to conceal the mysteries from the un-initiated, and what the priest explained from the *ambo* to the crowd gathered in the *naos* below, the painter could now freely reproduce on the inner walls of the *ecclesia,* the common home of the Christian people. The church in this way became one vast Bible, one multiform Scripture, one immense united body in which the painter, the architect, the musician and the Levite each performed his part, while all united together to form one great and powerful symphony.

❋   ❋   ❋   ❋   ❋

The Roman Liturgy originated and developed in the classical Latin basilica, hence this type of building suits its form and peculiar character better than any other. The Christians in early days, under the influence of Asiatic art, did, indeed, sometimes adopt the circular or octagonal style, but plans which destroyed the inner meaning of the sanctuary and placed the altar in the centre of the rotunda, in the very midst of the people, offended too intimately that very delicate sense of æsthetic mysticism which everywhere pervaded the Roman basilica. Such buildings must, in fact, have appeared quite revolutionary and anti-liturgical, for they were mostly used only as baptisteries. Also the open apses, supported by columns and surrounded by post-apsidal galleries, used as the *matronaeum,* seen in Rome in the basilica of the Apostles *ad catacumbas,* and in those of Sicininus on the Esquiline,[1] of SS Cosmas and Damian in the Forum, and of St Severinus at Naples, etc., would appear to offend that fine sense of liturgical spiritualism which looked upon the *bema* as the mysterious and inaccessible seat of the Holy of Holies.

There are no short-cuts nor by-ways by which to come to the *Pantocrator* and the eucharistic dove, no private entrances nor back doors; the ordinary way of all redeemed humanity must be traversed. Therefore we must each pass through the *ecclesia* and come under the benign influence of her faith, her teaching, her sacraments, her priestly hier-

---

[1] S Maria Maggiore.

archy; thus only may we present ourselves at the *solea* of the *bema* to receive the eucharistic pledge of immortality.

In the pure basilican style, therefore, the open apse is almost always an exception, prompted not so much by an æsthetic or architectural sense as by some other necessity arising from its surroundings which called for such an opening. Thus in the basilica *ad catacumbas,* a building of the fourth century, the open arched apse was intended to place the *naos* and the sanctuary in communication with the apostolic tomb below, which was so surrounded by various ancient structures that it had not been possible to include it within the circumference of the basilica, of which, however, it constituted the true centre and sanctuary. In the basilica of the martyrs Cosmas and Damian in the Forum the open apse was an expedient of Pope Felix IV, in order to give the usual semicircular form to the church which he had built in the *templum sacrae Urbis,* while at the same time turning to account the other half of the disused hall of the Catastal Records Office of Rome behind the hemicycle. In the basilica of San Severino at Naples, and in that of Sicininus at Santa Maria Maggiore, the reason for the pierced apse may have been the same as that which we have just indicated; while in the basilica of Domitilla, on the other hand, and perhaps also in the early *titulus Chrysogoni* in the Trastevere, the apsidal opening had as its object the placing of the two sanctuaries in communication, the one with the adjacent sepulchral *cubiculum* of St Domitilla in the Via Ardeatina, the other with the Roman house underneath it, already sanctified as the home of St Chrysogonus.

The problem of side altars is no new one. It dates back at least to the sixth century, and has been solved in various ways, the least happy of which was to place such altars flat against the walls of the aisles, like so many little funeral monuments, or else against the peristyle of the nave, to the detriment of liturgical meaning and no less to that of æsthetic taste. For the faithful of early days the whole church enclosed, as in a frame, the one altar of the one true God, erected at the culminating and central point of the basilica, whereas the multiplying of altars sensibly weakened that oneness of idea which had until then pervaded the basilica, co-ordinating all its lines so harmoniously towards the sanctuary. This unity of conception was crushed and broken by all that confusion of small monuments which, especially when isolated in the *naos* or in the transept, caused the colonnades of the church to resemble the honorary memorials set up in the Forum or the suburban roads of Roman towns when bordered by tombs.

The Byzantines, faithful to the ancient principle of a single altar and a single sacrifice in each church, got out of the difficulty by surrounding the *naos* with other smaller oratories in which private Masses were celebrated. The Latins also were not unwilling to favour this solution of the problem, and, that period being the golden age of the Liturgy, the divine Office eventually became the richer, the more dramatic, the more eloquent for all that system of singing psalms on the way from chapel to chapel (described, for instance, in the *Ordines Romani*) and for all that alternating of oratories clustering round the Lateran, St Peter's, St Paul's and the great basilicas *ad catacumbas* of Constantine, to say nothing of the monasteries, where also other oratories or chapels multiplied around the abbatial church.

Even without resorting to the device of constructing smaller oratories on the outside of the basilica, the question of multiplying altars could be solved in the way in which it was sometimes done in the Middle Ages—namely, by making use of the existing outlines of the basilica. The ancient *cellae* or three-choired basilicas, like that of St Sixtus in the catacombs of St Callixtus, are well known. In these *cellae* the central hemicycle enclosed the bishop's throne and the sacred altar, while the two lateral apses contained the *mensa* of the Holy Scriptures and that of the consecrated vessels for the Sacrifice. It needed, then, but a step to transform these marble tables into altars, nor could the change be said actually to have violated any canons of liturgical or artistic taste. All that was necessary was merely to weaken the effect of those lesser centres of worship by adhering strictly to one style only in their decoration, and to such fitting proportions in the central semicircle as would prevent the smaller apses from becoming independent in themselves, but would cause them to radiate, as it were, from the central apse. With this standard in view, these lesser hemicycles were largely multiplied in some basilicas around the main semicircle, producing thereby a beautiful rose-like effect which lent an additional gracefulness to the holy place.

Of later date than these apsidal altars was the custom of placing chapels in the transept or along the aisles. In the later Middle Ages—that is, when the primitive social character of liturgical worship had become greatly weakened in consequence of that spirit of individualism which always marks a new age—these chapels created special requirements as to worship, increased popular devotion, an eagerness for heraldic display which demanded a private family chapel in the church, a spirit of solidarity bringing closer together the associations of workmen and the guilds of artists, who needed to find in the church a meeting-place on common ground. All these sprang from good and reasonable motives and, in providing religious art with an inexhaustible source of inspiration, enriched Italy with a vast treasure of altar-pieces, triptychs, frescoes and tapestries. The gain is so great as to make us almost forget the corresponding æsthetic loss due to the cutting up of the *naos*, which in modern churches has no longer any unity of conception, and resembles rather the house of an art collector who does not know how to arrange fittingly the treasures he has acquired. The Church of San Gioacchino in the Prati di Castello at Rome is a striking instance of the individualistic spirit which now permeates every phase of modern life.

* * * * *

The ritual laws of to-day are still inspired by the ancient classical mode of thought which made the eucharistic *mensa* the pledge and symbol of unity, both material and artistic, in the House of God. The existing *Caerimoniale Episcoporum* directs that the holy Eucharist, save in capitular churches where the Offices are recited in the sanctuary, shall be reserved upon the high altar. No other spot, however ornate, can equal this, which makes the throne of the eucharistic Emmanuel, as it were, the keystone of all basilican art. To assign any other altar to the Blessed Sacrament, adorn it as one may, would only be to mar the proportions and disturb the harmony of these classic lines by displacing the central point of its axis.

The *Caerimoniale Episcoporum* also considers the case of the altar being turned towards the east, so that the priest during the sacred *actio* has the people massed before him in the nave. Thus our forefathers were always very desirous of having the altar isolated and free, and bare of all accessories, whether crosses, candlesticks or reliquaries, so that the faithful might the more easily follow the manual acts of the sacred minister during the offering of the Sacrifice. The crucifix was placed at the side of the altar, as are the capitular crosses to-day, or else its huge form hung from the vaulting of the church just as we see it now in those churches which follow the Ambrosian rite.

In the present Latin Liturgy it is not permissible to reserve the Eucharist in an open tabernacle, within the wall of the transept, as formerly was the custom in the time of Mino da Fiesole, nor to place it in the golden dove that hung from the ceiling of the baldacchino. If, therefore, the liturgical regulations now in force are faithfully carried out—they were certainly intended to eliminate grave abuses which had taken root by the end of the Middle Ages—the altar will still keep much of its impressive austerity of early days, and the faithful may follow freely enough the actions of the officiating priest, always provided that the holy table has only its simple ritual adornment and is unencumbered with shelves, light-reflectors and artificial flowers; provided also that the eucharistic ciborium does not assume too large proportions; because in this kind of altar, isolated and covered by an artistic *tegurium,* it is the whole of the altar, with its splendid marble coping, which constitutes the true seat, the *tabernaculum Altissimi.*

Since the third century at least the Church has allowed various forms of altars, from the *mensa* supported by pilasters or small columns, to the slab of the *arcosolium* in the catacombs, or to the simple tomb with marble sides completely enclosing the urn of the titular martyr. Each one of these forms is beautiful, and each is authorized by liturgical tradition, but since the idea of the altar tomb is later in date than that of the simple and primitive *mensa Domini,* and introduces a quite secondary funeral element, so, if one had to select a type of altar suitable for the Blessed Sacrament, one would preferably choose the table form, as corresponding more closely to the spirit of the eucharistic liturgy. A *mensa* set upon a tomb seems a sad anomaly, and if it signifies the union of the bloody sacrifice of the martyr with the unbloody offering of the divine Victim, that does not appear to be any great argument in its favour, because, when the sacred *actio* is completed, our Lord still continues his sacramental life with us, in the tabernacle.

The altar, moreover, must be of stone or marble, according to the universal idea among ancient peoples. It is impossible, therefore, to conceive an altar of wood or of some other fragile material, for it would offend not only æsthetic sentiment, but also liturgical good taste. The seat of Jahveh must be fixed and eternal, and marble alone can express this thought. Christian tradition on this point is supported by precedents among the Jews, Asiatics and Egyptians, whose altars, *cippi* and votive *stelai* were always of solid stone.

The ritual laws prescribe, further, that before the eucharistic altar lamps shall burn continuously, which, their flame fed with the vegetable oil of the olive and kept always bright by the watchful care of a Levite, shall bear constant witness to the fervour of Catholic devotion towards the eucharistic Emmanuel. Mineral oils and electric light are therefore excluded, both in deference to liturgical tradition and also because these kinds of lighting, not originating from any living source, express but poorly the vital strength of our devotion to the sacred mystery. Oil and wax burn away, and are consumed in honour of almighty God, and thus represent a true sacrifice of light, *eucharistia lucernaris* in the graceful patristic phrase. With gas and electric light, on the other hand, the burning away of the combustible element is not so clearly seen; the electric lamp is instantaneously lit by a simple expedient, requiring no special care for its maintenance; so, for that very reason, electricity fails to symbolize the *devotio,* the assiduous, loving service of the Levite who keeps the sacred fire of faith alive before the altar of Jahveh.

Modern custom nevertheless admits of electricity in the church for purposes of illumination; but here, too, a lofty artistic and religious sentiment is necessary in order to preserve to the house of God its hieratic character, and not transform it into a mere secular assembly hall. A scheme of lighting, moderate and subdued, which reveals the architectural outlines of the *naos* without distorting them, and allows of the faithful assisting at the divine Offices by night as well as by day, this is permitted by the ritual laws, as long as there are no fanciful light effects thrown upon the tabernacle nor upon the sacred pictures and statues. It may be further added that even in the daytime a dim light in the holy place is helpful to deeper spiritual recollection and gives greater prominence to the mystical character of the *naos,* along which, guided by the torch of faith through the mysteries of dogma, we advance towards the Pantocrator of the Sanctuary.

One last word regarding altar-pieces. Sacred pictures in the nave and in the aisles of the church preceded by several centuries the side altars, for, when these were multiplied and placed against the walls, they found the latter already adorned with sacred paintings and biblical scenes. The ecclesiastical custom of the present day permits pictures of the saints to be displayed on the altars for the veneration of the faithful, on the understanding, however, that the *ikons* be worthy of the holy place both in material and in design, and that they shall be such as shall inspire devotion.

This condition, therefore, shuts out oleographs, photographs and ultra-realistic representations; in fact, any pictures that lack that sacred and liturgical stamp which all art should bear when it enters the house of God. Photography is not art; still less is it liturgical art, the function of which in the Church is to adorn as well as to illustrate, co-ordinating all its representations to the great eucharistic idea which pervades the whole religious edifice. Thus the idea of the artist at the tomb of Pius IX in the Campo Verano at Rome was not a happy one when he introduced, alongside of sacerdotal representations of the Pope proclaiming the dogma of the Immaculate Conception to the world, a picture showing the Holy Father, in ordinary dress, giving a private audience to some women of the people.

It is, above all, to be desired that the altar-piece of the altar on which the Blessed Sacrament is reserved should be in closest relation with this august mystery. The classical custom in the great Roman basilicas is to dedicate the eucharistic altar exclusively to the adoration of the Blessed Sacrament; hence pictures of the Madonna or of the saints are excluded in favour of representations of the most holy Trinity, the angelic choirs, or even those celestial beings who, lost in rapturous adoration, pay homage to the divine Guest in the Tabernacle. The adoration of the most holy Sacrament inspired the greatest artists of Christianity to achieve stupendous masterpieces in the past, and the subject remains to-day neither barren nor exhausted. How grand it would be, for example, to see the painters of our day turn to the Apocalypse of St John for inspiration, and represent, as did the great masters of old, the Lamb of God slain for the sins of the world standing before the golden altar of heaven in the presence of Jahveh. The patriarchs gathered round should cast down their crowns before the Thrice Holy, while angels swing their censers in unison with the alleluiatic song of the saints.

Far be it for us to deny that which Horace so graciously conceded : *Pictoribus atque poetis, quidlibet audendi semper fuit aequa potestas.*

We would, however, only say that a spirit of unrestrained liberty and individualism is contrary to true Christian art, which, like the Liturgy, is essentially social; and by social we here mean that art in the Church, whether it be painting, sculpture, architecture, etc., should not stand alone and be a mere end in itself. It should rather be subordinate in all respects to liturgical inspiration, which, employing all the resources of the Christian mind, seeks to make of the Church, as it were, a complete poem, a sort of Bible in real life, actually experienced, a *dominicum;* in a word, an *ecclesia Dei* which reflects and pictures that of which God himself in the highest heavens is the author.

CHAPTER XIII

RELIGIOUS CONSECRATION

IN the fourth century, when the ascetic life of the cenobite had come to be one of the most important of Christian institutions, the chroniclers of that day desired to assign its origin to remote antiquity, to a time earlier, almost, than any existing historical record, connecting it again with the preaching of the Apostles themselves, who, in the person of St Mark at Alexandria, and of St Peter and St Paul in the Greek and Roman world, are said to have sown the first seeds of Christian chastity, thus inaugurating the religious state. In as far as this claim is made for private discipline practised at home in the midst of one's own family —and this, in fact, was the earliest form of religious life in the primitive Church—it cannot be seriously contravened, but it is inaccurate to maintain that the cenobitic institution dates back to the first century. Not only do the early Fathers never mention it, but they take for granted spiritual surroundings wholly different from those visualized by the idea of a cloister. The Epistle of St Clement *ad Virgines* is at once seen to be a compilation of a date at least two centuries later than the pontificate of Clement, by the simple fact that the anonymous author addresses himself to regular communities of ascetics scattered through the desert, whereas, up to the fourth century, no such communities had ever existed within the Roman jurisdiction.

In the history of the religious life three different periods can be distinguished as those respectively of private asceticism, the eremitical state and the cenobitic life. Moreover, these stages do not merely follow one another in point of time; they embody an inherent and vital evolution, a development extending itself first in the East and then in the West. The followers of the religious life acquired a variety of names in different countries and at different times. They were known as ascetics, philosophers, eunuchs, *continentes, encratisti,* gnostics, children of the covenant, monks, confessors, religious, servants of God; while the women were called virgins, holy virgins, handmaidens of God and nuns. It is as well to make clear at the outset the special character which distinguishes this early monastic asceticism from the religious life of the mendicant orders who arose towards the end of the Middle Ages. For these latter the immediate object of their institution is some particular external work of benevolence, whether spiritual or corporal—the exercise of

173

the priestly ministry, for example, service in hospitals, or the ransoming of Christian slaves; while in the case of the earlier monks the ascetic life bears no necessary and immediate relation to any external mission, since it is essentially ordained for the sanctification of the soul in the *dominici schola servitii,* as St Benedict calls the monastery.

All Christians, in virtue of their baptismal vows, aim at perfection, even when they remain in the world. The monastery is, therefore, as it were, a school of greater sanctity, into which there enter only a chosen number of well-disposed persons desirous of making their salvation sure.

The idea of stainless virginal purity which prepares itself for Christ by means of spiritual espousals tended very early to restrict to the weaker sex the glorious name of *virgin,* notwithstanding that in the Apocalypse (xiv, 4) it is bestowed preferably upon men, and an organization of *virgines* under ecclesiastical authority necessarily preceded the rules and canons of the monks by at least two centuries. Tertullian, in his *De virginibus velandis,* testifies to the fact that at the end of the second century the virgins were already so numerous at Carthage that it became necessary to appeal to public opinion in order to induce them to wear a plainer style of head-dress. A little later St Cyprian shows in his *De habitu virginis* a similar cause of concern, while in the fourth century St Ambrose, St Jerome and indeed almost all the great ecclesiastical writers of the age, were fully preoccupied with the question of the virginal state of life, sketching out for the private use of the Demetrias, Marcellas and Eustochiums the first laws of the ascetic life of the cenobite, which formed the foundation and groundwork of successive regulations.

When, with the ever-increasing number of virgins, it was necessary for the Church to intervene formally and sanction their state, granting them an organization and a recognized position in the midst of the great Christian family, the intention or vow of virginity, supposed or implied, formerly of custom in the early Church, was no longer deemed sufficient. It was required that such a state should be professed publicly before the heads of the Christian community, and under such special conditions as would ensure the seriousness and perseverance of the candidate. Hence, notwithstanding Tertullian's opinion to the contrary, public vows were considered as being more stable and more complete than private ones, so that gradually the whole personal initiative of aspirants to the state of holy virginity came under the discipline of canonical legislation.[1]

---

[1] *Cod. Theod.,* l. ix, 25.

It is only in a very fragmentary manner that we know anything of the rite of these early consecrations to the virginal state. They took place, as a rule, on the most solemn feast-days; in Rome, for instance, at Christmas, on Easter Sunday, or the Monday following, when the Station was held at the Vatican basilica. The ceremony was carried out before the altar, very probably during Mass, the bishop presiding over it as of customary right.

St Ambrose gives us the discourse delivered by Pope Liberius in St Peter's on Christmas Day, when he consecrated Marcellina, the sister of the great doctor. It is probable that the bishop's homily always formed part of the ceremony, since in St Jerome and St Ambrose we often meet with allusions to the parable of the Wise Virgins and to Psalm xliv, pointing, no doubt, to a vague recollection of the *sermones* pronounced by the bishops at the consecrations of holy virgins.

Sometimes the vow of chastity was committed to writing, as in the famous Priscillian painting of the *velatio virginis,* and after the invocation of the bishop the people acclaimed *Amen,* as if to bear testimony to the solemn act of betrothal to Christ. From the days of St Ambrose the laying on of hands by the bishop also came to be considered as one of the characteristic features of the ceremony.

As late as the fourth century custom had not yet fixed the age at which virgins should be admitted to the rite of consecration, but about that time there was a much more marked tendency to defer the taking of the vow to a mature age, when there would be less risk of its being abused by a course of conduct quite other than chaste.[1] It is of importance to notice the very different mode of action adopted by the Church as regards men from that employed towards women; for ecclesiastical discipline, which was constantly becoming more and more strict with regard to the age of *nonnae,* as they were called, in the case of monks, on the other hand, allowed young boys, with the consent of their parents, to be consecrated to God.

It is to be regretted that no ancient ritual of the *Velatio virginis* has come down to us, for the Roman sacramentaries give us only the euchological portion of the rite. This usually included an *oratio* and a eucharistic preface, similar to the one used at ordinations, in which the Church's teaching upon the excellence of the virginal state as being far superior to that of matrimony is brought out with wonderful clearness. The profession itself is duly dwelt upon, but there is nothing to show that the cenobitic life was as yet organized for these

---

[1] Cf. *Lib. Pontific.* (Ed. Duchesne), vol. i, 239-41.

bands of virgins by uniting them under one roof and one rule of life.[1]

The Gallican Liturgy, on the other hand, is much less restrained than the Roman, and already in the *Missa Francorum* are seen the first tendencies towards all that liturgical display which prevailed later on and even found its way into the existing Roman Pontifical. The rite began with a kind of preamble, addressed to the people, to whom the bishop explained the trend of the prayer which he was about to recite; then followed the giving of the habit, which was likened to the *vestimentum Sanctae Mariae*,[2] the ceremony closing with a formula of blessing imparted to the newly professed, in which there is also explicit mention of the vows pronounced *coram Deo et angelis sanctis*.

It was only in later times and in the churches of the Gallican rite first of all that the actual ceremonial obtained as given in the Roman Pontifical, with antiphons taken from the Office of St Agnes, and the bestowal of the ring and the crown, all heterogeneous elements which finally penetrated into the Roman ceremonies, forming a strange liturgical conglomeration. It became worse still, however, when the conception of the *consecratio* was relegated to a secondary place, giving way to that other idea of the mystical death of the newly professed virgin with the bier, the funeral pall and the solemn tolling of the bells.

The benediction of widows and deaconesses had its special rite in the early Church. These latter had been instituted in the time of the Apostles, and one of their liturgical functions was to assist persons of their own sex at the time of baptism, as well as to guard the door into the church which was reserved for women. St Paul, in his pastoral epistles, when giving to Titus and Timothy precise instructions as to the choice of the clergy, does not fail to regulate the recruiting of deaconesses, who should preferably be widows, not less than sixty years of age, good mothers of families, hospitable and charitable. At the time of the Council of Chalcedon (451) their inaugural benediction was still accompanied in the East with the imposition of hands by the bishop, although at Nicaea (325) this ceremony had been definitely abolished. In the *Pastor* of Hermas a very honourable part is allotted to the deaconess Grapte, whose office it was to give instruction in Christian doctrine to widows and orphans, and to explain to them the apocalyptic writings of Hermas. Still, notwithstanding the importance of the duties assigned to Grapte, widows as a rule, even if they took the vow of perpetual

---

[1] Muratori, *Liturg. Rom. vetus*, vol. i, 444, 629; vol. ii, 174, 184.
[2] *Cf.* Duchesne, *Christian Worship, ed. cit.*, p. 427.

chastity, did not receive any benediction, nor did they make their profession publicly in church, but only privately in the *secretarium*.

* * * * *

Akin to the benediction of virgins and deaconesses were the blessing of monks and the consecration of abbots. This latter ceremony was performed by the bishop or bishops of the province, but within the Roman metropolitan province the actual confirmation of the appointment was reserved to the Pope. The Gregorian Sacramentary has only one *oratio ad faciendum abbatem,* and, in contrast to the Eastern custom of accompanying nearly all consecratory prayers with the laying on of hands, for a long time the imposition of hands by the bishop formed no part of the ceremony. Here, too, however, the Gallican rite, perhaps under Greek influence, surrounded the benediction of an abbot with so much ceremonial that it seemed almost the same as the consecration of a bishop.

In the *Penitential* of Theodore of Canterbury it is laid down that, in order to consecrate an abbot, the bishop is first to celebrate Mass; then, in the presence of a deputation of the monks, he is to present the abbot-elect with the pastoral staff and the special shoes, which mark his ecclesiastical rank. The pastoral staff was the true symbol of the abbatial office, so that, when there occurred a vacancy or an abdication, it was laid on the altar as if to give it back to God, to whose care the orphan flock was entrusted. The use of the mitre, and the custom introduced by the abbots of celebrating Mass with rites almost the same as those of the consecration of a bishop, make their appearance in the great monasteries of the Franco-Lombardic kingdom as early as the eighth century. They are connected with the canonical dignity to which these powerful prelates were raised when they began to exercise wide ecclesiastical jurisdiction over the secular clergy as well as over the numerous dependencies belonging to their monasteries. These were the beginnings of the abbeys *nullius dioeceseos* of the late Middle Ages, and the final phase of the development of the exemption and autonomy granted to the monasteries by way of concession and privilege.

* * * * *

From the fifth century onwards the consecration of monks took place before the altar, and in all probability during the celebration of the eucharistic sacrifice. The Gelasian Sacramentary,[1] indeed, has a whole series of Masses *in monasterio,*

[1] *Sacr. Gelas., Liturgia Romana vetus* (Ed. Muratori), pp. 742-3, 719-20.

pro renunciantibus saeculo, oratio monachorum, purely Roman in form and spirit, and it would prove a work of very great importance if one were to search out in the sacramentaries and ecclesiastical writers the origin and history of the early monastic liturgy. Here, however, we may fittingly confine ourselves to describing the profession of a monk as it is found in the Rule of St Benedict.

The ceremony took place in the oratory of the monastery, in the presence of the abbot and the monks. First, following in this the ancient Roman tradition, the novice promised in writing to maintain his perseverance in the monastic state and to render due obedience to the abbot. The deed was drawn up in the classical legal style, preserved later in the formulas for granting long tenures of property, *Peto a vobis . . . domne abba . . . ut mihi tradere debeatis,* whence it acquired the name of *petitio.* It was not, however, addressed exclusively to the abbot, but also to the patron saints of the monastery, since, according to the ideas of those days, the profession implied a kind of double contract between the monk and his heavenly as well as earthly superiors.

This *petitio,* or deed of oblation, was placed on the altar at the Offertory of the Mass, and when it related to children, in order to express more tangibly that the deed signified the offering of their persons to God, the *petitio* was wrapped in the altar cloth together with the hand of the child, who from that day forward was irrevocably consecrated to God, in virtue of the *patria potestas.* In such a case as this the *Regula sancta* allowed wealthier parents to accompany the offering of their offspring to God with alms, which might even take the form of real property.[1] Grown-up persons also, influenced by this example, showed themselves no less generous, for their ancient *petitiones* often mention gifts of land being made to the monastery on the occasion of their monastic profession.

After the *petitio* followed the antiphonal singing of the verse from Psalm cxviii, *Suscipe me, Domine, secundum eloquium tuum, et vivam; et non confurdas me ab exspectatione mea,* together with the doxology. The novice then prostrated himself before the community, begging them to pray for him, and, having laid aside his secular garments, put on the monastic habit, the girdle and the cowl, *cucullus* or μηλωτή. The rite developed greatly later on, and towards the end of the Middle Ages, especially in France, it involved a kind of scrutiny, with questions and answers, various prayers, a eucharistic supplication (Preface), the blessing of

---

[1] *Regula S Benedicti,* ch. lix.

the monastic habit, and, in more recent times still, even a bier covered with a funeral pall. The details and accessories have in the end obscured the main idea of the rite. The ceremonial described in the Rule of St Benedict, on the other hand, is far simpler, but at the same time, because of its Roman sobriety, far more dignified.

We may here remark upon the similarity which exists between the Gelasian Sacramentary and the rite as given by St Benedict. The prayer *pro renunciantibus saeculo* certainly preceded the reading of the Epistle, and must have had its traditional counterpart in the Secreta, in the prayer *Hanc igitur* immediately before the consecration, and in the Collect after the Communion. These were the prayers of the Church which accompanied the offering that the novice made of himself to almighty God. It is important to bring out this character of oblation, which was essential to the profession of a monk, for it came within the category of the sacred oblations which the faithful of old were accustomed to present at the altar; hence it was that the liturgical moment best suited to it was that of the Offertory in the Mass. The sacred *actio* suffered no extraordinary interruption thereby; the deed of petition was placed on the holy table just as was done with the other gifts, and either after, or in place of, the usual antiphonal Offertory psalm, the verse *Suscipe me,* with the doxology, was sung three times, after the manner of an antiphon. Then, while the Mass continued its usual course, the novice prostrated himself and implored the prayers of his new brethren. In this Roman use there is no room for a Preface—at least during the Offertory—and with a sublime simplicity of conception the oblation of the monk to God was intimately associated with the Oblation in the Eucharist, thus bringing out anew the thought of the Epistle to the Hebrews, that Christ *una oblatione consummavit in aeternum sanctificatos.*[1]

[1] Heb. x, 14.

CHAPTER XIV

THE CHURCH'S CONSECRATION OF STATES AND RULERS

IN fulfilment of that which was foreshadowed by Melchisedech, who united in his own person the dignity of king with that of priest of the Most High, our Lord, as the firstborn of creation, concentrated in himself the sum of all power and all dignity, and not only is he the priest of the New Testament, but is likewise the one supreme and true king, legitimate and universal, placed by God the Father over the whole created world. This union of priestly and royal rule is the only one befitting him, whether because it is the most perfect, since it is the direct reflex of the unity and simplicity of God's almighty power, or because it is the one best adapted to the unity of our composite human nature; which, although consisting of soul and body, yet constitutes but one person having but one supernatural end at which he aims—namely, God, the beginning and end of all beatitude.

The Church also, inasmuch as she is the constant reflex of her Lord, the *pleroma* of his glory, his Bride, his mystical Body, the members of which are all united to him and kept alive by his own Spirit, is seated as a Queen at his right hand. Equally with Christ, and directly through him, she is the key to the world's history, so that, in virtue of her sovereign state and supernatural mission to guide all humanity to eternal life, its true supernatural end, her power extends over all peoples and all kingdoms. She not only opens and closes the doors of heaven, but through the golden irradiation of faith in the Middle Ages, she could, with every right, claim for herself the power to take off the crowns from the proud heads of kings, to place them on her own brow, or to bestow them on those of her more worthy sons.

From this point of view the temporal power of the Popes and the creation of the Carlovingian Christian Empire must be reckoned as among the most important institutions in history, since, in virtue of the first, the Supreme Pontiff united in himself the sacerdotal and the regal power (although this last was exercised only over a small tract of territory, as much, that is, as the more urgent cares of the spiritual rule of nations permitted), while with regard to the second the Popes, without being themselves called to the direct exercise of supreme civil dominion over the Christian peoples, placed it in the hands of an Emperor who should be at once the armed defender of the Church, the devoted eldest son of the

Roman Pontificate, and the legitimate representative of divine justice. This is the ancient explanation of the two swords presented to our Lord by the Apostles : *Domine, ecce duo gladii hic.* Of these two swords, the one is wielded by the Church herself, and symbolizes her spiritual authority; the other is wielded through the Church, and represents the civil power committed by her unto Cæsar.

It is not to be wondered at, then, if the Byzantine Emperors, following the example of that which Samuel did in the case of David, inaugurated their reign with a solemn religious ceremony, designed to surround the majesty of the *Basileus* with something of a sacred character. The first Emperor crowned by Proclus, Patriarch of Constantinople, seems to have been Theodosius II (408-450), according to the narrative of Theodorus;[1] after him Justin II (568), Tiberius, Maurice, Heraclius, all alike received their crowns at the hands of the patriarchs. A similar rite made its way also into the West; and while in Ireland St Columba, though only a simple abbot, claimed the power of consecrating King Aidan,[2] in France, too, the bishops began to anoint with chrism the royal heads of the first successors of Clovis (465-511).

The historical genesis of the Italian states before the Carlovingian conquest, with their medley of improvised governments, made the administration of the rites of religious consecration impossible. Indeed, those governments must all have appeared illegal in Roman eyes, inasmuch as they represented the breaking up of the one truly lawful and sacred state, which was to last as long as the world itself, the *Imperium Romanum.* It was only later on, when the Roman Church, finding herself at enmity with the Greeks and Lombards, turned to the Franks for help, that the new Carlovingian Empire could receive a real consecration from Pope Leo III (795-816). The somewhat vague meaning attached to the rite in the first instance caused Popes and Emperors for many centuries mutually to contest the overlordship of the Roman territory, without arriving at any solution of the original misunderstanding. While the Franks claimed substantial regal rites over Rome, the Popes, on their side, strove to weaken the Frankish influence by every means in their power.

The episode of the coronation of Charlemagne in the Vatican Basilica at Christmas in the year 800 is well known, although the agreement previously arrived at between him and Leo III is far from clear. From that day forth a new era opened in the history of Christian Europe, issuing in a

---

[1] *Eclogue*, ii.   [2] *Vita S. Col.*, ii.

general revival of all the old Franco-Italian culture. Hence not only science and art, but even liturgical formulas felt the force of this universal renascence, and this through the uniting of the Carlovingian spirit with that of Pontifical Rome. The fact remains that we know the most important documents of the Roman Liturgy only through Frankish elaborations of them, and had not the *schola* of Charlemagne taken upon itself the initiative in spreading the Roman liturgical books in Gaul, we should perhaps find ourselves to-day with but a very small part of the rich literary heritage of the Pontifical See.

The rite of the imperial consecration, as it was used in Rome during the Middle Ages, offers one of the most curious examples of this liturgical intermingling of Frankish and Roman elements. France supplied the outline and the formulas of the rite, Rome localized and adapted them to her own temperament and surroundings, and the outcome of the fusion was one of the most splendid ceremonies in the whole of the Latin Liturgy.

The *Ordo Coronationis imperatorum* has come down to us in several different forms. The oldest, dating from Carlovingian times, is very simple and corresponds exactly to the style of the Roman consecratory rite. It consisted of a prayer and of a *consecratio,* also euchological but not eucharistic, as at Ordinations, at the conclusion of which the Pope placed the imperial diadem on the head of the newly elected Emperor. Then followed the bestowal of the crown and sword, accompanied by distinct and special formulas of non-Roman origin, after which the *schola* intoned the traditional *laudes* in honour of the Pope, the new monarch, and the armies, Roman, Frankish and Teutonic. These *laudes,* now heard only at the coronation of a Pope, have preserved almost unchanged the classical Roman manner. We have actual testimony that they were sung in the time of St Gregory the Great, when the official portrait of the new Emperor arrived from Constantinople, and we meet them again in Africa during the episcopate of St Augustine.

In the course of time the rite of the imperial coronation became very much more elaborate, and was even modelled upon the Papal consecration itself. Thus the liturgical conception of the ceremony developed wholly to the detriment of the theological idea, since it is never well to surround a purely euchological rite with ceremonies which are characteristic of the administration of the sacraments properly so called. The fusion of the Frankish and Roman Liturgies under the Carlovingians is responsible for several of these unsuitable combinations. The anointing with chrism is mentioned as obtaining in France from the eighth century onward, and, if we may believe the chroniclers, St Remigius himself anointed King Clovis.

Whilst, however, at Rome it is the Pope alone who places the crown on the head of the new sovereign—*Petra dedit Petro, Petrus dat diadema Rodulpho*—according to the Gallican idea, on the contrary, it is the whole body of the episcopate who perform the sacred rite, and, as the formula clearly shows, they are too conscious of their own weakness in the presence of the royal power to employ the strong and dignified language used by the Roman Pontiff on similar occasions. The Pope, as head of the Church, can confer the right to a throne, in virtue of the very power with which he is himself indued, while the Frankish bishops seem to be merely delegates from their dioceses, personally owning themselves to be miserable sinners, unworthy of honour, and making but a feeble show of authority by being altogether seven in number.

In fact, at the coronation of Charles the Bald there were seven bishops who each recited a prayer over him, the actual anointing being reserved to the Metropolitan. At Rome, on the other hand, when the custom of anointing the shoulders of the emperor-elect was introduced, no special importance was attached to the act, so it was not administered by the Pope, but by one of the Cardinals, as a simple ceremony preparatory to the rite itself of the conferring of the imperial insignia.

We know fully the ceremonial used at the consecration of Frederick I on June 10, 1155. The King, escorted by his troops, ascended the steps of the Vatican Basilica, and after laying aside his customary garb in the oratory of Sancta Maria in Turri, in the atrium of St Peter's, arrayed himself in new and much more splendid apparel. Before the altar of the Blessed Virgin there awaited him Pope Adrian IV, between whose hands the Teuton took the customary oath of fealty. Then the Pope made his formal entry into the basilica and went up to the altar of St Peter, while the Bishop of Albano, standing at the silver door, recited a preliminary prayer over the monarch. Near the great porphyry circle, which may still be seen close to the central door of the Vatican Basilica, the Bishop of Porto recited a second prayer, after which the King went up to the sanctuary and remained prostrate while the litanies were being sung. A third prayer was said by the Bishop of Ostia before the altar of the confession. This time it was accompanied by the anointing of the King's arm and shoulder with the oil of the catechumens, an anointing which used afterwards, however, to take place before the altar of St Maurice, the patron and leader of armies.

When these preparatory ceremonies were over, the Pope resumed the interrupted Mass, which was offered with all the usual pomp of solemn papal Masses. While the subdeacon read the Epistle and the *schola* sang the Gradual, the Emperor-elect withdrew to the altar of St Maurice. Then, returning once more to the foot of the altar of the confession, he received from the hands of the Pope a sword taken from off the tomb of the Apostle : *accipe gladium desuper beati Petri corpore sumptum.* Having girded himself with this weapon, *accingere gladio tuo super femur,* he unsheathed it, brandished it three or four times in the air, and then replaced it in its scabbard, desiring to indicate by these actions that he would always be ready to wield it in defence of the Church and of the Pontiff, from whom he was seeking the imperial dignity. Adrian IV then took the crown from the altar and placed it on the Teuton's brows, saying : *Accipe diadema regni, coronam imperii, signum gloriae, in nomine Patris et Filii et Spiritus Sancti.*

In sign of humble gratitude the newly crowned Sovereign prostrated himself and kissed the feet of the Pope, after which he finally took up his position upon a seat prepared for him on the right of the papal throne. The *schola* intoned the usual *laudes* in honour of Adrian and Frederick, the people and the army responding with enthusiastic shouts of joy. Had not the fierce factions, by which Rome was at that time torn in pieces, prevented it, the ancient ceremony would then have been carried out, by which the Pope and the new Emperor, each wearing his crown, would have proceeded in solemn state to the Lateran, there to partake of a sumptuous banquet in the Leonine Triclinium.

Although this twelfth-century ceremonial appears indeed at first sight majestic, yet, when closely examined, it is seen to be neither so fittingly expressed nor so clearly conceived as the ancient Roman coronation rite of the ninth century— before, that is, the Papal Liturgy yielded to Gallican influences. Thus the three Cardinals, who recite the three collects over the Emperor-elect, are an imitation of the Papal consecration, in which the Bishop of Ostia and two other suburbicarian Cardinal-Bishops regularly took part. The anointing with the oil of the catechumens recalls that of bishops and priests in the Frankish ordinal, but one must remember that in the latter case it is a question of imparting the Sacrament of Orders, while in the former the Church is merely bestowing an inaugural blessing upon a temporal sovereign.

The coronation rite of the Frankish kings is equally of very great importance. The bishops made the candidate promise beforehand to uphold the privileges of their respective sees, a first sign of weakness in the episcopal body thus anxious to secure their own diocesan patrimonies in the face of royal authority. The matter of the election was then put before the people, so that they, too, might give their vote. If the result were favourable, two bishops took the sovereign by the hand while the *Te Deum* was being sung, and, leading him to the altar, caused him there to prostrate himself until the canticle should be ended. Several prayers followed, recited by the various prelates in turn, the general and predominant conception of which was always the anointing— *unde unxisti sacerdotes, reges, prophetas et martyres*—thus making a most inopportune confusion between the spiritual gifts of the priesthood, those of prophetic inspiration, and the rite of the inauguration of kingly government.

After the anointing with oil mixed with sacred chrism the ring was bestowed upon the king, and the metropolitan girded him with the sword. We now come to the most solemn and decisive moment of the whole ceremony. The archbishop, assisted by all the bishops present, takes the crown and places it upon the head of the sovereign, bidding him observe that it is the Pontiffs of the Gallican Church who, although in themselves but erring mortals, are conferring upon him this mark of royal power. Then followed the giving of the sceptre and of the *ferula;* sometimes also of a palm in sign of victory, after which the prelates seated the sovereign on the royal throne and, exchanging with him the kiss of peace, acclaimed him : *Vivat rex feliciter in sempiternum.*

Next to the coronation of kings comes that of queens, for these also received their royal crown at the hands of the Pope and the bishops. In France the rite was not unlike the one just described, but the anointing was upon the head, although instances are not lacking of its being performed also on the arm, as prescribed in the existing Roman Pontifical. The imposition of hands by the metropolitan, though very unusual, recalls the ancient Irish rite adopted by St Columba in the case of King Aidan. The new queen received in due course the ring, and was crowned by the bishops in the same manner as her consort.

It was by a very special and peculiar ceremony that the kings of Germany, before being crowned emperor by the Pope, received the crown of the Lombard Kingdom of Italy at Monza or at Milan. The Archbishop of Milan presided at the ceremony as of right, but as Monza had been anciently regarded as the second Lombard capital, so the coronation took place from the first in that city, until the violent opposition of the Milanese overbore the rightful claims of the City of Monza. Ripamonti thus describes the coronation ceremony : The king first stationed himself before the atrium of the Church of St Ambrose, near the base of a great column, and there received from the Count *de gente Angleria* a volume in which were described the rites and the prayers peculiar to the Milanese Liturgy.

It is known that Charlemagne, with the object of securing liturgical uniformity throughout his vast dominions, attempted to suppress the Ambrosian Liturgy; but the tenacious attachment of the people to their traditional customs so completely prevailed over the king's desire that his successors, when they visited Milan in later times, were obliged to promise the Milanese, before everything, that they would make no attempt to change their own special liturgy.

With his hand upon the Ambrosian Sacramentary, the Teuton swore fealty to the Pope and to the Roman Church. The archbishop then placed the iron crown upon his head, and the cortège, preceded by the Count as cross-bearer, entered the Basilica of St Ambrose, where the sovereign received from the archbishop the royal benediction. The solemn enthronement of the new king on the seat of the Lombard sovereigns brought the ceremony to a close.

At imperial coronations in Rome in the later Middle Ages the mode of procedure is indeed strange, and shows considerable confusion of ideas regarding the mutual relations between the sacerdotal hierarchy and the ministers of the Christian states. The canons of St Peter's received the new sovereign as one of their Chapter, so he put on the dress of a subdeacon, and occasionally that of a deacon, in order to sing the Gospel and serve the Pope at Mass and later on at table. These rites betray a confusion between two wholly distinct orders of ideas, and are the outcome of pious exaggerations, which, however, show the intensely religious mind of the period that conceived them, and lead us to form a high opinion of that culture which could soar so high as to derive from God himself the principle of that kingly authority which at that time was the pivot of civilized society.

In Germany the rite of the coronation of the Kaiser was somewhat different from those above described. The Archbishops of Cologne, Mainz and Trèves, the three Grand Electors, clad in pontifical array, awaited the emperor-elect at the doors of Aachen Cathedral, and, having conducted him into the building, caused him first of all to prostrate himself on the ground. However lofty the royal power at that period might be, its representative began by acknowledging it to be derived from almighty God and from his Church, and by this devout and humble posture in the presence of the whole assembly confessed that there existed another tribunal, higher and far more imposing than his own, before which he himself was, like the least of his subjects, but mere dust of the earth.

The Archbishop of Cologne recited a prayer over him, and Mass followed, at which the King assisted from his throne, supported by the Archbishops of Mainz and Trèves. After the singing of the Gradual and the Litany of the Saints, the Archbishop of Cologne went through the formal scrutiny of the emperor-elect, and, putting a number of questions to him, caused him to promise that he would observe justice and uphold the laws of the realm. As soon as he had satisfied the demands of the prelate, the bishops presented him to the people, that they, too, might signify their consent to the coronation, and the two Electors of Mainz and Trèves cried out, *Fiat, fiat,* in the name of the whole German nation.

The Metropolitan of Cologne then proceeded to the rite of the imperial consecration, properly so called. With the oil of the catechumens he anointed the sovereign on the head, breast, shoulders, arms and hands; then the royal chaplains arrayed him in a white linen tunic, stole and sandals, exactly as if the *regale sacerdotium* imputed to monarchs of the Middle Ages were a real sacramental priesthood. Lastly, the three archbishops presented him with the sword, the bracelets, the mantle embroidered with eagles, the golden orb and the royal sceptre—symbolical gifts which the sovereigns often bestowed as an offering on some famous basilica or abbey in their dominions, as if to show that Christ is the only true sovereign of Christian peoples. The ceremony came to an end when the king, having laid his weapons on the altar, again swore to defend the Church and to keep the laws of the realm. If the monarch had his spouse with him, then she, too, was anointed on the breast with the oil of catechumens, crowned with the royal diadem and enthroned beside her consort.

Far removed as we now are, both in time and in ideas, from medieval society, these rites may perhaps seem to us strange and fantastic. Yet the altered conditions of the nations of to-day, which no longer call upon the Church to consecrate their sovereigns and their thrones by her divine authority, indicate something quite other than progress in the path of civilization. It is true that we still keep up the traditional formulas in the official titles of public documents and declare sovereigns to be such by the grace of God, but this solitary and bare conception is too vague to have any really practical efficacy, to cause men to reflect upon it, or, indeed, for it to influence their lives; hence the monarchists in the nations of to-day represent, at most, the preponderating party as opposed to the others—the socialist, the radical, the anarchist and such-like. Is this one, then, no more than a mere party? Surely if it be true that a legitimate sovereign is what he is by the grace of God, if it be true that his authority has as its source the authority of the "King of kings and Lord of lords," if his person and his rights be thus rendered sacred, intangible and inviolable, it follows therefrom that those parties which oppose him unjustly are not merely parties, but disloyal factions in rebellion against the supreme law of God and in enmity to the lesser laws of civilized society.

In the Middle Ages, when kings were brought to the foot of the altar in order to receive the crown and the sceptre at the hands of the Pope and the clergy; when the holy chrism was poured upon their heads; when they were vested in white tunic and stole; when a royal throne had its place in the church beside that of the bishop; when the codex of the Gospels was presented to monarchs for them to kiss during the solemn Mass; when they were honoured at the Offertory, like the clergy, with special incensings and ceremonies; when their arrival in a city was hailed by priests and people, who went out to meet them with uplifted cross and with smoking censers and holy water;—then, by means of all this ritual, the Church desired to train the minds of men not only to treat the reigning dynasty with respect, as being the representative of legitimate authority, but also to regard it with religious awe. It was not here a question of mere legal obedience, but of real religious devotion, since, according to Christian teaching, authority, having God himself as its source, bears a sacred character, and, as such, becomes an actual part of religion. St Thomas, St Bonaventure, Gregory IX and Dante attached no other meaning than this to the medieval *imperium,* and so in the *Divina Commedia* our Lord himself is hailed as a citizen of Christian Rome.

Nor should this view of the case be affected by the fact that in the medieval judgement the sovereign power either showed itself excessive and absolute, or else bowed down too obsequiously before the clergy. Nothing could be more incorrect.

While the Middle Ages looked upon all legitimate monarchs as so many depositaries of divine authority, they also upheld the principle that their rulers, both as sovereigns and as men, were subject to the laws of God and his Church, and would therefore have to render a strict account of their actions to the divine Judge and to his Vicar here on earth. Without dwelling longer on the well-known instance of Bishop Babylas of Antioch, who forbade the Emperor Philip to enter the church (244), we would point out that the Middle Ages were well accustomed to sovereigns giving examples of public penance when found guilty of great crimes. Thus did St Benedict reprove King Totila lying prostrate at his feet most severely for his cruelties, and thus did St Romuald impose penance upon Otto III (997) for the blood he had shed on the occasion of the rebellion in Rome of the partisans of Crescentius against Gregory V, sending him on pilgrimage to the Basilica of St Michael on Monte Gargano. When kings, instead of being the fathers of their people, became their tyrants, there was ever present a higher tribunal—that of Christ's Vicar on earth—to recall them to their duty, and, if need were, to remove the crown from their brows. Henry IV, accused not so much of simony as of political tyranny, had bitter experience of this, when, by the sentence of Hildebrand, the whole Empire refused him fealty and obedience until he should be reconciled with his own conscience and with the Pope (1078).

It must not, indeed, be concluded from the liturgical formulas here described that this high jurisdiction, which the Church claimed for herself over kings and their dominions, would result in the merging into one of this twofold power, ecclesiastical and lay, thus placing the destinies of society exclusively in the hands of the priesthood. The two powers, subordinate as the material must be to the spiritual, certainly remained distinct, just as their supreme depositaries and representatives, the Pope and the Emperor, were distinct. If at times the Popes summoned kings to their judgement-seat, it was not upon any political charge, but for moral and religious causes that they did so : *Non de regno, sed de peccato.*

This political conception which inspires the magnificent ritual of the *coronatio regis* finds its reflex in the whole of the Middle Ages, and can never be fully understood without first taking into account the mentality of the civilized society of that time. Indeed, the medieval period is mainly a religious age, in which faith and the sacred Liturgy permeate all social customs and cause them to reflect, so to say, its soul, so much so that it is impossible to eliminate it. Moreover, since the faith and the piety which inspired the Middle Ages belong to the realm of supernatural and revealed religion, therefore the political and social forms also, which sprang immediately from them, shared in their transcendence, and must be reckoned by us among the noblest and most perfect of earthly institutions.

Certain it is that the society of to-day has nothing better to take their place. While in the Middle Ages all nations bowed in reverence before the Church, took up arms or laid them down, accepting the truce of God at the mere word of his Vicar, to-day, after four years and more of deadly conflict in Europe, the nations, who recognize no higher tribunal than the battlefield or the commercial supremacy of the world, are still at a loss to discover the conditions upon which they shall be able to settle down to a lasting peace.

CHAPTER XV

THE NUPTIAL BLESSING

THE marriage contract is by its very nature a religious act, since it involves a sum of blessings quite beyond the ordinary competence of the civil power to bestow. Our Lord, furthermore, raised marriage to the dignity of a sacrament, and, by the seal of grace, rendered the nuptial bond so holy, strong and indissoluble as to symbolize that one chaste and eternal union between himself and the Church. From the simple fact that Christian marriage is a sacrament, the conditions of the contract and the rites connected with it are subject exclusively to the authority of the Church, and do not call for the intervention of any secular power.

We have here to distinguish between the sacrament of marriage, which in its essence consists simply in the matrimonial contract between the two parties concerned, and the nuptial blessing which ordinarily accompanies it. This blessing is ecclesiastical in origin, and did not exist from the beginning, and although later on it acquired a legal force, it never became an essential condition of validity. The contract, on the other hand, is of divine institution and constitutes a sacred deposit entrusted to the Church, which protects and guarantees its rights.

The oldest testimony concerning the intervention of episcopal authority in binding fast the marriage contract occurs in the Epistle of St Ignatius to Polycarp : *Decet ducentes et ductas cum sententia episcopi unionem facere, ut sit secundum Dominum et non secundum concupiscentiam.*[1] We cannot, indeed, infer from this that there existed as yet any euchological rite for the celebration of the sacrament of matrimony; but such a rite certainly dates from the second century at least, since Tertullian writes of it to a married woman, as if it were already universal: *Unde sufficiam ad enarrandam felicitatem ejus matrimonii quod ecclesia conciliat, et confirmat oblatio et obsignatum angeli renuntiant, Pater ratum habet? Nam nec in terris filii sine consensu patris rite ac jure nubunt.*[2]

Let us here note the two most important points in the declaration of the Carthaginian controversialist: (1) *Ecclesia conciliat*—this shows the matrimonial contract publicly entered into before the ecclesiastical authorities—and (2) *et*

---

[1] c. v; *P.G.* V, col. 723.
[2] Tertull., *Ad uxor.*, lib. II, c. ix; *P.L.* I, cols. 1415·16.

confirmat oblatio, the Mass pro sponso et sponsa which by the eucharistic sacrament ratifies the mutual giving of themselves to each other. Tertullian, indeed, takes us still further.

The ecclesiastical blessing and the concluding of the contract before the bishop are not, strictly speaking, essential to the legality of the marriage; but anyone who omitted them would justly incur great reprobation, and his union would be regarded as practically unlawful in the eyes of the faithful generally: Penes nos occultae quoque conjunctiones, idest non prius ad ecclesiam professae, juxta moechiam et fornicationem judicari periclitantur.[1] To avoid this contingency, therefore, it is necessary that this professio of conjugal troth should be made coram episcopo monogamo, presbyteris et diaconis ejusdem sacramenti, ac viduis,[2] a condition which, indeed, already existed in the Roman mentality, for Apuleius assures us that impares nuptiae et praeterea in villa sine testibus et patre non consentiente factae, legitimae non possunt videri.[3]

The old Roman law required, moreover, that marriage should be contracted between equals, and it punished with the forfeiture of patrician rank a union between one of the richer citizens and a plebeian. Such were the impares nuptiae of which Apuleius speaks. It happened that many persons, in order to evade the law and avoid incurring its penalty, preferred to live, unmarried, with a plebeian woman, and not contract any civil tie—an unsatisfactory state of things which was done away with by Pope Callixtus I (219-224), when he declared that such marriages, though irregular under Roman law, were legitimate in the eyes of the Church. This is the first act by which the Church, fully conscious of her autonomy as regards the State in matters essentially religious, legislates on her own account where the interests of souls are at stake, in a manner altogether independent and without taking account of the civil decrees.

The impediment of the state of slavery also falls within the scope of these impares nuptiae; it survived for so many centuries in the Canon Law that it was not unknown even to Manzoni's Don Abbondio. The Church retained this impediment to marriage, not indeed to degrade the condition of the slave, but in order to protect the ingenuus—i.e., free-born—partner in the union from a rude awakening, should the lack of liberty on the part of the servile partner have been unfortunately concealed from him.

St Augustine attests that marriages between blood rela-

[1] Tertull., De Pudic., c. iv; P.L. II, col. 1038.
[2] Tertull., De Monog., c. xi; P.L. II, col. 993.
[3] Apuleius, lib. VI.

tions were commonly tolerated almost down to his own time :
*Quia id nec divina prohibuit, et nondum prohibuerat lex
humana.*[1] It was Theodosius who first forbade, under severe
penalties, any marriage between relatives, and when his sons,
Arcadius and Honorius, confirmed their father's decrees, the
Church willingly embodied them in her Canon Law, and in
the Middle Ages extended them even to the seventh degree
of consanguinity.

The marriage of widowed persons, although declared lawful
and valid by the Apostle, has always met with strong aversion
and disapproval on the part of the faithful in general. The
reason for this lies in the fact that second marriages do not
perfectly symbolize the indissoluble union of Christ and his
Church; moreover, they break that bond of loyalty which,
even after death, links the surviving partner to the memory
of the deceased. Early ecclesiastical writers perceived,
further, in second marriages a sign of incontinency, and if
they did not actually condemn them, as did Tertullian, who
ranked them with bigamy and fornication, at least they disapproved of them and did not hesitate to blame those who
ventured to enter into such a state. Thus St Ambrose says :
*Non prohibemus secundas nuptias, sed non probamus saepe
repetitas ;*[2] and when St Paul's leniency in the matter was
quoted to St Jerome, the great Doctor of Bethlehem replied :
*Aliud est quod vult Apostolus, aliud quod cogitur velle. Ut
concedat secunda matrimonia meae est incontinentiae, non
illius voluntatis. . . .*[3]

Hence arose the ecclesiastical custom of denying the nuptial
blessing to widowed persons on marrying again, and also of
depriving them of the Church's monetary grants. *Non solum
ab officio sacerdotii bigamus excluditur, sed et ab eleemosyna
ecclesiae; dum indigna putatur stipe, quae ad secunda con-
jugia devoluta est.*[4]

The existing rite of bestowing the nuptial blessing indubitably preserves certain very ancient elements, which may
possibly go back to the third century, to the time when the
various blessings of oil, of fresh fruit, etc., were brought
together in the same eucharistic anaphora : *infra Missarum
solemnia.* We lack sufficient documents, however, from
which to try to reconstruct a complete description of the
ceremony. The Gelasian and the other Sacramentaries preserve only the Collects of the Mass *pro sponso et sponsa* on
the wedding day itself, and on the thirtieth day following, or
on the anniversary when another eucharistic *synaxis* was
held. The *Ordines Romani* contain nothing to the point, and

---

[1] *De Civit. Dei*, lib. XV, c. xvi ; *P.L.* XLI, col. 459.
[2] *De Viduis*, c. xi ; *P.L.* XVI, col. 268.
[3] *Ep. ad Ageruchiam; P.L.* XXII, col. 1050.   [4] *l.c.*

before we can find any fuller description we must come to the famous letter which Nicholas I wrote in 866, as a result of the conference with the Bulgarians. From this letter it appears that the sacrament of matrimony, according to the Roman rite of that time, included the following ceremonies, some of which preceded, while others accompanied, the sealing of the nuptial bond.

First of all took place the espousals, consisting of the mutual promise of intended marriage by the parties concerned, a promise, however, which required the consent of the parents for its ratification. Upon this followed the *subarrhatio*, or the giving of the ring—*annulum pronubum*—to the bride by her betrothed. The dowry was next agreed upon, and a legal act embodying it drawn up—*tabulae nuptiales*—to which, according to St Augustine,[1] the bishop often affixed his signature. Here it will be to our purpose to quote a passage from the saintly Doctor of Hippo, in which he argues from these same *tabulae* that the procreation of children is the chief end of matrimony : *Coeterum, qui uxoris carnem amplius appetit, quam praescribit limes ille "liberorum procreandorum causa," contra ipsas tabulas facit quibus eam duxit uxorem. Recitantur tabulae, et recitantur in conspectu omnium adstantium, et recitantur liberorum procreandorum causa, et vocantur tabulae matrimoniales.*[2]

All this preceded the celebration of the marriage, and shows the persistent survival of the former Roman usages in the very heart of medieval Christian society. The sacrament of matrimony, indeed, displays better than any other the conservative spirit of the Church, which, instead of excluding from her ritual the ancient classical forms of worship inspired by Juno *Pronuba* and Hymen, appropriates their harmless elements, baptizes them anew and gives them a higher and Christian meaning, thus endowing Latin civilization with the stamp of permanence and universality.

The day being fixed, the marriage took place *in facie ecclesiae*—that is to say, in the atrium of the church and in the presence of the bishop or of the priest. In later times the phrase *in facie ecclesiae* was taken for granted, and came to bear a purely legal signification, whereas at first it was merely a liturgical term and was understood in its literal meaning of the *façade of the church*.

According to St Augustine, it was the parents or a *paranymphus, amicus interior, conscius secreti cubicularis*[3] who presented the betrothed couple to the priest. In the presence of the sacred minister they expressed their mutual consent

---

[1] Serm. 332; *P.L.* XXXVIII, col. 1463.
[2] Serm. 51; *P.L.* XXXVIII, col. 345.
[3] Serm. 293; *P.L.* XXXVIII, col. 1332.

and joined their right hands, whilst he invoked the divine blessing upon their union. The Fathers frequently allude to this joining of hands, the first mention of which is to be found in the story of Tobias (vii. 15). It will be sufficient to quote Tertullian's *De velandis virginibus: Ad desponsationem velantur, quia et corpore et spiritu masculo mixtae sunt per osculum et dexteras, per quae primum resignarunt pudorem spiritus.*[1] The ceremony of the kiss is more rarely mentioned. After the bride and bridegroom had been brought into the church, the Mass followed, with the nuptial blessing, called in the Leonine Sacramentary *velatio nuptialis,* from the veil which was stretched over the heads of the betrothed during this benediction. St Ambrose also affirms that marriage is consecrated *velamine sacerdotali et benedictione,*[2] and Pope Siricius (385-398) witnesses to the same rule in his letter to Hymerius.[3]

One sees here how the classical tradition constantly appears through the whole of the Christian liturgy. The veil of which Tertullian speaks is really the *flammeum* that covered the head of the Roman maiden when about to be married. The eucharistic sacrifice takes the place of the Latin *confarreatio* or of the *mactatio* of a bull or of a pig on the altar of the Temple. The Christian clergy replace the ancient college of priests and soothsayers, and the *velum conjugale* is analogous in meaning to the sheep-skin which covered the bride and bridegroom as they sat on two stools fastened together, while a sacrifice of fruit and corn was being offered on their behalf.

The old sacramentaries prescribe that the bride and bridegroom should receive Holy Communion, and that, on coming out of the church, they should be crowned with flowers. This last detail, too, recalls the classical custom of nuptial crowns, such as are still in vogue among the Orientals. Nicholas I (858-867), in his letter to the Bulgarians, also lays down that the wedded pair *de ecclesia egressi, coronas in capite gestant, quae semper in ecclesia ipsa sunt solitae reservari,*[4] an ordinance which authorizes us to suppose that at Rome, as in the East, during the Middle Ages, they gave back their crowns to the priest at some time after the wedding—probably on the thirtieth day—so that they might be kept in the church, as if to be a future pledge of the matrimonial contract there entered upon.

It is a real liturgical loss that, during the later Middle Ages, the greater part of this grand marriage ritual, so classical in style and so fraught with meaning, should have

---

[1] c. xi; *P.L.* II, col. 954.
[2] *Ep.,* xix, 7; *P.L.* XVI, col. 1026.
[3] c. iv; *P.L.* XIII, col. 1136. [4] *P.L.* CXIX, col. 980.

disappeared, and that marriages are consequently now celebrated with such grave and dull severity.

This loss which we have suffered in the West should render all the more valued and precious in our estimation the nuptial rites of the Greeks and of the Eastern peoples generally, among whom the ancient Roman ecclesiastical tradition has undergone but slight modifications.

In the Byzantine Euchologion the marriage rite comprises two distinct ceremonies—the nuptial blessing and the crowning. The betrothed persons await the priest at the door of the church; he then brings them in, gives them each a lighted candle, and censes them in the form of a cross, while the deacon and the choir sing a litany: *Pro servo Dei N. et ancilla Dei N. sibi nunc invicem desponsatis et salute eorum Dominum precemur—Kyrie eleison. Ut honoratas nuptias, inviolatumque thalamum Dominus Deus largiatur, Dominum precemur—Kyrie eleison*, etc. The giving of the ring follows. The priest first places one of gold on the bridegroom's finger and a silver one on that of the bride, saying, *Subarrhatur servus Dei N. propter ancillam Dei N. in nomine Patris*, etc., but immediately the witness to the marriage, the *paranymphus*, exchanges the rings and gives the gold one to the bride.

The *coronatio* is quite distinct from the *subarrhatio* and may be postponed to some other occasion. The priest again receives the bridal pair at the church door, and brings them in while chanting the psalm *Beati omnes*, in which the choir insert an antiphon at each verse. The deacon intones the customary litany, after which the priest places a crown on the heads of the bride and bridegroom: *Coronatur servus Dei N. propter ancillam Dei N. in nomine Patris*, etc. Then is read a portion of St Paul's Epistle to the Ephesians, detailing the duties of married persons; next follows the passage from St John's Gospel which describes the marriage at Cana. The common cup is now blessed, to which the married pair approach their lips; they then kiss one another, and, after receiving the good wishes of the congregation, they are dismissed by the sacred minister with a final prayer. A week later, when they bring back their crowns, the priest recites other special prayers.

The ceremony of the common wine-cup which the priest presents to the bride and bridegroom is found, too, in some Western liturgies, and it was also usual in some parts of France to bless the bridal bed on the evening of the wedding. The influence of the Book of Tobias upon the origin of this last custom is evident, and from it is derived also the idea of the newly married remaining continent on the first night of their union.

A further remark seems called for in this connection. The various formulas for the nuptial blessing among the Latins have reference rather to the woman than to the nuptial pair in common. According to the Leonine Sacramentary, it is for her that the holy sacrifice is offered: *hanc igitur oblationem famulae tuae N. quam tibi offerimus pro famula tua N.;* so also does the *velatio conjugalis,* together with its special blessing before the Fraction of the Host, refer exclusively to the bride: *Sit amabilis ut Rachel viro, sapiens ut Rebecca, longaeva et fidelis ut Sara,* etc.

When one bears in mind the point of view of the ancient peoples regarding the inferior state of the woman as compared to the man, the wisdom of the Church in this matter cannot appear other than admirable. In her liturgical formulas she has constituted herself the guardian of the weaker sex; she has raised womanhood from the degraded condition to which paganism had reduced it, and has so ennobled it that through Christian chivalry it has become, as it were, the symbol of a devotion, which inspired the *Divina Commedia* of Dante and the muse of Petrarch.

We shall conclude this chapter with one last observation. Elsewhere we have sketched the rites which in early times accompanied religious consecration; now we have to add that the ceremony of the *consecratio virginis,* especially that described in the existing Roman Pontifical, bears a close relationship to the nuptial blessing of which we have just been speaking. The reason for this is as follows: St Paul had formerly compared the virginal state to the spiritual marriage of the soul with Christ; and Tertullian, taking this as his starting-point, maintained that Christian virgins should wear veils on their heads, after the manner of married women. These ideas, when subjected to the influence of the Gallican liturgy, developed more and more in a mystical direction, so that a strange combination of ceremonies, taken from the marriage liturgy, replaced the early rite of the *consecratio virginis,* described in the Roman Sacramentaries—a rite which implied a simple eucharistic prayer and the *velatio capitis.*

There we find the matrons, *paranymphae;* the consent to the profession of virginity; the *subarrhatio* with the ring, the *velatio* and the *coronatio;* from all of which there resulted a magnificent and perfected ceremony, somewhat too emotional perhaps, and certainly detrimental to the theological sense which should dominate all those scenic accessories. There we read of nuptials, of golden bracelets, of vines with sweet-scented blossoms, of precious rings, of milk and honey tasted by the lips of the bridegroom, of his blood dyeing the cheeks of the bride, and even of an ethereal marriage-bed—*ipsi sum juncta in coelis, quam in terris posita tota devotione dilexi—* all these allusions showing, it would seem, no cognisance of the fact that we have to live here on earth, and have, moreover, to guard the treasure of virginity in weak and fragile earthen vessels.

The Middle Ages, essentially mystical and deeply religious, are well reflected in these formulas, which may, perhaps, at that time have stood for something really genuine. To-day our point of view has changed along with the state of society, and it is therefore not surprising that the religious profession of nuns is carried out with a more sober ritual, and that, save in a few exceptional instances, the magnificent *Consecratio virginis* remains unused in the Roman Pontifical, the relic of an age which was at once more sincere, more religious, and more light-hearted than our own.

CHAPTER XVI

THE LITURGY ON THE THRESHOLD OF ETERNITY

IN the golden age of faith, when the Liturgy had so intimate an influence both upon the individual and upon Christian society at large that the whole of life was, as it were, supernaturalized thereby, the very sorrow and sickness which precede the descent into the tomb were comforted and sustained by a splendid array of sacraments and ceremonies which, besides sowing the seed of immortality in the heart, implanted the soothing balm of certain hope in the spirit. The loneliness and sadness of the supreme hour found effective solace in the inward anointing of the Paraclete, and it seems that the Church, kind and pitiful Mother that she is, desired, by the splendour of the ceremonies with which she surrounded the couch of her dying child, to emulate, as it were, the liturgy of the angels which he would soon behold in heaven above.

The rite of the *Sacramentum Olei*—only in later days termed Extreme Unction, thus helping to give it that frightening aspect as of certain death which it now possesses—is mentioned by St James in his canonical Epistle (v, 14-15), where the essential conditions regarding the form, the minister and the effects of this sacrament are all precisely laid down. " If any one fall into *grievous sickness,* let him be anointed by the *presbyters* with *oil,* and the *prayer* of faith shall save the sick man both from the disastrous consequences of *sin* and from the sickness itself " —if this be for his soul's health.

Consequently, persons in good health, even when condemned to suffer a violent death, were always excluded from participation in the benefits of the *oleum infirmorum,* because in them, as the Angelic Doctor points out, there is lacking the *ratio signi,* without which this sacrament cannot exist. In old days it was also denied to those whose supposed evil dispositions rendered them unworthy of sacramental absolution in the eyes of the Church; while, for an entirely opposite reason, young children and neophytes, who died before having laid aside the white garment of baptism, were equally excluded. Thus we read in the *Life* of St Adelard, Abbot of Corbie, that his monks, knowing the spotless innocence of his soul, hesitated whether or not to give him Extreme Unction : *quem procul dubio scieramus peccatorum oneribus non detineri.*

Formerly, Holy Anointing, the completion, as it were, of the sacrament of Penance, preceded as a rule the Holy Viaticum; but these three sacraments were commonly received, not indeed at the last hour of life, as is the corrupt custom of these later times, but even before the sick person's condition gave any cause for anxiety. Nor is the mind of the Church on this matter in any way changed to-day, as is shown by the Tridentine Decree, and the contrary abuse is justly condemned as harmful, for this reason also that the grace of the sacrament operates to the benefit of the bodily health of the sick; not indeed by effecting a miraculous resurrection of a dead body, snatched from the very jaws of death, but *per modum medicinae,* at a time when it is still humanly possible to cure the sick person and restore him to health. Thus it was that in the Middle Ages, as in the East to-day, the sacrament of Unction was very often conferred publicly in church, whilst the sick person remained seated or else knelt before the priest.

Sometimes the sacred rite was repeated for seven consecutive days by different priests, who anointed not only the chief organs of the senses, but also whatever parts of the body were afflicted by the malady. The earlier ages, in short, knew nothing of the present-day abuse of putting off Holy Unction to the last hour of life, thereby justifying the modern title of " Extreme " Unction which it now bears. This abuse seems to have originated, not only in the ignorance and tepidity of faith in modern times, but also in the superstition which became current about the thirteenth century that a person who had once been anointed with holy oil was no longer at liberty to eat meat, to dance, or to live in the married state.

In the Western liturgies the oil was specially consecrated by the bishop on Palm Sunday and on Holy Thursday. At Rome, as we have already seen, the Pope blessed several phials brought to him by the deacons; but since every family wished to keep its own *ampulla* of holy oil in the house, as we nowadays keep holy water, and to make use of it as private devotion demanded for the curing of fevers, migraines and the like, the bishops and presbyters who assisted the Pope repaired to the *podium* enclosing the *bema,* and there, at the same time as the Pontiff, consecrated other little phials of oil brought to them by the faithful for this purpose. One of the collects in the existing rite of the consecration of the *oleum infirmorum* refers directly to this private use made of it by the early Christians when it begs the grace of almighty God *omni ungenti, gustanti, tangenti,* etc.

For this purpose, in the third century, the oil of the sick was, according to the Canons of Hippolytus, consecrated every Sunday, and we can perceive in the final doxology of the Roman Canon of the Mass the point of contact of the *benedictio olei* with the eucharistic anaphora: *Per quem, Domine, haec omnia nobis dona sanctificas, vivificas, benedicis et praestas nobis.* The *haec omnia,* etc., cannot really be an allusion, as the rubric would seem to imply, to the holy Eucharist, but refers especially to the oil, the bread and the fresh fruits which were brought to the bishop to be blessed.

In the East the oil for Extreme Unction is usually blessed by the priests, from time to time, as required. The Eastern rituals, faithful to the actual words of St James, *inducat presbyteros,* prescribe that the ministers of this sacrament shall be regularly seven in number, and never less than three. The ceremony is a very grand one. It begins with long prayers in which our Lady is repeatedly invoked in the most tender terms that a fervid Eastern imagination can think of— the only pure one, the one surrounded by an ocean of peace, the most fruitful olive, she who is crowned with Christ as with a diadem, the palace of the great King, the seat of the sovereign Trinity, etc. Then, while the body of priests bless the oil for the sacred lamp, the singers intone various invocations to St James the Apostle, to the Holy Anargyri—*i.e.,* the martyrs Pantaleon, Cosmas and Damian—to St John the Evangelist and to others of the most popular saints among the Eastern Christians.

When the blessing of the oil is completed, the deacon reads some portions of the sacred Scriptures; then the priests sing in succession seven passages from the holy Gospels, interspersing these lessons with as many prayers and sacramental anointings, performed successively upon the forehead, chin, cheek, breast and back of the sick person, also upon the palms of his hands and the soles of his feet. The anointings being finished, the codex of the Gospels is placed on his head, and the priests superimpose their consecrated hands on the volume, invoking at the same time the divine blessing.

This rite was often carried out in church, and formed part of the Mass *pro infirmo,* as it did also among the Latins of the Middle Ages. The Rituals prescribe that in such a case the ceremony shall begin on the evening before, and that the night shall be spent in singing psalms and in invoking the saints. In the morning, at the conclusion of the Mass, the sick person receives sacramental Unction, and, after him, not only the sacred ministers and the faithful who are present, but also the very walls of the church are anointed with holy oil. In the East, indeed, those whose death was near often spent their last days in a hospice adjoining the church, so that they might die amid the chants and the splendours of the sacred Liturgy.

The Western mind was always of a more sober cast. Thus the Pontifical of Jumièges, for example, orders that the priest be clad in all the sacred vestments as if for Mass, not excepting the *fanon*,[1] and that he be accompanied not only by the deacon who carries the codex of the Gospels and the *ampulla* of holy oil, but also by acolytes with lighted candles and a thurible filled with incense. Here the rite of Extreme Unction appears to be closely intermingled with that of Penance; the formulas are deprecative, but they differ from those now in use.

The ceremony described in the Capitularies of Theodulph of Orleans is of greater importance. The sick man first receives sacramental absolution, and then, if he be able to bear it, he is dressed in his best clothes and carried into the church, where he is laid on a straw mattress covered with sackcloth and strewn with ashes. Three priests come to meet him, who first of all sprinkle the spot with holy water into which some drops of holy oil have been poured; next they sprinkle ashes on his head and breast, repeating the words from Genesis: *In sudore vultus tui vesceris pane tuo, donec revertaris in terram de qua sumptus es. Pulvis es, et in pulverem reverteris.* Then the sick man kneels or prostrates himself on the ground while the seven penitential psalms and the litanies are being sung; the priests now anoint him with the oil of the sick on the shoulders, face and head, on the organs of the senses and on the breast, altogether at least fifteen times, and on some occasions as many as twenty. It was ordered that if a drop of the sacred oil fell on any portion of clothing, this was, for greater reverence, to be buried with the dead body, and if the sick person, on the other hand, recovered, then the garment must be carefully washed before being worn again. The dying man was made to recite the Lord's Prayer and the Creed; he then bade a last farewell to his relatives and friends, so that his last hours might be occupied solely with the thought of his eternal salvation.

At Tours, after the singing of the penitential psalms, those standing around the bed laid their hands on the head of the sick man, saying: *Dominus locutus est . . . super aegros manus imponite.* The anointings were at least twelve in number, and were followed by Holy Communion, a ceremony which was repeated for seven successive days. During this week of prayer and penance certain of the clergy were charged with the duty of celebrating the Divine Offices day and night near the bed of the dying person. It was

---

[1] The *fanon*, worn only by the Pope when celebrating, was formerly a veil of white silk with interwoven coloured threads. It was placed upon the shoulders after the manner of the " ephod " of the High Priests of the Hebrews.—Tʀ.

customary in the West, too, for several priests together to administer Extreme Unction; sometimes one performed the sacramental anointings while the others recited the prayers.

Notwithstanding so great a variety of customs, we find, nevertheless, a common outline for this rite, comprising the penitential psalms, confession, the imposition of hands and Holy Communion. As a general rule the Mass *pro infirmo* followed, whenever it was feasible, while the sick man remained lying on the sackcloth and ashes, since it was a principle universally accepted by the Latin mind in medieval times that one born of Christian parents could die only *in cinere et cilicio*. The instance in the Ritual of Châlons, where we find a rite which approximates more to the Greek use, may be regarded as sporadic, for the priest, having come back into the church after the ceremony, signs the congregation with holy oil and sprinkles them with holy water.

In speaking of liturgy we must always give a special place of honour to the Abbey of Cluny, which in the eleventh century attained to such glory and magnificence that its grand basilica was justly entitled by contemporaries *deambulatorium angelorum*. According to the *Ordines* of that celebrated centre of monastic liturgical life, the sick monk had himself to petition the abbot to grant him the grace of Unction. As soon as his request had been announced to the monks in Chapter, the procession was formed; the community went first, then came the priest in alb and stole, while four lay brothers bore the holy oil, the thurible, the holy water and the cross. The sick bed was first incensed, and while the priest was performing the ritual anointings the choir chanted the penitential psalms. After the Extreme Unction there followed the Holy Communion, and the kiss of peace was exchanged with the whole community, of which the dying man now took his final leave. When his passing into the life beyond was seen to be imminent the Holy Viaticum was again brought to him, this being a relic of a very ancient Roman custom, according to which the dying were to receive the Blessed Sacrament for the last time when actually at the point of death, that they might enter into eternity fortified with the pledge of immortality.

The pagans used to place a piece of money in the mouth of the dead, with which to pay the toll of Charon's barque; and in some districts—in Africa and in Campania—we find the custom of placing the consecrated Host on the breast of dead persons in force as late as the sixth century. Various councils forbade such a use of the sacred Bread of Life, but the old Roman practice had nothing superstitious or reprehensible about it; nay, it betokened a very lofty idea of the Sacrament as being for us mortals the seed of a blessed immortality.

After the Communion the sick monk was laid upon a bed of sackcloth and ashes, which, at Cluny, was always kept ready in the oratory of the infirmary; then the *Lives* of the saints were read to him and the litanies and psalms were chanted. At the moment of death all the monks had to be present in order to recite at once the Vespers of the Dead, while the body was being washed in the presence of a priest chanting psalms. In accordance with the hierarchal rank of the deceased, priests laid out the body of a priest, deacons that of a deacon, and so on down to children, who were trained to wash and clothe the body of one of their own age, over-coming in this way their natural aversion.

The dead body was never left alone so long as it remained unburied, and one choir relieved another in the chanting of psalms. Usually, however, the burial was not long delayed, but took place on the same day, for until the dead monk was laid in the grave no one was allowed to speak, to partake of food, or to go outside the monastery. The abbot solemnly absolved the deceased monk in the chapter house from the punishment incurred by breaches of the rule—*Absolutio super defunctum*—then, when the Mass had been sung, the body was carried to the place of burial. In some parts the custom obtained of first covering the face with the hood, which sometimes was also sewn up. At Rome in the seventh century the bodies of dead monks were anointed on the breast with holy oil, and at Clairvaux, in the time of St Bernard, the abbot was the first to cast earth on the remains of his fellow-religious when they had been lowered into the grave. The holy doctor records the torture he went through when it fell to him to perform this pious office for his own brother.

*   *   *   *   *

Our subject now leads us to describe briefly the ancient rites of Christian burial, for though they do not properly belong to the sacramental Liturgy, they are, nevertheless, so closely connected with Extreme Unction and with the Mass *pro defuncto* that they form an integral and complementary part of it.

According to the usual custom of antiquity, as soon as the sick man had breathed his last his body was washed, and when his social position did not permit of his being em-balmed, as was the usual custom in Egypt, he was, never-theless, anointed with such an abundance of aromatic perfumes that Tertullian could testify in his *Apologeticus* that the Christians bought these in far greater abundance for their dead than did the pagans for fumigation of their gods. The dead person was then dressed in the insignia of his rank, those who were rich being arrayed in purple garments ornamented with gold, so that St Jerome asked ironically if their bodies could not return to dust unless clothed in purple. Only those who died a violent death were laid in the grave in the same clothes as they had been wearing at the moment they were killed. Thus St Cecilia's body, when found in the sixteenth century, was clad in the same bloodstained garments that she wore when she died. In the time of St Benedict it was still the custom at Monte Cassino to place the Holy Eucharist on the breast of the dead monk, so as to consign him to the tomb, fortified by the sacred pledge of future resurrection; and, notwithstanding the prohibitions of various Gallican councils and of St Boniface in Germany, this custom survived down to the eleventh century, for we read that a pyx was found in the tomb of St Udalric (died 973) containing *sanguis Domini et alia sancta*.

In some of the churches in France a wax seal sprinkled with holy water was sometimes placed on the head of the deceased to indicate his Christian faith; priests and other ecclesiastics were shaven and their hair cut to the shape of a crown. In the case of priests, moreover, towards the end of the Middle Ages, instead of the Host a pewter chalice was placed between their hands.

In Rome, before the pontificate of Gregory the Great, the body of a dead Pope was covered with rich dalmatics, which were afterwards torn to shreds by the faithful and kept as pious relics. The same thing occurred when the deacon Paschasius[1] was buried, and it was this which led St Gregory to forbid these unauthorized marks of veneration and to order that henceforth the Pontifical bier should not have any covering at all.

Eusebius describes the splendid obsequies of Constantine before his body was finally laid in a golden coffin in the portico of the *Apostoleion* at Byzantium. When the mausoleum of the Emperor Honorius in the Vatican Basilica was demolished in 1543 a large quantity of gold and gems was found among the ashes. We know, too, how Charlemagne was buried, seated on his golden throne and dressed in a hair-shirt over which were other rich garments, with the imperial diadem on his head, the Book of the Gospels in his hand, and his shield and other insignia of his high rank beside him.

The dead were often interred on the day of their death, but for more eminent persons the funeral would be postponed for three, four, or even seven days. This delay, in the case of a bishop's obsequies, arose from the custom sanctioned by the Council of Valence in 524, that a bishop should be accom-

---

[1] S Greg. M., *Dial.*, iv, 40.

panied to the tomb by his fellow-provincials; hence the priests were forbidden to inter the body in the grave until the bishops in the near vicinity had been convened, which rite was called by the Council *mos antiquus in sepeliendis sacerdotibus.*

According to Roman law, which inspired the canonical legislation also, it was forbidden to bury anyone within the cities or in the interior of a church. St Gregory the Great, every time he gave permission to dedicate an oratory or a baptistery within his metropolitan province, did so only on the understanding that no tombs should be allowed in such places. Yet during the Lombard period quite the opposite custom prevailed, so that even in Rome the titular churches gradually came to take the place of the suburban cemeteries. First the bishops desired to be buried in their cathedrals, so that by the seventh century this custom had become so generally accepted in Italy that St Gregory himself tells us that, notwithstanding the many perils to be incurred, sometimes even those prelates who had been driven into exile from their sees when devastated or destroyed by the fury of the Lombards, still sought to return in order to realize the same desire.

At Milan, St Ambrose prepared his tomb under the same altar on which he was accustomed to offer the holy sacrifice, regarding it as most suitable, for he used to say that the priest should lie in the very place where he had fulfilled his sacred ministry. We know of several similar instances, all inspired by the same sublime thought of associating the dead pastor with the company of his predecessors who were resting in peace beneath the table of Christ, in the confession of the same faith and in the hope of the same resurrection. At Rome also, Pope Damasus, in one of the famous inscriptions from St Callixtus which mark the tombs of the Popes of the third century, places them in close relation to the altar : *Hic numerus procerum servat qui altaria Christi.* He wished to show how forcible an argument could be drawn against the heretics—as Irenæus had already done—from the fact of the different generations of Pontiffs succeeding one another in the same Holy See, and resting together after death under the same altar, for the apostolicity of the doctrine taught by the Church and handed down by our Lord and his Apostles by means of an ever uninterrupted series of bishops and pastors.

The Christians in general recoiled from the pagan custom of placing dead bodies one upon another, or of burying them without any distinction in one common grave. In the cemeteries the *loci bisomi* or *trisomi* are divided within by marble slabs or by tufa partitions, while the *loculus* itself was dug out to the exact measure of the body, which was laid in the tomb in a supine position with the face turned heavenwards and with the feet to the East. We cannot determine the exact text of the oldest funeral prayers, but we know that from the times of persecution a fixed ecclesiastical tradition existed on the subject. Indeed, it has been already pointed out by archæologists that the scriptural cycle which recurs most frequently in the funeral paintings of the catacombs answers exactly to the prayers of the *Commendatio animae,* which savour so strongly of antiquity and point to Jewish inspiration, in which mention is made of Isaac, David, Daniel, Susanna and Thecla. St Jerome, speaking of the burial of St Paul the Hermit, narrates that St Anthony sang the psalms *ex christiana traditione,* and there are also allusions to a funeral liturgy, or reminiscences of one, to be found in the ancient sepulchral inscriptions and on the Christian sarcophagi, among which may be mentioned several very important epitaphs from Libya which have recently been discovered.

Some allusion is made to the primitive rite of Christian obsequies in the Acts of St Cyprian, who, when persecution was at its height, was honoured with a triumphal funeral *cum scolacibus, voto et triumpho magno.* St Jerome, in speaking of the funeral of Fabiola, says that Alleluias re-echoed through the streets of Rome, and in his *Life* of St Paula he relates that she *translata est episcoporum manibus et cervicibus feretro subjicientibus, cum alii pontifices lampades cereosque proferrent. . . . Hebraeo, Graeco, et Latino sermone psalmi in ordine personabant; et non solum triduo, donec supter ecclesiam, et iuxta specum Domini conderetur, sed per omnem hebdomadam. . . .*

In the ninth book of his *Confessions* St Augustine has left us a wonderful description of the death and burial of his mother Monica at Ostia. As soon as she had expired, Evodius intoned the hundredth psalm, to which those present replied with the refrain : *Misericordiam et judicium cantabo tibi, Domine.* A great concourse of people then gathered in the house, and when the body had been arranged on the bier *de more illis quorum officium erat funus curantibus,* it was borne to the cemetery. Mass was celebrated *juxta sepulchrum posito cadavere, priusquam deponeretur,* and Augustine himself followed the mournful procession and took part with dry eyes in the funeral rites.

Dom Cabrol remarks that the funeral cortège constitutes one of the oldest forms of procession. Among other psalms, the second and the fiftieth were sung because of the words, *Exultabunt Domino ossa humiliata,* and St Gregory of Nyssa, St Jerome, St John Chrysostom and St Augustine lead us to suppose that also Psalms xxii, xxxi, c and cxiv formed part of this funeral liturgy which has come down to us, though only in a fragmentary state, in the *Rituale Romanum.* The responsory *Subvenite sancti* and the antiphon *In Paradisum* are therefore among the most precious treasures surviving from this funeral liturgy which so often inspired the painters and sculptors of Christian antiquity and of the early Middle Ages. For them, imbued as they were with the Christian's faith in the Resurrection, death had not anything gruesome or terrible in its aspect; it rather resembled a placid slumber, during which the soul was carried away into the bosom of its heavenly Father.

The Office for the Dead which is still in use, lacking as it does the opening invocation, *Deus in adjutorium,* and without hymns, but containing the beautiful and appropriate lessons from the Book of Job, is also manifestly very ancient. The Mass—*sacrificium pro dormitione*—on behalf of the dead is mentioned by Tertullian and by St Cyprian. Originally its form could not have differed very much from the ordinary eucharistic anaphora, but it may be that, from the fourth century onwards, a special eucharistic liturgy for the dead had to be composed, of which the existing *Missale Pianum* preserves only a few precious remains. Besides the Masses offered on the seventh and thirtieth days and on the anniversary of the death, the piety of the survivors sought comfort in their grief by celebrating funeral feasts at the tombs of their dear ones, as well as by pouring out libations, kindling illuminations and sprinkling perfumed ointments, all of which rites the Church did not fail to forbid as soon as ever a superstitious meaning attached itself to them.

The funeral absolutions are apparently medieval in origin, and their meaning is wholly distinct from that of sacramental absolution, although the prayers are inspired by the same conception of the power of binding and loosing possessed by the Church. The *Statuta Cartusiensium* (III, c. 2) say in this connection : *Absolutio defuncti post sepulturam in claustro . . . non debet fieri per modum absolutionis sacramentalis, sed per modum orationis.* Yet the faithful of those days intended, by means of this rite, to remit to the dead person the punishment due for his sins, absolving him from ecclesiastical censures, and, with a signification analogous to the idea of privileged Masses and altars, were in the habit of granting to the deceased *per modum suffragii* a plenary indulgence for his sins.

Hence in the Roman Pontifical, among the reasons which determine the bishop to visit each year every parish in his diocese is also the necessity of imparting absolution to the dead. Of great importance is the absolution which St Peter the Venerable sent to Heloise, Abbess of the Paraclete, so that it should be placed over the tomb of Abelard : *Ego Petrus, Cluniacensis abbas, qui Petrum Abaelardum in monachum Cluniacensem recepi, et corpus ejus furtim delatum Heloissae abbatissae et monialibus Paracleti concessi, auctoritate Dei et omnium sanctorum absolvo eum pro officio ab omnibus peccatis suis.*

In the monastery of St Ouen at Rouen it was customary at a funeral for the precentor at the Offertory to hand the stole to all the priests present in turn, so that they also might absolve the deceased person. The Milanese funeral customs have been strongly influenced by the Roman, but one of their characteristic features is still the reading of the *Passio* according to St Matthew, together with a portion from St John's Gospel and the chanting of the Litany of the Saints. The Greeks still preserve four different funeral rites, for priests, monks, the laity and children respectively, but the prayers are of a form very similar to that for the dead contained in the Pontifical of Serapion (fourth century). Sometimes the bodies of bishops are brought into the church and placed on their own episcopal thrones. The sight thus afforded cannot be a very cheerful one, but we have to remember that at Aachen Charlemagne was buried in the crypt of the cathedral, seated on a golden throne and vested in the imperial insignia.

The enfeebled faith of modern days has constrained the Church to lay aside, in a great measure, the ancient splendours of her ritual, and to reduce the sacramental Liturgy almost to its bare essentials. But the loss has been entirely ours, since, besides the poorer spiritual fruits which we gather from this lessening of the public prayer of the Church, the human soul, too, finds with greater difficulty that comforting balm of hope, that interior consolation, which through the sacred rites and through the all-powerful intercession of the mystical Bride of Christ so effectively sustained our forefathers in the battle of life and especially in the agony of death. As faithful sons of the Church their inner life was nourished by her supernatural spirit, and so, with a simplicity and dignity which those of our day find difficult to realize, they passed from the earthly temple and its liturgy to that liturgy which the Lamb of God is for ever celebrating amid the Hosannas of angels and saints on the golden altar of heaven.

PART II

THE INAUGURATION OF THE KING-
DOM OF THE MESSIAH

(THE SACRED LITURGY FROM ADVENT TO SEPTUAGESIMA)

NOMEN MIHI ABERCIVS
DISCIPVLVS PASTORIS˙CASTI
QVI PASCIT OVIVM GREGES
IN MONTIBVS ET AGRIS
CVI OCVLI SVNT GRANDES
VBIQVE CONSPICIENTES.
IS ME DOCVIT
LITTERAS FIDELES
QVI ROMAM ME MISIT
REGNVM CONTEMPLATVRVM
VISVRVMQVE REGINAM AVREA—
STOLA AVREIS CALCEIS DECORAM.
IBIQVE VIDI POPVLVM SPLENDIDO
SIGILLO INSIGNEM . . .
. . . PAVLVM HABENS (comitem)

Epitaph. Abercii ant. ann. 216 post Christ.

INTRODUCTION

CHAPTER I

HIERARCHY AND WORSHIP IN ROME IN THE EARLY CENTURIES OF CHRISTIANITY

FROM the stem of Jesse, according to the prophecy of Isaias, there came forth a most fair flower, and that flower was Christ. It is therefore only natural that there should be a continuity between the liturgy of the synagogue and that of the Christian faith, such that the Gospel revelation, far from representing the revolutionary reaction of the Pauline Diaspora against Hebrew intransigence, is the intrinsic and living development of the worship revealed by Jehovah, now brought to its legitimate completion by the warm rays of the Sun of Justice arisen on the horizon of Jerusalem.

There was an early period when the Apostolic Church used every care in order not to precipitate its separation from the parent stock of the Sanhedrim. Peter at Antioch and Paul at Jerusalem pushed the spirit of concession to its utmost possible limit, but the spite of the Jews against our Lord was not to be overcome, and the synagogue, no mother then, but a hard stepmother, assumed the base part, which she was to play for the next three centuries, of inciting the pagan world to drown the infant Church in its own blood. It was but adopting anew the former tactics of the Sanhedrim, who through Pilate put Christ to death.

At the very outset the authorities of Imperial Rome, as St Luke attests, had confused the Christians with the Jews, so that, as Tertullian expresses it, the birth-wails of the newborn Church had been shielded *umbraculo religionis insignissimae, certo licitae*. It was during this transitional period that the Christian family, presenting the outward and legal appearance of a Jewish community, borrowed therefrom likewise various liturgical usages which still form part of her sacred patrimony, and, like her faith, are, so to speak, of the seed of Abraham and of Israel by origin and descent.

We have already seen in the preceding part how the general plan of the synaxis for the purpose of instruction in the Christian faith, with its system of the *psalmus responsorius* interpolated between two Scripture lessons, the homily of the leader and the final litany for all the various needs of the community, exactly follows the outline of the religious service of the Sabbath in the synagogues; but we now have to add that the outward aspect also of the Catholic worship and hierarchy, especially in Rome, where the Hebrew element was exceedingly strong, reflected in many respects the organization of the Jewish hierarchy in the great cities of the Diaspora, and would seem to have been modelled upon it.

The internal constitution of the synagogue is sufficiently familiar. In order to set up a new one, it was enough if ten persons or so came forward, and in Rome several different synagogues existed, each one presided over by a *gerousiarch,* or by an "angel of the Church," assisted by a *gerousia* or "council of elders." The financial administration of the common property was in the hands of seven persons, each of whom was also charged with the relief of the poor in his own quarter of the city. Each urban area occupied by the Jews possessed, moreover, its corresponding cemetery outside the city walls. The Jewish necropolis on the Appian Way is well known, as are also those of the Porta Portese, of the Esquiline, etc.; from which it is to be inferred that the plan of the Christian burial-places, with their *cubicula, arcosolia, loculi,* etc., was taken from the Hebrews, with whom the Christians had in common both the hope of a final resurrection and a shrinking from the cremation of their dead.

What do we notice, then, with regard to the outward appearance of the Roman hierarchy during the first centuries? The Christian community at Rome is, without any doubt, presided over by its own monarchical *episcopus,* the successor of Peter and the visible head of the whole Church, who has the divine mandate to exercise his episcopal authority over all Christendom. From the time immediately following that of the Apostles he is found teaching all Christians, and intervening to decide questions that arise in individual churches, as, for instance, in that of Corinth. Moreover, he threatens to excommunicate the bishops of distant Asia unless they fall in line with him in matters of mere ritual. He is the cause of a disciple of St John the Evangelist, St Polycarp, taking the journey from Smyrna to Rome in order to try to bend the Pope to his way of thinking; indeed, from every quarter of the globe there is a constant stream of Catholic and heretical teachers coming to Rome to solicit the support of the *papa benedictus,* who is not merely the point of convergence for the whole Church, as Irenaeus teaches us, but even, to quote Tertullian's sarcastic expression, as *Pontifex Maximus, Episcopus Episcoporum,* sets his authority above that of all bishops, all uses and all customs. These prerogatives of the papal primacy were felt both by Catholics and by heterodox in the early ages of the Church; they were freely exercised; nay, they were often invoked, without any question ever being raised; so much so that Irenaeus, when he would prove the apostolicity of the universal Church, simply recites the lists of the successive Bishops of Rome, adding that with her *necesse est omnem convenire ecclesiam*.

It is therefore a matter of the personal prerogative of the Pope, and not of the pre-eminence or prerogative of the Roman Church, although in some ancient documents—as, for instance, in the writings of Ignatius of Antioch and of Clement I—the person of the Pope remains half hidden behind the traditional collective form sometimes assumed by the Catholic hierarchy, just as St Paul, in his Epistles, associates the names of his disciples with his own. Thus in the Clementine Epistle to the Corinthians the Roman Church is the signatory writing to the Church of Corinth, in order to implore the cessation of that schism by which the latter was being rent asunder (this was the very same epistolary form as was employed by the various Jewish synagogues, who were in the habit of keeping up an active correspondence among themselves); but the recipients of the letter at Corinth understood perfectly the true value of such conventional and bureaucratic phraseology, so much so that nearly a century later Bishop Dionysius of Corinth assures us that Pope Clement's letter continued to inspire the greatest respect among his flock, and that it was still read from time to time at the liturgical synaxes.

In the exercise of his office the Pope, besides being assisted by seven deacons in the administration of ecclesiastical property and in the distribution of alms to the needy, had also the aid of a college of presbyters, composed under St Cornelius (251-2), of forty-two members. The ever-increasing number of the faithful had induced the Pontiffs, long before the time of Justin, to divide the parochial administration of Rome into different sections or districts, establishing in each *region* certain *titles* or centres for worship, each possessing clergy, property and cemeteries of its own. At Alexandria, in the time of Arius, a similar organization flourished to such an extent that the titular priests were almost in the position of bishops within the area of their own parishes.

The names of the Roman titles, as well as those of the cemeteries, give the key to their origin. They began usually as the private property of Christian matrons, and passed into the collective possession of the Church when she became legally capable of ownership. In the third century there were twenty-five titles, and later on their number rose to twenty-

eight. The full list of them can be made out from the
signatories of the Roman Council held under Pope Symmachus (498-514).

We shall naturally give precedence to the *domestica ecclesia*
of Aquila and Priscilla, on the Aventine, which claims for
itself the honour of having been mentioned by St Paul the
Apostle in his Epistle to the Romans (xvi, 3-5); and a certain
primacy over all the churches of Rome belongs also to the
titulus Pastoris, or *Ecclesia Pudentiana,* on the Viminal,
because, notwithstanding the intricacy of the tradition concerning the relations of St Peter with the family of Pudens,
it seems certain that the Apostle did for some time accept the
hospitality of their house. Indeed, the memories of St Peter's
connection with Aquila and Priscilla, and with the Pudentes
and the Pudentiani, all converge upon the history of the
Priscillian cemetery in the Via Salaria, which was certainly
inaugurated from the time of the preaching of St Peter and
received the mortal remains of his earliest followers among
the Roman patriciate.

Bearing in mind the division of the City of Rome into seven
ecclesiastical regions, each of which included two or more of
the fourteen civil regions instituted by Augustus, we here give
the list of the old urban titles, the greater number of which
are still recorded in the Roman Missal and Breviary.

Regio I corresponded at least in part to regions i, xii, and
xiii of Augustus, and included five titular churches whose
ecclesiastical jurisdiction extended over the cemeteries on the
Ostian, Appian and Ardeatine Ways:

1. *Titulus Sabinae.*
2. *Titulus Priscae.*
3. *Titulus de fasciola.*
4. *Titulus Balbinae.*
5. *Titulus Tigridis* (S Sisto).

The remembrance of this grouping of the clergy lasted a
long time, for the cardinal priests of these titles, down to the
eleventh century and even later, duly carried out in turn the
duties of *hebdomadary* at the celebration of High Mass in
the Basilica of St Paul.

Regio II, Coelium et Forum, corresponded to the second
and eighth of the Augustan regions, and comprised three
titles, with jurisdiction over the cemeteries on the Via Latina,
and over those of Praetextatus and *ad Catacumbas* on the
Appian Way:

1. *Titulus Byzantis* (SS Giovanni e Paolo).
2. *Titulus de Velabro* (S. Giorgio).
3. *Titulus Anastasiae.*

Regio III, Esquilinum et Coelium, corresponded to numbers iii and v of the Augustan regions, and had five titles, with jurisdiction over the cemeteries of Cyriaca, of Hippolytus on the Via Tiburtina, and also of SS Peter and Marcellinus on the Via Labicana:

1. *Titulus Clementis.*
2. *Titulus Eusebii.*
3. *Titulus Apostolorum (Eudoxiae).*
4. *Titulus Aequitii* (S Martino).
5. *Titulus Praxedis.*
6. *Titulus Matthaei in Merulana.*

Regio IV, Quirinalis et Viminalis, corresponded to iv and vi of the Augustan regions, with four titles, and exercised jurisdiction over the cemeteries of the Via Nomentana:

1. *Titulus Vestinae* (S Vitale).
2. *Titulus Cyriaci.*
3. *Titulus Susannae.*
4. *Ecclesia Pudentiana.*

Regio V, Via Lata, Pallacines, corresponded to the seventh and part of the ninth Augustan region, with two titles, exercising jurisdiction over the cemeteries of the Salarian, Pincian and Flaminian Ways:

1. *Titulus Marcelli.*
2. *Titulus Marci juxta Pallacinas.*

Regio VI corresponded to the ninth Augustan region, and, like the preceding, had only two titles:

1. *Titulus Lucinae.*
2. *Titulus Damasi.*

Regio VII, including the Vatican, the Trastevere, etc., possessed three titles, with jurisdiction over the cemeteries of the *Viae Triumphalis, Portuensis* and *Aureliae:*

1. *Titulus Chrysogoni.*
2. *Titulus Caeciliae.*
3. *Titulus Callisti (Julii).*

To these titles must be added several churches of lesser importance, such as the Churches of St Bonosa, of St Hippolytus, of St Saturninus, of St Rufina, etc., as also the private family chapels set up in the palaces of the patricians.

Almost all these urban titles go back to the first years of the fourth century, to a time a little before the Peace of Constantine. Several of them must certainly have suffered confiscation during the Diocletian persecution, since Eusebius asserts that it was only Constantine who could give back to the Christians the buildings in which they had been accustomed to assemble, and which were the property, not of private individuals, but of the community at large.

It would seem that originally two presbyters were assigned to each title, as at Carthage, one of them being the actual titular priest, while ·the other acted as his coadjutor. An inscription of the year 521-525, in the cemetery of San Pancrazio, mentions, it is true, priests entitled *prior, secundus, tertius* and *quartus;* but during the first three centuries the clergy were very few in number, and the forty-six presbyters of the time of Pope Cornelius would barely allow of each title having the services of even two priests.

In Rome, while the presbyters, acolytes and readers took the name of the church to which they were assigned, the deacons and subdeacons, on the other hand, were called after the region over which they were placed; hence, in the ancient inscriptions, along with presbyters *tituli Sabinae, Nicomedis, de Velabro,* etc., are recorded deacons *regionis quartae, secundae,* etc. It was only later that churches were built attached to the deaconries of the Byzantine period, at a time, that is, when the primary function of the diaconate, which was to serve as storekeepers and officials for the free distribution of corn—*frumentatio gratuita*—had lapsed during the Lombard period for lack of means, and the deacon's office had become wholly religious and liturgical instead of being purely philanthropic.

In the ordinary course of things the administration of the sacraments took place in the urban titles. For the first four centuries the catacombs were used only for burials, and in normal times no synaxes were held there save funeral gatherings, in which may also be included the festal commemorations of the martyrs, held on the anniversary of their death. Consequently the popular notion that the Christians of the first centuries worshipped in subterranean burial-places is wholly devoid of proof, as is also the idea that they concealed themselves there in time of persecution and lived like so many moles burrowing amid the shades of death. Moreover, besides the fact that such precautions would have been absolutely useless, since the government must certainly have been in possession of a list of ecclesiastical properties, together with the names of those who presided over the Christian community, it seems even more improbable when we consider the vast number of the faithful of every age, sex and condition who, from the time of Tertullian onwards, would have had to abandon their regular avocations in Rome in order to take refuge in the underground life of the catacombs.

We have, on the other hand, from historical sources a very different picture of Christian life and worship in Rome during the first three centuries. From the very beginning the patricians placed some hall or court of their palaces at the disposal of the *ecclesia fratrum,* and there, protected by the sacred right of private ownership and *sub titulo* of some great name and of the *jus domiciliare,* the faithful of the neighbourhood used to assemble at fixed times for the ceremonies of their worship. This is the explanation of the fact that the name of the early proprietor was in its legal aspect always connected with that of his title, *titulus Tigridis, titulus Nicomedis,* etc., without any dedication to a particular saint. It was only later that the Roman titles assumed the names of their heavenly patrons, and what partly contributed to their doing so was the circumstance that when several of the founders of the primitive titles had come to be looked upon as saints, as, for instance, the *titulus Eusebii, titulus Susannae, titulus Cyriaci, titulus Caeciliae,* etc., then the other churches, too, which had been named after private individuals —*titulus Sabinae, titulus Balbinae,* etc.—came in time to be dedicated to martyrs of the same name, whose relics, on account of this similarity of name, were translated to these ancient halls. In this way did the *titulus Sabinae, Balbinae, Anastasiae* become, in their turn, the *titulus Sanctae Sabinae, titulus Sanctae Balbinae, titulus Sanctae Anastasiae,* etc., although these saints had no connection whatsoever with the foundresses of their respective churches.

Since we are speaking of domestic titles called by the names of their first owners, it is worthy of notice that a good many of the ancient churches of Rome, including non-titular churches dedicated to the martyrs, still retain the memory of having once been private houses. In those early days the *cultus* of the martyrs was of a specially local character. Outside the city precincts we see this *cultus* almost entirely localized in the suburban cemeteries, at the actual tombs of the martyrs, while within the city, if we do find some church named after a martyr, it is always because the tradition of his having lived there has been preserved, so that the building itself came to be looked upon as a sanctuary and relic of the saint. The most recent researches and excavations only serve to confirm more strongly this ancient Roman liturgical principle which has been brought out clearly by De Rossi, so we may accept it as true that all the early urban churches dedicated to martyrs regularly mark the spot where they once lived.

The following is a list of the more important of those churches which have been built on the sites of the houses of their titular saints :

1. *Basilica Apostolorum ad Catacumbas*, on the Appian Way.
2. *Dominicum Clementis*, near the Lateran.
3. *Titulus Caeciliae*, in the Trastevere.
4. *Memoria S Martyris Hippolyti*, near the Pudentian titular church.
5. *Basilica S Bonosae,* ⎫
6. *Titulus Chrysogoni,* ⎬ in the Trastevere.
7. *Titulus Byzantii* (SS Joannis et Pauli) on the Coelian.
8. *Titulus Callisti*, in the Trastevere.
9. *Titulus Cyriaci,* ⎫
10. *Titulus Susannae,* ⎬ near the Baths of Diocletian.
11. *Titulus Praxedis,* ⎫
12. *Titulus Pudentis,* ⎬ on the Viminal.
13. *Oratorium ubi decollatus est Xystus*, in the cemetery of Callixtus.
14. *Ecclesia SS Rufinae et Secundae*, (?) near the titular church of Callixtus.
15. *Basilica S Bibianae*, on the Esquiline near the nymphaeum of Alexander Severus.
16. *Titulus Aequitii*, near the Baths of Trajan.
17. *Titulus Nicomedis*.
18. *Ecclesia S. Felicitatis*, near the titular church of Clement.
19. *Dominicum Eusebii*, on the Esquiline, near the nymphaeum of Alexander Severus.
20. *Titulus Lucinae*, in the Via Lata.
21. *Titulus Damasi* (S Laurentii), near the theatre of Pompey, where the ancient archives of the Church were kept, and where possibly the great archdeacon had his official dwelling.
22. *S Saturnini*, on the Quirinal, destroyed in the time of Paul V (1605-21).

*   *   *   *   *

In order that the principle of the Church's unity under a single *episcopus* might not become too much weakened by the multiplication of all these lesser centres of worship, with their own clergy and their own particular cemeteries, the Pope, on every feast-day, was wont to send by means of acolytes a particle of his own *eucharistia* to the titular priests, so that it should be placed in their consecrated chalice to symbolize a *sacrum fermentum*, which, by pervading the whole mass of the faithful, should impart to their sacrifice the realization of Catholic unity. This practice must have been already begun in the second century, with the rise of the Roman titles, and in all probability it is to this custom that the story of the acolyte Tarsicius refers, who, when carrying out his mission, fell a victim to pagan brutality because he would not reveal to the infidels the sacred mysteries which he was carrying hidden in his breast. This regulation was still in force in the fifth century, and it may have lasted to the late Middle Ages; at any rate, for the more solemn seasons of the year, such as Easter Week. We gather from a letter of Innocent I (402-17) to Decentius, Bishop of Gubbio, that this sending of the eucharistic particle by the bishop came to signify that without episcopal authorization ordinary presbyters were not allowed to celebrate the eucharistic synaxes within the city. This rule has its counterpart in that other regulation, which still holds good, obliging priests to administer the *chrismatio* and Extreme Unction with the oil consecrated every year by their own bishop.

Another ritual institution intended to safeguard the grand principle of liturgical unity in Rome was that of the stations. As Tertullian remarks, *Statio de militari exemplo nomen accepit, nam et militia Dei sumus.*[1] At Rome, indeed, from the time of Hermas, the arrangements for the stations included not only prayers in common, but also a fast lasting till None, when, the eucharistic synaxis having been celebrated, the faithful went home for rest and refreshment. The belief in the imminence of the *parousia* may perhaps have contributed to the giving of the special name of " station " to this custom of keeping watch on the part of the faithful while waiting for the coming of their Lord, who, when he comes, will do so unexpectedly like a thief in the night. In classical Rome we have the expressions *statio I cohortis, statio annonae, statio aquarum,* and by *statio* was designated *barracks,* or place where the officials in charge of administrative work had their headquarters, so that the στατίονα ἔχειν of Hermas would be taken in a spiritual sense and translated " to keep watch," " to be on the lookout."

     *   *   *   *   *

The triumph of Christianity under Constantine lent a powerful impetus to the development of these collective *eucharistiae* celebrated in the most venerated sanctuaries of Rome, and often presided over by the Pope in the presence of a vast concourse of the faithful.

About the year 460, Hilary (461-8) entrusted a special charge to the *ministeriales—constituit in Urbe ministeriales, qui circumirent constitutas stationes*[2]—which justifies us in the belief that the parochial clergy were not summoned to attend each station as it came round, for after the fourth century the station, having by then lost its primitive peni-

---

[1] *De Oratione,* c. xix; *P.L.* I, cols. 1287-88.
[2] *Lib. Pontific.,* Ed. Duchesne, I.

tential character, with its fast prolonged to the hour of None, meant no more than a procession with a litany, followed by the offering of the holy sacrifice. This popular procession really constitutes the new element in the later Roman station, as it developed after the Peace of Constantine. The litany and the procession are not, however, regarded as being something by itself, but as forming part of a whole complexity of rites, incorrectly called by the name of *antiphony,* and first inaugurated at Antioch as a measure of opposition to the Arian party in that city. This new form of antiphony comprised certain popular chants of Catholic propaganda, sung amid the waving of banners and the lifting up of crosses illumined with candles, with choirs of musicians and processions through the streets of the city. Here was the Liturgy moving out into the open to meet the new needs of God's family and attract popular attention by song and scenic effect. This happy innovation from the banks of the Orontes was introduced by Chrysostom into Constantinople, and came thence to Milan in the time of St Ambrose.

Furthermore, when we consider the influence which this holy doctor possessed over the mind of Pope Damasus, it is very probable that this Pontiff of the Martyrs—who devoted his gentle muse to hymning the praises of those witnesses to the Faith who lie buried in the catacombs, who carried out immense works of excavation, restoration and adornment in the cemeteries, so that forgotten tombs might once more be honoured, and who, finally, borrowed from Milan psalmodic prayer and the liturgical office and introduced them into Rome—derived from the Ambrosian Church not merely the chanting of the psalms, but the entire *mos orientalium partium,* as the biographer of Ambrose calls it—the stational procession, that is, and the Mass which followed it. Certain it is that the famous nocturnal torchlight processions through the streets of Rome on the vigils of the greater feasts of our Lady, with representations of the Blessed Virgin and stational crosses, described in the *Ordines Romani,* recall the customs of Antioch and Constantinople too vividly for us not at once to perceive that it was, indeed, from there that such rites as these were brought to the banks of the Tiber. But also the ordinary stational procession in Rome, which, setting forth from the church of the *collectio* with uplifted cross and with the codex of the Gospels, the casket containing the Holy Eucharist and the smoking censers, wends its way, to the chanting of the Litany, towards the basilica chosen for the station, does not essentially differ from the night processions mentioned above, for a strong strain of Eastern influence is clearly seen in the Roman stational rite as celebrated after the fourth century.

St Gregory the Great, in the seventh century, gave a fresh impulse to the observance of the stational processions and finally rearranged their order, so that with few exceptions the list of stational basilicas is to-day just as we find it in the Gregorian Sacramentary. The principle followed in arranging the different stations is not always clear, especially with regard to those in Lent, but for the greater festivals the compiler has certainly found it necessary to keep to the traditional and uniform plan.

The ancient and true Cathedral of Rome is St Peter's. There the chair of the Apostle was preserved, there baptism was administered, there on Ember Saturdays were held the night vigils and ordinations, there the Pope was consecrated, and lastly there, around the *Confessio* of the Apostle, were laid to rest the Pontiffs in their last sleep. In a word, it was the Vatican, with its historical and liturgical memories, rather than the Lateran, the usual residence of the Pope in the Middle Ages, which became the living and authoritative embodiment of the Roman Pontificate. This idea is well expressed in the following lines which the pious pilgrims of the twelfth century repeated in the baptistery of Damasus near the tomb of St Peter :

> *Auxit Apostolicae geminatum Sedis honorem*
> *Christus, et ad coelum hanc dedit esse viam;*
> *Nam cui siderei commisit limina regni,*
> *Hic habet in terris altera claustra poli.*

Another inscription from the same Vatican baptistery, in expressing the twofold thought of the laver of regeneration, administered by the successor of St Peter, and that of the wooden chair of the Apostle preserved in the baptistery, unhesitatingly gives to the Vatican church the title of *Petri sedes*, using it in the same signification as we have indicated above :

> *Una Petri Sedes, unum verumque lavacrum,*
> *Vincula nulla tenent quem liquor iste lavat.*

In accordance with this principle the stational Mass on all the greater festivals of the year—Christmas, Epiphany, Easter, Ascension, Pentecost, etc.—was always at St Peter's. To the Lateran belonged the honour of being the habitual residence of the Pontiff, who only exceptionally celebrated the great feasts in the Basilica of the Saviour—when, that is, there was some reason for sparing the people the fatigue of the stational procession. Thus, for instance, on the great *feria quinta in Coena Domini,* the three Masses, for the reconciliation of penitents, for the consecration of the chrism and for the Easter Communion respectively, were all celebrated at St John Lateran, because it would not have been possible for the faithful to repair three times in one day to St Peter's, which was then outside the circle of the city walls.

In the fourth century the Easter baptism was certainly administered in the Vatican, but later on, as the power and influence of the Popes gradually increased the splendour and prestige of the Lateran, it became customary to confer the sacrament of regeneration there in the baptistery of Sixtus III, which same rite we find having its definite place in the *Ordines Romani*. In order, however, to compensate St Peter's—as originally it was probably not intended that there should be any stational Mass in Rome on Easter Sunday because of the preceding all-night vigil—the station of the following Monday was allotted to the Vatican.

A further blow was dealt to the privileges of St Peter's about the eleventh century. In winter in the short, rainy days that make the end of December so dreary in Rome, the third Mass, or rather the only true stational Mass at St Peter's *in die sancto,* Christmas Day, must have been very inconvenient, and rendered all the more so when the schisms occasioned by the struggle regarding investitures made it wellnigh impossible for Hildebrand or his immediate successors to venture outside the city walls in order to go to St Peter's, without hazarding their lives and running the risk of finding the gates shut and barred against them on their return. For this reason the claims of the Vatican Basilica were passed over and the station definitely fixed at Sta Maria Maggiore, where the liturgical spirit of Christmas Day found an especial attraction in the *Praesepe* of Sixtus III.

From the very first there were held at the Lateran Basilica of the Saviour the celebrated stations of the *initium quadragesimae,* and of the commencement of the *hebdomada paschalis* (afterwards called Palm Sunday), the three Masses of Holy Thursday, and that of the conclusion of the Paschal feast, the Saturday *in albis*. It is a strange thing, on the other hand, that the station of Easter Sunday should be held in the Liberian Basilica and not at the Lateran, but probably this arrangement is not of ancient date, and the choice of Sta Maria Maggiore may have been prompted by a desire for suitable variety in the stations, this latter church being situated quite near to the Lateran Basilica, where it was the custom to keep the baptismal vigil from the sixth century onwards.

The Basilica of St Paul has always possessed the privilege of the stational Mass on one of the first days following the great festivals of Christmas and Easter. It is, however, a place too remote from the centre of population; so that though on the Wednesday following the Fourth Sunday in Lent the great baptismal scrutinies were held there out of special devotion to that Apostle who was the chief of all the converts, and although Gregory the Great, who possessed there his own family tomb, was the means, through his good-will, of establishing a penitential station there on Sexagesima Sunday, yet the long walk in Whit Week under the fierce June sun of Rome dissuaded the Popes from celebrating the station there, and it was transferred instead to the Byzantine title of Sant' Anastasia, near the Velabrum. In the Liberian Basilica, besides the solemn stations of the Christmas Vigil, the Feast of St John the Evangelist, Easter Sunday and the Assumption of the Blessed Virgin, is also celebrated the stational Mass on all Ember Wednesdays. On the Fridays the station was ordinarily held in the *Apostoleion* of Narses, while the *pannuchis* in preparation for the Sunday constituted an exclusive privilege of the Basilica of St Peter.

St Laurence *in Agro Verano* (without the walls), notwith-standing its distance from the centre of habitation, has a number of stational feasts, thus bearing witness to the antiquity of the veneration paid to this martyr, whose basilica, in preference to that of Sta Maria Maggiore, was always reckoned from very early days among the patriarchal churches. Thus at the beginning of Septuagesima, in the middle of the Lenten season and again on the Wednesdays of Easter and of Whit Weeks the Roman Liturgy was wont to guide the steps of the faithful in devout pilgrimage to the tomb of the *staurophorus* of the Church, to whose prayers, from the time of Prudentius, was attributed the triumph of Christianity which ushered in the age of Constantine.

That the *Apostoleion* of Narses, too, like the title of Anastasia, enjoyed a brief period of fame, was due in great measure to its connection with the Byzantine Court. Hence on all the Ember Fridays the station is assigned in the Missal to the Basilica of the Twelve Apostles, at the foot of the Quirinal, where also the synaxis of Easter Thursday was held. The medieval Sacramentaries allotted a stational synaxis on the Fourth Sunday of Advent (*vacat*) to the *Apostoleion,* but this was a later innovation, made with a view to the Feast of St Eugenia, whose relics were pre-served in that splendid church. As her anniversary fell on December 25, its commemoration was anticipated on the preceding Sunday.

The title of Sant' Anastasia practically occupied the position of a Court church in the Byzantine period. It is not strange, therefore, that special privileges were attached to this basilica, such as that by which, on the second day of the first week in Lent, after the synaxis of the Monday at San Pietro in Vincoli, there at once occurred the station at the Anastasian title. Another famous station at Sant' Anastasia was that on Whit Tuesday, when the Mass should properly have been at St Paul's, had it not been for the difficulty of going so far in the heat of summer.

After the dedication of the Pantheon by Boniface IV (608-15), the Rotunda of Sancta Maria *ad Martyres,* or of Sancta Maria *Martyra* as it was called, also become very famous. The station of the Octave of Christmas was held there, as also those of Friday in Easter Week and of the Sunday before Pentecost, on which occasion a shower of roses *in figuram Spiritus Sancti* was scattered down through the top of the immense dome over the people assembled below.

The title of Pammachius on the Coelian Hill also enjoyed the privilege of having three stational days in the course of the year—viz., one of the days after the Epiphany, the Friday of Quinquagesima and the Wednesday in Whitsun Week. The first and third of these stations, however, have long since disappeared from our Missal, which in the Middle Ages likewise deprived the ancient title *de fasciola* on the Appian Way of its stational feast, in order to transfer it instead on the Monday in Holy Week to the Esquiline title of Praxedes, which had for long in vain desired the honour of having a station.

Another instance of liturgical spoliation traceable to the present Missal is that which was inflicted on the Basilica of St Laurence Without the Walls, when the station of *Sitientes* Saturday was moved thence to S Nicholas in Carcere, a church which, about the eleventh century, had risen to great importance in the city through its connection with the neighbouring family of the Pierleoni.

In the Gregorian list of the stations we seek in vain for ancient sanctuaries of the martyrs in the suburban cemeteries. While the Leonine Sacramentary keeps an exact record even of the traditional Masses celebrated in the catacombs—at the tomb of St Sylvester, for instance, or at that of the Seven Brothers Martyrs—in the Gregorian Sacramentary, on the contrary, there is no indication whatever of these extra-mural synaxes; so much so that the four Masses for July 10, allotted in the Leonine Sacramentary to the four different cemeteries where lay the sons of St Felicitas, are reduced in the Gregorian Sacramentary, or rather in the Sacramentary of Adrian, to a single synaxis in memory of all the Seven Brothers together. Yet it is known that St Gregory the Great regularly kept the traditional feasts of the martyrs in the cemeteries, and, indeed, several of his homilies were actually delivered there on these solemn occasions.

We subjoin the list of those of his forty homilies which were pronounced in the suburban catacombs.

1. *Homil. III in Basilica S Felicitatis, die natal. ejus*—Cemetery of Maximus on the Via Salaria.
2. *Homil. VI in Basilica SS Marcellini et Petri, Dominica III Adventus*—Via Labicana.
3. *Homil. IX in Basilica S Silvestri, die natal. ejus*—Cemetery of Priscilla, Via Salaria.
4. *Homil. XI in Basilica S Agnetis, die natal. ejus*—Cemetery " Agelli," Via Nomentana.
5. *Homil. XII in Basilica S Agnetis, die natal. ejus*—Cemetery " Agelli," Via Nomentana.
6. *Homil. XIII in Basilica S Felicis, die natal. ejus*—Cemetery Via Portuense or S Felix in Pincis.
7. *Homil. XXVII in Basilica S Pancratii, die natal. ejus*—Cemetery of Calepodius, Via Aurelia.
8. *Homil. XXIII in Basilica SS Nerei et Achillei, die natal. eorum*—Cemetery of Domitilla, Via Ardeatina.
9. *Homil. XXXII in Basilica SS Processi et Martiniani, die natal. eorum*—Via Aurelia.
10. *Homil. XXXVII in Basilica S Sebastiani, die natal. ejus*—At the catacombs, Via Appia.

An examination of the Gregorian Homiliary leads us to a further conclusion. The stations mentioned in the headings of the sermons, unless there be some error in the manuscript—a matter not always easy to determine—very often do not correspond to those in the Sacramentary; which circumstance, added to the fact that the cemetery stations were certainly frequented by St Gregory, though not mentioned in his Sacramentary, would cause us to suspect that the existing list of stations handed down to us in the Missal is at least either later than the compilation of the Homiliary, or else that St Gregory did not keep to it very strictly. The very order of the Gospel extracts is not always the same, and points, indeed, to a final rearrangement made possibly in the last period of the pontificate of the great doctor. The list of these divergencies is not without importance for the history of the stational liturgy.

HOMILIARY OF ST GREGORY.	ROMAN MISSAL.
2nd Sunday of Advent : Sermon at SS Pietro e Marcellino.	Station at Santa Croce in Gerusalemme.
Ember Saturday of Advent : Sermon at the Lateran.	Station at St Peter's.
Thursday in Easter Week : Sermon at the Lateran.	Station at the Twelve Apostles.
Sunday " In Albis " : Sermon at the Lateran.	Station at S Pancrazio.
Ember Friday in September : Sermon at St Clement.	Station at the Twelve Apostles.

Sunday in the Autumn Season: Sermon at SS John and Paul.	The Gospel corresponds to that for the 3rd Sunday after Pentecost.
2nd Sunday after Pentecost: Sermon at the Twelve Apostles.	Nil.
19th Sunday after Pentecost: Sermon at St Clement.	Nil.
9th Sunday after Pentecost: Sermon at the Lateran.	Nil.
Sermon at St Laurence on the Gospel of Dives and Lazarus.	Gospel-extract out of place, and put back by Gregory II to the Thursday of the Second Week of Lent.

Whatever may have been the order of the stational synaxes in use before the time of Gregory the Great, the fact remains that the list given in the Sacramentary of Adrian systematically excludes the suburban stations of the cemeteries, which, for that matter, had from the time of the Lombards come to be very unsafe.

Under John III (560-573), in order to ensure in some way that religious services should be held at the tombs of the more venerated of the martyrs, the papal administration of the patriarchate had been obliged itself to take up the matter and to appoint priests in regular order for that purpose, bearing on its own account the expenses of these rural synaxes. The convenient proximity of the cemetery of Octavilla, on the Via Aurelia, and the widespread veneration of St Pancras, did indeed secure some degree of favour for this boy martyr of fourteen, who still retains in the Missal the privilege of the station on Low Sunday. Yet with the exception of the tombs of the Apostles Peter and Paul, and that of St Laurence, the rest of the extra-mural shrines—those, for instance, of St Sebastian, St Hippolytus, St Agnes, and even the ancient cenotaphs of SS Peter and Paul *ad catacumbas*—remained excluded from the list of stations.

It would be interesting to ascertain the system by which the order of the Lenten stations was arranged. At times it appears as though its object may have been to take into account the different urban regions, but the earliest list has certainly been altered, and the thread of the series is frequently broken.

For the benefit of students, we here subjoin the list of the Roman stations in poetical form, the work of a humanist of the Renaissance. The text is that of Marucchi in vol. iii of his *Eléments d'archéologie chrétienne*, taken from a manuscript in the Ambrosian Library (cod. sign. f. 36, sup. fol. 83-4).

Qui tua praesidio Sanctorum crimina tolli
  Quaesieris, voti, me duce, compos eris.
Festa quadragenae nec sit grave tempora serva,
  Quaeque dies veniam continuata dabit.

                                  Ash Wednesday.

Primus Aventinum labor est conscendere montem, — Reg. I.
  Audiat ut primas diva Sabina preces.
Proximus ut subeas quae templa Georgius offert, — of later introduction.
  Quae fora nunc etiam de bove nomen habent.
Hinc Paulum fratremque simul venerare Iohannem, — Reg. II.
  Inde Triphon humili voce rogandus erit. — of later introduction.

                                  1st Sunday in Lent.

Mox subeunda genu Laterana palatia flexo, — Reg. III.
  Templaque quae Petri ferrea vincla tenent. — Reg. II.
Sit tibi Anastasiae post hos venerabile numen, — Reg. II.
  Virgoque maiori culta sub aede parens. — Reg. III.
Teque in pansperna excipit Laurentius ara, — of later introduction.
  Dictaque Apostolico nomine fana petas. — Reg. V.
Et Vaticani venereris limina Petri,
  Huic dedit in terris iura superna Deus.

                                  2nd Sunday in Lent.

Hinc aedes Mariae templum cui Domnica nomen, — Reg. II.
  Cui iacet ante ipsas parvula cymba fores.
Clementis subeunda etiam delubra benigni, — Reg. III.
  Qua Nero deductas stare coegit aquas.
Et tibi Balbinae visenda est virginis ara, — Reg. I.
  Edita Aventini quam iuga montis habent.
Caeciliaeque sacrum flavas trans Tybridis undas — Reg. VII.
  Te vocat et Christi transtyberina Parens. — of later introduction.
Subque Quirinali Vitalis colle rogeris, — Reg. IV.
  Et Marcelline, tu quoque, Petre comes. — Reg. III.

Te sacer hinc extra videat Laurentius urbem, — 3rd Sunday in Lent. Outside the walls.
  Terreatque accessus nec via longa tuos. — Reg. V.
Inde colas Marcum cui celsa palatia surgunt,
  Fundata auspiciis, Paule secunde, tuis.
Est quoque patricio veneranda Pudentia vico, — Reg. IV.
  Et piscina fuit publica Xystus ubi — Reg. I.
Fratreque cum Cosma Damiani numen adora, — of later introduction.
  Quorum sunt sacrae fana propinqua viae.
Mox in Lucina Laurentius aede colendus, — Reg. VI.
  Flaminiae Triphali qua tegit arcus iter.
Inde Quirinalem cum sol remearit adibis, — Reg. IV.
  Annuat ut precibus virgo Susanna tuis.

Atque Crucis Domini sacras accesseris aras, — 4th Sunday in Lent.
  Post ubi Sanctorum quatuor ossa iacent. — Reg. II.
Et pete qua colitur Damasi Laurentius aedem, — Reg. VI.
  Huic fuerant Magni iuncta theatra loco.
Nec pigeat Tyberis per quam petis Hostia porta — Outside the walls.
  Efferre ad Pauli maxima templa pedem.
Quaeque tibi in summis fuerat, Martine, carinis — Reg. III.
  Silvestro nunc est rite dicata dies.
Fana quoque Eusebii, Marii vicina trophaeis, — Reg. III.
  Carcere sacratum Nicoleonque petas. — Reg. II.

	Passion Sunday.
Ecce autem Petrus revocat tua vota precesque,	Outside the walls.
Post quem Chrysogoni numina sancta colis.	Reg. VII.
Iulitam pro Cyriaco Quiricumque rogabis,	Reg. II.
Quis data sunt Nervae proxima templa foro.	
Et quod Marcello posuit Lucina sacellum	Reg. V.
In Lata tibi sit cura subire via.	
Mox in Flaminiis pratis pete Apollinis aedem.	Reg. VI.
Haec Apollinaris dicere metra vetant.	
Sphaerica dein Stephani studiosus fana requiras,	Reg. II.
Coelius in summo mons habet illa iugo.	
Templa Iohannis adi portae mox iuncta Latinae,	Reg. I.
	Palm Sunday.
Et Lateranensi tecta colenda solo.	Reg. III.
Confer in Exquiliis hinc te Praxedis ad aram,	Reg. III.
Priscaque Aventino colle roganda tibi est.	Reg. I.
Maioremque Parens te Virgo reposcit ad aedem,	Reg. III.
Et Laterana domus tertia vota petit.	Reg. III.
Crux repetenda etiam cui Nevia proxima porta est,	Reg. III.
Templa habeant quartas et Laterana preces.	Reg. III.
Adiice praemissis pascalia festa diebus,	
Ut veniae referas uberioris opem.	
	Easter Sunday.
Curaque maiorem sit tertio visere Matrem,	Reg. III.
Tertius et Petri templa subire labor.	Outside the walls.
Expedit et Paulum geminato accedere voto,	Outside the walls.
Est labor, at meriti gratia maior erit.	
Moenia teque etiam vocat Laurentius extra,	Outside the walls.
Et bis Apostolici nominis arca petit.	Reg. V.
Pantheon hinc aedes Mariae nunc templa rotundae,	Reg. VI.
Clarumque opus Agrippae conspicuumque decus.	
Et Lateranensi celebratus in aede Iohannes,	Reg. III.
Excipiat quintas qua prius aure preces.	
Ultimus e merito Pancratius ore rogetur,	Outside the walls.
Et tua sic tolli crimina posse puta.	

From this summary it is clear that the distribution of the stational synaxes according to regions too often proves a fallacious guide, so we shall probably have to content ourselves with knowing that the stations, though lacking in topographical and hierarchical order, alternate and succeed one another in such a way that all the most extensive and most important titles in the city were visited during the Lenten season.

This arrangement of liturgical services in the various sanctuaries of the city is not altogether peculiar to Rome. In the Middle Ages all the more famous towns of Italy, France and Germany had their own lists of stations, and this circumstance had much to do with impressing upon the Liturgy a certain dramatic, popular and living character which rendered it accessible and dear to the masses. In this way Christian worship has had only a beneficial effect upon all that already existed in the classical Latin tradition, since anyone who is acquainted with the old Roman Calendars knows well that alongside of the letters of the alphabet, corresponding to the days of the month, there were also indicated the religious ceremonies themselves, the sacrifices and the altars at which they were to be offered, just as in our Philocalian Calendar, which records the places where the feasts of the martyrs and Pontiffs were celebrated near their tombs in the cemeteries.

Thus it is that in every civilized nation—every one, that is, in which true liberty is understood and honoured—the religious problem is not something which merely concerns the individual in the hidden recesses of his own conscience, but is rather the fundamental postulate of all true social progress. It is therefore necessary that the Liturgy should not only emanate freely from the hearts of all the faithful, but should also constitute a social atmosphere, enveloping its very spirit.[1] It should therefore come forth from the church and the sacristy and take its majestic way through the streets and the squares of the city, educating and strengthening weak consciences thereby, and thus contribute, as powerfully as it did in the days of old, towards the work of christianizing the inner springs of modern life—a life which is wellnigh in total ignorance of the Christ from whom alone it can hope for eternal salvation.

[1] Prudence will dictate in individual cases at what point it is advisable to make a stand. Most certainly we would not give unconditional approval, in the case of the Catholic country districts of Italy, to a too easy-going and yielding policy; as exemplified by the growth, even in small out-of-the-way places, of the habit of carrying the Holy Viaticum to the sick in an absolutely private manner, just as if we were living in the midst of a heathen people.

CHAPTER II

THE ROMAN CALENDAR

THE essential object of the Liturgy's yearly cycle is to adore in spirit and in truth, to praise, to propitiate and to offer thanksgiving to the triune God for his great glory and goodness. This glory and this goodness are especially manifest in the twofold work of cosmic creation and human redemption; hence in early times these two *theophanies,* as we may call them, of the divine magnificence, while they afforded the central theme of the eucharistic anaphora, likewise gave inspiration to the liturgical cycle, as well for the week as for the year.

In the ancient Italic Liturgy at Rome and at Milan, not to mention other churches, the religious *cursus* both weekly and yearly constituted, however, two distinct cycles, each having its own marked characteristics. The days of the week commemorate the *Hexameron* of the Creator in framing the universe, while the annual cycle celebrates the work of our redemption. St Ambrose remains the classical exponent of the *Hexameron* with his splendid vesper hymns describing the work of each day of creation. The mysteries fulfilled by our Saviour in traversing the way of redemption are honoured, on the other hand, by a succession of feasts, which, beginning with Advent and going on to Christmas, Lent, Easter and the twenty-four Sundays after Pentecost, embraces the whole year, and always maintains a wonderful harmony between the logical order of ideas and the chronological sequence of events. The weekly round is, moreover, strikingly Trinitarian in character, while that of the year deals rather with our salvation and our last end, but both the one and the other have as their permanent objective the glorifying of God in his manifestations of power and of love.

Some few commemorations of martyrs stand out conspicuously on this early theological background, from the second century onwards, being especially distinguishable from the ordinary funeral rites for the dead by their triumphal and festive tone, so that, while for other dead persons the holy sacrifice was offered by way of suffrage, in the case of the martyrs it was celebrated in their honour and in thanksgiving to God who had triumphed in them and had finally crowned them. Prayers were offered for the ordinary dead, but as for the martyrs, as St Ambrose says, it would be

230

almost an insult if supplication were made on their behalf, seeing that it is they, united now in heaven with Christ, the Chief of Martyrs, who plead for the sins of all nations.

The first impulse towards the *cultus* of the martyrs being derived from the funeral liturgy of the catacombs, it is not to be wondered at if, during the first centuries, its characteristics were to some extent retained. We intend to speak here exclusively of the liturgical *cultus* which, unlike the veneration paid privately to the martyrs, bore from the first a local character, being confined to the cemetery wherein the particular tomb of a venerated confessor of the faith was situated. His feast-day, the *natalis,* was fixed and localized at the place of his burial, which is the reason why the old Philocalian Calendar, as a rule, takes no account of the martyrs of the first two centuries, nor of those who suffered in Nero's persecution, nor even of Justin and Ignatius, since ecclesiastical tradition had retained no memory of their tombs in the catacombs. For the instituting in such instances of a liturgical *cultus* there was lacking, so to say, any visible material upon which to establish and develop it.

This primitive, local and, we might add, sepulchral character of the martyrs' solemnities is seen very clearly in the early calendars, where each *depositio* or *natalis* bears regularly the indication of the place where the station was to be held: *Romae in Callisti, Xysti episcopi;* or *Via Ostiensi VII ballistaria, Cyriaci, Largi, etc.* Outside of the cemeteries —in the urban titles, for example—there was no particular reason for celebrating such feasts; so much so that while the faithful flocked beyond the *Pomerium* to take part in a commemoration in the catacombs, the clergy, whose duty it was to serve the titular church, remained in the city and went on with the celebration of the divine Offices in accordance with the usual weekly cycle. It was only afterwards, about the eighth century—when, that is, altars containing relics of the saints began to be multiplied also in the city churches— that the old principle of localizing the liturgical *cultus* of the martyrs and confining it strictly to their sepulchral sanctuaries took on a wider interpretation, so that the *depositio* came to be celebrated wherever there was an altar with the relics of any saint, such relics consisting in most cases merely of veils which had touched the original tomb. It was always required, however, that there should be an altar or some other memorial of the saint, so that the feast might have, if only by a kind of *fictio juris,* a sepulchral and therefore local character.

The *Ordo Romanus* of Montpellier echoes the ancient rule of the Apostolic See when, at the papal Mass, just before the Communion, it places this announcement in the mouth of the archdeacon: ILLA *feria . . . veniente natalis est* ILLIUS. . . .

Sancti, sive Martyrum sive Confessorum, IN ILLO LOCO.[1] Later on Gregory III (731-41) built at St Peter's a chapel, in which he desired that the monks should celebrate daily a supplementary office in honour of those saints *quorum natalicia fuerint*,[2] who were in danger of being forgotten now that the catacombs were abandoned. It was Adrian I (772-95) who ordered that *passiones sanctorum vel gesta ipsorum usque ad Hadriani tempora tantummodo ibi legebantur ubi ecclesia ipsius sancti, vel titulus erat. Ipse vero a tempore suo renuere iussit, ut (et) in ecclesia sancti Petri legendas esse constituit.* This was an extension of the rule and a kind of privilege granted to the Vatican oratory dedicated by Gregory III (731-41) *in honour of the Saviour, of the Virgin Mary, of the Apostles, of the Martyrs, of the Confessors and of all the just.* Other churches consequently profited thereby, but in a lesser degree, so that the Vatican Calendar of the twelfth century still remains an essentially Roman and local record, consisting almost entirely of the feasts of Roman saints, or of those saints who, because of their churches in Rome, had practically acquired the right to be considered as Roman citizens.

It would take too long to tell here the full story of the Roman Church Calendar. It will suffice for the scope of this work to supply the student, by means of the following tables, with a kind of synoptic outline of its formation and development down to the day when, mainly through the agency of the Mendicant Orders, it became in the thirteenth century the Calendar of the Universal Church.

We will preface our scheme with some remarks upon its documentary sources.

(a) *Sepulchral Inscriptions.*—It is not unusual, among the inscriptions in the catacombs, to find, in addition to the chronological notes, some mention of the saint on whose *natalis* the deceased person quitted this life. Sometimes also the salutations scratched by pilgrims on the walls of the catacombs contain very valuable information regarding the saints.

(b) *The Philocalian Calendar.*—The oldest Roman calendar which we possess is that embodied in the almanac of *Furius Dionysius Filocalus*, the amanuensis of Pope Damasus. It comprises two lists, one of the *depositiones episcoporum*, the other of the *natalitia martyrum*, both of which must have been compiled about the year 336, but were only definitely completed in 354, when the date (352) of the death of Pope Julius was added.

---

[1] Batiffol, *History of the Roman Breviary*, p. 62, n. 1.
[2] Batiffol, *op. cit.*, p. 62.

(c) *The Leonine, Gelasian and Gregorian Sacramentaries.*—
We are already cognizant of the value of the three Roman
Sacramentaries known up to the present, to which these
names have been given. In the following tables we shall
distinguish them by their initial letters, thus : *L* Leonine,
G Gelasian, *Gr* Gregorian; and we shall add to them the
names of the saints contained in the *Capitulare Evangeliorum*
of the Würzburg Codex of the eighth century, designating it
by the letter *W*.

(d) *The Calendar of St Peter.*—This comes from the famous
twelfth-century Antiphonary of the Vatican Basilica. It has
been commentated by Mgr. Batiffol in his *History of the
Roman Breviary.*[1]

The tables on pp. 234-253 show the formation and development of the Roman Calendar.

---

[1] *History of the Roman Breviary, ed. cit.,* p. 101 *sq.*

JANUARY

Epigraph. Coemeter.	Laterculus Philocalian.	
	Deposit. Episc.	Natalitia Martyr.
	10 Militiadis *in Callisti.*	
	15 Marcellini (?) *in Priscillae.*	
ann. 348, Jan. 16, Cemet. *ad Catacumbas* (S. Marcellus) STVDENTIAE Depositae MARCELLI · DIE Natali CONS SALLIES		
	20	Fabiani *in Callisti* et Sebastiani *in catacumbas.*
	21	Agnetis *in Nomentana.*

JANUARY

Sacramentaria	Kalend. Vaticanum
1 *G*. In Oct. Dñi. — *Gr*. In Oct. Dñi.	1 Oct. Dñi. — S. Martinae — *At her church in the Forum.*[1]
	2 S. Telesphori Pap. — *At S. Peter's.*
5 *G*. In Vigiliis de Theophania — *W*. Vig. de Theophania in eccles. S. Petri.	
6 *G*. In Theophania — *Gr*. Epiphania. — *W*. Theophania.	6 Epiphania.
	13 Octav. Epiph.
14 *G*. S. Felicis Conf. — *Gr*. S. Felicis Conf. — *W*. S. Felicis in Pincis.	14 S. Fel··is — *At his church in Pincis.*
	15 S. Mauri — *At various Roman abbeys.*
16 *G*. S. Marcelli Conf. — *Gr*. S. Marcelli Mart.	16 S. Marcelli — *At his title in the Via Lata.*
	17 S. Antonii — *At his church, formerly the basilica of Junius Bassus in Exquiliis.*
18 *Gr*. S. Priscae — *W*. S. Priscae.	18 SS. Aquilae et Priscae — *At their title on the Aventine.*
19 *G*. SS. Marii etc.	19 SS. Marii et Marthae — *At their cemetery in the Via Aurelia.*
20 *G*. S. Sebastiani, S. Fabiani—*Gr*. S. Fabiani, S. Sebastiani — *W*. Nat. S. Sebastiani, Nat. S. Fabiani.	20 SS. Fabiani et Sebastiani — *" Ad Catacumbas " on the Via Appia.*
21 *G*. S. Agnetis de passione sua — *Gr*. S. Agnae — *W*. S. Agnae de pass.	21 S. Agnetis — *At her basilica on the Via Nomentana.*
22 *Gr*. S. Vincentii — *W*. S. Vincentii, S. Anastasii.	22 SS. Vincentii et Anastasii — *At " Aquas Salvias " on the Via Ostiensis.*
	23 S. Emerentianae — *At the basilica Nomentana.*
	25 Conv. S. Pauli — *At the basilica of St. Paul.*
28 *G*. In nat. S. Agnetis de nativitate — *Gr*. S. Agnae II° — *W*. S. Agnae de nativit.	28 S. Agnetis secundo — *At the basilica Nomentana.*
	29 SS. Papiae et Mauri — *At the basilica Nomentana.*
	31 SS. Cyri et Johannis — *At their basilica on the Via Portuensis.*

[1] These topographical indications shew the local character of the feasts in the Calendar of St. Peter's.

FEBRUARY

Epigraph. Coemeter.	Latereulus Philocalian.	
	Deposit. Episc.	Natalitia Martyr.
ann. 401, Feb. 11, cemet. St. Paul (S. Soteris) HIC · POSITVS · EST BITALIS · PISTOR MIA HIC ES RG XII QVI BICXIT AN · NVS PL MINVS N XLV DEPO SITVS IN PACI . . . DEP · IN NATALE · D OMNE SITIRETIS TERT TIVM IDVS FEBR · CONSVLA TVM FL VINCENTI · VVC CONSS	22	Natale Petri de Ca- thedra.

MARCH

	5 Luci *in Callisti.* 7	Perpetuae et Feli- citatis Africae.

APRIL

	12 Juli *in via au- relia*, mill. III *in Calisti.*	
Cemetery of Callixtus (S. Gaius) Γαιο Υ ΕΠΙ σκοπ KAT ΠΡο . . . ι KAL ΜΑΙΩ ν	22 Gai *in Calisto.*	

FEBRUARY

Sacramentaria	Kalend. Vaticanum
2 *G.* Purif. S. Mariae — *Gr.* Yppapanti.	2 Purificat. B. M. V. — *S. Simeonis.*
	3 S. Blasii — *At his abbey " ad Captum secculae."*
5 *G.* S. Agathae — *Gr.* S. Agathae.	5 S. Agathae — *At her various ancient churches, amongst which the one called Gothorum, reconciled by Gregory the Great.*
	10 S. Scholasticae.
11 *G.* S. Soteris, SS. Valentini, Vitalis et Feliculae — *Gr.* S. Valentini — *W.* S. Valentini.	11 S. Valentini — *At his cemetery on the Via Flaminia.*
17 *G.* S. Julianae.	
	22 Cathedra S. Petri qua primum Romae sedit. — *At S. Peter's.*
	24 S. Matthiae Apost. — *At S. Maria Maggiore.*

MARCH

7 *G.* SS. Perpetuae et Felicitatis.	
	10 SS. XL. Martyr. — *At their church in the Trastevere.*
12 *Gr.* S. Gregorii.	12 S. Gregorii Pap. — *At S. Peter's and at S. Andrew's at the Clivus Scaurus.*
	21 S. Benedicti — *In various Roman abbeys.*
25 *G.* Adnunciat. S. Mariae — *Gr.* Adnunc. S. Mariae.	25 Annunc. B. M. Virg. — *At S. Maria Maggiore.*

APRIL

13 *G.* S. Euphimiae.	
14 *L.* S. Tiburtii etc. — *Gr.* S. Tiburtii etc.	14 SS. Tiburtii, Valeriani et Maximi — *At the title of St. Caecilia.*
23 *L.* S. Georgii ? — *Gr.* S. Georgii.	23 S. Georgii — *At his title in the Velabrum.*
25 *Gr.* Letania maior.	25 S. Marci — *At the title of St. Mark.*
	26 S. Cleti — *At S. Peter's.*
28 *Gr.* S. Vitalis — *W.* S. Vitalis.	28 S. Vitalis — *At his title at the foot of the Quirinal.*

MAY

Epigraph. Coemeter.	Latereulus Philocalian.	
	Deposit. Episc.	Natalitia Martyr.
Graffit. in the Cemetery of Callixtus		
III id. Febr. Partheni Mart. Caloceri Mart.	19 Natal. Mart. Partheni et Caloceri *in Calisti*, Dioclet. IX et Maximiano VIII *conss.* (*ann.* 304).	

MAY

Sacramentaria	Kalend. Vaticanum
1 G. SS. Philippi et Jacobi — Gr. SS. Philippi etc. — W. SS. Philippi et Jacobi.	1 SS. Philippi et Jacobi — At their title.
3 G. S. Juvenalis, Invent. S. Crucis — Gr. SS. Alexandri, Eventii et Theoduli — W. SS. Alexandri, Eventii et Theodoli.	3 Inventio S. Crucis — SS. Alexandri, Eventii et Theoduli — In their cemetery in the Via Nomentana.
	5 Translatio S. Stephani — In the Agro Verano.
6 Gr. S. Johannis ante portam latinam.	6 S. Johannis ante portam Latinam — In the Via Latina.
	8 Apparitio S. Angeli — In his basilica in Piscaria.
10 Gr. SS. Gordiani et Epimachi — W. S. Gordiani.	10 SS. Gordiani et Epimachi — In the Via Latina.
12 G. SS. Nerei, Achillei et Pancratii — Gr. S. Pancratii — W. SS. Nerei et Achillei, Nat. S. Pancratii.	12 SS. Pancratii, Nerei et Achillei — In their respective cemeteries in the Via Aurelia and the Via Ardeatina.
13 Gr. Nat. S. Mariae ad Martyres.	
	14 S. Bonifatii — At his church on the Aventine.
19 W. Nat. Pudentianae.	19 S. Pudentianae — At her title on the Viminal.
25 Gr. S. Urbani.	25 S. Urbani Pap. — At his basilica near the Via Appia.
	26 S. Eleutheri Pap. — At S. Peter's.
	27 S. Johannis Pap. — At S. Peter's.
	31 S. Petronillae — In the cemetery of Domitilla in the Via Ardeatina, then at S. Peter's.

JUNE

Epigraph. Coemeter.	Laterculus Philocalian.	
	Deposit. Episc.	Natalitia Martyr.
	29	Petri *in Catacumbas* et Pauli *Ostense.* Tusco et Basso Consulibus (*ann.* 258).

JUNE

Sacramentaria	Kalend. Vaticanum
1 *Gr*. Dedicat. S. Nicomedis.	1 S. Nicomedis — *At his own title.*
2 *G*. SS. Petri et Marcellini — *Gr*.SS. Marcellini et Petri — *W*. SS. Marcellini et Petri.	2 SS. Petri et Marcellini. S. Erasmi — *At their own title. The feast of S. Erasmus was kept at his own monastery on the Coelian.*
9 *W*. SS. Primi et Feliciani.	9 SS. Primi et Feliciani — *At S. Stefano, on the Coelian.*
	11 S. Barnabae.
12 *G*. SS. Cyrini, Naboris et Nazarii — *W*. S. Basilidis.	12 SS. Basilidis, Cyrini, Naboris et Nazarii — *At their cemetery on the Via Aurelia. The church of S. Basilides in the Via Merulana was restored by S. Leo III.*
15 *G*. S. Viti.	15 SS. Viti, Modesti et Crescentiae — *At their own diaconal title.*
18 *G*. SS. Marci et Marcelliani — *Gr*. SS. Marci et Marcelliani — *W*. SS. Marci et Marcelliani.	18 SS. Marci et Marcelliani — *At their title.*
19 *G*. SS. Gerbasii et Protasii — *Gr*. SS. Protasii et Gervasii — *W*. SS. Gerbassi Protassi.	19 SS. Gervasii et Protasii — *At their title of Vestina.*
23 *G*. Vig. S. Johannis Bapt. — *Gr*. Vigilia S. Johannis Bapt. — *W*. Vig. Joh. Bapt.	
24 *L*. Nat. S. Johannis Bapt. — *G*. Nat. S. Johannis Bapt. — *Gr*. Nat. S. Johannis — *W*. S. Johannis Bapt.	24 Nativ. S. Johannis Bapt. — *At the Lateran.*
25 *G*. In vig. Mart. Johannis et Pauli.	
26 *L*. SS. Johannis et Pauli — *G*. In nat. SS. Johannis et Pauli — *Gr*. SS. Johannis et Pauli — *W*. SS. Johannis et Pauli.	26 SS. Johannis et Pauli — *At their title on the Coelian.*
28 *G*. In Vigil. Apost. — *Gr*. Nat. S. Leonis — *W*. Vig. Apost.	28 S. Leonis secundo — *At S. Peter's in Vaticano.*
29 *L*. Nat. SS. Petri et Pauli — *G*. In nat. Apost. Petri et Pauli — *W*. Nat. Apost. Petri et Pauli.	29 SS. Petri et Pauli — *At the Vatican and in the Via Ostiensis, in their basilicas.*
30 *Gr*. Natal. S. Pauli — *W*. Ad S. Paulum.	30 Comm. S. Pauli — *At his own basilica in the Via Ostiensis.*

JULY

Epigraph. Coemeter.	Late.reulus Philocalian.	
	Deposit. Episc.	Natalitia Martyr.
Basilica of S. Maria in Trastevere, origin unknown 　　(SS. Seven Brothers Martyrs) 　　　　　　　P SCLEMINA INACE QVE VIXIT A ET HABE DEPOVSIONE DIE VO DIE MCVRII IRIDIE MARTVROrum. ORA IV IN PACE VIS VIXIT AN N		
Cemetery of SS. Processus and Martinianus[1] PECORI DVLCIS ANIMA BENIT IN CIMITERIO VII ID IVL DEP POSTE 　　　　　　MARTVRORV		RA DIE
	10	Felicis et Philippi *in Priscillae; et in Jordanorum* Martialis, Vitalis, Alexandri; *et in Maximi* Silani (hunc Silanum martyrem Novati furati sunt); *et in Praetextati* Januarii.
On the cornices of a sepulchral shrine in the cemetery of Priscilla. MARTIRVM FILICIS FILIPPI VITA(lis)　　MART(ialis) (natalis VI id) IVLIAS		
Graffito in the cemetery of Pontian DIE IIII NAT SC̄I MILIX MART etc.		
[1] The dead body was brought to the cemetery on July 9, but was buried on July 11, the day after the *natalis* of the Seven Martyrs. All the difficulties raised by certain archeologists who seek to prove July 9 to be the *dies martyrorum* on the supposition that SS. Processus and Martinianus have an Octave, are without real foundation. The body of Pecorius was certainly taken to the cemetery on July 9, but the actual interment took place two days later, on July 11.	30	Abdos et Semnes *in Pontiani*, quod est ad Ursum Pileatum.

JULY

Sacramentaria	Kalend. Vaticanum
2 *Gr.* SS. Processi et Martiniani. — *W.* SS. Processi et Martiniani.	2 SS. Processi et Martiniani — *At their own cemetery in the Via Aurelia.*
6 *G.* In Oct. Apostol. — *Gr.* Oct. Apost. — *W.* Oct. Apostol.	6 Octav. Apostol. — *At the Vatican and in the Via Ostiensis.*
10 *L.* SS. Mm. Felicis, Philippi *in coemet. Priscillae.* Vitalis, Martialis et Alexandri *in coemet. Jordanorum,* et Silani *in coemet. Maximi via Salaria,* et Januarii *in coemet. Praetextati via Appia* — *Gr.* SS. VII Fratrum — *W.* Nat. VII Fratrum, *Appia, Salaria.* Prima missa ad Aquilonem, secunda ad S. Alexandrum, ad S. Felicitatem.	10 SS. VII Fratrum. SS. Rufinae et Secundae — *At their respective cemeteries and for the two martyrs of Silva Candida, at the Lateran baptistery.*
	12 SS. Naboris et Felicis. S. Pii.
	13 S. Anacleti — *At S. Peter's.*
	15 SS. Cyri et Johannis — *In the Via Portuensis.*
	17 S. Alexii — *At his church on the Aventine.*
	18 SS. Symphorosae et filior. — *At S. Angelo in Pescheria.*
21 *W.* S. Praxedis.	21 S. Praxedis — *At the title of the same name on the Esquiline.*
	22 S. Mariae Magdal. — *At her own church at the Vatican.*
23 Nat. S. Apollinaris.	23 S. Apollinaris — *At his various churches at the Vatican etc.*
	24 S. Christinae.
	25 S. Jacobi.
	26 S. Pastoris — *At his own title on the Viminal.*
	27 S. Pantaleonis — *At his various churches.*
	28 S. Nazarii, S. Victoris — *S. Vittore in the Via Aurelia.*
29 *G.* SS. Simplicii, Faustini et Viatricis — *Gr.* S. Felicis. SS. Simplicii, Faustini et Viatricis — *W.* SS. Felicis, Simplicii etc.	29 S. Felicis. SS. Simplicii, Faustini et Viatricis — *At their basilicas in the Via Portuensis.*
30 *G.* SS. Abdo et Senis — *Gr.* Abdom et Sennem — *W.* SS. Abdon et Sennem.	30 SS. Addon. et Sennen. — *At the cemetery of Pontian in the Via Portuensis.*

AUGUST

Epigraph. Coemeter.	Laterculus Philocalian.	
	Deposit. Episc.	Natalitia Martyr.
	2 Steffani *in Calisti.*	
	6	Xisti *in Calisti et in Praetextati;* Agapiti et Felicissimi
	8	Secundi, Carpofori, Victorini et Severani *in Albano;* et Ostense VII Ballistaria, Cyriaci, Largi, Crescentianae, Memmiae, Smaragdi.
	10	Laurentii *in Tiburtina.*
	13	Ypolithi *in Tiburtina,* et Pontiani *in Calisti.*
	22	Timothei *Ostense.*
	28	Hermetis *in Basillae, Salaria Vetere.*

AUGUST

Sacramentaria	Kalend. Vaticanum
1 *G.* Nat. Machabeorum.	1 Dedic. S. Petri ad Vincula — *At his title on the Esquiline.* — SS. Machabeorum — *At S. Pietro in Vincoli.*
2 *L.* Stephani *in coemet. Callisti* — *W.* S. Stephani Pontificis.	2 S. Stephani pap. — *At the cemetery of Callixtus.*
	3 Inventio S. Stephani — *At S. Lorenzo al Verano.*
	4 S. Justini — *At S. Lorenzo.*
6 *L.* Xisti *in Callisti*, Felicissimi et Agapiti *in Praetextati Via Appia* — *G.* S. Xisti — *W.* SS. Xisti, Felicissimi et Agapiti.	6 S. Xysti, Felicissimi, et Agapiti — *In the Via Appia.*
7 *G.* S. Donati.	7 S. Donati — *At his own churches on the Aventine and near the Pons Ælius.*
8 *W.* S. Cyriaci.	8 S. Cyriaci — *At his own title on the Quirinal.*
9 *G.* Vig. S. Laurentii — *W.* Vig. S. Laurentii.	9 S. Romani — *At S. Lorenzo.*
10 *L.* S. Laurentii — *G.* S. Laurentii — *W.* S. Laurentii in prima missa. In missa publica.	10 S. Laurentii — *At his own basilica.*
11 *G.* S. Tiburtii.	11 S. Tiburtii — *At the cemetery ad duas lauros in the Via Labicana.*
12 *W.* S. Eupli.	12 SS. Eupli et Leucii — *At their own church in the Via Ostiensis, built by Pope Theodore* (642-49).
13 *L.* SS. Yppolithi et Pontiani — *G.* S. Yppolithi — *W.* S. Yppolithi.	13 S. Hippolyti — *At his own cemetery in the Via Tiburtina.*
14 *W.* S. Eusebii.	14 S. Eusebii — *At his own title on the Esquiline.* —
15 *Gr.* Assumptio S. Mariae.	15 Assumptio S. Mariae — *At S. Maria Maggiore.*
17 *G.* Oct. S. Laurentii.	
18 *L.* S. Agapiti — *G.* S. Agapiti — *W.* S. Agapiti.	18 S. Agapiti — *At his basilica on the Esquiline.* —
19 *G.* S. Magni.	
22 *W.* S. Timothei.	22 S. Timothei — *At the basilica in the Via Ostiensis.*
	24 S. Aureae — *At her own church.*
	25 S. Bartholomaei — *At his basilica on the island in the Tiber.*
27 *G.* S. Ruffi.	
28 *Gr.* S. Hermis — *W.* S. Hermae.	28 S. Hermetis — S. Augustini — S. Hermes, *feast at his cemetery.*
29 *G.* In die passionis b. Johannis B. —	

SEPTEMBER

Epigraph. Coemeter.	Laterculus Philocalian.	
	Deposit. Episc.	Natalitia Martyr.
Cemetery of Hermes (S. Hyacinthus, Martyr) DP. III IDVS SEPTEBR YACINTHVS MARTYR	5	Aconti *in Porto* et Nonni et Herculani et Taurini.
	9	Gorgonii *in Lavicana.*
	11	Proti et Jacinti *in Basillae.*
	14	Cypriani *Africae, Romae* (Cornelii) *celebratur in Calisti.*
Near the Baths of Diocletian (SS. Maurus and Papias) SANCTIS · MARTYRIBVS PAPRO · ET · MAVROLEONI DOMNIS · VOTVM · REDD. ☧ CAMASIVS QVI ET ASCLEPIVS · ET VICTORIN NAT · H̄ · DIE · IIIX · KAL · OCTOB [1] PVERI · QVI · VOT · H · VITALIS · MARANVS ABVNDANTIVS · TELESFOR	16	
Discovered in 1884 in the Trastevere (SS. Victor, Felix, Emerentiana and Alexander) XVI · KAL. OCTOB. MARTYRORVum in Cimi TERV MAIORE VICTORIS FELIcis EMERENTIANETIS ET ALEXANdri		
Cemetery of Hermes (S. Basilla, Mart.) DOMINA BASILLA COM MANDAMVS TIBI CRES CENTINVS ET MICINA FILIANOSTRA CRESCEN QVE VIXIT MENS X ET DES 🐟	22	Basillae, *Salaria Vetere;* Dioclet. IX et Maximiano VIII *conss.*
	26 Eusebii *in Calisti.*	

[1] The date of the death of the martyrs Papias and Maurus is an error. It should be *XVI Kal. Octobris.*

SEPTEMBER

Sacramentaria	Kalend. Vaticanum
1 *G.* In nat. S. Prisci.	1 S. Aegidi — *At his church near S. Pietro in Vaticano.* 2 S. Antonini.
8 *G.* Nativ. S. Mariae — *W.* S. Hadriani. 9 *G.* S. Gurgonii. 11 *W.* SS. Proti et Hyacinthi. 14 *L.* SS. Cornelii et Cypriani — *Gr.* Exalt. S. Crucis — *W.* S. Cornelii. 15 *W.* S. Nicomedis. 16 *L.* S. Euphemiae, Nat. S. Caeciliae[1] — *G.* SS. Cornelii et Cypriani — *W.* SS. Luciae et Euphemiae.	8 Nativ. B. M. Virg. S. Hadriani — *Feast at the basilica of S. Adrian in the Forum.* 9 S. Gorgonii — *In the Via Labicana " ad duas lauros."* 11 SS. Proti et Hyacinthi — *At the cemetery of Hermes in the Via Salaria.* 14 Exaltatio S. Crucis — SS. Cornelii et Cypriani — *At the cemetery of Callixtus and at the title of Cornelius in the Trastevere.* 15 S. Nicomedis — *At his own cemetery in the Via Nomentana.* 16 S. Euphemiae — *At her own churches at the " Vicus Patricius" and near the Forum of Trajan* — SS. Luciae et Geminiani. 21 S. Matthaei — *At his own title in the Via Merulana.*
	22 S. Mauritii — *At S. Peter's.*
	23 S. Lini, S. Theclae — *At S. Peter's.* 25 S. Eustachii — *At his own basilica.*
27 *G.* SS. Cosmae et Damiani — *W.* SS. Cosmae et Damiani. 29 *L.* Nat. basilicae Angeli *in Salaria* — *G.* S. Archang. Michaelis — *W.* Dedicatio Ecclesiae S. Angeli.	27 SS. Cosmae et Damiani — *At their own basilica in the Forum.* 29 Dedicatio S. Angeli — *At his own basilica near Castel Giubileo, in the Via Salaria.* 30 S. Hieronymi — *At S. Maria Maggiore.*

[1] This date is given both in the Martyrology of St. Jerome and in the Gelasian Sacramentary, but the latter has transferred it to November 22, on which day may have been celebrated the *natalis*, or anniversary of the consecration of the basilica. The Leonine Sacramentary, and together with it, all Roman liturgical tradition consider November 22 to be the true date of the feast of St. Cecilia. The tradition evidenced by the rubric of

OCTOBER

Epigraph. Coemeter.	Latereulus Philocalian.	
	Deposit. Episc. 7 Marci *in Balbi-nae.*	**Natalitia Martyr.**
October 11, Cemetery of S. Agnes (S. Marcus Pap.) IN PACE ABVNDANTIVS ACOL 🖋 REG QVARTE $\overline{TT}$ · VESTINE QVI VIXIT ANN · XXX DEP · IN · P · D · NAT $\overline{SCI}$ MARCI MENSE OCT · $\overline{IND}$ XII 🖋		
Cemetery of Commodilla[1] (S. Asterius) PASCASIVS VIXIT PLVS MINVS ANNVS XX FECIT FATV IIII IDVS OCTOBRIS ÇII AN TE NATALE DOMNI AS TERI DEPOSITVS IN PACE A 🜨 ∞	14	Calisti *in Via Au-relia* mil. III.

[1] The deceased died October 12, but was laid in the tomb October 14, eight days before the feast of S. Asterius which occurs October 21. *Apud Ostia Tiberina S. Asterii presb. et Mari.*

OCTOBER

Sacramentaria	Kalend. Vaticanum
7 *G.* SS. Marcelli et Apuleii — *Gr.* S. Marci — *W.* S. Marci.	7 S. Marci, SS. Sergii et Bacchi — *S. Mark at his title ; Sergius and Bacchus at their various churches in the Forum, on the Esquiline, etc.* 9 SS. Dionysii, Rustici et Eleutheri — *At the churches of S. Dionysius in Vaticano, at the Forum, etc.*
14 *Gr.* S. Callisti — *W.* S. Callisti Pontificis.	14 S. Callisti — *At the title of Callistus in Trastevere.* 18 S. Lucae — *At his church on the Esquiline, now destroyed.* 25 SS. Chrysanthis et Dariae — *At the cemetery of the Giordani in the Via Salaria and at the SS. XII Apostoli.* 26 S. Evaristi — *At S. Peter's.* 28 SS. Symonis et Judae — *At S. Peter's in the Vatican.* 30 S. Germani Capuani ep. 31 S. Quintini.

NOVEMBER

Epigraph. Coemeter.	Laterculus Philocalian.	
	Deposit. Episc.	Natalitia Martyr.
	8	Clementis, Semproniani, Claudii, Nicostrati *in comitatum.*
	29	Saturnini *in Trasonis.*

NOVEMBER

Sacramentaria	Kalend. Vaticanum
1 *Gr.* S. Caesarii — *W.* S. Caesaris.	1 Omnium Sanctorum — *Feast at the " Pantheon "* — S. Caesarii — *Feast at his churches at the Lateran, on the Palatine, on the Appian Way ; and at the monastery close to the basilica of S. Paul.*
8 *L.* SS. Coronatorum — *G.* SS. Coronatorum — *Gr.* SS. Coronatorum — *W.* Quatuor Coronat.	8 SS. Coronatorum — *At their title on the Coelian.*
9 *Gr.* S. Theodori — *W.* S. Theodori.	9 S. Theodori — *At his basilica near the Palatine.*
	10 S. Triphonis — *At his basilica.*
11 *Gr.* S. Mennae, S. Martini — *W.* S. Mennae.	11 S. Martini — *At his various basilicas.* — S. Menna — *At his church on the Via Ostiensis.*
12 S. Martini ep.	12 S. Martini pap. — *At his basilica on the Esquiline where originally the feast of the Wonderworker of Tours was kept on this day. Only later did the Pope of the same name come into consideration. He died September 16, 655.*
	13 S. Johannis Chrysostomi — *In Vaticano.*
21 *G.* Vig. S. Caeciliae.[1]	
22 *L.* S. Caeciliae — *G.* S. Caeciliae. — *Gr.* S. Caeciliae — *W.* S. Caeciliae.	22 S. Caeciliae — *At her basilica in Trastevere.*
23 *L.* S. Clementis, S. Felicitatis — *G.* S. Clementis et S. Felicitatis — *Gr.* S. Clementis, S. Felicitatis — *W.* S. Clementis, S. Felicitatis.	23 S. Clementis — *At his title.*
24 *L.* S. Chrysogoni et Gregorii (?) — *Gr.* S. Chrysogoni — *W.* S. Chrysogoni.	24 S. Chrysogoni — *At his title.*
	25 S. Catharinae — *At her churches in the Vatican, near the theatre of Pompey, etc.*
29 *G.* SS. Saturnini, Chrysantis, Mauri, Dariae et aliorum, Vig. S. Andreae — *Gr.* S. Saturnini, Vig. S. Andreae — *W.* S. Saturnini, Vig. S. Andreae.	29 S. Saturnini — *At the cemetery of Thrason, and at his church on the Quirinal.*
30 *L.* S. Andreae — *Gr.* S. Andreae — *W.* S. Andreae.	30 S. Andreae — *At his churches in the Vatican, at the Clivus Scaurus, etc. .*

[1] The original order has been altered, for the Gelasian Sacramentary has on November 22 the Mass *in Natali S. Caeciliae X Kalend. Oct.* The feast here in question is the "*natalis*" of September 16, so given in the Martyrology of S. Jerome.

DECEMBER

Epigraph. Coemeter.	Feriale Liberian.	
	Deposit. Episc.	Natalitia Martyr.
	8 Eutichiani *in Calisti.*	
	13	Aristonis *in Portum.*
	27 Dionysii *in Calisti.*	
	30 Felicis *in Calisti.*	
	31 Silvestri *in Priscillae.*	

DECEMBER

Sacramentaria	Kalend. Vaticanum
	2 S. Bibianae — *At her basilica.*
	4 S. Barbarae — *At her various churches —* S. Juliana.
	5 S. Saba — *At his monastery on the Aventine.*
	6 S. Nicolaus — *At his various churches —* S. Savini.
7 *G.* Oct. S. Andreae.	7 S. Ambrosii — *At his various churches.*
	10 S. Damasi — *At his title.*
13 *Gr.* S. Luciae.	13 S. Luciae — *At her various churches —* S. Eustratii.
21 *G.* S. Thomae.	21 S. Thomae — *At S. Thomas in Formis, on the Coelian and elsewhere.*
	23 S. Gregorii Spolet.
24 *G.* Vig. Nat. Dñi — *Gr.* Vig. Nativ.	
25 *L.* Pastoris, Basilei et Soviani et Victorini et Eugeniae et Felicitatis et Anastasiae — Natal. Dñi — *G.* Nat. Dñi — *Gr.* Nat. Dñi.	25 Nativ. Dñi, S. Anastasiae — *This latter feast at her own title —* S. Eugeniae — *At her cemetery in the Via Latina.*
26 *G.* S. Stephani — *Gr.* S. Stephani.	26 S. Stephani — *At his title on the Coelian and in the ancient oratory near the basilica of S. Paul.*
27 *L.* S. Johannis Ev. — *G.* S. Johannis — *Gr.* S. Johannis.	27 S. Johannis — *At S. Maria Maggiore and at the Lateran.*
28 *L.* SS. Innocentium — *G.* SS. Innocentium — *Gr.* SS. Innocentium.	28 SS. Innocentium — *At S. Paul's.*
31 *L.* S. Silvestri — *Gr.* S. Silvestri.	31 S. Silvestri — *At the cemetery of Priscilla and at his own basilica within the city.*

To these documents of great importance and wide interest it will not be amiss to add the twofold *notitia Nataliciorum* from the Basilica of San Silvestro *in Capite,* a most valuable source for the history of the *cultus* of many of the early martyrs who are not found in the Roman Calendar, although the old pilgrim itineraries bear witness to the early fame of their tombs in the catacombs.

We shall give the first place, on account of its erudition, to the splendid inscription placed by Pope Damasus in the papal crypt of the cemetery of Callixtus, which recalls all the records of the saints buried in that famous necropolis.

HIC · CONGESTA · IACET · QVAERIS · SI · TVRBA · PIORVM

CORPORA · SANCTORVM · RETINENT · VENERANDA · SEPVLCRA

SVBLIMES · ANIMAS · RAPVIT · SIBI · REGIA · CAELI

HIC · COMITES · XYSTI · PORTANT · QVI · EX · HOSTE · TROPAEA [1]

HIC · NVMERVS · PROCERVM · SERVAT · QVI · ALTARIA · CHRISTI [2]

HIC · POSITVS · LONGA · VIXIT · QVI · IN · PACE · SACERDOS [3]

HIC · CONFESSORES · SANCTI · QVOS · GRAECIA · MISIT [4]

HIC · IVVENES · PVERIQVE · SENES · CASTI · QVE · NEPOTES

QVIS · MAGE · VIRGINEVM · PLACVIT · RETINERE · PVDOREM

HIC · FATEOR · DAMASVS · VOLVI · MEA · CONDERE · MEMBRA

SED · CINERES · TIMVI · SANCTOS · VEXARE · PIORVM [5]

[1] The four deacons who, together with Pope Xystus, were surprised by pagan soldiers while celebrating the Eucharist, and all killed in the same cemetery of Callixtus; the other two deacons, Felicissimus and Agapitus, were buried in the neighbouring necropolis of Praetextatus, while Laurence the archdeacon, who was killed three days later, was laid in the cemetery of Cyriaca.

[2] *Numerus procerum*—that is to say, the series of Pontiffs of the third century who were buried near Xystus II in what was on that account called the papal crypt.

[3] *Longa qui vixit in pace sacerdos*—that is, Pope Melchiades, who lived to see the triumph of the Church under Constantine.

[4] *Quos Graecia misit,* a special group of Greek martyrs buried in the catacombs of Callixtus—to wit, Eusebius, Marcellus, Hippolytus, Maximus, Adria, Maria, Neone, Paulina, etc.

[5] *Sed cineres timui.* Pope Damasus, in order to lie near the martyrs, although not in the holy ground of the cemetery itself, built a little distance away a sepulchral vault for himself.

† IN N̄ D̄N̄Ī · HAEC NOT NAT S̄Carum

HIC REQUIESCENTium

MENSE MART · D̄ XVIIII N̄ S̄CAR DARIAE [1]

ET HILARIAE V

MENSE ĀVG · D̄ · VIII · N · S̄CAR MEMMIAE [2]

ET IVLIANAE ✿

DIE VIIII M̄ · S̄S̄ N · S̄CAE ARTHEMIAE [3]

DIE XII M̄ · S̄S̄ N̄ S̄CAE CONCORDIAE [4]

MENSE S̄EPT · D · XXX N · S̄CAR · SOFIAE [5]

PISTIS · HELPIS ET AGAPE ✿

MENSE ŌCT · D̄ · XIII · N̄ · S̄CAE · CONCHYLE [6]

D · XVIII M · S̄S̄ · N̄ · SCAE TRIFONIAE [7]

D · XXVIII · M · S̄S̄ · N̄ · SCAE CYRILLAE

[1] Daria is the companion in martyrdom of Chrysanthus; Hilaria is one of a group of several martyrs. Both were buried in the cemetery of Thrason in the Via Salaria Nova.

[2] These two saints form part of a group of martyrs recorded on this day in the Martyrology of St Jerome as being buried in the Via Ostiensis.

[3] This saint has not been identified.

[4] This is the martyr buried in the cemetery of Hippolytus.

[5] These were venerated in the cemetery of Callixtus, and John the priest was commissioned by St Gregory the Great to convey the oils from their tombs to Queen Theodolinda at Monza.

[6] Is this a second reference to the S Concordia buried in the cemetery of Hippolytus?

[7] This is the martyr buried in the cemetery of Hippolytus and called in the old Itineraries the wife of the Emperor Decius. She suffered martyrdom together with her daughter Cyrilla.

IN N̄ D̄N̄I HAEC EST NOTITIA NATALICIORVM

S̄C̄ORVM HIC REQVIESCENTIVM *✿*

MENSE IANVARIO · DIE III · NAT · S̄C̄I ANTHERI PAPAE [1]

DIE X M̄ S̄S̄ N · S̄C̄I MILTIADIS PAPAE [2]

MENSE FEBR · DIE XI N · S̄CORUM CALOCERI ET PARTHENII [3]

MENSE MARTIO DIE II N · S̄C̄I LVCII PAPAE *✿* [4]

DIE VIII · M̄ S̄S̄ N̄ SCORVM QVORVM NOM · D̄ SCIT [5]

DIE XVIII · M̄ · S̄S̄ N̄ · S̄C̄I PYMENII PB ET M̄ART [6]

DIE XVIIII · M̄ · SS · N S̄CORVM CHRYSANTHI [7]

ET THRASONIS *✿*

DIE XXIIII · M̄ · S̄S̄ · N̄ S̄C̄I · QVIRINI · MART · [8]

MENSE APRIL · D̄ · XXII · N · S̄C̄I CAII PAPAE [9]

DIE XXV · M̄ · S̄S̄ · NA · S̄C̄I · MILITI · MART · [10]

MENSE · MAIO D̄ XII · N · S̄CORVM TROFIMI [11]

ET CALOCERI *✿*

MENSE IVLIO · DIE · XXVI · NAT S̄CORVM ZEFIRINI PAPAE

ET TARSICII MARTYRIS [12]

MENSE · AVGVSTO · DIE · VIII · NA SCORUM

QVIRIACI · LARGI · ET SMARAGDI A²CEL [13]

[1] Buried in the papal crypt of the cemetery of Callixtus and entered on this day in the Martyrology of St Jerome.

[2] Buried in the cemetery of Callixtus and entered on this day in the Martyrology of St Jerome.

[3] Buried in the cemetery of Callixtus and entered on this day in the Martyrology of St Jerome.

[4] Buried in the papal crypt of the cemetery of Callixtus and entered on this day in the Martyrology of St Jerome.

[5] These cannot be identified unless they are a group of martyrs buried in the cemetery of Callixtus and entered in the Martyrology on the fourth day of the month.

[6] Mentioned on this day in the Martyrology; he was buried in the cemetery of Pontian.

[7] This seems to be the companion of Daria, buried in the cemetery of Thrason.

[8] This is the martyr buried in the cemetery of Praetextatus.

[9] He was buried in the cemetery of Callixtus; his feast falls on this day in the Martyrology.

[10] This is the *Milix* buried near Abdon and Sennen in the cemetery of Pontian.

[11] This is the third of the group of martyrs—Quartus, Quintus and Trofinus—buried in the Via Latina near S Gordianus. S Calocerus is the martyr interred with Parthenius in the cemetery of Callixtus.

[12] These were buried together in the cemetery of Callixtus. The martyrology of St Jerome, however, places the *natalis* of St Zefirinus on December 23.

[13] This is a group of martyrs buried in the Via Ostiensis.

DIE · XIII M̄ S̄S̄ N̄A S̄CI YPPOLITI 🖋 [14]

MENSE · SEPTIMBRIO · DIE · X · N̄ S̄CI GOR

GONII ET ALIOB · QVOB · NOM̄ D̄S SCIT 🖋 [15]

DIE XX · M̄ · S̄S̄ · N̄ · S̄CI IANVARII [16] D̄ XXII N̄

S̄CORVM PAMFILI [17] ET PAVLIMITIS

MENSE · OCT · DIE · VIIII · N̄ · S̄CORVM · MVLTOR · MART̄ [18]

DIE XIII M̄ · S̄S̄ · N̄ S̄CORVM · PROIECTI ET SEBERI 🖋 [19]

MENSE NŌV · D̄ XXVII N̄ S̄ · OPTATI ET POLYCHAMI [20]

D · XI · M̄ · S̄S̄ · N̄ · S̄CORVM · VIGINTI QVINQVE 🖋 [21]

MENSE DĒC · D̄ · XXVII · N̄ S̄CI DYONISII · PAPAE [22]

D̄ · XXVIIII · M̄ · S̄S̄ · N̄ · S̄CI · NEMISI · DIACONI · [23]

[14] After being confined in the convict prison of Sardinia, his body was brought to Rome together with that of Pope Pontian, his former rival. The lawful Pontiff was buried in the papal crypt of the cemetery of Callixtus; the anti-pope, having been reconciled to Catholic unity, was interred in the Agro Verano, where his admirers afterwards raised a statue to his honour.

[15] Gorgonius was put to death at Nicomedia, and his relics were placed in the Via Labicana near those of a nameless group of martyrs to whom Pope Damasus alludes in the sepulchral inscription relating to this same Gorgonius.

[16] Since this cannot be the famous Bishop of Naples we may identify the Januarius of this day's date with the martyr of the same name buried in the crypt of Praetextatus.

[17] St Pamphylus is the name of a celebrated cemetery in the old Via Salaria; Paulinitis is unknown, unless this be a mistaken reading for Paulina, who was buried in the cemetery of Thrason.

[18] There are no means of identifying these martyrs.

[19] These are not mentioned in any of the Roman sources of the history of the saints.

[20] Both were buried near the papal crypt of the cemetery of Callixtus.

[21] The data for the identification of these saints are lacking.

[22] Buried in the papal crypt of the cemetery of Callixtus, and commemorated on this day in the Philocalian Calendar.

[23] Recorded in the Martyrology of St Jerome on October 31; he was buried in the Via Latina.

Though leaving the analysis of the various feasts mentioned in these calendars until we come to the Missal itself, we must, however, begin now to consider their general features. Above all, they are local in character. Down to the twelfth century the Roman Calendars did not ordinarily contain any but Roman saints—Roman, that is to say, either by their martyrdom or in the quasi-domiciliary sense explained above; and as, from the first, no churches were built in honour of the martyrs, save for the purpose of enclosing their relics, the ancient canon was satisfied, which ordered that the feasts of the saints, the *depositio* and the *natalis* were not to be celebrated except at their tombs. It was only after the thirteenth century, when the Roman Calendar had been spread abroad more especially through the Mendicant Orders, who had no fixed dioceses nor sees, that it became the Calendar of the Latin world, and had, in consequence, to adopt a certain international appearance which caused it to lose its primitive character.

The existing divisions of the Missal and of the Breviary, with the Proper *de tempore* and *de sanctis,* date from the end of the Middle Ages. In the old calendars the solemnities of the saints kept on fixed days are found mixed up with those offices which are movable in the course of the year—an arrangement of which we still have a typical instance in the train of feasts that come after Christmas. Both the general order and the subdivisions of the liturgical year are in like manner inspired by this same unity, or fusion, between the Sanctorale and the weekly office of the year, as may be seen from the following table :

(*a*) Christmas, and the series of Christmas feasts up to the third day after Epiphany.
   (*b*) Eight weeks[1] *post Theophaniam.*
   (*c*) Five weeks of Lent.
   (*d*) A fortnight of Passiontide.
   (*e*) Easter, with its prolongation of fifty festival days. The Ascension is kept on the fortieth day, but without a vigil (since the joyful character of Eastertide did not permit of this) and without an Octave, as all the fifty days after Easter constitute one single solemn cycle.
   (*f*) Pentecost.
   (*g*) Sundays after Pentecost, before the Feast of SS Peter and Paul. The number of these Sundays differs in different systems. The Würzburg Codex (*W*) reckons two, as does

---

[1] It is so in the Würzburg Codex (*W*); but the three weeks preparatory to Lent, introduced about the time of St Gregory, considerably shortened this cycle of Sundays after Christmas.

the Calendar of Fronteau; the Homiliary of Charlemagne, on the other hand, has three.

(h) Sundays after the Feast of the Apostles, usually seven in number.

(i) Sundays after the Feast of St Lawrence, often four or five.

(l) Sundays after the Feast of St Cyprian, or after the autumn Ember days. Sometimes there were six up to Advent, but in several lectionaries the following cycle is also found :

(m) Sundays *post S Angeli* (*dedicationem*) up to Advent.

Between Pentecost and Advent there are usually only some twenty Sundays provided for in the sacramentaries; if others were needed, they were borrowed, as is done nowadays, from the cycle of Sundays after the Epiphany.

Since the modern Calendar prefixed to the Roman Missal has no longer a purely local character, it is not to be expected that in a representative series of the saints of the universal Church the hagiographical traditions of Rome will meet with special consideration. For this reason, certain feasts which appeared in the oldest liturgical records of the Roman Church, such as those of the martyrs Calocerus and Parthenius, St Soter, SS Papias and Maurus, St Priscilla, etc., have disappeared from the Calendar of the Roman Missal without leaving any trace, their places being taken by feasts of more recent origin but of more general hagiographical importance. We cannot say merely that the *proprium de tempore* has shown a great development from the sixth century down to our own time; but some feasts have been added to it, such as the Feasts of the Holy Trinity, Corpus Christi and the Sacred Heart, to say nothing of the numerous Octaves that fill the Roman Calendar to-day, although originally the Octave, following a purely Hebrew tradition, was a special characteristic of the Paschal feast alone.

The other great feasts of our Lord, Epiphany and Pentecost, had a train of two or three festal days only, and nothing more, while towards the eighth century, in order to raise the rank of the festival of Christmas, a kind of Octave was assigned to it, consisting, however, merely of a simple stational Mass on January 1. In the Roman Missal of to-day the Octaves instituted in the Middle Ages can be all easily distinguished from those introduced at a later date. The former enjoy the privilege of a Mass proper to each day of the seven, whilst the latter monotonously repeat the same formulary, as at the Epiphany, the Ascension, Corpus Christi, etc. There are also a certain number of vigils marked in the existing Missal which were not there originally. The vigils preceding the Epiphany and the Ascension belong to this category, the reason being that the festive season in which they fall excluded such vigiliary rites with their fasts and their penitential character.

The *Sanctorale* of the Roman Missal calls for many comments, which may, however, be more suitably deferred until we come to examine the text of the Sacramentary. For the present we shall content ourselves with remarking that certain feasts occurring in the Calendar do not mark the day of the martyr's death, but that of the consecration of his church within the city, as is the case with the Churches of SS Philip and James, St Peter *in Vincoli,* St John before the Latin Gate, St Hippolytus, St Cecilia, the Machabees, etc. In Rome, indeed, at the consecration of any church it was a matter of tradition to celebrate both Mass and Office in honour of the saint from whom it took its name, a custom which differs from the modern liturgical use, in that the latter reckons the feast of the consecration of a church as among the feasts of our Lord.

However strange it may seem, the liturgical commemoration of St Agnes, on January 28, had in view, not indeed the octave of her *natalis,* as recent liturgists have imagined, but the actual birthday of the martyr. This is a liturgical anomaly, difficult to explain and only to be accounted for by the popularity of the *cultus* of this saint and the great veneration with which the early Christians regarded her.

The Feast of the Chair of St Peter on February 22, unlike the other Gallican feast of January 18, is certainly Roman in origin. It appears in the fourth century in the Philocalian Calendar, but is omitted in all succeeding Roman Sacramentaries and Roman Calendars, probably because it usually came in Lent, and therefore could not be kept at such a time. The translation of the Chair of the Apostle, too, from the cemetery *ad nymphas ubi Petrus baptizabat* to the Vatican Basilica, by displacing the topographical centre where the people were wont to meet for the celebration of that festival, may have helped to make the feast less popular, so that in the later Middle Ages it had come to be looked upon simply as a local feast of the Vatican Church.

On June 28 occurs the anniversary of the translation of the relics of St Leo the Great from the portico of the Vatican Basilica to the altar within the church which had been erected in his honour by Sergius I (687-701). This is the second liturgical commemoration kept at Rome in memory of that great Pope—*Sancti Leonis secundo;* hence it is an unfortunate misunderstanding of modern writers to assign this Feast of *Leonis secundo* to the Pontiff Leo II, whose whole reign lasted only some twelve months.

The Feast of St Cecilia on November 22 merely marks the

dedication of her titular church in the Trastevere; the anniversary of her martyrdom was kept on September 16, a festival of which traces still remain in the sacramentaries.

It is more difficult to account for the presence of St Anastasia in the morning office of Christmas Day. The saint in question is the famous martyr of Sirmium, whose *cultus*, after the translation of her relics to Byzantium, spread rapidly throughout the Byzantine world. Since the anniversary of her martyrdom fell on December 25, the festival of the martyr was celebrated in Rome at the *titulus Anastasiae* on the morning of Christmas Day itself, imitating all that took place at Constantinople, which had not as yet adopted December 25 as the feast-day of the Nativity of our Lord. In Rome the Mass at daybreak was wholly dedicated to St Anastasia, a fact which explains the apparent peculiarity of that day with its threefold stational Mass, and brings it into harmony with the liturgical rule. The midnight Mass at the Praesepe of the Liberian Basilica, *ad galli cantus*, is the vigiliary Mass; that at the title of St Anastasia forms a kind of interlude, a thing apart; it is the Byzantine commemoration of the martyr of Sirmium introduced by the Greeks into the Court Church at the foot of the Palatine; while the third Mass at St Peter's is the only true Mass of the great Christmas festival.

CHAPTER III

THE ORIGIN AND EVOLUTION OF THE "ORDINARIUM MISSAE"

LET us picture to ourselves a great palace of the Renaissance, which, through having been continuously occupied, has, in the course of centuries, suffered a succession of changes, restorations and adaptations to the tastes and habits of its various inmates. Everyone has gone to work in his own way to suit himself, so that the building, although it has preserved intact the main outlines of its early style, shows a number of later elements, reflecting all the modifications which it has undergone.

This sketch will help us to understand the history of the *Ordinarium Missae* from the day on which the Apostles gave it forth extemporaneously under the influence of the gifts of the Holy Ghost down to the present time, in which the Sacred Congregation of Rites constitutes itself the guardian and defender of its fixed and immutable form. We will now proceed to give a brief but comprehensive account of the origin and development of this important formulary.

In nomine Domini. Incipit Liber Sacramentorum de circulo anni, expositum a sancto Gregorio Papa Romano, editum ex authentico libro bibliothecae Cubiculi, scriptum: Qualiter Missa Romana celebratur.

Hoc est, in primis Introitus, qualis fuerit statutis temporibus, seu diebus festis, sive quotidianis. Deinde Kyrie eleison. *Item dicitur* Gloria in excelsis Deo, *si episcopus fuerit, tantummodo die dominico, sive festis diebus. A presbyteris autem minime dicitur, nisi solo in Pascha. Quando vero* Letania *agitur, neque* Gloria in excelsis Deo, *neque* Alleluia *canitur. Postmodum dicitur oratio. Deinde sequitur Apostolus. Item gradalis, seu Alleluia. Postmodum legitur evangelium. Deinde offertorium et dicitur oratio super oblatam. Inde dicit sacerdos excelsa voce: Per omnia saecula,* etc. . . . *Sursum corda* . . . and the consecratory anaphora follows, which includes the existing Preface with the Canon as far as the Fraction of the Host.

Such is the *Ordinarium Missae* of the Gregorian Sacramentary, which represents the Roman use in the time of Adrian I (772-795).

We notice, first of all, the absence of Psalm xlii, *Judica me,* with the versicles which follow. These owe their origin to the *Apologiae Sacerdotis* and to other prayers of private devotion which it became customary in the Middle Ages for the sacred ministers to recite, partly before approaching the altar, and partly before ascending the steps, whilst the singers were chanting the Introit. This came about naturally. The Introit was designed to give greater solemnity to the processional entrance of the Pope into the stational church, and when the Roman Liturgy spread beyond the city itself, and it thus became no longer possible to carry out the procession, the priest preferred to occupy the time during which the Introit was being sung by the cantors in reciting private prayers on his own account.

The two following prayers, *Aufer a nobis* and *Oramus te, Domine,* which the priest now recites while going up to the altar and kissing the sacred table, also take their rise in private devotion. The first of them occurs in the rite for the consecration of churches, but is of Gallican origin.

At High Mass, when the singing of the Gospel and the Creed is finished, the choir sits down, and remains seated during all the long ceremony of the Offertory and of the censing of the oblations and the altar. While offering to God the host and the chalice, the priest recites two beautiful prayers for himself; but this offering, which is of somewhat late Frankish origin, and arose from a mistaken idea of the truly preparatory character of this part of the sacred *actio*— *offertorium* signified originally merely the presentation to the priest of the offerings made by the people—seems a strange anticipation of the oblation of the Victim which, in all liturgies, takes place after the *anamnesis.* It is, first of all, necessary that the Victim should be present on the altar. This is effected through the transubstantiation of the sacred species, by which it becomes possible to make the offering to almighty God.

The existing prayers, and, generally speaking, the whole of this rite of oblation with which we are dealing, originated under the influence of the Gallican Liturgy and are found partly in the ancient Mass described in the Codex of Ratoldus, Abbot of Corbie, and partly in that other Mass edited by Menard from the Codex Tilianus.[1] Rome only accepted these prayers very late—the seated choir still seems to ignore their existence; indeed, in the fourteenth century, the *Ordo Romanus* which goes by the name of Giacomo Gaetani knows nothing at all of the great development to which the ceremony afterwards attained during the decline of the Middle Ages.

We come now to the matter of the Canon, so much discussed by liturgists, without, however, any very clear light

---

[1] *P.L.* LXXVIII, cols. 239 *sq.*

being thrown upon the subject. Less qualified even than others to attempt a solution of this problem, we shall confine ourselves to a brief examination of the documentary material available for its investigation.

The consecratory anaphora, before it was cut up and altered by so many later interpolations, preserved (as we saw in Part I of this work) from beginning to end a complete literary unity, and in those countries which followed the Roman rite bore the name of *prex, mysteria, Canon,* or *agenda.* It is *prex* in the well-known passage from St Gregory the Great: *Orationem vero Dominicam idcirco mox post* precem *dicimus . . . et valde mihi inconveniens visum est, ut* precem *quam scholasticus composuerat,* etc.[1] The word had already been used by St Cyprian in this sense in the third century.

St Ambrose calls the consecratory anaphora *mysterium: Nos autem quotiescumque Sacramenta sumimus, quae per* sacrae orationis mysterium *in carnem transfigurantur.*[2]

The word *canon* duly occurs in the writings of St Gregory the Great—*Orationem dominicam mox post* Canonem *dici statuistis*[3]—but there are earlier traces of it in those of Pope Vigilius (538-55): *Quapropter et ipsius* Canonicae precis *textum direximus.*[4]

The question now arises, What are the limits of the Canon? Does it include the Preface, as in the Gelasian Sacramentary, which has the words *Incipit Canon actionis* before the invitation *Sursum corda,* or does the Canon begin only with the prayer *Te igitur* after the Trisagion and continue as far as the *Pater Noster?*

Here we have to distinguish between the medieval tradition, represented by several codices of the Gregorian Sacramentary, and the primitive custom of Rome. The secret character, the special rhythm and the authority of not a few manuscripts certainly tend to place the commencement of the Canon at the words *Te igitur;* but this use is, without any doubt, later than the primitive patristic tradition, according to which the invitation of the priest, *Sursum corda,* is the true preface to the *prex,* which both in the countries of Latin rite and in the Eastern anaphoras included the present Preface, the Trisagion and the following prayers. We will quote St Cyprian by way of example: *Quando autem stamus ad orationem, fratres dilectissimi, invigilare et incumbere ad preces toto corde debemus. . . . Ideo et sacerdos ante orationem, prefatione praemissa, parat fratrum mentes dicendo: Sursum corda, ut*

[1] *Epist.,* lib. IX, Ep. xv; *P.L.* LXXVIII, cols. 956-7.
[2] *De Fide.* IV, c. x, n. 124; *P.L.* XVI, col. 667.
[3] *Epist.,* lib. IX, Ep. xii; lib. II, Ep. lix; *P.L.* LXXVII, col. 956.
[4] *P.L.* LXIX, col. 18.

dum respondet plebs: habemus ad Dominum, admoneatur nihil aliud se quam Dominum cogitare debere.[1]

St Augustine, in commenting upon that passage in St Paul's Epistle to Timothy (1 Tim. ii, 1) where he thus addresses him, *Obsecro itaque primum fieri obsecrationes, orationes, interpellationes, gratiarum actiones,* adapts it with much ingenuity to the different parts of the eucharistic liturgy: *Eligo in his verbis hoc intelligere quod omnis, vel pene omnis frequentat ecclesia; ut precationes (obsecrationes) accipiamus dictas, quas facimus in celebratione sacramentorum* (the litany after the Gospel homily of the presiding ecclesiastic) *antequam illud quod est in Domini mensa incipiat benedici* (all this—*antequam . . . incipiat benedici*—falls outside the Canon, and thus forms no essential part of the sacramental *actio.*)

Orationes cum benedicitur (that portion of the Canon which precedes the consecratory formula, which St Augustine, at any rate, considered as a part by itself—consisting of so many different prayers) *et sanctificatur* (consecration) *et ad distribuendum comminuitur (oratio in fractione) quam totam petitionem* (*i.e.,* the Canon, which, notwithstanding all these different elements of which it was composed, preserved its literary unity almost intact, and formed one single prayer or *petitio) fere omnis ecclesia Dominica oratione concludit* (the *Pater Noster* which was not originally included in the Canon, but was recited after the Fraction of the sacred species). *Interpellationes, autem, sive, ut vestri codices habent, postulationes, fiunt cum populus benedicitur; tunc enim antistites, velut advocati, susceptos suos per manus impositionem misericordissimae offerunt potestati* (blessings given by the bishop before the Communion—found also in the Gallican Liturgy) *quibus peractis, et participato tanto sacramento,* gratiarum actio cuncta *concludit.*[2]

This extract from St Augustine sketches, as it were, the general outline of the Canon, but precisely because it is so general in its terms it is of little use to us in ascertaining the inner structure of this ancient prayer.

A passage from Pope Innocent (about 410) addressed to Decentius, Bishop of Gubbio, takes us a step further. The Bishop had consulted the Pope regarding various liturgical usages in which his church differed from that of Rome, and especially concerning the right place to be allotted to diptychs and to the kiss of peace in the Mass, *De nominibus vero recitandis* (*i.e.,* the names on the diptychs read by the deacon) *antequam* (*i.e.,* before the Canon and at the time of the

[1] *De Dominica Oratione,* c. **xxxi**; *P.L.* IV, col. 557.
[2] Augustini, *Epist.* CXLIX *ad Paulinum,* n. 12-17, edit. Maur., t. II, c. 508 *seq.*

Offertory), as was the Gallican custom, and also, according to Justin, the primitive use. The diptychs are, indeed, nothing else than a later development of the intercessory litany which is found in all the ancient liturgies from the very first, immediately after the reading of the Gospel and the dismissal of the catechumens : *Precem sacerdos faciat* (the eucharistic Canon) *atque eorum oblationes quorum nomina recitanda sunt* (by the deacon, while the priest goes on independently *sub secreto* with the anaphora) *sua oratione* (thus showing the twofold part of the deacon and the priest, as we still find it to-day in the East) *commendet* (here should be noticed a very important element of the Canon—viz., the *commendatio* of the offering and of the offerers, which was deeply embedded in the Canon itself) *quam superfluum sit, et ipse pro tua prudentia recognoscis, ut cujus hostiam necdum* (thus, no *offertorium,* and no *oratio post nomina* before the Preface, as in the Gallican rite) *Deo offeras* (by means, that is to say, of the *prex* uttered in the first part of the Canon) *ejus ante nomen insinues, quamvis illi incognitum sit nihil. Prius ergo oblationes sunt commendandae* (in the very body of the *prex: ut accepta habeas et benedicas haec dona,* etc. ; *Hanc igitur oblationem . . . quam tibi offerimus . . . pro his quoque,* etc. . . . *eorumque nomina adscribi jubeas in libro viventium*) *ac tunc eorum nomina quorum sunt edicenda, ut inter sacra mysteria* (*i.e.,* in the Canon and probably after the consecration) *nominentur* (*Memento, Domine, famulorum,* etc.) *non inter alia quae ante praemittimus* (the litany) *ut* (in such a manner that) *ipsis mysteriis* (by means of the consecration) *viam futuris precibus* (the intercessory prayer of which from early times one portion was recited after the anamnesis) *aperiamus.*[1]

The passage is not very clear. At the time of Pope Innocent I (402-17) the diptychs were recited at Rome by the deacon *inter sacra mysteria,* during the Canon, but apparently in two separate parts. One portion came before the prayer *Hanc igitur*—as witnesses the Leonine Sacramentary—while a second followed the consecration of the divine mysteries, *ipsis mysteriis viam futuris precibus aperiamus,* precisely as in the Roman Missal of to-day. We shall return to this subject later on.

The extract which follows is from the same Pontiff, and refers to the Kiss of Peace : *Pacem igitur asseris ante confecta mysteria* (that is, before the termination of the anaphora and the Fraction of the eucharistic Bread) *quosdam* (the Gallican and Milanese Churches, etc.) *populis imperare* (with the Ambrosian formula, *Pacem habete,* or the like) *vel sibi inter*

---

[1] Innoc. I, *ad Decentium, Ep.* XXV ; *P.L.,* t. XX, col. 553.

se sacerdotes tradere, cum post omnia (the whole of the anaphora) *quae aperire non debeo* (because of the *disciplina arcani*) *pax sit necessario indicenda* (with a formula equivalent, therefore, to those which we find in other liturgies) *per quam constet populum ad omnia quae in mysteriis aguntur atque in ecclesia celebrantur, praebuisse consensum, ac finita esse* (The anaphora is the sacrificial *actio*. The Communion, indeed, remained, but it was considered as something distinct from the sacrifice, so much so that at Rome the Pope now left the altar and returned to his throne, where he received the holy mysteries. In France, those who did not intend to approach the holy table received the bishop's blessing and left the church at this point of the Mass) *pacis concludentis* (as the conclusion of everything) *signaculo demonstrentur*.[1]

No less important for the history of the Roman Canon is a passage in a letter written by Pope Vigilius to Bishop Profuturus of Braga in 538 : *Ordinem precum in celebritate Missarum* (Canon) *nullo nos tempore, nulla festivitate significamus habere diversum, sed semper eodem tenore oblata Deo munera consecrare. Quoties vero Paschalis, aut Ascensionis Domini, et Pentecostes et Epiphaniae Sanctorumque Dei fuerit agenda festivitas singula capitula diebus apta subjungimus* (Where? Probably not at the Preface, which, from the time of Leo the Great, had been a composition complete in itself, distinct from the consecratory prayer and varying with every feast, but at some other prayer analogous to, if not identical with, our *communicantes*) *quibus* (*et memoriam celebrantes . . .*) *commemorationem sanctae solemnitatis, aut eorum facimus, quorum natalitia celebramus ; caetera vero ordine consueto prosequimur. Quapropter et ipsius canonicae precis textum direximus subter adjectum, quem, Deo propitio, ex apostolica traditione suscepimus. Et ut charitas tua cognoscat quibus in locis aliqua festivitatibus apta connectes* (phrases or formulas, therefore, to be interpolated, exactly as those which are still inserted to-day in the *Communicantes*) *paschalis diei preces* (probably the *Communicantes* with the prayer *Hanc igitur* in which intercession is made for the newly baptized) *similiter adjecimus*.[2] Thus, unlike the Frankish and the Mozarabic rites, in which every feast has its own special consecratory prayers, the Roman Canon, resembling in this respect the anaphoras of the churches of the East, is always identical and unchangeable without any really variable parts.

We will now quote other passages of lesser weight, yet not without value for the history of the Roman Canon. First in order of importance come those from the *Liber Pontificalis*.

[1] Innocentii I, *idem*.
[2] Vigilii Papae, *Epist.; P.L.* LXIX, col. 18.

(a) *Hic* (Pope Alexander I, 105-115?) *passionem Domini miscuit in predicatione* (precatione) *sacerdotum quando missae celebrantur.*[1] Many liturgists, possibly through an anachronism, have identified this insertion with our *Qui pridie quam pateretur,* or with the *anamnesis* in which there occurs also the commemoration *beatae passionis.* May not the notice in the Pontifical perhaps refer to an anaphora—that, for example, of the Egyptian Ecclesiastical Ordinances in which is celebrated the triumph of God's goodness through the Passion of his only-begotten Son?

(b) *Hic* (Sixtus I, 115-125?) *constituit ut intra actionem* (thus the Preface at that time formed part of the Canon) *sacerdos incipiens, populus hymnum decantaret: Sanctus, Sanctus,* etc. . . .[2]

(c) *Hic* (Leo I, 440-61) *constituit ut intra actionem sacrificii* (in the oblation which follows the *anamnesis*) *diceretur: Sanctum sacrificium,* etc.[3]

(d) *Hic* (Gregory I, 590-604) *augmentavit in predicationem Canonis: diesque nostros in tua pace dispone*[4]—that is, in the prayer *Hanc igitur* in which the priest customarily made mention of the special intention for which the holy sacrifice was being offered. The sentence which Gregory added permanently to the Canon was no new one; it is found almost word for word, at the same place, in the Leonine Sacramentary at the *natali episcoporum.* . . . *Hanc igitur oblationem . . .* placatus accipias *. . . diesque meos clementissima gubernatione disponas.*[5]

(e) *Hic* (Sergius I, 687-701) *statuit ut tempore confractionis Dominici Corporis Agnus Dei . . . a clero et populo* (at Rome the *fractio* was made by the bishops and priests as well as by the Pope, and therefore occupied a certain amount of time. Hence the reason for the singing by the people at this point. Originally the Fraction of the sacred species took place at the doxology of the Canon) *decantaretur.*[6]

(f) *Presbyter qui in hebdoma fuerit* (at St Peter's in the Chapel of All Saints erected by Gregory III) *in eundem oratorium in honorem Salvatoris, Dei Genitricis,* etc., *missam faciet. Communicantes et memoriam celebrantes imprimis gloriosae semper Virginis . . . et omnium Sanctorum . . . sed et natalicium celebrantes Sanctorum tuorum Martyrum ac Confessorum, perfectorum justorum, quorum solemnitas hodie in conspectu gloriae tuae celebratur.*[7] This passage is important because, from the tenor of Pope Vigilius's letter to

---

[1] *Lib. Pontif.*, ed. Duchesne, p. 127.   [2] *idem*, pp. 56, 57.
[3] *idem*, p. 239.   [4] *idem*, p. 312.
[5] *Sacr. Leon.*, in Muratori, *Liturgia Romana Vetus*, col. 426.
[6] *idem*, p. 376.
[7] *Concil. Roman. anni 732 Decret. Cf.* Duchesne, *op. cit.*, 422.

Profuturus, it shows that in the eighth century the ritual tradition still in part survived by which an insertion was made in the *Communicantes* for the purpose of calling to mind the feasts of those saints whom it was desired to commemorate.

(*g*) *Vis scire quia verbis coelestibus consecratur? Accipe quae sunt verba. Dicit sacerdos. Fac nobis, inquit, hanc oblationem ascriptam, ratam, rationabilem, acceptabilem, quod figura est corporis et sanguinis Jesu Christi. Qui pridie quam pateretur, in sanctis manibus suis accepit panem, respexit in coelum ad te, Sancte Pater omnipotens, aeterne Deus, gratias agens benedixit, fregit, fractumque apostolis suis et discipulis suis tradidit dicens: Accipite et edite ex hoc omnes. Hoc est enim corpus meum quod pro multis confringetur. Similiter etiam calicem, postquam coenatum est, pridie quam pateretur, accepit, respexit in coelum ad te, Sancte Pater omnipotens, aeterne Deus, gratias agens, benedixit, apostolis suis et discipulis tradidit, dicens: Accipite et bibite ex hoc omnes: hic est enim Sanguis meus.*[1] (This work *De Sacramentis* is often attributed to St Ambrose, but it was more probably written by some contemporary scholar.)

Et sacerdos dicit: Ergo memores gloriosissimae eius passionis et ab inferis resurrectionis et in coelum ascensionis, offerimus tibi hanc immaculatam hostiam, hunc panem sanctum et calicem vitae aeternae; et petimus et precamur, ut hanc oblationem suscipias in sublimi altari tuo per manus Angelorum tuorum, sicut suscipere dignatus es munera pueri tui justi Abel, et sacrificium patriarchae nostri Abrahae et quod tibi obtulit summus sacerdos Melchisedech.[2] This quotation is of great importance, both because it is of the fourth century and is the fullest we possess concerning the Canon, and still more because, on comparing it with the actual text of the eucharistic prayer, it would seem that both are derived from the same Greek original, to which the *De Sacramentis* has adhered the more closely, while the Roman compiler translates it more freely and even on occasion modifies it.

(*h*) (Pope Vigilius, 538-555) *Antiqua in offerendo sacrificia traditione deposcimus, exorantes* ut catholicam fidem adunare, regere Dominus et custodire toto orbe dignetur. It is to be noted that Pope Vigilius, in quoting these words of the Canon, appeals to the ancient tradition—an indication that at Rome in his day the modifications introduced into the text of the anaphora were still unknown.[3]

(*i*) (Pope Gelasius I, 492-496) *Nam quomodo ad divini Mysterii consecrationem coelestis Spiritus invocatus adveniet?*

---

[1] *De Sacramentis*, l. IV, c. v, 21 ; *P.L.* XVI, cols. 463-4.
[2] *idem*, col. 464.
[3] Vigilii, *Epist. ad Justinianum* ; *P.L.* LXIX, col. 22.

—by means, that is, of the epiklesis which originally preceded the words of the institution of the Holy Eucharist, but which in the East in later times was placed after the *anamnesis*. The passage from Pope Gelasius in favour of the pre-consecratory epiklesis in the Roman Canon is not absolutely conclusive, since the Pontiff, in writing to Elpidius, may very well have been using an argument *ad hominem* and basing his reasoning on the anaphora of his correspondent. However, everything leads us to believe that Rome, too, like the liturgies of the Alexandrian Patriarchate, originally possessed her pre-consecratory epiklesis, and that the last relic of it is contained in these words of the prayer : *Quam oblationem . . . ut nobis fiat Corpus et Sanguis Unigeniti Filii tui*. We may here compare the Epiklesis of the three anaphoras—of Serapion, of St Mark and of the Egyptian eucharistic papyrus (published by Crum and annotated by Dom De Puniet)[1]—with the corresponding invocation in the Roman Canon.

De Sacramentis	Roman Canon	Egyptian Papyrus	Anaphora of S Mark
(*Coelestis Spiritus invocatus adveniet*) . . . fac nobis *hanc oblationem adscriptam, ratam, etc. quod figura est Corporis et Sanguinis Domini nostri Jesu Christi. Qui pridie etc.*	*Quam oblationem . . . benedictam etc. facere digneris ut nobis fiat Corpus et Sanguis Domini Nostri etc. Qui pridie etc.*	*Mittere dignare Spiritum Sanctum tuum in has creaturas et fac panem quidem corpus Domini . . . Calicem autem Sanguinem Novi Testamenti. Quia . . . qua nocte etc.*	*Reple, Domine, et hanc oblationem tua benedictione per illustrationem Spiritus Sancti tui. Quia ipse Dominus etc. . . . qua nocte tradebatur etc.*

Anaphora of Serapion	Coptic Liturgy of St Mark	Oratio Ambrosii Autperti
Reple etiam hanc oblationem tua virtute et acceptione tua, tibi enim offerimus hanc salutiferam oblationem . . . quia Dominus . . . qua nocte etc.	† R̶. *Amen. Et benedictione benedicas.* † R̶. *Amen. Et purificatione purifices.* † R̶. *Amen. Haec dona tua veneranda proposita coram te, hunc panem et hunc calicem.*	*Peto clementiam tuam, Domine, ut descendat super panem tibi sacrificandum plenitudo tuae benedictionis, et sanctificatio tuae divinitatis. Descendat etiam, Domine, illa Sancti Spiritus tui invisibilis . . . majestas . . . qui et oblationes nostras corpus et sanguinem tuum efficiat.*

We must notice, however, that the invocation of the Holy Ghost of which Gelasius speaks has no precedents, neither has it left any trace in the history of the Roman Canon. He is alluding, perhaps, to an epiklesis from some Eastern source which may have been introduced for a short time into the anaphora of the Apostolic See, and, not meeting with a

---

[1] *Cf.* Cabrol, *Dict. d'Archéologie Chrétienne et de Liturgie*, t. II, Part II, cols. 1882 *sq*.

favourable reception, quickly passed into oblivion. Certain it is that the statement made by Gelasius concerning the Holy Spirit in the Canon has undergone alteration; for we know that the existing prayer, *Quam oblationem . . . fiat nobis Corpus,* etc., addressed to God the Father rather than to the Paraclete, represents a very ancient liturgical tradition, the intention of which was essentially that of calling down the grace of transubstantiation through the intervention of almighty God. The invocation might, strictly speaking, be addressed to any one of the three Persons of the Blessed Trinity, Father, Son or Holy Ghost; however this may be, it certainly soon disappeared from the Roman formulary; but the prayer for the transubstantiation of the oblations is there and still retains its original position.

Seeing that the nature of these simple notes forbids us to go further into a discussion on the various passages, what conclusion is to be drawn from those which we have already passed under review? First of all, we have to admit that if the existing Preface originally constituted the beginning of the eucharistic anaphora and of the Canon, it does so no longer, even though in its form and in the declamatory melody with which it is clothed the Preface preserves more distinctly than the Canon itself the characteristics of a hymn of praise and thanksgiving (*tibi gratias agens*) which this prayer anciently possessed. From the time of Leo the Great, the Preface, as is clearly seen in his Sacramentary, had already become a composition complete in itself, a fixed and self-contained entity without any real literary connection with the Canon which followed. Unlike the immutable Canon, the Preface varied with every feast; so that when Pope Vigilius wrote to Profuturus that in Rome the consecratory prayer was always the same on all the festivals of the year, he had necessarily to exclude the Preface as outside the limits of the Canon.

However, the Canon began, as it does now, with the *Te igitur—igitur* is here probably a word inserted to form an arbitrary connection with something preceding; somewhat like the *vere Sanctus* of the Gallican rite, for the purpose of sustaining, in some degree, the traditional continuity of the *prex*—and all the first part (*ut accepta habeas et benedicas*) corresponds quite well to the first distinction pointed out by St Augustine in the Canon: *Orationes cum benedicitur.* Furthermore, the passage from Vigilius addressed to Justinian, *Ut catholicam fidem adunare, regere Dominus et custodire dignetur toto orbe terrarum,* quoted above, being without any doubt taken from this first part of the Roman anaphora, confirms its primitive authenticity. Moreover, there is even a fragment of an ancient Preface, quoted by an anonymous Arian writer, and published by Mai with Mercati's comments,[1] which seems to refer (without the interpolation of any Trisagion between the Preface and the Canon) to the opening sentences of our prayer : *Te, igitur . . . sacrificium istud quod tibi offerimus . . . per Jesum Christum Dominum et Deum nostrum per quem petimus et rogamus*, etc.

We come now to the mention of the Pope : *Una cum famulo tuo papa.* . . . That the Pope in his Western Patriarchate was usually mentioned by name in the Mass is beyond doubt, but the question turns upon the original place assigned to this commemoration in the Roman Canon. This extract from Pelagius I (555-60), addressed to the schismatic bishops of Tuscia[2] should be noted : *Quomodo vos ab universi orbis communione separatos esse non creditis, si mei inter sacra mysteria, secundum consuetudinem, nominis memoriam reticetis ?*[3] The commemoration of the Pope in the Mass is also mentioned in the Acts of the Roman Council assembled under Pope Symmachus (498-514); and in the discourse held by Ennodius on this occasion he thus questions the Fathers of the Council : *Deinde pro quaestionum tormentis venerabilem Laurentium* (of Milan) *et Petrum* (of Ravenna) *episcopos a communione Papae se suspendisse replicatis . . . ullone ergo tempore, dum celebrarentur ab his sacra Missarum a nominis ejus commemoratione cessatum est? Unquam pro desideriis vestris sine ritu catholico et cano more, semiplenas nominatim antistites hostias obtulerunt.*[4]

St Leo I alludes in like manner to the custom of calling to mind in the Mass the most eminent bishops with whom he was in communion : *De nominibus autem Dioscori, Juvenalis et Eustathii ad sacrum altare recitandis . . . iniquum nimis est atque incongruum eos . . . sanctorum nominibus sine discretione misceri.*[5] There is a parallel to this in the letter of the Egyptian bishop to Anatolius of Constantinople : *Etiam in venerabili diptycho, in quo piae memoriae transitum ad coelos abeuntium episcoporum vocabula continentur, quae tempore sanctorum Mysteriorum secundum sanctas regulas releguntur, suum posuit* (Timothy of Alexandria) *et Dioscori nomen.*[6]

Another quotation from St Gregory, bearing on the same custom, must not be omitted : *Quod autem . . . fratrem et coepiscopum nostrum Johannem Ravennatis Ecclesiae inter missarum solemnia nominetis, requirenda vobis consuetudo*

---

[1] G. Mercati, *Antiche Reliquie liturgiche*, Roma 1902.
[2] " Tuscia " was that part of the " Patrimony of St Peter " which was contained in Etruria (Tuscany).—Tr.
[3] Pelagii I, *Epistol.* V; *P.L.* LXIX, col. 398.
[4] Labbe, *Sacr. Conc. Nova Collectio*, t. VIII, col. 282, Venetiis 1767.
[5] Leonis I, *Epist.* LXXX; *P.L.* LIV, cols. 914-15.
[6] Cf. *P.L.* LIV, col. 1397.

antiqua est. . . . Sollicite perquirere studui si idem Johannes . . . vos ad altare nominet, quod minime dicunt fieri. Et si ille vestri nominis memoriam non facit, quae necessitas cogat ignoro, ut vos illius faciatis.[1]

The chief point arrived at from an examination of these authorities is the particular meaning given to the commemoration of the Pope in the Canon of the Mass, corresponding importance in due proportion being attached outside Rome to the mentioning by name of the other bishops with whom each prelate maintained special relations. This commemoration of the Pope was quite distinct from the diptychs—recited by the deacon—of those who made the offerings, since it was pronounced by the celebrant himself before commending to God the offerings of the people. Pelagius I said that to omit it would be equivalent to declaring oneself outside the Church, while according to Ennodius of Pavia it would render the sacrifice mutilated and incomplete. All this leads us to the conclusion that the actual position allotted to the mention of the Pope in the Canon is indeed the original and primitive one, since it exactly agrees with the evidence furnished by ancient writers. The words would run thus, *Quam tibi offerimus pro Ecclesia tua*, etc. . . . *toto orbe terrarum una cum famulo tuo Papa nostro N.*, but without the words *et omnibus orthodoxis*, etc., which represent a later addition found only in one set of manuscripts.

The next subject is that of the *Memento*, which brings us at once to the much debated question of the diptychs. These, as we saw when discussing the testimony of Pope Innocent I, were preceded by a *commendatio* spoken by the priest. They formed part of the Canon : prius *ergo oblationes sunt commendandae, ac tunc eorum nomina quorum sunt edicenda, ut inter sacra mysteria nominentur . . . ut ipsis mysteriis viam futuris precibus aperiamus.* Innocent has here two different things in mind : (1) that the priest's *commendatio* comes first of all, and (2) that the reading of the diptychs is carried out in two different parts, *inter sacra mysteria*—that is, in the body of the Canon, both before and after the Consecration.

It has been supposed that the *Memento* represents the formulary of the diptychs recited by the deacon while the priest continued the Canon at the *Communicantes*. This is a likely hypothesis, since also at Alexandria the reading of the names preceded the Consecration, although everywhere else in the East the intercessory prayers are found regularly after the *anamnesis*. In the Roman Canon we have a kind of compromise between the Alexandrian use and that of the Patriarchate of Antioch, since the diptychs of the living read

---

[1] Gregorii I, *Epistol.*, lib. IV, *Ep.* XXXIX *ad Constantium Episc.*; *P.L.* LXXVII, col. 714.

by the deacon precede the Consecration, while those of the dead come at the end of the anaphora. Both the intercessory prayers, however, betray a common Eastern origin, and still show traces of the separation which they had to undergo when at Rome it was desired to recite them in two parts, so as to complete the twofold list of the commemorations of the living and of the dead.

But how was this separation arrived at? We can only hazard hypotheses in reply. After the mention of the Catholic Church and of the Pope, *in primis quae tibi offerimus*, there should logically follow other names and other secondary commendations. We know, however, from the passages already quoted of Leo I, from the letters of the Egyptians to Anatolius, and from those of St Gregory the Great, that one of the diptychs contained the words *piae memoriae transitum ad coelos abeuntium episcoporum vocabula continentur, quae tempore sanctorum mysteriorum, secundum sanctas regulas, releguntur.* Now, this list in the Roman Canon is to be found in the *Communicantes,* and is the more important, as in this prayer alone occur the names of the first successors of St Peter, Linus and Cletus, who in early days had no other special *cultus* in Rome.

A certain harmony, too, was sought in the drawing up of the list; so, in order to give precedence to Peter and Paul, the Baptist was omitted and placed in a secondary list, that of the *Nobis quoque.* The same thing befell Matthias, for otherwise an alteration would have been made in the symbolical number twelve of the Apostles. Barnabas and Stephen, who should have taken precedence over the early Pontiffs of Rome, were also passed over and relegated to the *Nobis quoque,* so that the primitive Roman form of the episcopal diptychs was probably arranged as follows: First the Blessed Virgin, then Peter and Paul and the other ten Apostles, then Linus, Cletus, Clement, Sixtus and Cornelius, with the addition afterwards of other martyrs whose inclusion deprived these purely episcopal diptychs of their primitive character.

While the priest is commemorating the Apostles and the deceased Popes, the deacon proceeds to read out the list of those of the laity who are making the offerings, and both ceremonies come to an end together at the prayer *Hanc igitur.*

In the existing Roman Missal the *Communicantes* stands alone and is somewhat disconnected, on account of the insertion of the diptychs read by the deacon: *Memento, Domine.* It is true that this is an instance of the *lex talionis,* since the *Communicantes* in the Roman Canon is itself an interpolation of Eastern origin; but in any case there is a connection between the prayer *Te igitur* and the *Communicantes*, and the participle *communicantes* depends on the preceding verb *tibi offerimus*, while after the insertion of the *Memento*, the prayer, which, so to speak, framed in the episcopal diptychs, was left stranded and unsupported. But this is not all. The *Communicantes* underwent interpolations in its turn, interpolations so intrinsic that, according to the tradition of the manuscripts, it soon acquired the character of a variable part of the Liturgy, with the special title *infra actionem*, and that by reason of the famous *capitula diebus apta* of which Pope Vigilius speaks, which varied with each feast of the year.

The *Communicantes* still fittingly fulfils, even after so many centuries, the function of which Pope Vigilius wrote to Bishop Profuturus, and on days of great solemnity proclaims in a few words the precise aim of the festival which is being celebrated. The formula of this announcement occasionally presents features of very great antiquity, a fact which leads us to trace back its origin far beyond the time of Vigilius. This is the case with the Feast of Epiphany, on which day, scarcely any notice being taken of the Roman tradition which places the birthday of our Saviour on December 25, are used the words—corresponding exactly to the primitive conception of the festival in the East—*diem sacratissimum celebrantes, quo Unigenitus tuus in tua tecum gloria coaeternus, in veritate carnis nostrae visibiliter corporalis apparuit.* The Gelasian Sacramentary, perceiving the anachronism involved in this early formula, has attempted to correct it by simply adapting it to the particular episode of the Manifestation of our Lord to the Wise Men, but this later alteration has only succeeded in weakening the force of the original antithesis between the pre-existence of the Word in the glory of the Eternal Father, and his manifestation in time in the reality of his sacred Humanity. The Three Kings in the Gelasian Sacramentary represent a very small detail of the compiler and cause us greatly to prefer the strong primitive antithesis preserved by the Gregorian Sacramentary.

The Missal of to-day maintains almost unbroken the christological series of these *singula capitula diebus apta*, but there are wanting those relating to the feasts of the martyrs, of whom, according to Pope Vigilius, *commemorationem . . . eorum facimus, quorum natalitia celebramus.* The ancient writers, however, have preserved to us some important traces of them—for example, in that decree of Gregory III promulgated in the Roman Council of 732, in which he ordains that additional mention shall be made in the Canon : *Communicantes . . . et omnium sanctorum, sed et natalicium celebrantes sanctorum tuorum Martyrum ac Confessorum, perfectorum justorum, quorum solemnitas hodie in conspectu tuo celebratur.*

The order of these *capitula diebus apta* was as follows: The feasts of our Lord came before the mention of the Blessed Virgin, as in the present Missal, while those of the martyrs were inserted either in the text or at the foot of the page, just as in the *Communicantes* of Gregory III quoted above. Pope Vigilius alludes to the different position occupied by the insertions concerning the saints when he tells Profuturus to send him the Canon with the additions of the Easter festival, in order to show him *quibus in locis aliqua festivitatibus apta connectes.* Occasionally, however, this connection is so studied and artificial that it at once shows itself to be an interpolation. The *Communicantes* remains at times strangely disconnected, and as ill-adapted to the *capitula diebus apta* as to the list of saints which follows it.

To the early Christians the idea of being *in communione* with the Pope and with one's own bishop was very familiar. This is the ordinary and legal signification of the word *Communicantes.* Therefore the being in communion with the blessed in heaven may pass as one of its meanings, for everyone, whether Catholic or heretic, would greatly desire to be of that blessed company; but a *communicantes et diem sacratissimum Pentecostes celebrantes, quo Spiritus Sanctus Apostolis innumeris linguis apparuit, sed memoriam venerantes imprimis gloriosae semper Virginis,* etc., is hardly natural; it has a strange appearance, and looks like a passage which has been adapted to an end. We must, therefore, conclude that the mention of the feasts, the *capitula diebus apta* of Vigilius which are interpolated between the *Communicantes* and the *memoriam venerantes,* and which sometimes cause the meaning to be involved, are either not primitive, or else that it is as well, perhaps, to separate the *Communicantes* from the list of saints, so as to join it to the name of the Pope with whom communion was maintained, especially as the Canon adds *sed et memoriam venerantes* for the special purpose of emphasizing the more the distinction between the two absolutely separate ideas—*tibi offerimus pro Ecclesia tua . . . una cum famulo tuo Papa nostro communicantes sed et memoriam venerantes imprimis gloriosae,* etc.

Nor should we be surprised that the Pope's name here takes precedence even of that of the Mother of God herself. The mention of the Pope in the Canon is a proof of the orthodoxy of the offerer, and completes *ex parte subjecti,* as the scholastics would say, his priestly action—let us here call to mind the *semiplenas hostias* of Ennodius, so named because they were unaccompanied by the name of the Pope—while *ex parte objecti* the first person in whose honour the holy sacrifice is offered after God himself is she who is blessed above all other creatures.   By harmonizing the *Communicantes* with the mention of the Pope and of the bishop of the diocese, as was customary, one would have also the advantage of giving to this participle (translated, in all probability, from a Greek text in which it took the place of the subject of the sentence) the support of a finite verb, *tibi offerimus . . . communicantes, sed et memoriam venerantes,* a support which is now lacking to it and therefore causing it to be disconnected and isolated.

The series of saints mentioned in the *Communicantes* is also worthy of notice.   Peter and Paul come first after the Blessed Virgin; then, instead of following the list of the Apostles as given by St Mark, who places James and John next, we have Andrew, as in the Gospels of St Matthew and St Luke.   Thomas and James follow, although in St Mark and St Luke they are put after Philip, Bartholomew and Matthew.   Furthermore, disregarding the traditional linking together of the names of Philip and Bartholomew, Matthew and Thomas, James and Jude, the Roman Canon couples together instead Thomas and James, and closes the list of Apostles with Simon and Thaddeus.   The order followed in these last two names is that of St Luke; but the brother of James, while he is called Jude of James by the Evangelist Luke, the disciple of St Paul, here, on the other hand, is named Thaddeus, as in the Gospel of St Mark.   As may be seen from this, the plan followed by the compiler was distinctly eclectic, and no clear reason appears why the list of the Apostles inserted by him in the Canon should not wholly agree with one or other of the four lists handed down to us in Holy Scripture (Matt. x, 2; Mark iii, 16; Luke vi, 14; Acts i, 13).

After the twelve Apostles there follows a list of twelve other martyrs, representing a later compilation in which, however, it is easy to discover the original nucleus.   First come the four immediate successors of St Peter, Linus, Cletus, Clement and Sixtus, the first two of whom were inscribed among the number of the martyrs, only at a much later date, and have therefore left no trace of any *cultus* during the early centuries.   Their names are found in the *Communicantes,* as witness of that which the compiler was really desirous of inserting in that place—namely, the episcopal diptychs of the Roman Church.   We do not know if the series of St Peter's successors was at first complete, or whether, as is more likely, it was merely representative with four or five names only, as at the present day.   Because of the late origin of the *Communicantes,* we incline towards this latter hypothesis, which has the advantage of not unduly prolonging the Mass.

The Sixtus (Xystus) mentioned in the Roman Canon is the second of that name, the one who was beheaded with his six deacons in the cemetery of Callixtus while celebrating the eucharistic Synaxis. His *cultus* was very popular in Rome, as is proved by the numerous salutations scratched on the entrance wall of the papal crypt in the Appian Way. Cornelius is always accompanied by Cyprian in ancient liturgy, both by reason of the relations which the famous Carthaginian primate had with St Cornelius, and also because of the circumstance that they both died on the same day, though in different years. There is a representation of Cyprian to be seen near the tomb of Pope Cornelius, so that the medieval pilgrims used to believe that both saints rested together in the catacombs of Lucina in the Via Appia.

Lawrence, who was the archdeacon of Xystus, is only separated from him out of consideration for the episcopal dignity of SS Cornelius and Cyprian, which gives them the precedence over the staurophoros of the Roman Church. Chrysogonus, like SS John and Paul, would seem to have been inserted in the Canon at a later date, when, during the Byzantine period, the *cultus* of the great Dalmatian martyr had become widely spread even in the Eternal City itself. His body was translated from Aquae Gradatae in the district of Aquileia, where he was put to death, to Zara in Dalmatia, but the titular Church of San Grisogono in the Trastevere at Rome is certainly contemporary with the Peace of Constantine. The *cultus* of the martyrs John and Paul acquired fresh vitality in the time of Bisante and of Pammachius, when the building on the Coelian in which they were martyred, and where also they lay buried, was turned into a church. The Leonine Sacramentary bears witness to the fame of their festival in Rome, so that the insertion of their names in the Roman diptychs must with certainty date from the fourth century.

Last of all come the two holy *anargyri*, the physicians Cosmas and Damian, who at once recall the Byzantine epoch when Felix III (483-92) transformed and dedicated in their honour the *eroon* of Romulus Augustulus in the *Sacra Via*, together with the adjoining temple of the *Sacrae Urbis*. These were the last saints to be inscribed on the episcopal diptychs of Rome, which henceforth remained resolutely closed against any further insertion whatsoever, no exception being made even for St Caesarius, St Theodore, St Sebastian or St Pancras, all of whom attained to great renown in the Holy City.

After the *anargyri* should be inserted—to judge by the

tenor of Pope Vigilius's letter to Profuturus—the commemoration of that martyr whose *natalis* it was ; and that this
was actually put into practice is proved by the *Communicantes*
of Gregory III quoted above. The prayer has its usual form
of ending, *protectionis tuae muniamur auxilio*, etc., so that it
constitutes something quite complete in itself, separate and
distinct from that which follows. This, concluding the first
part of the prayer of intercession with the episcopal diptychs,
also confirms its later origin with respect to the anaphora,
which, from a literary point of view, is cut off from it.

A rubric directing the priest to place his hands on the
oblations separates the *Communicantes* from the prayer *Hanc
igitur oblationem*. The substance of this rubric is already
found in the Canons of Hippolytus, so that we can be certain
that here we have to do with a very ancient eucharistic rite.
It is necessary, first of all, to realize the full significance of
this imposition of hands, which is to be seen in a representation of the Eucharist of the third century in the cemetery of
Callixtus. The scene shows a preparatory offering and the
sanctifying of the oblations destined for the sacrifice ; and as,
in ancient times, any prayer or blessing whatsoever *super
hominem* was accompanied by the imposition of hands on the
part of the priest, it naturally was the same with the *oratio
super oblata*. In the *Hanc igitur*, indeed, we must recognize
just the most essential part of the *commendatio oblationum*
of which Innocent I writes, a part, moreover—though this is
contrary to that which his letter to the Bishop of Gubbio
might lead us to believe if it were interpreted apart from the
other Roman documents—which was so closely connected
with the recital of the diptychs that in some formularies this
recital is especially mentioned, as may be seen in the following
extracts :

SACRAMENT. LEON.	SACRAMENT. LEON.	SACRAM. GELASIANUM
Vigil. Pentec.	*Conjunctio oblationum Virginum Sacratar.*	*Vigil. Pentec.*
Hanc igitur obla-tionem . . . quam tibi offerimus pro his quos ex aqua et Spiritu Sancto regenerare dig-natus es . . . quae-sumus placatus acci-pias eorumque nomina ascribi jubeas in libro viventium.	*Hanc etiam obla-tionem . . . Virginum Sacratarum quarum ante sanctum altare tuum* nomina recitan-tur, *quaesumus placa-tus accipias*, etc.	*Hanc igitur obla-tionem . . . quam tibi offerimus pro his quoque quos ex aqua,* etc. . . . *ut* nomina eorum *adscribi jubeas in libro viventium.*

Even without always referring expressly to the reading of
the diptychs, we find that anciently the prayer *Hanc igitur*
occupied the position of a true *oratio post nomina*, so that
this was precisely the moment at which the special intentions

of the faithful, for whom the sacrifice was being offered, were presented to God by the priest. The tradition of the Sacramentaries has retained many traces of this. We will here give some examples.

SACRAM. LEON.	SACRAM. LEON.	SACRAM. GELASIAN.	SACRAM. GREGOR.
In consecr. Episc.	*Super Defuncto*	*Miss. in Monasterio.*	*Miss. votiva*
Hanc igitur oblationem quam tibi offerimus pro (Illo) famulo tuo quem ad pontificalem gloriam promovere etc. quaesumus, Domine, placatus accipias etc.	*Hanc igitur oblationem quam tibi offerimus pro anima famuli tui (Illius) quaesumus, Domine, propitiatus accipias etc.*	*Hanc igitur oblationem, Domine, famulorum tuorum quam tibi offerunt ... pius ac propitius ... suscipias etc.*	*Hanc igitur oblationem quam tibi offerimus pro famulo tuo (Illo) ut omnium peccatorum suorum veniam consequi mereatur, quaesumus, Domine, placatus accipias etc.*

All this, therefore, leads us to maintain that this prayer brings to an end the *commendatio oblationis* of which Innocent I speaks to Decentius of Gubbio, so that in the Roman Canon it would have a signification more or less corresponding to the other prayer *post nomina*, or *super oblata*, which the Frankish liturgies and the Sacramentary of Adrian give to the prayer that precedes the Preface. The connecting link, however, between the *Hanc igitur* and the preceding part of the Canon still remains to be established, the more so as, notwithstanding the force of the *igitur,* there is apparently no connection between the end of the *Communicantes* and the prayer over the oblations. We must take into account, however, the fact that in the existing Canon the prayers of the priest are strangely intermingled with those recited by the deacon, so that in order to replace them in their proper connection and sequence it is necessary first of all to distinguish the parts allotted to each of the sacred ministers.

We will begin by assigning the *Te igitur*, at the outset of the Canon, to the priest. This represents the prayer *cum benedicitur* mentioned by Augustine, and its antiquity is shown, not only by the passages which we have already cited, by also by the ancient Preface not later than the fifteenth century, quoted by an anonymous Arian and published by Mai. In this Preface there is no trace of any *Trisagion,* but the *prex* is continuous and, after mentioning our Lord, goes on at once to the Canon: *Per Jesum Christum . . . Dominum . . . per quem petimus et rogamus . . . (ut accepta habeas,* etc.). While the people were singing the *Trisagion,* the celebrant was, perhaps, continuing the Canon undisturbed, asking God to accept and bless the gifts—*prius ergo oblationes sunt commendandae*—which were being offered to him in the name of his holy Church, spread abroad throughout the world, in communion with the Pope and with their own bishops, and in honour and commemoration of the Ever-Blessed Virgin, of the Apostles and of the martyrs. When the singing of the *Sanctus* was ended, the deacon began the *Memento*, thus causing the list of those who made the offerings to coincide with that of the saints commemorated by the priest; both the sacred ministers thus arrived simultaneously at the end of the *Communicantes* and of the *Memento*, at which point the celebrant, taking up word, and making allusion to the last sentence of the deacon—*qui tibi offerunt hoc sacrificium laudis pro se suisque . . . tibique reddunt vota sua*, etc.—added on to it, with an impressive *igitur*, his prayer over the oblations, *Hanc igitur oblationem*, and thus brought to a conclusion the solemn prayer of intercession for the living.

In this way the connection seems to be re-established and the various parts of the Canon appear to be coherent and really united to each other. The fundamental outline and rhythm of that eucharistic anaphora which papal Rome of the fifth century deemed apostolic in origin and therefore immutable, are again clearly manifested, and the ancient prayer comes to us to-day surrounded by a very much brighter halo of antiquity than we had hitherto supposed possible.

We cannot omit to draw attention to the expression *servitutis nostrae*, which in the Latin text is ambiguous and needs to be taken in connection with its context in order to arrive at its exact signification, whilst in the original Greek it would certainly be strictly accurate. The matter in discussion concerns the *Dominicum servitium*—λειτουργίας—in the sacerdotal state, which both here and in the *anamnesis* is distinctly marked off by this epithet from the mere body of the faithful.

Hanc igitur oblationem servitutis nostrae *sed et cunctae familiae tuae*, etc.	*Unde et memores sumus, Domine,* nos servi tui *sed et plebs tua sancta*, etc.

In the one case, as in the other, the *servitus* refers to a body of clergy and is therefore in the plural, because the sacrificial action of the priest was originally collective. This thought takes us back to remote antiquity, to a time when the sacerdotal body was not as yet dispersed among the different titles and churches of the city and of the country, but remained together, in regular attendance on the bishop when offering the holy sacrifice. This is precisely the position of the hierarchy as described by Justin in his *Apologia*. The *servi tui* and the *servitus nostra* of the Canon include in a single phrase both priests and bishop, just as in the times of Clement and of Tertullian and throughout the first two centuries of the Church, when the priestly body, following the Jewish Sanhedrim, was the representative of the entire hierarchy, so that the Popes themselves are styled presbyters by Irenæus. It became, in fact, the rule that on more solemn occasions the Pontiff associated with himself the entire body of presbyters, and thus all the priests, assembled together as at a council, transacted business and made laws as one body.

The addition of *diesque nostros in tua pace disponas* to the prayer over the oblations is attributed by the Pontifical to St Gregory the Great, and historians have sought to see in it an allusion to the siege of Rome by the Lombards, which the inhabitants were then enduring. Possibly, however, the Pontiff meant to refer to the calamitous condition of things obtaining generally in Italy at that time, seeing how the country was being ravaged by pestilence, famine, and war; and in his choice of this particular insertion he was doubtless inspired by the words of that other in the Leonine Sacramentary at this same place in the *Hanc igitur* for the anniversary of the consecration of a bishop—*Hanc igitur oblationem*, etc. . . . *diesque meos clementissima gubernatione disponas*. Some writers have suspected that the rest of the passage following St Gregory's insertion—*atque ab aeterna damnatione nos eripi,* etc.—was also added by him, and that by this ending he separated the prayer *Hanc igitur* from the invocation *Quam oblationem,* which originally formed one with the prayer *super oblata.*

This hypothesis, however, seems very improbable, since we are dealing with two traditional prayers bearing quite distinct characteristics. The first fulfils the requirements laid down by Innocent I—*prius ergo oblationes sunt commendandae*— and constitutes the prayer *super diptycha*—the natural conclusion, that is, of the deacon's prayer over the diptychs. The second prayer begs almighty God to grant consecratory efficacy to the words of the eucharistic institution, an efficacy which is invoked (epiklesis) in all liturgies, and especially in the Roman rite, in which the Gospel account of the Last Supper proceeds, from its bare historical signification, to assume the character of a sacramental formula precisely by virtue of the intention proclaimed by the sacred minister in uttering the words of the epiklesis—*ut nobis fiat corpus et sanguis dilectissimi Filii tui.*[1] This pre-consecratory and deprecative formula—the only one which is found in several Eastern eucharistic anaphoras—must be studied also in connection with the other deprecative sacramental formulas

---

[1] It is significant that the *De Sacramentis,* desirous of proving that the transubstantiation *verbis coelestibus consecratur. Accipe quae sunt verba: Fac nobis hanc oblationem adscriptam, ratam,* etc., makes the epiklesis part of the consecratory formula.

occurring in the rites of Confirmation, Penance, Holy Orders, Extreme Unction, as used in the Roman Church down to the late Middle Ages.

The prayer *Hanc igitur* must therefore be considered as something by itself, wholly independent of the *Quam oblationem,* and consequently in its present form it is provided with its own normal conclusion *per Christum,* etc., the same as that which we find in all Roman liturgical tradition as represented by the three sacramentaries, the Leonine, the Gelasian and that of Adrian I.

We have said that the intention of the prayer *Quam oblationem* is to beg for the sacramental grace of the transubstantiation of the eucharistic species, and that it is found in all liturgies, having among the Greeks the special name of *epiklesis.* The same unchanging conception always dominates the most diverse formularies, whether the prayer is addressed (as ordinarily it is) to God the Father, whether (as is sometimes the case) it calls upon the divine Word graciously to come down from heaven and change the elements, or whether, again, it solicits to this same end the descent of the Holy Ghost. It will prove advantageous to quote some instances.

Liturgy of St Mark	Eucharistic Papyrus (Crum)	Anaphora of Serapion
Mitte super hos panes et super haec pocula Spiritum tuum Sanctum, ut ea sanctificet et efficiat panem quidem corpus, poculum vero sanguinem testamenti novi ipsius Domini *Dei et Servatoris.*	*Mittere dignare Spiritum Sanctum tuum in has creaturas, et fac panem quidem corpus Domini et Salvatoris nostri Jesu Christi, calicem autem Sanguinem Novi* (Testamenti).	*Reple, Deus, hanc oblationem tua virtute et tua acceptione . . . Veniat, Deus veritatis, sanctum* Verbum *tuum super panem hunc, ut panis fiat Corpus Verbi, et super hunc calicem, ut calix fiat sanguis veritatis.*

The natural and traditional place for these epikleses is before the account of the Last Supper, as it is actually found in Rome, in Egypt and formerly also in Antioch. Afterwards, however, the traditional form underwent a change in the East, especially at the time of the Macedonian controversies regarding the divinity of the Paraclete, and because the descent of the Holy Ghost was also invoked after the *anamnesis,* in order to obtain thereby the effective participation of the faithful in the eucharistic feast, the one epiklesis was confused with the other, and the pre-consecratory invocation thus became post-consecratory. The immediate effect of this transposition was to postpone the mystery of the transubstantiation until after the *anamnesis* and the offering of the sacrifice; in fact, it came about eventually that in the East, contrary to the ancient patristic tradition, all consecratory efficacy was denied to our Lord's words, and exclusively assigned instead to this later and misplaced epiklesis of the Holy Ghost.

That Rome also at one time had adopted an epiklesis, in which the descent of the Holy Ghost was invoked for the consecration of the holy mysteries, seems to be clearly evident from the passage of Pope Pelagius, already quoted : *Nam quomodo ad divini mysterii consecrationem coelestis Spiritus invocatus adveniet, si sacerdos et qui eum adesse deprecatur, criminosis plenus actionibus reprobetur?*[1]

We can infer the same from that which St Ambrose says— *Quomodo igitur (Spiritus Sanctus) non omnia habet quae Dei sunt, qui cum Patre et Filio a sacerdotibus in baptismo nominatur, et in oblationibus invocatur?*[2]—and also from the fact that the epiklesis of the Holy Ghost regularly occurs in all the other consecratory anaphoras adopted in the various sacraments.

We add here some examples :

BENEDICT. OLEI INFIRMOR.

Sacram. Gelas.

(Fer. V in Ccena Dni.).

Emitte, quaesumus, Domine, Spiritum Sanctum Paraclitum ...in hanc pinguedinem olei ... et tua sancta benedictione sit . . tutamentum animae et corporis, etc.

CONSECRAT. EPISC.

Sacram. Gelas.

... Comple, Domine, in sacerdotibus tuis ministerii tui summam ... ut tui Spiritus virtus et interiorum ora repleat, etc.

CONSECR. DIAC.

Sacram. Gregor.

Emitte in eum, Domine, quaesumus, Spiritum Sanctum, quo in opus ministerii fideliter exsequendi, septiformis gratiae munere roboretur.

CONSECRAT. CHRISMATIS

Sacram. Gelas.

Te igitur deprecamur, Domine sancte ... per Jesum Christum . . . ut hujus creaturae pinguedinem sanctificare tua benedictione digneris et ei Sancti Spiritus immiscere virtutem, etc.

CONSIGNAT. INFANT.

Sacram. Gregor.

... Deus ... quique dedisti eis remissionem omnium peccatorum, emitte in eos septiformem Spiritum Sanctum Paraclitum de coelis, Spiritum sapientiae, etc.

CONSECR. ECCLESIAE

Sacram. Gregor.

Descendat quoque in hanc ecclesiam tuam quam ... indigni consecramus, Spiritus Sanctus tuus, septiformis gratiae uberitate redundans, etc.

CONSECRAT. FONTIS

Sacram. Gelas.

Descendat in hanc plenitudinem fontis virtus Spiritus Sancti et totam hujus aquae substantiam regenerandi foecundet effectu, etc.

CONSECR. PRESBYTERI

Sacram. Gregor.

Da, quaesumus, Pater, in hunc famulum tuum presbyterii dignitatem, innova in visceribus eius Spiritum sanctitatis, etc.

CONSECR. ALTARIS

Sacram. Gregor.

. . . Dignare hoc altare coelesti sanctificatione perfundere et benedicere. Assistant Angeli claritatis et Sancti Spiritus illustratione perfulgeat, etc.

---

[1] Gelasii I, *Epist. ad Elpidium. Cf.* Thiel, *Epist. Rom. Fontif.* vol. i, p. 486.

[2] S Ambrosii, *De Spiritu Sancto,* iii, 16; *P.L.* XVI, col. 837.

MISSAL. GALLIC. VETUS	MISSAL. GOTHIC.	MISSAL. GOTHIC.
Miss. S. Germani	*In Assumpt. B. Mariae*	*Bened. Fontis*
Post Secret.	Post Mysterium	*Benedic,*
Descendat, precamur, omnipotens Deus, super haec, quae tibi offerimus Verbum tuum Sanctum; descendat inaestimabilis gloriae tuae Spiritus . . . ut fiat oblatio nostra hostia spiritualis, etc.	*Descendat, Domine, in his sacrificiis tuae benedictionis coaeternus et cooperator Paraclitus Spiritus; ut . . . translata fruge in Corpore, calice in Cruore, proficiat meritis quod obtulimus pro delictis,* etc.	*Domine Deus noster, hanc creaturam aquae, et descendat super eam virtus tua; desuper infunde Spiritum tuum sanctum Paraclitum, Angelum veritatis.*

We could multiply such instances, but those here cited make it abundantly clear that the epiklesis of the Holy Ghost, or the appeal to the *Logos*, regularly furnished the indispensable theme of every anaphora, and particularly of that of the Eucharist, in which, according to the Eastern Fathers, not only the efficacy of the sacrifice for the faithful who took part in it, but also the transubstantiation itself of the bread and wine into the substance of the body and blood of our Lord was to be attributed in a special manner to the grace of the Holy Ghost, just as from the first that same body and blood had been conceived in the virginal womb of Mary by the operation of the Paraclete, so upon the cross it was the Holy Ghost who out of the fulness of his sanctity consecrated the divine Victim and rendered that Victim acceptable to the Father.

Nevertheless, although the pre-consecratory epiklesis in the Roman anaphora is primitive, we cannot say the same of the version in which it has come down to us. The prayer of the priest over the oblations recorded by Pope Innocent I, contrary to the use customary in the churches of his suffragans, must here have so broken the completeness and continuity of the anaphora that the relative *Quam oblationem* has now no antecedent to which to refer. It may well be that the *Quam* now represents an infelicitous attempt to connect the acephalous Roman epiklesis with the preceding prayer *Hanc igitur oblationem,* just as in the case of *Te igitur* and this same *Hanc igitur* of which we have already spoken.

Certain it is that we have to do with a prayer which has suffered alteration, since in the existing text of the epiklesis there is lacking the formal invocation of the Holy Ghost mentioned by Pope Pelagius. Further, in the *De Sacramentis*—which preserves to us a version of the Canon at once older and nearer to the Greek original—instead of the *Quam oblationem . . . facere digneris,* we have the direct expression: *Fac nobis hanc oblationem adscriptam, ratam, rationabilem, acceptabilem, quod figura est corporis et sanguinis Jesu Christi. Qui pridie, etc.*

It will be useful at this point to compare the divergencies in the two texts:

DE SACRAM.	CANON ROMAN.
Fac nobis hanc oblationem:	*Quam oblationem tu, Deus, in omnibus:*
(a) *adscriptam,*	(a) *benedictam,*
(b) *ratam,*	(b) *adscriptam,*
(c) *rationabilem,*	(c) *ratam,*
(d) *acceptabilem, quod figura est Corporis et Sanguinis Jesu Christi.*	(d) *rationabilem,*
	(e) *acceptabilemque facere digneris, ut nobis fiat*
	(f) *Corpus,*
	(g) *et Sanguis Filii tui Jesu Christi.*

We notice that the prayer, according to the version of it given in the existing Canon, contains practically a repetition of the other *Te igitur,* which is without doubt ancient, and to which St Augustine was, perhaps, alluding in the passage quoted above—*Orationes cum benedicitur, et sanctificatur et ad distribuendum comminuitur.* We have, in fact—

CANON MISSAE	EPICLESIS
Te igitur . . . et petimus ut . . .	*Quam oblationem . . .*
(a) *accepta habeas*	(a) *in omnibus benedictam*
(b) *et benedicas haec dona ; . . . quae tibi offerimus.*	(b) *adscriptam*
	(c) *ratam*
	(d) *rationabilem*
	(e) *acceptabilemque facere digneris.*

Did the two prayers invoking in almost similar terms the acceptance and the blessing of the oblations form, from the very first, part of the same anaphora? Might they not perhaps have been exchanged, then placed together and made into one by the last compiler of the Roman Canon? It is true that in some of the Mozarabic Masses the *Te igitur* comes after the Consecration, just at that point where the Eastern rite has the solemn prayers of intercession for the living and the dead, but for many reasons we are inclined to think that the *Te igitur* in the Roman Canon actually retains its primitive position. We will here quote a somewhat curious instance from the Mozarabic Liturgy, in order to show how its compiler has impoverished the Roman anaphora. Beside it we will place the text of the Canon, together with that of the Preface edited by Mai, which has been quoted above:

POST PRIDIE[1]

Credimus, Domine sancte, Pater aeterne, omnipotens D e u s, Jesum C h r i s t u m Filium tuum Dominum nostrum pro nostra salute incarnatum fuisse et in substantia deitatis tibi esse aequalem.

Per quem te petimus et rogamus omnipotens Pater, ut accepta habeas et benedicere digneris haec munera et haec sacrificia inlibata, quae tibi in primis offerimus pro tua sancta Ecclesia Catholica, quam pacificare digneris per universum orbem terrarum in tua pace diffusam.

Memorare etiam, quaesumus, Domine, servorum tuorum qui tibi in honore sanctorum tuorum (Illorum) reddunt vota sua Deo vivo et vero pro remissione suorum omnium delictorum. Quorum oblationem benedictam, ratam, rationabilemque facere digneris, quae est imago et similitudo Corporis et Sanguinis Jesu Christi Filii tui ac Redemptoris nostri.

PREFACE (ED. MAI).

Dignum et justum est . . . mittens nobis Jesum Christum . . . qui nostrae salutis causa humiliando se ad mortem usque subiecit . . . Per Jesum Christum Dominum et Deum nostrum, per quem petimus et rogamus. . . .

CANON ROMAN.

Vere dignum . . . per Christum Dominum nostrum. Per quem majestatem tuam, etc.

Te igitur . . . ut accepta habeas et benedicas haec dona, haec munera, haec sancta sacrificia illibata. In primis quae tibi offerimus pro Ecclesia tua sancta Catholica; quam pacificare, custodire, adunare et regere digneris . . . Memento, Domine, famulorum, famularumque tuarum . . . qui tibi offerunt . . . pro redemptione animarum . . . tibique reddunt vota sua aeterno Deo vivo et vero . . . Quam oblationem . . . benedictam, adscriptam, ratam, rationabilem, acceptabilemque facere digneris, ut nobis Corpus et Sanguis fiat dilectissimi Filii tui Domini nostri Jesu Christi.

The comparison is suggestive, for the Preface quoted by the anonymous Arian is without any interpolation of the Trisagion, but proceeds at once to the prayer *Te igitur . . . petimus et rogamus ut accepta habeas et benedicas,* which shows that its position is truly primitive. It is also to be noticed that the compiler of the Mozarabic *Post Pridie* seems to have made use of some text of the Roman Canon different from the one now existing, and perhaps nearer in date to the version cited in the *De Sacramentis.*

Returning to the subject of the Roman epiklesis, the expression *in omnibus benedictam* seems to have been inspired by the doxology in the Epistle to the Ephesians, *Qui est per omnia et in omnibus nobis; qui est benedictus in*

[1] Dom Ferotin, *Liber Ordinum,* pp. 321-22.

saecula, thus clearly explaining the entire character and special meaning of this first part of the Canon (*orationes cum benedicitur*) before the Consecration.

We are speaking here of a blessing fraught with deep significance, similar to that given by our Lord to the bread and to the eucharistic chalice, so that the Apostle forthwith terms this latter *calix benedictionis cui benedicimus.*[1]

The oblations are blessed, first of all, in thanksgiving to God for having bestowed them upon us—this was the meaning of the chalice of benediction which was passed round among the guests at the Jewish paschal supper—then the divine grace is invoked upon them, as if to prepare and arrange the matter of the sacrifice, so that the offering may be pure and worthy of the divine Majesty and of the devotion of those who make it. There is evidently no question as to the oblation in itself, treated objectively, since this cannot but be pleasing to God, being the very Word of God made man, but as regarded in relation to the dispositions and merits of the offerers, according to which their offering can be acceptable or otherwise in the sight of the divine Majesty.

Adscriptam: A petition is here addressed to almighty God that he will deign to accept the sacrifice as meritorious on the part of those who offer it. The idea of the *adscriptam* is recalled not only by the image in the psalms *in libro tuo omnes scribentur,* but also by the prayer in the Canon which immediately preceded the epiklesis—*Nomina eorum (offerentium oblationem) adscribi jubeas in libro viventium.*

Ratum: This expression, if it be not borrowed from Ignatius of Antioch, where he speaks of a valid and irreprehensible Eucharist,[2] is, at any rate, inspired by the same idea, and has always reference to the efficacy and ratification in heaven of the homage that we pay to God on earth, a conception which is also developed later on in the Roman Canon. In the meantime it is helpful to compare the Roman epiklesis with the following *Post Secret* of the Gothic Missal: *Hoc sacrificium suscipere et benedicere et sanctificare digneris, ut fiat nobis Eucharistia legitima.*[3]

Rationabilem: This is the word used by St Paul, who employs the phrase *rationabile obsequium*[4] with the meaning of spiritual religion—*i.e.,* the interior worship of the soul. The Fathers, also, of the first three centuries speak to us of

[1] 1 Cor. x, 16.
[2] *Una illa Eucharistia legitima est, quae fit sub episcopo. Ad Smyrn.,* viii, 1-2. *Quidquid agitis, irreprehensibile sit et ratum.* P.G. V, col. 713.
[3] Cf. *Missal. Gothic. In Circumcisione Domini.* Edit. Tommasi, p. 246.
[4] Rom. xii, 2, 4.

the Eucharist as being a sacrifice and a nourishment which is λογικός—that is to say, spiritual.

Acceptabilem = Ut accepta habeas, meaning the divine acceptance of the oblation, not for what it is in itself, for it is equal in dignity to God himself, to whom it is offered, but inasmuch as it is the gift of the offerer. It will be of advantage to us to compare these attributes in the Roman epiklesis with that which St Paul writes to the Romans— *Ut exhibeatis corpora vestra hostiam viventem, sanctam, Deo placentem, rationabile obsequium vestrum*—and in another place when addressing the Philippians : *Hostiam acceptam, placentem Deo.*[1]

Ut nobis fiat Corpus et Sanguis = quod figura est Corporis et Sanguinis Jesu Christi. The *De Sacramentis,* agreeing with the Mozarabic Liturgy, keeps the original expression of the epiklesis, which the compiler of the existing Canon has modified, whether in deference to its orthodoxy or to its clearness of statement we do not know. The two expressions, however, bear the same meaning, for Tertullian, even in his time, had said, in speaking of the eucharistic bread, *Hoc est corpus meum, id est figura corporis mei,*[2] in the sense of the Sacrament of the Body and Blood of Christ, inasmuch as the Body of Jesus Christ lies mysteriously hidden in the Eucharist under the sacramental species. The following is a similar phrase from the same writer : *Corpus ejus in pane censetur.*[3]

The expression *figura Corporis et Sanguinis Christi* is very often applied to the Eucharist by the Fathers of the Church— as, for example, by St Augustine—*Convivium in quo Corporis et Sanguinis sui figuram discipulis commendavit;*[4] by Gaudentius of Brescia—*Rationabiliter in eo (pane) figura accipitur Corporis Christi;*[5] by the unknown author of the *De Sacramentis*—*Sed habes similitudinem . . . similitudinem pretiosi Sanguinis,*[6] in several prayers of the Mozarabic Liturgy—*Sint tibi sacrificia haec . . . in similitudinem Corporis ac Sanguinis Domini . . . translata, ut cunctis proficiant,*[7] and again—*Quaesumus . . . ut hanc hostiam in similitudinem corporis et sanguinis ejus tibi oblatam,* etc.[8]

Origen, too, speaks of the Eucharist as τοῦ τυπικοῦ καί συμβολικοῦ σώματος[9] meaning a true body, but one existing in

[1] Phil. iv, 18.   [2] *Adv. Marcionem,* iv, 40; *P.L.* II, col. 491.
[3] *De Oratione,* 6; *P.L.* I, col. 1263.
[4] *Enarr. in Psalm.,* iii, 1; *P.L.* XXXVI, col. 73.
[5] *Serm.* II; *P.L.* XX, col. 860.
[6] Lib. IV, 20; *P.L.* XVI, col. 462.
[7] Dom Ferotin, *Liber mozarabicus Sacramentorum,* p. 197 (Paris 1912).
[8] *id.,* 321, 342.
[9] *In Matth. Comment.,* xi, 14; *P.G.* XIII, col. 952.

a sacramental state—veiled, that is, *sub specie aliena.* An identical expression occurs in the anaphora of Serapion; the eucharistic bread is τὸ ὁμοίωμα τοῦ σώματος τοῦ μονογενοῦς and the chalice τὸ ὁμοίωμα τοῦ αἵματος,[1] just as in St Cyril of Jerusalem, in the Apostolic Constitutions and in the Didascalia, where the Blessed Sacrament is called ἀντίτυπον τοῦ βασιλείου σώματος.[2]

This language, which would be ambiguous to-day—for Catholic theology, thanks to more than nineteen centuries of toil, is now in possession of an absolutely exact terminology in which to express its dogmas—was understood by the early Christians in an absolutely orthodox sense, since the Fathers, in calling the Blessed Sacrament a figure, a type, an antitype or a symbol of the Body of Christ, did not deny its reality, for they indeed acknowledged it, even as we do, but merely desired to give expression to the sacramental condition in which it is imparted to us. In speaking as they did, they were supported by the liturgical tradition of the Church; so much so that while the Latin and African Fathers, in agreement with the Canon of the Mass and with the Alexandrian anaphora, called the Eucharist a *figura, similitudo,* ὁμοίωμα of the body of Christ, the Syrians and Cappadocians termed it ἀντίτυπον, σύμβολον, exactly as in their own liturgies.[3]

After the prayer for the transubstantiation of the oblations there follows immediately in the Roman Canon the Gospel narrative of the Last Supper, together with the words of the institution of the holy Eucharist—words to which the Church, speaking by the mouths of the Fathers, has always attached a sacramental efficacy. We are here speaking of the culminating point in the anaphora—εὐχῆς λόγου τοῦ παρ' αὐτοῦ, as Justin teaches us—and marvellous indeed is the agreement with which all the different liturgies, even those of the Eastern rites, which seem to postpone the mystery of transubstantiation until after the anaphora and the epiklesis, faithfully reproduce—except in a few instances which admit of a plausible explanation—the consecratory formula, *This is my body; this is my blood* (the only one made use of by our Lord).

When we consider that the early Church took advantage, so to speak, of its liturgical freedom to compile a large number of anaphoras of the most varied form and conception —not omitting the epiklesis—and that still, even in the midst of such great variations and changes of prayer and of rite,

---

[1] *Cf.* Funk, *Didascal. et Constitut.,* t. II, p. 174.
[2] *id.,* pp. 412, 381; S. Cyrilli, *Catech. Mystagog,* v. 20; *P.G.* XXXIII, col. 1124.
[3] In the liturgy entitled of St Basil we have : προσθέντες τά ἀντίτυπα τοῦ ἁγίου σώματος καὶ αἵματος.

the one thing which has remained really immutable is the sacred words of the institution of the Eucharist—after which the people, both in the East and at Milan, used to cry out *Amen*—we cannot fail to realize that the reason of this unchanging formula lay in the faith of the Church which believed, then as now, that only in virtue of those divine words is transubstantiation effected and the sacrifice offered—*Sacramentum . . . Christi sermone conficitur*,[1] as St Augustine has it, or as St Chrysostom expresses it : οχῆμα πληρῶν ἐστηκεν ὁ ἱερεύς, τά ῥήματα φθεγγόμενος ἐκεῖνα, ἡ δέ δύναμις καί ἡ χάρις του Θεοῦ ἐστι. Ὁ Χριστός " Τοῦτό μου ἐστί τό σῶμα " φησί. Τοῦτο τό ῥῆμα μεταρρυθμίζει τά προκείμενα.[2]

The Gospel account of the Last Supper begins, in the Roman Canon, with the words *Qui pridie quam pateretur*, which are generally believed to date back to the time of Pope Alexander I (105-115 ?), who, according to the Pontifical, *Hic passionem Domini miscuit in praedicatione sacerdotum, quando missae celebrantur.*[3] We have already given our opinion as to the meaning to be attached to the words of the historiographer of the Pontifical, writing at some later date, with regard to Pope Alexander. We may, nevertheless, observe that while all the Eastern liturgies derive their formula from the text of St Paul, ἐν τῇ νυκτί ῇ παρεδίδοτο, the Latin liturgies, on the other hand, always keep or kept, as did the Mozarabic rite, the Roman formula, *Qui pridie quam pateretur,* which expression is not, however, taken literally from any passage of Scripture.

This singular harmony among the Latin liturgies as regards the words *Qui pridie* substantiates the statement in the *Liber Pontificalis,* and causes us to regard it as probable that Alexander or some other of the early Popes may have inserted in the eucharistic anaphora a passage, a sentence, some interpolation, in short, deemed to be of primary importance, having reference to the Passion of our Lord. We are ignorant both of the circumstances and of the motives of such an insertion, but it is perhaps not without significance that theologians should be preoccupied at that particular period with the necessity of opposing and protesting against the Docetes, the Gnostics and other heretics who were denying the reality of our Saviour's sufferings. However this may be, it is certain that the simple words *Qui pridie quam pateretur* do not fully correspond to the statement in the *Liber Pontificalis: Hic passionem Domini miscuit in praedicatione sacerdotum.* There must therefore have been something else which has now disappeared, leaving only a slight trace of itself in the

---

[1] S Ambrosius, *De mysteriis*, 52; *P.L.* XVI, col. 424.
[2] S. Joh. Chrys., *In prodit. Judae*, hom. i, 6; *P.G.* XLIX, col. 380.
[3] *Lib. Pontif.* (Edit. Duchesne), vol. i, p. 127.

existing *Qui pridie.* Might not this something to which we are seeking a clue have been an expression of special thanksgiving for the mercy of God, shown to us in the Passion of his Son?

It is true that in the *anamnesis* all the liturgies commemorate the Passion, but this commemoration is altogether primitive and essential by reason of the command given by our Lord himself, so that the innovation of Pope Alexander cannot refer to this, but must necessarily be understood of some other eucharistic commemoration of the sufferings of Christ, inserted in the anaphora before the formula of consecration. Without in the least claiming to have discovered the primitive formula, may we not suppose that its tenor approximated to the very suggestive passage[1] in the anaphora of the Egyptian Ecclesiastical Ordinances? *Qui . . . extendit manus cum pateretur, ut a passione liberaret eos qui in te crediderunt. Qui cumque traderetur voluntariae passioni, ut mortem solvat . . . accipiens panem,* etc.

With regard to the consecratory formula, as Dom Cagin observes,[2] no liturgy, whether Eastern or Western, has kept strictly to the Gospel text or to that of St Paul. The most ancient rites have a formula for the compilation of which various texts have been fused and combined, but it was not long before further additions were made of other elements derived from traditional sources. We will place the two formulas of the *De Sacramentis* and of the Canon in parallel columns, drawing especial attention to those words taken from the Gospel text.

De Sacramentis	Canon Roman.	
In sanctis manibus suis	*Accepit panem* in sanctas	Cum accepisset panem sanctis et ab
Accepit panem	ac venerabiles manus suas	omni labe puris
respexit in coelum		manibus suis
ad te, sancte Pater omnipotens,	et elevatis oculis in coelum	et sustulisset oculos ad te Deum suum ac
	ad te Deum Patrem suum omnipotentem	Patrem — *Lit. Clement.*
aeterne Deus	*tibi*	
gratias agens	*gratias agens*	
benedixit,	*benedixit*	
fregit	*fregit*	
fractumque	*deditque*	dedit sanctis suis
Apostolis suis	*discipulis suis*	discipulis et apostolis
et *discipulis suis*		—*Lit. Grec. S. Jac.*—
tradidit		Sanctis suis discipulis
dicens:	*dicens*	et apostolis suis tribuit
Accipite	*accipite*	—*Lit. Grec. S. Joan.*
et edite	*et manducate*	*Chrys.*

---

[1] *Cf.* Cagin, *L'Euchologie Latine,* II : *L'Eucharistie,* pp. 148 *sq.*
[2] *idem,* p. 79, note.

DE SACRAMENTIS	CANON ROMAN.	
ex hoc omnes :	*ex hoc omnes:*	
hoc est enim corpus meum	*Hoc est enim corpus meum.*	
quod pro multis confringetur.		
Similiter etiam calicem	Simili modo	
postquam coenatum est, pridie quam pateretur	postquam coenatum est	
accepit,	*accipiens et hunc*	Accipit et hunc
respexit in coelum ad te,	praeclarum *calicem* in sanctas ac venerabiles manus suas,	praeclarum calicem— *Stowe Missal.*—Accepit
Sancte Pater omnipotens, aeterne Deus,		et hunc praeclarum calicem in sanctas, etc.
gratias agens benedixit,	item *tibi gratias agens benedixit*	— *Bobbio Missal.* —
Apostolis suis *et discipulis suis tradidit*	*deditque discipulis suis*	Accipit et hunc praeclarum calicem—
dicens:	*dicens*	*Missal. Aanc.*
Accipite et bibite ex hoc omnes:	*Accipite et bibite ex eo omnes:*	
Hic est enim sanguis meus. . . .[1]	*Hic est enim Calix Sanguinis mei, novi*	
	et aeterni *Testamenti,*	Eduxit . . . in
	mysterium fidei, *qui*	sanguine testamenti
	pro vobis et pro	aeterni.—Heb. xiii, 20.
	multis effundetur in	—Habentes mysterium
	remissionem peccatorum.	fidei in conscientia
		pura.—1 Tim. iii, 9.

The amplification of the phrase already found in Hippolytus, *Holy and uncontaminated hands,* is common to many Eastern liturgies, as, for instance, the Greek Liturgies of St Mark and of St James, the Liturgy of St Basil, the Ethiopian Liturgy of the Saviour, etc. The tautology involved in the expression *of his Apostles and disciples,* corrected in the present Roman text, but found in the *De Sacramentis,* has its counterpart in the Liturgies of St Chrysostom, St Basil and St Mark, and also in the eucharistic papyrus edited by Crum. The epithet *aeterni* applied to the word *Testamenti* is evidently inspired by the Epistle to the Hebrews, and is common to the whole group of Latin liturgies, whether Ambrosian, Frankish or Roman, together with the Missals of Bobbio and Stowe, the Mozarabic Liturgy forming the sole exception. The *Mysterium fidei* represents another scriptural addition, taken from the first pastoral Epistle to Timothy, which found its way into the Roman Canon through Gallican influence.

After the Consecration there follows that which the Greeks call the *anamnesis,* and which we Latins might designate as the commemoration of our Lord's death. It is a primitive element common to all liturgies, fulfilling the command of the Saviour, who wished that we, when offering the

---

[1] *De Sacramentis,* iv, 5; *P.L.* XVI, col. 463.

eucharistic sacrifice, should make a memorial of him, or, as St Paul explains it, of his death : Ὁσάκις γαρ εσθίητε τὸν ἄρτον τοῦτον καί τὸ ποτήριον πίνητε, τον θάνατον τοῦ Κυρίου καταγγέλλετε ἄχρι οὗ ἐλθε.[1]

The *anamnesis* is joined on to the final words of the eucharistic Consecration, *in mei memoriam facietis*, by means of the somewhat artificial link of the word *unde*, which barely succeeds in lessening the feeling of disconnection which now dominates the whole of our present anaphora. The commemoration is thus made both by all the clergy who are assisting at the Mass, *nos servi tui*, also by the people present, *sed et plebs tua sancta*—an indication of a very early period of the Liturgy when the Eucharist was offered collectively by the *episcopus* surrounded by his *presbyterium*. Further, the explicit mention of the sacerdotal hierarchy, upon whom our Lord has bestowed the signal honour of offering the divine Victim upon the altar, is a feature peculiar to one whole class of liturgies, its place being immediately after the Consecration. We meet it for the first time in the anaphora of the Egyptian Ecclesiastical Constitutions—to which anaphora Dom Cagin assigns a quasi-pauline origin—emanating from these; it appears in the anaphora of the *Testamentum Domini,* in the Ethiopian Liturgy of the Saviour and in that of the Apostles, in the Greek and Syrian Liturgies of St Basil and in many others. The primitive text, according to the Ecclesiastical Constitutions of the Egyptians, is as follows : *Memores igitur mortis ejus . . . gratias agentes tibi qui nos dignos habuisti stare coram te, et tibi ministrare.* The *nos servi tui* of the Roman Canon thus appears to be the last echo of a very ancient liturgical tradition commemorating the divine gifts of the priesthood, the *servitium Dominicum,* immediately after the Consecration.

The commemoration of the Passion is primitive and common to all liturgies; it may even be regarded as explained, where he applies indifferently to the eucharistic really is—the commemorative sacrifice of the Passion of our Lord. St Luke's want of grammatical sequence is thus explained, where he applies indifferently to the Eucharistic species of the bread and the wine that which should in reality be referred to the victim of Calvary : Τοῦτό ἐστιν τό σῶμά μου τό ὑπέρ ὑμῶν (διδόμενον) · τοῦτο τό ποτήριον ἡ καινή διαθήκη ἐν τῷ ᾿ις τί μου, τό ὑπέρ ὑμῶν ἐκχυννόμενον. The body, indeed, was delivered up to death for us on Calvary, and the ποτήριον . . . ἐκχυννόμενον was only shed in reality upon the cross.

The addition of the Resurrection to the *anamnesis* is fairly ancient; it may even be said that it is necessitated by the

---

[1] Cf. *Lib. Pontif.*, t. I, p. 127.

mention of the Passion, from which Christian people never separate it. Our Lord himself said at the Last Supper that he would taste no more of the fruit of the vine until the mystery of the Messianic redemption should be fulfilled. Now, the Messianic kingdom of the Saviour was formally inaugurated on the day of his resurrection, and it is because of this that we drink with him of the chalice of salvation, seeing that this redemption through the blood shed upon the cross is not merely prefigured by the chalice of the precious Blood consecrated at the Last Supper, but has become an historical fact, a real and true sacrament celebrated on the altar.

In the *anamnesis* of the anaphora of Serapion we have merely the bare record of our Saviour's death—ὁμοίωμα τοῦ θανάτου—but in that of the Der-Balyzeh papyrus edited by Crum, as also in the Egyptian Ecclesiastical Constitutions and in the later liturgies, we find explicit mention of the Resurrection, from which was afterwards developed the commemoration of our Lord's ascension into heaven, his sitting at the right hand of God, his second coming in glory, etc.

In the Canon of the *De Sacramentis* mention is made of the Passion, of the Resurrection and of the Ascension, as in the existing text of the Roman Missal; but from certain quotations made by Arnobius in his commentary on Psalm cx,[1] and from Bernold of Constance,[2] we infer that formerly there had been inserted a commemoration in the Roman Canon of the nativity of our Lord—*tam venerandae nativitatis, quam beatae passionis*—as is seen also in the traditions of many particular churches.

After the *anamnesis*, which forms an integral part of the consecration of the eucharistic victim, in commemoration of his bloody sacrifice on the cross, there follows at once the offering up of the victim himself to the Father at the hands of the priest. This is indubitably one of the most important and solemn moments of the liturgical *actio*; it is found in all the ancient liturgies in almost identical terms, even to the phrase τὰ σὰ ἐκ τῶν σῶν, *de tuis donis ac datis*. The matter is important also from the point of view of the Eastern epiklesis which follows this oblation, because, according to the view of the Greeks, who assign consecratory efficacy to the invocation of the Holy Ghost, it is incomprehensible how the *anamnesis* and the *prosphora*, or offering to the Father, can precede the transubstantiation, which constitutes the Host an actual Victim. We must therefore conclude that the

---

[1] *Cf.* G. Morin, *L'anamnèse de la messe romaine dans la première moitié du Ve siècle*, in *Rev. Benedict.*, vol. xxiv, p. 407.
[2] *P.L.* CLI, col. 985.

existing post-consecratory epiklesis of the Eastern Church, which—after the *anamnesis* and the offering of the sacrifice— still invokes the descent of the Paraclete, in order to effect the transubstantiation of the eucharistic species, is a theological contradiction in terms, and represents a strange and later deviation from the original liturgical conception of the Fathers of the Church and also of the Byzantines, who all of them—as St Chrysostom, for example—attributed the efficacy of the transubstantiation solely to our Lord's own words.

The prayer *Supra quae*, with all its eucharistic symbolism of the gifts of Abel, the sacrifice of Abraham and the offering of Melchisedech, has been made a subject of study by Baumstark, and is found in nearly all the liturgies of the great patriarchates. It inspired the artist who adorned with mosaics the apse of San Vitale at Ravenna, but without necessarily deriving the prayer from a common liturgical but unknown prototype, we can say that—granted the accuracy of its symbolism—this same symbolism passed from one anaphora to another until it became, in the fifth century, the common inheritance of every eucharistic Canon.

The author of the *Quaestiones Veteris et Novi Testamenti*, identified by Dom Morin as Isaac, the converted Jew, who would thus be the same person as Ambrosiaster, falls out with those who in the Canon give to the Holy Ghost, symbolized by Melchisedech, the title of High Priest of God : *Similiter et Spiritus Sanctus, quasi antistes, sacerdos appellatus est excelsi Dei, non summus, sicut nostri in oblatione praesumunt.*[1] Indeed, the idea that the King of Salem who went forth to meet Abraham and offered a sacrifice of bread and wine after his victory was really a manifestation of the Holy Ghost was widely spread in the fifth century at a time when there came unexpectedly the Manichean *gnosis* which proclaimed that material sacrifice to be impure. Thereupon St Leo I, as in protest, added to the words of the Canon, *Summus sacerdos tuus Melchisedech*, the further phrase : *Sanctum sacrificium, immaculatam hostiam.*[2]

In the *De Sacramentis* the *anamnesis* and the two prayers *Supra quae* and *Supplices te rogamus* are strikingly interwoven, and preserve that sense of continuity which is now wanting in the Roman Canon, where, despite their meaning, they appear as three separate prayers. The *Supplices te rogamus*, indeed, which the priest to-day recites bowing low over the altar, is only the continuation of the preceding oblation ; it begs God to grant that the earthly liturgy may be ratified in heaven in as far as regards the personal fruit of the sacrament and its substantial efficacy. In order, there-

---

[1] *P.L.* XXXV, col. 2329.　　　[2] *Lib. Pont.* I, 239.

fore, to express this in a striking manner, a beautiful figure
is borrowed from the book of Tobias, and we ask almighty
God that the sacrifice of the Church militant may be offered
up by the hands of his angels upon the golden altar which
St John saw before the throne of God in Paradise.

Some liturgists have found this passage very strange and
obscure, yet the prayer, as Baumstark has demonstrated, is
common to all the ancient liturgies of the great patriarchates
of the fifth century. Furthermore, it is couched in figurative
and symbolical terms, and was never meant to be taken as
literally as a formula in geometry. The Eucharist is here
considered not only as a sacrament, but also as a sacrifice,
and in both the one and the other aspect its substantial
efficacy is conditional on the good dispositions of the offerer;
hence we pray to our Lord that through his grace these may
become living realities. As holy Scripture extols the faith of
Abraham, Isaac and Melchisedech, whose offerings typified
and prefigured that of our altars, so we beseech the divine
mercy to grant that our sacrifice—*sacrificium nostrum*—may
be equally acceptable, seeing that the holy Eucharist is not
only the sacrifice which the eternal High Priest offers of
himself, but according to the teaching of the Church is also
the joint sacrifice of the priest, of the people present, of those
who make offerings, of those for whom it is offered, etc.

Since, then, in the holy Scriptures it belongs to the
ministry of the holy angels to present to God the prayers and
the merits of the saints, we pray that they may perform the
same office for the sacrifice which we offer upon our altars,
so that it may abundantly bless all such as participate in it
through the Holy Communion. This is the true meaning of
the *Supplices te rogamus*. Unlike the Eastern liturgies,
which at this point have so distorted the primitive invocation
of the Paraclete as to turn it into an epiklesis—that is, a
sacramental formula of transubstantiation—the Roman
Canon, on the contrary, retains its original meaning as a
prayer in preparation for Communion, as it is also seen to be
in the Ecclesiastical Regulations of the Egyptians.

There is no question of invoking the Holy Ghost in order
to obtain the transubstantiation of the sacred gifts, for in the
anamnesis, in the oblation and in the presentation upon the
heavenly altar, such transubstantiation is taken as already
accomplished, but only of entreating the grace of the Paraclete that the communion of the divine Victim may bear fruit
in the souls of those who partake thereof.

The explanation of the anaphora of the Egyptian Regulations is as follows : *Petimus ut mittas Spiritum tuum sanctum
in oblationem sanctae ecclesiae, in unum congregans* (this is
the firstfruit of the Eucharist—Catholic unity) *des omnibus qui*

percipiunt sacra, repletionem spiritus tui (here is the second fruit, the nourishing of the interior life according to the promise) *qui manducat me, et ipse vivet propter me—ad confirmationem fidei in veritate* (this, lastly, is the third fruit of Holy Communion, inasmuch as the *Mysterium fidei* strengthens the faith which is an earnest of the truth).

Like authorities such as the *Testamentum Domini*, the apostolic statutes, etc., agreeing with the Roman Canon, have preserved the original character of this invocation of the Paraclete as of a prayer preparatory to Holy Communion; it was only later that the Eastern liturgies, influenced by the preoccupation of the theologians with the progress of the Macedonian heretics, distorted it into the form of an epiklesis, which, however, resulted in giving it a completely contrary meaning.

How, then, did this distortion come about? It was quickly done. The Eastern Fathers, in probing the depths of the mystery of eucharistic transubstantiation, while they acknowledged that the change took place through the words of our Lord, nevertheless had recourse to the operation of the Holy Ghost in order to account for its efficacy, since it was through the power of the Paraclete that the Word of God took upon himself that human flesh which he afterwards, in the fervour of an ineffable sanctity, *per Spiritum Sanctum semetipsum obtulit*, offered for us upon the altar of the cross.

In the anaphora of Serapion the Holy Ghost is called the witness of the Passion of Jesus. As, however, in the Eastern anaphoras the invocation of the Holy Ghost was more commonly met with after the *anamnesis*, its object being to implore the outpouring of the grace of the Spirit upon the holy offerings, so that *from the resulting effect might be seen that which they really are,* namely, the Body and Blood of the Saviour—we have here precisely the mission of the Holy Ghost on the Day of Pentecost, of which our Lord prophesied, *Ipse me clarificabit*—so from the conception of the eucharistic mystery as a manifestation of the grace of the Holy Spirit, ἀναδεῖξαι, or, rather, ὅπος ἀποφήνῃ τὸν ἄρτον τοῦτον σῶμα τοῦ Χριστοῦ κ.τ.λ., as in the Apostolic Constitutions, it easily passed into that of the ποιήσῃ, according to which the transubstantiation was considered to be accomplished by virtue of the epiklesis of the Holy Ghost.

The wish to approximate the prayer *Supra quae* of the Roman Canon as nearly as possible to the Eastern epiklesis has rendered several writers desirous of seeing in the angel who presents the gifts on the heavenly altar a type of the Holy Ghost. Such an interpretation, however, does not accord with the Eastern anaphoras, in which the office of presenting the offerings in heaven is expressly assigned to the holy angels. Furthermore, instead of the present reading, *Per manus sancti angeli tui*, the *De Sacramentis* has *Per manus angelorum tuorum*, which clearly excludes any allusion to the Holy Ghost in this connection.

After the *anamnesis* and the oblation, which are much earlier in form, there follows, in the existing text of the Roman Canon, which goes back at least to the sixth century, the second part of the prayer of intercession, at the conclusion of the recitation of the diptychs for the dead. Amalarius tells us : *Hic orationes duae dicuntur, una super dyptitios (diptycha), altera post lectionem nominum, et hoc quotidianis, vel in agendis tantummodo diebus.*[1] Concerning the diptychs of the living, he had already observed : *Hic nomina vivorum memorentur, si volueris, sed non dominica die, nisi caeteris diebus.* The custom, therefore, in the ninth century was to regard the diptychs as something apart; they might, or might not, be recited on ferias and at funerals, but they were wholly omitted on Sundays, together with the prayers in which reference is made to them. This division at Rome of the prayer of intercession does certainly appear strange, one part being recited before the Consecration and the other before the Fraction.

Such a state of things shows the uncertainty, as regards the diptychs, that we meet with in all the ancient liturgies, where they never keep to one and the same fixed place. Thus in the Alexandrian they come before the Trisagion; in the Antiochene and in nearly all the Eastern liturgies they are to be found after the Consecration, between the *anamnesis* and the epiklesis, as in the anaphoras of Theodore of Mopsuestia and of Nestorius; between the epiklesis and the final doxology, as in the Greek and Coptic Liturgies of St Basil, the Greek Liturgy of St John Chrysostom, the Greek and Coptic Liturgies of St Gregory and the anaphora of Serapion; immediately after the Consecration, as in the Liturgy of the Apostles Addai and Mari; and after the epiklesis, but partly before and partly after the final doxology, as in the Apostolic Constitutions and in the Liturgy of St James.

Amid such diversity of tastes Rome, too, ended by combining all these differences in a compromise. One part of the diptychs was placed between the Trisagion and the Consecration, where the commemoration of the Pope and of all the orthodox faithful scattered throughout the world naturally called for the recital of the names of the offerers, while the remaining part was postponed until after the *anamnesis* and the offering, in imitation of the Syrian Liturgy of the Patriarchate of Antioch, which had a very wide range of influence even in the West.

[1] *Eglogae de off. Miss.; P.L.* CV, cols. 1130-1.

This compromise may, perhaps, have been prompted by practical reasons rather than founded upon abstract principles. The reading of the diptychs required time, and perhaps neither the celebrant nor his hearers were always disposed to listen to that long litany of names; hence, in Rome, it was eventually found necessary to omit it on feast-days. Therefore, so that the priest should not be obliged to suspend the recital of the anaphora in order to read the diptychs, this duty was entrusted to the deacon, so that when the latter came to the end of the list of the living, the celebrant should have already reached in his prayer the *Commendatio oblationis* and the pre-consecratory epiklesis.

The priest, as a matter of course, said his part of the anaphora in silence, while the deacon recited aloud—this would seem to be the beginning of the custom of the reciting of the Canon of the Mass *sub silentio*—forming a rite parallel to the rule concerning the *secretum,* the *oratio post nomina* of the Gallican liturgies; whenever, that is to say, the reading of the diptychs took place, as at Gubbio, before the Canon. The eucharistic Consecration obliged the deacon to cease the reading of the names, but he resumed it after the words of institution from the Gospel, in such a way as to end the list of the dead just as the celebrant reached the final doxology of the anaphora.

All this is set down here simply by way of hypothesis, and not with any idea of its being positive and absolute, since we are treating of obscure questions, for the elucidation of which very little documentary evidence is forthcoming.

It will be interesting here to outline the structure of the prayer of intercession in the Roman Canon. It is divided into two parts—for the living and for the dead—and each of these parts comprises two prayers—*una super dyptitios,* as Amalarius phrases it, and *altera post lectionem nominum*—entirely separated from the anaphora and forming a part to itself, with its own doxology and conclusion; in short, absolutely distinct from the Canon. For this reason the commemoration of the dead corresponds exactly to that of the living, just as the *Nobis quoque* corresponds to the *Communicantes,* which resumes the interrupted list of martyrs whose intercession is to be invoked.

Nor should this double litany of saints appear strange to anyone; it is a purely literary device in order to give honour to the two tables of the *diptycha* by accompanying each list of names to be presented before God with the powerful advocacy of their heavenly patrons. In the Armenian Liturgy also, in the Ethiopian liturgies of the Saviour and of the Apostles, etc., similar lists occur; indeed, in this last there is a double list of saints, one placed after the commemoration of the living, and the other after that of the dead, just as we find them at Rome. We are inclined to consider, therefore, that the whole Roman formulary of the prayers *super diptycha* was brought to the banks of the Tiber from beyond the seas, probably from Syria and from the Patriarchate of Antioch, whence Rome borrowed so many liturgical elements. We are confirmed in this supposition by the fact that in the prayer *Nobis quoque,* besides the Apostles Matthias and Barnabas, who were for many centuries wholly unknown to the Roman Calendar, Ignatius of Antioch is also invoked; he, too, notwithstanding that he died at Rome, having passed into almost entire oblivion in the ancient liturgical tradition of the Apostolic See.

The John who heads the list in the *Nobis quoque* is the Baptist, who, together with the protomartyr Stephen, precedes—evidently out of respect to the chronology—this same Apostle Matthias. Similarly, in the Ethiopian Liturgy of the Saviour, Stephen, John and the Evangelists come before the Blessed Virgin and the Apostles. It is significant that in the Roman prayer of intercession Matthias is not inserted among the Apostles in the first list, but that we meet with his name, on the other hand, in the *Nobis quoque* after the diptychs of the dead. This must certainly have come about through the fact of St Paul being placed among the twelve Apostles in the *Communicantes;* consequently later on it was not thought necessary to alter the symbolical number of the first twelve pillars of the Church by adding the successor of Judas, whose name does not occur in any scriptural list of the Apostles.

Barnabas, who follows Matthias, comes next to him also in the Ethiopian Liturgy of the Saviour, in which we find also the names of St Paul's first companions, Timothy, Silas, Titus, Philemon and Clement. The Roman *intercessio,* on the other hand, commemorates Ignatius the Antiochene, who was usually considered by the early Christians as a disciple of St Peter, ordained bishop by him, and consequently deserving of a place in the list of apostolic personages.

The Alexander who comes next is, in all probability, the one of that name buried in the cemetery of Ficulea at the seventh milestone on the Via Nomentana, who has been identified, without much ground, with the first of the Popes of that name. Perhaps because of this identification, his *cultus* enjoyed a good deal of popularity in Rome, in consequence of which his name came to be inserted in the prayer of intercession, together with those of the martyrs Peter and Marcellinus, who also belong to the suburbicarian district of Rome, and were buried at Silva Candida.

Felicitas and Perpetua were Carthaginians, but so famous

were the *Acts* of their martyrdom that we find their feast already noted in the Philocalian Calendar. It is not surprising, therefore, that the two names were inserted in the *Nobis quoque* of the Roman Canon. They are placed together now, but originally Felicitas, as a married woman, was preceded by the Roman virgins, Agnes and Cæcilia. The order used to be as follows :

Perpetua, Agnes, Cæcilia, Felicitas, Anastasia, Agatha, Lucia.

The last two martyrs in this list, Sicilians, come, although virgins, after Anastasia of Sirmium, who was so greatly venerated in Rome during the Byzantine period, because they represent a later addition to the *intercessio* made, very probably, in the time of St Gregory, as St Aldhelm of Sherborne attests : *Sanctae Agathae rumores castissimae virginis Luciae praeconia subsequantur, quas praeceptor et paedagogus noster Gregorius in Canone quotidiano quando Missarum solemnia celebrantur, pariter copulasse cognoscitur.*[1] The conclusion of the prayer *Intra quorum nos consortium* is to be found in the *Breviarium in psalmos* wrongly attributed to St Jerome, though it is certainly of great antiquity : *Ad capescendam futuram beatitudinem cum electis ejus; in quorum nos consortium, non meritorum inspector, sed veniae largitor admittat Christus Dominus noster. Amen.*[2] The fact that the prayer of intercession has its own ending is sufficient to show that it is something complete in itself, without any real connection with the Canon. Moreover, its very phraseology, so humble and meek—*nobis quoque peccatoribus, partem aliquam, non aestimator meriti*—ill accords with the stately and solemn tones of the Roman anaphora— *haec sancta sacrificia illibata, pro Ecclesia tua sancta, oblationem servitutis nostrae sed et cunctae familiae tuae, nos servi tui sed et plebs tua sancta*, etc.—and perhaps betrays a different mode of thought and a different compiler.

The solemn doxology of the eucharistic anaphora follows, during which the *fractio panis* took place up to the time of St Gregory I, this being the characteristic act by which our Lord at the Last Supper wished to express in a tangible way the relation between the sacrifice of the Mass and that of the cross : " This is my body which is broken for you "—τὸ ὑπέρ ὑμῶν κλώμενον—as much as to say that as the eucharistic bread is broken to be distributed to the communicants, so is the Body of the Son of Man to be broken by his death, but after a bloody manner.

However suggestive the doxology of the anaphora may be, and however much it may hide a deep theological meaning,

---

[1] *De Laud. Virginit.*, cap. xlii ; *P.L.* LXXXIX, col. 142.
[2] *P.L.* XXVI, col. 1094.

even if we have to admit that the connection *per quem* conceals in a somewhat artificial manner the fact that there is little or no relation between the doxology and the ending of the prayer of intercession—two consecutive endings—there is, nevertheless, a treacherous *haec omnia* which, passed over unnoticed down to the last compiler of the Canon, has done him a bad turn and brought to light his deceptive acts. This *haec omnia creas, sanctificas, vivificas, benedicis et praestas nobis* has nothing to do with the sacred eucharistic species, to which, moreover, it would hardly be feasible to allude again in so abrupt a manner, but refers to the fresh produce of the earth, to the oil for the sick and to the other firstfruits which had just been presented on the altar in order to receive the blessing of the priest. Only of these can it be said, *All these things dost thou create, hallow, quicken, bless and bestow upon us,* language which would be, at the least, strange and incomprehensible if it were meant to be applied to the Blessed Sacrament.

This place, reserved in the eucharistic anaphora to the various blessings—including the nuptial benediction—was most appropriate, and served to emphasize that deep sense of unity which anciently pervaded the Liturgy, when the sacrifice of the altar was the central point of Christian worship, with which all other rites were connected and from which they all took their rise as from an overflowing source of grace. The priest invoked the blessing of the Holy Ghost upon the sacred gifts, that as many as partook of them might be filled *omni benedictione coelesti et gratia,* and it was here that in certain circumstances a parenthesis, as it were, occurred in the Canon and the different blessings were bestowed which are mentioned in the ancient sacramentaries.

It would seem that the blessing of the oil for the sick, restricted later to the chrismal Mass of Holy Thursday only, was formerly quite commonly bestowed, since the Canons of Hippolytus speak of it as being one of the ordinary rites of the eucharistic synaxis. The *velatio nuptialis* cannot have been less frequent, its place to-day being before the *fractio* of the sacred mysteries. If the consecration or *benedictio* of bishops, priests and deacons took place before the Mass, it was in order that the newly ordained might at once enter upon their sacred ministry by celebrating the holy sacrifice.

Before, however, coming to the solemn act of the fraction of the sacred species, which in Rome was performed collectively by the whole *presbyterium,* the rite required that the chalice with the Host should be raised up in the sight of the people so that they might adore the eucharistic Presence. This was the true and solemn elevation, though wellnigh atrophied to-day in the rubric of the Roman Canon, and still more so by the custom of the priests, introduced about the twelfth century, of another famous " showing " of the sacred species immediately after each part of the Consecration—a custom for which the heresy of Berengarius was largely responsible.

From the time of Justin the people were wont to answer *Amen* to the final doxology of the anaphora, and here the eucharistic liturgy, properly so called, came to an end. In the Gallican rite blessings were actually introduced at this point of the Mass for those who, not intending to partake of the holy mysteries, now left the church. At Rome also the Pope quitted the altar when the *fractio* was completed, and returned to his own seat, where he recited the Lord's Prayer before receiving Holy Communion. In both cases, however, the Mass was regarded as essentially finished. *Post sanctificationem sacrificii . . . dicimus orationem Dominicam,*[1] says St Augustine : the oblation had been offered and the sacrifice accomplished. The Holy Communion, indeed, which by divine law is obligatory upon the celebrant, according to the teaching of the theologians, alone belongs to the integrity of the sacrifice ; the faithful might partake of it in their own homes, or they might postpone it to another occasion, or they might receive it only spiritually. This was actually the line of thought of St Gregory the Great, when regarding it as a grave abuse that *precem quam scholasticus composuerat super oblationem diceremus, et ipsam traditionem quam Redemptor noster composuit, super ejus Corpus et Sanguinem non diceremus,*[2] he desired that the Lord's Prayer should be recited by the celebrant immediately after the Canon, and that the people should make the response *Sed libera nos a malo.*

A very widely spread liturgical tradition had, indeed, made the *Pater Noster* a popular prayer of immediate preparation for Holy Communion. St Augustine bears witness to this *quam totam petitionem fere omnis Ecclesia dominica oratione concludit.*[3] The *Pater Noster* was recited before approaching the Lord's table, just as it is still recited by the faithful before partaking of ordinary food : it bore a special significance when said before Holy Communion, because of the petition *Give us this day our daily bread,* in which the Fathers saw a special reference to the eucharistic bread. St Gregory was of the belief that the Apostles, from the beginning, had added in the consecration of the divine mysteries no other

[1] St August., *Serm.* CCXXVII *in die Paschae,* IV ; *P.L.* XXXVIII, col. 1101.
[2] *Reg.,* lib. IX, *Epist.* XII ; *P.L.* LXXVII, col. 957.
[3] *Ep.* CXLIX *ad Paulinum,* n. 1 ; *P.L.* XXXIII, col. 636.

anaphora to the consecratory formula save the *Pater Noster;*
he therefore wished to restore to this Lord's Prayer its former
character of anaphora by making it the continuation of the
anaphora then in use at Rome, which, according to him, was
merely the compilation of some scholar (*scholasticus composuerat*).

When the Fraction of the sacred mysteries was postponed
until after the prayer which follows the *Pater Noster,* this
latter came to be linked up with the Canon by means of its
introductory formula, *Oremus, Praeceptis salutaribus,* etc.,
and that very beautiful prayer—its position changed—lost
some of its force in ceasing to be the epilogue, as it were, of
the eucharistic liturgy now completely finished.   This is the
original meaning of the words of the existing version—
Praeceptis salutaribus moniti; they refer to our Lord's twofold
precept—to pray according to the formula which he taught
us, and to offer the holy sacrifice in memory of his death (*et
divina institutione formati*).   This alludes to the divine
oblation which brings grace upon the people and confers on
the Christian flock the divine image and likeness (*audemus
dicere*), only, that is to say, after so great a preparation by
grace, after such divine efficacy of initiation as sons of God,
who are about to approach the holy table, there to share the
children's bread; only then do we dare to raise our eyes to
heaven and call upon God our Father.   The oldest version of
this formula in the Missal is simply *Divino magisterio edocti
et divina institutione, audemus dicere.*

After the *Pater Noster* the priest, taking as starting-point
the acclamation of the faithful, *Sed libera nos a malo,* adds
the embolism *Libera nos,* in which, through the merits of the
two Apostles Peter and Paul—the mention of the Blessed
Virgin and of St Andrew is more recent—and in connection,
perhaps, with the Kiss of Peace exchanged by the faithful at
this point, public peace is invoked upon the City of Rome—a
peace so often disturbed in that era of barbarian invasions.

The Fraction of the divine mysteries, thus separated from
its primitive doxology—*Per ipsum est tibi Patri omnipotenti
omnis honor et gloria*—has now no other accompanying
formula than the priest's acclamation : *Pax Domini sit semper
vobiscum.* In the Middle Ages, however, when the *Fractio
panis* at the Pope's Mass still retained all its own liturgical
importance, and while the assistant bishops and priests aided
the Pontiff in performing the rite and placed the particles for
the Communion of the people in the linen bags held by the
acolytes, the *schola cantorum,* in order to occupy the
interval, introduced about the time of Pope Sergius I (687-
701) the invocation *Agnus Dei qui tollis peccata mundi,
miserere nobis,* as corresponding in some degree to the con-

fractorium of the Milanese rite. When the custom of breaking the eucharistic bread for the people had fallen into
disuse the *Agnus Dei* also came to be looked upon as mean-
ingless, an unnecessary addition, and to-day, thanks to the
posthumous addition of *dona nobis pacem,* it has lost its
original sense of a *confractorium* and taken on instead that of
a *collectio ad pacem,* similar, to some extent, to the prayer
thus designated in the Gallican Sacramentary.

The position assigned to the Kiss of Peace in the Roman
rite is different from that which it holds in the Frankish,
Milanese and Eastern Liturgies, where the fraternal embrace
is given either before or after the general litany following the
homily of the presiding priest, but in any case it always takes
place before the anaphora. This is precisely the order of the
Kiss of Peace in the liturgy described by Justin, and it
harmonizes with the Gospel maxim, *If therefore thou offer
thy gift at the altar, and there thou remember that thy
brother hath anything against thee; leave there thy offering
before the altar and go first to be reconciled to thy brother:
and then coming thou shalt offer thy gift.*[1]

Notwithstanding these considerations, the faithful, both at
Rome and in Africa, postponed the Kiss of Peace until the
moment of Communion. St Augustine attests this most
clearly: *Post sanctificationem sacrificii . . . dicimus Orationem Dominicam. . . . Post ipsam dicitur: Pax vobiscum,
et osculantur Christiani in osculo sancto: Pacis signum est;
sicut ostendunt labia, fiat in conscientia. Id est: quomodo
labia tua ad labia fratris tui accedunt, sic cor tuum a
corde ejus non recedat. Magna ergo sacramenta, et valde
magna. . . . Ecce accipitur, comeditur, consumitur, etc.*[2]

As regards the papal custom, we have the testimony of the
letter from Innocent I to Decentius of Gubbio, already quoted
above: *Pacem igitur asseris ante confecta mysteria quosdam
populis imperare, vel sibi inter se sacerdotes tradere, cum post
omnia quae aperire non debeo pax sit necessario indicenda,
per quam constet populum ad omnia quae in mysteriis
aguntur atque in ecclesia celebrantur praebuisse consensum,
ac finita esse pacis concludentis signaculo demonstrantur.*

This Roman custom of deferring the kiss until the end of
the eucharistic anaphora is extremely ancient, since it is
mentioned by Tertullian: *Jam alia consuetudo invaluit: jejunantes, habita oratione cum fratribus, subtrahunt osculum
pacis; quod est signaculum orationis.*[3] Moreover, we know
the real meaning of this embrace; both Innocent I and

---

[1] Matt. v, 23-24.
[2] S August., *Serm.* CCXXVII *in die Paschae; P.L.* XXXVIII,
col. 1101.
[3] *De Oratione,* c. 18; *P.L.* I, col. 1280.

Augustine regard it in the light of a *signaculum*, a seal or conclusion of the anaphora and of the Lord's Prayer already recited, so that after having said *Dimitte nobis . . . sicut et nos dimittimus*, the faithful exchange the Kiss of Peace as a pledge of perfect reconciliation. In the minds of the early Fathers, therefore, the Lord's Prayer, the embrace and the Holy Communion were three intimately connected rites, or rather they constituted but one single rite, which, in modern phrase, we might call *Ordo communicandi*.

Further, the Kiss of Peace was so closely bound up with the Holy Eucharist that in many places, including Rome, the custom obtained of offering the kiss in the very act of receiving the sacred mysteries, a custom which only survives to-day when canons receive Communion at the hands of their bishop. St Augustine speaks of it in his writings against Petilianus : *Cui pacis osculum inter sacramenta copulabatis, in cujus manibus eucharistiam ponebatis, cui vicissim danti porrigebatis.*[1] St Gregory, in his notice concerning St Cassius, Bishop of Narni, points out the same use when describing the death of the saint : *In episcopii oratorio missas fecit et manu sua Corpus Dominicum pacemque omnibus tribuit.*[2] St Jerome had already drawn attention to the same custom at Jerusalem when writing against John, the Bishop of that city : *Quisquamne tibi invitus communicat? quisquamne extenta manu vertit faciem et inter sacras epulas Judae osculum porrigit?*[3]

In Spain also there was a similar rite, as Paul of Merida shows in the words addressed to Bishop Felix : *Vade, communica et da nobis osculum.*[4] It is not difficult to explain the origin of this second Kiss of Peace, especially in the East, where the first embrace took place before the commencement of the eucharistic anaphora. To receive the Holy Communion at the hands of one's bishop or priest signified to communicate with him, to be at peace with him ; so much so that the bishops and priests and the Pope in Rome used often to send the sacred eucharistic bread to one another as a sign of mutual love and concord. To grant Communion to a penitent sinner was equivalent to pardoning his sin. It was thus that St Benedict, when he wished to absolve at their death certain persons who had departed this life in his disfavour, sent to their relatives at times *oblata* to be offered on the altar for the repose of their souls, and at other times the Blessed Sacrament to be placed on the breast of the dead

---

[1] *Advers. Epist. Petiliani*, Lib. II, c. 23; *P.L.* XLIII, col. 277.
[2] Hom. 37 *in Evang.*; *P.L.* LXXVI, col. 1281; *P.L.* LXXVII, col. 424.
[3] *Epist.* LXIII.
[4] *De Vitis Patrum*, c. vii; *P.L.* LXXX, col. 135.

person before filling in the grave with earth. In the act of
receiving the consecrated Host from a bishop it was
customary to give him the Kiss of Peace on the face, just as
the faithful of to-day kiss his hand, and this meant that they
were in communion with him, that they shared the same
catholic faith, and that they lived under his obedience.

St Augustine speaks of another rite before Holy Communion : *Postulationes fiunt cum populus benedicitur: tunc
enim antistites, velut advocati, susceptos suos per manus
impositionem misericordissimae offerunt potestati.   Quibus
peractis, et participato tanto sacramento gratiarum actio
cuncta concludit.*[1]   These are the famous episcopal blessings,
found also in the Gallican and Mozarabic Sacramentaries, but
never, so far as we know, made use of in Rome, where they
were even censured by Pope Zacharias (741-52) in a letter
written in reply to St Boniface : *Pro benedictionibus autem
quas faciunt Galli, ut nosti, frater, multis vitiis variantur.
Nam non ex apostolica traditione hoc faciunt, sed per vanam
gloriam adhibentes sibi damnationem. . . .   Regulam itaque
catholicae traditionis, quam a sancta Romana Ecclesia, cui,
Deo auctore, deservio, accepisti, omnibus praedica.*[2]

The three beautiful prayers to be found in the Missal before
the Communion belong to that period of fervent devotion
which characterized the later Middle Ages; they appear also
in the Codex of Ratoldus of Corbie—with some variants—as
eucharistic collects.   Rome placed them in her sacramentary
codex at a very late period, and, as the *Micrologus* notes,
derived them *non ex ordine Romano, sed ex religiosorum
traditione;*[3] whilst they appear in fact for the first time in the
Ordines in the fourteenth century.

Ancient custom prescribed that the faithful should receive
the Holy Eucharist in their hands, and should place their
lips to the consecrated chalice held by the deacon.   The rite
is thus described in the Mystagogic Catecheses attributed to
St Cyril of Jerusalem : *Adiens igitur, ne expansis manuum
volis, neque disjunctis digitis accede; sed sinistram velut
thronum subjiciens dexterae, utpote Regem susception; et
concava manu suscipe Corpus Christi, respondens: Amen.
Postquam autem caute oculos tuos sancti Corporis contactu
sanctificaveris, illud percipe, advigilans ne quid ex eo tibi
depereat. . . .   Tum vero post communionem Corporis
Christi, accede et ad Sanguinis poculum; non extendens
manus, sed pronus et adorationis ac venerationis in modum
dicens: Amen, sanctificeris, ex Sanguine Christi quoque
sumens.   Et cum adhuc labiis tuis adhaeret ex eo mador,*

[1] *Epist.* CXLIX *ad Paulinum,* n. 16; *P.L.* XXXIII, col. 637.
[2] *Epist.* XIII; *P.L.* LXXXIX, col. 651-52.
[3] cap. xviii.

manibus attingens, et oculos et frontem et reliquos sensus sanctifica.[1]

But earlier than this, in the inscription of Pectorius, which is of the first half of the third century, we find an allusion to the custom of receiving the Holy Communion on the palm of the hand : Ἔσθιε πινάων ἰχθὺν ἔχων παλάμαις.[2]

The *De Sacramentis* gives us the formula pronounced by the priest when distributing the sacred particles : *Ergo non otiose, cum accipis tu dicis Amen, jam in spiritu confitens quod accipias Corpus Christi. Dicit tibi sacerdos: Corpus Christi, et tu dicis: Amen, hoc est, verum. Quod confitetur lingua teneat affectus.*[3]

Anciently the faithful used to receive Communion under both species. To provide for this the Pope consecrated the wine in several chalices, and, in order to emphasize the close affection which bound the faithful to their pastor through the *sacramentum unitatis et pacis,* he poured some drops of the Blood of the Lord from his own chalice into the two-handled cup[4] destined for the communion of the people. However, about the ninth century it became customary, even in Rome, not to give the consecrated chalice for the communion of the faithful, but merely ordinary wine in which some drops of the precious Blood had been infused in order through them to sanctify the whole draught.

The *Ordo Romanus* III bears witness to the antiquity of this rule.[5] This was made in order to obviate the grave inconveniences of Communion under both kinds, which arose in the days of diminished faith, notably the risk of spilling the sacred Blood, the possibility of the wine turning sour if at any time some of it still remained in the chalice after the Communion of the people, and finally the nausea which many were already beginning to experience at having each one to place in his lips one common reed. From giving the people a chalice, no longer consecrated, but only sanctified, it was but a step to suppress it altogether. Cardinal Robert Pullo wrote thus about the middle of the twelfth century : *Qualiter a laicis eucharistia sumi deberet (Christus) sponsae suae commisit judicio. Cujus consilio et usu pulchre fit ut Caro Christi laicis distribuatur. Nimirum periculose fieret ut Sanguis sub liquida specie multitudini fidelium in ecclesia divideretur; longe periculosius, si infirmatis per parochiam deferretur.*[6]

The custom of imbibing a few drops of wine after Holy Communion is not mentioned in the *Ordines Romani* before

[1] S. Cyrilli Hieros., *Catech. Mystagog.* V; *P.G.* XXXIII, cols. 1123-26.

[2] De Rossi, *Inscription.,* t. II, p. xix.
[3] lib. IV, c. v; *P.L.* XVII, col. 464.
[4] *P.L.* LXXVIII, col. 982.   [5] The Scyphus (σκύφος).—Tr.
[6] *In Sententiar.,* Pars VIII, c. iii ; *P.L.* CLXXXVI, col. 163-64.

the fourteenth century, but there are many traces of it in antiquity. It arose from the great reverence of the early Christians, who feared lest through coughing or expectoration some particle of the sacred species should be profaned.

The habit of washing the hands after giving Holy Communion to the people is met with as early as the *Ordo Romanus VI*,[1] but not so the prayers which now accompany the first and second ablutions in the Missal, for the prayer *Quod ore sumpsimus* appears in the Gregorian Sacramentary as a collect of thanksgiving.

The following prayer, *Corpus tuum, Domine, quod sumpsi*, belongs to that development of private prayers for the use of the priest in the Mass, which we find in the sacramentaries from the ninth century onwards. The same applies to the invocation *Placeat tibi sancta Trinitas*, at the end of the liturgical *actio*, which is already noted in the Mass in the Codex of Abbot Ratoldus of Corbie.

Very ancient, on the other hand—we had almost said primitive, in the sense that it has given its name to the whole sacrificial rite—is the eucharistic collect of thanksgiving, as also that other *ad complendum* which is faithfully reproduced in the best manuscripts of the Gregorian Sacramentary, whilst in the Roman Missal of to-day it only survives in the ferias of Lent. We are referring to the very beautiful prayer of praise and thanksgiving preceded by the deacon's words of invitation : *Humiliate capita vestra Deo*. Anciently—that is, before the papal custom of blessing the people after the Mass with the formula *Benedicat nos Deus* had been adopted by bishops and priests—this collect *ad complendum* embodied a true and final benediction, to which the assembled faithful assigned peculiar efficacy. We have already narrated the story of the tumult raised by the Roman people against the Byzantine soldiery who had been sent to arrest Pope Vigilius because they would not even allow him time to recite the collect of benediction *ad complendum*.

At length the sacrifice has been offered, the thanksgiving has been rendered and the divine blessing invoked upon all present; it is now time for them to return home to their social duties, carrying away with them from the church that breath of sanctity which lingers about the altar of the Eucharist. *Ite, missa est*, therefore exclaims the deacon, it being his function to dismiss the faithful, just as it fell to him to send away before the Offertory the penitents and the catechumens with the words *Fit missa catechumenis. Si quis catechumenus, procedat. Si quis paganus, procedat. Si quis haereticus, procedat. Cujus cura non est, procedat.* The faithful,

---

[1] *P.L.* LXXVII, col. 994.

with the Eucharist in their hearts, went back in silence to
their respective avocations, armed with supernatural courage
for the battle of life, ready for love of Christ to let those
limbs be stretched upon the rack, and to pour out generously
that blood which had been strengthened and enriched by the
body and blood of their Lord in the eucharistic sacrifice.

To what date does the Roman anaphora take us back?
The answer to this question is neither easy nor simple, since
we are dealing with a text the compilation of which was not
definitely completed until the seventh century, and which
shows traces of successive growths, while it involves the
study of documents of varied sources and epochs. It is
highly probable that the original prototype was Greek, since
on this supposition alone can we explain the different readings
which distinguish the Canon quoted in the *De Sacramentis*
from that handed down in the Gelasian and Gregorian
Sacramentaries. Furthermore, in the same manuscripts of
the Roman Canon two different forms are clearly discernible,
each having distinct readings and peculiarities of its own.

The existence of this common Greek prototype, of which
there would have been an early literal version, followed by
another showing alterations and corrections, becomes a still
more likely hypothesis when we consider that the primitive
liturgical language of the Roman Church down to the third
century was Greek, in which idiom are set forth all the papal
documents of that period, the works of the great writers, of
Pope Clement, Hermas, Justin, Hippolytus, Cornelius, etc.,
the papal epitaphs in the necropolis of Callixtus, as well as a
considerable number of the inscriptions in the catacombs.
Certain it is that when Pope Anicetus granted to St Polycarp
the privilege of celebrating the eucharistic sacrifice in the
Roman synaxis, the anaphora could only have been in the
Greek tongue : Ἐν τῇ ἐκκλησία παρεχώρησεν ὁ Ἀνίκητος τὴν
εὐχαριστίαν τῷ Πολυκάρπῳ κατ' ἐντροπὴν δηλονότι.[1]

The Diocletian persecution wrought irreparable harm to
the Church of Rome, since besides causing the destruction
and confiscation of the ecclesiastical archives and buildings,
it wellnigh severed the thread of ancient liturgical tradition,
rendering impossible the stations, the vigils for the Sundays,
and the *natales* at the tombs of the martyrs—concealed or
previously covered up—so that they consequently fell into
complete disuse. When peace was restored not every portion
of the shattered vessel came to port ; more than one, and
among these Greek as the liturgical language, with great
difficulty reached the shore, only, after a brief struggle, to
disappear for ever.

The traditional eucharistic anaphora thus began to be

[1] Euseb., *H. E.,* v, 24; *P.G.* XX, col. 508.

translated into Latin, at first perhaps only for the use of the parochial synaxes, and then later on for the papal Curia also. Certainly Victorinus (died 363), in his work *Adversus Arium*, written at Rome between the years 357 and 358, quotes both the Greek and Latin texts of the Canon indiscriminately—a proof that both of them were in use at that time. *Sicut et in oblatione dicitur: Munda tibi populum circumvitalem, aemulatorem bonorum operum, circa tuam substantiam venientem;*[1] *Oratio oblationis intellectu eodem precatur eum:* Σῶσον περιούσιον λαὸν Ζηλωτὴν καλῶν ἔργων—words which do not answer to anything in the existing Latin text of the Roman Canon, but must have probably belonged to one or other of the forms then in use of the prayer of intercession after the *anamnesis*.

However this may be, the Latin version of the Greek anaphora made in Rome in the fourth century speedily caused the original prototype to be forgotten. On the other hand, the alterations must have been very few, for the succeeding Popes, Vigilius, Innocent I and St Gregory, to be able to call (with good reason) the Roman Canon a prayer of apostolic tradition : *Qua propter nos ipsius canonicae precis textum dirigimus supter adjectum, quem, Deo propitio, ex apostolica traditione suscepimus.*[2]

Thus Vigilius wrote to Profuturus of Braga, and the Roman writers of succeeding centuries all say the same thing. They were, indeed, so strongly convinced of the apostolic inviolability of their eucharistic Canon that the *Liber Pontificalis* has taken note of the smallest additions made to it by Alexander I, Sixtus I, Leo the Great and Gregory I, in order to preserve a record of them, so striking a novelty did it seem to lay a finger upon the traditional anaphora. Thus we may be certain that the existing Canon in the Roman Missal is textually the one which the Popes of the fifth century regarded as being of apostolic origin, nor have we any evidence to show that it has undergone any appreciable alteration since that time.

Certainly this apostolicity of the Canon is to be understood in a somewhat wide and general sense; for have we not ourselves just remarked upon the lack of continuity, the several lacunas, the various interpolations in the Roman anaphora? Moreover, the very rhythm of the *Canon Missae* of to-day is so changed from that which must originally have dominated the *Eucharistia,* as in early times was called the consecratory hymn of thanksgiving to God for all his benefits —a free paraphrase of the great Hallel of the Last Supper and of the *tibi gratias agens* of the Gospel narrative—that in

---

[1] *Advers. Arium*, i, 30; *P.L.* VIII, col. 1063.
[2] *P.L.* LXIX, col. 18.

the end we should have to own that the only text which to-day retains intact in the Mass this lyric character of the ancient consecratory prayer is really that part which falls outside the *Canon Missae*—viz., the Preface. To the Preface, therefore, rightly belongs the primitive title of *Eucharistia;* to it, both on account of its rhythm and also of its form, truly appertains the designation of apostolic, seeing that still to-day, as in the time of Justin, the Preface gives thanks and glory to God through Jesus Christ, whose coming into the world was the crowning blessing bestowed upon that world by its Creator : *Tibi gratias agens . . . hymno dicto.*

Although the prayer *Te igitur, clementissime Pater,* both because of its form and of the lateness of its compilation, cannot rise to the same apostolic rank as the Preface—which ought more accurately to be called the first part of the consecratory eucharistic *Hymnus*—nevertheless it can claim in its favour a creditable period of service, since it was considered traditional and even apostolic by the Popes of the fifth century. Moreover, its dissemination through the greater part of Italy must date from the time of the actual founding of the various episcopal sees through the initiative of the Roman Pontiffs, since this liturgical unity could scarcely have been accomplished as late as the fifth or sixth centuries ; at a period, that is to say, when the Arianism brought in by the barbarians, the schism of the Three Chapters, the ever-increasing power of Ravenna and Milan, and the internal dissensions among the Roman clergy themselves threatened seriously to endanger that primitive liturgical unity which the Popes Vigilius, Innocent and Gelasius were called upon to foster so carefully.

Notwithstanding so great a variety of rites and ceremonial customs in the divine Offices and at processions, we find, in the fifth century at Rome, Ravenna, Milan, Pavia and Gubbio, in the church of the anonymous author of the *De Sacramentis,* etc., that there was one eucharistic Canon used and revered—the Canon which all acknowledged as having been received from Rome—*Ecclesia Romana . . . cujus typum in omnibus sequimur et formam,* as the author of the *De Sacramentis* writes,[1] and this dating from time immemorial. We must therefore admit that this Canon, so that it may claim the veneration of all, goes back at least to remote antiquity, and that it really forms part of the sacred deposit transmitted to the other Italian sees by the Apostolic Chair.

But this same text of the Roman *Eucharistia,* even in the state of disconnection in which it has been handed down to us, shows very satisfactory evidence in favour of the antiquity

[1] lib. III, c. i; *P.L.* XVI, col. 452.

which we claim for it. The very fact that its epiklesis is pre-consecratory, just as in the papyrus of Crum, and that it is not addressed to the Holy Ghost—as in the Eastern epikleses from the fourth century onwards—nor to the Word, as in the anaphora of Serapion and in the writings of Athanasius, but exclusively to the Father, *fac nobis . . . quod figura est Corporis et Sanguinis Domini nostri Jesu Christi,* gives to the Roman invocation a genuine appearance of antiquity.

Further, in the place of the post-consecratory epiklesis, common to the anaphoras of St Mark, of Serapion, and in general to all the Eastern liturgies, the Roman Canon— agreeing in this with the anaphora of the Egyptian Ecclesiastical Statutes—has the prayer in which petition is made for the obtaining of the gifts of grace in the Holy Communion : *Ut quotquot ex hac altaris participatione sacrosanctum Filii tui Corpus et Sanguinem sumpserimus, omni benedictione coelesti et gratia repleamur.* The meaning of this ancient prayer, as Dom Cagin[1] has so well demonstrated, was very soon changed. Whilst in the Egyptian Statutes the Holy Ghost is still spoken of as overshadowing the sacred oblations and as granting his gifts to the communicants, in the Ethiopian Liturgies of the Saviour and of the Apostles the Holy Ghost, through a treacherous interpolation, becomes the agent of the transubstantiation of the mysteries. The other later liturgies, not only in the East and in Africa, but sometimes even in Spain, have all been altered in this same fashion, so that the Roman anaphora, together with that of the Egyptian Ecclesiastical Statutes, which for many reasons is to be regarded as very ancient, are the only witnesses extant to this primitive condition of things before the post-consecratory epiklesis of the Eastern liturgies obtained its present position. A comparative table of the various texts is here given.

VERONA PALIMPSEST	EGYPTIAN ECCLESIASTICAL CONSTIT.
Petimus ut mittas Spiritum tuum Sanctum in oblationem Sanctae Ecclesiae, in unum congregans, des omnibus qui percipiunt Sanctis in repletionem Spiritus Sancti ad confirmationem fidei, etc.	*Oramus te ut mittas Spiritum tuum Sanctum super oblationes hujus Ecclesiae, pariterque largiaris omnibus qui sumunt de his (ut prosint eis ad) sanctitatem et repleantur Spiritu Sancto, et ad confirmationem fidei, etc.*

TESTAMENTUM DOMINI	LITURG. ETHIOPICA SALVAT.
Domine, Spiritus Sancte, adfer potum hunc et escam hanc sanctitatis tuae, fac ut nobis sint non	*Rogamus . . . ut mittas Spiritum Sanctum et virtutem super hunc panem et super hunc calicem, (ut*

---

[1] Cf. *L'Anaphore Apostolique et ses témoins,* pp. 239 sq.

in judicium, neque in ignominiam . . . da deinde, Deus, ut tibi uniantur omnes qui participando accipiunt de sacris tuis, ut Spiritu Sancto repleantur ad confirmationem fidei, etc.

efficiat Corpus et Sanguinem Domini et Salvatoris) . . . da nobis conjunctionem animorum qui accipimus sacra tua, satiemur Spiritu Sancto et robore fidei, etc.

CANON UNIVERS. ETHIOP.

Rogamus . . . ut mittas Sanctum Spiritum et virtutem super hunc panem et super hunc calicem. (Faciat utrumque Corpus et Sanguinem Domini et Salvatoris nostri) . . . da omnibus illa sumentibus . . . sanctificationem et plenitudinem Spiritus Sancti et ad robur fidei, etc.

CANON ROMANUS

Supplices te rogamus . . . ut quotquot ex hac altaris participatione sacrosanctum Filii tui Corpus et Sanguinem sumpserimus, omni benedictione caelesti et gratia repleamur.

We can see another sign of the antiquity of the Roman Canon in the phrase from the epiklesis of the *De Sacramentis*, afterwards corrected in the Roman version : *Quod figura est corporis et sanguinis Domini nostri Jesu Christi.* . . . *Figura* is here equivalent to *sacramentum*,[1] but that which is especially worthy of note is that the term corresponds exactly to the ὁμοίωμα of the anaphora of Serapion, and agrees with the expression so repeatedly used by Tertullian : *Hoc est Corpus meum, id est figura Corporis mei.*[2] Moreover, Drews has surmised that the fiery controversialist of Carthage may have borrowed this word *figura* directly from the eucharistic liturgy of his own church.[3]

But this is not all. The Roman Canon reveals no special theological preoccupation, for it stands completely aside from the doctrinal disputes which agitated the Christian schools from the third century onwards. In the prayer *Communicantes* for Ascension Day, for example, mention is made simply of the human nature united to the Word, without saying anything about the conditions of such a union : *Unitam sibi fragilitatis nostrae substantiam in gloriae tuae dextera collocavit.* Would not something more exact have been said in the time of St Leo?

The entire *Eucharistia* is addressed to the Father through Jesus Christ our Lord, without any regard for the Arians. Possibly the heresy of the Pneumatomachians may have influenced St Leo, for at that point, where many then considered the Holy Ghost as foreshadowed by the offering of Melchisedech, he altered the text somewhat and added the words *sanctum sacrificium, immaculatam hostiam.* We do

[1] *Cf.* Battifol, *L'Eucharistie. La présence réelle et la transubstantiation.* (5me edit., pp. 362 *sq.*, Paris 1913).

[2] *Advers. Marcionem,* iv, 40; *P.L.* II, col. 491.

[3] *Untersuch. über die sog. Clement. Liturgie,* p. 141.

not know what was the original reading of this passage, but certainly we shall look in vain in the existing text of the Canon for that which the author of the *Quaestiones Veteris et Novi Testamenti* found there when he wrote : *Similiter et Spiritus Sanctus, quasi antistes, sacerdos appellatus est excelsi Dei, non summus sicut nostri in oblatione praesumunt.*[1]

Placing these words of the anonymous author of the *Quaestiones* beside that which the *Liber Pontificalis* remarks concerning the addition made to the Canon by St Leo—*sanctum sacrificium, immaculatam hostiam*—and regarding this, again, in relation to the fact that the invocation of the Holy Ghost, of which Pope Gelasius speaks in the passage above quoted, has no counterpart in the Roman Canon, we must conclude that at the time of the Pneumatomachian controversies our *Eucharistia,* too, like the Eastern anaphoras, probably underwent successive corrections and modifications, with the object of emphasizing the divinity of the Holy Ghost.

These corrections and modifications, happily, did not meet with success, and so may perhaps supply us with the reason why the famous Gelasian epiklesis has neither forerunners nor successors in the different manuscripts nor in liturgical history, but remains isolated, a sporadic fact which disturbs the whole harmony of the liturgical development of the Roman Missal. Neither St Ambrose, nor the author of the *De Sacramentis,* nor the entire tradition of the sacramentaries of all the Latin rites, ever knew any other consecratory formula than the words of the eucharistic institution, for which they claim exclusively all transubstantiatory efficacy. They certainly knew nothing whatever of the invocation of the Holy Ghost of which Pope Pelagius writes, who—if when addressing Elpidius he does not use an argument *ad hominem*—surely refers to some short-lived addition made to the Canon under the stress of Pneumatomachian troubles.

One other point still remains to be considered in reference to the history of the Roman Canon. The beginning of the doxology *Per quem haec omnia creas,* etc., reveals, as we have said, a lacuna or hiatus which nevertheless is easily filled in. We allude to the blessing of the oil and of the new fruits of the earth, etc., which took place at that point in the *Eucharistia,* and which is spoken of in the *Canones Hippolyti,* although it must have fallen into disuse at Rome at an early date for it to be wholly lost to the existing tradition of the sacramentaries. This fact signifies, therefore, that the hiatus in the Canon must be very ancient—earlier than the

[1] *P.L.* XXXV, col. 2329.

tradition itself—and herein we see a fresh argument for the antiquity of the Roman *Eucharistia* in its earliest form.

A certain importance is also attached to the collective formulas *oblationem servitutis nostrae, nos servi tui,* used by the clergy when offering the holy sacrifice, so as to distinguish themselves from the people in general. These formulas arose from circumstances then existing, and were true only of the first 150 years of Christianity, when the small number of the faithful allowed of their being present at the sacrifice celebrated by their own bishop surrounded by his band of priests. At that time in Rome one person only—the Episcopus—offered up the *Eucharistia,* or, speaking more correctly, the whole body of the clergy offered it up with him and through his hands; hence the formula was, and had to be, collective, like the formulas of letters and decretals to which we have already referred.

With the increase in the number of the faithful, and with the establishment of titular churches and country parishes, the primitive unity of altar, sacrifice and collective celebrant had to yield before the necessities of the faithful who claimed to have Mass in the church of their own quarter of the city; and the collective terms *Nos servi tui, oblatio servitutis nostrae,* became mere formulas, in no way corresponding to the reality, but testifying to a much more ancient condition of things, and hence also to the antiquity of the Roman *Eucharistia.*

To the reasons above stated for seeking the primitive prototype of the Roman Canon in a Greek text a further confirmatory observation may be made. The *servi tui* and the *oblatio servitutis* are ambiguous in the Latin and do not clearly express the idea of the *ministerium altaris* which they are intended to convey. In the Greek, on the other hand, the terms λειτουργίας or διακονίας adopted purposely in the ecclesiastical language, in order to designate the completeness of the levitical and sacerdotal offices, involve no ambiguity. The further circumstance, too, that in several ancient anaphoras—beginning with that of the Egyptian Ecclesiastical Statutes—mention is made of this *dominicum servitium* immediately after the consecration of the holy mysteries, at the same point as the Roman *Eucharistia* has it also, leads us to infer that the *Servi tui* of our *anamnesis* represents the very last remnant of this primitive liturgical custom, expressed in its simplest terms.

Let us now sum up that of which we have been speaking. A Roman tradition, which we find already fully established in the fifth century, unquestioned, nay, reverently accepted by the whole papal Patriarchate, assigns an apostolic origin to the Canon. In harmony with this belief, the Roman historians considered that in the *Liber Pontificalis* they had succeeded in noting even the smallest modifications introduced by the early Pontiffs into the text of this traditional *Eucharistia.* Moreover, the Popes and the writers who treat of the Canon regard it as a prayer unaltered and unalterable, the acceptance of which is incumbent upon all the churches. The documentary evidence of the various parts of our Canon goes back at least to the fifth century, and obliges us to identify it in its main outline with that which the early Christians held to be of apostolic tradition. A closer examination of this evidence, far from weakening our contention, only reinforces it, giving to our Roman *Eucharistia* the glory of such great age that when, to-day, after the lapse of so many centuries, we repeat the consecratory prayer of the Mass, we can be sure of praying, not only with the faith of Damasus, of Innocent and of Leo the Great, but in the very same words which they uttered at the altar before our day, and which thus sanctified that pristine age of doctors, confessors and martyrs.

THE SACRED LITURGY
FROM ADVENT TO SEPTUAGESIMA

THE FIRST SUNDAY OF ADVENT

Station at St Mary Major.

UNLIKE the old sacramentaries, in which the year began with the feast of Christmas, the Roman Missal enters to-day upon her liturgical cycle. The reason for this is that the Incarnation of the Word of God is the true central point—the *milliarium aureum*—which divides the long course of the ages of humanity. In the designs of divine Providence the Incarnation either prepares that fulness of time which heralds the coming of the *year of redemption,* or, from the cradle of Bethlehem, directs its steps towards the Valley of Josaphat, where the Babe of the Manger awaits the judgement to be pronounced on all the seed of Adam, redeemed by his precious blood. The order of our present Missal is more logical, and corresponds more closely to this lofty conception of history, by which the Incarnation is made the true central event in the world's drama. The early Christians, on the other hand, when they began their sacramentaries with the festival of Christmas, were following, in so doing, the primitive liturgical tradition, which, down to the fourth century, knew nothing as yet of a period of four or six Sundays of preparation for this, the greatest of all solemnities.

It was towards the middle of the fifth century, when, consequent on the christological heresies of Nestorius, the commemoration of the birth of our Saviour rose to great prominence, that a special season of preparation for Christmas began to make its appearance in the Liturgy, at Ravenna, in Gaul and in Spain. The controversy with Nestorius and Eutychius, and the great Councils of Ephesus and Chalcedon—in which was solemnly proclaimed the dogma of the two natures, divine and human, united in the one Person of Christ, and in which the glories and prerogatives of the *Theotokos* were consequently highly exalted—these all gave to Catholic devotion a powerful impulse towards that mystery of Redemption, through the Incarnation, which found in St Leo the Great and in St Peter Chrysologus its most able and enthusiastic exponents.

As the first portion of the Leonine Sacramentary is mutilated and incomplete, it can tell us nothing concerning the early sources of the Advent liturgy in Rome; but in all probability the rite of the papal metropolis, in this as in other respects, was practically identical with that of Naples and with the suffragan see of Ravenna, where Chrysologus—even if he be not the author of the Advent collects in the famous Ravenna Roll—delivered to the people on four different occasions four splendid homilies in preparation for the feast of Christmas.

For many centuries the Roman Church has set aside four weeks for the keeping of Advent. It is true that the Gelasian and Gregorian Sacramentaries, as well as several other ancient lectionaries, reckon five weeks, but the lectionary lists of Capua and Naples, and the custom of the Nestorians, who know only four weeks of Advent, bear witness in favour of the antiquity of the pure Roman tradition on this point also.

Unlike Lent, with its predominant thought of penance and grief for the *deicide* about to be consummated in Jerusalem, the spirit of the sacred Liturgy during Advent, full of the joyful announcement of approaching freedom, *Evangelizo vobis gaudium magnum quod erit omni populo,*[1] is one of holy enthusiasm, tender gratitude, and an intense longing for the coming of the Word of God in the hearts of all the children of Adam. Our hearts, like that of Abraham, who, as our Lord says, *exultavit ut videret diem meum, vidit et gavisus est,*[2] must be full of holy enthusiasm for the definite triumph of humanity, which, through the hypostatic union of the two natures in Christ, is raised above to the throne of God on high.

The chants of the Mass, the responsories, the antiphons of the divine Office, are all for this reason bedight with Alleluias. It would seem that the whole of Nature, looking forward, as the Apostle describes it, to the final *parousia, expectatio enim creaturae revelationem filiorum Dei expectat,*[3] feels herself uplifted by the Incarnation of the Word of God, who, after so many ages of waiting, comes at length into this world to bring his greatest handiwork to its final perfection. *Instaurare omnia in Christo.*[4] The sacred Liturgy, during this time, gathers from the Scriptures all those passages which are most forcible and best adapted to express the intense and joyful longing with which the holy patriarchs, the prophets and the just men of the Old Testament hastened by their prayers the coming of the Son of God. We cannot do better than associate ourselves with their pious feelings, and pray the Word made Flesh that he will deign to be born in the hearts of all men and spread his kingdom likewise throughout those many lands where his holy Name has not hitherto been made

---

[1] Luke ii, 10.   [2] John viii, 56.
[3] Rom. viii, 19.   [4] Eph. i, 10.

known, and whose inhabitants still sleep in darkness and the shadow of death.

To-day's station at the Liberian Basilica—in which, from the time of Sixtus III (432-40), a Roman reproduction of the Nativity at Bethlehem has been venerated—seems as if it would point out to the faithful the true meaning and aim of this season of prayer. It is there that the *Praesepe Domini* awaits us, the crib of the Incarnate Word, which, while it demonstrates the reality of his human nature, is at the same time the throne and the chair whence he will give us his first Gospel lessons upon obedience, poverty, and the mortification of the senses, whilst condemning pride, sensuality and the deceptive pomp of this world.

The *Ordo Romanus* of Cencius Camerarius attests that in the twelfth century the Pope was still wont to repair on this day to St Mary Major, there to celebrate the stational Mass.[1] It is probable that this custom goes back to the time of St Gregory I, the great reorganizer of the stational liturgy, especially as several of the ancient manuscripts of his works contain the information that to-day's homily on the Gospel, which is read in the Breviary, was actually delivered at St Mary Major.

The Introit *Ad te levavi,* with its continuation from Psalm xxiv, gives eloquent expression to the feelings of humanity, cast down, yet full of hope, and begs the Saviour to bring it back into the path which leads to Bethlehem, along the way of truth and justice. The Angelic Hymn is omitted, so that it may be taken up again the more jubilantly on Christmas night; yet at Rome in the Middle Ages the Pope intoned it on this day at St Mary Major with great solemnity, this act being in perfect harmony with the festive character of all the Advent Office. In the Collect which follows we ask our Lord to come to our aid and to save us by his power from the dangers to which we are exposed through our sins.

The Epistle is taken from that of St Paul to the Romans, xiii, 11-14. After the slackness and spiritual lethargy in which we have been, as it were, immersed by a long period of temporal peace and prosperity, now, at the end of the year, the Church rouses us at last from sleep by those inspired words of the Apostle which once wrought the conversion of Augustine. The night of the world, of ignorance and of sin is almost wholly spent; the light of the Gospel, like the first ray of early dawn, already gilds the summits of the *colles mundi;* and it is fitting that our deeds also should be worthy of this new era of light and holiness inaugurated by Christ.

[1] *P.L.,* vol. LXXVIII, col. 1063.

That deeply ingrained phrase of St Paul, *Put ye on the Lord Jesus Christ,* is too profound to be easily translated or expounded. Our divine Saviour, as the sacred doctors show, must be to us, through his example, his merits and his spirit, as it were, a secret and supernatural garment of the soul, which may live again in him, and may continue mystically on earth his Incarnation and his most holy life, to the glory of the Father.

The Gradual, following an old liturgical rule, is from the same Psalm xxiv from which the Introit is taken. The alleluiatic verse, which originally followed the second *lectio* (the Gospel was the third), is derived from Psalm lxxxiv, and expresses our desire that the Father will now show us his pity and his salvation—which is Jesus Incarnate.

The Church, in the Gospel for to-day (St Luke xxi, 25-33), connects the second coming of our Lord at the end of the world, *in gloria majestatis suae,* with his first appearance at Bethlehem as our Redeemer, *in humilitate passionis.* In both instances he calls upon his elect to lift up their heads, for the day of their redemption and deliverance is now at hand. The Church has remained ever faithful to her trust; the first generations of Christians brought their synaxes to a close with the fervent prayer that our Lord would hasten the hour of his final appearing—*Amen, veni, Domine Jesu*[1]—and to-day the same ardent faith still sustains the whole Catholic family, *hi qui diligunt adventum ejus,*[2] in their struggles and in their sorrows.

St Gregory the Great expounded to-day's Gospel to the faithful at Rome in this same stational Basilica of St Mary Major, where we, too, are still assembled; and in order to depict the final catastrophe of the world in more striking colours he takes as the groundwork of his description an earthquake which only three days before had destroyed churches and houses, filling all hearts with terror.

The Offertory also is borrowed from Psalm xxiv—the typical psalm of the first Sunday of Advent—and shows clearly the reason of such a choice in the words: *He who with watchful trust waits upon the Lord shall never be confounded.*

The Secret expresses with most admirable sobriety and terseness of language in its own words the ancient idea that runs through the Roman epiklesis, and beseeches the Saviour that the tremendous virtue of the eucharistic sacrifice may so purify our minds that we may worthily receive him who is its Author.

The Communion is a song of gladness and thanksgiving,

[1] Apocal. xxii, 20.   [2] 2 Tim. iv, 8.

taken from Psalm lxxxiv, from which we have also the alleluiatic verse. Our Lord has given us in the Eucharist a pledge of his infinite goodness, and our hearts, so long rendered arid and sterile by sin, but now refreshed by the dews of grace, are about to bring forth fruit in due season.

The Post-Communion—the true *Eucharistia* in its etymological sense—is inspired by Psalm xlvii. The divine virtue of the heavenly bread of which we have partaken will help us more than anything else to prepare ourselves suitably for the approaching feast of our common ransom.

In the later Middle Ages there was a widely spread custom, at the opening of the liturgical year, of singing certain verses before the Introit in honour of St Gregory the Great, the inspired compiler of the *Antiphonarium* which bears his name : *Sanctissimus namque Gregorius, cum preces effunderet ad Dominum ut musicum tonum ei desuper in carminibus dedisset: tunc descendit Spiritus Sanctus super eum in specie columbae, et illustravit cor ejus. Et sic demum exorsus est canere ita dicendo: Ad te levavi*, etc.

The famous fourteenth-century sequence, also, *Dies irae, dies illa*, before it was taken to form part of the Office for the Dead by the addition of the final verse—*Dona eis requiem. Amen*—used to be sung on this day before the Gospel, as if to prepare the minds of the hearers for the awful narrative of the final catastrophe described by St Luke.

Man is made up of spirit and flesh, and whilst the former is desirous of being drawn towards truth and love, the latter understands only such good or evil as he can perceive with his senses, and must therefore be held in check by penance and by a salutary fear of the judgements of almighty God.

THE SECOND SUNDAY OF ADVENT

Station at Holy Cross in Jerusalem.

After Bethlehem and the Manger comes Golgotha with the cross already shining far off over the peaceful country of Ephrata, where the Incarnate Word first appeared upon earth. The station is therefore at the Sessorian Basilica— the Roman counterpart of the *Martyrium* at Jerusalem. Here was kept the holy cross which the Empress Helena had presented to the Church in Rome. It is indeed necessary, in order to bar the way to sentimental illusions, to emphasize clearly and betimes the character of this first appearance of the Messiah in humility and poverty. Our Lord comes to offer himself as an expiatory victim for the sins of the world, and we must realize this if we are not to fall into the sin of the Jews, who in their worldliness and pride refused to accept Jesus as the Messiah, merely because he did not respond to the grandiose conception which they had formed of him. How many souls to-day still find the cross a stumbling-block ! How many say, indeed, that they seek Jesus, but when they meet him crowned with thorns and carrying on his shoulder the cross of Calvary, fail to recognize him, and pass by on the other side !

The Introit is taken from Isaias xxx and from Psalm lxxix, in which we ask that our Lord will show himself at last to the faithful tribes of Israel. This is the psalm of the *Apparitions,* so often repeated by the Church during the Christmas season, because it expresses the supreme longing of the patriarchs and of the just men of old that the power of the Most High might come to redeem mankind and destroy the empire of Satan, the *fortis armatus* who so jealously keeps guard over his prey.

The Collect is inspired by the famous cry of the Baptist, *Prepare ye the way of the Lord;* so we pray to God to pour his grace into our hearts. This preparation consists in the spirit of contrition purifying the soul and in the sincere purpose of obedience to the divine precepts.

In the Epistle, St Paul (Rom. xv, 4-13) sketches with a few touches the mission of the Redeemer, which is to level the wall of division between the fleshly seed of Abraham and the rest of humanity, in order to establish one single family, the Church. Jesus is indeed the fair flower blossoming upon the stem of Jesse, according to the promise made by God to the patriarchs; but at the same time he is the universal monarch in whose name all the nations of the earth are to be blessed, in fulfilment of the covenant already sealed with Abraham, who thus became, through faith, the father of all believers.

The Gradual is from Psalm xlix, in which the *parousia* is depicted in vivid and glowing colours. The divine Judge comes into the world surrounded by all the heavenly host of the saints, to render to each one according to his works. There is a close connection, and one which the Church does not fail to point out, between the first appearance of the divine Infant and the last coming of the supreme Judge of the living and the dead. They represent the beginning and the end of the Messianic era.

The alleluiatic verse is taken from Psalm cxxi, and expresses, with a graceful allusion to the *Sancta Hierusalem* where the station of to-day is held, the joy of the soul at the announcement of its not far distant homecoming to the heavenly Jerusalem.

John is the messenger who precedes the advent of God made Man, and so to-day, taking note rather of the logical connection of events than of their chronological sequence, the Gospel (Matt. xi, 2-10) tells us of the holy forerunner sending his own disciples to our Lord so that they may learn from his lips the good tidings that he brings. Christ testifies to his Messianic mission by deeds rather than by words, and, pointing to his miracles, teaches us that the greatest of all the wonders which bear witness to his divine nature is that of the conversion of the world in spite of the offence of the cross. This, indeed, which to the Jews was a stumbling-block, to the Gentiles was a source of happiness in their adoration of the divinity of him who hung upon the tree.

The offertory is from Psalm lxxxiv, which is conspicuously Messianic in character. After long ages of wrath, almighty God at length inaugurates an era of grace, and looks down with pity upon his people, as they hope and pray that Jehovah will speedily reveal to the world his *Misericordia*, Jesus, our Saviour.

The Redemption, the χάρις, which is the spirit of the New Testament, is not a thing merited, but is the free gift of God's loving-kindness. In the Secret, therefore, we acknowledge our own insufficiency and adduce our poverty and wretchedness as the reason of our imploring this heavenly grace.

The Communion is taken from Baruch iv and v, and invites the soul, under the figure of the stational *Hierusalem*, to prepare itself to-day for the joys which our Lord has in store for it at the feast of Christmas.

The eucharistic grace for which we beg in the Post-Communion is that the holy bread, the memorial of the death of our Lord, may destroy in us the germs of evil and may nourish us unto everlasting life.

In the Middle Ages the venerable Sessorian Basilica was called simply *Sancta Hierusalem;* this explains the several graceful allusions to this title which occur in the liturgy of this day.

THE THIRD SUNDAY OF ADVENT

Station at St Peter's.

Seeing that in Rome on the fourth Sunday of Advent there was no station—because of the great ordinations of priests and deacons *mense decembri* which took place on the preceding night—this third station preparatory to Christmas was celebrated at St Peter's, with unwonted splendour of rites and processions, as if it were the mind of the Church to introduce us at this moment to the holy joys which belong to the season of our Lord's birth.

This, in fact, is the week of the great scrutinies and of the solemn fasts preceding the ordinations; hence the faithful also on this day assemble at the tomb of the Prince of the Apostles, in order to obtain for themselves his heavenly protection, and to share with the *Pastor Ecclesiae* the joy which fills the hearts of the flock at the glad news of the approaching *parousia: Prope est jam Dominus. . . .*

Formerly the Pope used to repair to the Vatican Basilica at sunset on the Saturday, and, being present at Vespers, intoned the first and last antiphons which were indicated to him by one of the canons. The *Ordines Romani*[1] tell us that in reward for this service the Pontiff was accustomed to place a gold coin in the mouth of the worthy ecclesiastic.

It was the duty of the Vatican Chapter to provide the Pope and the cardinals with supper and sleeping accommodation for the first part of the night; this latter, however, was not required for long, since the Office of the Vigil began shortly after midnight. The Pope, preceded by acolytes with candles and torches, went first to incense the altars of St Leo I, St Gregory the Great, St Sebastian, St Tiburtius, the Apostles SS Simon and Jude, the Holy Face, the Blessed Virgin and lastly that of St Pastor. This being done, he went down into the crypt of the Confession of St Peter, and after he had offered incense at the tomb of the Apostle the first Offices of the Vigil began. Three psalms and three scriptural lessons were chanted by the clergy, then the *primicerius* intoned the *Te Deum,* the Pope recited the collect, and so ended the first part of the night psalmody *ad corpus.*

The procession then returned to the basilica above in the same order in which it had come down, and after the altar under which the body of St Peter rested had been incensed, began the Office of Matins, properly so called. This proceeded without there being anything special to be noted. The Vatican canons chanted the lessons of the first nocturn; in the second, the first two lections—extracts from the letter of St Leo I to the Patriarch Flavian—fell to the bishops; the third lection and the first of the third nocturn to two of the cardinals; the last but one to the senior canon of the Vatican Chapter; and the last one of all to the Pope. The Office of Dawn followed, in which the Pontiff intoned the antiphon preceding the Canticle of Zachary, and last of all recited the final collect.

The stational Mass for this day, as it immediately precedes the Christmas season, had originally a strikingly festive

---

[1] *Ord. Rom. XI; P.L.* LXXVIII, col. 1029.

character. We know that *novenas* and *triduums* in preparation for the greater feasts are of later origin, and in the golden age of the Liturgy these weeks before Easter and Christmas, with their vigiliary Masses and stational synaxes at the most famous basilicas of the Eternal City, were intended to prepare the souls of the faithful and to obtain for them from heaven the grace to profit by the various solemnities of the liturgical cycle.

At the Mass the Pope intoned the Angelic Hymn, which was then taken up by all the clergy. After the Collect, the singers, led by the cardinal deacons, the apostolic subdeacons and the notaries, recited the *Acclamations* or *Laudes,* in honour of the Pontiff, the clergy and the Roman people, a custom still observed at the coronation ceremony of the Sovereign Pontiffs. At the termination of the holy sacrifice the deacons replaced the tiara on the head of the Pope, and, having mounted their horses, the whole cavalcade proceeded with all due solemnity to the Lateran, where the banquet took place.

To-day's ceremonial has preserved very little indeed of all this brilliant ritual setting; joy is, indeed, by no means the dominant note of modern society. At the Mass, it is true, the sacred ministers are clothed in rose-coloured vestments in place of the customary ones of violet, and the organ once again fills the aisles with its strains. The divine Office itself has not undergone any change; it preserves intact its primitive spirit of festivity and eagerness aroused by the nearness of the coming of the Saviour.

The Introit is derived from St Paul's Epistle to the Philippians (iv, 4), and is well adapted to the occasion. The Lord is now very close at hand, and at this announcement the heart overflows with joy. Yet this joy is in complete contrast to that to which the world gives itself up, for it is the fruit of that inward peace which the Holy Ghost communicates to the soul when it remains faithful to God's holy will. Such fidelity—the careful fulfilling, that is, of the duties belonging to one's state, is here called by St Paul *modestia;* the exact measure and form, as it were, of all the virtues. Interior peace might well find an obstacle in the sorrows and anxieties of the outward life; but St Paul would have us banish from our hearts all excessive solicitude, having recourse in humble confidence to God in prayer, and laying all our needs trustingly before him whom he calls the Father of mercies and the God of all consolation. Psalm lxxxiv, which forms the concluding portion of the Introit, is in a special manner the canticle of the Redemption.

In the Collect we pray God to incline his ear to our sighs

and speedily to disperse the shadow of sin by the brightness of his coming.

The Epistle is drawn from the same passage of St Paul's letter to the Philippians as is the Introit (iv, 4-7). The Apostle concludes by wishing that the ineffable peace of the Holy Ghost may keep the faithful of his flock in the love of Christ. This supernatural peace, which is one of the fruits of the Paraclete, is the serene steadfastness of the soul in the service of its Creator.

The Gradual comes from Psalm lxxix, which we have already seen in the Introit of the preceding Sunday. He who sits tranquil above the Cherubim of his glory, and guides the destinies of mankind, is about to come in all his power to subdue his agelong enemy.

The alleluiatic verse belongs to the same psalm.

In the Gospel (St John i, 19-28) the Baptist continues his mission of preparing the way of all hearts for Jesus, so that they may become fruitful ground for the sowing of the holy seed. The world seems weary of long waiting, and by the mouth of its most authoritative representatives questions John if he be at last the prophet who was promised by Moses, whose coming has been so long announced. But the friend of the Bridegroom does not usurp his rights; nay, he abases himself still further in his humility, in order to proclaim the Messianic dignity of the Saviour and his existence from all eternity. As for himself, he says that he is merely an echo, a shadow, unworthy to render to Jesus even those menial services which slaves were then accustomed to perform for their masters. Such humility is truly in keeping with the greatness of the forerunner, of whom it was said, by the mouth of the divine Word himself, that none greater had arisen among the sons of men. In the first days of apostolic preaching, the testimony borne by John to our Lord's divinity greatly facilitated the spread of the faith among the priests and among the disciples and admirers of the austere preacher of the Jordan. At Ephesus, even, St Paul found whole groups of believers who had received only the baptism of the Precursor.

The Offertory is taken, like the Introit, from Psalm lxxxiv. The coming of our Lord on earth is the blessing promised by Jehovah to Abraham; it is freedom from slavery, it is the remission of sins.

In the Secret we ask God so to help us that we may renew the unbloody sacrifice by constant devotion, and that the eucharistic mystery now about to be accomplished may be for us a pledge of eternal salvation.

In the Communion comes a last invitation to timid souls: " Fear not : it is no longer a prophet, a lawgiver, a scribe, as under the old Covenant, but God himself who comes to save you " (Isa. xxxv, 4).

In the Post-Communion—the *Eucharistia*—we pray God that the sacred gift may so purify us as to prepare us fittingly for the coming solemnity.   To dispose our souls for the worthy reception of divine grace demands suitable preparation before approaching the sacraments, by giving due care to prayer and meditation.   If Jerusalem rejected the Messiah, it was precisely for want of preparation for the receiving of the Messianic grace.   Wholly immersed in vain and worldly desires, she was indeed ill-prepared to see the King of Glory in the Man of Sorrows.   Ritual and external practices of worship are praiseworthy and necessary, but preparation for the right use of grace is something far more searching and needful.

WEDNESDAY IN EMBER WEEK

Collecta at the Title of Eudoxia.   Station at St Mary Major.

The solemn fast of the three days in Ember Week seems to have been originally peculiar to the Roman Church, whence it was afterwards borrowed by the other Latin dioceses.   St Leo I explains its meaning clearly, especially on the occasion of the December fasts, when he remarks that, at the end of the year, and before beginning to draw upon the winter resources, it is very fitting that we should dedicate the firstfruits to the divine Providence by a freewill offering of abstinence and almsgiving.   In this case there was a further motive.   An ancient tradition reserved the ordinations of priests and deacons to the month of December, and the faithful—following a custom introduced by the Apostles themselves—felt constrained to unite with the bishop in prayer and fasting, in order to call down from God an abundance of priestly gifts upon the heads of those newly chosen to minister at the altar.

In truth the highest interests of Christian people are bound up, to a great extent, with the holiness of the clergy ; and since Holy Scripture teaches us that the most terrible chastisement which almighty God inflicts upon perverse nations is to give them pastors and leaders of their own kind, it is evident that the ordination of the sacred ministers is not a matter which concerns merely the bishop and his seminary, but one which is of supreme importance to the whole Catholic body.

For this reason the Acts of the Apostles record the solemn fasts and public prayers which preceded the ordination of the first seven deacons and the mission of Paul and Barnabas as Apostles to the Gentiles; and to-day, after so many centuries, this rule has undergone no substantial relaxation. The rites and their outward setting are, perhaps, somewhat simpler now than they were at the height of the Middle Ages in Rome, but the fasts, the preparatory stations, and the solemn prayers of the Christian community still precede in their due order the sacramental imposition of hands upon those elected to the priesthood.

To-day's station—following the custom for Ember Wednesdays—is at the Liberian Basilica, in order that the new Levites may be placed under the heavenly patronage of her whom the Fathers of the Church sometimes call the *virgin-priest,* in whose temple the Incarnate Word himself was anointed priest by the divine Paraclete. Formerly the procession of clergy and people, chanting the Litany, went from St Peter in Vinculis to the Liberian Basilica by way of the Suburra, the Viminal and the Esquiline. After the Collect on entering St Mary Major, one of the keepers of the papal archives announced to the people from the *ambo* the names of those about to be ordained. *Auxiliante Domino et Salvatore nostro Jesu Christo, eligimus hos N.N. diaconos in presbyteratum. Si igitur est aliquis qui contra hos viros aliquid scit de causa criminis, absqu⹂ dubitatione exeat et dicat; tantum, memento Communionis suae.*

These solemn proclamations took the place at Rome of the ancient custom—very widely spread in other parts—of popular suffrage at ordinations. In some localities the people were consulted, with the idea that they would yield obedience more readily to those whom they themselves had chosen as their pastors. Rome, however, from very early days—so we learn from the Epistle of St Clement to the Corinthians—looked upon this privilege as being too dangerous and compromising, easily open to misinterpretation and not in keeping with the divinely authoritative character of the sacred hierarchy. The sacred ministers should be chosen by Christ himself through his Apostles and bishops, and not by popular suffrage, as if it were a matter of electing public officials in the Forum. Rome, therefore, in her sacred ordinations, granted a part to the people, honourable indeed, but secondary and merely confirmatory; they could make a deposition, that is, concerning any of the candidates, if they knew them to be legally guilty in any matter, and consequently unworthy. It is just this which the Apostle requires when he writes to Timothy, that it is necessary for those chosen to the priestly office to have *testimonium . . . bonum ab his qui foris sunt, ut non in approbrium incidant.*[1]

---

[1] 1 Tim. iii, 7.

The whole of the Mass for this day is one deep sigh of the most heartfelt desire for the Messiah who is to come. Isaias is the great prophet of Advent, hence the Church reads at this season the finest passages from his writings, so that the faithful, too, may hasten by their prayers the coming of the kingdom of Jesus Christ.

The Introit is from Isaias xlv, 8, in which the meek and peaceful character of this first coming of the Word of God upon earth is wonderfully expressed in two brilliant figures of speech—namely, the heavens distilling refreshing dew upon Gedeon's fleece, and the earth producing the little flower of the fields upon the mystic stem of Jesse. Psalm xviii follows, wherein all created things—the heavenly bodies, the sun, the moon and the stars—join in glorifying their Maker. To these the Psalmist adds the praises of the Law, the clear reflection of the eternal Word of the Father.

Originally, on the days of the stational processions, when the great Litany was sung on the way, the Introit was omitted, and the Pope, on reaching the church, recited the Collect after the last Kyrie. The deacon first invited the faithful to prostrate themselves so that they might pray for a while in secret—*Flectamus genua;* then, after a few moments spent in prayer, he gave the signal to get up again, and the Pontiff summed up the petitions of the assembly in a brief formula—*collecta*—and presented them to God. In to-day's *collecta* we beseech the divine clemency that the approaching Christmas solemnity may be to us fruitful in grace for this present life, and so prepare us to receive the reward of final blessedness.

The Mass for to-day still keeps the rite of the threefold scriptural lesson which in early times usually preceded the Offertory; the first lesson was as a rule from the Old Testament, the second from the New Testament, and the third from the Gospel. But the primitive order was frequently upset. Thus to-day the first two lessons are both from Isaias. In the first (Isa. ii, 2-5) the Church is compared to a high mountain, up which all the peoples of the earth are making their way; the Messianic times are described, the universality of redemption, and the tranquillity and peace of the nations when they shall finally be united in the ties of a common faith. The Gradual which follows is taken from Psalm xxiii, and describes the triumphal entry of Christ into his kingdom.

The second lesson (Isa. vii, 10-15) announces in formal terms the wondrous event which will shortly come to pass. The more almighty God is grieved by the wickedness of the world, the greater is his mercy towards all poor sinners. He desires to give them a pledge of this pity, and behold a virgin shall bring forth a son who shall be called simply that which he truly is—*God with us.*

The Gradual, from Psalm cxliv, tells us that the Lord is very nigh to those who trust in him. God is near to the man who wishes him to be near and who loves him; but he is far from those who do not desire him. He treats souls according to their inward dispositions. As, however, God is good, he often turns to good our bad dispositions by the working of his grace.

The Gospel (Luke i, 26-38) contains the message of the Angel Gabriel to the Blessed Virgin Mary, and her consent to fulfil her mission as the Mother of God. What treasures of generosity, of humility and of devotion are hidden in those words: *Behold the handmaid of the Lord; be it done to me according to thy word!*

In the monasteries during the Middle Ages it was the duty of the abbot to give a special address to his monks on this Gospel, and we still possess a whole collection of homilies *super Missus Est* delivered by St Bernard to his monks in Chapter at Clairvaux.

The Offertory comes from Isaias, and contains the announcement of the imminent approach of the Messiah. The Church insistently repeats this good news, so that the soul may rouse itself from the lethargy into which spiritual sloth has cast it, and may fully realize this nearness of Jehovah.

The Secret presents to our Lord the fruit of the solemn fasts that are being kept during this week by the whole Christian flock. Their object is to expiate past sins and to prepare us fittingly for that holy *newness of life* which is about to be inaugurated at the coming of the Incarnate Word.

The Communion is taken from the prophecy of Isaias to King Achaz : " A virgin shall conceive and bear a son : and his name shall be called Emmanuel, that is, *God with us.*" Here we find clearly expressed the dogma of the two natures in Christ which was so much disputed during the period preceding the Council of Ephesus, at which was solemnly proclaimed the Catholic doctrine giving to Mary the title of *Mother of God.* The son born of a virgin cannot indeed be otherwise than *Man,* as we are, but the Holy Ghost calls him, at the same time, *Emmanuel*—that is, *God* with us. Thus in the single person of Jesus Christ we have to recognize and adore the two natures, divine and human. Without the divine nature the expiation offered by Christ Jesus would not have sufficed to satisfy God's justice, affronted by the sins of the world; without the human nature God would have been incapable of suffering. It was therefore necessary that the human nature should be hypostatically united to the person of the Word, so that the reparation presented by Christ might be the reparation rendered by God himself to God.

In the Post-Communion we pray our Lord that he will grant us not to rest satisfied with that pleasure in outward devotion which is sometimes kindled by partaking of the heavenly food, but to aim at laying a firm foundation of virtue. Visible consolations are like the blossoms on a tree. But the husbandman is not satisfied with flowers alone; he desires to see the fruit as well. So it should be with us. We must not allow ourselves to be too much attracted by the outward delights of devotion, but must look to the acquisition of the solid qualities of a virtuous life, to gain which we need to separate ourselves from the things of this world, and to take off our thoughts wholly from ourselves, so as not to desire aught else than God.

During this season of immediate preparation for Christmas the Church invites us to attach ourselves with special love to Mary, for it is from her that our Advent has its beginning during those nine months in which she bore our Lord within her. What must have been the feelings of faith, of love, and of zeal which then animated the Virgin so closely united to that God who in the Scriptures is called a *consuming fire?* Prefigured by the burning bush of Moses, Mary, aflame with Jesus, is the model of all who love him truly.

FRIDAY IN EMBER WEEK

Collecta at St Mark's. Station at the Twelve Holy Apostles.

The station preceding the solemn ordinations in Rome is always at the *Apostoleion* of Pelagius I (555-60), partly in homage to the holy Apostles whose mission to evangelize the world is to be carried on by the Levites of to-morrow, and partly on account of the great celebrity to which this venerable basilica attained during the first Byzantine period. The Pontifical makes Julius I (341-52) its original founder, but the building, thanks to Byzantine money, must have undergone thorough restoration during the pontificates of Pelagius and John III (560-73), so that when the records of Pope Julius were lost, the basilica was commonly regarded as the work of Pelagius I, erected as a votive memorial of the victory of Narses over the Goths (554).

In 1873, in the course of excavations made under the high altar, a casket was discovered containing fragments of the bones of the Apostles SS Philip and James, mixed with the remains of balsam, doubtless placed there on the occasion of the second dedication of the basilica. In the ninth century several bodies of early martyrs, brought from the cemetery of Apronianus on the Via Latina, also found a resting-place in this church, amongst them being the highly venerated body of St Eugenia, which was therefore placed in a special oratory adjoining the *Apostoleion.*

The *collecta,* or place of assembly, whence the stational procession used on this day to start on its way to the *Apostoleion,* must have been in the ancient titular Church of St Mark *in Pallacinis,* which is quite near by. It is so prescribed, at least, in the stational lists for the Friday of Ember Week in Lent, although these lists of the stations contain nothing actually concerning to-day's Advent-tide ceremony.

The Mass is once again an impassioned longing of the soul for the coming Emmanuel, who is to redeem Israel by the tremendous power of his arm. The Introit has been adapted from Psalm cxviii: "Thou, O Lord, art already near, and truth makes plain for thee the way. I have learnt from the beginning, from thine own lips, this ineffable mystery of thy Messianic *parousia.* Born in time, according to the flesh, thou art, nevertheless, eternal in thy divine generation."

In the Collect we implore our Lord to gird on the sword of his might and come to succour us. Mankind has already confidently awaited this redemption for many ages, and the world has long ago sounded all the depths of depravity and wickedness. It has learnt by sad experience of what human nature is capable without the grace of God. It is now time for the hope to be realized which the chosen people of the race of Adam have been nourishing for so many centuries.

Isaias (xi, 1-5) speaks in the Epistle, and describes for us in glowing colours the future emancipator of Israel. He shall blossom, he says, as a flower upon the stem of Jesse, and all the fulness of the grace of the Paraclete shall rest upon him like a sweet-smelling unction which shall consecrate him the judge of his people. Yet he will not judge according to outward appearances, nor decide upon the mere testimony of the senses. He it is for whom Job sighed when, crushed beneath the imputations of his enemies, he said to God: *Hast thou eyes of flesh? or shalt thou see as man seeth?* (Job x, 4). The eye of God shall search into the innermost depths of the heart, and by the might of his Word he shall put all his adversaries to confusion. He shall array himself with justice as with a cincture, and bind up his loins with faithfulness as with a girdle.

Such is the plan of redemption put forth by the Messiah. The servitude to which Satan has condemned humanity for many centuries is indeed burdensome. He relies on his weapons of pride and cunning, but God will entangle him in the very same snare which he has set for mankind. A son of Adam stronger than the Evil One shall soon come, who like David, the lowly little shepherd, shall overcome with the weapons of humility and patience the pride of Goliath, this false giant, and shall set his captives free.

The Gradual is derived from Psalm lxxxiv, which is wholly a hymn of thanksgiving for the blessings of redemption. Like Abraham and the patriarchs of old, the prophet begs God to show us at last the radiant light of Christ, the sweet face of the Saviour, who shall come in meekness, breathing forth grace over the waters of redemption.

The Gospel takes up again the thread of St Luke's narrative (Luke i, 39-55), which was begun two days ago. Mary, saluted by the angel as full of grace, hastens to begin at once her work as the dispenser of grace, and so takes her Jesus into the house of Elisabeth, in order that he may initiate his redeeming work by sanctifying John in his mother's womb. The Blessed Virgin enters the home of her cousin and humbly salutes her; all at once, at Mary's word, the being of the Forerunner is filled with grace, and the spirit of prophecy possesses his aged parents. Thus the priestly house of Zacharias in Hebron becomes the first sanctuary of Mary, wherein the Mother of God begins to spread abroad her mercies by pouring out their firstfruits upon the greatest of those born of woman. Thus is John the first among the saints to owe all his gifts of grace to Mary, and there, under the humble roof of Zacharias, is sung for the first time that sublime canticle, the *Magnificat,* which shall form the dedication hymn of the first church of our Lady, and shall be the daily prayer of the Church through all the ages.

The verse *ad offerendum* is also from Psalm lxxxiv : Thou, O Lord, who hadst turned away thy face from us on account of our sins, mayst thou be appeased and turn again and look upon us, and the light of thine eyes shall restore us once more to life. Show us thy mercy, O Jehovah, and reveal to us now the Saviour whom thou hast promised and in whom the patriarchs of old fell asleep full of trust and hope. The face of Jesus in heaven is the cause of joy to the angels, but on earth it is the token of God's pity for sinners. We say to the Father, *Respice in faciem Christi tui,* but let us, too, fix our own gaze on that face, lest we lose sight of it. As the eternal Father, when he beholds the face of Jesus, is touched with compassion for the wretched children of Adam, so let us also show a holy reverence for that sacred face and for those pure eyes that look on us so tenderly ; let us take care that all our actions are worthy of the ineffable sanctity of that divine regard.

By means of the prayer which, in the Roman use, serves as an introduction to the Preface, we beseech almighty God to accept our humble supplications, together with the holy sacrifice, so that, being purified by the mystery of redemption, we may deserve that our petitions be granted. Indeed, we know that our sins have too often forfeited the divine grace, which has thus been so sadly abused; the eucharistic sacrifice, therefore, must above all things be for us a sacrifice of propitiation, increasing in us that faith and charity *quae prima datur, ut caetera impetrentur,* as St Augustine says.

The Communion, as is often the case in Advent, is taken from the prophetic books instead of from the Psalter. To-day the choice falls upon Zacharias, who comes to warn us that now very near at hand is that bright day when our Saviour, followed by all his elect, will enter into his Messianic kingdom (Zach. xiv, 5). This prophecy, indeed, refers rather to the second coming of Christ at the end of the world than to the first; but both these appearances form part of one single plan of grace, of one and the same mystery of salvation. The Messianic kingdom has already been inaugurated in the obscurity of the cave at Bethlehem, but it will not be fully and finally established until the day of the general resurrection.

The coming of the Incarnate Word puts an end to a former state of things which had become intolerable, and inaugurates instead a new era. The sacrament by which we are consolidated into this new kingdom is the sacrament of Redemption itself, and thus most beautifully in the Post-Communion we pray our Lord that the sacred outpouring of the chalice of salvation, while it cleanses us from old stains, may renew our interior life and make us partakers of the mystery of salvation.

Gabriel also, on behalf of the heavenly hosts, salutes Mary, full of grace, higher than all living creatures. Elisabeth, too, the favoured mother of the greatest of all those born of woman, as representative of all the human race, proclaims her to be the Mother of the Lord, blessed above all the seed of Adam, the fertile tree about to bear a blessed fruit. But why such an outpouring of grace and such high praises bestowed upon Mary? The answer is that she is humble, and that is why God exalts her; that she believes and puts her trust in him, therefore God fulfils in her his glorious promises. The *Magnificat* is the crowning utterance of this sublime prophetess filled with the Holy Ghost. It voices her humility, her faith, her gratitude, her love, graces which have so entranced the Church of God that she has never found it in her heart to forbid the joy of singing this canticle, even in days of bitterest grief. Thus in the Office for the Dead, and on the last three days of Holy Week, when alleluias, doxologies, hymns and all other joyous utterances are silenced, the sacred Liturgy never omits the *Magnificat,* whose privileged strains resound through the arches of God's temple even amid the mournful sadness of Good Friday itself.

SATURDAY IN EMBER WEEK

Station at St Peter's.

At first the ordinations of the sacred ministers in Rome took place only in the month of December—when, that is to say, the Christian family at the approach of the Christmas festival made an offering, as it were, to God, by a solemn three days' fast, of the fruits now gathered in, taking this opportunity to beg the bestowal of his gifts upon those whom the Holy Ghost had chosen to carry on the work of the Apostles and to guide the flock of Jesus Christ. It was the usual custom for the ordinations of the sacred Levites to be celebrated at the tomb of St Peter, but as we have had to point out, although all the members of the clergy take their origin from the Apostle from whom they derive their power as from a living source, nevertheless the Pope alone inherits from him the plenitude of the pontifical power and the universal primacy of the Church. Thus in the twelfth century it came to be the rule that the papal consecration alone was carried out at the altar over the tomb of the Apostle, while all other ordinations took place usually in the adjoining rotunda of Sant' Andrea, or in the oratory of San Martino.

Formerly this Saturday was non-liturgical in Rome, like Holy Saturday and the other Ember Saturdays, so that the fast which began after supper on the Friday evening lasted until dawn of the following Sunday—until the end, that is, of the vigiliary Mass which was being said in the Vatican Basilica. In those early days of which we are speaking, the primitive idea was still prevalent of the convivial *agape* being closely bound up with the celebration of the Eucharist. For this reason the ecclesiastical fast did not admit of even the Mass which from the time of Tertullian marked the end of the period of abstinence. It was therefore very natural that, as the sacred ordinations had to be celebrated at St Peter's during the vigil for the Sunday, the people should abstain from food throughout the preceding day, and that in consequence the Saturday had no Mass of its own.

In the old sacramentaries the Ember Saturdays are often called the *Saturdays of Twelve Lessons,* the origin of which is as follows : Originally, in Rome—and many other Western

22

churches followed this example—there were three fast-days in the week; that is to say, Wednesday, Friday and Saturday; and during the night preceding the Sunday the nocturnal vigils were held in preparation for the Sunday sacrifice. Here we have the primitive manner of sanctifying the Christian week, as contrasted with that of the Pharisees, which had only two fast-days—Monday and Thursday. As time went on, this strict evangelical rule was relaxed, and that which was at first the customary rite for the weekly cycle ended by becoming, in the fourth century, the peculiar feature of certain special weeks—*i.e.,* those of the three solemn fasts of June, September and December, which took the place of the old Latin *feriae* of harvest, vintage and the drawing off of the new wine.

The form of the ancient Roman vigil has been fairly well preserved for us in the Roman Missal, in the first part of the ceremony which now precedes the blessing of the baptismal font on Holy Saturday. This archaic form is derived in the first instance from the custom of the synagogues of the *Diaspora,* in which, on every Sabbath day, the people alternated the responsorial chanting of the psalms with the reading of fixed portions of Scripture, commented on by the rabbis. As Paul, Barnabas, Silas and others used to frequent the sabbatical gatherings in the synagogues, the Christian synaxes could begin only at sunset, after the liturgical service of the Hebrews was over. When the timid followers of the Gospel assembled *circa domos ad frangendum panem,* Venus was already shining in the heavens, and, as the function would last all the night, it opened with the ceremony of the *lucernarium,* by which the flickering flame designed to disperse the shadows of the sacred vigil was dedicated to the uncreated Light. Herein we see a true image of the infant Church.

Long before the monks transplanted from Egypt the form of the psalmodic vigil in use in those monasteries and introduced it into the liturgy of the Roman basilicas, the nightwatch of the Church in Rome adopted a complete intermingling of twelve lessons, repeated in Latin and Greek, for the benefit of the cosmopolitan population of the Eternal City, and alternated with the responsorial chant of the famous morning *Hymns* and with the collects of the priest. Possibly from the first the lessons—as also in the East—were successively explained to the people by the priests or by the Pope; but about the fifth century all the explanation given was summed up in the collect pronounced by the person presiding over the assembly. At the end of each portion read the deacon invited the people to prayer—*Flectamus genua*—and all the people prostrated themselves to meditate on what they had heard. After a few minutes the Levite gave the order *Levate,* and everyone rose up, stretching out his arms in the form of a cross, in the attitude of prayer. Then the priest, in the name of all present, recited the short prayer to be found in the Missal of to-day, called the *Collect* because it *collected* the particular petitions of each of the faithful and presented them, thus summarized, before the heavenly throne.

At the end of the vigils, at daybreak, the canticle of the three youths of Babylon, commonly called the *Benedictiones,* brought the psalmody to a close, and served to fill in the time between the vigiliary office and the offering of the eucharistic sacrifice. Before, however, the sacred gifts were brought to the altar, the ordination of the new ministers took place. The main outline of the rite was the same for bishops, priests and deacons. A short preparatory collect was followed by the chanting of the eucharistic prayer of consecration (Preface), accompanied by the imposition of hands. Originally there was no conferring of the insignia of office, no anointing, no clothing; these were introduced later on under Gallican influence. The consecratory anaphora proceeded with the same rhythm as that of the Mass, to which the rite of ordination constituted, as it were, a short preparatory prelude. In that golden age of the sacred Liturgy the Eucharist was the true central point of Catholic worship, the setting of every other religious act. It was with a view to its consecration that the new ministers were ordained; hence it was peculiarly fitting that this rite should form the preliminary part of the anaphora itself. This is the reason why the oldest liturgical documents put before us the text of the eucharistic anaphora when they come to treat of the ordination of new priests : " When you shall have chosen someone for the dignity of bishop or presbyter, recite over him the prayer of consecration; then, when he shall have received the kiss of peace from the people, the deacon shall give him the bread and wine, and the new *sacerdos* shall recite the anaphora of oblation over these elements." So in general terms say the Canons of Hippolytus and the oldest texts of Canon Law which have come down to us.

To-day the rite of ordination, as prescribed by the Roman Pontifical, is much more intricate. The judicial Frankish mind, with its distinction between the law itself and the outward forms required for its actual administration, has introduced into the Roman ceremonial such a complexity of reduplicated prayers, of bestowals of insignia, of clothings and anointings with the oil of the catechumens and with chrism, that theological scholars have sometimes failed to disentangle the essential matter and form of the Sacrament of Orders. It must be said that Rome adapted herself most unwillingly to this network of ceremonial, and then only at the very end of the Middle Ages. Throughout the long centuries of the medieval period she preserved intact her original anaphoras for the ordination of the sacred ministers —as the *Ordines Romani* testify—and these, when compared with the anaphoras which we find embodied in the oldest liturgical documents of the Patriarchates of Alexandria and Antioch, such as the so-called Canons of Hippolytus, the Ecclesiastical Ordinances of the Egyptians, the *Didascalia* of the Apostles, the Apostolic Constitutions, the Testament of our Lord, etc., are seen to be closely connected with all these, and to be taken together with them from one common primitive source of inspiration.

As space does not allow of our giving in their entirety the Roman formulas for the consecration of the sacred ministers, we shall merely sum them up briefly.

After a short introductory collect, which for their greater honour always preceded, in ancient times, both the eucharistic anaphora and the Lord's Prayer, there follows the prayer for the consecration of bishops and of the Pope himself, which expresses the underlying conception that—unlike the ancient levitical priesthood, whose privileged position consisted wholly in outward splendour of apparel—the Christian priesthood possesses no special dress. We thus find ourselves in a period in which no distinctive type of priestly vestments as yet exists; but just as in Rome at the beginning of the fourth century the sacred Levites, when ministering at the altar or at the burial of the martyrs, are barely distinguishable by the greater whiteness of their *pallia,* thrown on over the Latin *toga,* from the common dress of the rest of the citizens.

The ornaments of our priesthood, as the anaphora, on the other hand, proclaims aloud, are those virtues which were symbolized and prefigured by the gold and the jewels on the ancient *ephod* of the high priest. As during the first three centuries—to the exclusion of the presbyters, who merely presided over the painful confessions made by the penitents— the usual minister of sacramental absolution, as well as of baptism and first Communion, was the bishop, so in the anaphora of which we are speaking a petition is addressed to God that he will grant to the bishop the keys of the heavenly kingdom, so that what he binds and looses on earth may also be bound and loosed in heaven.

In those early times, so much troubled by heresies, the ministry of preaching also belonged in so great a degree to the bishop rather than to the priest, that, notwithstanding St Jerome's disapproval of this rigid limitation of pontifical power, Rome had for a time to behold, though with a mistrustful eye, the diverse custom of the Gallican churches, in which presbyters had full liberty to preach. Hence, in the anaphora for the consecration of bishops, allusion is made to this duty of preaching the Word of God, so all-important and so especially the function of the Pontiffs, who were regarded as the successors of the Apostles in the ministry of evangelization.

Taking into consideration, therefore, all these duties assigned to the bishop in the first four centuries, and seeing that the anaphora for the consecration of bishops—according to the Roman Pontifical—clearly reflects this order of ideas and this primitive rule of the church, its compilation cannot be carried back further than the fifth century, and to a period in it rather early than late.

Next to the more important extracts from the text of the present Pontifical, we will here place the parallel passages from the Apostolic Statutes and from the so-called Canons of Hippolytus.

Pontif. Roman.	Statut. Apostol., Latin., Veron.	Canon. Hippolythi
Huic famulo tuo quem ad summi sacerdotii ministerium elegisti, hanc, quaesumus, Domine, gratiam largiaris . . . ut tui Spiritus virtus et interiora eius repleat. . . . Sint speciosi munere tuo pedes ad evangelizandum . . . Da ei . . . ministerium reconciliationis, in verbo, in factis, in virtute signorum et prodigiorum . . . Da ei, Domine, claves regni caelorum . . . quodcumque ligaverit super terram, sit ligatum et in caelis, et quodcumque solverit super terram sit solutum et in caelis. Quorum retinuerit peccata retenta sint, et quorum remiserit, tu remittas. Tribue ei, Domine, cathedram episcopalem, ad regendam ecclesiam tuam.	*Da . . . super hunc servum tuum quem elegisti ad episcopatum, pascere gregem sanctam tuam, primatum sacerdotii tibi exhibere. . . .* *. . . habere potestatem dimittere peccata . . . solvere etiam omnem colligationem, secundum potestatem quam dedisti Apostolis.*	*. . . Ratione hujus episcopi qui est magnus Abraham . . . respice super servum tuum, tribuens virtutem tuam et spiritum . . . quem . . . tribuisti sanctis Apostolis. Tribue illi episcopatum . . .* *. . . et potestatem ad remittenda peccata, et tribue illi facultatem ad dissolvenda omnia vincula iniquitatis.*

It is noteworthy that in the Roman consecratory formula the power to remit sins is placed in direct relation with the sovereign power of the keys committed to Peter. This is true of the Roman Pontiff, but it is not altogether accurate in the case of other bishops. This peculiarity would cause us to suspect that the anaphora of the Pontifical was originally compiled for the consecration of the Pope exclusively, and was only adapted later for that of the suffragan bishops of Rome, who had to receive their consecration at the hands of the Sovereign Pontiff as being their metropolitan.

The office of the presbyters, according to the ecclesiastical rule of the first centuries, was to act as counsellors to the bishop and to replace him in the administration of the sacraments, with the exception of those which were reserved to him by divine institution or by Canon Law. Therefore, conformably to the Roman Pontifical, in the anaphora for the consecration of priests, the bishop, having first called to mind that Moses in the wilderness was aided by a council of seventy elders, that Aaron made use of the ministry of his own sons, and that, finally, Christ granted even to the Apostles the help of teachers, begs our Lord to give to him, too, as their consecrator in the person of the new candidates to the priesthood, assistants filled with the spirit of all holiness.

In keeping with the position anciently occupied by the presbyters, who, although they formed a priestly assemblage around the person of the bishop, yet in ordinary circumstances had no especial function assigned to them; they neither baptized, nor celebrated Mass, nor absolved penitents, except in the absence of the bishop and at his personal delegation; so in the anaphora of the Roman Pontifical for the ordination of priests no particular charge is mentioned as being distinctively allotted to them; prayer is offered merely in general terms, that the gift of grace to the new priests may render them *providi cooperatores ordinis nostri*. This exactly corresponds with the practice of those very early times when the only *sacerdos* and minister of the sacraments was the Pontiff, while the priests, except in the case of the Sacrament of Holy Orders, took his place only on such occasions as, for some reason, he was unable to be present.

The deacon of antiquity was the bishop's inseparable companion; it may even be said that if the body of presbyters represented the wisdom of the Church and the mainstay of episcopal authority, the deacons were her right hand. Thus at Rome in the third century it was the invariable custom for the deacons, and never for the priests, to succeed to a deceased Pontiff. Unlike the priests, who aided the bishop by their knowledge and authority in the spiritual régime of the Church and in the administration of the sacraments, the office of the deacons, although of greater responsibility, was at the same time more humble.

The priests, for the reason that they shared, though in an inferior degree, a common priesthood with the Pontiff, sat beside him in the sacred synaxes. Sometimes they celebrated together with him and broke with him the eucharistic bread, while the characteristic posture of the deacons was to stand the whole time, awaiting orders, as it were, and confining themselves to the material duties of the sacred ministry. What were these duties? They were not merely to accompany the bishop when he preached or celebrated the sacred mysteries or attended councils; but it was their particular charge to administer the ecclesiastical patrimony, to supervise the cemeteries, and to care for the poor, the orphans and the catechumens, and for those who were thrown into prison for confessing the name of Christ, as well as to attend to the correspondence of the episcopal chancery, etc.

For this reason the anaphora for the consecration of deacons expresses the great importance attached by the Church to the office of her Levites. Their moral qualities must be such and so many that the bishop almost hesitates to make himself surety for their merit to the faithful, so he appeals to the inscrutable wisdom of almighty God, who alone can penetrate the consciences of the candidates and heal the wounds which are invisible to human eyes and beyond human cure. The celebrant, therefore, prays that the deacons may be a shining example of all virtue, chaste, constant and modest in the exercise of their authority. This last recommendation was especially opportune in the case of the Roman deacons, who would sometimes so exceed their powers as to oblige councils to place a check upon their arrogance: *De diaconibus Urbis, ut non sibi tantum praesumant.*

With the help of the various *Ordines Romani* we are enabled to follow step by step the whole course of development of the ordination ritual in the Eternal City. At first there was a simple *oratio* in the form of an anaphora, accompanied by the imposition of the bishop's hands, constituting a very short parenthesis, as it were, in the usual order of offering the holy sacrifice. It occupied but a few minutes—*jejunantes et orantes, imposuerunt eis manus,* just as the ordination of Paul and Barnabas is described in the Acts of the Apostles. The parenthesis being ended, the Mass went on from the point at which it was interrupted, and the Eucharist placed the final seal on the whole rite.

In the Middle Ages the ceremonial became more complex. Then were introduced the official conferring of the *oraria,* which had been placed the previous day on the tomb of St Peter; the clothing with the *paenulae;* the litanies and the solemn procession on horseback of the new priests and deacons to their respective titular churches. With these

rites, which are described in the *Ordines Romani* of the ninth
century, were afterwards interwoven the other Gallican
ceremonies, of the anointings and of the consignment of the
insignia of office symbolical of the Order which had been
conferred. All this accretion of ritual leaves something to be
desired from the point of view of liturgical æsthetics, which
demands in worship a strict theological order of formulas,
harmonized and proportioned in all its parts. Nevertheless,
the combination formed by the fusion of the two ceremonials,
the Roman and the Gallican, is effective and pleasing to
anyone not too exacting and critical. The Church speaks,
and her words, even when they are hindered by excess of
tender feeling, and therefore do not come forth in strict
methodical order, always awaken a lively impression, since
they are the words of the Holy Ghost, and God's word is
never without effect, nor is it ever a thing of naught.

In the Mass the dominant note is the immediate approach
of the Incarnate Word, rather than the holy ordinations
themselves. Perhaps originally on those nights when the
sacred vigils were held in Rome, and still more when the
sacred ministers were ordained, the whole of the first part
of the eucharistic liturgy—the so-called Mass of the Catechumens, which is nothing else than an abbreviation of the
first vigiliary rite—was omitted, so as to begin at once with
the presentation of the *oblata* and the consecratory anaphora.
Such was the custom in the afternoon of Holy Thursday,
the *missa chrismalis* and the reconciliation of the penitents
having already taken place in the morning. This is, perhaps,
the reason why to-day in the *Ordines* so much importance is
attached to the chanting of the *Benedictiones* after the lesson
from Daniel, since these praises were to take the place of the
Angelic Hymn, the customary morning doxology, as directly
preparing the souls of the faithful for the consecratory anaphora. However this may be, if we wish to understand fully
the present text of the Missal we must take into account the
successive stratifications of these rites. Their actual amalga-
mation undoubtedly goes back at least to the time of St
Gregory the Great.

We know as a matter of fact that it was St Gregory who
shortened the primitive vigiliary rite, which originally included the recitation of the twelve lessons in Greek as well as
in Latin. The holy Pontiff reduced these by half, but such
was the force of habit that outside the immediate surroundings of the papal Curia not only did the old name of
Saturday of the Twelve Lessons, already given to the Ember
Saturdays, remain unchanged, but, thanks to the Gelasian
Sacramentary, which was in use in very many places in
France and elsewhere, the famous twelve lessons of the

Easter vigil also escaped destruction. These lessons, driven out by Rome through the door, as it were, came in again by the window after the lapse of nearly a century, for though they were suppressed in the Gregorian Sacramentary, they regained the rights of citizenship in the Gelasian during that Frankish period when the latter was in general use among the clergy, together with the Codex of Gregory I.

The Introit of the Mass is taken from the usual psalm (lxxix), whose theme is heard as a continuous refrain during these days of holy expectation : *Come, O Lord, and show us thy face, thou that sittest upon the Cherubim.* God had already said to Moses and Elias, the two great contemplative minds of the old Testament, that they would never be able to see him face to face, but that he would show them his glory from behind. This, however, occurred in a religion of fear and servitude, when all worship was but a type of the reality to come.

Now, on the other hand, the divine economy of things is changed, and in a little while we, more blessed than the patriarchs and prophets of old, who sighed in vain for the graces imparted to us, shall contemplate the gracious countenance of a newborn infant, breathing forth all love, and laid between two dumb beasts in the straw of a manger. With Mary and Joseph let us, too, reverently fix our gaze upon that face which reflects the splendour of the divine nature and is the express image of the Father's loving-kindness. For us that face, the shining of those eyes, is as a guiding star which, in the ocean of this present life, points us to our true haven. Happy shall we be if, on the day of judgement, we also are able to look with confidence on that divine countenance, made human for us, and in his Passion disfigured, abused and defiled with blood and spittle for our sakes. If that face smiles upon us then, the battle of life is won and heaven's golden gates will open before us for all eternity.

The short litany, immediately after the Introit, is a last relic of the procession to the stational church which formerly took place. The collect which follows is conspicuously penitential in tone : " O Lord, thou seest, alas ! how we groan under the scourges which our sins have deserved; come and visit us that we may be comforted." The essential conditions of all holiness are a spirit of humility and contrition, for it is the measure of all true asceticism.

The first lesson is drawn from Isaias (xix, 20-22). Israel groans under the yoke of the Egyptians and cries aloud to Jehovah. He intervenes and punishes the oppressors, not from hate, nor from a spirit of revenge, but in order to heal them, so that the servants of Pharaoh, too, may build altars to the God of Jacob and have their part in the Messianic kingdom.

The chosen people, confined within the narrow boundaries of Judea, and groaning under the oppression of the Gentiles, are a type of all mankind under the bondage of sin. The divine Emancipator comes and punishes the oppressors, destroying the kingdom of Satan and his confederates. The Gentiles are converted; they enter the bosom of the Church, and, acknowledging the power of Jehovah and of his Christ, the Saviour, they erect altars and offer from the East even unto the West one pure oblation, just as was predicted by Malachias the prophet.

The Gradual which follows this lesson is from Psalm xviii, that great song in praise of the *Torah*. The sun appears from the highest heavens and fulfils its circuit, to set in the farthest extremity, plunging into the ocean as into a bath of gold. This sun is the Word of God. His beginning is before the daybreak, since he is begotten from all eternity. There is the true starting-point of his triumphal course. The opposite boundary, the place of his setting and disappearance, whence he will rise again on the morrow, is the ignominy of the cross, which here, in the psalm, is called by anticipation the highest point of the heavens, because the God who dies on the cross on Good Friday is at the same time adored by angels and saints as the great and glorious King, conqueror over death and hell. This is why, during the Adoration of the Cross on Good Friday, the Church chants the Trisagion and exclaims: *Crucem tuam adoramus, Domine, et sanctam resurrectionem tuam laudamus et glorificamus. Ecce enim propter lignum venit gaudium.*

At the conclusion of the Gradual the deacon invites the faithful to prayer, and the priest adds the petition : " Grant, O Lord, that as we are now bowed down under the old yoke of sin, the birth of thy only-begotten Son may be for us the beginning of redemption."

In the second lesson from Isaias (xxxv, 1-7) the prophet launches forth into a description of the golden age of the Messianic era, when the blind and the maimed shall be healed, when the arid deserts shall be watered by refreshing streams and clothed again with verdure and with flowers, rivalling the slopes of Lebanon, of Carmel and of Saron. The fearful shall then take courage and open their hearts to hope, since Jehovah is nigh at hand and is ready to take upon himself their defence.

The Gradual is formed from other verses of Psalm xviii, which holds a place of honour in to-day's feast : " The Lord hath set his tabernacle in the sun, and he is as a bridegroom coming out of his bride-chamber." The sun here symbolizes the eternal Father in whose bosom the Word is begotten from all eternity. This figure may also be applied to the ineffable holiness and love of Mary, who for nine months bore within her Jesus her Redeemer. He, like a fair flower blossoming on a verdant stem, comes into the world breathing love as a bridegroom; but the espousals which he wishes to contract are not, indeed, those of the body, but of the soul, which he desires to unite to his own heart that it may share in the ineffable treasures of his divine nature.

In the Collect the priest asks God that the joy at the coming of his only-begotten Son may finally banish the mourning which has oppressed us for so long by reason of our past misdeeds. This is the effect of sin or, as the Apostle expresses it, *stipendia peccati*—viz., death and sorrow. The age in which we live, on account of its apostasy from almighty God, has become enfeebled and wretched beyond all others. Notwithstanding its unbridled eagerness for pleasure, it has dried up the well-springs of joy, for joy is a gift which the Holy Ghost bestows only on those souls who fear God. The Paraclete gives to the just his gladness, in order to counterbalance the gift of the holy fear of God, which by itself might easily cause them to become faint-hearted and servile.

Isaias continues in the third lesson (xl, 9-11) to proclaim the coming Messianic deliverance. This announcement of the son of Amos is the prelude to the glad news of the Gospel, and is to be proclaimed to the sound of trumpets from the tops of the mountains, so that the knowledge thereof may be the more easily spread abroad to all peoples. May his liberating cry reach the ears of those also who would gladly stifle it! The Messiah will come to them in spite of themselves, and, like a good shepherd, will gather the scattered flock and take on his shoulders the young lambs and the weary sheep. Ancient Christian art had a special predilection for this symbolical figure of Jesus as the Good Shepherd, and reproduced it, not only in sculpture and painting on the walls of the cemeteries and on sarcophagi, but even upon eucharistic chalices, as we learn from the reproof addressed by Tertullian to Pope Callixtus.

The Gradual is taken from Psalm lxxix: "O God of all power, show us openly thy countenance and we shall be saved." In the Old Testament the face of God, like that of Moses the lawgiver, was veiled and hidden under the symbols and figures of the bloody sacrifices and of the prophecies. But this condition of things did not satisfy the love of those souls who, like Abraham when he *exultavit ut videret diem meum*, longed for better things. It was not sufficient for them to be the servants of Jehovah; they desired ardently the Honour of being his children and friends. Temporal rewards do not fill the emptiness of the heart; instead of a land flowing with milk and honey, they wished to possess heaven and to receive the kiss of God, saying, in the words of the canticle: *Osculetur me osculo oris sui.*

In the Collect is admirably put forth the desire that the advent of the Redeemer, now close at hand, besides being a remedy to assuage the bitterness of our present life, will bring us also the pledge of an eternal reward.

The Seer of Juda continues in the fourth lesson to develop his favourite theme of the Messianic era (Isa. xlv, 1-7). This time one of the types chosen to symbolize the Redeemer is Cyrus the Great, who gave the Jews permission to return home at last after seventy years of captivity in Babylon, and to rebuild the ruined cities of Juda. Almighty God had long pre-ordained the Persian king for this mission, and had led his hosts to victory, humbling the Babylonian rulers and unlocking for him the doors of their treasure-houses. Yet Cyrus learnt nothing from his good fortune in all these events. He never perceived the invisible hand guiding his footsteps, nor did he recognize the power of him whose mere instrument he was. Even this incredible ingratitude entered into God's plan and served to bring his good time to maturity. The world, in all these thousands of years of experience, has learnt nothing. Indeed, all hope in man has now become vain; it is necessary for the heavens themselves to open and like dew to distil, as it were, the Saviour upon the parched-up soil of our hearts.

The Gradual which follows is also from Psalm lxxix : " O thou who keepest the feet of Israel, who guidest the destinies of Joseph like a lamb, thou that sittest upon the Cherubim, show thyself to us, and let thy light shine upon Ephraim, Benjamin and Manasses." These tribes, reckoned the last in all Israel, well exemplify the nature of the *joyful news* of the Messiah, for these tidings are addressed, above all, to the poor and the humble.

The Collect, which here gathers up the prayers of the people after the singing of the Gradual, acknowledges that we are justly punished on account of our sins, but at the same time it gives utterance to the hope that the Saviour's coming will fill the world once more with joy. Though expressed in varied terms, the main idea which runs through to-night's solemn vigil is always the same : Sin brings with it sorrow, but grace unlocks the springs of joy.

The final place in the sacred vigils is always reserved for Daniel and for the moving scene of the three youths cast into the furnace of Babylon, which serves as a prelude to the grand canticle of the *Benedictiones*, freely adapted from the

Great Hallel of the Psalter. In this hymn, which was later imitated by the Seraphic Teacher of Assisi in his *Canticle of Brother Sun,* Ananias, Azarias and Misael praise God for all the blessings which he has showered down upon the work of his creation, for the forethought with which he rules it, and for the power with which he guides it to its final end—that is, to the greater glory of God. The eucharistic anaphora, in its original form of the second century, merely takes up and develops this theme of tender thanksgiving which was traditional in the synagogue and used by our Lord himself in the *tibi gratias agens* of the Last Supper.

The Collect which brings the *Benedictiones* to a close refers to the three youths cast into the Babylonian furnace; as God delivered them from the flames of the fire, so may he now deliver us also from the raging of evil passions.

The Epistle of St Paul to the Thessalonians (2, ii, 2-8), together with the ensuing Gospel, represent to-day a later reduplication, given that the vigil for the Sunday—that of the Twelve Lessons—first took place. Evidently when the rule as to the vigils began to be relaxed in Rome, and when—with the exception of St Peter's—the custom obtained in the other urban titular churches of saying Mass for the parishioners of each title, this Mass had to be abbreviated and adapted to the usual Roman type with lessons from the Epistles and Gospels. In the time of St Gregory, when the ancient vigil had been reduced to a mere sequence of six prophetic lessons, the two forms came to be placed together in the sacramentaries and ended by being happily merged into each other.

St Paul, in his Epistle to the Thessalonians, deals with the eschatological problem which at that time was troubling so many of his correspondents. The faithful of Salonica are not to let themselves be frightened; the *parousia* is not quite so close at hand as some would have them believe. There must first come a general apostasy of the nations, and the mystery of iniquity must first reach its climax in the profanation of the very temple of God. This mystery has indeed already begun to develop itself, but it is being kept back by an opposing force—an angel, a heavenly power—who at last will have to withdraw his help, although only for a short time. In the end Christ will reappear and will gain a decisive victory over the enemy whose kingdom of iniquity shall be brought to destruction at the breath of his word.

During Advent the sacred Liturgy often brings together the two comings of Christ on earth, the first in the humility of the flesh, the second in the majesty of his power. This is done because this twofold divine manifestation in reality only represents two distinct aspects of one single plan of redemption. The Messianic era does not move with the rapidity of lightning : it begins humbly at Bethlehem, it unfolds itself slowly through all the ages of the Church's life, and it reaches its culminating point only on the day of judgement, when, death and hell being conquered, the faithful among mankind shall rise again in glory with their mystical head Christ Jesus, the firstfruits of them that sleep. All this future happening, since it is evolved, according to the Scriptures, during the interval between the eleventh and the twelfth hour, constitutes but one single Messianic appearance, which, nevertheless, denotes a process of gradual development.

The Tract is taken from Psalm lxxix, some of its verses having been already recited after the fourth lesson. It seeks to hasten by prayer the coming of Jesus the Good Shepherd who guides the footsteps of Israel, who leads Joseph like a sheep, and who like a star will shine over the humble tribes of Ephraim, Benjamin and Manasses.

The Gospel is drawn from St Luke (iii, 1-6), who, having first clearly fixed the chronology of the beginnings of Christian preaching, sketches in bold strokes the mission of John the Forerunner in the desert.

Christianity is not merely a theosophical speculation evolved from the needs of our inner consciousness, a thing of which the mind cannot give a full explanation; it is a revelation of faith, and at the same time an historical fact making an appeal to human reason. Regarded as an historical fact, Christianity is presented to the world with all the safeguards that the most exacting historical critic can demand—genuine and truthful documents, miracles carefully authenticated and doctrine divinely higher than any mere human wisdom. It is for this that St Luke begins the narrative of the Gospel of Jesus with chronological notes concerning the rulers who were then controlling the destinies of Palestine.

The Offertory is from the prophet Zacharias (ix, 9). It bids us take heart from the near approach of the Saviour. Here is the purest, the most genuine source of joy, the spreading of God's kingdom in the soul, the realization of the daily petition in the " Our Father "—*adveniat regnum tuum.*

The Secret petitions almighty God of his loving-kindness to accept the sacrifice, so that the devotion of the faithful may attain the end which it has in view—namely, eternal salvation. Here again is the object of the whole of our life, towards which all our actions must be directed. What would it benefit us to set up any other aim, even though we should gain the whole world thereby, if we failed to save our souls?

In the Communion the glad tidings of Isaias are repeated.

Behold a virgin shall conceive and bear a son, and his name shall be called Emmanuel—that is, *God with us.* In the Middle Ages rabbinical tradition sought to obscure the meaning of this Messianic prophecy by maintaining that the Hebrew word *alma,* which the Vulgate translates by *virgo,* signifies merely a young girl. Exegetists have remarked, however, that every time this word is found in the sacred text it always refers to a maiden not yet given in marriage, and therefore a virgin. Moreover, the prophet speaks of a sign which the Lord will give to King Achaz and to his people, and there would be nothing out of the ordinary in a young maiden giving birth to a child, especially in the East, where such a one might be married at twelve years of age. The wonder, however, consists in this, that it is a virgin who, though remaining spotless and inviolate, is to conceive by divine power, the fruit of whose womb is to be that which alone befits such virginity—a Man-God.

The Post-Communion finely expresses the prayer that the frequenting of the holy table may be the means of our bringing forth the fruits of salvation always more abundantly. We see here how the doctrine of the Church concerning the Eucharist is always the same, always consistent with itself and with tradition. From the Acts of the Apostles, in which the faithful are described to us as intent upon the frequent breaking of the eucharistic bread, to our Collect in the Roman Missal and to the Decree of Pius X on Daily Communion, there is not only no break of continuity, but complete identity of teaching, so that we can apply to Catholic doctrine that which Paul says of Christ: *Jesus Christus heri, hodie, ipse et in saecula.*

Emmanuel, *God with us.* What a consoling name the Messiah is about to assume! Formerly sin had raised up, as it were, a wall of brass between the creature and his Creator, and the name of God could not even be uttered by the children of Israel. But now the Word himself will soon come to make his dwelling-place amongst us and to redeem us, and, in order to show by his very name all this merciful plan of salvation, he will be called Emmanuel and Jesus—that is, Saviour. Earth will then have no longer cause to envy heaven; we shall be for ever with our God, and he with us; he will be our salvation, and, if God is with us, who then can prevail against us?

THE FOURTH SUNDAY OF ADVENT

Station at the Twelve Holy Apostles.

To-day, according to the ancient *Ordines Romani,* there should, strictly speaking, be no station—*Dominica vacat*—since the Mass of this Sunday was the one which concluded the night vigil at St Peter's. This was the earliest arrangement; but later on, when the Sunday *pannuchis* had been shortened and anticipated on the Saturday afternoon, it did not seem fitting to let the Lord's day go by without offering the holy sacrifice. Hence the custom gradually grew up of having a second stational Mass at the Basilica of the Holy Apostles. This was done also to bring Rome into agreement with the use of other churches where the vigil was not kept, but where the Sunday sacrifice was wont to be offered in order to satisfy the devotion of the people.

The choice of the stational church, the same at which the eucharistic synaxis had been held only two days before, was not due to chance. We have already seen that in an oratory at the *Apostoleion* of Narses veneration was paid in the Middle Ages to the relics of St Eugenia, the famous martyr of the cemetery of Apronianus on the Via Latina. Now, the *natalis* of this saint falls on December 25, and as no commemoration can be made on Christmas Day, the feast, in accordance with the ancient Roman custom, was anticipated on the previous Sunday.

The Mass—like the synaxis at St Eusebius on the second Sunday after Epiphany, a few days before the Feast of St Vincent, who was venerated at that ancient title—contains no allusion to the saint who gave her name to the oratory, nor has it any connection with her. It sufficed to the faithful of those early times that the eucharistic synaxis itself was held in her honour, without there being any need for adding collects or other memorials of the martyr.

A tradition, widely accredited, contributed to this marked liturgical reticence, to the effect that in Rome the compilation of the Gregorian Antiphonary was to be attributed to the inspiration of the Holy Ghost. Consequently this work was deemed to be intangible, so no alterations nor additions could be permitted. Hence the chants of to-day's Mass were borrowed from other preceding Masses, so that the fourth Sunday of Advent possesses nothing peculiar to itself save the Offertory, the Epistle and the three collects.

The Introit is that of the previous Wednesday. The figure of the dew and rain, softly falling to refresh the parched earth, is derived from the well-known story of Gedeon; it was beautifully applied by the Psalmist, and then taken up again by the prophet Isaias, who made use of it to describe the benign and loving character of the first coming of the Messiah into the world. The Messianic kingdom is not inaugurated by a sudden stroke of the sword, nor by an earthquake shattering buildings and destroying whole provinces; it rather resembles a little plant, which, watered by the dews of heaven and kissed by the warm rays of the day-star, grows and flourishes in despite of every obstacle. The second coming of Jesus upon earth will, on the contrary, be sudden and unexpected. On that day he will annihilate in a flash with all the might of his arm the glory of the kingdom of Satan, and the kingdom of God will attain its full extent and its crowning splendour.

We beg God, in the first collect, that he will rise up in all his power and come to our assistance, and that, although our unworthiness would deserve that he should delay his coming still further, yet it may be hastened by his infinite mercy. The sacred Scriptures, indeed, constantly dwell on the wholly gratuitous character of the gift of the Incarnation, and this with the express object of stimulating still further our love and gratitude towards that God who, when offended, still loves us, when scorned and shunned still follows us and seeks us again, and when condemned to death gives his life freely for our sakes.

In the lesson from the first Epistle to the Corinthians (1, iv, 1-5) St Paul withdraws his actions from the open criticism and judgement of the dissentients of that Church which was always contentious and a prey to conflicting parties, reminding them that, as the Apostle and minister of Jesus Christ, it is to him alone that he is answerable for his apostleship. His conscience, indeed, reproaches him with nothing, but in spiritual matters one has constantly to fear the illusions of self-love, so it is as well to keep back all decisive judgement until the final *parousia* of Christ, when he will come to dispel the darkness of every conscience and give to each one that which he deserves. How fitting, therefore, it is that we should be slow to judge, not only our neighbour, but also ourselves! Men are welcome to call us good or bad as they will; their judgement will not in any way affect that of our Lord. We are in reality that which we are before God, and nothing more.

The Gradual is that of the preceding Wednesday. The alleluiatic verse is inspired by Isaias, and has been set to a marvellous melody in the Gregorian collection; it makes us feel all the loving eagerness of a soul who can no longer bear to be far from God. "Come, O Lord, and tarry no longer to deliver thy people from the bondage of sin." Who is this fortunate people? Certainly not any one particular people, taken in a narrow geographical sense, but the whole of believing humanity, all those who live by God through faith and therefore belong to the people of God. It is in this sense that the Apostle contrasts the Jews—*Israel secundum carnem* —with the true sons of Abraham according to the spirit, those, that is, who share in the faith of Abraham and who are co-heirs with him in his blessings.

The Gospel is the one already given us on the previous Saturday night, which makes it clear that the Sunday Mass for this day is, in substance, merely a repetition of the morning sacrifice offered in St Peter's at the close of the *pannuchis*.

We should note the place where God's voice is most often heard and where the Forerunner also listened to it *in deserto*. Weak and dissipated souls, and those who pass their lives absorbed in the rush of mundane things, do not very readily lend an ear to God. It is necessary, then, to withdraw into ourselves, to shut out the greater world around and also the little world of our own passions, to banish all illusions of the mind—and there are few souls without illusions—so that we may know ourselves as we are in secret before God and may show ourselves docile and ready to listen to the heavenly voice. This was the beautiful prayer of Solomon in his youth: *Dabis servo tuo cor docile.*

The Offertory is from St Luke, and repeats the gracious salutation of the angel to Mary, interwoven with the blessings addressed to her by the happy mother of the Forerunner. The history of the prayer *Ave Maria,* so dear to the piety of the faithful, and grown so familiar to us especially through the rosary, begins with this splendid Gregorian Offertory which gives us the text of the *Ave* in its original form as it was used throughout the Middle Ages. The second part of the prayer, *Sancta Maria, Mater Dei,* does not come from Holy Scripture, like the first; it wells up out of the very heart of that Christian piety which, in the time of the first Franciscans, was so especially distinguished by its tender love for the Blessed Virgin.

During Advent the Church surrounds the Immaculate Mother of God with special devotion, because she, during the nine months in which she bore our Lord in her womb, made it her first thought to sanctify by her love, her humility, her entire consecration to Jesus, this period of glad expectancy and of preparation for the birth of the Son of God. The disposition proper to this Advent season is the *preparation* of the soul for the coming of the Word of God with his gifts of grace; and Mary is our mistress and our model in this heavenly school of preparation. It is enough to open the first pages of the Gospel of St Luke to see at once all the sublimity of Mary's office in this *dominici schola servitii.* Prudent and humble with the angel, solicitous and helpful with Elisabeth, obedient to Joseph, poor and detached from all save God, she, the Blessed Virgin, causes the holiest dispositions to shine forth in her actions as she dedicates herself unreservedly to the service of the Lord, not seeking to please herself, but only him who chose her for his handmaid and his mother.

In the Secret we ask our Lord to accept the sacrifice so that its grace may foster our devotion and may assure unto us the merit of eternal salvation. It should be pointed out, in this connection, that the full meaning of the Latin word *devotio,* as used in the sacred Liturgy, is very imperfectly rendered by our word *devotion. Devotio* comes from the verb *devoveo,* and signifies the full consecration to almighty God of a person, who seals this offering of himself by means of a vow. *Devotion* is therefore not synonymous with *piety,* and strictly speaking we ought not to apply the word to anything but our consecration to God in baptism, through the promises then made to him, to the religious profession, and to holy ordination.

The Communion is identical with that of the preceding Wednesday. In contrast with the old Covenant, Jesus, in the New Law, takes the name of Emmanuel to emphasize the indissoluble character of the friendship now established between God and man. Sin will no longer be able to destroy this order of things, since as long as Jesus shall be Jesus— and this he will be for ever—he will also always be our advocate with the Father and all-powerful to wash away our sins in his Blood.

In the Post-Communion we pray God that our attendance at the eucharistic table may increase in us also that grace of which we stand in such dire need in order to continue in the way that leads to everlasting life. It is for this that Jesus teaches us in the *Our Father* to ask every day for our *supersubstantial* bread, without which we cannot repair the daily losses that we incur through our habitual faults, nor preserve for long the supernatural life of the soul. Christianity lies wholly in this—to take Jesus as our example, to live as he lived. It is Holy Communion which bestows on us the life and the mind of our Lord, in conformity with his promise. *Qui manducat me, et ipse vivet propter me.* As God in heaven, in the brightness of his glory, feeds the blessed from himself, so on earth he anticipates this his gift to his faithful pilgrims, and imparts himself to them as nourishment under the sacramental veils. The manner and the conditions of the reception differ, but the gift is substantially the same. The

Eucharist is paradise upon earth; this we can see from the etymology of the name; it is the one true *Eucharistia*—that is, the *bona gratia* of God.

Why is it that when the Word of God came upon earth and appeared among his own people, and this after so many thousand years of anxious waiting, they refused to receive him? It was from lack of suitable preparation. The Jews did not seek the glory and the kingdom of God; they desired their earthly kingdom and their own national and economic interests. They looked, therefore, for a victorious Messiah who would free Israel from the yoke of the nations and make them tributary to the seed of Abraham. Instead of this, Jesus Christ appeared poor, suffering and despised. He himself paid tribute to the Romans and preached an inward and spiritual kingdom. The carnal-minded Jew understood nothing of this new kind of divine manifestation, and in spite of all the miracles wrought by the Saviour, rejected it with scorn. How all-important is it, then, to prepare fittingly for the grace of God !

CHRISTMAS EVE

Station at St Mary Major.

Properly speaking, this Mass of the Vigil on December 24 ought not to exist, for the original vigiliary Mass is that which used to be celebrated on this night after the night office in the oratory *ad praesepe*. But after the Councils of Ephesus and Chalcedon the feast of our Lord's Nativity rose to such importance that the ancient Roman rite of Christmas had to be modified, and by analogy with Easter came to include a fast and a month of preparation. Moreover, the actual solemnity of December 25, instead of consisting of two Masses, one of the vigil and the other of the feast, with a third inserted in commemoration of St Anastasia, ended by allowing of four Masses, all of them in honour of the Christian mystery—viz., one in the evening of December 24 at the beginning of the night office, one at midnight at the first cock-crowing, one in the early morning, and one, finally, at the hour of Terce. In the time of St Gregory, St Anastasia came to take a secondary place, and at most retained only the privilege of a simple commemoration.

Thus the Mass appointed for to-day in the Missal is not the vigiliary sacrifice which always involved a preliminary *pannuchis;* it rather represents the Mass of the *preorte,* as the Greeks call it, the sacrifice of the day before the feast, when, None being over, the Mass of preparation was offered and the nocturnal solemnity at once began. This was the exact custom followed by the Milanese Church in the Middle Ages. The station of December 24 is at St Mary Major, as is that for the first Mass on Christmas night. Thus we have two, and, with the third Mass of to-morrow, three consecutive stations at the same church—a fact which, since it is quite contrary to the spirit of the ancient Roman Liturgy, of itself shows that the order followed in the present Missal is no longer the primitive one, and at once betrays a later revision. In fact, to-day's Mass also is merely supplementary to that of the coming night's celebration *ad praesepe,* and it constitutes a sporadic example in the Roman Liturgy of a feast with two vigiliary sacrifices, one before and one after the night office.

The Introit for to-day is from Exodus xvi, and repeats the words of Moses when, in order to pacify the murmuring people, he promised them from God that manna should be rained down on them out of heaven on the morrow. This manna typified the Incarnate Word who is the true food of souls. He comes like rain out of heaven because his virginal conception is not according to the common laws of Nature, but is purely the work of the Holy Ghost.

In the Collect we beg almighty God that even as we go forth joyfully to-day to meet our newborn Redeemer who comes to us as a little child, meek and humble, so at the end of life we may be able to await with a peaceful conscience his coming in splendour and majesty as our Judge and our Rewarder. The two manifestations are really so closely connected that they form part of the same plan of salvation. The birth of Jesus in time marks the beginning of the Messianic kingdom, but his second coming on the day of final judgement signalizes its decisive consummation. He, therefore, who would have part in the Messianic kingdom of the last day must receive the Christ-Child in his heart now and allow him to grow up there through faith and good works. He must embrace willingly the humility, the poverty, the zeal of Jesus, for thus only can he hope to realize the promised glory and possession of Jesus in eternity.

With to-day's lesson the Church begins the reading of the Pauline Epistles (Rom. i, 1-6), and, as we are in Rome, commences at once with the letter of the Apostle to the Romans, which, though it is not the first in order of time, is none the less the most important as regards its subject matter and the copious style in which the Apostle develops his theme. He prefaces this Epistle, according to his usual manner, with a long dedicatory passage, in which, very appropriately to the feast we are about to celebrate, he explains the general characteristics of the Incarnation of the Son of Man. The Incarnation, already announced by the prophets in the Scriptures, has come to pass by the operation of the Holy Ghost, through the royal line of David.

The dogma of the two natures, divine and human, united in the one person of Jesus Christ, ought to fill us with hope and consolation. Each time that we think of the sacred humanity of Jesus, which we adore in the holy Eucharist and see represented in pictures and statues, we feel our hearts glow with gratitude, and exclaim : " This body, these tender limbs, this human nature, destined to suffer the cruel torments of the Passion; all this is for my sake. O my God, how greatly thou hast loved me ! Thou hast humbled thyself for me even so far as to put on the livery of my servile condition, so that I, in coming to thee, may clothe myself in the garment of thy divine nature and become as the Apostle Peter teaches me, a sharer in thy very nature."

The Gradual adds to the verse from Exodus, already recited for the Introit, the Messianic Psalm lxxix which we find repeated again and again throughout this Advent season. The faithful soul by its prayers hastens the blessed hour of the *parousia* when the ancient shepherd of Israel, who led the gentle Joseph like a sheep, will appear to his people and will enlighten them.

It is, however, to be noticed that the rays of this Sun of Justice, instead of rising upon all the twelve tribes of Israel, are especially invoked upon the three little families of Ephraim, Benjamin, and Manasses, so as to mark the repudiation with which the great majority of the chosen people will treat the worship of Jehovah and of his only-begotten Son.

On Sundays, according to the practice established by Pope Damasus on the advice of St Jerome, and afterwards confirmed by St Gregory the Great, the alleluiatic verse is added to the Gradual. " To-morrow the sin of the world shall be blotted out and the Saviour of mankind shall reign over us." The birth of the Saviour initiates, indeed, the expiation of sin and the redemption of the human race. The manger, the poor swaddling-clothes, the hay, the cave, the warm breath of the two animals—all these condemn by anticipation our pride, sensuality and spirit of independence, and teach us to treasure the poverty of the Christ-Child and to follow out the apostolic teaching : *Propter nos egenus factus est cum esset dives, ut nos illius inopia divites essemus.*

In the Gospel (St Matt. i, 18-21) we are told of Joseph's hesitation in taking Mary into his home when he knew only that she was with child, but had not penetrated any further into the mystery of her divine fecundity. Commentators upon Holy Writ teach us that Joseph was fully convinced of the stainless purity of Mary, and therefore would not denounce her to the Sanhedrim as guilty of a broken troth; but at the same time he was so humble that he deemed himself unworthy of having Mary in his house and of sharing the secret of such a Virgin. Thus it was that he entertained the idea of withdrawing voluntarily from those espousals which he regarded as so much above him, and committing the whole matter to God's care.

But the same Lord who had chosen Joseph so that his person might in a certain sense justify before the world the temporal birth of the Word and guard Mother and Son from ignominy, neither left him long in doubt nor failed to reward his deep humility. He esteems himself unworthy to render service to Mary, the handmaid of the Lord, and yet he is to be the foster-father of the only-begotten Son of God, bearing simply the title of father, and exercising paternal authority over him in the name of the heavenly Father. The first act of this paternal authority will be to bestow upon the Incarnate Word the adorable name of Jesus, through which alone all mankind may gain salvation. Thus does God exalt the humble, and while every creature in heaven, on earth and under the earth bows the knee in fear at the most holy Name of Jesus, Joseph, on the other hand, invested with authority from him by whom all paternity in heaven and earth is named, gives this name to the Saviour, and with it all that the name implies—the carrying out of the whole plan of redemption.

The Offertory is taken from Psalm xxiii. The gates of a blessed eternity, closed after the first sin, and guarded by an angel with a flaming sword, are at last to be opened for the triumphal entry of the Saviour of the world. He, indeed, as St Paul teaches us in his letter to the Hebrews, has, through the merits of his precious Blood, the right to enter once for all into the sanctuary of heaven, and bring all believers with him in his train. Yet, according to the present plan of salvation, glory is closely bound up with humiliation; hence the supreme exultation of redeemed humanity begins when its leader and firstborn abases himself, and, making himself of no account, puts on the poor garments of our human nature.

In the Secret we ask God that, even as we anticipate by our prayers the adorable birth of his only-begotten Son on earth, so we may one day receive from him in heaven our eternal reward with great joy. Christ indeed is to be born to-night in a cave, not certainly for himself—for what need of birth has he who is the source of all life?—but for thee, that thou mayest be born again to heaven. He becomes the son of woman in order that thou mayest cease to be the son of woman and become the son of God.

In the Communion, Isaias announces to us for the last time in this Advent season the near approach of the Messiah. God will show forth his glory, and then not only Judea, but all mankind, shall look upon the divine Saviour clothed in human flesh. Religion will cease to be the monopoly of a tribe or clan that takes up arms against another for worshipping Bel or Astarte; rather will it become the precious patrimony of regenerated humanity, conscious of one common origin and possessed of one identical end and aim.

In the Post-Communion, mankind, oppressed now for so many centuries under the shameful yoke of sin, implores sorrowfully the grace of a short breathing-space, if no more, in its headlong onrush towards eternity. But suddenly the news of the Deliverer's approaching birth uplifts its heart and opens it to the brightest hopes. No longer throbbing painfully like that of a condemned criminal, it begins to beat quickly with the affectionate joy of a son, of one who, through the efficacy of the eucharistic mystery, already feels the very blood of the Incarnate Word of God flowing in his veins.

According to the ancient *Ordines Romani,* two vigiliary offices were sung to-day by the papal choir, as was usual on the most solemn feasts of the yearly cycle. In the first, three psalms were recited with five lessons and as many responsories. In the fourth of these the Jews were reproved because they would not acknowledge the Messiah, now about to be born, and in the corresponding responsory were sung the famous Sibylline verses, *Judicii signum, tellus sudore madescit,* so that even the pagan muse might rebuke that obstinate people for their unfaithfulness to God. After None, the Pope, surrounded by the high officials of his Court, celebrated the stational Mass at St Mary Major, followed by the supper provided by the Bishop of Albano, to which the Pontiff himself sat down, together with the accompanying prelates. After this Vespers were sung, but as the vigils were to begin again at midnight, the Pope, instead of returning to the Lateran, arranged to spend the first part of the evening in the Liberian Palace, not, however, before he had with his own hands administered a cup of wine to each of the clergy, including the youthful singers of the Lateran *schola.*

In quite recent times Pius IX used to go to St Mary Major on the evening of the Christmas vigil, and there begin the first Mass early, so as to be in time to return to the Quirinal before the hour should have struck at which the ecclesiastical fast commenced preparatory to the following day's Communion. Unlike the other vigils, in which the penitential character and a sense of sadness predominate, that of Christmas, like the rest of Advent, is full of vivacity and holy joy. This is fully in accordance with the nature of the heart of man. After so long a period of anxious and painful expectation the sudden news of our approaching deliverance lightens the heart, while a common joy unites us and makes us forget for a moment the hard conditions of our life here below. We feel that we are all brothers, the sons of one Father; we are born again with the Christ-Child to the beauteous simplicity of a holy and spiritual infancy, and are brought back again by love to the perfect happiness of un-fallen man in paradise.

CHRISTMAS DAY

The First Mass—at Midnight. Station at St Mary ad Praesepe.

As the historical date of our Saviour's birth was unknown in the early days of the Church, the different manifestations of Christ in his mortal nature, his birth, his baptism in the Jordan and his showing to the Magi were celebrated just after the winter solstice during the first ten days of January, in accordance with an ancient tradition already current about the beginning of the second century. This conventional date had already gained credit in all the Churches when, for some unknown reason, Rome on her own account divided the Feast of the *Manifestations,* and anticipated on December 25 the anniversary of our Lord's temporal birth.

When and how the Mother of all the Churches arrived at fixing this date we do not know, for, setting aside a very doubtful passage from the Commentary of Hippolytus on Daniel, the oldest document which assigns Christmas Day to December 25 is the Philocalian Calendar of the year 336, in which we find the following notice: *VIII Kal. Jan. natus Christus in Betleem Judee.* Clearly the chronologist is not putting forth anything of his own, but is merely repeating an earlier Roman tradition which claims, in the *Liber Pontificalis,* to go back to Pope Telesphorus. In the discourse delivered by Pope Liberius in St Peter's on that Christmas Day when he gave the veil of virginity to Marcellina, the sister of St Ambrose, there is no indication of any novelty about the feast; the whole context rather confirms the impression that we are dealing with a solemnity of ancient date to which the people were wont to flock in great numbers from the earliest times.

The feast of Christmas was from the first peculiar to the Apostolic See. St John Chrysostom, who introduced it into Antioch about 375, appeals to the authority of the capital of the Latin world, where, according to his belief, were still preserved the records of the census of Quirinus (Cyrinus), giving December 25 as the exact date of the birth of our Lord at Bethlehem.   From Antioch the celebration of the feast spread to Constantinople; then, under Bishop Juvenal (424-58), it was introduced into Jerusalem, whence it penetrated to Alexandria about the year 430, and from these famous patriarchal sees it was gradually extended throughout their diocesan dependencies.   The Armenian Monophysites are the only ones who still celebrate the birth of Christ on January 6, its primitive date.

We must not, however, omit to mention a coincidence. The civil calendar of the Philocalian compilation gives on December 25 the *Natalis invicti*—that is to say, the birthday of the sun, which thus coincides exactly with the winter solstice.   In an age when, through the Mithraic mysteries, the worship of the golden orb of day had assumed such proportions that, according to St Leo, the very same worshippers who frequented the Vatican Basilica allowed themselves also to practise the superstitious custom of first saluting the solar disc in the atrium of St Peter's, it is not unlikely that the Apostolic See, in anticipating our Lord's birthday on December 25, intended to oppose the *Sol invictus,* Mithras, to the true Sun of Justice, desiring in this way to turn away the faithful from the dangerous idolatry of the Mithraic festivals.   In another parallel instance on April 25, the festival of the *Robigalia,* Rome adopted a similar measure of prudence, and substituted for the pagan cortège to the Pons Milvius a Christian procession, which passed over the same ground, but turned off from the Flaminian Way and the Pons Milvius to the Vatican Basilica, so as to offer the holy sacrifice at the tomb of the Apostle.

The characteristic feature of the feast of Christmas in the Roman rite is the custom of the three Masses, one at the first cock-crowing—*ad galli cantum*—the next at dawn, the third in broad daylight.   St Gregory bears witness to the custom, but it is certainly older than his time, for the biographer of Pope Telesphorus, in the *Liber Pontificalis,* claims that it was this latter Pontiff who first introduced the singing of the *Gloria in Excelsis* into the midnight Mass at Christmas.

The Christmas *pannuchis* with the Mass at its close, besides being the natural outcome of that solemn occasion, was also suggested in part by the circumstance that Christ was born in Bethlehem at midnight.   As at Jerusalem, so also at Rome it was desired to reproduce in liturgical form the scene of that night, especially as Pope Sixtus III (432-40) had erected in St Mary Major a sumptuous oratory *ad praesepe,* and one which was considered by the Romans to be a copy of the original at Bethlehem.

This vigiliary Mass, however, did not originally constitute, as it does now, a special feature of the Christmas solemnity; it was simply the customary sacrifice which always ended the sacred vigils. Moreover, if we are to judge of the number of worshippers by the size of the place in which the station was celebrated, we must conclude that the little crypt *ad praesepe* would accomodate but very few persons; so few, indeed, that on a certain Christmas night while Pope Gregory VII (1075) was celebrating Mass therein it was possible for him to be actually seized by the armed ruffians of Cencio, who were placed in ambush for the purpose, carried off from St Mary Major, and held a prisoner in one of the towers of the Parione quarter, without the Roman people knowing anything until the next morning of what had befallen the Pope during the station.

The true solemn Mass of Christmas, *in die sancto,* was the one celebrated in broad daylight at St Peter's. It was at this Mass that Pope Liberius, on the testimony of St Ambrose, bestowed the veil of virginity upon Marcellina, in the presence of a great concourse of people. On that occasion the Pontiff delivered the famous address preserved by the saint in his *De Virginitate,* from which it will suffice for our purpose to quote these words : " Thou, my daughter, hast aspired to most lofty nuptials. Thou seest how great a concourse of people is gathered together for the birthday of thy spouse, and how no one of all these goes away unfed." If indeed all these people still remained to communicate at the papal Mass, it shows that the attendance at the vigiliary Mass and at the Mass at dawn must have been very small.

On Christmas Day of the year 431, Pope Celestine received the letters which informed him of the successful issue of the Council of Ephesus. He caused them to be read out " to the assembly of all the Christian people at St Peter's."

Between the vigiliary Mass *ad praesepe* and the stational Mass at the Vatican there took place, about the fifth century, another eucharistic synaxis at the foot of the Palatine, for the benefit of the Byzantine colony dwelling in Rome. Its object was to celebrate the *natalis* of Anastasia, the martyr of Sirmium, whose body had been translated from Constantinople under the Patriarch Gennadius (458-71). The *Titulus Anastasiae* at Rome was chosen for the ceremony because the *Acts* of the martyr identified her with the foundress of the Church. With the passing of the Byzantines the popularity of the *cultus* of St Anastasia also declined. The station indeed survived, though it now no longer represented the *natalis* of the martyr as at first, but introduced a second Mass at dawn of day in commemoration of our Lord's birth as man.

Originally the triple offering of the holy sacrifice on Christmas Day was the special privilege of the Pope or of the ecclesiastic who presided over the stational synaxis, nor was this triplication altogether unknown in Rome. The feast of the Apostles Peter and Paul also enjoyed the privilege of three Masses; that of the sons of St Felicitas included four, and, generally speaking, all the other great festivals of martyrs admitted as many Masses as there were sanctuaries in their honour. There were always two Masses in any case, one *ad corpus* in the sepulchral vault of the saint, and the other, the *missa publica,* as it was called, in the basilica above.

This custom is somewhat similar to that which regulates the celebration of conventual Masses in the collegiate chapters of to-day. There are many days to which the Calendar assigns two or even three conventual Masses; this, however, does not mean that the same priest shall offer the holy sacrifice for the second or third time on the same day; still less that every priest out of choir is authorized to say several Masses on such days. It simply indicates the number of Masses at which the collegiate Chapter is called upon to be present. It was the same also in ancient times on days of triplication of Masses; they were celebrated in the various sanctuaries which bore the name of the feast, and the Pope often presided there in person and himself offered the holy sacrifice. But apart from those sanctuaries where the feast was being kept, there was no question of triplication for the priests attached to the different urban titular churches, and everything went on in the customary manner as described in the sacramentaries.

The liturgists of the later Middle Ages took pleasure in seeking out deep reasons why there were three Masses on Christmas Day, but instead of exploring the field of archæology in which they would certainly have found traces of the three different Roman sanctuaries where December 25 must certainly have been kept, they concentrated their attention upon the ascetic and mystical reasons for this circumstance, good indeed in themselves and well calculated to foster piety, but wholly irrelevant to the early origin of this Roman triplication, the very idea of which was wholly unknown in the East.

The midnight Mass—called *ad galli cantus* by the early Christians because, from the time of St Ambrose, the daily morning office began only at that hour—commemorates the eternal birth of the Word of God amid the magnificence of his Father's glory; the Mass at dawn celebrates his appearance in time in the humility of the flesh, and lastly, the third

Mass, at St Peter's, symbolizes his final coming on the day of the *parousia,* to judge both the living and the dead.

According to *Ordo Romanus XI,* the two separate vigiliary synaxes of which Amalarius speaks were still celebrated in the time of Celestine II (1143-4) at St Mary Major on Christmas night, in the presence of the Pope. At first the lessons were sung by the canons, the cardinals and the bishops, just as on the third Sunday of Advent at St Peter's, and after the Office the Mass was celebrated *ad praesepe,* followed by the second Matins and by Lauds.

In the fifteenth century the Pope assisted at the vigils, clad in a cappa of scarlet wool with a hood to it, fastened under the chin *propter frigus* as is described in *Ordo Romanus.*[1] If the Emperor also were present he was vested in a cope, and, brandishing his sword, was called upon to sing the fifth lesson, the ninth being reserved to the Pope.

During the Mass all the offerings placed by the people on the altar or at the feet of the Pontiff went to the papal chaplains, except the bread, which was the portion of the acolytes. Contrary to his wonted custom, the Pope did not receive Communion on Christmas night at his throne, but at the altar, and drank of the consecrated chalice without making use of the customary golden reed, while the clergy waited until the next morning to receive Holy Communion.

The Introit is taken from the second psalm, and may be applied to the several generations of the Word—to his eternal and divine generation in the bosom of the Father, to his humble and mortal generation in the virginal womb of Mary, and finally to his glorious generation from the depths of the earth when he rose again on Easter Day to triumph for ever over sin and death. During the holy Christmas season it is fitting that we should often strengthen our faith by a fervent realization of the divine nature which lies hidden under the poor exterior of the little Child of Bethlehem. The Word has created us by his power and has redeemed us by his weakness, but this weakness would have availed nothing unless it had been joined to a power at once almighty and divine, by means of the hypostatic union.

In the Collect we call to mind that our Lord has dispelled the darkness of this holy night by the rays of his ineffable light. May he grant that, after having been initiated here below into the mystery of his Incarnation, we may one day have part also in the brightness of his heavenly glory. The connection is a very close one—faith here below, light in heaven above; here grace, there glory. Before the coming of the Word of God on earth mankind was groping in the

---

[1] *P.L.* LXXVIII, col. 1181.

dark places of sin and ignorance; then when Jesus came, the grace of the Holy Ghost shone into the hearts of men, and humanity, preserved intact in the Catholic Church by means of the Christian revelation, is now alive and is nourished by the light of Eternal Wisdom.

The lesson is from the Epistle to Titus (ii, 11-15), and it is important to note that when, in Rome, it was read in the Greek text as well as in the Latin, the first word, *apparuit*—ἐπιφάνη—recalled the name Epiphany, originally applied to the Christmas festival.

The Apostle points out very clearly the purely gratuitous character of the Incarnation of the Son of God, the reason for which is to be found entirely in God's infinite mercy, and not at all in our prayers or good works. We are still at Christmas, but according to the teaching of the early Fathers the Paschal sacrament has already begun. The gracious Babe of Bethlehem is the innocent victim to be slain for the sins of the world. Three-and-thirty years, indeed, have to pass before the Fraction of the mysteries will take place, but the sacrifice is begun to-day; the eternal High Priest is already at the Introit of his Mass.

The Gradual comes from Psalm cix, and begins by describing with rapid strokes the eternal *to-day* in which the Father has begotten, is begetting, and always will beget the Word, without beginning, succession of time, or end. The Psalmist then touches upon Christ's temporal mission of subduing all his enemies under his power, who are, therefore, also the enemies of God. He will win a final victory over them and will place them as a footstool for his golden feet, when he shall judge them on the day of the *parousia,* not only as God, but also as the firstborn of creation. When he shall have led captive all the rebels to God, then, as the Apostle explains, the temporal mission of Christ will be complete and will come to an end, so that God may be *omnia in omnibus.*

The alleluiatic verse, which ought to have followed the second lesson before the Gospel, repeats in like manner the verse from the second psalm: " Jehovah hath said unto me: Thou art my Son, for this day I have begotten thee." The Word repeats this phrase, not indeed amid the splendours of heaven with the angels singing Alleluia round about him, but in the infirmity of his flesh, amid the calumnies and blasphemies of his foes. It is against such enemies that Jesus has most often need to invoke his Messianic privileges, and thus he calls upon the infallible testimony of that Father who had begotten him already in eternity, and who then, in time, bestowed on the Word his most sacred humanity which is hypostatically united to him.

The Gospel, from St Luke (ii, 1-14), describes the birth of

Jesus at midnight in Bethlehem. The Holy Ghost has himself deigned to comment upon this sacred text through the Evangelist St John, and we shall read his words to-day in the third Mass. Hence any other merely human explanation would be superfluous. Jesus is born in a stable and sets up his throne and his seat in a manger, between two lowly beasts of burden. Come hither, therefore, Christian soul, and kneel before this crib. It is from this lowly spot that Jesus condemns thy vain pomp, thy pride, thy self-indulgence, and teaches thee instead obedience, humility, penitence and mortification.

The Offertory is taken from Psalm xcv, in which heaven and earth are bidden to rejoice because the Lord is come. Truly the coming of Jesus on earth has " consecrated the world," as the Church said yesterday in her Liturgy. This consecration affects in some degree even the brute creation and inanimate nature, both because the Incarnate Word willed to make use thereof during his mortal life, and also because some created things, such as water, wine, bread and oil, have been raised to the dignity of *materia* for the holy sacraments, while all join in helping man towards the attainment of his supernatural end and aim.

In the Secret—the real beginning of the ancient eucharistic anaphora—we ask God that as Jesus has willed to become partaker of our human nature through the merits of the divine sacrifice, so we, too, may happily become like unto him by means of the supernatural garment of grace which bestows on us an inward conformity to Christ.

In the Preface, during this Christmas season, in accordance with that which Pope Vigilius wrote to Profuturus of Braga, is inserted the following passage in commemoration of the mystery of the Incarnation : " . . . because, by the mystery of the Word made flesh, a new ray of thy glory has shone upon the eyes of our minds ; that while we know our God visibly, we may by him be drawn to the love of things invisible."[1]

In the first part of the diptychs also a commemoration is made of the Saviour's birth. " Communicating with and celebrating that most sacred night in which the undefiled virginity of blessed Mary brought forth the Saviour into this world."[2] These insertions are very ancient and go back at least to the fourth century.

The Communion is from Psalm cix, which is distinctly

---

[1] " *Quia per incarnati Verbi mysterium, nova mentis nostrae oculis lux tuae claritatis infulsit: ut dum visibiliter Deum cognoscimus, per hunc in invisibilium amorem rapiamur.*"

[2] " *Communicantes, et noctem sacratissimam celebrantes, qua beatae Mariae intemerata virginitas huic mundo edidit Salvatorem.*"

Messianic. The Father has begotten the Word in the brightness of his holiness, so that the tender infant who lies to-day in the crib, clad in the garments of a servant and a sinner, is co-eternal and consubstantial with the Father. A medieval painter in a Greek abbey has most ingeniously expressed this co-eternity of the Incarnate Word, representing him in the form of a child on the knees of the Father, but with a long white beard, just as the prophet Daniel describes the *Antiquus dierum*—with a beard and with hair like white wool.

In the Post-Communion we pray our Lord that our attendance at the sacred mysteries in commemoration of his birth may obtain for us grace to show forth these mysteries in our lives, and so come to our reward in heaven. This is the real object of Holy Communion—to make us sharers of the life of Christ, grafting us on to the tree of his Passion, that we may live no longer to ourselves, but to him and for him.

St Alphonsus, after having meditated on all the tenderness and love which the Christ-Child shows us in the cave of Bethlehem, ends one of his well-known hymns with this cry: " Ah, how much it has cost thee to love us !" At the foot of the crib this is all that we can say. When a God is so consumed with love for his creatures as to make himself of no account, to face dire poverty, persecutions and a most opprobrious and cruel death, then is there naught else to do but to shed tears of gratitude at his feet—*procidamus ante eum, ploremus coram Domino*—and to deplore that we have loved him so imperfectly and so tardily, exclaiming with St Augustine: *Sero te amavi, pulchritudo tam antiqua, sero te amavi.*

The Second Mass—at Dawn. Station at St Anastasia.

The *natalis* of St Anastasia falling on this day—her *cultus* had become very celebrated in Rome, especially during the Byzantine period—the Church instituted this solemn station at her basilica at the foot of the Palatine. The Leonine Sacramentary does, indeed, mention St Anastasia in the list of the December feasts, but the manuscript is so mutilated that we can gather nothing further from it. In the Gelasian Sacramentary there is nothing, while in the Gregorian—these names, Leonine, Gelasian and Gregorian, are no guarantee whatever of the matter contained in these documents—the collects of the famous martyr of Sirmium precede those of the second Mass of Christmas Day.

Although the Sacramentary which passes under the name of St Gregory covers a comparatively late period of liturgical development in Rome—about the time of the pontificate of Adrian I (772-95)—nevertheless, to-day's station at St Anastasia gives an impression of considerable antiquity, for it apparently dates back to a time before the feast of the Nativity of our Lord was deemed in Rome to be of such great importance, and when the custom still obtained of keeping several feasts of martyrs at different stations on the same day in different sanctuaries. In a later age the feast of St Anastasia would certainly have been transferred to another day.

Among the Sermons of St Leo I there is one delivered in the Basilica of St Anastasia against the Eutychian heresy. It is altogether about our Lord, and would therefore be quite suitable for Christmas, but we lack evidence for declaring with absolute certainty that it was preached at to-day's station in the basilica of the martyr of Sirmium.

Originally—as we can see from the Gregorian Sacramentary—the stational Mass at St Anastasia was wholly in honour of the martyr of that name, but later on, as the feast of Christmas gradually gained in importance, that of St Anastasia dwindled down to a mere commemorative collect.

The hour of dawn at which this station was celebrated in Rome had originally no mystical meaning connecting it with the birth of our Saviour, such as the medieval liturgists afterwards saw in it. Since the solemn Mass at St Peter's was fixed for the hour of Terce, only the very earliest morning hour remained available for the assembly at the foot of the Palatine, the night vigil at the Liberian Basilica being then barely over. The existing rubric in the Missal—*ad secundam missam in Aurora*—is therefore, archæologically speaking, not quite accurate, nor is that of the midnight Mass, which in reality was celebrated at the first cockcrowing.

The *Ordines Romani* prescribed that the Pope, when he was in Rome, should himself hold the station at St Anastasia; if he were absent, the *presbyter tituli*, or the senior cardinal priest, took his place. The last Pope to conform to this ancient rule was Leo XII (1823-29).

In the Middle Ages, when the Mass in the crypt *ad praesepe* was ended, the Pontiff repaired at once to the titular church of St Anastasia, without even taking off his *paenula;* but in the fourteenth century, when the ancient stational rule had wellnigh fallen into disuse owing to the sumptuous papal festivals which were then celebrated within the pontifical chapel, it became customary to have a short interval between the one ceremony and the other. In more recent times, before 1870, Pius IX used to celebrate the Mass

24

in nocte at St Mary Major during the early part of the evening, so as to be able to return to the palace for supper before midnight. The Communion of the cardinals and of the Roman clergy, which originally took place at St Peter's at the third Christmas Mass, was anticipated in the fourteenth century in the Mass at St Anastasia at dawn, and with the cardinals there also took part the other prelates of the papal court who were not of episcopal rank.

This Mass draws its chief inspiration from the thought of the sun, whose rising already begins to dispel the shades of night and leads us to the contemplation of him who was begotten, *Light of Light,* from the bosom of the divine Father before the rising of the day-star.

The Introit is taken from Isaias (ix). A people that walked in darkness, the hapless Gentiles, unenlightened by the Mosaic revelation or by the prophecies, have to-day seen a great light, for he who is born is the Father of a new generation, the Prince of Peace, in whose kingdom there are no distinctions of rank, no worldly prerogatives, no privileges of birth, since whoever receives his word becomes a son of God and a citizen of the new Messianic kingdom. The prophetic antiphon follows—Psalm xcii—which is properly the Easter psalm, but is very suitable also to Christmas, since, if the Resurrection marks the Saviour's final triumph over death and sin, his birth announces the dawning of that great day of victory.

In the Collect we call to mind that the Word was made flesh in order to illumine the world with splendours—not indeed materialistic nor of a purely abstract and speculative nature, but divine. The sublime truths of the faith must become realities in such a way that the Christian, as a living likeness of the eternal Word, in so far as he receives and makes his own the knowledge of the Father which Jesus reveals to him through the holy Gospel, lives the life of Christ again and works in him and for him.

To this collect is added the commemoration of St Anastasia, the titular martyr of the stational basilica, asking that we may have grace to experience the effect of her powerful intercession. The saints are grounded in love, and are therefore always full of compassion for all our needs, for which they constantly make intercession to God.

In the passage from the Epistle to Titus which follows, the Apostle emphasizes the wholly spontaneous, free and gratuitous character of the Redemption. He employs in this connection a word which is often misused nowadays, but which in the mind of St Paul expresses all that is most gentle, condescending and ineffable in the mystery of our redemption

—" God who loves man ;"—this is the *humanitas* of the Latins, and the φιλανθρωπία of the Greeks.

This love is eternal, even as the Holy Ghost is eternal, but the visible effect—we might almost say the kiss of God which testifies to his *philanthropy*—has been given to us, *novissime, diebus istis,* as St Paul expresses it, by means of the Messianic manifestation. Christ will come again at the end of the world, the inexorable judge of the living and the dead; but now, in his first coming, justice seems to retire into the background of the picture, where Satan and death lie chained, so that only the loving-kindness and *philanthropy* of the divine Saviour may appear.

The Gradual borrows from Psalm cxvii the joyful greeting of the redeemed to Christ on his first coming into the world : " Blessed is he that cometh in the name of the Lord." On Palm Sunday the children and the crowd went out to meet Jesus, who was making his triumphal entry into Jerusalem, and sang this psalmodic salutation. Their devotion was so pleasing to the Saviour that he announced to the Synagogue his intention of abandoning it for ever to its fate, until it should acknowledge his Messianic dignity and should salute him with the greeting : " Blessed is he that cometh in the name of the Lord." To come in the name of the Lord signifies to come as the messenger of God, or rather as that great Prophet already announced by Moses, to whom Israel should have given that obedience which formerly they had rendered to their deliverer from the bondage of Pharaoh.

The alleluiatic verse is from the Paschal Psalm xcii : " The Lord is clothed with strength and with grace, to inaugurate his Messianic kingdom." With grace towards us to whom he shows his human nature, in all things like unto the sons of Adam, *ut sit ipse primogenitus in multis fratribus;* with strength towards the Evil One whom he overcomes by the power of his divine nature, breaking his weapons and destroying his kingdom.

The Gospel, from St Luke (ii, 15-20), tells us of the visit of the shepherds to the crib, of their devout dispositions, and of the attitude of the Blessed Virgin towards the great mystery which was unfolding itself before her eyes. While the shepherds are doing the work of apostles, in relating to their companions what they have heard and seen, Mary is raised to the loftiest height of contemplation, and in the secret of her heart is already proclaiming the Gospel story. Half a century hence, when the four blessed Evangelists shall be moved by the Holy Ghost to undertake the narrative of the life and teaching of Christ, the holy Mother will pour into their writings the fulness of heart which had meditated and lovingly dwelt upon these things for more than fifty years.

The compilation of the holy Gospels certainly dates from the second half of the first century, but the work was already conceived and pondered over from those early days at Bethlehem in the most pure heart of the Mother of God.

The Offertory takes us back again to Psalm xcii, the special psalm of this festival. The Babe wailing in the crib to-day has a history as old as the ages. God has established the world that it shall not be moved and that it shall serve as a footstool to the throne of the newborn Messiah. This throne is reserved to the firstborn of creation from all eternity, since although in his human nature he can count but a few hours of life, yet in his divine nature he is called in the Scriptures the *Ancient of Days* and co-eternal with the Father.

In the Secret we pray God that our offerings may be worthy of the mystery which we are celebrating, and may reconcile us to him; and as the little Child born on this day is both God and Man, so the eucharistic elements, while outwardly they appear like any other earthly substance, may bestow on us *quod divinum est*—that is, Jesus Christ with his divine nature and all the treasures of his merits and graces.

The commemoration of St Anastasia follows, in which we beg our Lord to look favourably upon the oblations which we offer him, so that through the merits of the martyr they may help us to gain eternal salvation.

The Communion is taken from Zacharias (ix, 9), who bids the daughters of Sion and of Jerusalem go out to meet Christ Jesus with festive joy as, full of gentleness and mildness typified by the meek creature upon which he rides, he comes to take possession of his kingdom. This prophecy, as St Matthew observes, directly refers to the entry of the Redeemer into the Holy City on Palm Sunday, but the Church finds striking analogies of humility, meekness and benignity between the entry of Jesus into Jerusalem and his first coming into the world. In the cave of Bethlehem, as well as at the gates of Jerusalem, he was all poverty, grace and pity. Jesus was not indeed then seated upon the ass, but this same lowly beast warmed with its breath his tender, half-frozen limbs in the manger.

In the Post-Communion we ask God that the yearly recurrence of this Christmas sacrifice may renew our souls also, just as the wonderful birth of the Lord has initiated a new era for humanity grown old under the curse of sin.

With the Fathers we may discern a threefold *parousia*, very happily shadowed forth in the Christmas liturgy. At his first coming Jesus is born in poverty as a victim to expiate sin, and the throne whence he condemns pride and self-indulgence is the manger.   The second time he rises radiant in glory from the humiliation of the tomb, and by the sending down of the Paraclete upon the Apostles he infuses into his Church, together with the hidden " spirit of resurrection," all his treasures of grace and holiness.   The third time he will appear at the end of the ages, seated upon a fiery throne of holiness and justice in the majesty of his office as supreme Judge of the living and the dead, when he will bring all creation into subjection to God, and then at length shall be ended the epic struggle, which embraces all angelic as well as all human history—the great battle between Christ and Satan.   A close bond of connection runs through all this threefold *parousia,* and this is why the Church never separates them in her Liturgy.   Easter is the fulfilment of Christmas, and the Feast of All Saints is the fruit of the Sunday of the Resurrection.

The Third Mass—in Daylight.   Station at St Mary Major (at St Peter's).

Up to the time of Gregory VII (1073-85) the third Christmas station was held, as was usual in Rome on very solemn days, at St Peter's, as if to keep Christmas as a family feast around the *mensa Petri*—the table of the common father and shepherd.   The shortness of the winter days, however, and the difficulty of going in procession to the Vatican in those troublous times when the Pope was actually torn from the altar *ad praesepe* at the midnight Mass, and was dragged off as the prisoner of a hostile faction, caused the Liberian Basilica to be preferred as being nearer to the Lateran, the more so as during the eleventh century St Peter's several times fell into the hands of schismatics and their anti-popes.

This custom, which was first made necessary by the difficulties of the times, ended by becoming permanent, and the station at St Mary Major was substituted for that at St Peter's, with this difference, however, that whereas the midnight Mass was celebrated in the oratory *ad praesepe,* which could accommodate only a limited number of persons, the third Mass took place in the vast *aula* of Sicininus, which had been restored by Liberius (352-66) and Sixtus III (432-40).

When the Pontiff entered the church—so the ancient *Ordines Romani* describe the ceremony—the *cubicularii* received him under a kind of baldachino, and the Pope, holding a taper affixed to the end of a rod, set the tow alight which had been entwined in the capitals of the pillars.

This rite, which at the present day takes place only on the occasion of the consecration of the Sovereign Pontiff, typified festive joy, as well as providing a *figura finis mundi per ignem*,[1] but this secondary and symbolical meaning was not attached to it until later. In more recent times the primitive meaning has undergone yet another modification. As the Pontiff, in all his glory, approaches the altar of St Peter in order to put on the triple crown, a master of ceremonies displays the burning tow before him, saying : *Pater sancte, sic transit gloria mundi.* The lesson is a deep one, but the Humanists of the Renaissance, to whom we owe it, did not seem in the least to comprehend the unsuitableness of reciting it before the Head of the Faith just as he was in the act of taking possession of the papal throne.

When the procession reached the *presbyterium*, the *primicerius*, having removed the Pope's mitre, kissed him on the shoulder, and the Pope, in his turn, having kissed the Codex of the Gospels, exchanged the Kiss of Peace with the senior cardinal-bishop, and, surrounded by his seven deacons, began the liturgical *actio*.

After the Collect, the lesser clergy, under the direction of the archdeacon, sang a series of acclamations in the form of a litany—as is always customary at the coronation of a Pope —in honour of the Pontiff, who repaid this compliment by presenting each of them with three pieces of silver. At the Offertory seven other ecclesiastics—bishops and cardinal-priests—went up to the altar and celebrated with the Pope ; in fact, this rite of the eucharistic concelebration at a solemn papal Mass was maintained in Rome for a very long time.

At the conclusion of the holy sacrifice the Pontiff was crowned by the archdeacon with the *regnum*—the second and third crowns were added during the period of the papal exile at Avignon—and the splendid cortège set out on horseback to return to the Lateran, where they dined. Before getting off their horses the cardinals drew up in order in front of the little Basilica of Zacharias, where—like the *Polichronion* of the Byzantine Court at the Christmas festival—the archpriest of St Lawrence similarly intoned : *Summo et egregio ac ter beatissimo papae N. vita.* His fellow-priests answered three times : *Deus conservet eum. Salvator mundi*, or *Sancta Maria, omnes sancti*, replied the archpriest, and at each invocation the others answered in chorus : *Tu illum adjuva.* The Pope gave thanks for these good wishes and distributed three pieces of silver money to each of the cardinals. The judges then came forward, and the *primicerius* intoned *Hunc diem*, upon which the rest repeatedly exclaimed : *Multos annos.* The archpriest then continued, *Tempora bona habeas*, and the others sang in conclusion : *Tempora bona habeamus omnes.*

[1] *Ord. Bened. Canonici, P.L.* LXXVIII, col. 1032.

Then at last the Pope dismounted, and, having entered one of the halls, made the customary distribution of money to his attendants, following, in so doing, an ancient tradition of the Cæsars. It is very interesting to note how the papal court of the Middle Ages preserved so many traditions of the imperial era of Rome and Byzantium. In addition to the customary gratuities received by all alike, twenty pieces of money went to the Prefect of the city, four to the judges and to the bishops, three to the cardinal-priests and deacons, and two to the lesser clergy and to the singers. When everyone present had been gladdened by this largess, they sat down to the banquet which was spread in the great *triclinium* of Leo III (795-816), the mosaic apse of which is still to be seen on the piazza of the Lateran in a building of later date, completed in the time of Benedict XIV (1740-56).

Near the Pope at table there sat—in their sacred vestments —on the right the cardinal-bishops and priests, on the left the archdeacon and the *primicerius* with the high officials of the Court. In the middle of the hall stood the lectern with the book of homilies, from which, halfway through the banquet, a deacon read a passage from one of the Fathers. The reading did not last long; the Pope sent an acolyte to invite the *schola* to perform some sequences from their collection in commemoration of Christmas, from which we learn the position allotted in Rome to the sequence as being a devout and popular but extra-liturgical chant. After the singers had given proof of their musical skill, they were admitted to kiss the Pope's foot, while he graciously offered to each one a cup of wine and a piece of money (*bezant*). What poetry lay in these ancient ceremonies of papal Rome, and, above all, what an influence the sacred Liturgy exercised over the whole religious life of the people !

The Introit is from Isaias (ix, 6), " Behold a child is born to us, and a son is given to us," who, notwithstanding the infinite nothingness to which he stoops, is God eternal, the Creator of the universe, who rules and governs all things in the power of his Word, and upon whose shoulder rests the divine and universal monarchy. He, as the brightness and express image of the Father, will reveal him to men and will be to them the envoy of the most holy Trinity, the angel or messenger of the glad tidings of redemption. Psalm xcvii follows, bidding us sing a new song unto the Lord, in thanksgiving for the new wonder of mercy which he has wrought in the Incarnation of the Word.

In the Collect we beseech almighty God that the new birth of his only-begotten Son in the flesh may deliver us from the old slavery of sin.

In the lesson, from the Epistle to the Hebrews (i, 1-12), St Paul demonstrates, by means of a profound exegesis of Old Testament texts, the divine nature of the Messiah and his infinite superiority over the angels, who indeed adore him and offer him, in fear and trembling, their humble services. Although he appears as the Babe in the manger, he is still the eternal God; everything in the world passes away and is renewed, and he creates new forms in succession to the old, as one may change a worn-out garment, but " he is always the self-same, and his years shall not fail."

The Gradual is taken from Psalm xcvii. God has manifested the divine Saviour to the world, and all the nations have shared in this revelation. It is no longer Judea alone who is bidden to praise Jehovah whom at first she alone knew. The new redemption needs to be universal even as the fall was universal, and the national barriers dividing Jews, Greeks and Romans shall be of no account in God's sight; the Church shall be one and Catholic—that is, Universal.

The alleluiatic verse is borrowed from the Byzantine Liturgy. " A hallowed day hath shone upon us." As the Father begat the Word from all eternity amid the splendours of his own substantial holiness, so to-day the Blessed Virgin gives birth to the Redeemer who through his Incarnation consecrates the world and sanctifies the Church. " This day a great light hath descended upon the earth;" not merely a material, but also a spiritual, light. Christ Jesus, *Light of Light,* has come to dispel the darkness of the world. We have to remember that anciently, in the East, the feast of Christmas was joined to that of the Epiphany and called the " Festival of the Holy Lights "; hence the figure of material and spiritual light is a very natural one on such a day. This influence of the Eastern liturgies on the Roman recalls to our minds the golden age of monasticism at Rome, when, in the capital of the Catholic world, side by side with the Roman monasteries, there dwelt communities of cenobites from Greece, Syria, Cilicia, Armenia, etc, who all took their part in the papal solemnities.

The Gospel, from St John (i, 1-14), contains, perhaps, the most sublime page to be found in the whole of the Scriptures. It speaks of the twofold begetting of the Word in his divine and in his human nature. As the image of the supreme Artificer, the Word is at once the prototype and the pattern of all that is created; but in him this image is identical with his own substance, so that all things live in him. As a creature his birth does not proceed from the will of the flesh, nor from the will of man; the Immaculate Virgin Mother conceives him by the power of the Spirit of God, a divine begetting in which we also are allowed a share as often as, by faith, we receive Jesus into our souls. In becoming man and setting up his tent amongst us he loses nothing of his divine attributes, so that we, through the veil of his Humanity, see all the divine *pleroma,* the infinite fulness of grace and truth. This word *pleroma* should be noted as being opposed to the false learning against which the Evangelist is here speaking.

The Offertory comes from Psalm lxxxviii : " Thine are the heavens, thine is the earth and the universe which thou hast created; justice and judgement are the preparation of thy throne." How beautiful is this insistence of the Church upon the divine attributes of the Babe of Bethlehem on this very day when he, with infinite pity for our wretchedness, deigns to hide his splendours under the poor swaddling-clothes which enwrap his limbs benumbed with cold.

In the Secret we ask God to sanctify our offerings in commemoration of the temporal birth of his only-begotten Son, so that we also may be purified from all stain of sin.

In the Communion, taken from Psalm xcvii, we give thanks to almighty God for manifesting the divine Saviour to all nations. Generosity, magnificence and light, these are always the marks of God's handiwork. Sin is generally committed in darkness and in secret, for the wicked hate the light, but the Redemption is wrought upon Calvary in sight of the whole world, so that all people, through the light of faith, may recognize and adore the crucified Saviour.

In the Post-Communion we pray that the newborn Babe, as he is the author of our new birth in the sublimity of the divine regeneration, may also be the bounteous rewarder of our merits in the glory of eternity.

Jesus is born of woman in order that we may one day cease to be the children of woman and may be raised to the dignity of sonship to almighty God. The Word joins our human nature to his Person, to make us sharers in the divine grace. He stoops to the very dust of earth, in order to raise up his creatures to the highest heavens. What mysterious antitheses are here presented to us ! What force of eloquence in that visible poverty which surrounds the cradle of Jesus ! Those frozen limbs, that manger, that straw, that penury, that utter humiliation; what a condemnation are these of our self-indulgence and our pride !

ST STEPHEN THE PROTOMARTYR

Station at St Stephen's on the Cœlian Hill.

The basilica where to-day's station is held was begun by Pope Simplicius (468-82), but only finished under John I (523-26) and Felix IV, by whose direction the mosaic decoration was carried to completion. The feast of St Stephen, on the other hand, is much more ancient, and appears even in the *laterculus* of the Arian martyrology, which goes back to the last twenty years of the fourth century.

It would, indeed, seem as if, in order to give additional grandeur to the Christmas festival, the greatest saints had wished to gather around the cradle of the Christ-Child, especially those who had some particular connection with the mystery of his Incarnation. St Gregory Nyssa records them in the following order: Stephen, Peter, James, John, Paul and Basil,[1] while later Greek documents give in addition David, St Joseph and the Magi.

From the first half of the fifth century, shortly after the discovery of the relics of the protomartyr, several basilicas dedicated to him were built in Rome. There were two of them near St Peter's, St Stephen *Katà Galla patricia* and St Stephen *Katà Barbara patricia*. Another one was erected on some land in the Via Latina belonging to Demetrias, which was bequeathed by her to St Leo I. This Demetrias, the daughter of Sextus Anicius Hermogenianus Olibrius, besides being a friend of St Augustine, who presented her with some relics of the protomartyr, was the recipient of a celebrated letter from Pelagius on the devout life.

During the Middle Ages the piety of successive Popes multiplied sanctuaries dedicated to St Stephen throughout the city until they numbered at least thirty-five, including several monasteries, Latin as well as Greek. When we consider, therefore, the popularity of the *cultus* of the first martyr, the solemnity with which to-day's station on the Cœlian was celebrated will cause us no surprise.

The Pope, accompanied by the cardinals and the Court, all gorgeously apparelled in silken garments, set off on horseback from the Lateran for the Cœlian Hill. The trappings of the papal charger were of rich scarlet, while the Pontiff wore the tiara and the white *paenula* which was the travelling dress of the ancient Romans. At the Church of St Stephen *Rotondo* he laid aside the tiara and the white garments in order to put on the red vestments in which he celebrated Mass. When it was over he remounted his horse, and the

[1] *P.G.* XLVI, cols. 790 *sq.*

procession returned to the *patriarchium,* where the customary distribution of money took place—*presbyterium*—and the ritual banquet in the *triclinium.* The *Ordo* of Peter Amelius prescribes that it should be served with all decorum, and that the chaplains, acolytes, auditors and penitentiaries should take part in it, to each of whom a measure of pepper also was distributed.[1] In the case of the indisposition of the Pope, the Mass for to-day was allotted to the Cardinal-Priest of St Clement, since the Cardinal of St Stephen took by right the place of the Pontiff on Christmas Day. Vespers were sung in the afternoon in the Lateran, the Pope taking part therein, vested in a mitre and a red cope.

The Introit is from Psalm cxviii, and describes the leaders of the Sanhedrim taking counsel against the just man. The wicked persecute him solely because of the rectitude of his ways; their long pent-up spite is about to vent itself upon him, and he feels the supreme moment of open conflict to be imminent. He is wholly conscious of his own weakness, and therefore, in fullest confidence, he begs almighty God to help him bear his martyrdom.

In the Collect we pray to God that we may imitate the example of Stephen, not only by forgiving our enemies, but by even loving them and asking for them the grace of conversion.

The passage which follows, from the Acts of the Apostles, paints in vivid colours the trial of Stephen by the Sanhedrim and his being stoned to death outside the walls of Jerusalem. St Luke must have learnt the details from St Paul, upon whose mind that dreadful scene remained indelibly imprinted. The protomartyr, against whom the synagogues of the Diaspora in the Holy City are now especially inflamed, falls a victim to his own propagandist zeal for the universality of the Gospel ideal, even beyond the national barriers of Israel. As a Hellenist he addresses himself openly to the Hellenists, Alexandrians and Cyrenians, hoping to find them less narrow and hostile than the Jews in their conception of the Messiah; but the Christian seed must first germinate in the earth and be watered with blood, so Stephen meets with his death because of the mistaken religious ideas of the Sanhedrim. Yet God's work goes forward in spite of men, and Saul, his most fierce persecutor of to-day, has already in his heart, to his own despite, that divine plan which will make him to-morrow an apostle even unto the ends of the earth.

The Gradual is borrowed, as is the Introit, from Psalm cxviii. The martyr invokes help from on high, thus attribut-

---

[1] *P.L.* LXXVIII, 1281.

ing his victory to the compassion of almighty God whose grace sustains him in his hour of trial.

The alleluiatic verse comes from the Acts of the Apostles (vii, 55), where Stephen, standing undaunted in the midst of the Sanhedrim, confirms his scriptural proofs of the divine nature of Jesus Christ by his own personal testimony which directly led to his being condemned to death. It is not alone the prophets who bear witness that Christ is God, for Stephen himself now sees him as he is in heaven, seated on the right hand of the Father, consubstantial with him and equal to him in majesty and in power.

Stephen is not only a martyr; he is one of the most striking personages of the apostolic age; so much so that as the Greeks give him the title of Apostle, so the Roman Liturgy places him in the category of the prophets, doctors and masters, whose cruel fate is described to us in the Gospel for to-day. Jerusalem, the chosen of Jehovah, stones *eos qui . . . missi sunt;* in other words, his Apostles. But the measure of her ingratitude is now full. The Lord withdraws himself from her and leaves her to her own precarious fate. We say precarious, since the " Shepherd of Israel " can never altogether forget his people. Indeed, he is ever ready to return to the sons of Jacob *in misericordiis,* if only they be not too obdurate to accept him as their Redeemer. The acclamation refused to Christ by the Jews and laid down as the condition of a new reconciliation— " Blessed is he that cometh in the name of the Lord "—is the festive cry of the Church when the divine Lamb comes down upon her altars.

The Offertory, taken from various passages in the Acts of the Apostles (vi-viii), tells of Stephen's election by the Twelve. The Jews stoned him who was filled with faith and the Holy Ghost, while he, kneeling down in prayer, bore his final testimony to the " Lord " Jesus—this was the whole point at issue between him and the Sanhedrim—calling upon him to receive his spirit into heaven.

The Secret is of typical form, but it acquires a special significance in view of the commemoration of the proto-martyr. The Host which is being immolated joins the sufferings of the martyrs with our Lord's own sacrifice, whence we pray that, as their violent death became for them the title of endless glory, so our devotion may avail to keep us far from all sin.

The Communion antiphon sung by the *schola cantorum*—the Lateran *schola* was dedicated to St Stephen, which accounts for their wishing to honour their titular saint on this day by so splendid an office—unites the last two testimonies of the protomartyr. He beholds Jesus at the right hand of the divine Majesty, and therefore commends his spirit to him, praying him to forgive his murderers, blinded as they were by ignorance and passion. The prayer of Stephen was heard, and its wondrous answer was Paul. The piety of the early Pontiffs led them to emphasize this connection between the protomartyr and the Apostle by building, about the sixth century, beside the tomb of St Paul in the Via Ostiensis, a notable oratory, with a monastery attached to it, in honour of St Stephen.

In the Post-Communion we ask that our participation in the eucharistic mystery may bring forth fruit in us and may sustain our frailty by its divine strength.

In an age of such enfeebled energy, of so many compromises with conscience, of such regard for human respect and opinion, what an example of Christian fortitude is given us by Stephen when, confronting the Sanhedrim, he declares to the Jewish people the most unpalatable truths. Like deaf adders, they stop their ears and refuse to hear more; they gnash their teeth against him, but he, unperturbed, endures his long examination to the end and finally seals it with his blood.

On this day, then, let us beg, through the intercession of St Stephen, the grace of fortitude, which is one of the seven gifts of the Holy Ghost.

ST JOHN, APOSTLE AND EVANGELIST

Station at St Mary Major.

Of all the feasts of Apostles which anciently formed part of the Christmas cycle, the only one now remaining is that of St John, who was commemorated in the East conjointly with St James, the first Bishop of Jerusalem. The station is at the Liberian Basilica, for the reason that the Lateran church is dedicated to the Saviour. To St John the Baptist and to St John the Evangelist were dedicated respectively on the right and the left of the Baptistery merely two little oratories which had been erected by Pope Hilary (461-8), in memory of the danger he escaped when fleeing from the violence of the followers of Dioscorus at the so-called *latrocinium Ephesinum*.[1]

The Basilica of St John, before the Latin Gate, is of much later origin, and was not included in the list of stational churches until long afterwards. There was left, therefore, only the Liberian church. This basilica, however, seemed

---

[1] This occurrence took place at the time of the Second Council of Ephesus which Hilary was attending as Legate of Pope Leo I.—Tʀ.

the most suitable place for the celebration of the Christmas station in honour of St John, both on account of the Saviour's crib there preserved, and of the mosaics of Sixtus III commemorating the Council of Ephesus, held near the tomb of the Evangelist.

Later on the Lateran oratory of the Evangelist attained to great celebrity, and thus it is not impossible that the two Masses marked for to-day in the Leonine Sacramentary really refer to two separate stations, one at St Mary Major and the other at the Baptistery of the Lateran.

Down to the eleventh century the Roman stations maintained all their solemn traditional rites, but after that time, schisms and faction fights having prevented the Popes from taking part in them in person, the later *Ordines* prescribe that the feast of St John also, like many others, shall be celebrated simply in the papal chapel. A cardinal sang the Mass, and one of the procurators of the new Mendicant Orders delivered the homily in the presence of the Pontiff, who was vested in a scarlet cope and a mitre. At the second Vespers—an office adopted in Rome at a very late date, Vespers being originally the prelude to the vigiliary office which did not follow, but preceded, the great feasts—there were present the palatine clergy, together with those who sat at the same table as the Pope; also the auditors of the palace, the subdeacons, the acolytes and the chaplains.

The Introit of the Mass is an echo of the use of the Eastern Christians, who give to St John the title of *Theologos,* since he penetrated more deeply than any other mortal into the mysteries of the divine nature. John was the favourite disciple of Jesus, consequently the divine Master had no secrets from him. The ineffable inner life of the august Trinity, the beatings of the loving heart of the Incarnate Word, the future history of the Church and the ultimate destiny of the world, the Liturgy of the Church triumphant; all these things were pondered over in the divine light by the Eagle of Patmos, the true " son of thunder," who in the brief pages of his Gospel and Apocalypse has left us a complete treatise on theology—the story of the eternal Godhead. Well may the Church repeat to-day in the Introit in praise of St John those words of Ecclesiasticus (xv, 5): " He opened his lips in the midst of the church, for the Lord had filled him with the spirit of wisdom and understanding, clothing him with a robe of glory." Then follows a passage from Psalm xci, which speaks of the happiness of those who worship Jehovah and sing his praises upon the psaltery.

The Collect begs from almighty God a greater outpouring of inward light, so that by entering deeply into the teachings of John the blessed Apostle, we may obtain the grace of everlasting happiness.

To-day, as on all the greater feasts of the year, the Würzburg Lectionary makes mention of two lessons before the Gospel in both the Masses for the feast of St John the Evangelist. In the first Mass the lesson from the Old Testament is the same as that which is read in the present Missal, while the New Testament lesson is taken from St Paul's Epistle to the Ephesians (i, 3-8). In the second Mass—with its grand collects and its splendid preface, preserved to us in the Leonine Sacramentary—the Old Testament reading is again taken from the Book of Wisdom (c. x), while the second lesson is also from the Epistle to the Ephesians (ii, 19-22). This arrangement would appear to have been deliberately made for its appropriateness, if we consider the relations existing between Ephesus, St John and the Liberian Basilica, the votive memorial at Rome of the great Council which assembled in Asia near the tomb of the Evangelist.

The present lesson from Ecclesiasticus (xv, 1-6)—in the Missal all such books as Ecclesiasticus, Proverbs, the Canticle of Canticles, etc., are classed under the general heading of the Book of Wisdom—praises the truly wise man who, building his spiritual edifice upon the unshakable foundation of the holy fear of God, does good and practises justice. Grace is poured out freely upon a soul so well disposed. The Lord, the Just One, goes forth to meet him and unites himself to him as a bridegroom to a bride, illuminating his mind and bestowing on him the gift of true wisdom so that he shall light up the whole Church with the rays of his teaching.

The Gradual is drawn from that passage of St John's Gospel (xxi, 23) in which reference is made to the popular belief current in the first generation of Christians in Asia that the beloved disciple should not die before the *parousia*. The advanced age of the Apostle, on the other hand, seemed to lend credit to this opinion. So St John, in the very last chapter of his Gospel, desired—as a sort of final postscript—to rectify this erroneous interpretation of the Saviour's words. " So I will have him to remain till I come, what is it to thee?" The words were uttered by our Lord merely as an hypothesis. " So (if) I will;" but in the several oral versions of the episode the conditional and hypothetical particle " if " was easily passed over; hence St John felt the necessity of explaining the misunderstanding and setting the matter right.

The alleluiatic verse (John xxi, 24) is the continuation of the preceding text. The churches of Asia which had prayed and fasted that the Evangelist might compose his sacred volume, now associate themselves with him and present him

to the world as the true author of the fourth Gospel. Here
is the anticipatory confutation of all those ideas devised by
modern rationalistic exegesis which would deprive St John
of the authorship of his holy Gospel, or deny it any solid
historical basis.

The chants which follow the Epistle have already prepared
us, as it were, for the Gospel (John xxi, 20-24). Peter and
John are linked together by a special affection, and, notwithstanding the difference of their characters, they have many
traits in common. Hence the Gospel narrative nearly always
speaks of them together, whether on apostolic journeyings,
preparing the Paschal supper, in the house of the High
Priest, fishing in the Sea of Tiberias, or at evening prayer in
the Temple, etc.

On the present occasion, after the meal on the shores of the
Lake of Genesareth, Jesus takes Peter apart in order to tell
him his ultimate fate, while John stands aside, tactfully
refraining from any importunate disturbance of their colloquy.
His companion, however, who knows his desire, now repays
the good service rendered to him at the Last Supper by the
beloved disciple, when the latter asked for him of the Lord
who should betray him. So Peter asks : " Lord, and what
shall this man do?" The divine Master, alluding to the
diversity of vocations, offices and graces in the Church,
replies : " So I will have him to remain till I come, what is it
to thee? Follow thou me." He would thus teach us that the
calling and the merit of others ought not to distract us from
giving due attention to the claims of our own work and
station. This it is which our Lord requires of us, and not to
concern ourselves with that which others may or may not
accomplish.

The Offertory is from Psalm xci, in which the just man is
compared to a flourishing palm-tree and a great cedar crowning the slopes of Lebanon.

In the Secret we beg almighty God graciously to receive
the gifts which we offer him on the feast of this so powerful
advocate in whom we place all our trust.

The Communion returns to the misunderstanding of the
early Christians that the beloved disciple should not die.
This, however, is not the true meaning of the promise made
by Jesus to those who love him, and especially to those who
feed upon his eucharistic sacrament. Death will indeed
exercise its power for a time over their bodies, but grace will
nourish their spirit unto life everlasting, and this immortal
life will one day so completely inundate the soul as to free its
mortal habitation from the bonds of death and make it partaker of its own happy state.

The Gospel of to-day's Mass contains clear proof of the

authenticity of the fourth Gospel, so much called in question by the rationalists that it needs to be constantly reasserted. If St John is to remain always hale and hearty until the second coming of Jesus—so argued the faithful of the last ten years of the first century—that is the same as saying that the *parousia* will find him still living. Such a misapprehension was not possible before the death of all the other Apostles, for they certainly could not have misunderstood the Master's words, nor would they have failed to rectify the interpretation of them; nor would the error have continued after the death of John, as that event would at once have discredited the report. Only the last quarter of the first century, therefore, remains for the development of this strange interpretation—a time when St John was still able personally to explain the mistake. *Donec veniam* refers, then, to the *parousia* only in a conditional sense—merely " if " our Lord should have willed so to dispose the course of events.

The vigorous old age of the Evangelist was, moreover, fully in keeping with his spotless virginity. If, in fact, the married state is ordained to ensure the preservation of the race against the infirmity of the flesh, which ever tends to dissolve itself in dust, virginity, on the other hand, expresses the condition of the saints in everlasting glory, who, being no longer subject to bodily weakness and corruption, are therefore free from the necessity of contracting any conjugal tie : *In resurrectione autem non nubent neque nubentur, sed erunt sicut angeli Dei in coelo. . . .*

THE HOLY INNOCENTS

Station at St Paul's.

The choice of to-day's station at the basilica of the Apostle would seem to have been influenced, not so much by association with the relics of the Holy Innocents—said, according to tradition, to have been preserved in that splendid church—as by the delicate feeling of the ancient liturgy that the great solemnities of the year should always be celebrated by a station at the tombs of SS Peter and Paul. We have instances of this in the three weeks before Lent, as well as at the baptismal scrutinies, at Easter, at Pentecost, and now at Christmas. Moreover, it is not unlikely that this station at St Paul's, following on that of December 25 at St Peter's, still preserves a last remnant of a very ancient festival in honour of the two Princes of the Apostles, as is attested by several Oriental calendars and ferial records of the fourth century.

We do not know at what date Rome included the Holy Innocents among her liturgical feasts. They already appear for to-day in the Calendar of Carthage (fifth to sixth century) and in the Leonine and Gelasian Sacramentaries, while in the Syriac Calendar they are commemorated on September 23. It is certain that the feast of Christmas, at a very early date, revived and drew to itself that of the Innocents massacred by Herod; hence in Rome this day was observed as a day of mourning and penance. The *Ordines Romani* prescribe that the Pope and his assistants should be arrayed in purple vestments, that the deacons and subdeacons should put on the processional *paenula,* and that the Pontiff should wear a mitre of plain white linen. The *Te Deum* was not sung at the night office, nor were the *Gloria* and the Alleluia at the Mass, unless it were a Sunday, while the faithful were bidden to abstain from flesh meat and from foods cooked in fats.

In the fifteenth century, however, the pontifical court used to celebrate this feast in the papal chapel, a sermon being preached for the occasion; but little by little this tradition died out, as the *Ordines Romani XIV* and *XV* sadly lament. It may be that as yesterday it was desired to commemorate the Evangelist of Ephesus in the Basilica of Sicininus amid the memories of the Council, so there may have been a similar wish to commemorate to-day Rachel weeping for her children in the basilica of the most illustrious scion of the tribe of Benjamin, and so to find oneself in the home, as it were, of those innocent victims.

The Introit comes from Psalm viii, which was quoted by our Lord when the chief priests found fault with him for allowing the young children to acclaim him in the Temple as the Messiah : " Have ye never read : Out of the mouths of infants and sucklings thou hast perfected praise because of thy enemies ?"[1] The antiphon is from the same psalm.

In the Collect we remind our Lord that the innocent martyrs proclaimed his glory rather by their death than by their lips, and we pray him to uproot all evil passions from our hearts, so that we may testify by our lives to that faith which we confess with our mouths.

The lesson from the Apocalypse (xiv, 1-5), which speaks of a hundred and forty-four thousand virgins singing in heaven the *epithalamium* of the virginal Spouse, gave rise in the Middle Ages to a curious misinterpretation, according to which the symbolical number—intended to indicate quite in a general way the twelve tribes of Israel from among whom the divine Lamb gathers his lilies—signified that of the inno-

[1] Matt. xxi, 15-16.

cent victims of Bethlehem. But however rigorously the slaughter may have been carried out in the City of David and in the surrounding country, it is difficult to imagine that it could have included so many male infants. The Liturgy, however, is not concerned with this misapprehension, which doubtless arose from a too literal interpretation of the sacred text.

The magnificent Gradual of the Martyrs now follows. It is taken from Psalm cxxiii, which really belongs to the collection of the fifteen Gradual psalms of the Hebrews. " Our soul hath been delivered as a sparrow out of the snare of the fowlers. The snare is broken and we are delivered. Our help is in the name of the Lord who hath made heaven and earth."

Instead of the alleluiatic verse, " Praise the Lord, ye children, praise ye the name of the Lord " (Psalm cxii, 1)— which is used only when this feast falls on a Sunday—is sung the Tract from Psalm lxxviii, referring to the massacres which took place in Palestine before the time of the Machabees. "They have poured out the blood of thy saints as water round about Jerusalem, and there was none to bury them. Revenge, O Lord, the blood of thy servants which hath been shed."

The Gospel from St Matthew (ii, 13-18) describes the flight of the Holy Family into Egypt and the massacre of the Innocents. How short-sighted is human scheming ! At the very time that it tries to thwart the designs of almighty God, it is just then that it merely serves them the better. Herod is desirous of slaying the newborn Messiah; this he fails to do, but sends instead a number of innocent babes into Limbo, there to proclaim his coming, while the Saviour goes forth to enlighten and to bless the land of Egypt.

The Offertory is practically the same as the Gradual. The victims of Herod's persecution, having attained their freedom, have gone up to heaven without ever realizing the wondrous manner of their going. At God's word the net is broken and they, like birds set free from a snare, have at once flown away.

In the Secret we pray God that the intercession of his saints may never fail us, but that it may render our oblations more pleasing to him and may call down upon us his infinite mercy.

The Communion (Matt. ii, 18) recalls the lament of Rachel in Rama, inconsolable because her children are led away captive into slavery. The Evangelist applies this verse of Jeremias in a symbolical sense to the slaughter of the Innocents, who were snatched violently out of life by an even worse act of cruelty than that of the destroyers of Jerusalem.

In the Post-Communion we ask that, having shared in the sacrifice offered for the feast-day of the Innocents, we may obtain through their prayers both consolation now and eternal life hereafter.

We ought to look upon those who do us injury in the light of the Faith, evincing towards them the sincerest gratitude. They are as surgical instruments in the hands of the heavenly Physician, with which he performs upon our souls incisions and amputations such as we ourselves would never have the courage to accomplish.

SUNDAY WITHIN THE OCTAVE OF THE NATIVITY

The holy feast of Christmas, like Easter and Pentecost, possessed in Rome its own cycle of Sundays, and in the ancient lectionary lists this particular Sunday was marked as being the first Sunday after the Nativity of our Lord. The station is not indicated, either because it was perhaps announced each time to the people, or because it was left to the titular priests on these lesser Sundays to celebrate Mass in their own parish churches without it being necessary for their people to go in procession to the church where the Pope himself was celebrating.

The Introit is from the Book of Wisdom (xviii, 14-15), and refers directly to the coming of the destroying angel in the dead of night to slay the firstborn of the Egyptian oppressors of Israel. "While all things were in quiet silence, and the night was in the midst of her course, thy almighty Word, O Lord, came from heaven, from thy royal throne." To this are added, from Psalm xcii, the words: "The Lord hath reigned, he is clothed with beauty: the Lord is clothed with strength, and hath girded himself."

The destroying angel passes over the houses of the Hebrews on whose doorposts the blood of the paschal lamb has been sprinkled. This heavenly envoy, the minister of divine justice for the one people and the loving Saviour of the other, is a type of the Incarnate Word. Hence the Church, following in this the authoritative interpretation of the Apostle St Jude (verse 5), applies this passage from the Book of Wisdom to our Lord himself. Both the deliverance from the Egyptian bondage and that from the ancient yoke of sin through the operation of the Messiah took place in the dead of night—the hour of closest and most recollected prayer— when all surrounding creation kept silence, and the civil and political world itself was enjoying the immutable *pax romana* of Augustus. The darkness of night is also a symbol of the ignorance and sin in which mankind was plunged when our Lord, the glorious morning star, appeared upon earth.

In the Collect, now that the High Priest and Teacher of our Faith has come into the world to show us by his example the way to all good, we pray God to direct our actions in accordance with his holy will, so that in the name of his Son Jesus we may deserve to abound in good works.

When once the original order of the stational Masses had been changed, the sequence of lessons suffered a corresponding dislocation. To-day's lesson is from the Epistle to the Galatians (iv, 1-7), although the Epistle to the Romans should continue until the Epiphany. However, either by a fortuitous coincidence or through an intended anticipation, this passage from the Apostle is quite in keeping with the mystery of our Lord's infancy which the Church is celebrating during these days. St Paul wishes to show that Jesus is the Son of God; he therefore brings forward an argument at once deep and intimate, yet one of wide and far-reaching import, inasmuch as it appeals to all Christians. The Holy Ghost, he says, places upon our lips the filial cry: "Abba, Father." But the divine Paraclete is the Spirit of Jesus, hence it is Jesus who grants us a share in his own divine sonship and gives us the right to call God our Father, he himself being the Firstborn and the rightful heir of the Father's riches.

The Gradual follows, from Psalm xliv. "Thou art beautiful above the sons of men: grace is poured abroad in thy lips. My heart hath uttered a good word, I speak my works to the King: my tongue is the pen of a scrivener that writeth swiftly."

The alleluiatic verse is also from Psalm xcii, which has become in these days the special song of the inauguration of the new Messianic kingdom.

The Gospel (Luke ii, 33-40) is very ancient, dating back at least before the feast of the Purification. Originally, before the mysteries of the holy infancy came to be observed with separate solemnities in accordance with their chronological development, the Roman Liturgy had grouped them around the feast of Christmas, following the order of the lessons from the holy Gospels.

The most natural feeling of a soul that contemplates the things of God is one of holy wonder. The Christ-Child was a source of constant study and increasing marvel to Mary and Joseph. As yet he had not opened his lips nor performed a single miracle. What will it be when the blessed Mother contemplates him on the cross? If the mysteries of the unspeakable condescension, the self-effacement and gentleness of the sacred infancy of Jesus are so profound that even the enlightened minds of his holy parents are perplexed thereat, what ought not we to do in order constantly to study Jesus and so get an intimate knowledge of him?

An ancient writer called this the *magna quaestio mundi,* and so indeed it is. Our Lord is a consoling mystery to the good and a tormenting problem to the wicked. They would fain disregard him, they would gladly belittle his claims to universal sovereignty, but in vain. They acknowledge his divine Nature by the very fact of their attacking it, for if Jesus were simply man and not God, they would not give themselves so much trouble to persecute him. *Signum cui contradicetur;* here in three words we have the whole story of Jesus and that of his Church. Persecution may vary in form and manner, but throughout the centuries, whatever of hatred and oppression may be vented upon the Church, it is always Jesus who is the persecuted One.

The Offertory is the same as that for the second Mass on Christmas Day.

In the Secret we pray God to accept our oblations so that they may obtain for us the grace of that holy fervour which shall finally bring us to everlasting life.

The Communion is an extract from St Matthew (ii, 20), but from a Gospel reading different from that which we have already had to-day, thus showing that the order of the antiphons and of the scriptural *pericopes* has been disarranged. " Take the child and his mother, and go into the land of Israel : for they are dead that sought the life of the child."

The Post-Communion describes in a few words the fruits of the Eucharist. " By the operation of this mystery, O Lord, may our vices be cleansed away and our just desires accomplished."

God loves self-effacement and humility, and even when he manifests himself, it is only to hide in a new way, unrealizable by human perceptions. Thus the Word of God appears on earth, but hides himself under the outward wrappings of the flesh; he is seen of men indeed, but in the guise of a poor artisan, and to-day, too, if the Gospel bears witness that our Lord grew in strength and gave daily more wondrous proofs of his divine knowledge, it goes on at once to say that he hid this substantial and divine wisdom, spending thirty years in the workshop of a carpenter, always obedient and subject to Mary and Joseph.

DECEMBER 29. ST THOMAS OF CANTERBURY, BISHOP AND MARTYR

This feast was placed in the Calendar of the Roman Curia and thence in the Missal only as late as the thirteenth century—that is to say, when the *cultus* of the holy Primate of England had become widely spread, even in Italy. It was, however, never included among the stations, notwithstanding that to-day's office belongs to the *Proprium de Tempore* and not to the *Proprium de Sanctis*.

The Mass is imposing, pathetic, and eloquent of the impression made upon Christian Europe by the murder of the Archbishop of Canterbury at the hands of a small band of assassins in his own cathedral at the hour of Vespers. After the red blossoms with which the Innocents decked the crib of the Babe of Bethlehem, it is most fitting that one of the most powerful prelates of the Middle Ages should come to place thereon a chaplet of roses in the name of the whole Catholic episcopate. We shall find this Mass constantly laying stress upon the gifts and the duties of a bishop and pastor of souls.

The Introit is borrowed from a Greek text originally destined for use on the feast of St Agatha. "Let us all rejoice in the Lord, celebrating a festival day in honour of the blessed martyr Thomas : at whose martyrdom the angels rejoice, and give praise to the Son of God." To this is added the opening verse of Psalm xxxii : "Rejoice in the Lord, O ye just; praise becometh the upright."

The Collect is expressive of devout grandeur : "O God, for whose Church the glorious bishop Thomas fell by the swords of the impious; grant, we beseech thee, that all who implore his assistance may obtain the salutary effect of their petition."

The lesson comes from the Epistle to the Hebrews (v, 1-6), in which the figurative priesthood of the Old Covenant is compared with that of Christ. The priestly calling is one of mercy and pity, wherefore God has willed that it should be exercised, not by the angels, for they are pure spirits remote from every weakness of the flesh, but by frail men whose very frailty renders them the more able to understand and compassionate the weaknesses of others. For this reason did Christ also put on our human nature, in order to show us his infinite condescension in a more tangible way. It belongs to God to choose those whom he destines to be his mediators and the ministers of his mercies. No one can arrogate this office to himself; even Jesus was chosen by his heavenly Father to be the High Priest of our Faith.

The Gradual is from Ecclesiasticus (xliv, 20). It praises the great prelate, who in his lifetime was chosen in preference to others as the special object of divine favours, which he merited by his fidelity to the law of God.

The alleluiatic verse is taken from the Gospel of St John (x, 11), where Jesus is likened to the Good Shepherd who knows his sheep and is likewise known of them.

The Gospel (John x, 11-16) is the same as that for the second Sunday after Easter, but to-day it bears a particular meaning. In the Paschal solemnity it is Jesus, the Good Shepherd, who gives his life for the flock; to-day, on the other hand, it is the faithful disciple who has closely followed the example of his Lord and has shed his blood for the liberty of the Christian family when threatened by the tyranny of a kingship degenerated into despotism.

The Offertory is from Psalm xx, 4-5. "Thou hast set on his head, O Lord, a crown of precious stones : he asked life of thee, and thou hast given it to him.   Alleluia."

In the Secret we beg God to sanctify the offerings dedicated to him, so that through the intercession of blessed Thomas, bishop and martyr, they may avail to call down upon us the benign glance of divine compassion.

The Communion is the same as the alleluiatic verse, and is taken from St John's Gospel; but here it is applied to our Lord, who feeds his flock with his own blood.

The Post-Communion is very ancient.   There has been added to it merely the mention of the martyr : " May this communion, O Lord, purify us from crime; and by the intercession of blessed Thomas, thy martyr and bishop, make us partakers of a heavenly remedy."

How sublime is the pastoral office, and what unfailing virtue it calls for !   In explaining that passage in St Paul's Epistle to Timothy (iii, 2), where he says that " it behoveth therefore a bishop to be blameless," the Fathers commonly teach that he ought to be already so far solidly established in a state of perfection as to have extirpated the last roots of self-love, so that he may no longer seek anything but the glory of God and the salvation of souls.   Love is indeed a going forth of the soul out of itself towards God and towards all that concerns him.   When the soul is wrapped up in itself, then does it come short of the perfect law of love and fall into the evil defect of self-love and self-worship.   *Charitas non quaerit quae sua sunt;* hence the pastoral office, which is one of supreme and disinterested love, requires such forgetfulness of self as to see nothing before it save God and his glory in the sanctification of the faithful.

DECEMBER 31. ST SYLVESTER, POPE AND CONFESSOR

Station at the Cemetery of Priscilla.

To-day's station was celebrated in the Via Salaria, at the Basilica of St Sylvester in the cemetery of Priscilla, where the great Pontiff of the Church's triumphant peace lay resting beside the martyrs Felix and Philip, two of the sons of St Felicitas, and at a short distance from Pope Marcellus and the martyr Crescention. St Gregory the Great delivered one of his forty homilies there; indeed, for many centuries that spot was the goal of pious pilgrims when visiting the holy places of the Eternal City.

St Sylvester was one of the very earliest saints to receive public veneration, even though he was not a martyr, but only a *confessor a Domino coronatus,* by reason of his exile in the caves of Soracte. This title *prope martyribus,* joined to his extraordinary personal virtues and to the circumstance of his having inaugurated a new era of splendour and prosperity for the Church, availed to surround the brow of Sylvester with the aureole of the blessed and make his name famous even in the far-off East. Legendary fancy did not fail to take advantage of the popularity of the great Pontiff: thus he became the destroyer of the famous dragon which used to poison the air with its breath, a curious but very impressive figure of the Church's victory over idolatry.

In the Middle Ages St Sylvester was regarded as being the typical representative of the Roman Pontificate and the glorious originator of that series of pontiff-kings who perpetuated in Rome the idea of universal monarchy, the eternal dream of the *Urbs aeterna.* One might, indeed, look upon him as the founder of the dynasty of papal sovereigns, since his memory was associated quite early with the famous but apochryphal Donation of Constantine and with the first establishing of the Papal States.

The memory of Sylvester remained highly honoured for many centuries, not only in Rome, but throughout the whole Christian world. His festival, partly because it coincides with the last day of the civil year, was considered as a feast of obligation, and even now it is incumbent on pastors of souls to offer up the holy sacrifice for their own flock on this day. According to the *Ordines Romani,* it was customary for the Pope to be present at the Mass of St Sylvester, wearing the tiara as on solemn feast-days, and also for him to grant for the occasion a holiday to the Consistory.

The Introit comes from Psalm cxxxi, which is pre-eminently Messianic. "Let thy priests, O Lord, be clothed with justice, and let thy saints rejoice: for thy servant David's sake turn not away the face of thy Anointed." The first verse of the psalm follows: "O Lord, remember David, and all his meekness."

The Collect in honour of the saint has become, in later times, common to all holy bishops. "Grant, we beseech thee, almighty God, that the venerable solemnity of blessed Sylvester, thy confessor and bishop, may increase our devotion and promote our salvation."

The lesson is taken from St Paul's Second Epistle to Timothy (iv, 1-8), in which are set forth the duties of a preacher of the Gospel, especially when called upon to oppose false teachers, who spread errors against the faith while assuming an empty show of knowledge. The Apostle knew that only too many such harmful disseminators of evil would quickly spring up in the Church of God, men who tickle the ears and excite the curiosity of their hearers, and who stray from the path of truth in order to give themselves over to the intellectual fantasies of a proud but distorted mind. Sylvester's own life, with its disputes against the Arians, fully confirms these predictions of St Paul.

Although this portion of the Epistle to Timothy is so applicable to the great Pope who confirmed the *Homoousion* of Nicæa, the Würzburg Lectionary assigns two different *pericopes* to to-day's feast, both taken from the Epistle to the Hebrews. This may, perhaps, be due merely to there being alternative lessons, but it may also be that St Sylvester enjoyed the honour of two stations in Rome, one *ad Corpus* in the cemetery of Priscilla, and the other at his titular church of Equitius, or at the ancient *domus Faustae* at the Lateran.

The Gradual is the same as that for St Thomas of Canterbury, while the alleluiatic verse is from Psalm lxxxviii: "I have found David my servant; with my holy oil I have anointed him." This mysterious anointing is the grace of the Holy Ghost, which the Church calls *spiritalis unctio,* and, when spoken of in reference to priests, is the special gift of their sacred office, symbolized by the holy oil which is poured on their hands and head.

The Gospel from St Luke (xii, 35-40) has special reference to bishops and sacred pastors whom our Lord bids be watchful, in order that they may not be taken unawares either by robbers who would attack the flock, or by their Lord who would desire to have proof of their faithful solicitude. The Würzburg Capitulary assigns the lesson *Vigilate* to this day, with which, on the other hand, the *Communio* also agrees, and thus establishes its own antiquity.

The Offertory repeats in part the alleluiatic verse. The Lord has consecrated his servant David with his holy oil; therefore he will not leave him alone in the arduous work for which he is destined. God's hand will come to help him, and his untiring arm will be his strength.

In the Secret we pray that the memory of the saints may ever be to us a source of consolation, so that while we venerate their memory, we may also experience their protection.

The Communion is from the same part of St Matthew (xxiv, 46) as that which is appointed for to-day's Gospel in the Würzburg Lectionary: " Blessed is that servant, whom, when his Lord shall come, he shall find watching : Amen, I say to you, he shall set him over all his goods."

In the Post-Communion we beseech almighty God that, while we render him thanks for the sacramental gifts which we have received, the intercession of the blessed Pontiff Sylvester may obtain for us still more abundant grace. The *beneficia potiora* for which we ask after Holy Communion are the effects of the sacrament, and, above all, eternal glory —the ultimate goal to which tends the grace of God in our present life. In order to grasp the full meaning of this prayer—a meaning frequently recurring in other eucharistic prayers, in which, in reference to the sacramental offering, gifts yet more abundant are asked for—we must distinguish, with the angelic doctor, the sacrament itself from the *res et virtus sacramenti*—that is, from the grace signified by the sacrament and from its supernatural effects.

The Eucharist is indeed the sacrament of the body and blood of the Lord, but it also signifies and brings about in us our union with him. Bad dispositions can render these effects subjectively null and void, just as green and damp wood resists the action of fire; therefore, when the Church in her eucharistic collects implores after Communion graces still more abundant, she has in view the full effects of the blessed Eucharist and, above all, the close interior union of the soul with God under the sacramental form.

JANUARY 1. OCTAVE OF OUR LORD

Station at St Mary in Trastevere.

Such, in the Roman Calendars, was the original designation of to-day's synaxis, until, through the influence of the Gallican liturgies, was added to it that of the Circumcision. Indeed, in the early days after the Peace of Constantine, the idolatrous feasts of the New Year, and the indecorous dances which accompanied them, prevented the Popes from

holding a station on this day, the more so as the entire fortnight between Christmas and the Epiphany was looked upon
as one continuous festival of the Manifestation of the divine
Infant; and besides, the Octave was a special privilege of
the Paschal solemnity.

When finally, about the end of the sixth century, it became
desirable to oppose the expiring struggles of the pagan rites
which were fighting desperately in their death-throes—instead of instituting the feast of the Circumcision of the Holy
Child, as was done in the countries of the Gallican rite—
Rome preferred to solemnize the eighth day after the
Nativity of our Lord.[1] It was not, in fact, an uninterrupted
octave, like that of Easter and later that of Pentecost, which
both terminated on the following Saturday, but was a festival
of a somewhat undefined type and of quite peculiar character,
occurring almost in the middle of the Christmas cycle, like
the solemnity of the *mediante die festo* which was kept by
the Greeks halfway through Eastertide.

We are in ignorance as to which was the primitive stational
basilica for this day. In the Würzburg Lectionary is indicated St Mary *ad Martyres,* in the Pantheon of Agrippa, but
after Gregory IV (827-44) had erected a crib at St Mary in
Trastevere—in imitation of the one at the Liberian Basilica—
the station was transferred to that basilica, thus making it a
sort of cathedral church across the Tiber.

In the fourteenth century the pontifical Mass took place
in St Peter's, and the Pope presented himself before the
people clad in a white cope and wearing a mitre; if he were
prevented from being present, one of the cardinals took his
place, and in this case the Bull of delegation remained
fastened throughout the day to the railing which enclosed the
Confession in the Vatican Basilica.

The Mass and Office for to-day's feast show a mixed
character and are of no great originality. At first it was
merely a question of the Octave of our Lord; then, in
connection with the Basilica of our Lady, where the station
was held, a special commemoration of the virginal mother-
hood of Mary most holy was inserted, the Circumcision and
Presentation in the Temple being afterwards added, although
this last, doubtless through Byzantine influence, was afterwards expunged from the office of January 1, so that it
should be celebrated on February 2.

The Introit is the same as that for the Third Mass of
Christmas Day, but the Collect is different. " O God, who
by the fruitful virginity of blessed Mary, hast bestowed on

[1] The present designation being : " The Circumcision of our Lord
and Octave of the Nativity."—Tr.

mankind the rewards of eternal salvation; grant, we beseech thee, that we may experience her intercession for us through whom we have been made worthy to receive the author of life, Jesus Christ thy Son our Lord."

The Epistle from St Paul is identical with that of the Mass on Christmas night. The Gradual is the same as the Gradual of the Third Mass of Christmas Day, but the alleluiatic verse is a different one, for it corresponds with the beginning of the Epistle of that Mass, being probably out of its proper place. "God who diversely spoke in times past to the fathers by the prophets; last of all, in these days, hath spoken to us by his Son."

The dignity of the New Testament is incomparably greater than that of the Old. In the latter, almighty God, through inspired men and by symbols and typical figures, deigned to reveal to the patriarchs a part only of the truths relating to the plan of our redemption; in the New Testament, on the other hand, it is no longer a few scattered rays of light, but the Sun of Justice himself, who shines upon his Church. The Church is initiated into the whole of eternal truth, not indeed in an indirect and typical manner, but by the Son of God himself made Man, and by the Holy Ghost who follows up and brings to final perfection the work of our eternal salvation.

The passage from St Luke which follows (ii, 21) formerly included the narrative of the Presentation of the Child Jesus in the Temple (22-32), before, that is, Rome adopted the Byzantine feast of the *Hypapante*[1] of our Lord. A deep mystery lies hidden under the symbolical name of Jesus bestowed on our Saviour to-day by Joseph and Mary, each acting independently of the other—he in virtue of the *patria potestas* which he exercised in the name of the eternal Father, she in virtue of her rights as mother. The name points out a complete scheme of free and universal salvation; it is the supreme title of glory for the Incarnate Word to whom God has given *nomen quod est super omne nomen.* How fitting, too, it is that the Redeemer should take such a name on the day of his Circumcision, when, by shedding the first drops of his precious blood, he inaugurates his sacrifice of redemption.

The Offertory is a repetition of that at the Third Mass of the Christmas feast, of which to-day is the Octave.

In the Secret we pray to God that while he accepts our gifts and our prayers, he may cleanse us by means of the heavenly mysteries and may mercifully hear us when we call upon him.

---

[1] The Feast of the Hypapante = the Feast of the Purification (Candlemas).—Tr.

The Communion is that of the Third Mass of Christmas Day.

The grand Post-Communion, terse and forcible, yet perfectly balanced and rhythmical, implores through the prayers of Mary our purification from sin and our attainment of celestial bliss.

Jesus in heaven, in the essential brightness of his glory, is seated at the right hand of the Father, but here below his more fitting throne of mercy and grace is in the bosom of the Virgin who holds him a little babe in her arms.

JANUARY 2. OCTAVE OF ST STEPHEN

The custom of extending the Paschal solemnity over a period of eight days is borrowed from the Synagogue, and it remained for several centuries the exclusive prerogative of the Easter festival. About the eighth century it became usual in Rome to keep an octave also after Christmas and Pentecost, and later on after the feasts of various saints. The Octaves of St Stephen, St John and the Holy Innocents occur as early as the eleventh century in the Statutes of Cluny, and the *Ordines Romani* of the fourteenth century expressly mention them.

The Mass for the Octave of St Stephen is identical with that for the feast, except as regards the Collect, which is always different in the ancient Roman octaves.

" O almighty and eternal God, who didst dedicate the firstfruits of thy martyrs in the blood of the blessed Levite Stephen, grant, we beseech thee, that he may be an intercessor for us, even as for his persecutors he besought our Lord Jesus Christ thy Son."

JANUARY 3. OCTAVE OF ST JOHN

The Mass is the same as that for the feast, but with the Preface of the Apostles.

JANUARY 4. OCTAVE OF THE HOLY INNOCENTS

The Mass is that of the feast, except that the Angelic Hymn and the Alleluia are sung, and, according to the Roman use, the vestments, instead of being purple, are red.

JANUARY 5. VIGIL OF THE EPIPHANY

Station at St Peter's.

The festive character which originally pervaded the whole fortnight after Christmas Day necessarily forbade the keeping of this vigil, which, however elaborate, must always bear a penitential character. When, about the eighth century, the stational afternoon Mass was introduced—at Milan, too, in the Middle Ages the great feasts began with Mass in the evening—it was assigned to the Vatican Basilica, whither the Pope was accustomed to repair from the Lateran on that afternoon with his Court for the celebration of Vespers and of the Night Office. This explains why the station is noted in the Missal as being at the Basilica of St Peter on two days in succession.

The Mass is that of the Sunday within the Octave of the Nativity, because—there being no primitive station—the faithful had so great a reverence for the Gregorian Antiphonary and Sacramentary that they did not venture to make any change in them by fresh additions. Not even the Gospel reading, with the account of our Lord's return out of Egypt, is original, since it formerly occurred in the Mass of the Holy Innocents. The peculiar character of this vigil is also shown by the fact that the Mass and Office have no connection with the feast of the Epiphany. In the twelfth century the Canon Benedict appoints in his *Ordo* that in Rome the Office of the Nativity should be recited on this day.

In the Gospel (Matt. ii, 19-23) it is narrated of Joseph that, being admonished by an angel in a dream, he returned with the Child Jesus and his most holy Mother to Palestine, whence, however, for fear of Archelaus, Herod's son and successor, he withdrew to Nazareth in Galilee.

Humility is the mother of order and justice, and portrays the full beauty of the divine perfection. In the Holy Family of Nazareth authority and personal dignity are seen in inverse order. Jesus is the last in the house and is obedient to all. Mary, indeed, commands her divine Son, but yields obedience to Joseph; and he, out of obedience to the eternal Father who so ordains it, serves both Jesus and Mary, giving them commands, thus setting an example of the manner in which all prelates and superiors should act in the Church of God. The virtue of St Joseph, although proportioned to his high office as foster-father of Jesus and spouse of the Immaculate Virgin, is very much less than that of those who are subject to him; yet almighty God maintains the order of rank which he has established, and communicates his will, not to Jesus nor to Mary, but to Joseph as being the head of the house.

Following on the afternoon Mass, the Pope in the Middle Ages began the real vigiliary solemnity in the Vatican Basilica, observing the ceremonial already described for the Third Sunday of Advent.

JANUARY 6. THE EPIPHANY OF OUR LORD

Station at St Peter's.

Epiphany means "appearance" or "manifestation," and among the Eastern Christians had originally the same significance as Christmas in Rome. It was the festival of the eternal Word, clothed in the flesh, revealing himself to mankind. Three different phases of this historical manifestation were especially venerated—viz., the adoration of the Magi at Bethlehem, the changing of the water into wine at Cana, and the baptism of Jesus in the Jordan.

In the East special emphasis was laid on the scene at the Jordan, when the Holy Ghost overshadowed the Saviour in the form of a dove, and the eternal Father proclaimed him from heaven as his beloved Son. From the time of St John the Gnostic heresy attributed great importance to this episode on account of its christology, maintaining that only then was the divine nature united to the human nature of Jesus, to leave it again at the moment of his Crucifixion. That baptism was, therefore, according to the Gnostics, the true divine birth of Jesus; consequently it was celebrated by them with the greatest splendour. It was against this doctrine that St John wrote in his first Epistle: *Hic venit* (Jesus Christ) *per aquam et sanguinem, non in aqua solum, sed in aqua et sanguine;*[1]—that is to say, Jesus came into the world as the Saviour and as the Son of God, and this not merely in the waters of the Jordan, but from the very moment of his Incarnation, when he took upon himself our human body and blood.

In all probability the Catholics, following the example of the Evangelist, wished from the first to set against the Gnostic baptismal manifestation the temporal birth at Bethlehem; hence the feast had a very complex signification, inasmuch as it was desired to retain also the Gospel dates of the baptism and of the marriage at Cana, relegating them, however, to a secondary place as being similar solemn and authentic manifestations of the divine nature of Jesus. At Rome, in an atmosphere extremely practical and altogether

---

[1] *Epist.* I, v, 6.

foreign to the mystic etherealism of the Eastern world, the historical recurrence of the Nativity of our Lord came to occupy so prominent a place in the popular mind that it is still the predominating idea throughout the whole of the Christmas Liturgy.

There was, it is true, some uncertainty regarding its date, which led to a partition of the festival. On the banks of the Tiber the feast of January 6 was anticipated by two weeks, to the greater honour of the Nativity; but the ancient *Theophania* retained its place, although deprived of its full significance, since the Crib of Bethlehem, by its power of attraction, gave greater prominence to the Adoration of the Magi, at the expense of the original idea of the baptism in the Jordan.

It is probable that in the third century Rome was still faithfully following the primitive Easter tradition and administering solemn baptism on the day of the *Theophania*. Hippolytus, in fact, delivered an address to the neophytes εἰς τὰ ἅγια Θεοφάνεια, just as in the very ancient Coptic Calendar in which to-day's feast is called *dies baptismi sanctificati*. In the time of St Gregory Nazianzen the Greeks named it the Feast of the Holy Lights—*In Sancta Lumina*—because baptism constitutes the supernatural illumination of the soul.

The third commemoration assigned to to-day's feast is of the first miracle performed by our Lord at the marriage at Cana. It is reckoned among the manifestations of Christ because the Gospel miracles supply the visible proof of the divine nature of Jesus. St Paulinus of Nola[1] and St Maximus of Turin[2] draw attention to the threefold aspect of the feast of the Epiphany in terms exactly similar to those which the Roman Church employs in the grand antiphon of the Office at dawn. *Hodie coelesti Sponso juncta est ecclesia*—mystical nuptials typified by those of Cana—*quoniam in Jordano lavit Christus ejus crimina*—baptism for the remission of sins—*currunt cum muneribus magi ad regales nuptias*—the Adoration of the divine Infant—*et ex aqua facto vino laetantur convivae*—the miracle of Cana.

That which surprises us is that these primitive features of the Eastern Epiphany feast are found to have penetrated more or less in Rome into the festival of December 25 itself, so much so that Pope Liberius (352-66), in a sermon delivered at St Peter's on Christmas Day, on the occasion when Marcellina, sister of St Ambrose, received from his hands the virginal veil, said to her, among other things: " Thou, O daughter, hast desired an excellent marriage. Thou seest

---

[1] *Poem.* XXVIII, *Nat.* IX, 47. *P.L.* LXI, col. 649.
[2] Hom. VII *in Epiph.*; *P.L.* LVII, col. 271 *et seq.*

what a multitude of people is here assembled for the birthday of thy Spouse, and no one of them all goes away unsatisfied. He indeed it is who, being invited to the wedding feast, changed the water into wine, and who with five loaves and two fishes fed four thousand men in the desert."

The station at St Peter's is inspired by the same thought as that of Christmas Day. In Rome the greater festivals— always excepting the very lengthy ceremonies of the Easter baptism—are celebrated at the *Pastor Ecclesiae* whose basilica is the sheepfold of the Roman flock. The *Ordines Romani* prescribed down to the thirteenth century that after Mass the Pope should put on his tiara and return on horseback to the Lateran. Later on, however, the Pontiffs preferred to remain at the Vatican for the second Vespers also, at which they were present in a scarlet cope and wearing a golden mitre. The custom of the Pope himself celebrating the stational Mass on this day is witnessed to, down to the end of the fourteenth century, in the *Ordo* of Bishop Pietro Amelio of Sinigaglia, in which the sole exception to the rule is in the case of the Pontiff being prevented from officiating either by some malady or by the rigour of winter weather.

The Introit is a free rendering of Malachias iii, 1, and was sung by the Byzantines when they went forth to meet Pope John (523-26). It is used also as a responsory verse on the Second Sunday of Advent, but the immediate source from which it comes is unknown. " Behold the Lord the Ruler is come : and a kingdom is in his hand, and power and dominion." The psalm (lxxi) is that of the feast, and foretells the kings offering their gifts to Christ. It is to be noted, and we shall see it clearly in the Canon, that in the Roman Liturgy the entire feast of the Epiphany still keeps something of its primitive Eastern significance, so that, regarding it apart from the Nativity, it sometimes seems as though the principal mystery which it has in view were actually the first manifestation of the Word of God made flesh.

In the Collect we pray God that as on this day he has revealed his only-begotten Son to the Gentiles by the shining of a star, so we who already know him by faith may be brought to contemplate the beauty of his majesty.

The lesson is drawn from Isaias (lx, 1-6), where he describes the calling of the Gentiles to the Faith and to the citizenship of the Messianic kingdom. The darkness of sin does indeed cover the earth, but in the Church there shines the living light divine, towards which all nations shall turn their gaze. The peoples shall vie with one another to enter into the great Catholic family, and the praise of the Lord shall resound over the whole world.

The Gradual is taken from the same portion of Isaias, and tells of the nations hastening to the cradle of the Messiah, bringing gold and frankincense. The alleluiatic verse, on the other hand, comes from that chapter (ii) of St Matthew in which the Magi relate how, through the appearance of a star, they are come to adore the Messiah. It is always faith that lights up our path to God, so that without it it is not possible for us to please him.

The Gospel is taken from St Matthew (ii, 1-12), and narrates the arrival of the Magi at Jerusalem, the anxiety of Herod and of the Sanhedrim, and, finally, the offering of the gifts to the Infant Jesus seated on Mary's lap. It is noteworthy that the Evangelist tells us nothing about St Joseph, as if he were someone entirely unconnected with the story. Yet the holy patriarch must certainly have been present, for, in his capacity as *paterfamilias,* he played a very important part on this occasion.

St Matthew's silence and his insistent precision in giving Mary the title of Mother of Jesus exclusively shows us that, over and above the mere historical recital of facts, we have here also a profoundly dogmatic representation of the incarnate Word being acknowledged and adored on his Mother's knees by the great ones of the earth. St Joseph has no indispensable part in this mystery, whereas Mary has. Thus the Evangelist has sketched for us his marvellous picture of this manifestation, excluding from his canvas all those secondary figures who, not being necessary to the scene, might have confused or weakened its essential conception.

The Offertory recalls that prophecy of Psalm lxxi, in which it is said that " the kings of Tharsis and the islands shall offer presents : the kings of the Arabians and of Saba shall bring gifts : and all kings of the earth shall adore him : all nations shall serve him."

The original intention of the Secret differs in the Roman and the Gallican Liturgies. In the first it serves as an introduction to the eucharistic anaphora, while in the second it closes the reading of the diptychs bearing the names of the offerers. These names were recited in some places after the Consecration, hence some of the Roman formulas for the *secreta* found their way into the Gallican Liturgy *post mysterium.* In the Roman rite the Collect, which serves as the prelude to the eucharistic anaphora, anticipates to some extent the *commendatio oblationum,* and thus its meaning practically corresponds to the *oratio post nomina* of the Frankish liturgies.

The text of the Secret for to-day's feast occurs, with slight differences, in various liturgies. The version given in the

Gregorian Sacramentary, and consequently in the existing Roman Missal, runs as follows: " Graciously regard, O Lord, we beseech thee, the gifts of thy Church, in which are offered now no longer gold, frankincense and myrrh; but he whom those mystic offerings signified is immolated and received, even Jesus Christ thy Son our Lord."

The special addition which, according to the letter of Pope Vigilius to Profuturus of Braga, was inserted in the text of the eucharistic hymn—*i.e.*, the Preface—is the following: " Because, when thy only-begotten Son appeared in the substance of our mortality, he repaired us with the new light of his immortality."[1]

In the original version of the prayer called by the Greeks the " Great Intercession," which in the Roman rite contains the episcopal diptychs of the Apostolic See, express mention is made of the solemnity of the *Theophania,* in such a way as to show clearly that at first this feast was one and the same as the Christmas festival. The actual words used are these: " Celebrating the most sacred day on which thy only-begotten Son, co-eternal with thee in thy glory, appeared among us in a visible body like unto our own."[2]

The Communion is a repetition of the alleluiatic verse.

In the Post-Communion we pray for the subjective realization of to-day's mystery, observed by the Church with such profound and solemn rites; in other words, for the manifestation of Jesus in our souls.

The interior life of a Christian is the reproduction of the life of Jesus; thus the object of the Church in placing before us the annual cycle of feasts is not merely to commemorate the great historical epochs in the history of our redemption, but also to reproduce in our souls their spiritual teaching. Hence in the Night Office of this feast of the Epiphany we do not so much adore the Christ who showed himself twenty centuries ago to the Magi, but rather the Christ who has revealed himself to us, too, who are now living. In a word, it is not alone the historical Epiphany which we desire to celebrate, but we associate ourselves also with that other subjective and personal Epiphany which is manifested in the soul of every believer to whom Jesus appears by means of our holy Faith.

[1] " Quia cum Unigenitus tuus in substantia nostrae mortalitatis apparuit, nova nos immortalitatis suae luce reparavit."
[2] " Communicantes, et) diem sacratissimum celebrantes, quo Unigenitus tuus in tua tecum gloria coaeternus, in veritate carnis nostrae visibiliter corporalis apparuit."

SUNDAY WITHIN THE OCTAVE OF THE EPIPHANY

Station at the Title of Pammachius.

The Octave of the Epiphany, with its one Mass repeated on every day of this week, is of comparatively late origin, the ancient Roman lectionaries indicating a prolongation of the feast extending to two or three days at most. On the day following the Epiphany, the station was on the Coelian Hill at the title of Pammachius, where once the martyrs John and Paul were beheaded and buried in their own *domus;* but about the eighth century, when this stational rite had fallen out of use owing to the feast having become a working day, it was transferred to the Sunday.

The Introit is taken out of the apocryphal books of Esdras, which sometimes found their way into the Roman Liturgy through Byzantine influence. " Upon a high throne I saw a man sitting whom a multitude of angels adore singing together : Behold him the name of whose empire is to eternity." Psalm xcix which follows is better suited to the joyfulness of this Christmas-time.

In the Collect we pray God of his heavenly mercy to grant the prayers of his suppliant people that they may not only see by the divine light that which they ought to do, but may also have strength to carry it out.

This little prayer of the Church is a true theological gem. It was invoked, among many others, by Celestine I (423-32) in the discussions regarding grace, when, in appealing to the authority of the liturgical formulas, he wrote : *Legem credendi lex statuat supplicandi.* In order to do right we need, first of all, to know what is right, and that not merely in a general way nor after a purely speculative fashion, but through a practical understanding of the mind which, illumined by grace, sees in detail that which God desires of his children in any particular circumstance. When the right course is known, it must be followed, and God will effectively stir the will by his grace, without disturbing in any way our freedom of judgement. As the Church teaches us in her sacred Liturgy, this divine touch *adspirando praevenit et adjuvando prosequitur* in such a way as to rouse the will out of its state of passive indifference, giving it at the same time its natural liberty of action.

The Epistle has no special characteristic; it is merely the continuation of the Epistle to the Romans which was begun on the vigil of the Nativity. It fits in, however, wonderfully well with the spirit of the sacred Liturgy during this Christmas cycle. Just as Jesus, in the obscurity of the home at Nazareth, inaugurates the world's redemption by becoming a little child obedient to Mary and Joseph, so must the Christian reform himself after the manner so well expressed by the Apostle by entering upon a new spiritual infancy of humility, simplicity, obedience and filial trust in God, after the example of the Child Jesus. This state of spiritual infancy leads us each to remain content in the position in which Providence has placed us, without wishing to raise ourselves, or without desiring, as St Paul says, " to be more wise than it behoveth to be wise." We are simply the mystical members of the one Body which is Christ. It matters little that every member has not the same office as every other; all, however, share in the same divine life which pervades every part of the Church.

The Gradual, from Psalm lxxi, is a cry of joy breaking forth instinctively at the mystery of peace and justice accomplished in these days by our Lord.

The alleluiatic verse is taken from Psalm xcix, as is the Introit. It is thoroughly in keeping with the festive spirit of holy gladness which characterizes to-day's station.

The Gospel from St Luke (ii, 41-52) tells us of Jesus being lost in the Temple and found again after a three days' search, and of his going down to Nazareth, where his wondrous home life from the age of twelve to thirty years is summed up by the Evangelist in the simple words: *Et erat subditus illis.* What depth of wisdom lies in that one sentence! The most holy Virgin—a prey to such woe as was the foretaste of her desolation upon Calvary—brought face to face with those resplendent rays of divine wisdom irradiating the fair head of Jesus as he sat among the doctors, causes us to realize to the full the truth of his human nature by the solemn exercise of her maternal rights over him.

To him whom the angels adore in silence, veiling their faces with their wings, she, a simple human creature, gives the name of Son, and asks him the reason of his three days' absence. *Quid fecisti nobis sic?* What creature, however holy, can arrogate to himself such an authority over the only-begotten of the Father? Yet Mary not only can do so, but has to do so, in virtue of her office as his Mother, which imposes on her the duty of watching over and guarding Jesus until the day on which the victim must be given up for sacrifice.

The answer of Jesus throws so great a light from his divine generation that it dazzles even his Mother's enlightened eyes. *Nesciebatis quia in iis quae Patris mei sunt oportet me esse?* Mary had claimed her rights over his human nature; Jesus points out other and higher rights over his divine nature—a mystery which could not but confuse the minds of both herself and St Joseph, by the very fact of the great light with which God was flooding their high calling. *Et ipsi nihil horum intellexerunt.* It is always so in this present life, and the light which God sheds upon our prayers serves only to make us realize the more his infinite majesty.

There is yet another circumstance which calls for notice. Mary and Joseph were perplexed when confronted by the depth of wisdom revealed in the simple answer of the youthful Jesus. It was not that they were ignorant of so obvious a truth as that every creature is bound to dedicate himself wholly to the service of the Creator, but they did not as yet fully understand the particular manner nor the circumstances in which this perfect " servant of Jehovah," as Isaias calls him, would accomplish his obedience to the Father. If it needs such sublime wisdom to penetrate this mystery, which baffled even the very parents of Jesus, who can flatter himself that he has nothing more to learn at the foot of the cross?

The Offertory, like the Introit, is from Psalm xcix, and is a real musical masterpiece. The rich melody belongs to the golden age of the Roman *schola,* and it is evident that its composer, in accumulating all those chants of the *Jubilate Deo omnis terra,* repeated even a second time, wished to linger over and draw therefrom its full spiritual sweetness.

The Secret is at once terse and graceful. "May the sacrifice we offer thee, O Lord, ever enliven and defend us."

The Communion is drawn from the Gospel, where the Blessed Virgin asks her divine Son why he thus left his parents. Jesus answers: "And how is it that you sought me? Did you not know that I must be about my Father's business?"

The Post-Communion humbly begs almighty God that, after having strengthened us with the divine sacrament, he will also enable us to correspond thereto by a life worthy of so great a gift.

Nesciebatis quia in iis quae Patris mei sunt oportet me esse? Here is a fitting pattern of priestly life after the example of Jesus. The priest, indeed, like Melchisedech, of whom the Apostle remarks that he appears suddenly in the Scriptures *sine patre, sine matre, sine genealogia,* has no longer any family ties nor mundane interests to bind him to the world. His country is the Church—*presbyter de Catholica,* as the ancient presbyters were sometimes called in the catacombs—his family is God's family, his interests vast and wide, for they transcend heaven and earth and even purgatory itself, seeking the supreme glory of God alone.

OCTAVE OF THE EPIPHANY

The Roman Sacramentaries know absolutely nothing of this Mass, which was compiled at some later date, use being made of the alternative collects noted in the Gelasian Sacramentary, as also of the Gospel originally belonging to the eucharistic synaxis of the Wednesday after the *Theophania*, but which has long ceased to be in use. The rest of the Mass is that of the feast of the Epiphany.

The Collect is a very fine one, breathing the true spirit of the Leonine era. " O God, whose only-begotten Son appeared in the substance of our flesh, grant, we beseech thee, that as we confess him to have been outwardly like unto us, so we may deserve to be inwardly created by him anew."

The Gospel from St John (i, 29-34), recounting the manifestation on the banks of the Jordan, takes us back to the very oldest and earliest signification of the feast, opposed by Catholics to the Gnostics who used to commemorate the birth of Jesus as being effected at his baptism in the Jordan through the infusion of his divine nature. Yet the Church regards the baptism of the Redeemer in the waters of penance as one of the most important of the manifestations. Jesus there takes the place of sinful man and humbles himself in order to partake of the mystery of the Baptist; at the same time, however, the Father and the Holy Ghost proclaim his divine nature, and the whole august Trinity sanctifies the baptism of the New Covenant, endowing it with true power to regenerate the adopted sons of God *ex aqua et Spiritu Sancto*. It is, therefore, not so much the birth of Jesus as our own rebirth to supernatural life which we celebrate on this day; hence in the Night Office we fittingly exclaim : *Christus apparuit nobis; venite adoremus.*

The Secret is in a very ancient and classical strain. " We bring thee offerings, O Lord, for the appearance of thy Son born for us; humbly beseeching thee, that as he is the author of our gifts, so he may mercifully receive the same, Jesus Christ our Lord."

The " Eucharistia," or thanksgiving for the sacred gifts (Post-Communion), draws its inspiration from the old Byzantine name for to-day's solemnity—viz., the Feast of the Holy Lights. " Let thy heavenly light, we beseech thee, O Lord, go before us always and in all places, that we may behold with pure eyes, and receive with worthy affection, the mystery of which thou hast been pleased to make us partakers."

The Christian is the child of light; hence it is fitting that in his actions there should never be any darkness, crookedness or prevarication. To go forward with truth, as St John says, signifies to live according to the fulness of the Christian ideal, carrying its divine meaning into daily life and thus following in the footsteps of Jesus Christ.

SECOND SUNDAY AFTER THE EPIPHANY

Station at St Eusebius.

According to the early Roman custom preserved to us in the ancient lectionaries, the Sundays which follow up to Lent were reckoned either from Christmas or from the Epiphany, and the Würzburg Capitulary enumerates as many as ten of them. That is to say, in this list of Sundays, nothing was as yet known of the three Sundays of preparation for Lent, which were very probably instituted by St Gregory the Great.

Originally to-day's station—it constituted an exception, for the ordinary Sundays of the year are never characterized by any stational solemnity—was appointed to be held at the Basilica of St Eusebius, near the cemetery in the Via Merulana, where the saint of that name died of misery and want in the time of the Emperor Constantius, on account of his confessing the faith of Nicea. We find the *dominicum Eusebii* already mentioned in an inscription of the fourth century, so it is probable that the transformation of the house into a titular (parish) church took place immediately after the martyr's death in the time of Pope Liberius (352-66).

We are in ignorance of the reasons why this day was chosen for a station. Seeing that certain documents indicate the station at St Eusebius as being, not on this Sunday, but on January 22, the day on which the *natalis* of the martyr Vincent of Saragossa is celebrated, Tommasi has supposed the choice to have been inspired by the similarity of name existing between the Spanish deacon and another martyred Vincent, the deacon of Sixtus II (260-66), whose body, moreover, reposed in the Basilica of St Eusebius. Others, again, have been inclined to see in this station the last remnant of an ancient commemoration of the dead which was observed in the cemetery on the Esquiline, and which has left scattered traces here and there in the different liturgies. Possibly, though, the reason is a much more simple one.

Generally speaking, the Sundays throughout the year had no fixed station. As, however, after the Epiphany there followed two or three other feast-days with a station at the title of Pammachius, and another at St Eusebius, when these processions were abandoned on working days, they were transferred to the Sunday, so as not to be wholly forgotten.

The Introit is from Psalm lxv, and calls upon the whole earth to worship the Lord and to sing praises to his name.

The Collect begs him who governs all things in heaven and earth mercifully to hear the supplications of his people and to grant them his peace in their days.

The Epistle is taken from that of St Paul to the Romans (xii, 6-16). In it we learn the precious lesson of the necessity of using the various gifts of grace for the edification of all.

The diverse distribution of these graces ought to inspire us with the greatest respect for the vocation of others : without our claiming that our individual form of spirituality shall determine the conditions of the supernatural life of the Holy Ghost in the souls of others. Each has his own place and his own gift, but both the one and the other are co-ordinated to the common good, which is the building up of the mystical body of Christ.

The Gradual comes from Psalm cvi. God has sent his Word to heal the world, therefore a canticle of gratitude bursts forth from every heart.

In the alleluiatic verse from Psalm cxlviii—probably this was originally merely an acclamation following upon the reading of the Gospel—the angels and powers are invited to give praise to the Lord God.

In the Würzburg list of Gospels the passage containing the account of the miracle at Cana is duly assigned to the Mass for this day, but there is nothing to prevent us from maintaining that the three Gospel *pericopes* of the Adoration of the Magi, the Baptism, and the changing of water into wine, which are now read on the feast of the Epiphany, on the Octave, and on the following Sunday respectively, really represent the readings of the early threefold station which denoted in Rome the feast of the *Theophania,* at a time when the Octave had not yet come to be observed.

The whole scene described in to-day's Gospel, besides recording our Lord's first miracle, veils a deep meaning into which the human mind can with difficulty penetrate. How sweet and consoling it is for the children of Mary to know that Jesus, at her bidding, hastens the hour of his manifestation to the world ! *Quid mihi et tibi est, mulier? nondum venit hora mea.*

Whatever explanation may be given to these words with which the Saviour—in the truthfulness of his human nature which caused him to be the obedient Son of his Mother— asserts his own divine perfection, it is certain that they are to be understood in an affirmative and sympathetic sense, as Mary, his most holy Mother, herself understood them. *Nondum venit hora mea.* But did our Lord really anticipate *hora sua* on this occasion and change the wondrous plan of his manifestation to mankind? It would seem that the meaning of his Mother's request was far more complex than appears at first sight. She asked for wine, not merely for the needs of the wedding feast, but also for that other wine of which the miraculous draught at Cana was but a symbol—that is, for the Holy Eucharist. Three years had to elapse before the type was fulfilled in the antitype, so our Lord, in full response to the prayer of his blessed Mother, changed the water into wine, and announced, with regard to the Eucharist, that the time for its institution was not yet come.

The Offertory for to-day is a *Jubilus* drawn from Psalm lxv. The prophet invites the whole world to praise God, and would make known to all mankind the blessings which he has received from on high.

In the Secret we pray God to sanctify our oblations and to cleanse us from the stains of our sins.

The Communion tells of the miraculous changing of the water into wine and of the surprise of the ruler of the feast, and brings out fully the meaning of the miracle by connecting it with the Holy Eucharist. Our Lord has kept *bonum vinum usque adhuc,* because only in this last age of the world, the Messianic age, as St John calls it, has he given to men the good wine of his Blood in the Blessed Sacrament. Furthermore, the sweetness of the holy love of God is an inebriating draught which he keeps until the last for those who serve him faithfully.

In the Post-Communion we beseech almighty God to increase in us the power of his grace, so that, being nourished by his sacrament, we may also be prepared to receive what it promises.

The world's storehouse is soon depleted. *Vinum non habent.* Moreover, *omnis homo primum bonum vinum ponit;* that is to say, the world is wont to give its followers the good wine only at the beginning of their feasts; for, when passion shall have gained the mastery and the mind shall have become intoxicated, as it were, with mundane pleasures, *cum inebriati fuerint, id quod deterius est,* then it is that it brings forth the wine which is worse—that is, the bitter dregs of that cup of which the Psalmist says: *Bibent omnes peccatores terrae.*

THIRD SUNDAY AFTER THE EPIPHANY

Formerly in Rome, besides the Sunday synaxis, there were those of the Wednesday and the Friday in each week, and thus several passages from the Scriptures, now assigned to the Sunday, belonged originally to these weekday Masses. This explains why the lesson from the Epistle to the Romans (xii, 16-21) is continued on this day, while in the old Roman lists the Epistle to the Galatians began at once on the first Sunday after the feast of the Nativity. The same is to be noted with regard to the Gospel readings which in the Middle Ages—according to certain arrangements of lessons—were drawn up for the week in a regular scheme, so that the parallel passages from all the four Gospels were read in succession. The catechetical instruction of the faithful has suffered a great loss by the falling into disuse in the Missal of these Wednesday and Friday synaxes with their relative lessons.

The Introit is from Psalm xcvi, and is the same for the remaining Sundays of this cycle. It is characterized by a holy joyfulness and by fervent gratitude towards God.

In the Collect we present our prayers to God with all humility, begging him to stretch forth the right hand of his power and come to aid us.

In the Epistle (Rom. xii, 16-21) St Paul dwells upon the necessity of our mutually forgiving injuries, pointing out to us that the best means of rectifying the wrong we may have suffered is to commit ourselves in all quietness to the judgement of God who is the sure avenger of all injustice.

The Gradual is taken from Psalm ci. In rebuilding Sion the Lord hath clothed himself with power and laid fear upon all the kings of the earth.

The alleluiatic verse is also from Psalm xcvi, which is a true hymn of triumph for the inauguration of the new Messianic kingdom, no longer merely national in character, like that of Israel, but truly universal and worldwide.

The Gospel (Matt. viii, 2-13) places the healing of the leper and that of the centurion's servant at Capharnaum as a prelude to the conversion of the Gentiles, who, like the lepers and those connected with the opprobrious rule of heathen Rome, were despised by the proud Israelites as unworthy of the Messianic heritage promised to the seed of Abraham. We ought not to despise anyone, since no one is so far outcast from the divine mercy that he may not be drawn to God and converted. We ourselves, as the Apostle says, were once afar off, but now *facti sumus prope in sanguine Christi*.

The Offertory is a song of triumph. "The right hand of the Lord hath wrought strength, the right hand of the Lord hath exalted me. I shall not die, but live, and shall declare the works of the Lord."

This thrice-repeated glorification of the divine right hand, the text of which we find in Psalm cxvii, symbolizes the mystery of the all-holy Trinity, and is repeated by the Church in the Mass for the Finding of the Holy Cross. Jesus, by his own death, finally crushes the power of death, and, rising again, he tells the world of the wonders wrought by Jehovah for the benefit of all humanity redeemed and made to share in the blessing of the Resurrection.

The Roman Liturgy gives us this very beautiful Offertory again on the Tuesday in the third week of Lent, on which day the synaxis was held in the *domus Pudentiana* on the Esquiline, which by ancient tradition was venerated as the abode of the Apostles Peter and Paul and of their immediate successors in the Roman See. The material edifice, therefore, of the Pudentian title typifies the Roman Church and the supreme pontificate, so that in the chant *non moriar, sed vivam et narrabo opera Domini* one rightly saw an allusion to the privileges and prerogatives of the Apostolic Chair.

The Secret asks God that our oblations may avail to purify us from all stains of sin, so that we may offer him the unbloody sacrifice with pure hearts and minds.

The Communion is taken from St Luke (iv, 22). "They all wondered at these things, which proceeded from the mouth of God." This verse, however, is out of place, for it no longer bears reference to the corresponding Gospel lesson of our Lord's discourse in the synagogue at Nazareth, which was originally assigned to one of the Wednesdays or Fridays after the *Theophania*. The disappearance of these weekly stations from the Gregorian Sacramentary leaves a great blank and also disarranges the order of the readings which now follow one another only at irregular intervals.

The Post-Communion is as follows : " Grant, O Lord, we beseech thee, that we to whom thou vouchsafest the use of such great mysteries, may be truly fitted to receive effective benefits therefrom."

How is it that sometimes souls who are not so privileged by grace have, nevertheless, greater faith and deeper humility than even persons professing the religious life? It is because these latter too often resemble the Jews, who show a distaste for the heavenly manna. They see themselves chosen out by God, and a subtle sense of inward pride enters into them, producing indolence and a disinclination for the things of the spirit.

FOURTH SUNDAY AFTER THE EPIPHANY.

The Sunday Masses up to Septuagesima have no special psalm-chants; they merely repeat those of the Third Sunday after the Epiphany. This is an anomaly which finds its explanation in the very uncertainty which dominates this latter part of the cycle after the Epiphany. As everything depends upon the date of the beginning of the Lenten fast, so in some of the Roman lectionaries it comprised as many as ten weeks, while others enumerate no more than three. The last Sundays after Pentecost are in a similar position, so that we have every reason to believe that, in the absence of special chants for these supplementary Sundays, the Gregorian version of the antiphonary really represents the Roman use of the seventh century.

The Collect takes us back to the times of St Gregory the Great, when the Lombards were threatening the very capital itself of the world. Throughout the fifth and sixth centuries the Eternal City was repeatedly taken and sacked, and it is to such a state of things as this that this prayer of the Church alludes: "O God, who knowest that we are beset by perils greater than our human frailty can withstand; grant us health of mind and body, that those things which we suffer for our sins we may with thy help successfully overcome."

A passage from the Epistle to the Romans (xiii, 8-10) follows, in which the Apostle shows that the love of our neighbour is the synthesis of all other social duties, and that it is the spirit of the whole Law and the immediate outcome of the precept enjoined upon us to love God.

The Gospel, with its account of the miracle of our Lord stilling the tempest, is drawn from St Matthew (viii, 23-27). How pleasing is this picture of Jesus, weary, and composing himself placidly to sleep in the bottom of a simple fishing-boat! Thus does he preach the spirit of mortification, of humility and of simplicity in the exercise of the sacred ministry. He slumbers indeed, but his heart still beats for us. If the waves do not overturn the boat, it is because he is supporting it, so that he may awake and come to succour his Apostles just when all hope of human help is lost.

In the Secret we beg for grace that the offering of the divine sacrifice may free us from all evil and may be a protection to our weak nature.

The Post-Communion implores from God that his mysteries may detach us from worldly pleasures and ever renew our strength with the heavenly nourishment of grace.

Why dost thou tremble in adversity, O my soul? It is, as

it were, a storm arisen upon the small and sinuous sea of thy heart, but the winds and the waves obey the voice of God almighty.

FIFTH SUNDAY AFTER THE EPIPHANY

The Roman Lectionary of Würzburg enumerates only four weeks after the Epiphany; hence, when the reading of the Epistle to the Romans is finished in Christmas week, that to the Galatians is begun at once on the following Sunday. The existing Missal still keeps the lesson *ad Galatas* for the Sunday within the Octave of the Nativity, but for the following Sundays the interrupted Epistle to the Romans is resumed and continued until to-day, when the Epistle to the Colossians begins—assigned in the Würzburg Codex to the second Sunday after the Nativity. Thus there are two courses of lessons which have become interwoven the one with the other, a fact which goes far to prove the great antiquity of the Liturgy of the Apostolic See.

After last Sunday's cry of anguish, we have in to-day's Collect an act of serene confidence. " Keep watch, we beseech thee, O Lord, over thy household in thy unceasing mercy; that, as it relies only upon the hope of thy heavenly grace, so it may ever be defended by thy protection."

The passage which follows from the Epistle to the Colossians (iii, 12-17) is a short treatise upon the inner life, in which are put before us mutual patience and love, brotherly counsel, continuance in prayer, and above all, that close union with Jesus from which all our actions must draw their living force.

It is noteworthy that the Roman Liturgy for the Sundays goes rapidly through the Apostolic Epistles, reading only short portions of them at the Mass. It is probable, however, that before the time of St Gregory the readings were longer and that the scriptural portions which had been omitted were read during the night vigils and in the synaxes of the Wednesdays and Fridays.

The Gospel is from St Matthew (xiii, 24-30) and relates the parable of the cockle. The problem of the origin of evil has exercised the most acute minds from time immemorial. *Unde habet zizania?* No one has ever solved the question so decisively as our Lord in to-day's lesson. *Hoc fecit inimicus homo;* that is to say, it is a consequence of Satan's envy, the malice of him who did not persevere in the truth and who became, from the beginning, the destroyer of the whole human race. The householder leaves the cockle to grow up together with the wheat, so that it may not damage the harvest. But at the right moment, when the wicked shall have fulfilled their mission as instruments of purification for the just, when they shall have received their own reward in the consolations of this world, and when the sanctification of the elect shall be completed, then the angels of God will root out the cockle, and the Church, without spot or wrinkle, shall celebrate her eternal nuptials with the immaculate and heavenly Bridegroom.

In the Secret, while offering to almighty God the victim of propitiation, we beg him to absolve us from our sins and direct our inconstant minds in the way of salvation.

In the Post-Communion we pray that we may be led unto that eternal salvation of which we are offered a pledge in this holy banquet.

How profound are the mysteries of Providence! If the Lord does not punish and destroy the wicked in this life, it is in order that the good may not be involved in the same doom, who by ties of blood, of fellow-citizenship and of country are associated together with the sinners. The world never reflects upon the great and important part fulfilled by the saints, whose merits ward off from the world its well-deserved chastisements.

SIXTH SUNDAY AFTER THE EPIPHANY

On this last Sunday of the Christmas cycle the series of lessons from the Pauline Epistles is continued with that addressed to the Thessalonians. This sequence of the Epistles will, however, be broken in order to give place to the Easter cycle, and only taken up again some time about the month of June.

In the Collect we beg almighty God that, ever fixing our thoughts on reasonable things, we may both in our words and works do what is pleasing in his sight.

In the Epistle (1 Thess. i, 2-10) the Apostle reminds the faithful of Thessalonica of the first days of Christianity in that city, when the Gospel seed, scattered upon a soil fertile and well prepared, had borne fruit a hundredfold. From Thessalonica, in fact, notwithstanding all the persecutions and difficulties to which the faithful were exposed, the Faith spread through Macedonia and Achaia. This preaching of the Gospel was by no means isolated, for we know that one of the most effective means for the diffusion of Christianity in the Greek and Roman world was the insistent and widely-spread propaganda by the laity, especially by the women.

The Apostle gives thanks to God for all this splendid growth which was confirming the supernatural character of his message, while he himself, having suffered sickness and scourging, and having been put in chains at Philippi, had sought refuge at Thessalonica, where he worked a great number of miracles.

The parables which follow in the Gospel (Matt. xiii, 31-35) —the continuation of that of last Sunday—show that God has no need of an elaborate apparatus with which to work his wonders; on the contrary, he chooses means and instruments to all appearance unsuitable, so that no one should claim for himself the merit of having effected the result. Of all his miracles, the most stupendous is most certainly the Church, which, from humble beginnings in the tortuous passages of the catacombs, has for more than nineteen centuries been extending her universal dominion over all the earth.

The most powerful dynasties, the greatest empires, are no more; of the stupendous power wielded by the ruler of the *sacra urbs* and his *basileus porphyrogenitus* on the shores of the Bosphorus nothing now is left. Dozens of barbarian dynasties, whether of Gauls, Germans or Britons, arise and set again; Charlemagne brings under his sway the greater part of Central Europe; after him come the imperial German dynasties, the communal republics of the Renaissance, the universalism of Napoleon and the modern worship of the State. The Church, in the exuberant vigour of her eternal youth, beholds with serenity the rise and fall of all these peoples. She cradles them in their infancy, she sustains them in their decrepitude, and while all the generations of mankind pass in review before her, she, with her own gaze fixed on heaven, meditates on eternity.

The Secret clearly points out the different effects of the sacrifice: " May this oblation, O God, we beseech thee, cleanse, renew, govern and protect us."

To-day's Post-Communion is finely conceived. " Being fed, O Lord, with heavenly delights, we beseech thee that we may ever hunger after those things by which we truly live."

There is nothing greater than the Church, the " Great Church," as Celsus called her in the third century, in order to distinguish her from the heretical self-styled " churches." She is likened to a tree in which the birds build their nests. Indeed, since the sanctification and glorification of the Church are the ultimate end of all created things, it is necessary that social institutions, kingdoms and families should derive their strength and their permanence from her. At Rome, in the pontificate of St Clement, she was called the firstborn of all creatures, for whom all other things were made. Therefore liberalism, the theory that the Church and the State are two irreducible parallels, is an anarchical idea, which resolves itself in pure atheism. History, life's great teacher, demonstrates but too clearly the truth of that which was said by the ancient author of the Epistle *ad Diognetum*—namely, that the world without the spirit of Christianity is no more than a decaying corpse from which the soul has fled.

Printed in the USA
CPSIA information can be obtained
at www.ICGtesting.com
LVHW020720070124
768171LV00086B/543/J